'Jews and other foreigners'

MANCHESTER
1824

Manchester University Press

'Jews and other foreigners'

Manchester and the rescue of the victims of European fascism, 1933–1940

Bill Williams

Manchester University Press
Manchester and New York

distributed in the United States exclusively
by Palgrave Macmillan

Published by Manchester University Press
Oxford Road, Manchester M13 9NR, UK
and Room 400, 175 Fifth Avenue, New York, NY 10010, USA
www.manchesteruniversitypress.co.uk

Distributed in the United States exclusively by
Palgrave Macmillan, 175 Fifth Avenue, New York,
NY 10010, USA

Distributed in Canada exclusively by
UBC Press, University of British Columbia, 2029 West Mall,
Vancouver, BC, Canada V6T 1Z2

British Library Cataloguing-in-Publication Data
A catalogue record for this book is available from the British Library

Library of Congress Cataloging-in-Publication Data applied for

ISBN 978 0 7190 8549 9 hardback

First published 2011

Edited and typeset
by Frances Hackeson Freelance Publishing Services, Brinscall, Lancs
Printed in Great Britain
by TJ International Ltd, Padstow

Contents

Abbreviations

AAC	Academic Assistance Council
BA	B'nei Akiva
BEN	*Bolton Evening News*
CM	Committee Meeting
EC	Executive Committee
EZF	Zionist Federation of Great Britain and Ireland
GM	General Meeting
GEC	Germany Emergency Committee
GMCRO	Greater Manchester Record Office
HATS	Manchester Home for Aged, Sick and Incurable Jews and Temporary Shelter
ISC	International Service Committee
ISF	International Solidarity Fund
ISS	International Students Service
JC	*Jewish Chronicle*
JG	*Jewish Gazette*
JRC	Manchester and Salford Jewish Representative Council
JT	*Jewish Telegraph*
KHE	Kershaw House Executive Committee
KPD	Kommunistische Partei Deutschlands (Communist Party of Germany)
LIDC	Lancashire Industrial Development Council
MCL	Manchester Central Library
MCN	*Manchester City News*
MFA	Archive of the Manchester Society of Friends
MG	*Manchester Guardian*
MGJAC	Manchester German-Jewish Aid Committee
MH	Machzikei Hadass
MJRC	Manchester Jewish Refugees Committee
MSWC	*Manchester and Salford Women's Citizen*
NCW	National Council of Women
NJCSR	National Joint Council for Spanish Relief
MY	Manchester Yeshivah
ORT	Organisation for Resettlement and Training
PPU	Peace Pledge Union
QM	Quarterly Meeting
QRC	Manchester and District Refugee Committee of the Society of Friends
RCM	Refugee Children's Movement

SA	*Stockport Advertiser*
SCR	*Salford City Reporter*
SCRC	Salford Committee for Refugees from Czechoslovakia
SPSL	Society for the Protection of Science and Learning
SRAC	Springfield Refugee Aid Committee
TVA	Torah Va'Avodah
WAEC	War Agricultural Emergency Committee
WCML	Working Class Movement Library
WILPF	Women's International League for Peace and Freedom
WLMBB	Manchester Women's Lodge of the Order B'nai Brith
WVS	Women's Voluntary Service

Glossary

Agudas Israel (adj. Agudist)   Council of an orthodox Jewish movement
Agudas Lomdei Torah   Organisation of the alumni of the Manchester Yeshivah

Aliyah   Jewish migration to Israel
Austreit Gemeinde   independent community
Bachad (-niks)   religious Zionist organisation
Barmitzvah   ceremony for boys reaching their religious majority

Bayyit   (lit. house) headquarters
Beth Chalutz   House of Zionist pioneers
Brocha   blessing
Chalutzim   Zionist pioneers in training for settlement in Palestine

Chanucah   festival celebrating the re-dedication of the Temple

Chaverim   fellow-members
Cheder (pl. Chedarim)   private school for the teaching of religion and Hebrew

Daven   to pray
Eretz Israel (alt. Yisroel)   Land of Israel
Eruv Shabbos   eve of the Sabbath
Hachsharah/oth   Zionist training camp/s plural: Hachsharoth
Halacha   Jewish Law
Haredi/m   strictly orthodox Jew/s
Hashomer Hatzair   (lit. Young Guards). Left-wing Zionist organisation

Hechalutz   organisation of Zionist pioneers
Ivrit   modern Hebrew
Kaddish   prayer for mourners
Kehilla   Jewish community
Kiddish/kiddush   blessing
Kinder   German for children
Kultusgemeinde   Jewish communal organisation
Macher   communal activist
Madrich/im   leader/s
Merkaz Limmud   Zionist study centre
Mezuzah   cased portions of the Torah attached to the doors of a Jewish home

Minyan	quorum of ten males required for the holding of a religious service
Mizrachim	religious Zionists
'Movement Children'	children from the Kindertransport
Oneg Shabbat	religious meeting on the Jewish Sabbath
Poalei Zion	Socialist Zionist organisation
Rav	Rabbi
Rebbe	cheder teacher
Seder	ceremonial meal on the eve of Passover
Shabbat	Jewish Sabbath
Shekhol (pl. Shekholim)	contributions to the Zionist movement
Shiur (pl. shiurim)	religious study session
Shivah	seven days of mourning
Shochet	qualified ritual slaughterer.
Sichoth	discussion on matters of religion
Sidra Shiur	lessons drawn from the current portion of the Law
Snif	branch of Bachad
Stiebl (pl. stieblich)	small synagogue
Tarbut	central group
Tephillim	phylacteries worn by orthodox Jews during prayer
Yeshiva	academy for higher Jewish learning
Yishuv	settlement in Palestine
Yom Kippur	Day of Atonement

Preface

'Jews and other foreigners' is a phrase used in an article in the *Manchester Mercury* of 12 March 1774, on the very cusp of Manchester's emergence as a modern centre of industry and commerce, to warn its citizens of the presence amongst them of conspirators said to have come to Manchester under assumed names to steal the secrets of the cotton industry and convey them to Britain's overseas competitors. A Committee of Trade created to detect such persons offered a reward of twenty guineas to anyone providing information leading to an arrest. There is no evidence of any such arrests and the article, apart from suggesting the early presence of Jewish hawkers and pedlars, reflects panic rather than reality.

To the confident elite which emerged in the following decades from Manchester's industrial and commercial success, and to the editors of *Manchester Guardian*, founded in 1821 as their mouthpiece, such xenophobia was unpalatable. These 'new Athenians' saw themselves as quintessential liberals who welcomed to the city anyone, regardless of race, religion and nationality, who contributed to the city's economy and well-being. In doing so they created the image of a 'liberal city' which was to remain central to Manchester's sense of identity throughout the nineteenth and twentieth centuries.

This book does not so much seek to dismantle such an image as to suggest some of the flaws and ambiguities which, at the very least, complicated the cherished tolerance of 'outsiders'. In a sense it complements my earlier attempt to assess the responses of Mancunians to the 'mass immigration' of the late nineteenth century. It poses the question: how liberal were Mancunians in the face of those seeking refuge from oppression in Fascist Europe?

It represents the first result of research conducted at The Centre for Jewish Studies of the University of Manchester with the generous support of the Association of Jewish Refugees. The first draft of the results, which embraced the experiences of the 8,000 or so refugees from Fascist Europe, Jewish and non-Jewish, who reached the Manchester region, including refugee industrialists and academics, and the political and national organisations which refugees created for themselves, proved too long for a single book, although a full draft, some part of which may later be published in an amended form, is available for consultation in the Local Studies section of Manchester Central Library.

The present study focuses on 'rescue': that is, the role of Manchester people in facilitating the arrival in Britain of the victims of European Fascism, Jewish and non-Jewish, between Hitler's accession to the Chancellorship of Germany in January 1933 and May 1940, when the last body of refugees arrived in Manchester in the wake of the German occupation of Amsterdam.

I am grateful to the Association of Refugees for their support and forbearance and to its representative in Manchester, Werner Lachs, for his advice, his patience and for making possible the contacts with refugees; to the many refugees who submitted themselves to my interviews; to Rosalyn Livshin, Professor Anthony Grenville and the Jewish Refugees Visual Recording Project, for permission to quote from the interviews which formed part of their programme; to Kevin Bolton and his colleagues for their efficiency and empathy in providing access to records in the archive of Manchester Central Library; to Professors Bernard Jackson and Philip Alexander, the joint directors of the Centre for Jewish Studies, for their support and the space they allowed me to complete this work; to Professor Tony Kushner and Dr Daniel Langton, without whose advice, critiscism and support this book could never have been written; and to my partner Hilary for surrendering the space that this research took up in our home and for leaving me with the time to complete it.

Introduction: Jewish refugees in Manchester

In June 1933, five months after Hitler's appointment to the Chancellorship of Germany, nearly 500,000 people of the 'Mosaic faith' lived in Germany.[1] An unknown further number of those of Jewish origin who had either abandoned their beliefs or been converted to some branch of Christianity, were soon to be defined by Nazi legislation as Jewish by race, and therefore as the proper subject of official discrimination. The number of Jews of both kinds under Nazi control was increased by the Nazi occupation of Austria, with its 190,000 Jews, in March 1938 and of Bohemia and Moravia, in the March of the following year, which brought the total number of Jews under Nazi rule to approximately 913,000.[2] Although it took time for the Jews of Germany and Austria to become fully aware of the dangers Nazi rule entailed for them, or to overcome what Joseph Roth has described as an inherited 'tradition of endurance', for the growing number who sought an escape by emigration, their likelihood of success depended largely not only upon the openings for their resettlement but on their ability to gain access to such openings. Many were restricted in their choice not only by the strict immigration policies of the potential receiving countries, but by their lack of the knowledge, the horizons, the contacts and the resources which would have enabled them to turn those policies to their own advantage.

This in turn depended in large part on the existence overseas of those ready to facilitate their entry, in the case of Britain by identifying the economic opportunities, the cultural openings, the work placements and the guarantees of maintenance which might steer them through the barbed wire of British aliens legislation. Ultimately, that is, would-be refugees from Fascist Europe were dependent on the active goodwill of British people and institutions, including those of Manchester. In January 1939 the *Manchester and Salford Woman Citizen*, the organ of the Manchester branch of the Association of Women Citizens, provocatively entitled 'Seasonal Ill-will', raised the issue of whether in Manchester there existed the degree of sympathy 'for human suffering in any part of the world' which would engender practical aid for the Jewish victims of Nazism. 'Protests on behalf of the vindictively tormented and persecuted Jews in Germany' were, it believed, 'of little avail unless they are associated with offers of help to the victims who can escape (there are many channels for offers of hospitality, maintenance, or small contributions of money) … That in a so-called civilised country a subject race can with impunity be cruelly used as a political pawn must burden the consciences as well as the heart of the rest of humanity.'[3]

This book seeks to assess the degree to which, in a city which prided itself on its liberality and housing the largest Jewish population in provincial Britain, the consciences of people and organisations, Jewish and non-Jewish, were sufficiently 'burdened' to elicit practical measures of help for refugees from Germany, Austria and Czechoslovakia, the vast majority of them Jewish.

Since it began to develop a distinctive identity after the debacle of Peterloo in 1819, Manchester came to be seen by its new middle class of merchants, manufacturers and professional men as the quintessential 'liberal city'. The *Manchester Guardian* became its mouthpiece, the Free Trade Hall its political fortress, the Cross Street Chapel its spiritual home and the Athenaeum its proof of the cultural sophistication of the new captains of industry and trade. Typically the *Manchester Guardian* contrasted the civilised liberality of the town towards outsiders, including Jewish outsiders, with the vulgar xenophobia and barbarous anti-Semitism of other people in other places. Those foreigners who settled in Manchester, chiefly to profit from its expanding economy, were portrayed as tangible proof that newcomers were judged not by their origins or beliefs but by such qualities as enterprise, benevolence and commitment to the urban good. Manchester, Disraeli believed, was a New Athens, the centre of a liberal civilisation hewn out of industrial and commercial rock.

Successive Manchester historians and antiquarians bought into these notions to develop the myth of a benevolent cosmopolis. So Louis Hayes could write in 1905:

> Our foreign trade brings us into contact with almost all nationalities, and makes us probably more cosmopolitan in our views. We welcome to our shores … men from all part of the world – Parthians, Medes, and 'the dwellers in Mesopotamia, Jews Cretes and Arabians'. Manchester makes no distinction as to creed or race. She opens her portals and offers an equal chance to all those who wish to settle here to trade and get gain … . We have attracted to our city very many foreigners who have settled amongst us and been a strength to us in every sense of the word – men who having made Manchester their adopted home, have been ready and willing to give liberally of their time, their money, and their energies to the promotion and furtherance of all good works, and have supported with no niggardly hand the various charitable institutions for which we are honourably distinguished.[4]

Such a view sits easily with a reading of British refuge history in which, with varying emphases, refugees, under the guidance of well-intentioned British, including British Jewish, supporters, and in an essentially benevolent British society, are seen to have rapidly and effectively accommodated themselves to 'the British way of life', to have transferred their loyalties to the country of their adoption, and to have amply 'repaid' the British nation by the levels of their contributions to British life.

These are the central themes, for example, of Malet and Grenville's *Changing Countries*, the first study of the adult refugee experience to be based upon the oral testimony of the refugees themselves. Analysing interviews conducted with thirty-four refugees, supposedly from 'a wide range of backgrounds', Malet, Grenville and their co-authors have concluded that most refugees were able, once in Britain, 'to continue the processes of assimilation' (into non-Jewish society) which they had begun in their countries of origin.[5] The refugees were 'remarkable', in Malet and Grenville's view, 'for their strength in surmounting the traumas of persecution and exile, as well as for their achievements in their adopted homeland, which was and continues to be greatly enriched by their presence'.[6] They were 'overall … an unusually gifted and resourceful group of men and women':[7] their testimony offers, the authors believe, 'living proof of their commitment to British society'.[8]

It is in these senses that the history of Jewish refugees has been readily accommodated within what, until relatively recently, has been the dominant Whig interpretation of British Jewish history. The history of the British Jewish 'community', it has been argued, has been one of steady and often spectacular progress, achieved through the medium of a self-propelled cultural integration encouraged, managed and monitored largely by a wealthy and beneficent communal elite. In Britain, successful integration has relegated anti-Jewish sentiment to the social and political margins and provided the Jewish people with the space and opportunity to create institutions based upon their own special and specific needs. It was an interpretation of British Jewish history which at one and the same time stroked the egos of British Jewish leaders, reassured members of the Jewish mainstream and so excited politicians like Margaret Thatcher that they saw the path chosen by the Jews as the one to be urged upon all subsequent immigrant settlers in Britain. During the 1930s it was Nathan Laski's view of the Manchester Jewish community, or, at any rate, his view of what the Manchester Jewish community ought to be.

The history of those refugees who arrived in Britain from Fascist Europe between 1933 and 1945 has been set in a very similar frame. Their rescue has been portrayed as proof of the continuing strength of Britain's liberal tradition, their integration and their subsequent contributions to British life both as evidence of the transforming power of liberal toleration and as its just reward. Once in Britain, they were seen, by and large, to have accepted the kinds of leadership, to have subscribed to the forms of integration and to have conformed to the kind of values on which the acceptance of the established community was seen to be based. The refugee narrative has effectively been incorporated into the success story which is the history of British Jewry, a process, it must be said, aided and abetted by many of the refugees themselves, inevitably grateful in the first instance, for their removal from Nazi soil.[9]

In compiling a review of the activities of the Manchester Jewish Refugees Committee in August 1942, its then chairman, Morris Feinmann, placed some emphasis on this notion of the reciprocal relationship between Britain's liberal tradition and refugee contributions. 'For centuries', he wrote, 'Great Britain had had its doors wide open to the persecuted peoples of France, Germany, Russia and other countries. In every case the generous hospitality of the British people was ultimately repaid by the rich contribution the new arrivals made towards the country's progress in industry, commerce, science and art ... What has been true of the past is even more true today ... Refugees, whether in HM Forces, industry, science or other sphere, already hold a fine record of service and, I think, the Government has every reason to congratulate itself on its decision to admit refugees in reasonably large numbers and, later on, on giving them the opportunity to make themselves useful.'[10]

A similar scenario was constructed by leading refugees soon after the Second World War. In a volume published in 1951 to commemmorate the tenth anniversary of the foundation of the Association of Refugees in Great Britain, Hans Reichmann, the vice-chairman of the Association, suggests the way in which Britain's 'welcome to the outlaws' – a 'great humanitarian act by the British government', in his view, and one compounded by 'a general atmosphere of kindliness and solicitude' – would be followed by the 'modest contributions' of the refugees themselves and by 'the future achievement of our young generation'. The 'debt' owed by 'the flotsam and jetsam' to whom Britain 'opened its doors' would thus be 'repaid'.[11]

The result is, at best, a partial history of the refugee experience. It is a history from which the more ambiguous response to refugees of the British government and the British people has been excised. It is a history which gives little, if any, space to those who, for reasons political or religious, failed to pursue the goal of ultimate integration: members of the political Left, some of whom maintained their Socialist or Communist ideals to the extent of returning to their homelands after 1945 to participate in their reconstruction, all of whom were likely to find fault with aspects of the capitalist society which was their new home; young Zionist refugees, like those brought to the Manchester region by Bachad and Hashomer Hatzair, who single-mindedly pursued their object of training in Britain for future participation as skilled pioneers in the creation of a Jewish state, and who never saw their presence in Britain as anything but a passing phase on their route to Zion; religiously Orthodox refugees, like those who arrived in Manchester through the efforts of Rabbi Dr Solomon Schonfeld, by the Manchester Women's Lodge of B'nai Brith and by the Manchester Yeshiva, who sought with equal single-mindedness to ensure that opportunities existed in Britain for the pursuit of the kind of strict religious observance to which acculturation was seen to pose a threat; those too damaged by their experiences to formulate positive goals of any kind; and those who, for reasons both aspirational and perverse, led lives which failed to match up to the preferred values of a conforming Jewish mainstream. It is a history from which the dark, the discordant and

4

the damaged have been excised: a history without nonconformity, deviance or, for that matter, failure.

As questionable as the ease of refugee integration is the benevolence of the society which received them. Manchester, in particular, was proud of its 'liberal tradition in the whole field of human endeavour'.[12] The liberal press believed that the city had 'long identified itself with movements to remove barriers and to safeguard the right and well-being of the individual'.[13] A 'letter of thanks to the Refugees living in our city', published in the *Manchester City News* early in 1944, and written by the local Congregationalist minister, William Hodgkins, ends with these words: 'Through all the inconveniences and tragedies of your coming here, and your stay, you will have seen deep down into the hearts of English people and you will have reason to know that the finest social and Christian influences of which this country is capable have been exercised on your behalf'.[14]

Central to this reading of refugee history is the 'gratitude' to be expected from refugees. The way in which the preferred outcome of Jewish communal history (for some) may determine the reading of its content, may also affect the way personal experience is reconstructed, especially if the instrument for its reconstruction is the human memory. What is seen by an individual as the successful or desirable outcome of his or her life may prompt the memory to construct the personal past as its inevitable precursor: as a series of experiences, that is, leading inexorably to a desirable and inevitable outcome. This may be particularly true of a personal history intersected by such traumatic upheavals as the involuntary, and perhaps isolated, departure from the homeland, knowledge of the tragic fate suffered by loved ones left behind before which the refugee was impotent. The problem with refugee history is that, like Jewish communal history, it is framed in terms of what is seen as ultimate success. And as with communal history, what this may mean is that the privations, the losses, the failures experienced en route are, at best, glossed over as tiny glitches in a personal progress leading, in the case of refugees, to personal, cultural and economic success. Or that the experiences of those whose personal trajectory through the refugee experience deviated from the desirable are either minimised as exceptions or altogether ignored. Such tendencies will inevitably be increased in the case of refugees who were told in the past, and reminded in the present, that a failure to conform to recipes of success is, at best, a risky undertaking.

'Gratitude' is also explicable in terms of the genocidal fate of European Jewry, a fate which could in no way have been anticipated by refugees of the 1930s as the probable outcome of Nazi anti-Semitism. Their gratitude is essentially retrospective. It was only after 1942 that they came to know of the tragedy from which they had been saved and before which the privations they suffered in Britain could readily be written off. The Holocaust casts a shadow over the memories of those whose admittance to Britain spared them its consequences. It was only in this context that 'for those coming from the Continent', Britain was, in Fred Uhlman's memorable phrase, 'a haven and a heaven'.[15]

This study seeks to restore a sense of balance to Manchester's role in refugee history: to assess the degree to which the people and institutions of a supposedly liberal British city like Manchester actually reached beyond their everyday concerns to help the victims of European Fascism find a haven of safety. It throws questions around the view of Manchester as a 'liberal city'. It asks what it was about those who did reach out which caused them to do so; which differentiated them from an indifferent majority. In Holocaust history, the Manchester population might have been designated 'bystanders' to the unfolding tragedy wished by the Nazis upon those judged to have been unworthy of membership of the Third Reich. There is now no way of knowing how these Manchester bystanders might have responded to a Nazi occupation and the implementation in Britain of Nazi policies of exclusion. All that is possible is to try to understand why certain people and particular institutions played roles in the work of rescue, while others did not, and to explore the constraints, external or self-imposed, which limited the scope for action even of the genuinely well-intentioned.

Since the late 1980s, aspects of the experience of refugees from Fascist Europe have attracted the interest of British historians. Marion Bergahn's *Continental Britons: German-Jewish Refugees from Nazi Germany* (Oxford 1988) represented a pioneering, if controversial, analysis of the impact of the refugee experience on the Jewish identity. In *Second Chance: Two Centuries of German-speaking Jews in the United Kingdom* (Tubingen 1991), Werner Mosse brought together a number of important academic studies on the refugee experience and particularly on the role of refugees in British life. The impact of refugees on British culture was the subject of Daniel Snowman's *The Hitler Émigrés* (London 2002). No one has done more to remind the British people of the centrality of the refugee heritage than Tony Kushner in his ground-breaking studies (with Katherine Knox), *Refugees in the Age of Genocide* (London 1999) and, more recently, *Remembering Refugees* (Manchester 2007). What this book shares with Kushner is a critical stance towards Britain's liberal tradition, a stance evident in Kushner's first book, *The Persistence of Prejudice, Anti-Semitism in British Society during the Second World War* (Manchester 1989) and accorded a wider frame in *The Holocaust and the Liberal Imagination* (Blackwell 1994).

The response of the British government to refugees of the Nazi era has been explored by A.J. Sherman in *Island Refuge: Britain and Refugees from the Third Reich 1933–1939* (London 1973), by Bernard Wasserstein in *Britain and the Jews of Europe 1939–1945* (Oxford 1979) and, most recently, in Louise London's classic study, *Whitehall and the Jews 1933–1948: British Immigration Policy, Jewish Refugees and the Holocaust* (Cambridge 2000). What is lacking in the growing literature around the subject is a consideration of those responses from the perspective of the places in Britain in which refugees sought settlement or to which they were directed by the agencies of refugee support. It is this gap in the historiography which this book addresses. London's emphasis is on the considerations of national self-interest which limited the British government's willingness to rescue the Jews of Europe: the fear, for example, that the arrival of an unlimited number of Jewish immigrants at a time of economic depression was likely to arouse the sleeping giant of anti-Semitism, or that undue concessions to refugees would undermine the British policy of appeasement. The evidence used for the present study does not lend itself to a critique of London's thesis. What it does is suggest the degree to which British policy towards refugees filtered down to people and institutions in a particular city and the ways in which local conditions reinforced (or, less frequently, contradicted) its messages.

There is no attempt to assess the collective responses of 'Manchester', a subject as elusive as the collective anti-Semitism and xenophobia of the 'British people', and which might well lead to an image of the city as equally stereotypical as its liberality.[16] Anecdotal evidence cited by refugees ranges from perceptions of Britain as a nation of ingrained anti-Semitism and anti-foreign feeling to the view of it as a benevolent and humanitarian haven of saftey. All that is attempted here is to define the responses of relatively well-defined sectors of the Manchester population: the Jewish and Quaker communities, the University of Manchester, the Lancashire Industrial Development Council, the Manchester branch of Rotary International, the Catholic hierarchy of Salford Diocese, the German Lutheran Church, Manchester's 'Little Italy', the fee-charging schools in the Manchester region, and the 'exceptional people' who stand out from the crowd in the personal initiatives they took to ensure the safety of refugees. It may be that this is as far as the historian can realistically reach in seeking a 'popular' nation-wide or city-wide response.[17]

Notes

1 Saul Friedlander, *Nazi Germany and the Jews 1933–1939: The Years of Persecution* (London 1997), p. 338 fn30.
2 Bernard Wasserstein, *Britain and the Jews of Europe 939–1945* (Oxford 1979), p. 7.
3 *Manchester and Salford Woman Citizen*, No. 243 (January 1939), p. 1.
4 Louis M. Hayes, *Reminiscences of Manchester and Some of its Surroundings from the Year 1840* (Manchester 1905), p. 286.
5 Marian Malet and Anthony Grenville (eds), *Changing Countries: The Experiences and Achievement of the German-Speaking Exiles from Hitler in Britain from 1933 to Today* (London 2002), p. 4.
6 *Ibid.*, p. vii.
7 *Ibid.*, p. 148.
8 *Ibid.*, p. x.
9 *Britain's New Citizens: The Story of Refugees from Germany and Austria* (London 1951), celebrating the tenth anniversary of the Association of Jewish Refugees, is set in this reciprocal framework.
10 Report of the Activities of the Manchester Jewish Refugees Committee, 14 August 1942, by Morris Feinmann (Manchester City Archives M533/1/2/2/6).
11 Hans Reichmann, 'Tribute to Britain', in *Britain's New Citizens*, p. 9.
12 Leader in MCN 30 July 1943.
13 MCN 26 March 1943.
14 MCN 4 February 1944.
15 Fred Uhlman, *The Making of an Englishman* (London 1960), p. 203.

16   For a recent statement of the negative view, see Milena Roth, *Lifesaving Letters: a Child's Flight from the Holocaust* (Seattle and London 2004), pp. 5, 121, 164. Milena left Prague with the Kindertransport in July 1939. For her, the British people, 'some shining examples' apart, responded to refugees with racism and xenophobia. For a strongly positive view, Hanna Behrend, *Autobiography* (unpublished 2004), p. 1.

17   For a broader approach, however, see Tony Kushner, *The Persistence of Prejudice: AntiSemitism in British society during the Second World War* (Manchester 1989).

2

Speak no evil: Manchester Jewry and refugees, 1933–1937

Early in 1938 the Manchester Ladies Lodge of B'nai Brith, probably the most influential women's organisation in Manchester's Jewish community, persuaded the director of Manchester Central Library to stage a 'Jewish Book Week' on 4–9 April of that year.[1] The prime mover was almost certainly Collette Hassan, president of the lodge and the wife of a Sephardi cotton merchant, Victor Hassan. It was Collette Hassan who became chairman of a Jewish Book Week Committee of thirty-four prominent members of the Jewish community and who wrote the introduction to the brochure associated with the event. Preparations were proceeding smoothly in March 1938 as in Europe Nazi anti-Semitism, which had already excluded Jews from the political, academic and economic life of Germany, reached an early peak following the German occupation of Austria. The entry of the German army into Vienna on 15 March was followed by anti-Semitic violence on an unprecedented scale. And yet the introductory brochure makes only one passing reference to events in Europe: a note of the German-Jewish architect, Erich Mendelssohn, as being 'amongst many distinguished exiles from Germany now giving of their best on Britain's upbringing'. The articles in the brochure, on 'The Jew and the Book' by the Manchester Hebraist and Zionist, Isaiah Wassilevsky, on 'Objects of Ceremonial Service and Ritual' by Revd Joseph Pereira Mendoza, minister of the Withington Congregation of Spanish and Portuguese Jews, on art and music by Mrs A.P. Simon, also the wife of a Manchester Jewish cotton merchant, make no reference to events in Europe. It might be assumed that the emphasis on the Jewish contribution to civilisation and on the Jewish religious experience, and the inclusion of ten works by prominent Zionists in a list of fifty 'recommended books', were counter-blasts to the Nazi treatment of Jews, Judaism and Jewish aspirations, but nowhere is this stated.

It was not as if the organisers of Jewish Book Week were unaware of what was happening in Germany and Austria or of its significance for their co-religionists. The anti-Semitic policies and actions of the Nazis had been reported in detail since 1933 by the judeophile *Manchester Guardian* and in the *Jewish Chronicle*, the national Jewish paper most commonly read by members of the Manchester community. As a member of the B'nai Brith

Ladies Lodge, Collette Hassan was well aware of young Jewish women leaving Nazi Germany as domestic servants: since 1935 the Lodge's Hospitality Committee had given at least sixty of them a degree of financial and social support. She was also a Manchester representative on the Grand Lodge of B'nai Brith in London which was equally giving sustenance to young refugees. There had been in Manchester a fund-raising Committee of the Central British Fund for Germany Jewry since 1933; by the April of 1938, Manchester contributions to the fund exceeded £200,000. It was almost as if, while knowing precisely of the anti-Semitic disaster that was unfolding in Germany, and empathetic towards its victims, the Jewish Book Week Committee, which included two prominent and otherwise articulate Jewish City Councillors, Leslie Lever (Labour) and Abraham Moss (Liberal), felt constrained not to talk about it in public.

This was certainly true of Nathan Laski, president of the Manchester Jewish Representative Council for all but one of the years between 1930 and 1941 and of his barrister son, Neville, president of the Board of Deputies of British Jews between 1931 and 1939. In an article published in the weekly *Manchester City News*, on 4 November 1939 and entitled 'The Man Who Knew But Would Not Tell', Laski is reported as saying 'My son [Neville] and I have felt it our duty as loyal British citizens to respect the Government's desire and keep our silence'. Although some stories had leaked out despite their efforts, the 'worst stories' of those who bore 'physical and mental scars of their treatment at Hitler's hand' had not yet been told. Although he had 'lain awake night after night weeping over these horrible things' and one of 'his closest helpers in the work of relief' had 'broken down and is now a mental case', Nathan Laski had judged it to be disloyal to endanger the British Government's policy of appeasement at least until the outbreak of war had rendered it obsolete. It was not lack of concern or compassion that had informed his silence, that is, but his sense of patriotism.

It had equally prevented him from giving too open a welcome to those seeking to flee Germany after 1933, who, in large numbers, might have been seen as a threat to the British workforce, and who, in whatever numbers, could be construed, as were their co-religionists from Eastern Europe at the turn of the nineteenth century, as a threat to a supposed 'British identity'. This was not so much a response invented by Laski as part of a tradition of communal leadership deferential to the British state and culturally subservient to what it saw as the British identity. Since the struggle for political equality in the 1830s and 1840s the leaders of the community had been persuaded by the currency of discourse around emancipation to believe that the acceptance and safety of the community depended on the offer of proof of its loyalty and its intent on integration into respectable and orderly sectors of British society. Such a belief had been pressed home by the adverse publicity accorded to Jewish immigrants arriving from Eastern Europe in the late nineteenth and early twentieth centuries. In responding to press attacks on the alien habits, supposed exclusivity and 'threat' to native welfare posed by the immigrants, the community had created or reinforced agencies of 'anglicisation' designed, in the language of the time, to 'iron out the Ghetto bend' by 'converting Polish into English Jews'. The arrival of more Jewish immigrants was a particular concern for Laski, himself a member of a family which had fled Russia for Britain in the 1870s, and who had been party to the abuse of his co-religionists. He was worried equally that the acceptance of refugees from Germany, like outright critiscism of German anti-Semitism, would mock the government's policy of appeasement. It was his expectation that the funds collected by the Central British Fund (CBF) in Manchester would be used primarily to improve the 'absorbent capacity' of Palestine, the yardstick by which Britain, as the Mandatory authority, determined the scale of Jewish immigration.[2]

The truth is that, under the leadership of Laski, the Manchester community, numbering perhaps 40,000 people in 1933, was ill-equipped to respond other than financially, to the crisis of German Jewry. The response to refugees of the Representative Council of Manchester and Salford Jews (otherwise the Jewish Representative Council), the only communal body which might have orchestrated collective communal support,[3] was very largely conditioned by the Council's interpretation of its overall role in the community and particularly by the interpretation pressed upon it by Nathan Laski.[4] Already over seventy when the refugee influx began, Laski's constitutional authority was reinforced by an impressive personal charisma, striking oratorical powers, prestige and respect as a merchant and JP in the city, marriage to the prominent and popular Liberal City Councillor, Sarah Frankenstein, his own leadership of the Liberal Party in north Manchester, political skill in mobilising and manipulating allies within the community, and dictatorial inclinations which few, if any, of the community's lesser activists were prepared to challenge. According to his successor, Abraham Moss, he had deliberately confined his interests to the Jewish community, when he could have reached 'the highest public honours'.[5] In the political world of British Jewry he never sought more than membership of the Board of Deputies. When, in 1932, he signalled his desire to relinquish the presidency of the Representative Council, temporarily as it turned out, he was pressed to accept an honorary Life Presidency; according to one Council veteran 'his association with the Council was so valuable that it was essential to have his name as being at the helm'.[6] He was, in the words of one obituarist, 'King' of the Manchester Jews.

The Council which he dominated had been founded in 1919, and remained in 1933 essentially as a mechanism of communal defence, designed to ward off the threat of anti-Semitic assault, in part (to use Samuel Finburgh's phrase) by defending 'the fair name of the Jew',[7] in part by mediating with the civic authorities on the community's behalf. The aim was 'to counter anti-Semitism wherever possible'.[8] This was thought to be achievable in large part by massaging the communal image. The Council worked, for example, 'to prevent Chillul-Hashem [communal shame] by reducing the number of Jewish disputes appearing in the courts'; it intervened privately to settle literally hundreds of civil cases involving everything from domestic disputes to conflicts between Jewish employers and their workers, or Jewish landlords and their tenants, in a private court in Laski's home on Smedley Lane, Cheetham Hill.[9] Competition between communal institutions was resolved before it undermined the image of 'cohesion' on which the effectiveness of the Council's mediating role depended.[10] This role it saw as one to which it was exclusively entitled: a running battle was fought with communal mavericks, lay or clerical, who rushed into print or into action on issues of concern to the community without first seeking its assent.[11] The Council's Press Committee, set up in June 1933 and chaired by Laski, was defined as the only means of access for the press to 'official and authoritative' information 'relating to Jewish matters'.[12] The Council saw anything but a measured response to the anti-Semite as a potentially 'disastrous';[13] knee-jerk reaction by individuals, Laski believed, itself 'breeds anti-Semitism'.[14]

Two assumptions underlay such strategies. One centred on the perceived role of Jewish behaviour in anti-Semitism: the belief that supposed Jewish 'failings', large and small, played a crucial part in generating hostility towards the community, a supposition apparently intensified by the 'vices' attributed to Jews in Nazi propaganda. In January 1934, Samuel Finburgh, then the Council's vice-president, warned his colleagues of 'the fault of ostentation among our people'.[15] In May of that year, the Council's executive became anxious that 'so many Jewish boys [in Manchester] were limiting their professions to two or three only ... a vital factor in the German-Jewish problem'.[16] Their solution was to set up a Juvenile Employment Advisory Bureau which, inter alia, encouraged the Manchester Jewish young to take up work as motor or wireless engineers, bricklayers and plasterers, telegraph and trolley boys, policemen, nurses, gardeners and cinema projectionists.[17] During 1937 the Council took special steps to prevent Jewish builders from 'sweating' their workers, Jewish bakers from baking on the Jewish Sabbath and Jewish shopkeepers from ignoring the regulations imposed by the Sunday Trading Bill: 'it was necessary', Laski told the Council, 'for us to be 100% perfect employers'.[18] Manchester Jewish shopkeepers preparing a militant response to the Sunday Closing Act of 1937, which, in its draft form, would have compelled the closure of all shops at 2p.m. on Sundays, were urged by Laski to exercise 'patience': the difficulties, he believed would be resolved.[19] During 1934–35 Laski even denounced the appearance of 'unauthorised [Jewish] collecting boxes' on the streets of Manchester as a 'scandal' which 'ought to be stopped'.[20]

The second of the Council's assumptions was of a generally benevolent non-Jewish society, in which the anti-Semite was a marginal figure and, for this reason, a militant response to anti-Jewish sentiment was inappropriate and potentially counter-productive. The isolated anti-Semite might be better silenced by more or less gentle persuasion, by sensitive diplomacy, or, in the last resort, by mobilising the civil authorities in the community's defence. To over-react to hostility would also be to question the depth of an integration on which the community prided itself and on which it believed its welfare to ultimately depend, and to throw unwarranted aspersions on the goodwill of the

Christian majority. It was only when he felt sure that he had the Manchester public on his side that Laski settled for a more robust response to the anti-Semite.[21] Fearful of traditional perceptions of Jewry as 'separate' or 'exclusive', the Council found it necessary to constantly reiterate the degree to which the community's interests coincided with those of the city and the nation. Laski viewed Manchester Jewry's Memorial Service for King George V which the Council mounted in the Great Synagogue in February 1936 as 'one of the highest manifestations of loyalty of any portion of the citizens of the Empire'; the synagogue itself was so crowded that at least 1,000 people had to be turned away.[22] During 1936–37, after appeals had been launched for German Jewry, the Council joined forces with the Jewish Literary Society to raise £600 for the Lord Mayor's Unemployment Fund.[23]

By deploying these essentially deferential, even apologetic, and certainly cautious, strategies of defence, Nathan Laski believed that, in and outside the Council, 'he had at all times worked hard to keep the prestige of Jews high in the estimation of his fellow citizens'.[24] But within his thinking, and particularly within his distaste for projects within the community not sanctioned by its Representative Council, there were also more mundane considerations: matters, that is, of money and manpower. Neither Laski personally nor the Council as a whole could look favourably on 'unauthorised' departures which ran the risk of over-stretching or misapplying the limited human and financial resources of a voluntary community already committed, by 1933, to the provision of funds and resources for thirty-six synagogues, twenty-eight charities, eighteen Zionist societies and another twenty or so communal organisations vital to its religious identity and the welfare of its members.

In these circumstances, and with these priorities, the arrival of refugees from Nazi Germany presented the Council with a serious challenge. Sympathetic as it naturally was to the plight of German-Jewry, could it afford to lend its support to the entry of Jewish refugees whose presence was seen by the British people as likely to adversely affect the prospects of the native unemployed and so foment anti-Jewish feeling? Laski himself, brought to Manchester as a child by his Russian immigrant parents and as an emerging communal leader in the 1890s, had been put on the defensive by the vehemence of anti-alien sentiment in Manchester. Would not the encouragement of refugees constitute a classic example of the Jewish community pursuing its 'particular' interests at the expense of the well-being and order of the nation? Although the issue was never debated, the evidence suggests that, in these years, the Council did everything it could for German Jewry, short of publicising its suffering and open support for a refugee settlement in Manchester which might have disturbed the valuable equilibrium which was seen to exist between the city and the community.

There is no doubt that local communal leaders shared the compassion of their London counterparts for their German co-religionists and their desire to offer help. At a special meeting of the Council convened by Laski on 21 May 1933, Laski characterised 'the tragedy that was being enacted in Germany' as worse even than its depictions in the British press. 'Sacrifices

must be made', he told the meeting, to help German Jews and it was necessary to demonstrate to the world that 'the Jewish community was prepared
to make a sacrifice'. It was necessary to establish a Manchester Fund, which
he was himself prepared to open with a donation of £500.[25] After attending
the public launch of the CBF in London, where he became one of its vice-
presidents, he called a second Special Meeting of the Council in Manchester
on 25 May at which a committee of leading local activists was set up under his
chairmanship as the Manchester Committee of the Central British Fund for
German Jewry.[26] Four Manchester appeals raised a total of well over £225,000
between May 1933 and July 1938.[27]

While committing itself financially to the cause of German Jewry, however,
the Council was less anxious to encourage refugee settlement in Manchester.
It shared with the CBF a belief that the ideal destination for refugees was
the Holy Land. Palestine, Laski believed, was 'the only place ... that the Jew
could enter without reproach and with security'; there was no longer any
excuse for non-Zionists not to contribute to Zionist funds.[28] In the face of
growing fears from 1936 that the Mandatory Power intended to restrict,
even to suspend, Jewish immigration into Palestine, the Council was ready
to back protests to the British government and send deputations to the MPs
of Lancashire and North Cheshire.[29] In 1936 the annual Palestine Bazaar, a
regular fund-raising mechanism for Manchester Zionists, described itself as
the 'German-Jewish Refugee Palestine Bazaar Fund'. In January, an anonymous Lancashire sportsman staged a midnight matinée at the Manchester
New Hippodrome, with Robert Donat and George Formby, to raise money
for a fund of that name: Palestine was 'the sole avenue for the rescue of those
co-religionists who are suffering untold miseries under the Nazi iron heel':
it offered the only 'permanent and constructive' solution to 'the German
problem'.[30] If Germany was an example of the fate of diaspora Jewry, according to Rabbi S.M. Lehrmann, minister of Manchester's prestigious Higher
Broughton Synagogue, then the only way forward was to Palestine.[31]

Refugees in person, and in Manchester, were another matter. Of the
£12,700 collected in Manchester for the second German Appeal, only £48 was
set aside for 'local relief'.[32] The Jewish community at large was not (openly)
encouraged, let alone pressed, to gear itself for refugee support. On two occasions between May 1933 and early November 1938, the Council Executive
praised the efforts of Jewish individuals who, in their private capacities, were
affording some hospitality to refugees, although without offering them its
backing or according them the official status they desired.[33] In March 1934
it refused Joseph Mamlock's request that a small Hospitality Committee set
up by the Manchester lodges of the Order B'nai Brith should be taken on
by the Council as one of its sub-committees.[34] The Council's caution with
regard to refugees was intensified after May 1934 by its long engagement
with the British Union of Fascists (BUF) and with what it interpreted as an
escalation in the number of anti-Semitic incidents in Manchester, most of
them fomented, it believed, by Fascist propaganda. This was also the view of
perceptive and sympathetic non-Jewish citizens. In November 1936, in a City

Council debate on an application from the BUF to demonstrate in Hulme, the Manchester Labour Party Alderman, Wright Robinson, accused BUF activists of using 'all kinds of epithets' to 'outrage the feelings and sentiments of an important section of the community' and so provoke it to violence.[35] In reality, the reluctance of the Representative Council to condone anything like a violent response to the BUF arose from that same fear of provoking an anti-Semitic backlash that inhibited its support of refugees. After March 1934 the fate of refugees did not come up for discussion within the Council Executive until July 1938. By April 1937 Laski had even run out of patience with the raising of funds for causes beyond the Manchester community. The Jews of Manchester, he believed, 'had done their duty by the German and Palestinian funds'; it was time to focus on 'local causes'.[36]

There were only two official exceptions. One was a contribution from funds raised by the German appeals to support a programme set up by Manchester University which enabled selected German academics to obtain temporary fellowships, an exception rendered innocuous in his eyes by the respectability of the small number of applicants, and perhaps a reciprocation for the honorary MA conferred on Laski by the university senate in December 1932 in recognition of his active association 'with many public movements both of Jewish and non-sectarian character' and of his long chairmanship of the Manchester Victoria Memorial Jewish Hospital.[37] Laski's other exception, in fact, was the making use of refugee expertise to shore up the Jewish hospital. During 1936–37 the hospital employed at least two German refugees: Charlotte Sochaczewer in November 1936, as a technical assistant in its X-Ray department, and Werner Kupperman, who had arrived in Britain in 1933 and attended the Medical School at Edinburgh University to validate his qualifications before joining the hospital in March 1937.[38]

In responding 'loyally' to events in Germany and the needs of refugees, it was the image of the community that mattered to a man like Laski. For the leaders of the Jewish community, it might be argued, there was a clear distinction between the private and the public spheres. What could not be said by Jews in the public arena of Manchester society, for fear of threatening the repute – and therefore the well-being – of the community, could be said with safety within the bounds of communal life. So Laski could confess to his Council, but not to the public, his horror at what was happening to the Jews of Germany. And what, for the same reason, could not be done in public, Jewish leaders might well choose to do in private. This was true, for example, of support for refugees.

In the light of Laski's attitude to refugee settlement and the jealously guarded authority of the Representative Council, it is otherwise difficult to explain the rudimentary agency of refugee support set up, apparently in 1933, by a relatively obscure local jeweller and communal worker (but a long-time member of the Jewish Representative Council), Isidore Apfelbaum. Eight years later, on the point of his retirement from work with refugees, Apfelbaum offered a brief account of his early involvement to a reporter from the *Salford City*

Reporter, which published it under the title, 'Saved Hundreds of Refugees: Broughton Man's Outstanding Work'.[39]

When Nazi persecution began, Apfelbaum told the *Reporter,* he had been 'approached by a number of people in the district with relatives in Germany … to see if there was any way of bringing them over to this country … Soon the appeals became an overwhelming spate which meant throwing everything up and working day and night seven days a week … The stories we heard from the men, women and children who came over were so terrifying that it was beyond anyone with human feeling to withdraw'. While claiming that 'an organisation of some kind was hastily put together' with the cooperation of Nathan Laski in Manchester and Otto Schiff in London, he added that 'the work for five long years remained our personal responsibility'. Apfelbaum claimed to have brought 'hundreds of families out of Germany' by persuading his 'friends and sympathisers' to act as their guarantors, and, 'when the government gave permission for young people to be found jobs as trainees, I myself placed over 1,000 youths in such jobs'.[40] 'Many of Salford's best known employers,' he added, 'were kindness itself in making room for these unhappy young people, many of whom did not know where their parents or relatives were, and in every case we took the greatest care to see that no Salford worker or youth was displaced'.

On the face of it, this was a very private venture. Its affairs were conducted from Apfelbaum's house at 17 Wellington Road East, Higher Broughton, and from the offices of his firm at 42 Bull's Head Yard, a dreary alleyway off Market Place, in central Manchester. In spite of Apfelbaum's subsequent claim, there is evidence to suggest that Apfelbaum's maverick work with trainees was conducted without reference to the Jewish Refugees Committee in London and to the occasional embarrassment of Otto Schiff, anxious as he was to keep refugee work under his own control and within the limits set by the British Home Office. What Laski was later to describe as 'stories [of Apfelbaum] which make "thrillers" seem tame', to Schiff threatened the diplomacy which characterised his link with the Home Office. Apfelbaum intervened in person at the Home Office when young refugees who had smuggled themselves on to a KLM plane which landed at Manchester's Ringway, were ordered back by the Immigration Officers at the airport. Finding 'nobody at the Home Office', and learning that the plane was refuelling at Prague, Apfelbaum 'rushed' to the Czech Ambassador, and when he 'refused to do anything', phoned a friend in Prague to ensure that the boys would be detained. In the week which followed he obtained permits from the Home Office for the boys' entry to Britain as trainees, allowing them to return to Manchester 'and so escape certain death'.[41] What to Apfelbaum was (if true) an adventure, to Schiff was a risk too far.

Laski himself, however, appears to have tacitly condoned the work of a man some saw as his 'right-hand man' in his pursuit of communal power.[42] On at least one occasion he praised Apfelbaum's work at a meeting of the Representative Council. In later years he was to depict Apfelbaum as the leading figure in what became the Manchester Jewish Refugees Committee

(MJRC), much to the consternation of those who were, in reality, its official leaders. It is just possible, although now beyond proof, that behind a public image of deterring refugee settlement in Manchester, Laski was prepared to sanction, even to initiate, a secret operation. This would have been in keeping with Laski's approach to communal politics. Opinions of Apfelbaum as a person differ. Rae Barash, with whom he was later to work on the MJRC saw him as 'pompous, bumptious and unpopular, but hard-working'. His pursuit of personal kudos was later to provoke a crisis within the Committee which led to his resignation. No statistics remain of his achievements before November 1938.

One of the only two practical responses by Manchester Jewish institutions to the refugees in these early years came from the Manchester Women's Lodge of the Order B'nai Brith, founded in April 1926 as the first women's branch of the Order in the English provinces and only the second in Anglo-Jewry.[43] It was a response apparently stimulated, independently of Laski and the Representative Council, by the Grand Lodge in London of an autonomous Order with branches throughout Europe and with wide international contacts.

Members of the influential Manchester men's lodge, the Dr Moses Gaster Lodge No. 720, itself the second branch of the Order in England, saw the role of the Manchester sisterhood they helped to create as being 'to assist the Men's Lodge in their activities' and 'to co-ordinate Women's Work in Manchester'.[44] Its membership initially confined to fourteen 'near relatives of the Brothers of the Order', it was accorded the right to co-opt 'any woman whose help would be to the advancement of the Order' and, in fact, its founder-members, at the prompting of their first president, Nathan Laski's daughter-in-law (Neville's wife), Cissie Laski, set out immediately to recruit 'certain influential women' from local Jewry.[45] Drawing members from, in particular, the wealthy and influential Sephardi families of the south Manchester suburbs – the Hassans, Florentins, Dweks, Nahums, Leons and Shabetais amongst others[46] – the lodge evolved rapidly into what was almost certainly the community's most powerful women's organisation. Working always in cooperation with the men's lodge, and its policies subject to the ultimate control of the male-dominated and London-based District Grand Lodge of Great Britain and Ireland, in practice the Manchester Women's Lodge enjoyed a sufficient degree of autonomy to afford its sisters wide scope for independent action. They, in turn, had all the confidence of a select middle-class sisterhood of culture, respectability, intelligence and material comfort.

The lodge's main activities lay within the general parameters of what, by the mid-1920s, had become the Order's priorities: the promotion of communal philanthropy, communal 'harmony', communal defence, and the furtherance of the Zionist enterprise. It raised funds, provided donations and supplied volunteers to local Jewish charities. In particular, in the late 1920s, it adopted the cause of the new Lymm Holiday Home for (Jewish) Mothers and Babies, providing regular donations of £50–60 towards its annual overheads and maintaining some of its 'convalescent Jewish children'.[47] It helped in cases of individual need brought to its attention. Its 'Social Workers Bureau' maintained a pool of young Jewish women ready to serve as 'willing workers' for any local Jewish charity. It arranged outings, 'treats', entertainments and holiday camps for children from poor Jewish homes. It regularly protested at the incidence of anti-Semitism and, in the same mood, mounted public lectures on Jewish history, formed panels of speakers 'to address non-Jewish audiences', and identified itself closely with the Zionist cause. It contributed financially to Jewish institutions in Palestine, offered its services to such local Zionist events as the Zionist Central Council's Annual Bazaar (at which it regularly ran a profitable Fruit and Flower Stall) and gave its unreserved backing to the Zionist leadership in 'pressing on towards the goal of its 2000 years old aspiration'.[48] It functioned as part of an international organisation in its own right, linked by formal channels of communication and by personal contacts with continental lodges, particularly those in Germany. Its members offered hospitality to German-Jewish students. In July 1931 a Manchester sister brought back greetings from a women's lodge she had visited in Carlsbad.[49]

The sisters of the lodge saw themselves, perhaps, as a Jewish segment of a wider movement of self- assertion by intellectual women of progressive and liberal inclinations; the organisations to which they affiliated included the National Council of Women, the Manchester and Salford Women Citizens Association (WCA) and the Jewish Peace Society. Collectively, they stood for the extension of the rights of women, particularly of a social background similar to their own. The lodge's affiliation to the WCA in June 1933 was partly 'to represent Jewish opinion' on its counsels and to find sympathetic platforms for 'explaining the Jewish position' in Germany; but it was also used to promote wider causes. Invited in December 1933 to compose a resolution to be put to the WCA's annual conference, the lodge chose one which pressed for the appointment of more young women to the children's courts.[50] The early outside speakers to the lodge included the secretary of the Council for the Amelioration of the Legal Position of the Jewess.[51] A prominent lodge member, Flora Blumberg, was active in the Manchester, Salford and District Mother's Clinic, a campaigning organisation which successfully countered the refusal of municipal clinics to offer birth control advice.[52]

In the case of support for German-Jewish refugees, whose interests first came up for discussion at the lodge in May 1933, self-assertion was more problematic. Word came down from the District Grand Lodge 'that the name of the Order might not be used in any scheme for helping refugees' for fear of Nazi retaliation against the German lodges, none of which had yet been closed down by the regime.[53] 'In the event of our brothers and sisters in Germany requiring hospitality in England', members were asked 'to provide for such a contingency', but in their private capacities.[54] A similar stance was taken towards the boycott of German goods: while the boycott was 'not recognised officially', 'all members of the Order were asked to boycott all German goods'.[55] It was the Grand President's view that 'nothing could be done in connection with the trouble in Germany by members of the Order as such. Whilst he wished all members to help individually it was obvious that the name of the B'nai Brith must not be used.'[56] B'nai Brith's inadvertently named 'General Refugee Committee' was rapidly transformed into its 'Hospitality Committee'.[57]

The Manchester Women Lodge's first move in support of refugees was in response to the decision of this London Hospitality Committee to open a hostel in London for young German women students, 'so that those who could not offer hospitality in their own homes might contribute weekly amounts to the upkeep of the hostel'.[58] The idea was well received in Manchester, where a subscription list was opened.[59] It was only when a refugee doctor staying with one of the lodge members was denied status as a student by the Home Office that a decision was taken in July 1933 'to earmark all money given [for the hostel] by members in south Manchester to Golda Susman's private fund for the use of this doctor and his wife'.[60] It was not until October, after the District Grand Lodge had again 'stressed the necessity of finding hospitality and assistance for German refugees', and after the two Manchester lodges had been adressed by fleeing German Jews, that such private efforts began to give way to collective action by the Manchester Women's Lodge. By early November steps were already being taken by the lodge president, Henrietta ('Etty') Myrans, to form a local 'Hospitality and Advisory Committee',[61] and the process was completed on 4 December, when, at Myrans' invitation (Sister) Schwab, a B'nai Brith representative on the German-Jewish Aid Committee at Woburn House, spoke to the lodge of 'the necessity for a Hospitality Committee in Manchester'. The 'nucleus' of a committee, of men and women, under the chairmanship of Golda Susman, was put together at the same meeting and the decision taken to transfer for its use whatever remained of the local collection for the London hostel;[62] Joseph Pereira Mendoza, minister at the Withington Congregation of Spanish and Portuguese Jews, was taken on as the committee's honorary secretary.[63]

The evidence does not exist to prove how long the committee remained in existence, or to assess its achievements. From the start it appears to have lacked consistent financial support from members of the lodge. Reporting on its work in June 1934, Susman appealed for subscriptions 'in place of those who had ceased to contribute'. Some 'girls' had been placed, her report read, and changes made when the homes to which they had been assigned were found 'incompatible'. Five people were then being supported by the committee at a total cost of £8 6s 0d a week.[64] English classes and social events were being held, very probably at the home of one of the more active committee members, Rae Barash, in Withington in south Manchester, whose housekeeper gave talks to refugee domestics on such English mysteries as cleaning the grate and stoning the front step.[65] In December 1934 Susman made a further appeal for subscriptions, as 'money was still very much needed to meet the demands made on the Hospitality Committee'.[66] The committee remained active in November 1935, but by the time a luncheon was held 'in aid of German-Jewish women and children' in March 1936[67] such aid as the lodge was giving to refugees had become piecemeal and sporadic; occasional responses to particular cases of need rather than a consistent strategy. The work of the Hospitality Committee, if it still existed, no longer appears amongst the reports of the lodge's other sub-committees. When, in the following November, the lodge was called upon by the District Grand Lodge to 'adopt a [refugee] child', its decision was that it 'could not do anything in this matter at this date'.[68] In the two years which followed, there were signs of apathy not only towards refugees, but towards the general work of the lodge. Attendance was falling off, subscriptions not being regularly paid, promises made at the ceremony of initiation not being kept.[69] It was none the less the memory of Rae Barash that in its active phase the Hospitality Committee had found placements as domestic servants for sixty refugees.[70]

The declining activity of the lodge was accompanied by what read like indications of a lodge driven onto the defensive by anxiety (not unlike that of the Communal Council) that the escalation of anti-Semitism in Germany was having repercussions in England. One reason why the lodge decided, in February 1934, to invite all German-Jewish refugees in Manchester to its Purim Social was because 'it was considered undesirable to concentrate these people in large numbers in any non-Jewish place'.[71] In April that year, in what appears to be fear of the exact replication in Manchester of anti-Semitic diatribe in Germany, there was serious concern at the lodge at the number of Jewish students in England training for the legal and medical professions. Discussion of 'the means of diverting them from professional to other occupations' was followed by a lodge member (Sister Sless) being deputed to collect relevant statistics from the University of Manchester. Although Sless found that no such statistics were available, she drew attention to alternative openings for Jews in courses for chiropody and engineering for which few Jewish students had enrolled. There was, she added, a 'tendency amongst Jewish professionals to treat their professions as businesses and thus ... lower the dignity of them'.[72] In a similar vein, in December 1935, the lodge passed by 17 votes to 16 an internal motion 'that the spread of anti-semitism in England is largely brought about by ourselves'. It may be that in such an atmosphere, while it was acceptable for the lodge to press 'both actively and publicly for the restoration of the rights of Germany Jewry', to discuss 'the Refugee Question', to lend some help to particular refugees, even to initiate a refugee member who had belonged to a German B'nai Brith lodge,[73] systematic action to facilitate the entry of refugees was judged to be unnecessarily provocative.

The only Manchester Jewish institution which in the early 1930s was in a position to facilitate the entry to Britain of German-Jewish students of religion, the Manchester Talmudical College (otherwise the Yeshiva), was in these years heavily preoccupied with problems of its own, and particularly with the establishment, in a community undergoing critical cultural and physical change, of an identity which would render it financially viable without surrendering its religious integrity.

Founded in 1911 in 'small cramped premises' in Broughton Street, Cheetham,[74] on the initiative of three Russian immigrant rabbis,[75] the Yeshiva had provided the community with its first internal facilities for a higher religious education. From the start, its managers had seen themselves, quite consciously, as countering the assimilatory pressures of the Manchester (and, by extension, the western European) milieu. They were the self-conscious guardians of a 'spiritual lighthouse'[76] of Eastern European *Yiddishkeit* in the dangerous high seas of assimilation, secularity and apathy which threatened to engulf the communal young. According to one of them, 'hardly 5% of the Manchester Jewish community ... could be said to have a real knowledge of the Torah and Talmud'; it was 'to bridge the gap, daily growing wider, between the older generation of Jews who had had the advantages of a proper Jewish education in their youth, and the new generation, who had little, that the Yeshiva was a vital and indispensable necessity'.[77] Although generating a small but steady stream of 'graduates' as 'Rabbis, Ministers, Shochetim and Teachers', the main purpose of the Yeshiva had always been 'to produce lay orthodox Talmidai Chachomim in the full orthodox traditional sense';[78] in the words of the chairman of its Education Committee, 'to make 100% Jews'.[79] This was as much a matter of the ambience of the Yeshiva as its teaching: 'knowledge was itself not sufficient, it must be combined with practice'.[80] In 1933 full-time and part-time students were being taught (chiefly in Yiddish) by a small body of teachers headed by Rabbi Moshe Yitzchak Segal, the saintly and inspirational Rosh HaYeshiva (Principal), who had been recruited from the staff of London's Etz Chaim Yeshiva in 1913.[81] The administration of the Yeshiva (including its financial management) was in the hands of a 'general committee' of laymen, some of its members elected by the subscribers, some representing Manchester's more orthodox congregations,[82] of which the long-standing president in 1933 was Israel Libbert.

The Yeshiva ranked itself with the major centres of Jewish learning in continental Europe. One former student of the Telzer Yeshiva in Lithuania, who in the 1930s served as chairman of the Education Committee of the Manchester Yeshiva, believed that it 'compared quite favourably with continental Yeshivas as regards learning and more than favourably as regards the care it took of the students'.[83]

Given the Yeshiva's aims, a majority of the students were on full or part-time course which began when they were aged thirteen and ended at sixteen; only a selected few went on to a more specialised professional training. The Yeshiva was a religious institution with a religious head but a lay management. No student could be admitted without first being examined not only by the HaYeshiva, but by the Education Committee. The few who could readily afford it paid fees and met some or all of the cost of their board and lodging; most attended free of charge and were fully maintained from funds collected from regular subscribers. The structure of life for the full-timers resembled that of European Yeshivoth. Morning prayers at 8a.m. were followed by a 'time of learning' which stretched on weekdays from 10a.m. to 1p.m. and from 3.30 to 7.30p.m., with only the Friday afternoon free. There was no sleeping accommodation at the Yeshiva. The students were boarded out with carefully selected orthodox families, taking only their meals on the Yeshiva premises. On Sabbaths and Holy Days, however, in the style of European *bocherim*, students were expected to identify families which, as a mitzvah, would provide meals freely. Student discipline was solely in the hands of the HaYeshiva, with the single reservation that students were to be dismissed only with the approval of the committee. Appointments, however, even of rabbis and teachers, were the responsibility of the lay committee.[84]

But while modelling themselves on institutions central to the kehilloth of Eastern Europe and utterly convinced of – and constantly reiterating – the indispensability of their institution to the religious well-being of the Manchester community, the Yeshiva's managers were engaged in a more or less continuous rearguard action against those, very probably a communal majority, who, at best, saw no reason to give it their personal support and, at worst, perceived it as the symbol of a reactionary religious culture in a modernising, anglicising and suburbanising community. Those identified by the Yeshiva's committee as indifferent or inimical to its interests included parents 'apathetic to Jewish learning',[85] communal leaders who failed to 'bring home to the community' the importance of Yeshivas,[86] mainstream Jewish clergy 'who should really have been the first' to come to its assistance, and local *chedarim* (amongst which, with some irritation, it included the communal Talmud Torah) which failed to encourage their pupils to seek out its higher religious education.[87] It was said that only one local cheder teacher, the Yeshiva's own graduate, Jonah Balkind, regularly directed his more talented pupils to the Yeshiva's preparatory classes.[88]

This was a good deal more than the paranoia of a caucus of religious idealists. The Yeshiva came under sporadic attack in the early and mid-1930s as a cultural anachronism both in the local Jewish press and from local communal leaders like the Lancashire County Councillor, Samuel Taylor, who believed he had a justifiable 'grievance' against the Yeshiva (and attended a committee meeting to voice it) in that Yiddish was being used as the main medium of instruction.[89] Influential communal figures who were known to hold similar views included the architect, Joseph Sunlight,[90] and Rabbi Dr. Simon Lehrman, minister of the highly anglicised and communally powerful Higher Broughton Synagogue;[91] in all probability they were held, if in varying degrees, by most, if not all, the leaders of the community's mainstream. The local weekly, the *Jewish Gazette*, called the Yeshiva authorities to account for failing to provide their students with the secular knowledge, professional skills and fluency in English necessary for their survival and the exertion of influence in an Anglo-Jewish community.[92] It was only in the Eastern European communities of the past, the *Gazette* believed, that the Jewish young could secure 'their material future' without the advantage of secular learning.[93] Another common formulation of the attack on the Yeshiva's supposed cultural backwardness was that it 'occupied itself too much with the mind and too little with the body'. [94] The Yeshiva itself believed that those who failed to subscribe to its funds used its supposedly 'old-fashioned' methods as their excuse.[95] Dr. Israel Slotki, the long-standing director of the communal Talmud Torah (religious school), who saw himself as providing the religious education best suited to 'English boys'[96], spoke of the Yeshiva with some contempt, not simply as un-English, but as lacking 'system' in its administration and as failing to impose due discipline on its students, whom, he professed to believe, 'fight and do not study'.[97] He not only failed to encourage his boys to go on to the Yeshiva, Rabbi Segal believed; he actively discouraged them from doing so.[98]

In the Yeshiva's view, the Talmud Torah, with its 700 boys and girls, in 1933 'the largest Hebrew Schools in the country',[99] failed to provide 'the proper orthodox atmosphere' in which an authentically Jewish life might be nurtured; the boys leaving the school 'were not observing Jews'.[100] Its exclusive use of English was a barrier to true Jewish understanding; only through the medium of Yiddish might the Talmud be properly understood Slotki's proposal, in January 1937, that a teacher-training course be set up for Yeshiva students wishing to teach at the Talmud Torah received short shrift from Segal: the Yeshiva students 'required no training from the Talmud Torah'; the Yeshiva itself 'gave all the necessary training and had turned out many good teachers'.[101] The Yeshiva Committee, which had sought the compromise of a joint training course, came to the conclusion that collaboration with the Talmud Torah had been 'discussed and rediscussed almost ad nauseam' and was now impossible 'as the religious ideology of the two institutions and of their respective principals were not compatible'.[102] The Yeshiva's perceived need to fight such endless and fruitless rearguard actions on behalf of 'true Judaism' was as potent a distraction from the 'refugee problem' as its constant need to seek funds in a community 'beset and besieged from all sides by appeals'.[103] Nor did such actions help to resolve its perennial financial problems: plans for a fund-raising concert to be held jointly by the Yeshiva and the Talmud Torah at the end of 1937 almost came to grief when the latter was found to have booked female performers.[104]

It was because it differed so markedly from the Talmud Torah that the Yeshiva attracted a particularly withering assault on its 'policy, curriculum and administration' from Nathan Laski, for whom it was one of the last strongholds of Jewish cultural insularity. On one occasion, Laski sought to insist on the Yeshiva submitting itself to a 'commission of enquiry' made up of his own rabbinical nominees, all reliably integrated into the Anglo-Jewish religious establishment, threatening the alternative of a critical letter to the press.[105] Laski's verbal 'violence' the Yeshiva was able to evade, if only after angry correspondence.[106] More difficult to deal with were the financial impications of the community's perennial indifference and occasional hostility. The Yeshiva was, it believed, the Cinderella amongst communal institutions,[107] its 'sorry financial position'[108] entailing the periodic suspension of rabbinic salaries and student maintenance, incessant public appeals and canvasses for new subscribers, searches for new means of raising funds, repeated reminders to (hard-pressed) committeemen to respond to moments of crisis with a greater sense of urgency, and delicate negotiations with bank managers pressing for a reduction of (usually) increasing and unsecured overdrafts.[109] In 1933 its debts stood at over £700.[110]

These were hardly the circumstances in which the Yeshiva might have reached out for refugee students whose arrival seemed likely to further increase the demands on its resources. This was particularly true after March 1934, when the Yeshiva committee began its search for 'new and more dignified premises'[111] which might enhance its communal credibility and, subsequently, its appeal for the funds necessary for the purchase, refurbishment and furnishing of two houses in Seymour Road, Crumpsall, that might ultimately be 'a source of pride to Manchester'[112] and a 'turning point in the Yeshiva's history'[113]. Months of intensive fund-raising, rendered no easier by Laski's hostile intervention and by the Yeshiva's own decision, on religious grounds, to rule out both the card parties suggested by its Ladies Committee and female entertainers from its fund-raising concerts[114], ended only on 6 September 1936 with the opening of new premises to replace the dilapidated building at 215 Cheetham Hill Road which the Yeshiva had occupied since 1919.[115] The *Jewish Gazette* commented that although Nathan Laski would not appear at the consecration ceremony 'because of differences of opinion about the curriculum', the rumour that he had pressed the Chief Rabbi to absent himself was unfounded.[116] Set in its own grounds, the new building, comprising two solid Victorian mansions, was said to contain 'a Synagogue, large, airy classrooms, a library, a dining room, offices and kitchens' and to be 'centrally heated throughout'.[117]

The Yeshiva's earliest engagement with the issue of refugees was on 21 January 1934, when the committee considered an application for entry from a fourteen-year-old Berliner, Nathan Lindenberger. After deciding to seek a reference for Lindenberger from Berlin, the committee went on to discuss, for the first time, 'the possibility of admitting students from Germany'. The decision was that five such students might be admitted 'as a beginning', and that Rabbi I.J. Yoffey, the Yeshiva's secretary, should get in touch, for this purpose, with the German rabbinate.[118]

The fact that the decision was not followed up for over two years may perhaps be put down primarily to the Yeshiva subsequently according priority to the planning and financing of its new premises. It may also have been the case, however, that the project lost the inspirational guidance of Rabbi Yoffey, a leading Mizrachi Zionist and the well-loved and highly respected minister of the Central Synagogue, who died in April 1934 in Alexandria during an intended visit to Palestine. Later evidence suggests that in the affairs of the Yeshiva, rabbinical idealism might occasionally override the natural priority accorded by the laity to its financial viability. Lindenberger was in fact admitted for the summer term of 1934,[119] but the combined evidence of the Yeshiva's committee minutes and surviving lists of entrants suggest that only four other foreign applicants were considered between 1934 and March

1938 and that, of these, only three actually arrived, two from Germany (one of them via the Gateshead Yeshiva), one from Czechoslovakia. Their support did not involve the Yeshiva in any significant financial outlay. The committee agreed to pay for the board of one of the German boys, Rosenheim, who arrived in September 1936, but called upon him to meet his own costs of accommodation in private lodgings;[120] in the case of the second, Rosenbaum, who had perhaps arrived a little earlier, the Yeshiva accepted the financial burden of his board and lodging, but in return for some teaching duties.[121] Joseph Weis, a Rumanian residing in Czechoslovakia, was accepted in April 1937, only after he had been 'given a good character' and the Manchester businessman Philip Allweis, one of the representatives of the New Synagogue on the Yeshiva committee, had undertaken to underwrite all his material requirements.[122] In supporting refugees in these early years, the Yeshiva's expenditure was increased by perhaps 16s a week.

The imperatives of its internal development probably provide only part of the explanation of the Yeshiva's lukewarm response to refugee applicants before 1938. It was also, perhaps, an outcome of the Yeshiva's perception of its priorities in the face of the escalating forces of assimilation in both Manchester and Germany. In Manchester, what Walter Wolfson saw in 1937 as the Yeshiva's indispensable role in fostering religious knowledge and observance, was no doubt reinforced by the escalating movement of Jewish families from a close-knit 'Jewish Quarter', in which they comprised a majority and in which Jewish religious traditions provided a strong force for cohesion, to a more scattered, a more privatised and potentially a more materialistic existence in northern suburbs dominated by non-Jews. A minor symbol of the potentially corrosive effect of suburban Englishness was the creation in 1932 by a group of Jewish businessmen, most of them living in Prestwich, of a golf club open to its exclusively Jewish members on Saturdays.

In their perceptions of events in Germany, it may be that for the strictly observant orthodox, such as those who managed the Yeshiva, the religious apathy of German Jewry was more a matter of immediate concern than its insecurity. In May 1936 the lay president of the Manchester Yeshiva, reflecting on the growth of anti-Semitism in Britain and Germany, informed a *Jewish Chronicle* reporter that 'the answer to anti-semitism was more semitism, the answer to anti-Judaism was more Judaism'.[123] The Sephardi solicitor, Reuben Barrow Sicree, president of the Manchester Shechita Board, and one of the Yeshiva's most powerful friends amongst the communal leadership (he was often called upon to preside over its public meetings), informed the audience at a Yeshiva prize-giving ceremony in January 1936 that 'he brought a lesson from Germany, where … the Jews had tried to out-German the Germans and what had followed – persecution. He had come into contact with German Jews, and many of them did not have a spark of Jewishness in them. Judaism was heading for a landslide and its only salvation lay in educating its youth in the Torah and Talmud and raising it to have a greater respect for the Jewish faith and the observance of its tenets.'[124]

Another 'escape route' for the Jewish orthodox was provided by the recruitment of German religious functionaries to posts in the Manchester community. In the context, Germany provided as useful a source of Jewish religious learning and rabbinical experience as the more traditional recruiting ground of Eastern Europe. British universities could draw upon a pool of academics displaced by Nazi policies, so British Jewish communities could now fill religious vacancies from a German rabbinate increasingly beleaguered by Nazi anti-Semitism.

The first was Rabbi Dr David Feldman, a man of Eastern European origin, recruited from Leipzig in 1934 by the nascent Manchester orthodox pressure group, Machzike Hadass (literally, 'those who strengthen the law'), the creation of a body of immigrant businessmen from Brody in Austrian Galicia to counter what they saw as 'the fire of assimilation raging furiously'.[125] In August 1925 nine men had met at the house of the Jewish fent dealer, Herschel Heilpern, to inaugurate the Machzikei Hadass Society (MH), with the initial object of reforming the local structure of *shechita*, but with the longer-term aim of converting the community to what they saw as 'authentic' orthodox practices. The appointment of Feldman as their rabbi in 1934 marked a new stage in their development completed when, in the spring of 1938 a prominent MH member, the furniture dealer, Abraham Jacob Pfeffer, purchased a mansion at 17 Northumberland Street in Higher Broughton (ironically, from the BUF which had used it as their headquarters) as a 'strictly orthodox synagogue', Yesode Hatorah ('foundations of the Torah'), which became the focus of MH's missionary endeavour. Feldman, a man of deep religious learning, personal charm and administrative ability provided MH with a status which, in the long term, created in Manchester one of the leading orthodox *austritt gemeinde* (independent communities) of western Europe.[126]

In parallel with the development of MH was an attempt by Reuben Barrow-Sicree, the Sephardi president of the Manchester Shechita Board, beginning in 1934, to consolidate the structure of Manchester's less extreme orthodoxy by the appointment of a 'Communal Rabbi', a post unknown in Manchester since the first decade of the century.[127] The person appointed, who would become 'Chief of the community in all matters spiritual', head of the Manchester Beth Din (religious court) and adviser to the community on religious education, 'must be (in Sicree's words) a man of distinguished orthodox renown, a profound Talmudical scholar and possessing an equally profound English secular knowledge'. If the stated object was to raise the general standard of religious orthodoxy in Manchester, from the subsequent discussions it is possible to detect less lofty motives. One was to increase the Manchester community's bargaining power with the Chief Rabbi in London, the supreme religious authority in British Jewry; another to counter the local influence of MH. It may be that this was also part of a personal power struggle between Barrow-Sicree and Nathan Laski. By enhancing the status of the Shechita Board, to whom the Communal Rabbi would be responsible, Sicree might effectively undermine the authority claimed by the Manchester Jewish Representative Council under Laski's presidency. It was perhaps for this reason that for four years, in spite of several communal conferences on the issue, the matter was unresolved.

It was probably the departure of three Manchester rabbis for posts elsewhere during 1936–37 that had induced sufficient harmony between the Shechita Board and the Representative Council to set up a Selection Committee. After considering and rejecting a number of local candidates, in mid-July 1938 the committee decided that, if he 'could be brought out of Germany, the post might be offered on probation to Rabbi Dr. Alexander Altmann', a thirty-two-year old rabbi in Berlin, then 'in daily fear of [the] Concentration Camp'. Given £50 to meet his travelling expenses, Altmann arrived in Manchester in mid-September 1938. He was officially inducted by the Chief Rabbi, with whom a modus vivendi had also been worked out, on 4 December 1938. His appointment, Sicree believed, would mark the opening of a 'new epoch in the history of Anglo-Jewry'. In fact, a man of high secular and religious learning and, like Feldman, of Eastern European origin, Altman brought to Manchester a commitment to 'modern' German orthodoxy which was ultimately to lead him into conflict with MH and to divide the community religiously along lines still visible within the Manchester community.

Although neither Feldman nor Altman were 'refugees' in the normal sense, both welcomed their Manchester exile. Feldman had already been planning his departure from Germany before he received the call from MH (which he accepted in preference to a similar call from Antwerp), while Altman's acceptance of the Communal Rabbinate might also be seen as part of an escape plan for himself and his family.

Refugee academics and industrialists, trainees supported by Isidore Apfelbaum's 'private' operation, German domestic servants placed by the Ladies Lodge of B'nai Brith, the two or three foreign students accepted by the Yeshiva, the two German 'refugee' rabbis, and the handful of pacifists and Jewish 'Friends of Friends' supported by the Quakers represented the only known refugees from Nazism to have arrived in Manchester before November 1938. A now unknown number may have arrived by their own devices, some as students, or with their families, although the total number of refugees in Manchester probably did not exceed 500 in November 1938 and may have been considerably less. In any event, in these years only 10,000 Jewish refugees in total had left Germany and Austria for Britain. In spite of an escalating 'war against the Jews', many had delayed their departure in the belief that the Hitler regime would be as short-lived as its predecessors or, at any rate, that his anti-Semitism had been no more than a device for the achievement of power. Others were naturally reluctant to uproot their families, disrupt their livelihoods and leave the towns and villages of which they had come to feel a part. Nazi policies came as a shock to those who had come to see themselves as German and Austrian as their Christian neighbours. To depart would have meant a radical ideological shift which few of them were as yet prepared to make.

While Laski found difficulty with any action on behalf of refugees which seemed likely to injure the repute of the local community or which ran counter to the wishes of the British government for a rapprochement with Germany, there was one category of refugee whose evident respectability and whose potential contribution to British life was acknowledged by the government, to whom, while not taking the initiative, he was prepared to offer a degree of patronage: those German academics, most of them Jewish, who, from 1933, were being driven from their posts by the Nazi regime and whose experiences are the subject of the next chapter.

Notes

1 The brochure which accompanied the exhibition, with some correspondence relating to it, is in the archive at Manchester Central Library.
2 Laski had risen gradually through the hierarchy of Manchester Jewish institutions from the presidency of the Manchester Great Synagogue in the 1890s. In 1933, apart from his presidency of the Representative Council, he was president of the Jewish Board of Guardians, the central charity of the community, and of the Manchester Jewish Hospital, and a Manchester delegate to the Jewish Board of Deputies;, the parliament of British Jewry in London, of which his son Neville, a barrister, was elected to the presidency in 1933. His other son, Harold, was a Professor at the London School of Economics, a writer on Communist theory and chairman of the Labour Party.
3 This is not to suggest that the Council's writ was universally accepted within the community. It had no powers of coercion and was given to periodically 'reaffirming' its authority (JRC EC 18 September 1932, QM 17 May 1936).
4 Laski resigned the presidency to make way for the Salford Alderman, Samuel Finburgh, in 1934, only to return to the position following Finburgh's death in March 1935. Elected 'Life President' at the time of his resignation, from 1935 he assumed both titles.
5 MCN 23 February 1940.
6 JRC EC 18 September 1932.
7 JRC EC 28 January 1934.
8 *Ibid.*
9 JRC EC 28 January 1934 and 20 June 1934, 23 July 1936.
10 JRC EC 18 September 1932.
11 E.g. JRC EC 28 June 1933, 14 March 1934, 18 September 1935.
12 JRC EC 28 June 1933, 14 March 1934.
13 JRC EC 25 May 1933. The word is used here in relation to the proposed boycott of German goods.
14 JRC EC 28 June 1933.
15 JRC EC 28 January 1934.
16 JRC EC 6 May 1934.
17 JRC EC 25 June 1935. The Bureau held its first sitting on 21 July 1935.
18 JRC AGM 25 April 1937. See also MCC EC 14 July 1937, QM 18 July 1937.
19 MG 4 May 1937.
20 JRC EC 23 August 1934, 13 March 1935.
21 For example, when in 1935 he issued a public rebuke to a candidate for the City

Council who had cast aspersions on his Jewish opponent, Leslie Lever (MG 1, 5, 6, 11 November 1935).

22 JRC QM 12 February 1936.

23 JRC Annual Report for 1935–37, p. 3.

24 JRC EC 28 January 1934.

25 JRC Special Meeting 21 May 1933.

26 JRC Special Meeting 25 May 1933.The committee was made up of Laski as chairman, Norman Jacobs as honorary secretary, Samuel Finburgh, a former Mayor of Salford and Conservative MP, and the businessmen S.H. Steinart, Louis Kletz, Dan Kostoris, Alphonse Nahum, Joseph Mamlock, Major E.C.Q. Henriques and Lionel Boyars.

27 JRC Special Meetings 21 and 25 May 1933; EC 13 March and 10 November 1935; QM 28 July 1938. The figures given in the minutes are incomplete. The second appeal raised £12,070, the third at least £3,000, the fourth (specifically for Austrian Jewry) at least £9,200.

28 JRC Special Meeting 25 May 1933.

29 JRC EC 15 July and 7 September 1936, 26 January 1938. MCC Annual Report for 1937–38, p. 4.

30 MCN 17 January 1936; Selig Brodetsky to the annual conference of the Zionist Federation in June 1933 (MG 19 June 1933).

31 MG 29 October 1934 in a talk at the Holy Law Synagogue, 'Whither Jewry?'

32 JRC EC 18 September 1935.

33 JRC EC 14 March, 1934; AGM 10 November 1935.

34 JRC EC 14 March 1934. For this committee, see Chapter 13.

35 MSWC No. 219, November 1939, p. 11. Wright Robinson was a trade union organiser who had been elected to the City Council in the Labour interest and who had now been elevated to the Aldermanic Bench. The outcome of the debate (by 53 votes to 48) was that the BUF should be allowed to hold its demonstration in St George's Park, Hulme, but only on condition that no uniforms were worn. The decisive factor was the fear of some leading councillors that the Council would otherwise be accused of interfering with the right of freedom of speech.

36 JRC AGM 25 April 1937.

37 Meeting of the University Senate 12 December 1932.

38 Salford Aliens Register 1602E and 1603E. Refugee doctors were required to undertake a further course before being placed on the British medical register.

39 SCR 10 April 1941. Apfelbaum's business premises were destroyed in the Manchester Blitz of December 1940. His son was killed in action early in 1941. He told the reporter: 'I feel I have done my duty for the refugees and that I deserve a rest to deal with my personal affairs.'

40 These figures must be treated with care. By the time the article was published in 1941, a Manchester Jewish Refugees Committee had been in operation for over two years, with Isidore Apfelbaum as the honorary director of its 'Industrial Committee', responsible for the placing of trainees. The figures in the article almost certainly include refugee families and trainees brought to Manchester after November 1938. This would not be the last time that Apfelbaum was to exaggerate the results of his work with refugees.

41 MCN 4 November 1939.

42 Unconfirmed information from the late Hymie Gouldman, whose father was a member of the Representative Council.

43 Records of B'nai Brith Women's Lodge of Manchester No. 87 (henceforth WLMBB) in Manchester Central Library's Local Collection (M341). Minutes of the Inaugural Meeting, 28 April 1926.

44 *Ibid.*

45 *Ibid.* Cissie was the daughter of the Sephardi Haham (Chief Rabbi) of the Sephardim in Britain.

46 By the mid-1930s it included members of leading Ashkenazi families from north and south Manchester, including the Meeks, Weisgards, Blumbergs, Blonds and Goldstones.

47 MWLBB CM 30 April 1928, 9 May 1929. Apparently it maintained those children chosen by the lodge for residence at the home.

48 MWLBB Lodge Minutes 3 November 1930.

49 *Ibid.*, 6 July 1931.

50 MWLBB CM 20 December 1933.

51 *Ibid.* 5 December 1932.

52 Blumberg was one of the three leading founders of the clinic in 1925 (the others were Clarice Frankenburg and Mary Stocks). She was its chairman in 1935 (Information from Clair Debenham).

53 *Ibid.* 12 June 1933.

54 *Ibid.* [May 1933].

55 *Ibid.* 12 June 1933.

56 *Ibid.* [May 1933].

57 *Ibid.* 3 July 1933.

58 *Ibid.* 12 June 1933.

59 *Ibid.*

60 *Ibid.*

61 *Ibid.* 6 November 1933.

62 *Ibid.* 4 December 1933. Another influence on the lodge was that of Cissie Laski, who had left Manchester for London and was there engaged in refugee work at Woburn House (MWLBB CM 22 November 1934, 17 January 1935, when she spoke to the lodge on 'Some aspects of the refugee problem').

63 JRC AGM 10 November 1935.

64 *Ibid.* 4 June 1934.

65 *Ibid.* 6 November 1933, 4 June 1934. Notes on a conversation between the author and Rae Barash c. 1971 (hereafter Rae Barash interview).

66 MWLBB Lodge Minutes 3 December 1934.

67 *Ibid.* 3 February 1936.

68 *Ibid.* 9 November 1936.

69 *Ibid.* 2 May, 13 June, 4 July 1938.

70 Taped interview with Rae Barash by Bill Williams, 1975 (J15 in the tape collection of the Manchester Jewish Museum).

71 MWLBB Lodge Minutes 5 February 1934.

72 *Ibid.* 9 April, 7 May 1934.

73 *Ibid.* 3 December 1934, 4 February and 3 June 1935, 3 February and 8 June 1936, 3 May 1937. The refugee member was 'Sister Tutuer', first referred to at a meeting of 3 May 1937.

74 MY EC 10 June 1942. A résumé of the Yeshiva's history by Rabbi M.I. Segal. Segal's account places the original building in Carnarvon Street. A more likely sequence given in *The Manchester Talmudical College 40th Anniversary Souvenir Report* (1951) places it in Broughton Street, from where it moved after a few months to Stocks Street and then, in 1918, to Carnarvon Street. In the following year it moved to a house at 215 Cheetham Hill Road donated by the Manchester businessman. Baruch Meir Bloom, which remained its premises in 1933.

75 JT 22 June 1956. The three rabbis were Mendel Dagutsky. Israel. J. Yoffey and H. Levein (*Manchester Talmudical College Souvenir Report*, p. 75).

76 JG 7 February 1936.

77 MY GM 18 April 1937. The speaker was Walter Wolfson, a Manchester solicitor, who first joined the Yeshiva committee in July 1936.

78 MY Joint Meeting of the Yeshiva's Education Committee and the Executive of the Talmud Torah, 21 October 1934. The speaker was Rabbi M.C.E. Golditch, then a teacher at the Yeshiva, later its salaried secretary. For comments to similar effect, MY Education Committee 7 March 1934.

79 MY Joint Meeting 21 October 1934.

80 *Ibid.*

81 JC 12 November 1937, JG 11 November 1955. Rabbi Segal died in 1947; he was buried in Manchester, but re-interred in Israel in 1954 at the request of his son, Rabbi J.W. Segal, who succeeded him as Principal of the Manchester Yeshiva. Other teachers at the Yeshiva in the mid-1930s included Rabbi M.C.E. Golditch and Rabbi Dubov.

82 Particularly, it seems, judging from the known allegiances of its committeemen, from the Roumanian, Rydal Mount, United, New, Higher Crumpsall and Central Synagogues.

83 MY GM 2 October 1938.

84 An incomplete and undated list of regulations is enclosed in the minute book of the Yeshiva for 1933 onwards. Other information (but from 1951) is enclosed in the *Manchester Talmudical College Souvenir Report*. From the minutes it seems clear that neither the General Committee, which met monthly, nor the Executive, which met irregularly, nor any of the Yeshiva's sub-committees (chiefly for education, finance and boarding-out) felt bound by any clear definition of their roles and jurisdiction.

85 MY Education Committee 7 March 1934.

86 *Ibid.*

87 MY Joint Meeting 21 October 1934.

88 *Ibid.* and MY Education Committee 1 November 1939.

89 MY Finance Sub-Committee 3 June 1934. The committee's reply was that English was used for the teaching of T'nach, Grammar and History, but that for Talmudical studies 'English was considered both inadvisable and practically impossible.'

90 MY Joint Meeting 21 October 1934.

91 MY Education Committee 7 March 1936. The Higher Broughton Synagogue was the chosen place of worship of an anglicising orthodox elite of Eastern European origin: its members in the 1930s included Simon Marks and Israel Sieff, the controlling partners of the Marks and Spencer empire.

92 JG 7 February 1936. All 1930s editions of the (Manchester) *Jewish Gazette* were destroyed by enemy bombing during the Second World War; the references here are to cuttings in a scrap book kept by the Yeshiva authorities.

93 *Ibid.* The argument was that in Eastern Europe there were adequate communal posts for the religiously educated, while Jews in their supposedly typical roles as middlemen required no professional training.

94 JG 10 April 1936. The *Gazette* believed that this criticism would be adequately dealt with by the recreational facilities provided in its planned new premises.

95 MY CM 21 January 1935, MG 3 February 1936.

96 MY Joint Meeting 21 October 1934 op.cit. In Slotki's view, ' English boys could only be given the education they were fit for, and the Talmud Torah gave the best education for such boys.'

97 MY Joint meeting 21 October 1934.

98 MY Education Committee 14 June 1936. Rabbi Segal believed Slotki was attempting to increase his sphere of communal influence to embrace the Yeshiva (MY EC 27 January 1937).

99 MCN 27 March 1933.

100 MY Joint Meeting 21 October 1934.

101 MY EC 27 January 1937.

102 MY 31 January 1937.

103 JG 10 April 1936.

104 MY CM 14 November, 12 December 1937; Finance Committee 16 December 1937.

105 MY CM 23 July 1937. His nominees were 'Rabbi Abramsky (London), Rabbi Dr. Herzog (Dublin), Rabbi J.J.Unterman (Liverpool), Rabbi Dr E.W. Kirznir (London) and the local Beth Din'.

106 MY CM 30 July, 6 August 1936. The correspondence itself has not survived. From the minutes it seems clear that, in spite of the intense anger of some of its members, the Yeshiva committee attempted a conciliatory response before opting for total silence.

107 MY CM 24 December 1933.

108 *Ibid.*

109 E.g. MY CM 2 and 22 April, 13 May, 2 September 1934, Finance Sub-Committee 22 and 29 April, 6 May and 3 June 1934 and *passim*. The Yeshiva was entirely dependent on funds raised through subscriptions, donations, (rare) legacies, fund-raising events such as concerts and raffles (many, like an annual 'American Tea', organised by its Ladies Committee), collections at funerals and unveilings, the placing of collecting boxes in Jewish homes and workshops, and public appeals, often promoted through the synagogues of the Yeshiva's supporters (e.g. see Balance Sheet attached to MY CM 24 December 1933). Unlike the Talmud Torah, whose teaching programme was more acceptable to the communal elite, the Yeshiva (although not without trying) failed to identify the kinds of major donor who might readily have sustained it. Amongst those whose support it sought to woo during the 1930s (all without success) were Israel Sieff, S.H. Steinart, George Rose, Isaac Wolfson, Montague Burton, B.J. Globe and 'a Sassoon' (e.g. MY CM 7 June, 12 July and 30 July 1936, Appeal Dinner Sub-committee 3 November 1938, FC 13 November 1938). Its precarious financial situation also persuaded the Yeshiva to seek to maintain cordial relations with Nathan Laski, whatever his known reservations about its objects and methods.

110 MY CM 30 September 1936: Libbert's comment on the financial position at the time he first assumed the presidency.

111 MY Education Committee 7 March 1934.

112 MY CM 8 March 1936.

113 MY GM 18 April 1937.

114 MY Building Committee 19 April 1936, CM 14 November 1937, Finance Committee 16 December 1937.

115 MG 7 September 1936.

116 JG 28 August 1936.

117 *Manchester Talmudical College Souvenir Report*, p. 75.

118 MY CM 21 January 1934.

119 List of entrants, Summer term 1934.

120 MY CM 27 September 1936.

121 MY CM 25 October 1936.

122 MY EC 25 April 1937.

123 JC 5 June 1936.

124 MY CM 21 January 1936.

125 From an article by Rabbi Israel Yoffey, one of the founders of the Manchester Yeshiva, in JC 16 July 1926, quoted by Zalkind Yaakov Wise, 'The Rise of Independent Orthodoxy in Anglo-Jewry: The History of the Machzikei Hadass Communities, Manchester', an unpublished Ph.D. thesis submitted to the Department of Religions and Theology, University of Manchester, in 2006, and on which these paragraphs are largely based.

126 *Ibid.* pp. 103–113, 148ff.

127 This and the following paragraph are based on the minutes of the Manchester Shechita Board between July 1934 and December 1938.

3

'Displaced scholars':[1] refugees at the University of Manchester

Amongst those in Britain who protested against Nazi anti-Semitism after the Nazi government launched a boycott of Jewish businesses on 1 April 1933 was a World Alliance Against Anti-Semitism, with its 'British Empire Headquarters' in London. In May 1933 the Alliance published a pamphlet *J'accuse!*, detailing anti-Semitic barbarity in Germany and encouraging a militant response in Britain. The pamphlet[2] included 'messages' from leading British churchmen, politicians and businessmen condemning Nazi atrocities in the name of the British humanitarian tradition and the values of western civilisation. The harassment and murder of German Jews, the circumstances in which others were led to take their own lives, the exclusion of Jewish children from state schools, and the attack of the Nazi regime on Jewish lawyers, doctors, businessmen and academics were all reported in circumstantial detail. The implication was that Germany was turning on its Jewish citizens, intent on their elimination from the body of the nation, the savagery of the attack and the extent of danger underlined by the occasional use of the word 'extermination', although without any real prescience of the real genocide which was to follow. 'Sentence of death', *J'accuse!* asserted, 'has been passed on the Jews of Germany'.

The Alliance saw itself as making the world 'fully aware' of the nature and magnitude of the attack upon the Jews in Germany and as evoking an effective response from the British government and the British people. The British government might 'relax a little the severe conditions of admission to this country'. The 'powerful weapon' which it proposed for the British populace was a retaliatory economic boycott. 'Boycott German goods!', it advised all 'right-minded' readers, 'Avoid travelling in German steamers! Don't take your holidays in Germany! Don't frequent cinemas where German films are exhibited! Avoid dealing in German products or materials! Refrain from purchasing German goods and help to bring to an end the Nazi terror against the Jews.' By such means the people of Britain would have demonstrated their 'detestation' of the Nazi programme and 'brought our struggle to a victorious end'.

These strategies and hopes were orchestrated in *J'accuse!* by Sidney Salomon, a barrister and journalist, then press officer of the Board of

Deputies of British Jews, the national representative body of the British Jewish community, and, incidentally, the son of Rabbi Dr Berendt Salomon, once the minister of the Manchester Great Synagogue, the oldest and most prestigious of Manchester's many synagogues. There was a degree of continuity between the attacks on anti-Semitism past and present in that Dr Salomon had been prominent amongst those in Manchester condemning the Tsarist persecution of Russian Jews in the 1880s, himself advocating (in this he was then in a minority) their resettlement in Palestine.

The 'little relaxation' in the immigration laws advocated by *J'Accuse* did not amount to the suggestion of anything like a full-scale rescue operation. A carefully worded message from the former Home Secretary, Sir Herbert Samuel, noted that the 'economic state of things' would prevent such action 'on a large scale'. This too was Laski's view. Nor was he likely to be favourably disposed to the kind of militant 'struggle' which *J'accuse!* proposed, any more than, at the same period, he favoured a confrontational response to the British Union of Fascists. The earliest refugees to reach Manchester did not do so through Laski's mediation. They were German- Jewish industrialists anticipating a Nazi attack on their enterprises and German-Jewish academics dismissed from German universities.

J'accuse had given a special place to Jewish academics, highlighting their contributions to German science and culture and depicting their harassment and dismissal as the most evident indication of Germany's return to barbarism. They were noted too as one of several ways in which Britain might benefit from German obscurantism.[3]

The 'cleansing' of German universities of the decadent and oppositional elements which were seen to be undermining the mission of the nation was part of the cultural revolution wished upon the German people by their Nazi rulers. At risk were those whose supposed racial inferiority rendered them unfit to share the Aryan future or 'whose previous political activities [did] not offer the assurance that they will invariably and unreservedly support the National State'. Thousands of Jewish academics, facing harassment and dismissal, sought to leave the country. Some who were already in temporary posts abroad decided not to return. A handful of non-Jewish German academics who had protested, without result, at the dismissal of their Jewish colleagues were also in danger. In refugee historiography this racially charged cultural totalitarianism has typically been contrasted with the 'spontaneous individualism' which rendered Britain 'the principal asylum' for those who sought an escape.[4] The story of Britain's reception of displaced German academics has thus been typically characterised as 'a story to restore faith in humanity and in the fraternity of brains'.[5] Against a backcloth of Nazi obscurantism has been set 'the spontaneous rising of our [British] universities and those who worked and lived there in defence of free learning'.[6]

By early May the vice-chancellors of British universities had been fully alerted to the crisis in the German academy by a flood of applications for posts, many from established leaders in their academic fields. Some responded with immediate measures of support within their own universities. Their collective response, however, orchestrated by William Beveridge, Director of the London School of Economics, was the launch on 24 May 1933 of the Academic Assistance Council (AAC), the most influential of a series of bodies designed to assist the displaced academics in finding alternative work in Britain.[7]

While at once offering practical assistance to academics, the AAC felt obliged to act with caution and, along with most other institutions, within the framework of British immigration law. The AAC, and the constituent universities through which it operated, for the most part limited their assistance to the provision of temporary research posts which could not be seen to threaten established university teaching staff, and confined the appointments made with their financial assistance to outstanding scholars for whose expertise, it could be argued, there was no 'native' alternative; the AAC thus limited the initial scope of its work to a displaced academic elite whose claims could readily be substantiated and whose arrival was unlikely to threaten the careers of rank-and-file British academics.[8]

Until the outbreak of war limited the possibilities of rescue, the AAC thus struck a delicate balance between, on the one hand, responding with urgency to the increasing desperation of German academics and, on the other, keeping in mind both the restrictions imposed by the Home Office and the interests of the participating universities. There was also an element of self-interest, perhaps a necessary component of practical idealism. The ready availability of German (and subsequently Austrian, Czech, Spanish and Italian) refugee academics offered British universities a means of enhancing their status and, in particular, of strengthening further those elements of their academic life upon which their prestige was already based. The reception of refugee academics was as much about selection as it was about rescue. It added to other forces at work in the British State and in the Jewish community which tended to prioritise the rescue of a social, economic and professional elite. This is not to deny the humane intentions of the AAC or of the British universities, like Manchester's, which offered places to refugee academics. It is only to suggest that the chances for refugees were at their best when a coincidence existed of refugee need and British advantage. Likewise, those who wished to rescue refugee academics could stress the benefits which would accrue to the British academy.

This was certainly the case in Manchester, where, in early May 1933, the University Vice-Chancellor, the philosopher Walter (later Sir Walter) Moberly, organised a series of 'informal meetings' between members of the Senate and prominent Manchester citizens 'regarding the possible opening of a fund with the object of offering hospitality and facilities for prosecuting their work in Manchester to Professors displaced for political reasons from posts in European Universities'.[9] Evidence does not exist to identify the source of the Vice-Chancellor's initiative. One of those refugees who later benefited from it believed that 'an important part' was played by Lewis

Namier, the Polish-born Professor of History, a man of international reputation, Jewish origin and strong Zionist affiliations.[10] Certainly Namier was to become both a key figure in the University's subsequent support of refugees and one of the two members of Senate who took on the specific and thankless task of seeking out financial support from the community at large. Active in local Zionist formations, including the Manchester Friends of the Hebrew University and the Manchester Commission of the Jewish National Fund, he was alive to the possibility of using Manchester as a stepping stone which might carry welcome European talent to the Jewish-State-to-be.[11] But other members of the Senate were, from the beginning, equally active in the refugee cause, not least W.L. Bragg, the enterprising Langworthy Professor of Physics, who, as the successor of Ernest Rutherford, grasped the opportunity of attracting to his department some of the able young German scientists then at the forefront of international research in the field of theoretical and experimental physics.[12]

Nor is it clear exactly how widely the Vice-Chancellor reached out for advice and support. One of the Manchester citizens involved was certainly the Liberal City Councillor, Sarah Laski, who went on to persuade her husband, Nathan, a textile merchant and the acknowledged lay leader of Manchester Jewry, to promise £1,000 to the Vice-Chancellor's fund from moneys collected in Manchester for the Central British Fund for German Jewry.[13] Although the Vice-Chancellor had laid emphasis on supporting those displaced for *political* reasons, Nathan Laski's contribution, made in the name of the Manchester Jewish Representative Council, turned out to be exactly half the total raised initially towards a local University Appeal Fund for the maintenance of German academics.[14] It seems likely that most of the other Manchester citizens consulted at this stage were those who were later to identify themselves with the project and who were already amongst the University's major (and wealthy) patrons: Sir Thomas Barlow, Sir Christopher Needham, Sir Ernest Simon, Dr (later Sir) Kenneth Lee, the flour magnate Robert (later Sir Robert) McDougall, and the prominent Manchester industrialist, the Swiss entrepreneur Hans Renold of Renold's Chains.[15]

Of these, none had displayed any earlier interest in either refugee or Jewish causes. Robert McDougall, whose wealth was built on the production of self-raising flour patented by his father, was already well-known as a major benefactor of causes in the north-west of England which ranged from the National Trust and the Youth Hostel Association to the Manchester Royal Infirmary (MRI) and his alma mater, the University of Manchester. In May 1923, following a gift of £5,000 to the MRI for the extension of its radiological department, he became a member of the University's Court of Governors, and, in October 1931, its Deputy Treasurer. In 1933, as he was being drawn into the University's plans for displaced scholars, he made the first of what were to become nationally renowned purchases of land for charitable purposes: a substantial acreage in Derbyshire (the first of many) for the National Trust and land bought for £20,000 which enabled the Quakers to launch a scheme for the provision of allotments to the unemployed.[16] Donations to the University included support for the construction of the 'differential analyser' (the forerunner of the analogue computer) then being developed by the Bryce Professor of Applied Mathematics, Douglas Hartree.[17]

Beyond Manchester, the Vice Chancellor sought advice from William (later Lord) Beveridge, the Director of the London School of Economics, who was then in the process of organising British support for 'displaced scholars', both within his own university and within the British academy as a whole.[18] 'What is being done elsewhere?' Moberly wanted to know, and what action 'can be taken which would enable the university to provide hospitality for a short time to some of the dispossessed German professors?'[19] Beveridge responded by sending Moberly the first draft of what was to become, a few days later, 'a public Memorandum and Appeal for establishing an Academic Assistance Council' (the AAC). Beveridge's plan was based on the assumption that, bearing in mind the prior claims on their resources 'for their normal development', British universities would be able to support from their own reserves only 'a small fraction' of those 'likely to be condemned to want and idleness'.[20] What was required, he believed, was a body which would raise funds specifically for this purpose and which at the same time would serve as a 'clearing house', collecting information on appropriate university vacancies in Britain and elsewhere and putting potential academic refugees 'into touch with the institutions that can best help them'. The objects of the Council's attentions would be those 'who, on grounds of religion, political opinion or race are unable to carry on their work in their own country'. The intention, the Memorandum noted, was 'to prevent the waste of exceptional abilities exceptionally trained'.[21]

The Memorandum made it clear that 'the issue raised at the moment' was 'not a Jewish one alone; many who have suffered or are threatened have no Jewish connection'.[22] In his earlier negotiations with the Royal Society, which subsequently lent the appeal its support and the Council its 'maximum of help' (including its accommodation), Beveridge had been dissuaded from his initial inclination to offer one of the two honorary secretaryships to 'a distinguished Jewish Professor'. Further than that, the Society had been 'strongly of the opinion that no signatory of the Appeal ... should be of Jewish origin'. In the event, Beveridge was later to reflect, only one of the forty-three signatories, all 'men of academic standing and interest', was 'definitely Jewish'; a second 'might have been treated as non-Aryan' on the basis of his name alone.[23] Neither the Royal Society nor Beveridge thought it necessary to explain these decisions. They appear to rest on the assumption that no public appeal on behalf of Jews alone, or which appeared to have strong Jewish support, was likely to succeed, although whether this was because Jews would be seen to possess adequate resources of their own, or because wide sections of a potentially donating public were judged anti-Semitic, is by no means clear.

What was clear, however, was that, with or without Jewish participation, Beveridge expected Jewish money to be put at the Council's disposal. In his letter to Moberly he wrote of 'the need to secure effective co-operation with

people raising funds in the Jewish community ... clearly some of these resources ought to be available for academic purposes'.[24]

The signatories to the Memorandum fought shy of politics. The AAC was
not conceived, at least in public, as an anti-fascist organisation: 'our action',
the Memorandum ended, 'implies no unfriendly feelings to the people of
any country; it implies no judgement of forms of government or on any political issue between countries. Our only aims are the relief of suffering and
the defence of learning and science.'[25]

In this, as in other respects, Moberly followed Beveridge's lead. There was
to be no diversion of the University's existing resources, no displacement of
existing staff, no specific reference to 'Jews', a word which nowhere occurs
in the subsequent minutes of the Senate or of its sub-committees, no politics.
The academics soon to be provided by Manchester with one route of escape
were simply 'foreign', 'displaced' or 'distressed'; in fact, most were also of
Jewish origin, and all were fleeing regimes in which the 'forms of government' were central to their decisions to depart.

On 18 May 1933, the Senate gave a 'cordial welcome' to 'the inauguration
of some scheme to alleviate the distress of foreign scholars by affording them
hospitality in Manchester and at the University'; the Vice-Chancellor was empowered to put together an advisory sub-committee of six members of the
Senate to formulate a plan of action.[26]

In the meantime, in mid-June 1933 the Council of the University took the
quite extraordinary step of inviting Michael Polanyi, a man of Hungarian
Jewish origin, who in May had resigned his Professorship at the Kaiser-
Wilhelm Institute of the University of Berlin as a protest at the treatment of
his liberal and Jewish colleagues,[27] to accept the Chair of Physical Chemistry,
created for him in Manchester. Seen as 'one of the most prominent physical
chemists of the present time',[28] in Germany Polanyi was in the middle of a
distinguished academic career. While his own move was clearly highly princi-
pled and it is tempting to interpret the University's action as evidence of its
exceptionally liberal outlook, it seems probable that the University authorities were moved at least equally by the prospect of further enhancing a department already made famous by the pioneering work of Ernest (by then, Sir
Ernest) Rutherford twenty years earlier. Polanyi rapidly made his mark, not
only as a researcher and teacher, but as a magnet for external funding and
as a visiting lecturer sought after by prestigious universities throughout the
world. At all events the 'violent attack' on the University in the national press
for its preference of a 'foreigner' over highly qualified native candidates[29]
almost certainly dampened whatever liberal enthusiasm it had displayed in
Polanyi's case or, at all events, forced it to take a more cautious response
to displaced academics. The German physicist Rudolf Peierls attributed the
rejection of his own application for an assistant lectureship in Manchester in
1933, in spite of the powerful support it received from Manchester's Professor
of Physics, W.L. Bragg, to the Polanyi affair.[30] Peierls' fellow physicist, Hans
Bethe, dismissed from the University of Tubingen in 1933 on account of
his Jewish ancestry, in the same year was found a temporary lectureship in

Manchester, apparently through the mediation of Arnold Sommerfeld, his former colleague at the University of Munich.[31]

By the end of June, the Vice-Chancellor's sub-committee was in a position to make concrete recommendations to the Senate. Central to them was the creation for displaced academics of 'Honorary Research Fellowships', each worth £250 a year and tenable in the first instance for two years, 'it being clearly understood that men and women elected to Fellowships were not displacing members of the University regular teaching staff'. The Fellows would thus be 'mainly confined to research', although 'some assistance might be given by them in seminar work'. They would be people who would fit without difficulty into the University's existing pattern of research: heads of university departments were invited to make 'suggestions for openings and proposals for the type of scholar who would be most acceptable'. These suggestions would be submitted to a new standing committee of the Senate – subsequently known as the Joint Committee of Council and Senate on Assistance to Foreign Scholars (JCAFS) – which would have the power 'to consider applications and recommend candidates'. The question of whether these candidates should be academics 'already widely known' or 'junior scholars' was left for further consideration (and in reality never again debated). A letter would be sent out inviting subscriptions to supplement the £2,000 'already provided'.[32]

Approving these proposals, the Senate appointed seven of its senior professors – W.L. Bragg, G.W. Daniels, C.H. Dodd, Barker Fairly, Lewis Namier, J.L. Stocks and John Sebastian Bach Stopford – to serve on the Joint Committee. These were no lightweights. J.S.B. Stopford (later Baron Stopford of Fallowfield), then Professor of Anatomy, was in 1934 to succeed Moberly as Vice-Chancellor, a post in which he was to guide the University successfully through a period of major expansion. W.L. Bragg, the Professor of Physics, was the son of Sir Lawrence Bragg, himself famous as the pioneer of X-ray crystallography, work for which he was to receive a Nobel Prize.[33] By 1933 Lewis (later Sir Lewis) Namier had already made his mark as a leading trail-blazer in the field of British constitutional historiography. J.L. Stocks, the Aristotelian scholar who had succeeded Samuel Alexander to the prestigious Sir Samuel Hall Professorship in Philosophy, and who was also a highly respected supporter of humanitarian causes in the city – 'a great figure in the public life of Manchester' and 'a leader in all progressive causes', according to one commentator[34] – and an influential figure in the University Senate, went on in 1937 to become Vice-Chancellor of Liverpool University.[35] The three Senate members[36] who in 1938 replaced those committeemen who had by then left their Manchester posts included Douglas Hartree.[37] But although these figures suggest the importance accorded to the Joint Committee by the Senate, its most consistently active members (and most regular attenders) were Namier, Bragg and Stocks. A handful of Manchester industrialists co-opted onto the committee attended only sporadically and without any evident effect on its strategies; their substantive contribution was to serve as links with potential donors in the Manchester business community.

An (undated) press release issued by the committee, and a public appeal issued on 27 July 1933, give a rather different twist to this course of events.[38] In this version, 'simultaneously' with the formation of the AAC in London, 'a group of Manchester citizens raised a fund with the object of enabling Manchester University to offer a temporary home to some of these [displaced] scholars'. The money raised, amounting to £2,000, was then placed 'unconditionally at the service of the University' which duly 'accepted its administration'. The JCAFS was set up to 'control its application'. This seems unlikely. The letters passed between Moberly and Beveridge in May 1933 all point to an initiative from above rather than to the pre-existence of any 'group of Manchester citizens'. On the whole, it seems likely that the narrative of the project's origin had been carefully 'adjusted', perhaps to secure for it the maximum public (and financial) support. What the two versions have in common is that the proposed fellowships offered to their holders only 'a temporary resting place', that 'the field of employment open to British graduates [would] not be narrowed in any sense by their presence' and that their funding would 'involve no burden on the general funds of the University'.[39] The fate of displaced academics in Manchester was thus dependent, in part, on the selectivity of the AAC, through whom most were introduced to the University, and on the availability of external funds. It depended equally on the University's perception of its own needs.

Although noting the desirability of these plans, whatever their remote origins, being implemented 'as soon as possible',[40] the Senate fell somewhat short of delivering the level of response which measured up to the severity of the German emergency. A cumbersome process of selection clearly subordinated the urgent needs of German scholars to the long-term interests of the University. Nothing was to be done which would disturb the academic equilibrium of the University or the career prospects of its staff. Nothing happened quickly: it took four months for the first Honorary Fellows to be appointed. After toying with the idea of giving preference to 'junior scholars who might find it more difficult to obtain University appointments outside Germany', the Joint Committee hedged its bets, selecting, over the next nine years, a mixture of relative newcomers to German academia (although all with international reputations) and established scholars of world renown who would more evidently enhance the quality of the University's research and its academic reputation. Young academics without existing posts at German universities were ruled out of contention.[41] The stipends attached to the Fellowships were meagre, half or less of the salaries of junior academics.[42] Some found their positions humiliating; one foreign scholar who spent two years at the University relished the opportunity of then moving on to a post (in Cambridge) which was 'an appointment and not a gift from charity' and which immediately doubled his income.[43] The Fellowships offered little sense of security to those already uprooted; although tenable for two years, the second year depended both on cash being available and on favourable reports being received of the first year's work. Extensions were by no means a foregone conclusion.[44] Foreign scholars were not assured of their continuance at the University once their Fellowships had ended. Nor did the Senate's appeal letter meet with a ready response from within the University: by mid-October only £200 had been added to the original £2,000.[45]

The Manchester JCAFS, like the AAC nationally, felt it necessary to construct procedures which lay within the framework of government's immigration policies. The committee possessed neither the power, nor perhaps the inclination, to challenge official attitudes towards foreign scholars based typically – and even in the face of an elite whose entry was likely to prove advantageous – on perceptions of Britain's self-interest. Applicants for permanent posts, seen as a potential source of competition with equally well-qualified British scholars, were generally not welcomed; those most likely to gain entry were applicants for temporary research positions who, on the completion of their tenure, were expected to re-emigrate. Rank-and-file academics, seen as the major source of competition, were less likely to gain a foothold than scholars who led their fields. All of this dovetailed neatly with the University of Manchester's contemporaneous perception of its own self-interest and with the procedures put in place in 1933 to achieve it. Nor did the University wish to be disadvantaged by British institutions which might hold out to refugee academics more attractive terms of employment: amongst the recommendations which the advisory sub-committee had put to the Senate, and which the Senate accepted, was that an attempt should be made to bring a degree of uniformity to the responses of British universities to German refugee academics, a uniformity achieved in the event by government edict.

While providing 'research facilities' in terms of laboratories, equipment and libraries for the Fellows, the University showed no inclination to dip into its own financial reserves; its decided preference was to supplement money raised locally for the University Fund with subventions from the Rockefeller Foundation,[46] the Academic Assistance Council and the Professional Committee for German-Jewish Refugees (also founded in May 1933), all national bodies centred in London.[47] Offers of Fellowships were often conditional on support being received from other sources. Individual philanthropists, like McDougall, such local bodies as the Manchester Committee on Cancer Research, and local Jewish agencies with access to the Central British Fund were drawn in to help in particular cases.

The link with the AAC proved particularly useful. Rapidly establishing itself as the official medium through which German academics made contact with British universities, and as the major source of small grants which tided them over as they sought posts, the AAC supplied Manchester with most of its applicants. In October 1933, after correspondence with the Vice-Chancellor, the Council declared itself ready, in some cases to bear part of a Fellow's stipend, in others to accept full financial responsibility for scholars accommodated by the University and drawing upon its facilities.[48] At the same time, in keeping with the Senate's self-interested caution, it undertook not to 'allocate' scholars to the University from its growing pool of applicants without first seeking the Joint Committee's consent.[49] For Manchester, as for other British universities, the AAC became a kind of clearing-house, receiving applications in its rooms at Burlington House, selecting those it judged to have a reasonable chance of obtaining an academic post in Britain, putting them in touch with appropriate institutions, offering universities help in negotiating their entry and work permits with the Home Office, providing them with temporary financial support on their arrival and, once they had found posts, supplementing, and sometimes paying, their University salaries and the maintenance costs of their families.[50] Manchester made rather more sporadic use of the Rockefeller Foundation, the Medical Research Council and the Professional Committee for German-Jewish refugees,[51] negotiating grants or supplements for particular scholars only when other sources of finance ran dry.

By such devices, Manchester was able to draw in members of Germany's academic elite – at least twenty-five in all by 1939[52] – at relatively low cost and with a minimium of disruption. There was no place for the un-tenured or the mediocre, no scope for collective rescue, and, critically, no apparent attempt to prioritise the imperative of escape. The yardsticks were the AAC's assessment of the absorbent powers of British academia as a whole, Manchester's judgement of its own capacity to absorb émigrés without disadvantage to itself, and the availability of the necessary funds. Finance was a major problem. The eight Honorary Fellows appointed in 1933 absorbed all but a tiny fraction of the Joint Committee's initial resources; only £250 was held back as an emergency reserve. Professors Stocks and Namier, deputed in 1935 to seek out private donations, met with limited success. Their major (perhaps their only) coup was to secure the offer, in October 1935, of £2,100 covenanted over seven years by a consortium of Manchester businessmen of whom the leading figure was the textile manufacturer Sir Thomas Barlow.[53] This did not resolve the committee's immediate cash-flow problems. Twice – in October 1935 and February 1937 – the Committee declined to recommend appointments in the light of its substantial deficits.[54] In February 1937 the Vice-Chancellor wrote to a colleague: 'the money which the University has had to support Foreign Scholars is running out, and we are unable to give any further support in the future'.[55] In December 1938 Lewis Namier, in the forefront of those pressing for the entry of refugee scholars, informed the Vice-Chancellor that the JCAFS 'was overwhelmed with requests from people in severe distress and even in danger, and have therefore to exercise the severest censorship of applications'.[56]

The committee's major external supporter, the AAC (its name changed in 1936 to the Society for the Protection of Science and Learning (SPSL)), 'always in financial difficulty' according to Beveridge,[57] was itself under particularly intense pressure following the Anschluss, Kristallnacht and the intensification of the Civil War in Spain. Its fourth report, issued in November 1938, noted that the 'series of disasters' which had overtaken Europe during 1937–38 had produced a rapid rise in the number of dismissals from German universities, the displacement of 418 academic workers from universities in Austria and the beginning of an exodus from Spain, Portugal, and from Italy, where Racial Laws on the German model had been introduced during summer 1938. By November 1938 the total number of teachers and researchers 'displaced' in Germany alone had exceeded 14,000; some of those whose first refuge had been in Spain were now persuaded by events to move on to Britain. In Italy more than ninety holders of professorial rank and a larger number of junior lecturers had been dismissed.[58] In view of its 'limited funds' the SPSL was exercising 'extreme caution' in inviting even the Austrians to take refuge in Britain; the fate of refugees from Chinese universities destroyed by the advancing Japanese was placed in the hands of the ISS.[59]

In the circumstances academic staff at Manchester University were persuaded to join a SPSL fund-raising campaign organised on its behalf by David Clayhorn Thomson: it was important to impress upon the public, Thomson had argued, that British colleagues were 'playing their part' in the support and rescue of refugee academics.[60] Stopford himself joined the National Appeals Committee.[61] On 8 February 1939 a Manchester sub-committee of the Appeal Fund, of which Ross Waller, the Director of Extra-Mural Studies, was a prominent member, and Patrick Blackett, who in the autumn of 1937 had succeeded Bragg as Professor of Physics, perhaps the chairman, organised a meeting in the university's Whitworth Hall, with a platform party which included the local president of the NUT and the President of the Manchester and Salford Trades Council.[62] Although no record exists of the amounts raised for the SPSL at this and other meetings in Manchester, it was certainly insufficient, taken with its own bankruptcy, to convince the JCAFS that its operations remained viable. Even before the outbreak of war rendered the project obsolete, the committee had effectively ceased its work of rescue; between February and September 1939, as the European situation worsened, only two further scholars were added to the University's list of Honorary Fellows, one from Italy and one from Spain.

From 1934 until the outbreak of war, as the outlook for German-Jewish academics became increasingly perilous, the Committee had been able to recommend only two or three appointments each year; of a total of sixteen appointees in this period, two were Spanish scholars endangered by the Franco regime following the Civil War in Spain, one a refugee from Fascist Italy. The Senate was reluctant to divert to the work of rescue monies from the University's own resources, which were seen as badly needed to upgrade some of its more 'inadequate and undignified makeshift premises', to provide new laboratories and lecture theatres for its 2,600 full-time students, and so both 'consolidate' the University's international reputation for original research and scholarship and 'give better service' to the local hospitals, clinics and industries with which it had long been linked.[63] In the spring of 1937, at a public meeting attended by 'friends of the University' and 'civic heads of the region', the University launched a new appeal for £300,000 for 'a comprehensive scheme of development' which would replace 'inadequate and undignified makeshift premises' with new laboratories and lecture theatres; in such circumstances, the funding of displaced scholars was not a priority.[64]

Anti-Semitism played no part in such a decision. Nor, with Namier so central to its operations, and in the light of the University's long-standing relationship with the Jewish community, does it seem likely that the Committee exercised any particular caution in the case of Jewish applicants. At the same time, the word 'Jew' is not to be found in the minutes either of the Senate or of the Joint Committee. It may well be that, at least in public, and in line with the decisions of the AAC's founders, the Committee felt it to be diplomatic to stress that those it was rescuing were the victims of political rather than racial persecution.

However, a sinister note pervades the Committee's attempts, beginning in May 1935, to persuade the German émigré pianist Dr Artur Schnabel to give a concert in aid of its funds.[65] While much of the long delays to which the negotiations were then subject might be put down to the logistics of a popular musician's busy schedule, Schnabel also made it clear from the beginning that he had personal objections to being publicly identified with the raising of funds for displaced German scholars. 'It has been, so far and for many reasons, my attitude', he wrote in April 1935 to J.L. Stocks, to whom he had initially expressed a willingness to appear in Manchester, 'not to participate directly in any public activity linked with present German conditions, thus I have not yet accepted one of the invitations to play for victims of the Nazi regime'.[66] He wished in the case of the present invitation, he continued, neither to deviate from this position nor to set a precedent which might encourage others to invite him to play for a similar purpose. On 17 October 1937, as negotiations neared a successful conclusion, he noted, 'My dislike to appear publicly in any connection with political matters or politically originated [sic] organisations has not become weaker since I wrote in 1935'. While it was acceptable 'to have some general reference to strengthen some funds instituted to help distressed conditions in the academic district [sic]', no mention was to be made 'as to the places where those Scholars had their activities before getting in want of help'.[67] In the event, in what might appear rather less than a complete deference to his wishes, the printed programme for Schnabel's recital, given in the Whitworth Hall of the University on 8 December 1937, read that it was 'in aid of the Fund for Distressed Foreign Scholars'.[68] Of the profit of £118 made by the event, half was added to the JCAFS fund, half to the International Students Service 'for the benefit of refugee students from Germany'.[69]

Schnabel's stance is not readily explicable, especially since he himself chose not to explain it, even in private correspondence. It may have been part of a general desire to keep music out of politics; perhaps he was understandably concerned for the fate of fellow musicians still performing in Nazi Germany; perhaps he feared the effect on his potential audience of supporting German exiles. He does not appear either to condone the activities of the Nazi regime or to lack sympathy for its victims: on one occasion he refers explicitly to 'the miserable fate of the exiles from Germany'.[70] On the other hand, it is difficult to rule out self-interest in a man who spent part of every year in his villa on Lake Como in Fascist Italy;[71] it may be that he did not wish at this stage to rule out the possibility of appearing in Germany.

Rather less baffling is the rampant Germanophobia and unabashed nativism of Humphrey Procter-Gregg, the recently-appointed Reader in Music (and later Professor) at the University,[72] whom the Vice-Chancellor had invited, along with H.P. Turner, the University's Director of Extra-Mural Studies, to make the arrangements necessary for Schnabel's recital. While declaring his ultimate concern to back the Vice-Chancellor to the best of his ability, Procter-Gregg found himself 'unable to share the Schnabel-worship of a big public in Manchester'. 'I have never been in sympathy with him or his aims', he wrote, 'my whole sympathies are with the furtherance of English scholars and English music and I feel he stands for the cause of his oriental [*sic*] compatriots really, which is no doubt admirable both for him and for them, but English music has had a lot of that to endure. *Our* unplaced scholars and unplaced concert hall [*sic*] can find no Schnabel to give a recital either to raise funds or bring credit and first-rate music into our English sphere; and such a content as he proposes [a programme of pieces by Bach, Beethoven and Webber] will make a big noise in Manchester and is bound to react on any efforts, enterprises and causes *of our own*. In Manchester music particularly there are many people to whom charity always begins abroad, and I don't blame them for feeling that way. But I don't feel that way myself'.[73]

Procter-Gregg had other reservations. It was his firm belief that music, which rightfully belonged only to the spheres of art and education, should not be 'utilised for political, national or even charitable purposes'. He found it difficult to accept responsibility for going along with Schnabel in not informing the public of the true purpose of the recital; the result, he believed, would be 'public speculation as to what it was really for'.[74] Nor would he accept responsibility for Schnabel's chosen programme; the 53-minute piece composed by Beethoven in his youth had subsequently been rejected (so Procter-Gregg claimed) by the composer himself.[75] It is difficult to escape the conclusion that what Procter-Gregg really objected to was what he chose to see as the un-English music used to promote an un-English cause.[76] For his part, the Vice-Chancellor used Procter-Gregg's obsequiousness to politely brush his objections aside.

Whatever the public face of the Senate, however, and whatever the meaning of Schnabel's prevarication and Procter-Gregg's critique, in 1933 alone the Committee found temporary places of safety for at least eleven besieged German-Jewish academics, all of whom were later able to establish successful academic careers in Britain or the United States, some on at least the partial basis of their work in Manchester. It was in his first year in Manchester that Rudolf Peierls, later to join the Manhattan Project, wrote his first published papers in the field of nuclear physics.[77] The Fellowships provided the time and space for the displaced to reassess their academic prospects and to seek out more prestigious, more appropriate or more permanent openings. Some did not remain long in Manchester. Peierls himself, one of the first Fellows, left in October 1935 to take up a research post at the Royal Society's Mond

Laboratory in Cambridge.[78] Hans Heilbronn, appointed to a Fellowship in the Department of Mathematics in 1933, also departed in October 1935, to a Bevan Fellowship at Trinity College, Cambridge.[79] In 1935 the psychologist David Katz, after two years in Manchester, accepted 'the hospitality of Professor Cyril Burt in the psychological laboratory of University College, London' and 'facilities for research on animal behaviour at the Royal Zoological Society's Gardens' provided by Julian Huxley.[80]

Other displaced scholars were apparently encouraged by their academic colleagues in Manchester to move on to the greater safety of the United States as the prospect of war with Germany increased. The eminent Italian-Jewish physicist Bruno Rossi, who was deprived of his professorship at the University of Padua in September 1938, and who had first taken refuge in Copenhagen as a guest of Neils Bohr, was, in December 1938, according to his own account, 'invited' to Manchester by Patrick Blackett, with the aid of 'a fellowship of the SPSL'.[81] After renewing his own experimental work on cosmic rays in Blackett's Manchester laboratory, which he found to be 'a very active research centre', and where he was accorded Blackett's personal guidance, he was 'strongly advised' by a 'worried' Blackett to move on across the Atlantic in view of the increasing international tension in Europe.[82] In mid-June 1939 he left for the United States, where in July he was offered a Research Associateship at the University of Chicago, paid for by the American equivalent of the SPSC, the Committee in Aid of Displaced Scholars.[83] His six months in Manchester had thus served, with Blackett's friendship and support, and what Rossi experienced as the 'human solidarity' of the Manchester population, as an interlude of peaceful renewal between a life in science in Italy broken by the Racial Laws and a distinguished career in American academia.[84]

While never veering from its strategies of self-interest and caution, the committee proved more flexible than its original remit appeared to demand. Most scholars who requested them received extensions to their two-year tenures, if only with the partial aid of AAC or some other external body. The tenure of the historian Martin Weinbaum who arrived in 1933, was extended until 1938, when he departed for the United States with the help of a small grant from the committee towards the cost of transporting his furniture and library.[85] From the beginning of 1935 the Fellows became eligible to study for the University's higher degrees and received occasional help with their fees.[86] In practice, most Heads of Department felt only partly bound by the official restrictions on teaching placed on the Fellows, often drawing them not only into 'seminar work' but into the regular lecturing, demonstrating and supervision programmes of their departments.[87] Only two, however – the physiologist Walter Deutsch and the economist Adolf Lowe – secured permanent posts in Manchester, both with the aid of external funding.[88] Most made the exits expected of them by the government and increasingly encouraged by the AAC.[89]

This was not always easy in the case of the less eminent of the University's refugee scholars. On occasion the JCAFS clearly felt obliged to secure the future of a Fellow the renewal of whose contract it had recommended more than once, but who was unable to find a post elsewhere. This was the case, for example, with Dr Arthur Lasnitzki, a displaced Jewish scholar from the University of Berlin, whose Research Fellowship in the Cancer Research Department of the Manchester University Medical School, originally assigned to him at the end of 1934, was renewed annually (with the help of the AAC, the Professional Committee for Jewish Refugees, the Manchester branch of the CBF and the Manchester Committee for Cancer Research) until November 1938, when, with the University lacking funds to further extend his stay, and other sources of support exhausted, an increasingly 'desperate' Lasnitzki himself had failed to find a permanent post.[90] His cause was taken up not only by Namier, as a member of the JCAFS, but by a 'terribly troubled' Vice-Chancellor, who wrote personally to Nathan Laski to seek his help in finding a post for Lasnitzki at the Jewish Hospital.[91] Raper wrote to a series of pharmaceutical chains, including Boots, Burroughs Welcome and British Drug Houses, seeking work for Lasnitzki 'even at a few pounds a week … to keep the wolf from the door'.[92] Namier left no stone unturned: those he approached on Lasnitzki's behalf included the A.D. Lindsay, Master of Balliol; Walter Adams, secretary of the Society for the Protection of Science and Learning; 'a millionaire academic' with whom he was working on a new edition of the letters of Horace Walpole; and, as a 'distant chance', 'an [anonymous] old Duke'.[93] Laski, unable to find Lasnitzki a post at the Jewish Hospital, where the financial situation was 'very bad', suggested to the Vice-Chancellor a lunchtime meeting with a 'gentleman' who 'with nice handling and a bit of flattery' might produce 'a fair sum'.[94] Meantime, Lasnitzki himself, having come to believe that funds were now available only for 'fresh refugees' became increasingly 'desperate'.[95] On the brink of impoverishment, and possible deportation, he was finally saved by the offer of a post at the University of Bristol.

While the efforts on Lasnitzki's behalf suggest a degree of altruism in the affairs of the JCAFS, his failure to secure tenure in Manchester re-emphasises the priority accorded to the University's own best interests. In this the University's private patrons, each naturally seeking a visible return for his money, were inevitably complicit. Approached by a University Professor in 1934 to support a pure mathematician whose work was unlikely to further the production of the differential analyser, McDougall replied that he was not prepared to give £175 'just to aid a particular scholar'; he would give support for one year only if he had an assurance that 'the coming here of a German scholar is of real service and importance', and for a second only if 'adequate results' had accrued from the first.[96]

Given the criteria of selection, it is hardly surprising that Heads of Departments who received 'Foreign Scholars' through the JCAFS had little doubt of their worth. The only report on their work to survive, presented by the Joint Committee to the Senate in October 1935, is effusive in its praise of the earliest recruits. All had conducted experiments or investigations and published papers in academic journals which were seen as 'valuable contributions' to their fields of study. Their research had been original, their attitudes cooperative, their work-rates impressive. Building on their work in Germany and elsewhere, they had enhanced areas of research and teaching in which the University already had a special interest: the pathology of anaemia and scurvy (Deutsch), respiratory dust diseases in the cotton industry (Prausnitz), cancer research (Lasnitzki), child psychology (Katz),[97] the mathematical treatment of nuclear physics (Peierls and Bethe), crystallography (Berg) and English constitutional history (Weinbaum).

The last refugee from Fascism to be offered a post at the university was Beniamino Segre, a mathematician of Jewish origin born in Turin, who in 1938 was forced by the Racial Laws out of his professorship at the University of Bologna. Arriving as a refugee in Britain in the following year, and surviving at first in temporary posts found for him by the SPSL, he was interned in 1940. Following his release, he was appointed to an assistant lectureship in mathematics at the University in 1942, possibly with the help of the Brentanos, a Quaker couple of Italian origin, the husband a professor of Physics at the university, his wife, Sophie, an active member of the Quaker Refugee Committee. The Brentanos were certainly amongst those who befriended him in Manchester.[98]

Refugee academics at the University of Manchester, 1933–42[99]

Dr Reinhold Baer (Halle/Mathematics) HRF/1933[100]
Dr W.F. Berg (Physics) Research for Ph.D./1933
Dr Hans Bethe (Physics) Temporary Assistant Lectureship/1933
Mr Jacob J. Bickerman (Colloid Chemistry) HRF/1935
Dr Walter Deutsch [later Dale?] (Düsseldorf/Medicine, Physiology) HRF/1933
Dr Valliesa Arturo Duperier (Madrid/Physics) HRF/1939
Dr Raphael Feinberg (Electro-technics) Lecturer
Dr Hans Heilbronn (Gottingen and Bristol/Mathematics) HRF 1935[101]
Dr Erich Herlinger (Tech Hochschule, Berlin/Physics) (Tech Hochschule, Berlin/Physics) HRF/1933
Dr H.C. Hilman (Economics)
Dr Kurt Jackel (Breslau/Philology) HRF/1934
Dr Anni Jacob (Frankfurt-am-Main/Organic Chemistry) HRF/1938
Professor David Katz (Rostock, Mecklenberg/Psychology) HRF/1933
Dr Arthur Lasnitzki (Berlin/Medicine, Cancer Research) HRF/1935
Dr Ulrich Lauterbach (Breslau/German) Assistant in German, 1939
Professor Adolf Lowe (Frankfurt/Economics) HRF/1933 Honorary Special Lecturer in Modern Political Philosophy, attached to the Department of Philosophy/1939[102]
Dr Juan Luis Madinaveitia (Madrid/Organic Chemistry) HRF/1938
Dr Kurt Mahler (Germany/Mathematics) HRF/1933 Assistant lecturer
Dr Rudolf Peierls (Leipzig and Cambridge/Physics) HRF/1933[103]
Dr Karl Prausnitz (Medicine/Bacteriology and Preventive Medicine) HRF/1933

Dr Erwin Rosenthal (Germany/Semitic Studies) HRF/1935
Dr Bruno Rossi (Padua/Experimental Physics) HRF/1939
Miss Eve Sansome (Botany) HRF/1938
Dr Beniamino Segre (Bologna/Analytical Geometry) Assistant lecturer
in mathematics/1942
Dr [Hans?] Weiner Singer (Germany, Bonn/Economics)) Assistant
lecturer/1939[104]
Dr Otto Skutsch (Germany/Classics) Assistant lectureship in Greek and
Latin/1939
Dr W.S. Sondhelm MacLaren Cotton Industry Research Fellow/1939
Dr Martin Weinbaum (Berlin/History) HRF/1933

Refugee scholars at the Manchester College of Technology (then Manchester University's Faculty of Technology), 1933–39

Dr Abraham Buraway (Germany/Chemistry)/1936
Heinz [?] Raudnitz (Germany/Chemistry)

In assessing the response of the University of Manchester to refugee scholars, it is difficult to avoid the benefit of hindsight. From that perspective,
the offer of thirty-three temporary academic posts between 1933 and 1939
seems less than generous. This is not, however, as it appeared at the time, or
to the beneficiaries. Manchester stood fourth to Oxford, Cambridge and the
LSE, although a rather distant fourth in the case of Oxbridge, in the league
of British universities which received displaced scholars.[105] Rudolf Peierls,
one of Manchester's refugee honorary fellows, concurs with Beveridge and
Bentwich in their celebration of Britain's generosity to the displaced. It would
have been 'very understandable', he believes, if, at a time of economic depression and a shortage of academic posts, 'the local scientists had resented
the arrival of so many refugees who would compete with them for posts'. As
it was, the refugees were treated 'with great kindness'.[106] For Bentwich, the
work of the SPSL in bringing a total of 2,600 scholars to Britain constituted 'a
story to restore faith in humanity and in the fraternity of brains'; as 'a spontaneous growth of British individualism' it was a 'precious grain of light' in a
world darkened by totalitarianism, 'gratefully recognised' by those who were
saved.[107] For Beveridge, 'the outstanding feature of the British experience
was the spontaneous rising of our universities and those who worked and
lived there in defence of free learning'. With the help of British universities,
including Manchester, the SPSL had eased refugee scholars 'through the
barriers of official delay'.[108]

For this they were duly grateful. When Arthur Lasnitzki, after several re-
newals of his Honorary Fellowship in Manchester, was finally found a permanent post as a Research Fellow of the Birmingham branch of the British
Empire Cancer Campaign, his wife Malka, who had also held a temporary
post in cancer research at Manchester, thanked the Vice-Chancellor for having 'enabled us to carry out further research work which is one of the greatest

parts of our life. We shall continue to do all in our power to be of benefit to the science of this country.'[109] In his memoirs the Italian physicist Bruno Rossi, who arrived in Manchester in December 1938 and left for Chicago in June 1939, is fulsome in his praise of the personal and professional support he received in Manchester from his professor, Patrick Blackett, and from other colleagues at the University.[110] They had enabled him to renew the momentum of his career as an experimental physicist.

There can be no doubting the gains made (although, for the most part, at no cost to itself) by Manchester's programmes of rescue for the academic and business communities of Britain, Europe, the United States and Israel. According to a list of 'Academic Refugees who have been at the University of Manchester' compiled by the Vice-Chancellor's office in February 1939,[111] perhaps as a form of self-congratulation, five of the former refugee honorary fellows remained in Manchester, Deutsch as a biochemist at Christies Hospital, E.I.G. Rosenthal as a special lecturer in the Department of Semitic Languages and History, Mahler as a temporary assistant lecturer in Mathematics. Three held posts on American campuses, Baer at Illinois, Bethe at Cornell, Weinbaum at Kent State. The physicist, Erich Herlinger, was a Research Professor at the Daniel Sieff Institute (now the Weitzmann Institute) in Rehoboth. David Katz was Professor of Psychology at the University of Stockholm. Peierls had become Professor of Applied Mathematics at the University of Birmingham, where, he boasted in his memoirs, his students included Fred Hoyle.[112] Three were engaged in research for major commercial concerns, Berg for Kodak, Buraway for Calico Printers of America, Bickerman, at Cambridge, for Metal Box. Beniamino Segre, who achieved international eminence in the fields of geometry and combinatronics as a teacher and researcher, returned to Bologna in 1946 and went on to a professorship in Rome in 1950.

Michael Polanyi, for whose appointment as Professor of Chemistry in 1933 the University had risked public disapproval, had already by 1939 begun to move from chemistry to the social sciences as an eminent critic of the 'intellectual tyranny' imposed by totalitarian regimes in Germany and the Soviet Union.[113] He was one of four former displaced scholars from Manchester – the others were Heilbronn (then H.O. Wills Professor of Pure Mathematics at Bristol), Mahler (then Reader in Pure Mathematics at Manchester) and Peierls (still at Birmingham) – who during the later 1940s were elected to Fellowships of the Royal Society.[114] Otto Skutsch, who during the 1940s was Professor of Latin at University College, London, and a Fellow of the British Academy, went on after his retirement to a Visiting Professorship at Princeton.[115] Peierls went on to a knighthood and the Wykeham Professorship of Physics at Oxford, following his work towards the production of the atom bomb at the Los Alamos Laboratory in New Mexico; in later life he became a crusader against the use of nuclear weapons. His former colleague in Germany, Hans Bethe, who worked with him in New Mexico, became a Nobel Laureate.[116] After also serving as a leading member of the Los Alamos team, Bruno Rossi, amongst the founders of Europe's 'new astronomy', went on to a Professorship in Physics at the Massachusetts Institute of Technology.[117]

Notes

1 An earlier version of this paper, with the same title, has been published in *Melilah*, the online journal of the Centre for Jewish Studies at the University of Manchester, 2005, 3, pp. 1–29.

2 *J'accuse!* (World Alliance for Combating Anti-Semitism, London n.d. (April/May 1933)).

3 *J'accuse!*, p. 30.

4 Norman Bentwich, *The Rescue and Achievement of Refugee Scholars: The Story of Displaced Scholars and Scientists, 1933–52* (The Hague 1953), pp. xiii and 13.

5 *Ibid.*, p. v.

6 Lord Beveridge, *A Defence of Free Learning* (London 1959) p. 12: the words are from a 'sermon' by Beveridge delivered in Carrs Lane Church in October 1935.

7 Others included the Jewish Professional Committee, founded in May 1933 to find places for such professionals as doctors, lawyers, teachers and social workers and for those on the borderline between professional and academic careers. It also worked with the AAC by providing for the maintenance of some of those in academic posts. (For this and others, see Bentwich, *The Rescue* pp. 15–17.) Lewis Namier character-ised it as 'a general reserve and insurance fund for all Jewish professional refugees' (VCA/7/144 Namier to the Vice-Chancellor 21 December 1938). I am grateful to Dr James Peters of John Rylands Library for his help in guiding me through the Vice-Chancellor's Archive at the University of Manchester.

8 London, *Whitehall and the Jews*, pp. 48–49.

9 Minutes of a Meeting of the Senate of the University of Manchester (hereafter cited as MUS), 18 May 1933.

10 Sir Rudolf Peierls, *Bird of Passage: Recollections of a Physicist* (Princeton 1985), p. 107. For Namier, Julia Namier, *Louis Namier: A Biography* (London 1971).

11 Kurt Heilbronn, a young German refugee who in 1939 sought Namier's help in find-ing a place on the university's course in dentistry was advised to instead seek entry to Palestine (author interview with Kurt Heilbronn, hereafter Heilbronn interview.) Heilbronn, who, in his own words, 'sat on the steps of the Medical Department' until he was granted a place, went on to share a university prize in dental prosthet-ics (*The Serpent* Vol. XX1V No. 2 (1940)) and to become a dental practitioner in Manchester.

12 Peierls, *Bird of Passage*, p. 96. In 1933 he encouraged Rudolf Peierls, a young German physicist, then a Rockefeller Fellow in Cambridge, to apply for an assistant lecture-ship in Manchester. Bragg succeeded Rutherford in 1919.

13 MJRC Special Meeting 25 May 1933.

14 Minutes of an Advisory Conference of Representatives of the Senate on Distressed Foreign Scholars, 20 June 1933. The Vice-Chancellor reported that £2,000 was then available to the Senate for the support of displaced academics.

15 Hans Renold died in May 1943 leaving £472,000 gross.

16 For a fuller account of his benefactions, tribute in SA, 23 December 1938. A Liberal in politics, he contested the High Peak constituency (without success) in 1923, 1924 and 1929. Other donations to the University included the Burlington Street Drill Hall for use by students as a centre for physical education. His donations to the National Trust for the purposes of purchasing land in Derbyshire continued during his involvement with displaced academics, over which they apparently took prec-edence. Beeston Tor in the Dovedale area was bought by the National Trust in 1937 from funds promised by McDougall (MG 28 September 1937). He was knighted in

the Coronation Honours List and awarded an Honorary LLD by the University, both in that same year.

17 In 1937 McDougall received from the University an honorary LLD.

18 For an account of these efforts and their results, see Beveridge, *A Defence of Free Learning*, Chapter 1; Bentwich, *The Rescue*, Chapter 2.

19 VCA/7/144/3 Vice-Chancellor to William Beveridge 8 May 1933.

20 The press announcement of the formation of the AAC, 22 May 1933, in Beveridge, *A Defence of Free Learning*, pp. 4–5.

21 *Ibid.*

22 *Ibid.*

23 Beveridge, *A Defence of Free Learning*, p. 9. The Jewish signatory was Samuel Alexander, the 'possible non-Aryan' Arthur Schuster.

24 VCA/7/144/3 William Beveridge to the Vice-Chancellor, 9 May 1933. For this reason, he went on, 'we probably ought to add a couple of good Jewish names to the appeal'. It was apparently the advice of the Royal Society which changed his mind.

25 Press announcement.

26 *Ibid.*, and the Minutes of a Meeting of formation of AAC, 22 May 1933 (hereafter MUS), 22 June 1933.

27 A biographical note attached to the abstract of his papers at the University of Chicago renders this (p. 5) 'prompted by repeated attacks on Jewish intellectuals'.

28 MG 20 June 1933. After studying medicine at the University of Budapest and chemistry at the Technical High School in Karlsruhe, Polanyi was awarded his doctorate by Budapest in 1917. In 1920 he was appointed to assist Professor Herzog at the Kaiser-Wilhelm Institute of Textile Chemistry, later transferring to the Kaiser-Wilhelm Institute for Physical and Electrical Chemistry. In 1926 he was appointed to the professorship at the Technical University in Berlin from which he resigned in May 1933.

29 Peierls, *Bird of Passage*, p. 96.

30 *Ibid.* VCA/7/144 W.L. Bragg to the Vice-Chancellor 21 June and 25 July 1933. On 21 June Bragg wrote to the Vice-Chancellor: 'I want to make sure that we leave no stone unturned in an effort to get Peierls here'.

31 Obituary of Bethe, who had a Jewish mother and a Protestant father, by Jeremy Bernstein in *Physics World*, Vol. 18, No. 4 (April 2005), p. 12. In 1934 Bethe was offered a permanent post at Cornell University, where he remained in post for the rest of his life.

32 MUS 22 June, 12 October 1933.

33 W.L. Bragg left Manchester in autumn 1937 to take up a post as Director of the National Physics Laboratory at Teddington (MG 6 May 1937).

34 MG 8 June 1937, reporting the comments of A.D. Lindsay, the Master of Balliol.

35 For details of Stocks' activities in Manchester, see obituary MG 14 June 1937.

36 Professors Atkinson (Dean of Arts), Hartree (Professor of Applied Mathematics) and Webster (MUS 3 February 1938).

37 Peierls, *Bird of Passage*, pp. 104–105. According to Peierls, Hartree's machine was based on an invention made earlier at MIT by Vannevar Bush.

38 VCA/7/144 typewritten, but undated, press release; notes of the Joint Committee, 27 July 1933.

39 *Ibid.*

40 Advisory Conference, 20 June 1933.

41 Meeting of JCAFS, 18 October 1933.

42 They were based on the levels of support offered by the AAC.

43 Peierls, *Bird of Passage*, p. 114.
44 E.g. Vice-Chancellor to Professor Edward Robertson 18 May 1936 (VCA/7/144) .
45 MUS 12 October 1933.
46 VCA/7/144/3 Rockefeller Foundation, New York, to the Vice-Chancellor 2 August 1933. The Foundation would be able to supplement Manchester's funds in 'particular cases' although not for engineers, applied scientists or classicists.
47 JCAFS 20 September 1933. The Vice-Chancellor reported that he had written to Mr Van Sickle of the Rockefeller Foundation about the possibility of help. Professor Stocks was said to be in correspondence with the AAC on the allocation to the University of persons receiving grants from the Council.
48 JCAFS 20 September 1933 and *passim*.
49 *Ibid.*
50 London, *Whitehall and the Jews*, pp. 7–50; Gerhard Hirschfield, 'A High Tradition of Eagerness' in Messe (ed.), *Second Chance*, pp. 599–610.
51 The Professional Committee was described by Namier as 'a general reserve and insurance fund for all the Jewish professional refugees' (Lewis Namier to the Vice-Chancellor, 21 December 1938 in VCA/7/144).
52 See list, p. 49. The University ultimately gave sanctuary to a total of thirty-three academics: twenty-five from Germany, one from Austria, two from each of Spain and Italy, three from Czechoslovakia. By mid-1935, 148 refugee academics had found temporary, and sixty permanent, posts in Britain. Britain provided the 'first refuge' for over 1,000 scholars who had emigrated from Germany by 1938 (London, *Whitehall and the Jews*, p. 8).
53 JCAFS 9 October 1935: the consortium included 'Barlow, £1,000, Barclay, £350, Renold £70, Turner, £250 over five years, Wolfson £20' (JCAFS 30 April 1936). The only other donation attributable to their efforts was £175 from Robert McDougall.
54 JCAFS 7 October 1935, when the deficit stood at £867, and 4 February 1937, when it was £200.
55 VCA/7/144 Vice-Chancellor to Dr E.M. Brockbank, 23 February 1937.
56 VCA/7/144 Lewis Namier to the Vice-Chancellor, 21 December 1938.
57 Beveridge, *Defence*, p. 24.
58 Giorgio Israel and Pietro Nastasi, *Scienza e razza nell'Italia fascista* (Bologna 1998), pp. 252–256. Of the two 'displaced' Italians taken on by the University of Manchester, Bruno Rossi (1905–93) was an experimental physicist and one of the pioneers of research on cosmic rays. Before coming to Manchester he had held a full professorship at the University of Padua from 1932 to 1938 (Israel and Nastasi, *Scienza e razza*, pp. 160ff., 173, 254, 316 and 358). Benaimino Segre (1903–77) had been Professor of Analytical Geometry at the University of Bologna since 1931 and one of the four members of the board of Italy's most prestigious mathematical journal (*ibid.*, pp. 159, 252, 302, 325–326).
59 Bentwich, *Rescue*, p. 23; VCA/7/369/14th Report of the SPSL. By 1939 the ISS had evolved separate sections for Austrian and Chinese Relief.
60 VCA/7/369/1 SPSL to the Vice-Chancellor 10 January 1939; R.M. Cooper, *Refugee Scholars: Conversations with Tess Simpson* (Leeds 1992), p. 93.
61 VCA/7/369/6 SPSL to the Vice-Chancellor, 7 November 1938.
62 VCA/7/369/1 David Clayhorn Thomson to the Vice-Chancellor, 26 January 1939; Ross Waller to the Vice-Chancellor, 8 December 1938; P.M.S. Blackett to the Vice-Chancellor, 8 December 1938.
63 'The University of Manchester' by 'a Manchester Graduate' in MSWC No. 225, May 1937, pp. 5–6. As examples of the University's growing international repute, the

article cites its Department of Organic Chemistry as the first to study public health and preventive diseases and the 'pioneer work' of its Department for the Education of the Deaf. Apart from the full-time students, the University's Extra-Mural Department organised classes for over 2,000 people.

64 *Ibid.* The University's student body is said to have doubled since 1913. Amongst the innovations of which the University was proud, but which required further funding was the first Chair in organic chemistry, the first department to study public health and preventive medicine and a 'pioneering' department for the education of the deaf.

65 The correspondence is in the University of Manchester Archives, VCA/8/162. Schnabel had been given an Honorary Doctorate in Music by the University in October 1937 (MG 13 October 1937).

66 Dr A. Schnabel to Professor J.L. Stocks, 15 April 1935.

67 Dr A Schnabel to the Vice-Chancellor, University of Manchester, 17 and 26 October 1937.

68 Copy of the Programme in VCA/8/162; Vice-Chancellor of the University of Manchester to Dr A. Schnabel, 3 June 1935, 12 October and 2 November 1937. The situation is summarised in JCAFS 16 May 1935 and MUS 20 January 1938.

69 H.P. Turner to the Vice-Chancellor, University of Manchester, 12 January 1938; MUS 20 January 1938. Turner's recommendation that 'organising expenses' of £22 8s 6d be paid out of the University's ordinary funds rather than those of the JCAFS was apparently rejected (Statement of the Foreign Scholars Fund, 11 January 1938, in VCA/8/162).

70 Dr A. Schnabel to Professor JL Stocks, 15 April 1935.

71 His letters to Manchester in July and October 1936 come from Tremezzo, Lago di Como, Villa Ginetta.

72 For Procter-Gregg's life and achievements, Michael Almond, Peter Hope and John Turner, 'Humphrey Procter-Gregg, 1895–1980: Two Memoirs and a List of Compositions' and Donald Steele, 'Recollections of Humphrey Procter-Gregg, 1932–1937', in *Manchester Sounds* Vol. 4 (2003–04), pp. 71–114. Neither piece throws light on Procter-Gregg's 1937 correspondence with the Vice-Chancellor. He retired from his Manchester professorship in 1962 to become the first Director of the new London Opera Centre; he was awarded a CBE in 1972.

73 Humphrey Procter-Gregg to the Vice-Chancellor, University of Manchester, 18 August 1937 (original emphasis).

74 Humphrey Procter-Gregg to Sydney Moss (the Vice-Chancellor's secretary), 11 October 1937.

75 Humphrey Procter-Gregg to Sydney Moss, 22 September 1937.

76 Greg became a passionate follower of the 'new Hallé', the Hallé Orchestra as it was 'reconstituted' by John Barbirolli (letter from Greg in MG 13 July 1943).

77 Peierls, *Bird of Passage*, pp. 102–103.

78 JCAFS 9 October 1935.

79 *Ibid.*

80 Report attached to JCAFS 9 October 1935. The same report notes that the mathematician Dr Mahler had left in 1934 after one year for the University of Groningen, Dr Rudolf Baer, another mathematician, in 1935, after two years, for the Institute for Advanced Study in Princeton, the physicist Erich Herlinger, in 1933, after only a few months in Manchester, for a post in Palestine.

81 Bruno Rossi, *Moments in the Life of a Scientist* (Cambridge 1990), pp. 38–41. The autobiography frames the event in personal terms: what seems more likely is that Blackett,

as anxious to enhance the status of his department as Bragg, used the mechanism of the JCFAS. Rossi's experience also suggests the degree of international solidarity of physicists engaged in the 'new astronomy'.

82 *Ibid.*, pp. 42–45. In Blackett's laboratory he worked with Ludwig Janossy, a Hungarian physicist 'who had left his own country for the same reason as I had left mine'. Their collaboration offered him 'a chance of starting some experimental work again'.

83 *Ibid.*, p. 49.

84 This included three years (1943–46) in Los Alamos as part of the Manhattan project. On leaving Los Alamos he became Professor of Physics at the Massachusetts Institute of Technology.

85 MUS 3 November 1938.

86 MUS 17 January and 7 March 1935; JCAFS 13 February 1935.

87 Report attached to JCAFS 9 October 1935 *passim*.

88 MUS: For Lowe 30 April 1936, 20 January 1938 and 3 November 1938, when he was granted £600 a year (paid in part by the Rockefeller Foundation) to remain at the University until 1941 as Lecturer in Modern Political Philosophy. For Otto Deutsch JCAFS 8 June 1936 and 5 November 1936, when he was able to supplement a part-time lectureship at the University with part-time work as a biochemist at Christie's Hospital and Radium Institute. £600 of his University salary during 1936–38 was paid from funds made available by Nathan Laski.

89 London, *Whitehall and the Jews*, pp. 49–50.

90 VCA/7/144 Lasnitzki to the Vice-Chancellor 6 October 1938.

91 The Vice-Chancellor to Nathan Laski,14 October 1938 (VCA/7/144).

92 H.S. Raper to the Vice-Chancellor 7 October 1938 (VCA/7/144).

93 Namier to the Vice-Chancellor 19 February and 29 June 1937; the Master of Balliol to Namier 22 June 1937; Namier to Walter Adams 8 July 1937 (VCA/7/144).

94 Laski to the Vice-Chancellor 14 October 1938 (VCA/7/144).

95 Lasnitzki to the Vice-Chancellor 6 October 1938; Dr Malka Lasnitzki to the Vice-Chancellor 22 December 1938 (VCA/7/144).

96 Professor Mordell to Robert McDougall 14 December 1934; Mordell to the Vice-Chancellor 17 December 1934; McDougall to the Vice-Chancellor 14 December 1934 (VCA/7/144).

97 See also correspondence about Katz between T.H. Pear, Professor of Psychology, and the Vice-Chancellor filed under 'David Katz' in VCA/7/144.

98 www.history.mcs.st.andrews.ac.uk/Mathematician/Segre Beniamino.html. (2006)

99 Based chiefly on the minutes and reports to Senate of the JCAFS, 1933–39. The list may well be incomplete: the minutes of the JCAFS after February 1937 have apparently not survived. Entries in brackets are taken from a poor reproduction of part of a list of refugee scholars prepared by Esther Simpson, secretary of the AAC, in Cooper (ed.), *Refugee Scholars*, p. 36. Other names are taken from the 'university intelligence' section of the student magazine, *The Serpent* and from Eric Rowley with Colin Lees, *The University at War, 1939–1946* (Manchester 2001), p. 5.

100 HRF: Honorary Research Fellowship tenable for two years at £250 a year. This was a post specifically created by the University at the suggestion of the Joint Committee.

101 At the time of his appointment to a Manchester Fellowship, Heilbronn, whose academic base was in Gottingen, was a visiting lecturer at the University of Bristol.

102 As an active member of the German Social Democratic Party, Lowe had been particularly aware of his vulnerability after 1933. He had already left Germany with his wife and children for Switzerland before obtaining his Temporary Fellowship in Manchester. Of all the displaced academics reaching Manchester, Lowe was the most

active in the support of other refugees, including members of his own extended family. Taped interview of Doris Angel (née Loewenstein, Felix's daughter) by Lynne Jesky 25 March 2002 (hereafter Doris Angel interview). Doris's brother, Otto, and sister, Eva, arrived in Manchester in April 1936 with places at Manchester Grammar School and Manchester High School for Girls. Doris and her mother, Helene, followed Felix to Manchester in December 1936, apparently with guarantees from Sir Thomas Barlow. Felix had originally intended to return to Stuttgart, but decided to stay in Manchester when he received news of his likely arrest.

103 At the time of his appointment, Peierls was on two years leave of absence from the University of Zurich as a Fellow at Cambridge funded by the Rockefeller Foundation. Born in Berlin, he was educated at the Universities of Berlin, Leipzig and Zurich. In 1933, he felt unable, on account of his Jewish origins, to return to Germany.

104 W.H. Singer arrived with his wife and young son from Bonn in 1938 and found accommodation in Cheadle. Early in 1939 he was employed by the University as lecturer in Economics (Rowley with Lees, *The University at War*, p. 5).

105 VCA/7/369/1 4th Annual Report of the SPSL, November 1938: Manchester had then taken in nine of the scholars placed by the society, Oxford thirty-seven, Cambridge twenty-five, the LSE eleven, Birmingham eight, and Edinburgh seven.

106 Peierls, *Bird of Passage*, p. 95.

107 Bentwich, *Rescue*, p. v, xiii and 40–41.

108 Beveridge, *Defence*, pp. 7 and 42.

109 VCA/7/144 Malka Lasnitzki to the Vice-Chancellor 22 December 1939.

110 Rossi, *Moments*, pp. 1–42, 163.

111 VCA/7/369/1. The list is undated, but the context suggests February 1939.

112 Peierls, *Bird of Passage*, p. 119.

113 For Polanyi (1891–1976), biographical note attached to an abstract of the Michael Polanyi papers in the Department of Special Collections pf the library of the University of Chicago. As a chemist in Manchester, he is said to have 'attracted students and established scientists from all over the world'. His *USSR Economics – Fundamental Data System and Spirit* (1935) marked the beginning of his life-long defence of individual creativity against the inroads of state planning. He retired from Manchester University in 1958 to accept a position as Senior Research Fellow at Merton College, Oxford.

114 Bentwich, *Rescue*, p. 99.

115 Cooper, *Refugee Scholars*, p. 70.

116 *Ibid.*, pp. 58–59, 102. Bethe was awarded a Nobel Prize for Physics in 1967. After witnessing the effects of the atomic bomb at its test on 16 July 1945, he spent the rest of his life trying to control the spread of nuclear weapons.

117 Rossi, *Moments*, pp. 67ff.

4

'Refugees and Eccles Cakes': refugee industrialists in the Manchester region

In September 1967 Dr Heinz Kroch, the German-Jewish refugee from Berlin who thirty years earlier had founded the Lankro Chemical Company in Eccles, an industrial town of some 45,000 people four miles west of Manchester, was presented by the Mayor of Eccles with a casket and scroll to honour his admission to the Roll of Freemen of the Borough.[1] It was an occasion notable, amongst other things, as the first on which the Freedom had been conferred on anyone who had not served on the aldermanic bench. The local councillor who introduced Dr Kroch to the audience in Eccles Town Hall felt that he had to justify the honouring of an industrialist. It was 'right' to do so, he argued, because 'unless we have industry and exports abounding, Lancashire will die again', as he presumed it to have done during the Slump, when Kroch had contributed to its revitalisation.

Kroch was only one example, he went on, of the way in which Eccles had been repaid for the welcome it believed it had always extended to 'people who have had to leave their own lands and own homes under adverse circumstances'. In Silk Street, then the site of one of Lankro's outbuildings, persecuted French weavers had once set up a weaving shed for the manufacture of silk goods. Bentcliffe Works itself, the disused bleachworks which Kroch had purchased and converted, was first built by the German immigrant father of Friedrich Engels. Kroch, like his predecessors, had fully repaid the generosity of his welcome. He had brought work to the town during 'a difficult trading period', made 'a significant and growing contribution' to its prosperity and produced goods for export which had helped save Lancashire from economic ruin. Others at the ceremony, including Kroch's first local employee, paid tribute to his 'humanity', 'generosity', 'modesty' and 'genuine love of the arts'; he was 'a highly cultured man who never sought the limelight'.

Kroch responded that he was 'particularly proud of being honoured by this borough in which I work and which I love'. His 'primary object' in settling in Eccles had been to obtain 'a livelihood for my wife and myself'. His success, for which he gave credit to 'the people of Eccles' who had worked for him and the local authority from which he had received the 'greatest support', was 'beyond his expectations'. 'I wanted freedom and I needed freedom. This England has given me freedom. I am proud to be British and to have become an adopted Lancastrian and an adopted Eccles cake [*sic*]'. In his button-hole, much to the councillor's pleasure, Kroch sported a Lancashire red rose.

How are such events to be interpreted? In the first place, the whole episode may perhaps be seen as a continuance of those ritual exchanges, engineered on both sides, which, from the mid-nineteenth century, sought to define the relationship between Manchester Jewry and the civic authorities of the locality. From the perspective of the city, Manchester tolerance was not only to be repaid by civic virtue; it was the alchemy which transformed strangers into citizens, foreigners into Britishers, Jewish aliens into British Jews. From the perspective of the Jewish communal leadership, social integration, acculturation and civic commitment were the acknowledged price for tolerance. That the contract of which such exchanges were the symbols was rarely more than fragile is clear enough from their very repetition, as each party felt the need to confirm its stance towards the other. In 1967 Eccles, a time and a place troubled by newer waves of immigration, the corporation and the refugee were effectively laying claim to a heritage of reciprocity. For its humanity, the town had been rewarded by the contributions of the stranger; by his contributions, the stranger had confirmed his right to be British; a Jewish German had become an Eccles cake.

The notion of reciprocity was, in fact, central, not only to such retrospective definitions of the local heritage, but to the liberal polemic which surrounded refugee settlement during the 1930s.[2] In May 1939 a writer in the *Manchester Evening Chronicle* saw Lancashire as being 'repaid a thousandfold for its generosity to refugees from Nazi persecution'. By giving 'sanctuary' to Germany's 'ablest chemists, industrialists, engineers, and businessmen … in spite of the fact that the county itself was in the throes of hardship and unemployment', Lancashire had been able to revitalise 'idle' factories, to 'revolutionize' local industry with the aid of newly imported 'secret processes', to provide employment, often in 'model conditions', for thousands of 'happy' local workers, some retrained by their refugee employers, to supply native manufacturers with local sources of raw materials, to capture overseas markets which had once been the sole preserve of German industry, and to introduce Lancashire to courteous and effective forms of salemanship to which it was previously 'unaccustomed'. Glycerine, paint colours, synthetic resins, kid leather, hand-painted silks and satins, collapsible metal tubes (for toothpaste and cosmetics), machine tools, rings and pulleys and the chemicals used in the higher class of tanning were said to be amongst the products introduced into the local economy or produced by 'patent devices' hitherto known only to their refugee inventors. They showed, according to their publicist, 'the indomitable spirit of an oppressed people, and illustrate the way in which so many refugees who have found havens of rest in this country are now repaying it for its generosity'.[3]

Without doubt the British government was quick to recognise the advantage to be gained from drawing upon a widening pool of German (and later Austrian and Czech) entrepreneurs dispossessed by the Nazi regime. The guiding principle, however, in this as in other official responses to refugees, was the national interest.

In April 1933 the British Cabinet came to the conclusion that it was in the public interest to admit to this country German Jewish refugees whose experience of manufacturing and the export trade was likely to ease the deep and sustained economic recession into which Britain had been plunged by foreign competition and the Wall Street Crash.[4] By spring 1936 this policy had been refined by the Ministry of Labour and the Home Office into a positive attempt to steer German industrialists seeking refuge into the areas of deepest depression: particularly into the districts designated by the Special Areas Act of 1934 for the creation of government-sponsored industrial estates (Tyneside, South Wales and the Clyde Valley of Scotland), but also into other parts of the country, including south Lancashire, in which unemployment was particularly high and the staple exporting industries particularly fragile. By the beginning of 1937, as the recession showed no signs of easing, this essentially reactive policy was itself giving way to a concerted effort by government agencies, Special Areas organisations and British consular officers in Europe to induce refugee manufacturers to transfer their skills to areas of Britain in which they might be most usefully deployed. As conditions for the Jews of Austria, Germany and Czechoslovakia deteriorated sharply during 1938–39 what was essentially a government strategy of deploying displaced (and chiefly Jewish) industrialists to ease Britain's economic and social ills was pursued with ever-increasing energy and a growing degree of success.[5]

While simultaneous attempts were being made to persuade native industrialists to relocate to the Special Areas, foreign firms were particularly welcome since, while equally eligible for the preferential terms relating to rent and rates offered to all industrialists, few of the refugees required the additional financial assistance (up to 50% of their capital costs) claimed by most native firms. According to one informed contemporary observer, most of the earliest refugee industries to be established were capitalised 'either out of funds already accumulated in this country and temporarily invested, or out of the moneys brought out of Germany in the early days of the Nazi regime before the imposition of crippling restrictions'.[6] Even after the Nazi regime made the transfer of capital virtually impossible after 1936, many German and Austrian industrialists were able to draw on the funds of friends and relatives in Britain or in other countries in which they had found refuge,[7] or even of British entrepreneurs, to satisfy the Home Office requirement that they possessed the means to establish viable concerns.

While no official inducements were held out to businesses re-establishing themselves in districts of economic depression beyond the designated Special Areas, a fact which was a source of constant irritation to those seeking the regeneration of Lancashire,[8] refugee firms in these areas might benefit from the resources of relatives and peers who had preceded them. In establishing Lankro Chemicals Dr Heinz Kroch was able to draw heavily on the capital of his father-in-law, C.S. Mahler, who had earlier escaped with it to Lichtenstein.[9]

While the British government saw in the establishment by 1939 of some 200 refugee industries outside the Greater London area[10] a sign of its success in easing unemployment in the 'distressed areas', for the promoters of the refugee cause the creation (by 1942) of a total of 300 factories employing up to 30,000 British workers was offered as clear proof of the benefits which accrued from refugee settlement.[11]

After 1933 the Lancashire Industrial Development Council (LIDC), the body founded in Manchester in April 1931 to coordinate the economic regeneration of the county in the face of a declining cotton trade,[12] saw in beleaguered German industrialists one means by which Lancashire's industrial base might be profitably extended and diversified.[13] Its lavish promotional booklet, *Lancashire, Industrial and Commercial,* first published in 1932 and setting out the virtues of 'the World's Greatest Manufacturing Area', was available in French and German editions 'for readers abroad':[14] it included a section entitled 'If you want a factory in Lancashire here's what you do.'[15] In 1932 it devised an 'Overseas Propaganda Scheme' which by 1936 included the placing of advertisements in the German press 'inviting people with skills and who wished to change their residence' to apply to the Board's headquarters at Manchester's Ship Canal House, from where they were escorted around the county in search of suitable sites and premises.[16] The LIDC saw its task as guiding newcomers to 'clearings' which were being made in the wood of the Lancashire economy by the felling of some of the 'oaks' of the cotton trade by Britain's competitors; the hollow remains of some of these 'oaks' dotted the Lancashire textile area in the form of empty, and sometimes derelict cotton mills and weaving sheds.[17]

These were not primarily acts of humanity; rather they were a continuation of policies being pursued long before the German crisis. Since 1931 the LIDC had seen itself as competing with the Special Areas and with London and the south-east in attracting to Lancashire both native and foreign industrialists. The first 'overseas industrialists' to take the bait were not escapees from persecution, but far-sighted German, Dutch and French firms reacting to Britain's departure from the Gold Standard and a new fiscal policy of erecting a high tariff wall around British markets. By June 1933, 23 'firms of overseas origin' had been set up in Lancashire 'either on their own account or in conjunction with local interests'.[18] Intensive publicity which achieved this result included advertisements, letters and articles in foreign newspapers and trade journals; promotional films 'in sound and silent versions'; a regular column in *Industrial Britain,* a periodical issued by the Travel and Industrial Development Association of Great Britain and Ireland; stalls at European trade fairs; and posters in continental ports of departure and British ports of arrival. Attempts to 'overcome prejudice' against a county traditionally seen abroad as caked with industrial grime included a booklet *This Surprising Lancashire,* which sought in words and pictures to 'whet the appetite' for relocation by spelling out Lancashire's historical heritage and rural charms.[19]

No special effort was made to draw in German-Jewish firms; the overriding consideration was the economic and social health of the county.[20] Although many of the 'factory enquiries and development proposals' which reached the Council during the first half of 1938 were said to 'emanate from the Continent and particularly from those countries in which political conditions are most difficult', most were ruled out by their lack of adequate capital or by their potential competition with 'established industries in Lancashire'.[21] On a Council of over sixty members – including representatives of local authorities, development committees and chambers of commerce, and co-optees from the University of Manchester, the Manchester Ship Canal Company, the Mersey Docks and Harbour Board, local banks, railway companies, trade associations and trade unions – between 1932 and 1940 there was not a single Jewish member.

It was none the less the case that many of the refugee industrialists who found their way into Lancashire between 1933 and 1938 did so through the medium of the LIDC. Dr Kroch's Lankro appears to have owed its Eccles base to advertisements placed by the LIDC in the German press. A list of new industries named in a 'pictorial survey' published by the Council in 1938,[22] in part to suggest the efficacy of its efforts, in part to advertise once again the superiority of Lancashire over other British locations, includes six firms set up by Jewish refugee industrialists: the Lancashire Tanning Company, established in Littleborough in 1936 (of which more later); the Manchester Oil Refinery, set up by two German-Jewish entrepreneurs on Manchester's Trafford Park Industrial Estate; Neuman's (later Newman's) Slippers Limited, established by Walter Neuman in a former weaving shed in Blackburn 'for the production of women's footwear of a type chiefly made on the Continent'; the Lancashire Handbag Company, which manufactured ladies' handbags at factories in Oldham and Burnley; M. Wolf's Universal Leather Good in Blackburn; and E.G. Wertheimer's Universal Metal Products, founded in Salford in 1935.

Wertheimer's experience was incorporated into the Council's propaganda, although not as the Jewish victim of persecution. He was used rather as part of the Council's attempt to give itself an edge over competitors in the Special Areas by suggesting the advantages of Lancashire over sites in Scotland, London and the Midlands. In Lancashire, he is quoted as saying, 'labour conditions' were particularly satisfactory: skilled workers were more readily available than elsewhere, his own workers 'efficient, keen and willing, and easy to get on with'. Transport facilities were excellent: 'all goods we are loading in the evening are delivered first thing next morning'. He had no regrets over choosing Lancashire: the vibrancy of his trade in 'collapsible metal tubes' had already caused him to build an extension to his factory in Salford.[23] They were only a small fraction of the Council's overall achievement. By 1938, notwithstanding some local comment that the Council was not acting with sufficient urgency, 200 derelict cotton mills and weaving sheds had been converted to other purposes, a number of London firms had been persuaded to relocate and spaces had been created in new industries for 25,000 of the region's unemployed.[24]

Other German-Jewish firms made their way to the region without recourse to the LIDC and probably without its knowledge. In 1934 the Nazi government, anxious to earn foreign currency for use in the German armaments industry, decided to allow between eighteen and twenty German clothing firms to establish branches in England, provided only that they were financed by foreign capital and that their profits were remitted to Germany. One of these was M. Wolfsky of Berlin, a firm of mantle-manufacturers owned by three Jewish partners, Leo and Fritz Wolfsky and Hans Cohen, at which, as it happened, one of the trainee managers was Rolf, the son of the supplier of their raw material, Leopold Lindemann. A major industrialist, with weaving sheds in Saxony and a spinning mill in Silesia, Leopold Lindemann was able to offer Cohen and his partners the capital they needed for starting their English branch from a Trust he had set up in Switzerland (it was said to keep his profits safe in the event of a Communist coup); his condition was that once established in Britain they would offer employment to his son at the end of his training in Berlin. In the summer of 1934 the firm of M. Wolfsky was thus set up in Dantzic Street, Manchester, under the management of Fritz Wolfsky and employing a young German-Jewish designer, Gusti Lewin, also from Berlin.[25] Leopold Lindemann – his own factory, Leopold Lindemann and Gotthard Kessler AG, having been sequestered by the Nazis – arrived in Manchester in 1936 with his wife and son, Rolf. There, in February 1939 he used some of his Swiss capital to buy a 75% shareholding in the long-established but then ailing waterproof garment factory of Philip Frankenstein and Sons at Newton Heath in east Manchester. With the help of his son, he revived the factory's fortunes, creating, amongst other things, a subsidiary plant in Salford for what became the profitable manufacture of anti-gas clothing.[26]

Board of Trade statistics indicate that the north-west of England was second only to Greater London in attracting new enterprises to its region in the later 1930s – 116 in 1936 and 120 in 1937 as against the respective figures for London of 256 and 215 – but of these only a small (but unknown) portion were from overseas, and of overseas firms not all were established by refugees.[27] Contemporary figures for refugee businesses set up in the Manchester region do not exist. A list of 'Refugee Industries' (which includes some commission agents and wholesale distributors, but only one retailer) was compiled by the Manchester Jewish Refugees Committee in May 1942, very probably for the purpose of finding places for refugee trainees; it includes the names of forty-eight enterprises founded by refugees then operating in the region: twenty-one in Manchester, five in Salford, the rest dispersed over a wide area encompassing Blackburn, Bolton, Burnley, Nelson, Oldham and Rochdale in south Lancashire; Glossop in Derbyshire; Cheadle, Timperley and Macclesfield in Cheshire.[28] This was an underestimate. Other sources reveal a further twelve businesses set up wholly or in part by refugees before 1942, including industrial enterprises in Colne, Darwen and Preston.

Nor does this estimate include either refugee industrialists and researchers working for British firms – a number larger, it was said, than in other parts of Britain[29] – or what was probably a substantial number of independent export companies, commission agencies, shops and wholesale warehouses created by refugees. Some of these arose out of links, commercial and familial, between Manchester agencies exporting clothing or cotton goods, many created by immigrants of earlier arrival, and their distributors in Germany. In 1936 Otto Hertz, a director of a large yarn and clothing factory in Chemnitz, and his fellow director, Oscar Leopold Einstein, gained entry to Britain through guarantees offered by Otto's brother, Charles, a naturalised British citizen with a clothing business in central Manchester. Soon after their arrival both set up their own businesses as agents in the garment and textile trades.[30] Otto Hertz was later to give a loan to his refugee sister-in-law, Sally Feibelmann, to enable her to set up a small dress-wear workshop in Manchester. There were other ways in which links were made between Jewish entrepreneurs in textiles in Germany seeking a means of escape and Manchester's extensive textile industry. Felix Loewenstein, who with his brother Arthur owned a mill near Tubingen manufacturing furnishing fabrics and a distributing agency in Stuttgart, their home town, was introduced to contacts in Manchester by Dr Adolf Lowe, a relative by marriage who in 1933, as a 'displaced academic', had accepted a temporary fellowship at the University of Manchester. It was Lowe, acutely conscious of the potential risks faced by Jewish businessmen in Germany, who persuaded Felix Loewenstein to visit Manchester in 1934 to meet a leading textile manufacturer, Sir Thomas Barlow (also a member of the Court of Manchester University), from whom he subsequently obtained the guarantee and offer of employment which brought him to Manchester in July 1936. Within the next three years Loewenstein established his own firm, 'Helio's', manufacturing ladies' clothing, in Bolton.[31]

Refugee shopkeepers rarely appear in the records. One exception is the butcher's shop set up in Leicester Road by the orthodox refugee, Jonah Halberstadt, probably in 1938, to serve the refined kosher needs of the newly-established ultra-orthodox community in north Manchester, Machzikei Hadass. Another is the 'Viennese Model House' set up in All Saints, Manchester, in mid-March 1939 by Flora Weiss, once 'one of the most famous dress designers in Vienna' with a model house 'known all over Europe', and her daughter 'Madame Kessler'. Her workroom, producing clothing at once 'flattering' and 'inexpensive', was, according to a reporter from the *Manchester City News*, 'an argument against the people who say that refugees are taking work that should go to our own people': apart from one expert embroiderer, also from Vienna, her workers were local people 'doing jobs that otherwise they would have had no chance of doing, learning to model patterns and do exquisite embroidery and bead work'.[32]

Few 'refugee businesses' owed even their origins, let alone their development, solely to refugee enterprise. From the earliest years of the Nazi regime British entrepreneurs came to recognise, as much as the British government, that in refugee expertise there existed a possible route to their own economic salvation: one means by which they might beat off the challenges of a depressed overseas trade, Britain's increasingly high tariff wall and the prospect of war. As often as not, Britain's door to refugee businessmen was opened by those who feared for their own survival and saw the harnessing of refugee enterprise as one means of achieving it. Many industries which might superficially be seen as 'refugee contributions' to the British economy, were, in reality, constructed out of the mutual self-interests of the refugee and the native entrepreneur, each playing a financial and managerial role in their creation. The refugee might seek rescue and the native prove willing to facilitate it; at the end of the day, both were also businessmen with an ultimate eye to profit. To the LIDC, to whom notions of rescue were irrelevant, and which had no particular interest in the sources of the capital deployed by incoming firms or their structures of management, the combination of 'British and Continental interests' was unexceptional;[33] British Depa Crepes, for example, was set up for the processing of rayon creping 'by a special continental system', by the purchase of a disused mill at Hollinwood by an 'Anglo-Austrian syndicate' led by the Austrian Jewish entrepreneur, K.K. Pacht.[34]

Nowhere is this coincidence of native self-interest and refugee need more evident than in the train of events which led to the creation of the Lancashire Tanning Company (otherwise Lanctan), which began the production of high quality 'full chrome leather' at the beginning of 1937 in Littleborough, an industrial village within the conurbation of Rochdale, a town previously best known for mills which produced woollen and, particularly, cotton textiles.

The people of Rochdale, a mill town of 90,000 people in south-east Lancashire, some twelve miles from Manchester, were first alerted to the potential arrival of 'foreigners' by the *Rochdale Observer,* which, in a news item of 11 March 1936, under the heading 'New Littleborough Industry', announced that the Atlas Works on the bank of the River Roch, once a thriving factory producing artificial silk, had been sold off and would 'be restarted as a tannery by an English company with a foreign technical staff'. An unnamed 'local gentleman' said to have been 'concerned in the negotiations' is quoted as saying that when the new industry began production, in 'five or six months' time', it would 'absorb a good deal of local labour, both men and women'. The implication was that its establishment would compensate for the closure of the Atlas Works, which event, ten years earlier, had been a 'big blow' to Littleborough, and so hasten the economic regeneration of Rochdale. On points of detail, the reporter was either ill-informed or deliberately reticent. Although an English company was certainly involved, the new industry was to be primarily the first British branch of the giant European leather-manufacturing conglomerate, Adler and Oppenheimer; its 'foreign staff', directors and managers as well as scientists and technicians, were all of them German Jews linked to one or other of the continental tanneries of the parent concern.

In the late 1920s Adler and Oppenheimer was one of Europe's leading producers of high quality, 'full chrome' leather[35] with substantial plants in Neustadt and Neumunster in Germany, Wiltz in Luxemburg and Oisterwijk in Holland, sales offices in Berlin, Paris and Amsterdam, and a world-wide export trade for which London was one important market. The company had been founded in Lingolsheim, a town south of Strasbourg in Alsace-Lorraine, by two German-Jewish cousins, Isaac Adler and Ferdinand Oppenheimer who, with other enterprising Germans, had moved into Alsace soon after its acquisition by Germany following the Franco-Prussian War of 1871. It was only after the restoration of Alsace to France after the First World War, and the subsequent sequestration of the Lingolsheim plant by the French authorities, that the Adler and Oppenheimer principals transferred their capital and expertise to other European sites. It remained very much a family concern, its control firmly in the hands of seven Adler and Oppenheimer cousins, voting shares passing down only to the direct patrilineal descendants of the founders.[36] In 1929 some 3,500 workers were employed in the firm's four major tanneries to process around 11,000 skins a day, chiefly of the kinds of 'heavy' bovine leather sought after by the world's manufacturers of high-quality footwear.[37] British shoe and leather goods manufacturers, with no local source of chrome leather, depended upon the supply of Adler and Oppenheimer skins by the firm's main London distributors, Bevingtons and Sons of Bermondsey. By 1929 Adler and Oppenheimer leather was said to have provided 'the lion's share of the turnover of [Bevingtons'] Foreign Leather Department',[38] Bevingtons' attempts to produce chrome leather in its own London-based Neckinger Mills had met with repeated failure.[39]

Looking back on the events which followed, Werner Treuherz, the man deputed by Adler and Oppenheimer in 1936 to organise the construction of their Littleborough plant, remembered them primarily as an episode in Hitler's war against the Jews. According to this version, Harold Power, then Bevingtons' Sales Director (later to become its Chairman), became aware of the full force of Nazi anti-Semitism during a visit to Berlin in 1934. Immediately he sought to persuade the Adler and Oppenheimer principals 'that they should not live under such conditions and should start a tannery in England'. 'They did not like it,' this account continues, 'but Power wrote a letter to the Home Office asking for permission for them to come to England and start a tannery, particularly as England had not enough leather in case of war.'[40]

This seems unlikely. What Treuherz's memories suggest, rather, is the way in which the notion of reciprocity had been assimilated by former refugee German-Jews whose perception of their place in German society, prior to the rise of Hitler, had been based on a similar premise, and whose retrospective perception of their rescue was coloured by their subsequent knowledge of the Holocaust: in Britain, and in later life, Treuherz required benefactors worthy of his gratitude.

In a more complex reality, the foundation of Lanctan has all the hallmarks of a marriage of economic convenience. Bevingtons' earliest efforts to persuade the Adler and Oppenheimer principals to set up a tannery in Britain had, in fact, long preceded Hitler's rise to power. They were, in the first place, an attempt to sustain the high profits of their own trade in Adler and Oppenheimer products, against a background of the protective tariffs imposed on imported leather by the British government after 1929, very probably to encourage local tanneries to branch into the production of full chrome.[41] By 1933 these tariffs had risen to 15% to 20% on calf skins.[42] The real effect of the rise of Nazi anti-Semitism was to render such an arrangement mutually advantageous. Even before 1933 Adler and Oppenheimer principals had apparently been aware of the risks of their over-dependence on their German production; it has been suggested that the setting up of the Oisterwijk tannery in Holland during 1929–30 'was the first attempt by the two families to build up assets outside Germany where the anti-Jewish feeling was already very much in evidence'.[43] Hitler's emergence confirmed these fears. In 1933 the young Heinz (later Henry) Lehmann, a patrilineal grandson of Ferdinand Oppenheimer, one of the 'seven cousins' (and therefore an heir to shares in the company), was sent to Britain to work in Bevingtons' Foreign Leather Department,[44] perhaps to gain experience of British conditions, perhaps also to lay the foundations of a joint enterprise on British soil.

It must have been in 1933 or 1934 that Power approached the Home Office on Adler and Oppenheimer's behalf to seek permission for them to establish a plant in Britain.[45] Although details of the negotiations which followed have not survived, it is said to have taken the Home Office, still undecided as to its appropriate stance towards refugee industrialists, eighteen months to give its assent.[46] At all events, by 1935 Bevingtons' Harold Power and Geoffrey Bevington were scouring the country for possible sites,[47] while Adler and Oppenheimer had despatched two of its own directors, Clemens Oppenheimer and Max Weil, to investigate locations acceptable to the British authorities.[48] Although details of the way in which the search was conducted are now also lost, it seems likely that it was the Lancashire Industrial Development Council which finally came up with an acceptable offer. To the Council, and equally to the Home Office, Rochdale, where high levels of unemployment had already generated social unrest,[49] must have appeared a particularly appropriate location for a new industry likely to absorb up to 500 workers. In its own report of the arrival of Lanctan, the LIDC congratulated itself on a coup; Adler and Oppenheimer had settled on Littleborough 'only after close inspection and consideration of many other propositions [*sic*] elsewhere in the country'.[50] Although some of the promises made to achieve this result were beyond fulfilment – not least the navigability of the Roch – the Atlas Works had the real advantage of being the kind of one-storey building most readily converted to tanning.[51]

Finally, Werner Treuherz, a matrilineal grandson of Lazarus Oppenheimer, another of the 'seven cousins', and then a member of the sales staff at the Adler and Oppenheimer plant in Neumunster, was sent to prepare the conversion of the Atlas Works. He arrived in Littleborough on 6 April 1936, his departure from Germany hastened, according to his own account, by his impending arrest by the Gestapo, and after an escape engineered by a senior member of the Neumunster SS who had once been one of his father's customers.[52] His choice for the task, apart from his family links, appeared to rest on a better working knowledge of the English language than his superiors: early in his university career he had spent six months at the London School of Economics.

Aided by the advice of Adler and Oppenheimer's German architects and engineers, and monitored by Dr Paul Oppenheimer, the only son of Ferdinand, and then director of the Neumunster plant, Treuherz then set about the repair and conversion of 'a shambles' of buildings, some of them derelict, all of them requiring re-equipment, between the River Roch and the LMS railway line into Littleborough, some two miles from the centre of Rochdale. These were massive operations. A borehole was drilled into the bank of the Roch to provide the 750,000 gallons of water a week required for production; a sewage plant was constructed which was ultimately to deal with the effluent equivalent to that of a town of 60,000 people.[53] In a little over a year, 'a huge hall of ruins'[54] was transformed into a modern tannery 'the size of about two and a quarter football pitches' capable of producing 'about six million square feet of leather each year'.[55] Starting production on a small scale during 1937, Lanctan was said to be in 'full swing' by the autumn of 1939, with an initial workforce of 400, rising rapidly to between 500 and 600.[56] Oppenheimer was its managing director, Treuherz its 'technical director', Lehmann the buyer of the quality skins from hide auctions throughout the country.

Clearly the Adler and Oppenheimer family had been active in promoting a development which was to its personal and economic advantage. For some members of the family – Paul Oppenheimer, Lehmann and Treuherz – it provided a route to safety; for others, who found a more distant haven of safety in the Argentine – chiefly descendants of the Adler branch – it secured the profitable investment of some, at least, of the family fortune.

Equally clear, however, were the advantages gained by Bevingtons'; for them, according to one of their later employees, it was 'a very good deal'. In effect, they secured three sources of profit: a local and cheap supply of raw materials; a home market in which, as 'the sole agency for [Lanctan] products in the Great Britain and Ireland', they could now undercut their (few) British rivals; and a return on their ownership of Lanctan shares. Some 65% of the £20,000 of Lanctan's initial share capital was invested by members of the Adler and Oppenheimer families in person, 10% by the Oisterwijk branch of the company, 25% by Bevingtons.[57] The composition of the Lanctan Board reflected these arrangements. Harold Power and Paul Oppenheimer became joint managing directors of a Board of Management which comprised Treuherz, Lehmann, Geoffrey Bevington (a grandson of Bevingtons' founder) and Charles Adler in the Argentine.[58] The British economy was the other beneficiary: a new industry had been created of immediate benefit to local manufacturers and with potential for expanding Britain's export trade, realised after the war, when Lanctan supplied high-quality leather to the world's leading producers of fashion footwear.

The LIDC interpreted the arrival of Lanctan as proof of the efficacy of its propaganda. A firm had been induced to buy 200,000 square feet of disused property and 90 acres of land.[59] It was in this way, rather than as acts of salvation, that the LIDC perceived its reception of Jewish refugee entrepreneurs. When, in 1936, another German-Jewish industrialist, Walter Newman (formerly Neuman), was persuaded to establish a factory in Blackburn, the LIDC reported that this success had been 'gained in [the] face of keen competition from the Greater London area'.[60]

Lanctan (and very probably other refugee firms) were also the beneficiary of the LIDC's attempts to attract the attention of government contracting departments to the manufacturing potential of Lancashire, as Britain's Rearmament Programme gathered pace after 1936. While accepting that war contracts were, in the end, a matter for negotiation between particular companies and the service departments, in its own eyes the LIDC 'exerted considerable influence towards securing a fair proportion of the work for Lancashire'.[61] Whether or not through the instrumentality of the LIDC, Lanctan was the recipient of two profitable service contacts. The uppers of the boots worn by members of the armed forces required the kind of high-quality leather of which Lanctan was one of the very few British producers; it is said that during the war the firm produced 60% of the total leather required by the British armed forces. According to one account, it was one of Bevingtons' salesmen, Sidney White, who later came up with the idea of using a self-sealing leather coating to solve the intractable problem of enabling the engines of Lancaster bombers to recover from damage caused by shell splinters. The idea was taken up by Lanctan's chemists and developed in its laboratories, securing the company the Air Ministry contract for the rest of the war.[62]

By this time, Lanctan had also (depending on the perspective) served as an ark for the rescue of other of Adler and Oppenheimer's leading German employees[63] and/or composed an effective managerial and scientific elite from staff already experienced in its continental plants. During 1938–39 at least six current or former Adler and Oppenheimer employees received through Lanctan the guarantees and work permits required for their settlement in England. The industrial chemist Dr Martin Abendstern was born in Stuttgart, where his father had been a senior salesman for Adler and Oppenheimer. Following his father into the firm, Martin spent seven years at the Neumunster tannery. It seems likely that it was for his own greater protection that during 1938 he was transferred first to Oisterwijk and then to Wijk before reaching Littleborough in the August of that year. Already an expert in the colouring of raw leather, at Lanctan he was given charge of the finishing processes at what was known as the 'dry end' of the tannery. The 'wet end', at which the imported skins were put through the initial tanning processes, became the responsibility of the tanner, Otto Taubmann, also a former Adler and Oppenheimer employee, who had spent some time

in Palestine (where he had helped to create a tannery in Jaffa) before settling in Britain during 1938. Charles David, another matrilineal grandson
of Ferdinand Oppenheimer, was taken on in the same year, his departure
from Germany said to have been hastened by the refusal of his wife to sing
for Hitler at a Nuremberg Party Rally. At Lanctan he was placed in charge of
'split-production', the process by which the raw leather was split horizontally
to create the napped surface which was suede leather. Balfried Jaffe, who
was to become Lanctan's sales manager, had worked since he was seventeen
or eighteen in the office of Adler and Oppenheimer in Berlin. During 1938
his father, Abraham Jaffe, already under suspicion for his left-wing political leanings, arranged, by various devices, the departure of his whole family for London. The guarantor found for Balfried himself was the Chinese
scholar, Arthur Waley. Arriving in London in January 1939, Jaffe moved to
Littleborough a few months later.[64] The managerial elite was completed by
two former Adler and Oppenheimer technicians – the Hungarian-born Jan
Schraeder and Eric Hueber, a young Swiss chemist and son of the manager
of the Oisterwijk tannery.[65]

The very existence of Lanctan appears to have eased the entry of German
entrepreneurs in the chemical industry specialising in the manufacture of tanning salts, or, at any rate, to have caused them to be directed by the LIDC or
the Home Office to the Manchester region. One was Heinz Kroch's Lankro,
of which more later. The other was the Lancashire Chemical Works, founded in 1937 by the German refugees, Dr Walter Hene and Rudolf Hecksher,
in a converted tram depot in Glossop, Derbyshire, which specialised in the
production of just those chrome tanning salts on which the high quality of
Lanctan leather depended.[66] There is insufficient evidence at present to pos-
it a (likely) chain development in which the founders of Lanctan (or their
partners in Bevingtons) persuaded German suppliers of the parent firm to
follow them to Britain.

An even more complex amalgam of native enterprise, refugee skills, national interests and personal need was represented in the creation of Anglofelt
Industries, a felt-making plant in Whitworth, an industrial village three miles
out of Rochdale on the road to Bacup, during 1938–39.[67] Considerations
of humanity were again complicated by economic self-interest. In 1929 two
brothers of Dutch-Jewish origin, Richard and Edmund Wolf, had set up
in business in Hull importing wool and hair, chiefly from South America,
for re-sale in a market which included some of the leading felt-makers in
Weimar Germany. In 1938 they were approached by one of their long-standing German-Jewish customers, Hans Neuhaus, a felt-maker from Hanover,
for help in leaving Germany and re-establishing his firm in Britain. Aware
that their own international trade was in danger of disruption by war, the
brothers Wolf approached one of their British customers, the Valley Supply
Company, which supplied accessories – thread, laces, heels and packaging
as well as felt lining – to the many slipper-makers who in the late 1920s and
early 1930s had taken over buildings vacated by the spinners of coarse cotton

in the Rossendale Valley. These new manufacturers of 'Slipper Valley' were at first dependent for slipper insoles on imported felt. With the assent of the Lancashire Industrial Development Council, a deal was now struck by which the Valley Supply Company provided the accommodation and much of the capital, the Wolf brothers the commercial skills and Neuhaus the industrial expertise for the establishment of a felt-making plant in a former cotton mill in Tong Lane, Whitworth. By the outbreak of war, the factory was in production with around forty local workers.

Thus Neuhaus made his escape; the Valley Supply Company acquired a local source of raw materials; the Lancashire slipper-makers survived the loss of their overseas suppliers, the Wolf brothers the loss of their overseas markets; Britain acquired a new industry based on refugee expertise and potentially useful to its war effort. During the war years, Anglofelt Industries supplied the Ministry of Munitions with felt linings for the containers of delicate military equipment, for the storage of which they were allowed a bonded warehouse on the Whitworth site.[68]

Lanctan and Anglofelt owed their origins, in part, at least, to the pressures being brought to bear on the British importers of German goods by protective tariffs and the approach of war; either way, native entrepreneurs were bent as much on salvaging their own economic fortunes as on saving the lives of their German-Jewish peers. Equally, the priority of the British government was the welfare of the nation; only those businessmen found entry easy whose enterprise was adjudged likely to remedy the economic and social malaise generated by the depression in world trade.

Refugee businessmen themselves were a good deal more, however, than the passive recipients of British aid, whether governmental or private. They were, for the most part, experienced and successful entrepreneurs: the arrangements into which they entered with British entrepreneurs were a route not only to their personal safety, but to the regeneration of their economic concerns and the restoration of their lost wealth. This was clearly the case with the Adler and Oppenheimer principals, with the Wolf brothers and Hans Neuhaus. Although the detail is lacking, the evidence suggests that other German industrialists were entering into the kinds of partnership with British entrepreneurs which would facilitate the relocation of their companies as well as of themselves. This would appear to have been the case during 1936–37 with a firm set up in Colne for the 'manufacture of rayon dress fabrics of Continental styles', with a company established in Manchester for the manufacture of 'crepe paper goods' and with a firm which in 1938 took over an empty mill in Darwen as a knitwear factory 'to supply established British and overseas clientele'.[69] Universal Metal Products is said to have been established in the Pendleton district of Salford partly on the basis of the capital, technical expertise and skilled staff brought to Britain by its founder, E.G. Wertheimer, partly through 'the support of an [unnamed] British chemical enterprise'.[70] Relocation was a means by which refugee industrialists retained control of their export markets. Walter Newman's slipper factory in

Blackburn was said to supply his 'existing clientele in Great Britain and the Empire'.[71]

Another way in which refugee entrepreneurs might seek their economic salvation was by drawing on the support of their German peers. While still in Germany this might take the form of seeking guarantees or employment from refugees who had preceded them. Once in Britain, it became a means for seeking out new opportunities which better befitted their experience, skills and ambitions. There are signs that by the mid-1930s such concerns had led to the emergence within the refugee community of a network of communications, which alerted newcomers to vacancies within existing refugee industries, and refugee industrialists to the arrival of potential new recruits.

The interconnections were for the most part informal. According to one young refugee, Franz Wolfgang Rosen, 'somebody knew somebody, this was how it worked'. His own father, Fritz Rosen, well-known as a commercial artist in Berlin, found clients amongst refugees in London, where he settled in 1939, on the basis of his contacts and reputation in Germany. He, in turn, was to find an opening for his son with a refugee industrialist in Lancashire whose logo he had been called on to design. It was Franz Rosen's view that 'refugees at that time … knew few other people. So when a new refugee appeared on the scene [he] got in touch with other refugees that [he] knew were there. And if a refugee arrived and needed a job then other refugees who had places of employment would try … to give that refugee a job, whether they were qualified or not really.'[72] This was the case, for example, with the refugee industrialist E.G. Wertheimer's Universal Metal Products in Salford. His system of production was said to have been put in place by 'experts from Austria and Czechoslovakia'. Once well-established, he found employment in his tool-making shed for at least three unemployed Jewish refugees: Harry Korischona from Vienna, Ludwig Simon, who had trained in metal work with Youth Aliya in the German Rhineland, and the young Berliner, Gerhard Zadek.[73] This was the way, Russell believed, in which his own future employer, Heinz Kroch, had laid the foundations of Lankro Chemicals; Kroch's first senior employees were chosen not for their outstanding abilities, but by chance contacts within the world of German refugees.

Heinz Kroch was born in Berlin on 29 March 1904, into a middle-class and substantially assimilated Jewish family already established, in a modest way, in the German chemical industry; in its plants in Hamburg and Berlin, his father's firm, Chemische Fabrik Siegfried Kroch AG, manufactured some of the chemical oils and pigments required by the German leather industry. Following a secondary education at the Herder Schule and the study of chemistry at the Universities of Freiburg, Berlin and Munich, Heinz joined the family firm as a research chemist soon after the award of his doctorate by the Kaiser Wilhelm Institute of the University of Berlin in 1926. By 1930 he had become one of its directors. Following the subsequent 'Aryanisation' of the company, he made a series of exploratory visits to Britain in search of possible sites, one of them, it seems, in response to an advertisement placed in the German press by the Lancashire Industrial Development Council. According to his own later account, Dr Kroch 'responded to the advertisement and was taken around Lancashire and eventually decided upon coming to Eccles to the Bentcliffe Works [a bleach works] which had been closed for about 12–18 months'. There, having obtained official permission from the Home Office in November 1936 for the setting up of a chemical plant, the Lankro (an amalgam of Lancashire and Kroch) Chemical Company went into production on 12 February 1937, with the help of a capital outlay of £5,000 provided by Kroch's father-in-law, C.S. Mahler, himself a successful German industrialist who had found early refuge (with his capital) in Liechtenstein and who now settled in Eccles as a director of Lankro. The company was at first 'a modest operation', with sixty or seventy workers, producing only the range of leather chemicals with which Kroch was already familiar and using recipes for oils and pigments he had learnt at his father's firm.[74]

Lankro began as 'a pure refugee enterprise'.[75] Three other dispossessed Germans – two industrial chemists and an engineer – were drawn in by Kroch through the refugee grapevine. Dr Arthur Wolf, who became Lankro's first production manager, was in 1937 employed as a research chemist in the Berlin laboratories of the Oranienburger Chemische Fabrik AG, a non-Jewish firm manufacturing auxiliary products for the textile, leather, detergent and fur industries. By then, although accorded some protection by non-Jewish colleagues in a firm for which he had worked since 1930, he was facing a sufficient degree of Nazi-inspired harassment and social isolation to seek opportunities abroad. This did not prove easy. Although supported by 'excellent references' from his managing director, he applied, without success, to the company's agencies in Italy, France, Czechoslovakia and Britain. In the case of Hexoran, the firm's English agency in Trafford Park, Manchester, with whose technical correspondence he had dealt with for many years, he was turned down by its head, a Mr Goedecke, 'a fanatical Hitler admirer of German origin'. Finally, in August 1937, by now facing dismissal, Wolff travelled to Manchester in some desperation for an interview with Kroch, himself in urgent need of research assistance; at Lankro he was offered employment on an initial salary of £7 a week, sufficient for the work permit which gave him the right to temporary residence in Britain.[76] His appointment, Tony Russell believes, like that of two other refugees – the pigment chemist, Dr Ernst Levy, and the engineer, Franz Schlesinger – was, for Kroch, a matter of expediency at a time when he lacked the capital and the contacts to look further afield.

Notes

1 The following account is based on the report in the *Eccles and Patricroft Journal* (hereafter *EPJ*) of 7 September 1967. The conferment of the honour is anticipated in a report in *EPJ* 15 December 1966. In both issues, it is front-page news. For a history of Lankro, see below. The population of Eccles in 1931 was 44,838; its industries included cotton-spinning, silk-throwing, engineering, soap-making and the manufacture of fustians and ginghams.

2   Cf. Sir Norman Angell and Dorothy Buxton, *You and the Refugee* (London 1939); *Are Refugees an Asset?*, published for Political and Economic Planning (PEP) (London [1945?]); Dorothy Frances Buxton, *The Economics of the Refugee Problem*, (London [1939?]).

3   Leaflet, 'How Refugees Help Lancashire: New Industries with Secret Processes, by A Special Correspondent. Reprinted by courtesy of the *Manchester Evening Chronicle* of 16 May 1939'.

4   Herbert Loebl, 'Refugees from the Third Reich and Industry in the Depressed Areas of Britain', in Mosse (ed.), *Second Chance*, p. 380.

5   A classic account of the evolution of British policy towards refugee industrialists and its outcome is provided by Loebl, 'Refugees from the Third Reich', pp. 379–404.

6   C. Salway, *Refugees and Industry* (London 1942), p. 13.

7   Loebl, 'Refugees from the Third Reich', p. 387. According to Loebl, British consular officials and the Home Office exercised considerable flexibility in handling applications for visas from German manufacturers.

8   From the its beginnings in 1931, the Lancashire Industrial Development Council (LIDC) sought a means of competing with the Special Areas and with London and the south-east by subsidising the establishment of new industries in the county. By the time it found a means of doing so in 1938 by the setting up of Lancashire Industrial Sites Company Ltd, a quarter of whose capital was provided by the government, the international situation had negated its value, while competition from the Trading Estates in the Special Areas intensified. LIDC 3rd Annual Report (1933–34), p. 6; 4th Annual Report (1934–35), pp. 12–14; 7th Annual Report (1937–38), pp. 10–11; 8th Annual Report (1938–39), p. 5.

9   Recorded author interview with Tony Russell (formerly Franz Wolfgang Rosen), hereafter Tony Russell interview. His father was a partner in the leading firm of commercial artists in Berlin, Bernhard-Rosen. In London he established a successful practice as an independent commercial artist largely on the basis of his refugee clients, who included Heinz Kroch, by whom he was commissioned to design the logo for Lankro Chemicals. There in 1945 Franz Rosen was employed as Kroch's personal assistant, subsequently succeeding him as chairman of the company.

10 Loebl, 'Refugees from the Third Reich', p. 389. Loebl (*ibid.*, p. 380) estimates the number of manufacturing firms established by refugees by 1947 as around 1,000.

11 Salway, *Refugees and Industry*, pp. 13 and 17.

12 The LIDC was founded on the initiative of the secretary of the Manchester Chamber of Commerce, Raymond (later Sir Raymond) Streat in April 1931 to attract new industries to Lancashire and to expand existing industries in the face of a sharp contraction in cotton manufacturing and 'to help [newcomers] choose a location within the county that would provide them with the best chance of success'. Its first president was the Earl of Derby, its chairman the cotton spinner T.D. (later Sir Thomas) Barlow, president of the Manchester Chamber of Commerce, with Streat serving as secretary and director. Later in 1931 an engineer, J. Bennett Storey, was appointed General Manager. The Council was composed of representatives of the 14 chambers of commerce within the county and co-optees from the University of Manchester, the Ship Canal Company, the Mersey Docks and Harbour Board, and Lancashire-based banks, railway companies, power interests, trade associations and trade unions. Over 70 local authorities subscribed to its Overseas Propaganda Scheme; the Council was otherwise supported by public appeal. In 1946 the LIDC became the Lancashire Industrial Development Association, in 1949 the Lancashire and Merseyside

Industrial Development Association, in 1969 the North West Industrial Development Association (NWIDA). (Leaflet *The NWIDA: 50 Years of Service 1931–1981*, published by the NWIDA in 1981).

13 The decline of the Lancashire cotton trade during the inter-war years, uneven but sustained, is put down by John Walton to foreign competition after the First World War, exacerbated by the impact of the slump (John K. Walton, *Lancashire, a Social History, 1558–1939* (Manchester 1987), pp. 329–332).

14 *Lancashire, Industrial and Commercial* (Lancashire Industrial Development Council, Manchester 1935) p. 55.

15 *Ibid.*, pp. 54–55.

16 This is my reading of comments by Dr. Hans Kroch in the *Eccles and Patricroft Journal*, 7 September 1967, on receiving the Freedom of the Borough of Eccles. By 1938, 76 Lancashire authorities were contributing to the Overseas Propaganda Scheme. The LIDC was not interested only in German entrepreneurs; the orbit of its propaganda, which included promotional films and radio broadcasts, embraced France, Belgium, Denmark, India, South Africa, Canada and the USA. Amongst those companies which enquired after LIDC brochures was Fried Krupp AG of Essen (LIDC Quarterly Report, August 1938, p. 3.)

17 *Lancashire, Industrial and Commercial*, p. 50.

18 LIDC 2nd Annual Report (1932–33) p. 37; 3rd Annual Report (1933–34), p. 5.

19 An undated copy (1935 or 1936) survives in MCL. Until 1938 Lancashire could take no advantage of the special terms held out to industries locating in the designated Special Areas. In January 1938, however, under a special act of parliament sponsored by the LIDC, a Lancashire Industrial Sites Company was set up with capital of £260,000, three-quarters of it provided by banks, insurance companies and the LMS, one-quarter by the government, to finance the purchase of sites and the modernisation of buildings for industrial tenants who would acquire them on lease or purchase them on hire-purchase terms. New tenants would also have access to special grants for development purposes. The act came into force only at the end of June 1938 (LIDC 7th Annual Report, pp. 10–11). Even then the Council had problems competing with the developing Trading Estates of the Special Areas (LIDC 8th Annual Report, p. 5).

20 It seems, however, that the LIDC chairman, the Manchester cotton merchant Sir Thomas Barlow, provided the guarantees which enabled Felix Loewenstein of Stuttgart to establish his clothing factory in Bolton in 1938 and for the remainder of his extended family to follow him to Manchester (Doris Angel interview).

21 Quarterly Report of the LIDC, August 1938, p. 5.

22 *Lancashire Builds: Being a Pictorial Survey of the Introduction and Development of many new Industries and Factories in the Lancashire area since 1930* (LIDC, Manchester 1938).

23 *Lancashire Builds ...*, p. 92.

24 *Ibid.*, pp. 45–46. Major British firms listed include the Ferranti Radio Factory at Moston, Fairey Engineering's aircraft factory at Heaton Chapel, Montague Burton's clothing works at Worsley, and new branches of Courtaulds and A.V. Roe. New factories established by *local* Jewish entrepreneurs include two furniture manufacturers in Trafford Park, a waterproofing factory in Salford and the United Leather Goods Company Limited, relocated from London to Blackburn. In commenting on the recent attraction of 62 businesses to Tyneside by the Tyneside Industrial Development Board, the *Rochdale Observer* (11 January 1939) asked why the LICD

had not achieved similar results: 'the answer has generally been that our empty mills are not adapted for industries seeking new sites: one wonders why and whether some of the premises could be made more suitable'.

25 Rolf Lindemann, *Be Careful in the Choice of your Parents* (Privately printed in Miami n.d.), pp. 11–12. Of the firms allowed by the Nazis to set up British branches, some found their way, with the help of government subsidies, onto the Darlington-Auckland Trading Estate in Durham, within one of the designated Special Areas, others to the Manchester region, where they required the kind of private backing provided by Lindemann. After arriving in Manchester in 1936 with his wife and their son Rolf, Leopold first found a manager's post for his son with the Calico Printers Association, of which the vice-chairman was a friend of his, a Mr McCulloch (Lindemann, *Be Careful*, pp. 23–36).

26 *Ibid.*, pp. 37–44. In the war years, Frankenstein and Sons, with Leopold Lindemann as its managing director, won government contracts for the supply of flying suits, battle-dresses, great coats, ground sheets, hospital clothing, bullet-proof petrol-tank fabrics for aircraft, balloon fabrics, arctic, jungle and bush-wear, and paratroop smocks (*ibid.*, pp. 43–44).

27 Quarterly Report of the LIDC, August 1938 p. 6. The annual reports of the LIDC include notices of new firms from France and Holland including one, its origins unknown, which manufactured 'Basque berets' (LIDC 6th Annual Report (1936–37), pp. 20–22). The word 'refugee' is never used, the preference being 'Continental'.

28 The list includes some commission agents and wholesalers, chiefly in clothing and textiles, but only one retailer.

29 MJRC: NWIA Memorandum 3 March 1944.

30 Taped interview of Grete Einstein, Oscar's widow, by Bill Williams (hereafter Grete Einstein interview).

31 Doris Angel interview. Barlow was principal of the long-established firm of cotton spinners, Barlow and Jones; during the war years he held important government posts for the mobilisation of local resources, including membership of the Industrial and Export Council. By the end of 1941 these roles, and his 'mastery of the economic problems of Lancashire', had made him 'one of the most outstanding leaders of the North' (MCN 19 December 1941). His home was Dene House, Didsbury.

32 MCN 1 April 1939. Sir Thomas Barlow also acted as guarantor for Felix Loewenstein's brother, Herbert, his wife, Martha, and son, Robert. Herbert Loewenstein found work in Blackburn with another refugee firm, Neuman's Slippers.

33 LIDC 6th Annual Report (1936–37), pp. 20–22; 7th Annual Report (1937–38), p. 15; 8th Annual Report (1938–39), p. 7.

34 LIDC 6th Annual Report p. 21. No details of this syndicate survive.

35 That is, leather tanned with chromium salts to give it the degree of elasticity and waterproofing necessary for the manufacture of shoe uppers. Most British tanneries used vegetable oils to produce the lower-quality and less flexible leather suitable for the belting of factory drive shafts and shoe soles. Those manufacturing a higher quality leather tended to use the tougher bovine (calf, cow or bull), as against sheep skins.

36 This outline is based on an undated 36-page offprint, 'Die Geschichte des Hauses Adler and Oppenheimer', by Wilhem Eberhard Wortmann, in the possession of Mr Julian Treuherz; *True Hearts: The Memoirs of Werner and Irmgard Treuherz* (privately printed, 2000); and Treuherz, 'Fifty Years in Rochdale'.

37 Geoffrey Bevington, *Bevingtons and Sons, Bermondsey, 1795–1950* (privately printed for the company, London 1993), pp. 161–163.

38 Geoffrey Bevington, *Bevingtons and Sons*, p. 161.
39 *Ibid.*, pp. 170, 173.
40 *True Hearts*, p. 39.
41 Taped interview with John Keith Wilson and Neil Roberts (hereafter Wilson and Roberts interview). Both the interviewees are former Bevingtons' employees, Wilson having been engaged in 1955 specifically to take charge of the warehouse in Leicester from which Lanctan products were distributed.
42 Wortmann, 'Die Geschichte des Hauses Adler and Oppenheimer', p. 34.
43 Bevington, *Bevingtons and Sons*, p. 162.
44 *Ibid.*, p. 178. Paul Oppenheimer, Heinz Lehmann, Charles David and Werner Treuherz, all employees of the Lancashire Tanning Company, were all members of the Oppenheimer-Adler family.
45 It is now impossible to reconstruct a precise chronology of events; the one suggested here is derived from marrying Werner Treuherz's comments with Wortmann's account.
46 *True Hearts*, p. 39.
47 *Ibid.*, p. 182.
48 Wortmann, 'Die Geschichte der Hauses', p. 34.
49 In January 1932 army reservists were called out to protect Rochdale Town Hall from demonstrators mobilised by the National Unemployed Workers Movement. Although unemployment in the town had passed its peak by 1934–35, and the local textile industry was showing signs of recovery during 1936–37, the long-term prospect remained bleak. In the winter of 1939, 3,696 people were unemployed in Rochdale, 663 in Littleborough; demonstrations by the unemployed were well-attended (RO 14 January 1939).
50 LIDC 5th Annual Report (1935–36) p. 21.
51 *Ibid.*
52 *True Hearts*, pp. 39–40. It seems improbable that such an escape was necessary in 1936, the year in which, in the interests of international relations, Nazi anti-Semitism was at its most moderate. The account may perhaps be seen as part of an 'escape narrative' within refugee testimony: a theme which lays stress on persecution rather than economic self-interest as the cause of flight.
53 Treuherz, 'Fifty Years in Rochdale', p. 9.
54 *True Hearts*, p. 39. The former Bevingtons' employee, Neil Roberts, has an album in his possession with photographs of the Atlas Mill site before, during and after the construction of Lanctan.
55 *True Hearts*, p. 41; LIDC 5th Annual Report (1935–36), p. 21.
56 *Ibid.*, p. 42.
57 Wilson and Roberts interview. According to Wilson, Adler and Oppenheimer were sufficiently confident of the safety of their Dutch plant to invest part of the company's capital; since they were less confident about the future of their German tannery, the remaining 65% came out of the family's own pocket.
58 The composition of the Board is taken from an undated Lanctan letterhead in the possession of George Abendstern. At some time late in the war, Charles Adler returned with his wife from the Argentine and took up residence in Rochdale (George Abendstern interview; Wilson and Roberts interview).
59 LIDC 5th Annual Report (1935–36), p. 21.
60 *Ibid.*
61 LIDC 5th Annual Report (1935–36), p. 13; 6th Annual Report (1936–37), p. 15.
62 Wilson and Roberts interview.

63 According to one account, almost certainly spurious, Adler and Oppenheimer pursued a calculated plan for the rescue of its senior employees, prioritising their departure from Germany on the basis of their age and family commitments. (Notes of a conversation between the author and the one-time solicitor to Lanctan, Aslan Hamwee. Hamwee's memories are of comments made to him to that effect by Werner Treuherz.)

64 Taped author interview with Mavis Jaffe, the widow of Balfried Jaffe (hereafter Mavis Jaffe interview).

65 In Bermondsey, Bevingtons also engaged at least three German refugees immediately before or during the Second World War: Max Weil, whose wife was an Oppenheimer and who had worked for the company in Germany; Harry Fleish, a partner in a Swiss firm; and Harry Susmann, who later set up a company on the Treforest Industrial Estate manufacturing watch-straps (Wilson and Roberts interview). Max Weil later spent some time at Lanctan before moving with his wife to New York (Treuhertz interview).

66 *Glossop Chronicle* 17 July, 11 September 1987. In July 1987 the firm was said to have been founded 'fifty years ago'. Hene, a qualified chrome chemist with a doctorate from the University of Hamburg, was from Hassloch, near Mannheim, in the Rhineland, where his grandparents had been cattle-dealers. On deciding to leave Germany in 1936 he first considered a site in France and another neighbouring the Lankro site in Eccles before settling on Glossop. His son, who now runs the Lancashire Chemical Works, believes that the partners received initial financial help from the British distributors of chemicals, Bush Beech and Company. (Notes of an interview with Ronald Hene (Walter's son) by Bill Williams on 10 March 2006.)

67 This account is based on notes of a conversation with Peter and June Lonsdale, both of whom have worked at Anglofelt, Peter since 1968, June since 1970; both knew Hans Neuhaus. The early records of the company have unfortunately been destroyed.

68 After Hans Neuhaus' retirement in 1964, the Valley Supply Company appointed as general manager his son, Rolph, who during the war years had remained in Germany with his non-Jewish mother. Rolph returned to Germany in 1981. In 1987 the Valley Supply Company sold Anglofelt Industries to Kingston Macaulay, whose son, Simon, still runs what is now a major producer of felt, some of it recycled, for a range of British manufacturers, including the producers of carpet underlay, furniture fabrics and car head-rests. The Wolf brothers had meanwhile moved out of the Anglofelt building to return to the export trade from offices in Champness Hall, Rochdale.

69 LIDC 6th Annual Report (1936–37) pp. 20–22; 8th Annual Report (1938–39), p. 7.

70 Gerhard and Alice Zadek, *Mit dem letzten zug nach England* (Berlin 1992), p. 171.

71 LIDC 5th Annual Report (1935–36), p. 21.

72 Tony Russell interview.

73 Zadek and Zadek, *Mit dem Letzten*, pp. 171, 206.

74 Information on the founding of Lankro is taken from two articles in the *Eccles and Patricroft Journal* (hereafter *EPJ*) recording the award of the Freedom of the Borough of Eccles to Dr. Hans Kroch, 15 December 1966, 7 September 1967. In his speech of thanks, Kroch commented upon 'a repetition of history': the Bentcliffe works had originally been set up in the early nineteenth century as a cotton mill by the immigrant German father of Friedrich Engels. Lankro is said to have supplied Lanctan with leather chemicals (Francis Treuhertz interview).

75 Tony Russell interview.

76 The story of Wolf's experiences in Germany and his search for employment overseas is told in his *Personal Recollections, 1930–38,* privately published in Manchester in 1976. A Curriculum Vitae in the possession of his daughters provides further detail: Wolf was born in Saarlauten in Germany on 27 November 1903 and educated at the High School at Saarlouis and at the Universities of Freiburg and Berlin before finding employment at the factory in Oranienburg, where, in time, he was placed 'in charge of the whole of the works production'.

5

'Something ought to be done': Manchester Quakers and refugees, 1933–1937

The Society of Friends (otherwise, the Quakers), which from November 1938 was going to share with the Jewish community the rescue and support of refugees, in earlier years was as slow off the mark as the Jewish community, although for very different reasons. The problem for the Quakers was that of reconciling their objective of international harmony with the rescue of Jews from Germany, one of the chief national fields of their welfare services and missionary endeavour. In their eyes, too, the rise of Nazism, and the economic crisis and sense of national humiliation which had helped bring it about, were largely a consequence of Britain's treatment of Germany at the Versailles conference. Germany's reaction to this treatment, even if part of that reaction was an unacceptable anti-Semitism, was a natural consequence. The Manchester Quakers sought to retain a friendly relationship with Germany, including an annual exchange of students, until the outbreak of war. While the London Quakers were prepared from 1933 to lend organised support to refugees seeking a way out, their Manchester co-religionists were reluctant to follow suit.

Manchester was one of the earliest centres of the Quaker movement in Britain. Quaker settlement is thought to date from the 1650s at the latest in what was then a small but thriving centre of the textile trade. The first meeting house was built in 1693 on land at the corner of Deansgate and Jackson's Row, in central Manchester, then the residential focus of Quaker families. After further moves within the same district, in 1830 a Quaker community then numbering over 500 built what has remained the Friends Meeting House at 6 Mount Street. While never achieving the numbers, the social weight or the political influence of the Unitarians, with the focus of their activities at the nearby Cross Street Chapel, the Quakers were an important segment of dissenting Manchester, attracting members from the commercial and professional middle classes and active as a body in such liberal causes as the anti-slavery movement, temperance, anti-gambling, the alleviation of poverty and prison reform. Prominent Quakers in nineteenth-century Manchester included the scientist John Dalton, 'the founder of modern chemistry'; George Bradshaw, who produced the first of his famous railway guides in Manchester; and Alfred Waterhouse, architect of Manchester Town Hall, the Assize Courts in Strangeways and the first buildings of what was to become the University of Manchester.[1]

A German refugee who made his first contact with Manchester Quakers late in 1938 saw them as made up of 'a considerable number of well-to-do people, mostly business people'.[2] This was perhaps an exaggeration. While the Manchester meeting certainly included a sprinkling of the well-to-do, from the professions as much as from business, a majority of members were probably from the lower middle classes: shopkeepers, small businessmen, teachers, GPs and social workers.[3] Although Manchester was portrayed in the local press as 'this great centre of the Quaker faith',[4] Quakers in the city probably numbered no more than 300 throughout the 1930s.[5] With its library, games room, small restaurant, a kitchen open to members, and meeting rooms available to a host of fraternal bodies, the Mount Street Meeting House was, for many of them, the major focus of their social and cultural lives; Quaker business people with offices in the city centre took their lunch at the Mount Street dining room.

By the 1930s Mount Street had become the administrative headquarters of the series of Quaker meetings stretching between Warrington in Lancashire and Sale in Cheshire – at Ashton-on-Mersey, Eccles, Leigh, Penketh, Westhoughton, Pendleton and Wythenshawe – which together made up the Hardshaw East Monthly Meeting.[6] Quakers from the Whalley Range area of south Manchester had formed an eighth meeting which came together in the upper storey of a private villa, Edinburgh House, near the gates of Alexandra Park. Hardshaw East had by then become the major centre of Quakerism in the north-west of England, with a total membership of around 560 and 280 'attenders'. To the west were a complex of meeting houses belonging to the Hardshaw West Monthly Meeting, centred on Liverpool; to the east, meeting houses which formed part of the Cheshire Monthly Meeting, with its headquarters in Chester. While each meeting house enjoyed a considerable degree of autonomy, each also looked for guidance, locally to the regional monthly meeting at which each had its representatives, nationally to the London Yearly Meeting and its executive arm, the Meeting for Sufferings, and to the coordinating body of the movement's international interests, the Friends Service Council.

Of all the Christian bodies in Britain, the Society of Friends was, on the face of it, probably the one best equipped, in terms of belief, organisation and experience, to respond positively to those displaced from their home countries by Nazi persecution. Dispensing with dogma and ritual, it was free to focus, without doctrinal distraction, on what it saw as a human equality arising from 'the Essential Divinity of Everyman'. For Quakers, the presence of God in every human being – the 'divine spark in every human heart' – rendered the superficial differences of belief, gender, race, politics and nationality irrelevant.[7] A fundamental objective of the Quakers, in fact, was to transcend such differences and so 'remake the world on the basis of harmony and mutual respect'. Moreover, the consequences of discrimination were part of the Quaker heritage: since their beginnings in seventeenth-century England, Friends had suffered both collective persecution as dissenters and personal oppression as pacifists. Soon after 1933 it became clear that Quakers in Nazi Germany were again at risk on both counts.

A feature of 'the Quaker Way' was the immediacy of the link between egalitarian belief and philanthropic action, of which conscientious objection to military service was only the most obvious public expression. In the early twentieth century British Quakers were active in the support of Belgian refugees and alien internees during the First World War and in work with the unemployed in inter-war Britain. Their involvement with non-combatant victims during the war years had led thereafter to what the Quakers themselves saw as 'the newer endeavour, largely confined to Europe … not merely to carry relief to the suffering people of the devastated countries, but to build up a new life of faith and friendship between the nations'.[8] To serve these 'newer' purposes, Quaker 'Centres' had been established by 1933 in Vienna, Paris, Geneva, Berlin, Frankfurt and Nuremberg not only to promote the Quaker ideal of international harmony and 'to live in the spirit of Truth' but 'to help materially when such help is needed'.[9] From its Berlin Centre, in particular, dominated, as it was, by British Friends, Friends House in London received detailed intelligence on the progress of the Nazi regime and the impact of its policies.

Quakers in Manchester shared both the practical outlook and the evolving international concerns of the London Friends; they put their principles into practice, it was said, 'in a simple unconventional way'.[10] They took 'Love thy neighbour' to be 'an absolute injunction against war'. Peace meetings held at Mount Street before and during the First World War led ultimately to the invasion of the Meeting House by an enraged patriotic mob. Sixty-seven local Quakers refused to fight, of whom twelve were imprisoned and others left at liberty to join the Friends Ambulance Corps; Harold Howard, in the late 1930s an elder at Mount Street, had joined the Quakers after his imprisonment as a Conscientious Objector during the First World War. An Emergency Committee was set up to work with the wives and children of interned Germans. By 1933 the activities at Mount Street included a weekly Meeting of Mothers, with a District Visitor 'who keeps in touch with the members and gives help in cases of sickness or distress'; an Unemployed Men's Centre, 'open daily throughout the winter … to provide a community life for men who would otherwise be lonely in lodgings or home, and to give them an opportunity for cultural activity and friendly intercourse'; and an Adult School at which, in an atmosphere of 'spiritual fellowship', 'a frank study of social and religious questions' was intended 'to deepen the approach to the problems of life'.[11] The Quakers were said to have helped the unemployed 'before the Corporation lifted a finger',[12] offering them not only a safe haven but lectures, concerts and 'free writing materials'.[13] The 'Friends Institute', a centre for lectures, debates and adult education, which had begin in 1858 in an extension of the Mount Street meeting house, but which by 1933 was

confined to the upper storey of the building, saw itself as 'a place for enabling those amongst us interested in works of benevolence to meet together
and concert their arrangements'.[14]

It is a tribute to the resources and energy of the Manchester Friends that
by 1882 they had created a student hall of residence of the University of
Manchester, as it happens, the University's first.[15] In 1872 what had begun as
a committee for the foundation of a Friends School in Manchester turned its
attentions instead to the creation of 'a scholastic institution … where young
men and eventually (when Owens College will receive them) young women
can be accommodated and their education conducted under the care of a
well-qualified Friend'.[16] The three rented houses in Lloyd Street, Greenheys,
'a few minutes walk from the college', which were opened in October 1876
as a hall of residence for nineteen students, were replaced in July 1882 by a
fine building in Victoria Park named, after the Manchester Quaker scientist,
Dalton Hall. A series of subsequent extensions, the last of which was the Nield
Wing, opened in October 1934, produced a hall capable of accommodating
around seventy undergraduates (all of them, in the event, men), together
with the six or seven 'resident tutors' who offered them 'special tuition in
most university subjects'. Perhaps one-third of the students were themselves
Quakers. Of the rest, drawn from a variety of religious backgrounds, a growing number were from overseas, and increasingly from Europe;[17] by 1933
Dalton Hall had probably become seen by students arriving at the University
from Germany, native Germans (including Nazi sympathisers) as much as
political refugees, as their natural home. The Scot, George Sutherland,
Principal of Dalton Hall from 1924, and his wife, Christine, both of them
active in Quaker affairs in Manchester and London, were viewed by foreign
students, to whom they gave their personal attention, as their natural allies
in Manchester society.[18]

As in London, the First World War had served to broaden horizons.
When the hostilities ceased, Manchester Friends had been amongst those
Quakers who went out from Britain to Germany, Austria and Russia 'with
a message of goodwill as well as material succour'; others helped fight the
post-war typhus epidemic in Poland. 'Packers' at the Friends Meeting House
in Mount Street sent food, clothing and bales of cloth to the victims of
war. A Manchester Quaker, Arthur Watts, became head of all Quaker relief
work during the Russian famine. According to one of Mount Street's leading members, Elfrida Vipont Foulds, writer and one-time chairman of the
Women's International League of Peace and Freedom (WILPF): 'ever since
the war the cause of peace and internationalism has been near to the heart
of Friends, and every effort is made to keep in friendly touch with members
of other nationalities and races'.[19] One way of achieving this was through
an 'International Group', 'open to all visitors from overseas', which met periodically at Mount Street or in the homes of its members for social events
or 'to discuss international problems and ways in which friendship between
members of different nations may be encouraged and developed'.[20] A more
formal International Service Committee (ISC) of eighteen members, drawn

from all the Hardshaw East meeting houses, and equally committed to reconciliation, linked Mount Street to Quaker missions in Asia and Africa as well as determining Mount Street's responses to events in continental Europe. 'That Quakerism should have an international message [was] inevitable', according to Foulds, 'Quakerism itself is as essentially international as was primitive Christianity.'[21]

In a celebratory volume, published in 1930, and commemorating the centenary of Mount Street, there is no hint that the domestic and international mission of Quakerism was anything but unambiguous in theory and possible in practice. Three years later such idealistic optimism was to be severely tested by the establishment of the Nazi regime and, in particular, by the emergence of policies discriminating against political opponents, Christian dissidents and Jews.

By that time Germany had become a major focus of Quaker policies of reconciliation. Three of its international centres were on German soil. In Manchester, two leading members at Mount Street – John Major, the headmaster of Leigh Grammar School and national chairman of the Youth Hostel Association, and his fellow Grammar School teacher from Eccles, Edmund Emson – were by 1933 organising annual exchanges of young people and 'scholars' from Britain and Germany which were to continue throughout the 1930s. There was a sense in Quaker circles, too, that the darker developments in Germany during the inter-war years – inflation, social distress, even the rise of Nazism – were in part a consequence of policies imposed upon Germany, by Britain amongst others, after the First World War. The Treaty of Versailles, according to one prominent London Quaker, had 'sowed dragon's teeth'.[22] There was thus a special obligation on Quakers, with meeting houses throughout the country, to restore Germany to the 'brotherhood of nations'. The question which emerged after 1933 was how British Quakers were to reconcile this object with a support for refugees, and particularly for Jewish refugees, which might be interpreted in Germany as an implicit attack upon the Nazi regime.

A further issue was how well the uncompromising egalitarianism of the Quaker Way would render Quakers immune from the prejudices at large in the British society of the 1930s, not least the prejudice against Jews. Most Quakers belonged to just that petit bourgeoisie in which anti-Semitism had most obviously taken root in Britain. In the early 1930s, while undoubtedly hostile to Fascist nationalism and militarism,[23] Quakers had some sympathy for a movement which could be interpreted, in part, as a natural reaction to the terms of the Versailles Treaty, to which Britain had been a party. There were Nazi students at Dalton Hall in 1933, one of whom, Hans Wegener, who confessed to having 'taken part in house to house searches for Jews and Communists', was given space in the hall journal, *The Daltonian*, for an article which set out 'to bring about some understanding of Hitler and his movement'. The article exonerated Hitler and other Nazi leaders from involvement in the temporary 'excesses' perpetrated by the SA and the SS, adding:

Jews in Germany form a nation within a nation, appearing as an unwholesome fruit; they are mainly international in their outlook rather than national ... they have sought, during the fourteen years succeeding the war, to repress the thought and feelings of our people; and this they have done shamelessly both in books and upon the stage. It seems to me that a people who have tried to drag the honesty of German soldiers in the mud, cannot hope to retrain anything in a well-ordered State ... [The Jews'] control of finance was not in the complete interest of the people, so that they thereby wronged the State; moreover they hoarded their money in foreign countries. One sees, therefore, that the Jews themselves are responsible for the suppression and the contempt which they have incurred and that our hatred of them is by no means without reason. A section of them, after their flight from Germany ... have worked by speeches and in writings, in opposition to the new Germany ... Much has been written in the foreign press concerning the expulsion of Jewish professors from our colleges ... It is impossible to imagine that German students [involved in] the renaissance and the awakening of German culture ... wish to be taught by Jewish and Marxist professors ... All that has been done against Jews, Communists and Social Democrats has been necessary, for Hitler, and with him the greatest part of the German people, desire a national fatherland, free from all Marxist and Jewish influence.[24]

Rather less easy to interpret is the selection for the annual 'Dalton Hall Play'. In 1933 the choice fell on J. Gillespie's *Great Expectations*, said to be based around a spoof meeting in Hyde Park to announce the Day of Judgement, and which included 'a Jew ... doing fine business selling brass crucifixes'.[25] In 1937 the hall mounted James Bridie's *The Switchback*, a piece with evident anti-Semitic undertones. The scenario centres on a country doctor who had discovered what is taken to be a cure for TB. Confined by illness to his home, he is approached in turn by a surgeon, a newspaper proprietor and a financier, all of whom wish to exploit his discovery for their own purposes. The 'Jew financier', Burmeister, adds insult to injury by running off with the doctor's wife, only for her 'to find the Jew less pleasing at close quarters than sitting at the other end of a divorce'. *The Daltonian* found the play, in which George Sutherland [*sic*] took the part of Burmeister, with an accent 'a heterogeneous collection of the outstanding features of Scottish, Hebrew and Welsh', 'entertaining and convincing'.[26] Hall plays, chosen, according to Sutherland himself, 'to promote discussion rather than ... designed simply to amuse', were amongst the very few occasions when Dalton Hall was open to Friends from the Mount Street Meeting, University staff, Old Daltonians and the friends of its student residents.[27] The Hall itself, while welcoming foreign students, developed no facilities for observant Jews.

There were also aspects of Judaism, and of Jewish communal politics in the 1930s, with which Quakers were unlikely to feel sympathetic. The ritualism and hierarchy of Judaism could have little inherent appeal for a group which owed its origins to a rebellion against the impediments which organised religion had placed between man and God. There were fundamental differences on the issue of the morality of war. While pacifism was central to the Quaker creed, the official view of orthodox Jewry, voiced by the Chief Rabbi, J.H. Hertz, was that no basis existed in Judaism for exemption from military service on the grounds of conscientious objection; on the contrary, Judaism ranked 'defence of country among the supreme duties'.[28] Nor were those for whom world harmony was a central tenet likely to have sympathised with a Zionist movement which might be seen to have generated serious disharmony in the Middle East. In these contexts, the main Jewish contacts of Manchester Quakers were likely to have been with a local community renowned for just those features for which Quakers had little stomach: traditional orthodox observance and a history of commitment to the Zionist cause.

In all these circumstances, just how were Mount Street and its satellites likely to react to German refugees, most of them Jewish? As events evolved, and anti-Semitism came to be seen as central to the Nazi enterprise, how did 'the Jew' come to be seen in Manchester Quaker circles?

Quakers in the Manchester region were first drawn into issues surrounding refugees in June 1933 by a circular letter addressed to Meeting Houses throughout the country by Bertha Bracey, secretary of the newly formed Germany Emergency Committee of the Society of Friends (GEC). Founded in London on 7 April 1933, following an 'Emergency Gathering' of twenty-six leading British Friends shocked at the turn of events in Germany, the GEC represented the first organised response of British Quakerism to events in Germany.[29] Although still groping for an appropriate rejoinder, the GEC defined its immediate operational aims as the raising of funds and the provision of aid to the victims of the regime.

Bracey's letter was sent on behalf of the GEC's 'small Case Committee', which had set itself the task of dealing with 'individual problems' faced by those refugee Germans 'who seem to us to have a claim upon our practical sympathy and guidance'. At this stage the GEC was still in the process of working out its remit. Many of the refugees who had applied to it for help, Bracey wrote, were being referred to other relief organisations, not least the Jewish Refugee Committee in London, but there were others who, because they had 'some connections with Friends through contact with one of our German Centres or through other means' the Committee felt obliged to help. Of these, according to Bracey, most were students 'cut off in the middle of their professional training because of their being pacifists, Jews or Socialists, and who have no hope for a future career in Germany'. Unless people could be found to vouch for them, however, most were 'liable to be summarily turned out of this country if they come to the end of their meagre resources'. The task 'laid upon us' by such need appeared to Bracey to be 'a growing one'.

Her modest request to Tom Ellis,[30] secretary of the Hardshaw East Monthly Meeting, of which the Mount Street Meeting House in Manchester formed a kind of administrative centre, was for help in tiding these 'poor exiles' over 'a difficult period' by providing them with temporary hospitality in private homes or, alternatively, by making small contributions towards the cost of their support. It was also a call for empathy. 'We think,' she wrote, 'that you will share with us a sense of the tragedy of these young lives, uprooted from their environment and set a-drift separated from their families, not wanted anywhere, with no definite prospects for the future and yet firm in their adherence to pacifist principles. Some of them are exceptionally fine characters indeed.' Friends, she added, would be 'demonstrating their Quaker beliefs in a vital and convincing way to those who may be in sore need of a restored or strengthened faith in God' by helping these young people until 'some more permanent and satisfactory solution may be found for their problems'.[31]

In response, a Hardshaw East Monthly Meeting held at the Friends Meeting House in Eccles on 12 July agreed to send copies of Bracey's letter to all members of the Monthly Meeting, asking if they were prepared to offer free hospitality, make donations, or, in the last resort, find places in their homes for paying guests. Answers were to be sent to the International Service Committee (ISC), the body at Mount Street which sought to coordinate its work in the international sphere, and which was asked to obtain from London a 'List of Typical Needs' which might help in 'arranging hospitality for a definite number of refugees in our Monthly Meeting area'.[32] At the meeting in Eccles, it was said, 'a good deal of time was taken up by Friends who felt a concern that something ought to be done'.[33] In his own reply to Bracey, however, Ellis made it clear that, in the straitened material circumstances of the early 1930s, he expected help to be provided only for 'a few' of those in need.[34]

In the event, even this modest hope was scarcely realised. There were few replies, thirteen in all,[35] from a membership which stretched between central Lancashire and the south Manchester suburbs. Amongst them were no offers of free accommodation for any appreciable length of time, no financial contributions of any substance. Four wrote that they were unable to provide either hospitality or money. The most generous offer came from Winifred Garnett of Fallowfield in south Manchester, who felt able to provide free hospitality 'to a German student, man or woman' for one month (the 'October or November' of 1933).[36] Five offered short-term help (one for 'a week around Christmas') in return either for payment or for help around the house; three enclosed contributions, two of £1, one of 5s. There were reservations about the kind of help which was being sought. One, who felt that the country was 'drifting towards the catastrophe of Bolshevism', believed that Quaker energy might be better spent in helping the unemployed; it seemed to him that people were more ready to help men and women in other countries than in their own.[37] Winifred Garnett believed that help should be confined to pacifists and those in touch with German Friends: 'we do not think,' she wrote, '[that] there is any need for Friends to help Jews as the various Jewish organisations are quite able to do this'.[38]

These were the earliest days of the Quakers' engagement with the new German regime. In London, with its strong contacts amongst German

Friends, let alone Manchester, it was not yet clear just how permanent that regime was likely to be nor how intransigent its persecution of Jews and political dissidents. The GEC itself had yet to settle on the extent of its brief. In 1933 it was committed only to limited case work amongst refugees in Britain, to monitoring the developing situation in Germany, to the raising of funds which the German Friends might use to protect their own members, and to taking 'any steps alone or in co-operation with the concerned non-Friends organisations that may be demanded'.[39] It was not yet at all clear how persecuted Jews figured in these plans. Moreover, the response of British Friends to events in Germany was muted both by their fears of retaliation against their German co-religionists and by their sense of the degree to which British policies at the end of the First World War might be held responsible for the rise of Nazism; in June 1934 the Quakers were still being approached by British organisations committed to the material help of Germans impoverished by an economic crisis of which reparations might be seen as one cause and the 'abnormal political situation' as one result.[40] British Friends attempted to strike a balance between the general Quaker objective of promoting 'peace and reconciliation' and the pragmatic, but diplomatic, protection of Hitler's potential victims.

In the circumstances, it is perhaps not surprising that a greater sense of urgency, as distinct from a sense of the duties imposed on Quakers by their beliefs, was neither being conveyed to the provinces by the GEC nor by provincial Monthly Meetings to their members. Moreover, those Monthly Meetings were fiercely independent, looking primarily for guidance to their own elders. In the case of international affairs, this came not so much from the Germany Emergency Committee in London (itself a joint sub-committee of the Friends Service Council and the Meeting for Sufferings),[41] or from the central Friends Service Council, but from its own International Service Committee (ISC).[42] For the Manchester ISC, even as the GEC intensified its protests at Nazi atrocities, the state of Germany, the fate of German refugees in general, and needs of German-Jewish refugees in particular, were not immediate priorities.

Mount Street's perceptions of Jews in general remained, at best, ambiguous. In February 1936 some concern was expressed at an ISC meeting at the setting up by 'a Jewish refugee dentist', Werner Levinski, of a practice near that of a Friend, a concern that was to drag on for several months, apparently without resolution.[43] Such a response suggests the existence within the Quaker microcosm of prejudices which at this same period informed the attitudes of English professional organisations and of the British state. In March a request by a committee member, Mary Goodwin, that consideration be given to 'a matter concerning the relations of English people with the Jews' was referred to the Manchester Friends' recently formed and more informal 'International Group', who placed it on their autumn list of speakers.[44]

Mary Goodwin's request itself may have arisen from personal rather than ideological considerations. Working in her husband Horatio's jewellery shop in Swan Street in central Manchester was Millie Uhland, one of Mount

Street's only three members of Jewish origin.[45] The other two were Arthur Behrens, the son of a German-Jewish textile merchant, Gustav Behrens, and Lily Long, who in 1932, as Lily Weiss, the daughter of a Viennese-Jewish wine merchant, had joined her non-Jewish pen friend, Percy Long, in Manchester and subsequently married him. According to her niece, who had known Lily in Vienna and visited her in Manchester in 1936, she had never been comfortable with her Jewish identity; she was 'very anti-Jewish; she didn't want to be a Jew'. In Vienna, she had converted to Catholicism; her husband Percy was an Anglican; in Manchester she became 'a staunch Quaker', attending regularly at Mount Street, occasionally joining the smaller meeting near Alexandra Park and forming a circle of close Quaker friends which included Millie Uhland.[46] It was not a Jewish connection likely to incline her Quaker friends to a more empathetic view of the Jewish religion.

The predominant Quaker response to Judaism, however, was not so much hostility as indifference. When Lily Long, her aunt, arranged a Quaker student exchange visit for Lisa Steinberg, who was from a Jewish family in Vienna which had not broken its links with Judaism, Lisa moved easily amongst her aunt's Quaker friends in and around Manchester, by whom she was accepted, she remembers, 'as a person, not as a religious person'. Lodging with a family with Quaker connections in Hazel Grove, Lisa was introduced to the home in Disley of George Benson, a Quaker and the Labour MP for Chesterfield. Cycling there from Hazel Grove, she was befriended by Benson's teenage children.[47] That her Judaism was irrelevant to the egalitarian Quakers she met may be seen, however, in the circumstances of the 1930s, as of dubious advantage to her fellow Jews in Germany, who owed their persecution to that very 'irrelevance'. Such attitudes may partially explain both the reluctance of Quaker Manchester in these early years to take up a specifically Jewish cause and the priority later accorded by Mount Street to the victims of political discrimination.

At all events, the responses of the Manchester Friends to the needs of German refugees in general were piecemeal. Tom Ellis dealt with several cases in person, usually without reference to the ISC, but occasionally liasing with London.[48] Most were not so much victims of Nazism seeking help with their entry to Britain as those who had already made their escape and who were now looking for some means of avoiding what one of them saw as a journey 'back to Hell'. They included Alfred Kring, a freelance journalist, who had left Germany for Switzerland in June 1934 following a search of his home by the Gestapo for evidence of his distribution of leaflets put out by a German peace society. With his resources in Switzerland running out, he now sought help in finding space for his articles and translations in the British press: 'my little typewriter,' he wrote, 'is my future now'.[49] Two young German domestic servants, in 'impetuous' flight in February from employers in Kent, where they had been 'badly-treated', and without means or prospects, had sought help from a Christian Holiday Home in Romiley, near Stockport. The Director of the Home wrote to Ellis that one of them, 'who was without anyone on whom she has any claim', was 'well-educated and pleasant but too inexperienced in the world's ways to be left as she is'.[50]

It turned out that in neither of these cases was Ellis in a position to help. Early in 1936, however, Gunther Lenssen and his fiancée, Auguste Palusseen, both perhaps also pacifists, arrived in the Manchester area with visitors' visas, apparently unaware of the restrictions they were about to face in seeking permanent employment in Britain and, with it, the hope of permanent settlement. According to their own account they had 'fled Germany' and 'descended', without warning, on a young man with whom Gunther had been corresponding: Gunther, according to Tom Ellis, whose help he now sought, 'imagined it would be possible to get work here and they could marry and settle down'. By the middle of June, with their legal right of residence nearing its end, and now married, they found themselves stranded, without money, in a lodging house in the Pendleton district of Salford. Ellis, himself at this stage ill-informed on the niceties of British immigration law, put them in touch with the pastor of Manchester's Lutheran German Church in Wright Street, Chorlton-on-Medlock, which, as events were later to show, was unlikely to have given them a sympathetic hearing. Ellis also contacted the GEC in London, whose secretary, Mary Ormerod, called upon the (British) League of Nations High Commissioner for Refugees to use his good offices to enable the Lenssens to emigrate to the Argentine. This, too, was a dead end. Gunther Lenssen was then left to his own devices to obtain extensions to his visitor's permit and finally, in April 1937, by means unknown, to obtain a Ministry of Labour permit to work as a draughtsman with an engineering firm in East Manchester.[51]

Another pacifist, Hans Kruger, a commercial clerk, arrived in London in flight from Berlin early in 1936, also with a visitor's visa. For the following six months Kruger badgered the Quakers in London and Manchester, by card, telegram and letter, for help in extending his stay, for material support in Britain and for securing a means of gaining entry to his preferred destination, the United States. Having failed, even with the help of London Friends, to have his name added to the quota list for the United States, he moved on early in 1937 to Manchester, where (whether legally or not) he found temporary work at the Berlitz School of Languages, and where, amongst other matters, he pressed Tom Ellis to further a petition to President Roosevelt. For a further ten months he looked to Ellis with increasing insistence for financial support, help in his tortuous negotiations with the Home Office and a means of emigrating, if not to the United States, then to South Africa. His last preserved letter to Ellis, written from London on 10 October 1937, informs him that he has been granted an extension until the end of March 1938, with a temporary work permit to act as a 'private German tutor and companion'. 'My situation is now critical,' he added in a postscript, 'and I would not know what to do if I had to leave this country.'[52] It was Ellis's view that Kruger's incessant importuning had 'queered the pitch amongst the Manchester Friends' for other refugees; in June 1938 the ISC washed its hands of him.[53]

It may be that the ISC had not yet recognised the scale of the problem. In April 1936 it decided that it had 'no use at present' for two cottages in the Lake District, one in Keswick, one above Ullswater, offered (through Bertha Bracey) for possible use by German refugees.[54] Two months later it declared that it had 'no way of alleviating [the] distress' of two German refugees whose 'pressing need' had been urged upon it by Tom Ellis.[55] The first draft report of the ISC's work during 1935–36 omitted all mention of the German refugees 'who from time to time find their way to this Meeting House'.[56] In its subsequently amended form, the report referred only to the 'few German refugees', all 'political exiles', who had 'left their country to come to Manchester'.[57]

This may have been no more than a matter of numbers; before 1938 refugees arriving in Manchester were few and far between, perhaps 500 in all throughout south-east Lancashire.[58] It may also be, however, that conspicuous and systematic help to refugee Germans was not seen to sit easily with the ISC's prior commitment to a policy of international reconciliation. In 1936 the ISC was still supporting the exchange visits between German and English students organised by John Major and Edmund Emson; in September 1936, eighty German children and their hosts are said to have 'spent a very jolly evening at Mount Street'.[59] In that year the ISC's secretary, May Elliott, spent two months visiting Friends and 'friends of Friends' in Switzerland, Denmark, Belgium and Germany; amongst other places of Quaker interest, she visited the Quaker School at Ommen, just across the German border in Holland and set up in April 1934 primarily as a haven of safety for children from persecuted German families (most of them Jewish) and their teachers. After hearing a report of her visit, the Committee commented simply: 'we are grateful to her for forging yet another link in the chain of love and understanding that we hope will one day bind the world together'.[60]

It was not until autumn 1936 that the ISC showed signs of a more urgent and coordinated response to refugees, although at first only to non-Jewish refugees, and that at London's prompting and apparently with some reluctance. In October 1936 Bertha Bracey called upon the ISC to arrange a public meeting in Manchester at which an appeal might by launched for the GEC's work with 'non-Jewish refugees'. The Committee was cautious: 'Having considered the matter we feel that we should like more light on the subject before undertaking a piece of work that would appear to need informed and skilful handling.' Bracey was asked to provide further details.[61] It is not easy to fathom what was in the Committee's mind. Given what we know of its attitudes, it seems unlikely that its concern was with the possible reaction of the Jewish community to an event in which the sufferings of their co-religionists was absent from the agenda. More probable was its continuing anxiety – which it appears to have harboured for far longer than the GEC itself – about the effect of such a public meeting on its continuing drive for reconciliation with Germany.[62] Further pressure was required from Mary Ormerod of the GEC, who came to Manchester later in the month as its emissary, before the ISC gave way and agreed to take part in organising the meeting, which was held on 1 December 1936.[63]

Even then it cannot be said that the ISC threw themselves wholeheartedly into work for refugees from Germany. Its more obvious international concern throughout 1937 and most of 1938 was for the civilian victims of the Spanish Civil War, amongst whom Quaker volunteers were active as relief workers, and particularly for the Basque children, who by March 1937 had begun to arrive in Britain.[64] In May 1937 the ISC issued an unprecedented appeal to all the Christian churches in the Manchester district on behalf of the Friends Relief Work in Spain;[65] thereafter it was engaged in constant fund-raising and propaganda, its support for the victims of the Civil War symbolised by the setting up of milk depots in the region's meeting houses and by the placing of a Milk Churn as a collecting box on the steps outside Mount Street.[66]

Help for Germans was less systematic. When, in March 1937, the leading British Quaker, Corder Catchpool, recently relieved for his own safety of his secretaryship of the Friends' Centre in Berlin, was in Manchester with his wife, Gwen, both were invited to speak at Mount Street 'on the present situation in Germany'.[67] Help for German refugees was pursued, none the less, largely on an individual basis. Tom Ellis continued to deal personally with the occasional request for help.[68] In May 1937 circulars from Mount Street informed local Friends of the need for hospitality of a young German, Ewold Holst, who intended studying at the Manchester College of Art.[69] Later that year, Mark Hupenden, a student at the Ommen School who had enrolled at the Salford College of Technology, was accommodated in Manchester, first by Frederick Haggerstone, then by Benia Hesford, both long-standing members of the Mount Street Meeting, and finally at Dalton Hall.[70] The fostering of good relations with Germany continued to complicate the Manchester Friends' perception of Nazism. In June 1938 thirty German scholars who came to Manchester on the Friends' annual exchange scheme were welcomed at Mount Street by Elfrida Vipont Foulds and given tea to add to their lunch packets.[71]

There were few signs of any significant change in the ISC's response to those refugees known to be Jews.[72] Most were passed on to Jewish organisations of relief, which in Manchester meant the informal mechanisms of support coordinated, probably at Nathan Laski's request, by Isidore Apfelbaum.[73] When Tom Ellis informed the ISC in June 1937 of the 'urgent need for help' of the German-Jewish novelist, Arnold Bender, then living in Manchester, he was asked to 'remind' Bertha Bracey of Bender's distress and 'to ask her to inform Nathan Laski'.[74] Bender was one of the very few prominent refugee writers to reach Manchester. Known for his poems, talks and articles for his 'democratic ideas', and thus 'a marked man', Bender migrated first to Sweden, where he spent several months before coming to Britain in 1934, at the invitation of the International Voluntary Service, 'to help make playing fields in South Wales'. After breaking his arm in a car accident, he made friends with some Manchester people and came with them to the city, at first on holiday to complete a novel, then as a resident in Woodlands Road, Crumpsall, in what was then a new area of Jewish settlement in north Manchester. He was the sort of man, like the academics arriving at the University of Manchester, who might just have won Laski's support, although no evidence of their encounter survives.[75]

There is some evidence, too, that some members of the ISC were ill at ease with the increasingly vocal Zionist enterprise, seeing in it, perhaps, a form of divisive nationalism at odds with Quaker notions of the Brotherhood of Man. In June 1938, when the Committee received from the Manchester Zionist Central Council the offer of an address from its chairman, the veteran Manchester Zionist, Dr Philip Isidore Wigoder, on 'Palestine, Great Britain and the Jews', it replied that 'we do not feel able to arrange a meeting for such an address'.[76] In September, after 'a concerned Friend' had intervened, the decision was reversed and Wigoder actually spoke to the ISC on 20 October. On 17 November, however, it was resolved that 'in view of the fact that Dr. Wigoder spoke to us about Zionist aspirations, we ask the Secretary to endeavour to secure a suitable Arab speaker for our next meeting'.[77] This could not have been easy. The only Arab in Manchester who had made a public challenge to the Zionist enterprise was the Syrian merchant, Saleh M. Haffar.[78] In the event, no Arab reply took place under Quaker auspices.

A notable exception to the inaction of the Manchester Quakers was the rescue of the Kurer family of Vienna, favoured by the Quakers as 'friends of Friends'.[79] A middle-class and highly acculturated Jewish family, the Kurer home was in Leinz, a model municipal estate in the suburbs of Vienna. Theodora, the wife of a Viennese Jewish dentist, Jacques Kurer, was the younger sister of Lily Long, the Jewish convert to Quakerism who had committed suicide in Manchester in 1936. It was when they visited Manchester to attend her funeral that Jacques and Theodora had met up with a Quaker family, Horatio and Mary Goodwin, with whom, on their return to Vienna, they had kept in touch. Jacques Kurer, rapidly aware of the danger posed by the Nazi regime in Germany, had been trying to persuade his wife to leave Vienna with their two sons since 1934. She was finally convinced only after the Anschluss and when, in June 1938, the Goodwins offered the guarantees which allowed their entry to Britain. It was while staying with the Goodwins in their large house at 165 Withington Road in Whalley Range that guarantors were found from within the Quaker community for another three members of the Kurer family: the Maddocks, close friends of the Goodwins, became guarantors for Jacques' grandmother, Elizabeth Kramphlichek, for Theodora's sister, Margarete Steinberg, and for Margarete's teenage daughter, Lisa. The Kurers were fortunate in their early arrival. Jacques and Theodora had all their possessions sent on from Leinz, including every switch and plug, Jacques' dental equipment, even a marble fireplace that was reinstalled in the Goodwins' house.[80]

Although brought up as orthodox Jews, Jacques and Theodora had settled in Vienna for a mildly idiosyncratic version of the Jewish identity. The rules of Kashruth had been entirely set aside. Although Friday evenings were seen as 'special' and their 'sparkle' maintained by the saying of the *brocha* and the breaking of the bread, the candles were not lit at the commencement of the Sabbath but when the family sat down to eat, and there was no prayer after the meal. Every Friday night, in a custom not ordained by *halacha*, the two young children, Hans and Peter, received a token 'gift', perhaps a packet of sweets or a balloon. Occasionally, when his father was visiting, Jacques might accompany him on the Sabbath to an orthodox synagogue; otherwise the family's attendance was limited to Rosh Hashana, Yom Kippur and Hanukkah. At the Goodwins the Kurers continued their Viennese Jewish observances, while becoming regular 'attenders' of the Quaker Meetings for Worship at Edinburgh House in Alexandra Park; their children were found places at Brookfield, the Quaker school at Wigton in Cumberland, where they too attended Meetings for Worship. At a Christmas Party laid on for refugees at the Mount Street meeting house, Jacques Kurer dressed up as Father Christmas.[81]

The Kurers were the earliest 'practising Jews' to be saved by the Manchester Quakers. Their religious identity, however, illustrates also the very real difficulty of differentiating the 'practising' from 'non-practising' Jews, and still more of predicting outcomes. Peter and Hans are now members of the Manchester Reform Synagogue and active workers in the Jewish community. Peter's son married an orthodox Jewish woman and lives with her in Israel, their household characterised by a strict observance of orthodox custom.

Notes

1 Historical information based upon Elfrida Foulds and A. Neave Brayshaw, *Mount Street 1830–1930: An Account of the Society of Friends in Manchester together with Short Essays on Quaker Life and Thought* (Manchester 1930).

2 Bruno Retzlaff-Kresse, *Illegalitat, Kerker, Exil: Erinnerungen aus dem antifaschistischen* (Berlin 1980), p. 225.

3 Exceptional were prominent professional and business people like Elfrida Foulds, the wife of a doctor with his surgery in Longsight and herself the author of childrens' books, the merchant E.W. Whitworth, and the industrialist E. Russell Brayshaw, managing director of Brayshaw's Furnaces and Tools Company. In December 1939 Brayshaw sought (and obtained) permission from the AEU to employ a twenty-one year-old German refugee, who in Germany had spent four years in construction work, in his Furnaces Department (Minutes of the Manchester District Committee of the AEU 21 December 1939).

4 MCN 10 February 1940.

5 In 1924, 300 persons are said to have attended a social at Mount Street to welcome George Sutherland as the new Principal of Dalton Hall. This possibly included non-Quaker well-wishers as well as 'attenders' at Meetings not formally accepted into the Quaker fold. Within each meeting house, there was an official differentiation between 'birthright Quakers', who inherited a right to membership, 'accepted members', made up of converts granted official admission to membership, and 'attenders', who attended Sunday Meetings for Worship but were not officially 'members' of the Society. The Year Book of Meetings in the Lancashire and Cheshire region gives a

figure for Mount Street in 1939 of 255 members and seventy-four attenders.

6   All Friends Meeting Houses were organised around regional Monthly Meetings, of which one was Hardshaw East, which met at one or other of the meeting houses in the circuit and at which each meeting house had the right of representation, and which offered guidance on matters of policy. Monthly Meetings were subject, in turn, to a Yearly Meeting in London, at which each was represented and at which national policy was determined. Each Monthly Meeting had bodies of Elders and Overseers and sub-committees (eight in the case of Hardshaw East) which organised its routine activities.

7   Foulds and Neave Brayshaw, *Mount Street 1830–1930*, pp. 35–40.

8   *Handbook of Information*, Manchester and Salford Council of Social Service (1936 edition), p. 303.

9   Foulds and Brayshaw, *Mount Street 1830–1930*, p. 38.

10   *Ibid.*, p. 43.

11   *Handbook of Information*, pp. 303–304.

12   MCN 10 February 1940.

13   *Ibid.*

14   *Souvenir of the Jubilee of the Manchester Friends' Institute* (Manchester 1908), n.p.

15   This paragraph is based on George A. Sutherland, *Dalton Hall: A Quaker Venture* (London 1963) and Foulds and Brayshaw, *Mount Street 1830–1930*, pp. 25–28.

16   Sutherland, *Dalton Hall*, pp. 10–11. It is not clear why the idea of a school was abandoned: perhaps because there already existed in Manchester schools, like Manchester Grammar School and Manchester High School for Girls, in which Quakers were well-received, or because Quaker Schools already existed within fairly easy reach of Manchester.

17   The number of 'students from abroad' increased from 13 between 1876 and 1897, to 73 between 1897 and 1924 and 167 between 1924 and 1957. Of the 167, some 92 came from Europe, the rest from various parts of the British Commonwealth and ten other countries in Asia and America (Sutherland, *Dalton Hall*, p. 109). In 1957 the administration of Dalton Hall was taken over by the University.

18   WCML Ehlert Papers: in seeking a way out of internment in 1940 Ehlert quoted George Sutherland as a referee to his good character and patriotic intent.

19   *Ibid.*, pp. 21–23.

20   *Handbook of Information*, p. 303. The 'International Group' was one of the founding constituents of the Manchester International Club in 1939.

21   Foulds and Brayshaw, *Mount Street 1830–1930*, p. 35.

22   Letter in MG 3 June 1940 from T.C.P. (Corder) Catchpool, secretary of the Quaker Centre in Berlin until 1937, when he was withdrawn for his own safety.

23   *The Daltonian* No. 112 (December 1933), p. 8 ('War and Peace'), p. 21 ('Britain under Fascism').

24   *The Daltonian* No. 111 June 1933, pp. 13–15.

25   *Ibid.*, pp. 11–13.

26   *Ibid.*, No. 118 (March 1937), pp. 33–38.

27   Sutherland, *Dalton Hall*, pp. 90–91.

28   Chief Rabbi J.H. Hertz quoted in MG 7 June 1940.

29   For a measured account of the Quaker response at a national level, see Kotzin, 'Christian Responses in Britain to Jewish Refugees from Europe, 1933–1939' (Ph.D. thesis, University of Southampton), Chapter One, 'Quakers'. The GEC was a joint committee of the Friends Service Council and the Meeting for Sufferings (p. 27).

30   Tom Ellis was a 'born Quaker' who, on leaving school in Manchester at the age of 14

became a commercial clerk, at one stage for the Manchester Ship Canal Company. During the First World War he served in the Friends Ambulance Unit in France. His wife, Dorothy (née Robson) was born into a Quaker family in Saffron Walden. After their marriage in Guildford in 1925 they settled in Didsbury and it was soon afterwards that Tom became a paid official at the Friends Meeting House in Manchester. He died in 1961 ('Dorothy Ellis' in Hunter Davies, *Born 1900: A Human History of the Twentieth Century for Everyone Who Was There* (London 1998) pp. 65–77).

31 Bertha L. Bracey to Tom Ellis, June 1933, part of correspondence preserved in the archives of the Manchester Society of Friends at the Friends Meeting House in Mount Street, Manchester (hereafter MFA, for Manchester Friends Archive).

32 MFA Tom Ellis to May Elliott, secretary of the International Service Committee, 14 July 1933.

33 *Ibid.*

34 MFA Tom Ellis to Bertha Bracey 15 July 1933.

35 All preserved in the MFA.

36 MFA Winfred A. Garnett, 13 Amherst Road, Fallowfield to May Elliott 22 July 1933.

37 MFA Oswald Gregson to May Elliott 20 and 27 July 1933.

38 MFA Winfred Garnett to May Elliott 22 July 1933.

39 MFA Bracey to Ellis, June 1933.

40 MFA Circular from the German Distress Relief Fund, June 1934. The circular pointed to the risk of charity being monopolised by the new German government. It was careful to point out, however, that none of the 'distress' could be attributed to Hitler's policies; the regime was doing what it could to alleviate the situation. The Fund's chairman was the British historian, Dr. G.P. Gooch.

41 One-third of its expenses were met by the Meeting for Suffering, one-third by the Friends Service Council, one-third from funds collected by the GEC itself (MFA ISC 19 March 1936).

42 The committee's proceedings suggest that eighteen members were appointed to serve for a two-year period. Its chairman had the right to a seat on the Friends Service Council in London.

43 ISC 20 February 1936, 15 April 1937 and an (undated) meeting in May 1937.

44 ISC 19 March and 23 April 1936. The Group met at the house of the Baker sisters in Ryebank Road, Chorlton-cum-Hardy.

45 Author interview with Elisabeth (Lisa) Wolfe (hereafter Elisabeth Wolfe interview).

46 *Ibid.* Lily was the eldest daughter of Hugo Weiss, who owned a prosperous wine-growing and wine-blending business outside Vienna. Percy Long was a senior partner and foreign correspondent for the Cotton Spinners Association. In Manchester, after her marriage, Lily studied for an MA in Modern Languages at the University of Manchester and went on to become a teacher of German at the High School of Commerce. Lily's niece, then Lisa Steinberg, stayed with her aunt during a visit to Manchester in 1936, by which time her marriage to Percy had broken up. Soon afterwards, 'desperately lonely' and diagnosed as having a brain tumour, Lily Long hanged herself in the office in Chapel Street, Salford, where she then worked as a translator (Elisabeth Wolfe interview; author interview with Dr Peter Kurer (hereafter Peter Kurer interview)).

47 Elisabeth Wolfe interview.

48 MFA W.H. McKellen to Tom Ellis 5 and 7 February 1935; G.W. Shipway to Tom Ellis 26 March 1935; Tom Ellis to Edmund Emson 8 June 1936; card from Gunther Lenssen to Tom Ellis 9 June 1936.

49 MFA Alfred Kring to George Mallalieu, Stretford, 10 August 1934: the letter was sent

on to Ellis by Mallalieu.

50   MFA Letter from H. McKellan, of Alvaney Mount, Romiley, home to 'The Comradeship of the CE Holiday Homes Ltd.' to Tom Ellis 5 and 7 February 1935.

51   MFA Card from G. Lenssen to Tom Ellis 9 June 1936; Tom Ellis to the GEC 8 June 1936, 4 January 1937; Mary Ormerod to Tom Ellis 4 and 5 January 1937; G. and A. Lenssen to Tom Ellis 20 April 1937. Gunther Lenssen applied for a work permit in April 1937. While there is no note of a reply, in 1938 the Lenssens were living at 30 Briarsfield Street, Heaton Chapel, on the edge of Stockport, from where they offered hospitality to other refugees (MFA File Cards of those offering hospitality to refugees). QL identifies the Lenssens as living in Stockport in 1947.

52   MFA Tom Ellis to the GEC 8 June 1936, 4 January 1937; Mary Ormerod to Tom Ellis 4 and 5 January 1937; Hans Kruger to Tom Ellis 12 July 1936, 22 June, 10 October 1937; Bertha Bracey to Tom Ellis 5 January 1937; Tom Ellis to Hans Kruger 6 January 1937; William Dick, Trinity Church, Poplar, to Tom Ellis n.d.; Tom Ellis to William Dick 20 October 1937. Kruger appears to have in the end secured his entry to the United States.

53   MFA Tom Ellis to the GEC 8 June 1936; ISC 24 June 1938.

54   ISC 23 April 1936.

55   ISC 8 June 1936.

56   ISC 15 October 1936. The meeting decided to add a paragraph on the subject.

57   MFA Annual Report of the ISC, following a meeting of the committee on 26 October 1936.

58   Only 700 people from south-east Lancashire were examined by the Aliens Tribunals which sat in Manchester during October 1939.

59   ISC 18 July, 17 September 1936. See also MFA Annual Report of the ISC for 1936.

60   ISC 18 July 1936.

61   ISC 15 October 1936.

62   As late as July 1937 the ISC refused an invitation from the Manchester and Salford Trades Council to join a boycott of German goods (ISC 15 July 1937). In January 1938 Edmund Emson was asked to arrange a pen friend for a German who had made contact with the Committee (ISC 20 January 1938); June 1938 he was arranging for a visit of 30 German scholars to south Lancashire, a venture in which the ISC was 'glad' to cooperate (MFA ISC 24 June 1938).

63   ISC 26 October 1936. The main speakers were the Manchester cotton merchant and Liberal politician, Leonard Behrens; Sir Wyndham Deedes, vice-chairman of the National Council for Social Service; and Mary Ormerod of the GEC.

64   ISC 18 March, (undated meeting in) May, 17 June, 16 September, 21 October, 1937, 20 January, 17 February, 24 March, 24 May, 24 June, 22 September, 20 October 1938.

65   ISC undated meeting in May 1937.

66   ISC 22 September 1938, when it was found to contain £65.

67   ISC 18 February 1937.

68   MFA J. Ernest Grime to Tom Ellis, 14 October 1936; Mr and Mrs Cross to Tom Ellis, 15 October 1936; Mary Ormerod to Tom Ellis, 5 January 1937; Tom Ellis to William Glynn (International Quaker Centre in Paris), 11 and 15 August 1938.

69   ISC (undated meeting) May 1937.

70   ISC 20 January, 24 June 1938. The intention was that he would then complete his studies in the USA.

71   ISC 24 June 1938.

72   One was an invitation to David Baumgardt in March 1937 to speak to the Manchester

Friends on 'The Psychology of Anti-Semitism'.

73 See Chapter 2.

74 ISC 17 June 1937.

75 MCN 23 March 1940. In spring 1940 his novel, set in Sweden, which is said to have taken him only twenty-eight days to complete, won him £1,000 from the American Guild of Cultural Studies, of which the president was Thomas Mann.

76 ISC 17 June 1937.

77 ISC 22 September, 17 November 1938.

78 Haffar's firm, 'Haffar and Company' is located in a trade directory of 1938 in Globe House, Bloom Street. It exported 'cotton and woollen goods, artificial silk and yarns' to Syria, Egypt, West Africa, Palestine and South Africa.

79 This was the formal category of persons outside their own communion who the Quakers were prepared to support.

80 Peter Kurer interview.

81 *Ibid.*

6

The forgotten refugees: Manchester and the Basque children of 1937

> In this city the cause of the [Spanish] Republic has been taken very much to heart; we have given our sons in surprising numbers, we have provided two ambulances and one and a half shipments of foodstuffs … money and gifts have poured into the many societies and groups organised for the purpose and Manchester people practically organised [in June 1937] the Watermillock home for the Basque child refugees … There are still [in March 1939] a few of these unhappy children in Manchester Catholic houses.
>
> From a column in the *Manchester City News* written by the editor, 11 March 1939

In applying immigration law, the British government made the occasional concession and its agents at the ports of entry their occasional mistake. Through negligence or persuasion, passports were not imprinted with the necessary restrictions. Refugees arriving at destinations other than the official ports of entry walked ashore without official intervention. Even at the specified ports of entry, it was occasionally possible to by-pass the immigration officers.[1] The first substantial and official departure from the regulations imposed under the Aliens Acts of 1905, 1914 and 1919, however, was effected by the Civil War in Spain, when, in May 1937, a powerful political lobby, backed by a wave of public sympathy for Franco's civilian victims, led the Home Office to concede temporary refuge to 4,000 children from the Basque region of northern Spain.

One effect of the arrival of the children in Southampton, their dispersal to small 'colonies' managed by volunteers, the necessity of raising private funds for their support, and the debate which surrounded their repatriation, was to generate a public discourse around the generosity of the British state and the humanitarian instincts of the British people which was subsequently to surround other refugees from Fascist Europe. This discourse, in turn, marked the beginnings of what evolved into a perennial form of national self-deception in which the actual restrictions on the entry of immigrants and the very real limitations of a voluntary effort unsupported by the government were accompanied by sporadic declarations of the British government's commitment to the right of asylum and of the overriding humanitarianism of the British people.

An evocative element of such declarations was the degree to which they suggest that the limited rights granted to immigrants under the Acts of 1905, 1914 and 1919 had come to rest upon a popular consensus first generated by responses to the 'alien invasion' of the late nineteenth century. The British public had apparently become persuaded by 1937 that the regulations contained in the Acts represented a valid and minimal defence of the 'national interest'. The temporary and conditional admission of the Basque children suggest the very limited impact which even as potentially explosive a mix of international events, popular sentiment and voluntary action, such as that which came to exist in the spring of 1937, might exert on public as well as governmental perceptions of the national interest. Even a body of lobbyists as powerful in its membership, as strong in its support and as politically experienced as the National Joint Committee for Spanish Relief (NJCSR)[2] felt constrained to press only for limited concessions and then to accept the conditions with which the government surrounded them. Behind the limited opening of the door of Britain which the admission of the Basques represented – a 'short-term humanitarian gesture' in the eyes of one historian[3] – the structure of immigration control remained unchallenged and intact.

From the perspective of the Home Office, the whole episode served as an object lesson in the degree to which the government needed to bend in order to appease political pressure around immigration, even when that pressure was accompanied by a wave of public sympathy for the potential refugee. And as such, it might be argued, it served as a precedent for the way in which governmental 'generosity' in allowing the temporary residence in Britain of vulnerable children (and at no cost to itself) was enough to head off any potential complaint at the stringency of British immigration controls. It suggested to officialdom and politicians how, in the context of modern warfare and Fascism, innocent Modern Orphans of the Storm[4] might serve as useful pawns in the government's determination to limit the damage to immigration policies it believed essential to the welfare and identity of the nation. It was not the least of the ways in which children were to be used iconically in the 1930s, as much by democratic regimes as by their Fascist enemies, to justify official policies and beliefs.

It seems clear from the imagery and language surrounding discussions of the Basque children that notions of Britain's humanitarian tradition floated freely within the whole of Britain's political spectrum. It was the typical currency of the liberal *Manchester Guardian*. What was, in fact, the characteristically reluctant and heavily conditional decision of the Home Office to admit the Basque children, was rendered by the *Manchester Guardian*: 'The Home Office and the Ministry of Health had to ensure that proper provision was available for [the Basque children's] reception. But no serious obstacles were put in the way of the voluntary organisations which worked hard to prepare for their coming.'[5] A visit by the Home Secretary to the transit camp established in Hampshire for the Basque children had, in the *Guardian*'s view, 'enabled [them] to receive a semi-official welcome'.[6] In a letter to the *Bolton Evening News*, Craven Ellis, the Conservative MP for Southampton, described the rescue operation as 'a simple humanitarian gesture' which all should welcome, 'if only in view of Britain's traditional policy in these matters'.[7] The *Manchester Guardian* professed to believe that in 1937 Britain remained committed to 'giving a home to men of industry and goodwill exiled from their own land', a form of generosity by which her 'industry and artistic life' had been 'immensely enriched'.[8] In responding to demands from sections of the British press in August 1937 that the children should be immediately repatriated, a *Manchester Guardian* leader argued that, given the risk the children would face in a war-torn Spain, to return them 'would be a startling abandonment of those humanitarian principles which we all believe to form a peculiar part of our national inheritance'.[9] Writing on the eve of the arrival of an estimated 250 Basque children in the Manchester region, the weekly *Manchester City News* wrote of 'a pitiful cargo of … fatherless, homeless, bewildered children' being rescued by 'the merciful arm of Britain': 'kindly folk' could be expected to care for them 'in the spirit of the [Christian] Master'.[10]

Men and women of all political persuasions voiced similar views. As chair of a public meeting in Manchester to raise support for the Basque children, the Labour Lord Mayor of Manchester, Joseph Toole, told his audience: 'this country was famous for many things, but one great thing was the right of asylum'.[11] In July 1937, at a party in aid of the Basque children in Ashton-under-Lyne, a local councillor, James Watts, citing Britain's reception of the Huguenots and 'Jews from Germany', reflected that 'We English have always been proud that our island has provided asylum for fugitives from other lands'. In the case of the Basques, he was convinced that 'by proving to the world that England is, even in these days of unrest, a welcoming and friendly country to whom the poor and the weak can turn … we shall have done good work towards the promotion of peace and goodwill among the nations of the world'.[12] In defending the Basque refugees against accusations that they were distracting attention from the sufferings of the native poor, the secretary of the Salford Branch of the Young Communist League argued: 'My reading of history convinces me that the British people have always welcomed refugees from political reaction, no matter the extent of poverty in our country.' To do otherwise, he went on, would be 'foreign to the people of our great country'.[13]

Such is the rhetoric of propaganda, often well-intentioned, occasionally self-serving. How well does it portray the realities of the national identity? What do the experiences of the Basque children and the degree of their support have to say about Britain's 'humanitarian inheritance'?

Manchester and the war in Spain

In Manchester, the outbreak of the Spanish Civil War in July 1936, and the subsequent threat to Spain's civilian population from Franco's insurgents and his German and Italian allies, aroused a level of popular sympathy for the Spanish Republic and its beleaguered citizens described by one historian as 'the most widespread and representative mass movement in Britain since the mid-19th century days of Chartism and the Anti-Corn-Law League'.[14] During the three years of civil strife, voluntary groups throughout the country collected money, food, clothing, vehicles and medical supplies for despatch to Spain; and while anti-Fascist organisations of the political Left, particularly the Communist Party of Great Britain (CPGB), played a central role in the effort, 'Spanish Aid' was embraced, on the grounds of religious belief and humanitarian sentiment, by the Society of Friends, by Christian clergy of every Protestant denomination, by politicians of all three major political parties, by pacifist bodies, by women's organisations, and by a substantial body of the religiously and politically uncommitted. Even within the Catholic Church, an institution inclined by its virulent anti-Communism and instinct for self-preservation towards sympathy for Franco's cause, there were many individuals who, on the grounds of humanity, were prepared to engage in Spanish Aid. On one calculation, while the British government persisted in its stance of non-intervention in the Civil War, the stance adopted by all of Europe's bystander states, by 1939 the Spanish Republic had received from British voluntary organisations and private donors a total of £2m in cash, twenty-nine foodships, and ambulances, as well as hundreds of volunteer relief workers, military personnel and medical staff. From the beginning it was an effort which had received powerful support in Manchester and Salford.

Politically, the Republican cause had been embraced at once by the Manchester branches of the CPGB and by its youth and fraternal organisations. It provided another means by which the Party's anti-Fascism, orchestrated by the Communist International in Moscow, and already given expression by the party's anti-Nazi propaganda and by opposition to the British Union of Fascists, might take a tangible form. It formed one target – others included the Means Test and mass unemployment – for the party's attack on a National Government which, fearing an early confrontation with the Axis powers, had adopted the stance of non-intervention, and which, in Harry Pollitt's view, had thus 'sullied the name of Britain throughout the world'.[15] As a potentially popular cause, it was one means by which the party might steal a march on an official labour movement equally wedded, at least officially, to non-intervention and so promote the notion of a British Popular Front under its own leadership which, in 1935, had become the party's official policy. It was a means of persuading the Labour Party to finally accept the CPGB as an affiliate. Finally, it was a way in which the party might increase a membership which by 1930 had fallen to below 3,000. At a national level, the party railed at the government, the Labour Party and the Independent Labour Party (ILP) for their failure to properly embrace 'the cause of Spanish democracy'.[16] Palme Dutt, the party's leading ideologue, and the British party leader most in tune with Comintern policy, called for the replacement of the National Government by government 'based on a united labour movement', one feature of which would be the united response to the Spanish question advocated by the CPGB.[17]

Given these considerations, the party's responses to events in Spain were rarely a matter only of principle and ideology. They were expressions, almost equally, of the need for strategies and for forms of propaganda which would bolster its standing in Britain. The party's decision to support the Spanish Republic took several forms, all represented locally. Manchester and Salford provided fertile ground for the party's recruitment of volunteers to fight in Spain, a programme opened by Harry Pollitt, the Party's General Secretary, in the *Daily Worker* in December 1936. Amongst the early Manchester recruits to the British Battalion of the International Brigade, most of them either Communists or sympathisers with the party, was Clem Beckett, a professional motorcyclist of international renown famous in Manchester as a rider on the Belle Vue speedway and for his performances on the 'wall of death' at Belle Vue Zoo. Fred Copeland, a commander of the Brigade's British Battalion, calculated that by September 1937 sixty-six men had left Manchester and Salford as volunteers in the International Brigade;[18] at least two joined the smaller contingent created by the ILP, one of them, Charles Justessen, from Cheetham Hill.[19] Their subsequent 'heroism', while real enough (seventeen of the local volunteers in the International Brigade were killed in action, many more wounded), was used also as a means of publicly enhancing the party's image, emphasising its good intentions and pressing the advantage of a popular front. Towards the end of May 1937 the CPGB organised a memorial meeting at the Coliseum Theatre in Ardwick for the eleven Manchester Brigaders, including Beckett, who had died in Spain at the Battle of Jarama, with speakers who included Dame Sybil Thorndike and the Manchester Unitarian minister and pacifist, Stanley Mossop.[20] In a letter to the *Manchester Guardian* on 10 July 1937, Pollitt wrote of George Brown, formerly the party's Manchester Organiser, who had recently been killed in Spain, that his role had 'helped to remove the stain that the policy of the National Government has placed on the name of democratic Britain'.[21] Two days later a crowd of 1,500, drawn from CPGB branches in Manchester, Salford and 'different Lancashire towns', gathered at Ardwick Green for a march to Debdale Park, where a band played in memory of Brown, banners were unfurled to depict early episodes of the working-class struggle in Britain, and Pollitt, who had led the procession, spoke once more of the benefits of a united front.[22] At a second memorial meeting at the Co-operative Hall in Downing Street, Ardwick, on 25 July, chaired by the local Communist engineer, Edmund Frow, the platform party included the president of the Manchester and Salford Trades Council, a representative of the Transport and General Workers' Union and a Labour city councillor with a letter from the Manchester Borough Labour Party approving his attendance.[23] Propaganda on behalf of Republican Spain flowed from a variety of local organisations dominated by the party.[24]

The CPGB was active also in the promotion of local committees in support of the Medical Aid for Spain Campaign which had been inaugurated nationally (and also partly on the party's initiative) in August 1936. The

North Manchester Spanish Medical Aid Committee, one of the most successful in the region, is said to have been formed 'on the initiative of Issy [Isidore] Luft, a Communist acting on instructions from his party branch'.[25] In keeping with the party's commitment to a united front, he then sought to assure it of a wide base of support. Dr Nathan Malimson, who was persuaded to chair its committee, was a Labour Party member; the secretary, Eileen Lewis, belonged to no political group; and the committee also included other local doctors and representatives from local trade unions. With Dr Malimson's surgery as its base, the Committee organised concerts, dances, jumble sales and public meetings which raised funds sufficient to send three ambulances to Spain and to channel medical supplies to the Ucles hospital in central Spain.[26] At the end of June 1937 the North Manchester committee staged a major public meeting at the Albert Hall in Manchester at which the speakers included Professor J.B.S. Haldane, Arthur Koestler, Isobel Brown and Katharine, Duchess of Atholl.[27]

By this time, Medical Aid had caught the humanitarian imagination of Manchester and Lancashire people. In mid-July 1937 another local body, the Manchester and District Spanish Medical Aid Committee, which embraced the cotton towns of south-east Lancashire, arranged a tour of the district by a second field ambulance built, it was said, on the generosity of 'thousands of contributors', prior to its camouflage and despatch to a British Medical Aid Unit in Spain. Blake Motors of Manchester, who had built it, as 'the most advanced and serviceable type sent out', were then constructing another ambulance paid for by the people of Rossendale, as 'a concrete expression of Lancashire's sympathy with a suffering people'.[28] By the end of September 1937 the committee had sent to Spain five fully equipped ambulances and £600 in cash and was still appealing for clothing, tinned milk, bandages and cash.[29] In Moss Side more than thirty women were engaged in making bandages for Spain.[30] The Manchester AEU built motor cycle units for use in Spain.[31]

Meantime, the CPGB's youth wing, the Young Communist League (YCL), was taking a local lead in bringing together other youth organisations behind the creation of 'Youth Foodships' for Spain. The motives were again mixed. As secretary of the largest local branch, the Salford YCL, M.Cohen sought both to coordinate the collection of money and goods and to promote the YCL as a 'non-party' organisation open to anyone 'prepared to organise in defence of peace, democracy and progressive development'. He limited his attack on mainstream local organisations to those youth bodies, like the local Scouts and Lads Brigades, which had failed 'to render assistance to the heroic people of Spain'.[32] In March 1938, disappointed with the contribution of his own branch (£30) to the foodship, he announced a youth rally at the Co-operative Hall, at which a film would be shown of the defence of Madrid.[33] By then, demonstrations on behalf of Spanish Foodships had become regular fixtures in Manchester parks.[34] At the end of August 1937, after three foodships had already sailed for Spain, six depots were set up in Manchester for receiving donations of milk and clothing: they included the YCL's Challenge Club at 96 Herbert Street, Hightown, made up chiefly of young Jewish Communists, and the Advance Club, the local headquarters of the Labour League of Youth at 103a Wilmslow Road in Rusholme.[35] By October 1937 the Manchester and District Youth Foodship Committee had become a sub-committee of the Communist-dominated Youth Peace Council.[36]

During summer 1936 the Labour movement as a whole, while officially continuing its support of non-intervention, also committed itself nationally and locally to humanitarian effort on behalf of the Republic. A Spanish Workers Relief Fund was inaugurated by the Labour Party and the TUC in July 1936 as the British section of the Labour movement's International Solidarity Fund (ISF). ISF money was used to help build a base hospital for the Republican forces at Onteniente, outside Madrid, and, with the help of the Co-operative Wholesale Society, to send consignments of food and clothing to the civilian population.[37] The Manchester May Day procession of 1937, one mile long, according to the *Manchester Guardian*'s report, was made up of fifty organisations, including ten Communist Party branches. One of the tableaux depicted a dressing station in Spain.[38] Although itself suspicious of the Communist Party's motives, fearing an attempt to draw the movement into a broad-based and Communist-led anti-government alliance, and, on this account, reluctant to join organisations like Spanish Medical Aid, the Voluntary Industrial Aid for Spain Campaign and the International Brigade's Dependents and Wounded organisation, all seen to be dominated by Communists, the Labour movement was anxious to mobilise those of its supporters who might otherwise have perceived Spanish Relief as part of a Communist conspiracy. When, on 10 May 1937, speakers at a joint meeting of the Manchester Borough Labour Party and the Manchester and Salford Trades Council at the Piccadilly Theatre, 'in aid of the sufferers from Spain', met with 'slight opposition', the chairman, John Jagger, the Labour MP for the Clayton Division of Manchester, responded with the hope that, whatever their political sympathies, 'all would surely at least wish to help in the humanitarian work of succouring the non-combatants'.[39]

It seems likely that the transfer from London to Manchester in July 1937 of a 'Spanish Exhibition' designed to present an unvarnished view of the Republican struggle against Franco's rebellion, was also the work of the local labour movement. In his speech at its opening, in a vacant shop on Oxford Road, Jagger described it as 'seeking to bring home to English democrats the possible consequences to themselves of allowing that struggle to fail'.[40] For one *Manchester Guardian* reporter the 'cumulative effect' of the exhibition, with its stark portrayals of children bombed in the streets. was 'one of revulsion and nausea'.[41]

On 23 January 1938, very probably through the influence of Communists still intent on using Spanish Aid as a route to a united front, a Manchester and District Joint Council for Spanish Relief was set up through which the medical aid and youth foodship committees and such 'other bodies' as chose to affiliate might 'co-ordinate' their work, facilitate the transport of goods, jointly propagate the cause of Spain, and initiate such joint fund-raising efforts as concerts and film shows.[42] In late February the Council organised an exhibition of photographs, posters and pamphlets at 40 Deansgate at which, on a coloured map of Europe, Fascism was depicted as 'a menacing octopus' and throughout which, according to a report in the *Manchester Guardian*, the words 'Fascism' and 'Capitalism' appeared as 'broadly synonymous'.[43] Following a 'Spain Week' organised by the Council towards the end of that month, a van-load of milk and medical supplies left Manchester on its way to Spain.[44]

Although such Communist-dominated organisations and activities attracted wider support, the momentum of a purely humanitarian effort for Spain was increased with the publicity given by the press during the winter of 1936–37 to the plight of civilians in the war zones, and particularly those suffering in the Basque country from Franco's advancing forces, his blockade of Spain's northern coast and, in April 1937, the aerial assault of Nationalist, German and Italian planes on the towns of the Basque country. Local Quaker interest, which had earlier been focused on the few refugees from Nazism, was aroused in January 1937 by direct reports from Friends in Spain and by pressure from individual Friends upon the International Service Committee (ISC), the body which determined the overseas interests of the Friends Meeting House in Mount Street, Manchester. In January 1937 the committee received a letter from Quaker member Elfrida Foulds, drawing attention to those 'suffering terribly' in Spain and offering to put on a recital to raise funds for their relief.[45] During the month which followed Mount Street hosted two speakers, one of them Spanish, on the deteriorating situation.[46] Rather than affiliate to the National Joint Council for Spanish Relief, the London-based cross-party and interdenominational committee which had set itself up in January 1937 to coordinate relief work, the Manchester Quakers, perhaps because, as pacifists, they feared too close an involvement with the Spanish combatants, perhaps because they wished to distance themselves from the Communists who were members of the committee, decided in May to work through the Friends' own relief agency in Spain and to appeal to all Manchester's Christian churches to lend it their financial support. A press statement to this effect was released on 17 June 1937.[47]

Throughout 1938 the Manchester Society of Friends was heavily involved in publicising conditions in Spain and, with its sister pacifist organisation, the International Voluntary Service for Peace (IVSP), in the collection, storage and despatch of milk, foodstuffs and clothing. At the end of January Jessie Moorhouse of the Manchester IVSP was allowed to give a lantern lecture at Mount Street on conditions in Spain.[48] The secretary at Mount Street, Tom Ellis, circulated the clerks of other Quaker meetings in the region, calling on them to approach local grocers for gifts and to use their meeting houses as milk storage depots;[49] while apparently retaining its independent chain of relief, in February 1938 Mount Street yielded to a request that it become a major transit depot for the despatch of goods from Manchester to London for forwarding to Catalonia.[50] By the end of that month, when the Milk for Spain Campaign was 'in full swing over many districts of Manchester', the ISC decided that while money collected at its own meetings should go only towards Friends' work in Spain, anything else collected would go to the IVSP.[51] From September 1938 the ISC kept a tally of the monies and tins collected each month towards the Milk for Spain Campaign and goods and money deposited in the 'Mount Street Milk Churn': in November alone, as the scheme drew to an end, the totals were £17 and 1,900 tins of milk.[52]

By this time, the Manchester Friends, although keeping their distance from national committees supporting Basque refugees,[53] had long been involved in what became a major feature of Spanish relief work: the evacuation of children from the beleaguered Basque country. For the Quakers, the Basque children were a striking exemplar of the impact of war. In May 1937 G.A. Sutherland, Principal of Dalton Hall, the Quaker hall of residence at Manchester University, in a letter to the *Manchester Guardian* used the bombing of Guernica to condemn the British armaments industry: 'for what are these [British-made] bombs intended except to terrorise civilian populations'.[54] Their cause was taken up by the ISC and by the Manchester Friends Peace Committee. In January 1938 Tom Ellis, clerk to the Mount Street Meeting, took steps to ensure that *Modern Orphans in the Storm,* a propaganda film on behalf of the Basque children, was shown in Manchester.[55] It was perhaps this which persuaded the Manchester executive of the National Council of Women in the following month to urge its members to 'give all individual help possible' to Spanish Relief.[56]

This also reflected a growing empathy in Britain (and Manchester) with the sufferings of the Basque children. 'Guernica', Dr. Hewlett Johnson, the 'Red' Dean of Canterbury, and another supporter of the Basque children, told a meeting at the Manchester Free Trade Hall, 'might well have been Knutsford'.[57] The *Manchester Guardian* put its weight behind the evacuation of the 'thousands of orphan children throughout Spain'. The British government, it asserted, had offered its support in saving as many children as could be brought over by voluntary effort; the British navy would protect ships 'engaged solely in the work of rescue'. The claims of the children 'transcend[ed] the issues of Spanish politics'.[58] Their cause had been taken up throughout the country by churches of every denomination, by pacifist organisations[59], trade unions, co-operative societies, members of every political party to the left of the BUF, and by a vast array of unaffiliated individual humanitarians and philanthropists. To pacifists of all sectarian shades the cause was particularly attractive. The *Manchester City News* reminded its readers that behind the privations of the Basque children in Bilbao lay 'fresh reminder that war is steadily becoming more bestial and barbaric, as well as more mechanically devilish': the problem which overshadowed all others was the search for 'a formula that will ensure peace for Europe'.[60]

The Basque children

The evacuation of the Basque children was thus another, if perhaps the most dramatic, expression of a popular, inter-denominational and cross-party sympathy for a Spanish people under threat from Franco's forces. The origins of the project lay in an appeal by the Basque government to foreign nations in April 1937 to accept children endangered by the blockade of Spain's northern ports, by the bombardment of Bilbao and other Basque towns by Nationalist forces under General Mola, and by aerial attack from German and Italian planes. In Britain the influential National Joint Committee for Spanish Relief (NJCSR) responded by calling upon the Home Secretary, Sir John Simon, to allow the entry to Britain of 4,000 Basque children. After some delay, as a reluctant Cabinet debated the impact of the evacuation on Britain's neutral status, weighed Franco's objections, and sought to limit the number of children admitted to 2,000, on 29 April, three days after the bombing of Guernica, Simon, impressed by the intensity of popular feeling, gave the project the government's conditional approval. There were to be more girls than boys; all were to be between five and fifteen years of age; they were to be accompanied by 200 adult women teachers and thirty priests; they were to include non-combatants of all political parties; they were not to arrive as family groups; they were to return as soon as conditions allowed; and the NJCSR was called upon to provide a guarantee that the children would not become a public charge and to take responsibility for their maintenance, welfare and eventual repatriation. Accepting these conditions, the NJCSR undertook to raise funds which would make possible the children's maintenance at 10s per child per week.[61] The Basque Government stipulated only that, rather than be found accommodation in private homes, the children should be kept in groups which would safeguard their national identity.

To achieve these purposes, on 5 May 1937 the NJCSR set up a powerful Basque Children's Committee (BCC), chaired by the Conservative (and pro-Republican) MP for Kinross and West Perth, Katharine, Duchess of Atholl, and including the Independent MP, Eleanor Rathbone, MPs from the Labour, Liberal and Conservative Parties, and representatives of the Quakers, the Catholic Church (which had declined to join the NJCSR on the grounds of the Communist presence), the Salvation Army, Save the Children Fund, Medical Aid for Spain and the TUC. For the Catholic Church in particular, support was based on the supposition of the early return of the children to their Catholic homeland. While at first, on the instructions of the Catholic Bishop of Salford, Thomas Henshaw, giving its backing to the support of the Basque children in Britain, the Protection and Rescue Society of the Catholic Diocese of Salford added: 'Let us pray that soon they may be able to rejoin their parents and resume normal life in their own land.'[62]

Representation on the BCC reflected the exceptionally broad appeal of the rescue operation. The TUC, for example, while typically indifferent to broad-based movements of humanitarian aid, and generally keeping its distance on political grounds from other bodies promoting aid to Spain (it even eschewed 'direct association' with the NJCSR), made an exception in the case of the BCC, to the foundation of which it was centrally instrumental.[63] The BCC's fund-raising campaign was launched with a £5,000 donation from Walter Citrine, who, as General Secretary of the TUC, remained in close touch with its activities.[64] While, to avoid accusations of political bias, the TUC stressed the humanitarian character of its effort, the project 'captured the imagination' of ordinary trade unionists, whose local branches raised funds with enthusiasm for those who became known throughout the movement as the 'Basque babies'.[65] The movement's largely dormant International Solidarity Fund is said to have been revitalised by the emergence of so popular a cause.[66]

The public response was immediate and impressive. Within a fortnight the BCC had raised £2m, more than sufficient to finance a tented reception camp at North Stoneham in Hampshire, from which the children were then, at the BCC's expense, to be distributed around the country in 'colonies' managed by the Catholic Church, by such 'non-denominational bodies' as the Salvation Army and the Peace Pledge Union, or by such other local agencies with which the BCC was able to make contact. On 21 May 1937, as these arrangements were being put in place, the cruise ship *Habana* and the yacht *Goizeka Izarra* left Bilbao with a cargo of 3,826 children, 219 women teachers (*maestras*) and helpers (*senoritas*), fifteen priests and some mothers. Docking in Southampton on 23 May the *Habana* carried 'the biggest single influx of refugees in British history';[67] 'a pitiful cargo', according to the *Manchester City News*, 'of fatherless, homeless, bewildered children'.[68]

The BCC had by then opened negotiations for their distribution throughout the country, a procedure eased by a Save the Basque Children Fund, sponsored by the TUC, which by 8 June had raised £2,840.[69] By the end of June 1937, when the Countess of Atholl and the Liberal Wilfrid Roberts MP (the NJCSR's national treasurer and the BCC's secretary) wrote a letter of appeal on their behalf to the *Manchester Guardian*, 'over a thousand' had been dispersed from North Stoneham to Catholic homes (provided by the Archbishop of Westminster, who took responsibility for the housing of 1,200 children) or to hostels organised by the BCC.[70] They noted, no doubt with some forbearance, that while in France Spanish refugees had been maintained at the government's expense, in Britain 'our government has not yet felt able to contribute anything at all in money'.[71] From the public, however, the children received a spontaneous welcome. Atholl spoke of 'the wonderful kindness shown all over the country': people would approach her to ask 'How many children can you spare us? Are they all gone?'

By the end of the year Basque colonies were to be found throughout the north of England and north Wales. In Merseyside, through a local refugee committee, the Committee acquired a mansion, Greenbank, at Upton, on the Wirral, on loan from a Liverpool cotton broker, for up to 100 children.[72] The Liverpool Catholic Protection and Rescue Society agreed to accept a further 180.[73] A former workhouse at Brampton in Cumberland, 'reconstituted, scrubbed and refurnished', was put at its disposal by volunteers led by Lady

Cecilia Roberts, Wilfrid Roberts' mother, and 100 children were staying there by early July.[74] In Yorkshire, places were found in Leeds, Wakefield, Harrogate and Shipley for a total of 200 children; the first contingent were to be housed in a disused hospital in Harrogate, rented by the BCC.[75] By mid-July fifty children were accommodated at Sutton, near Hull, eighty in a former Ministry of Labour camp at Harwood Dale, six miles from Scarborough.[76] Amongst the four homes for Basque children organised by branch committees of the BCC in Wales was one at Old Colwyn on the North Wales coast.[77] By the end of 1937 ninety Basque 'colonies' had been formed in Britain; only Jersey refused them a place, ostensibly on the grounds of the damaging impact of the French immigrants who had 'overrun' the island many years previously.[78]

Basque 'colonies' in the Manchester region

In the Manchester region, the BCC identified three sources of accommodation and practical support for an expected 250 Basque children:[79] for 'those with the strongest [Catholic] church association', the institutions run by the Catholic Protection and Rescue Society of the Diocese of Salford, on offer from the Bishop, Thomas Henshaw;[80] for the rest, a decaying mansion called Watermillock, at Astley Bridge, near Bolton, brought to its notice by the National Council of Women, and an orphanage recently established in the Seedly district of Salford by an independent missionary movement, the 'Christian Volunteer Force': a local alternative, it would seem, for work which elsewhere was placed in the hands of the Salvation Army.[81] All the Basque children were 'baptised Catholics',[82] and all were given access to the Catholic clergy, but in its wisdom the BCC appears, in allocating them to particular sites, to have graded the level of their beliefs. A *Manchester Guardian* reporter who visited the children at Watermillock was told by an interpreter that they were 'mostly atheists and Communists'. Around all three locations there arose an impressive degree of popular goodwill towards the refugees, while funds for the cost of their maintenance and volunteers for their support were raised with little difficulty. There seems little doubt of the high levels of public sympathy and goodwill that the rescue operation attracted. Numerous offers of hospitality in private homes had to be turned down in keeping with the Spanish government's insistence that the children should be kept together in groups of not less than twenty 'so that their health and education could be effectively supervised and religious difficulties avoided'.[83] Fund-raising targets were based on the general expectation that the children would be in the Manchester region for around six months, after which the hope was that they would return 'to a peaceful and contented Spain'.[84]

Watermillock, a large, rambling, 'somewhat neglected and formerly beautiful mansion' set in ten acres of wooded land off Crompton Way on the outskirts of Bolton, was built in the early 1880s as the 'Tudor-Gothic' fantasy of a family of entrepreneurs in the local bleaching industry. In 1919, long since abandoned by the family, and then in use as a military hospital, the building had been acquired by the Anglican Diocese of Manchester for use as a retreat house, a purpose it served until 1935, when a more convenient centre for diocesan retreats was established in Manchester. In the following year, as the diocese considered plans for expanding its religious facilities in the Bolton area, the house was purchased by Revd H.V. Morse, one of the two assistant curates of St Augustine's Anglican church in Tonge Moor, apparently with the object of demolishing the building and using the materials in the construction of a second church in Tonge Moor: in August 1936 a local newspaper speculated that 'it will probably be in the hands of the property-breakers very soon'.[85] Instead, in May 1937 Morse offered Watermillock as a hostel for Basque children.[86]

According to one account the offer was the result of a request from the BCC to Miss Leonard, the Manchester secretary of the National Council of Women to provide hospitality for fifty children.[87] Whether or not this was the case, the intermediary between Morse and the BCC was Annie Lockwood, secretary of the active Spanish Medical Aid Committee in Bolton, which on 19 May, after the offer of a Bolton woman to adopt a refugee had been re-fused by the NJCSR, had set up a sub-committee to deal with 'the care of ref-ugee children'.[88] Reporting this development, the *Bolton Evening News* added: 'No doubt there are in Bolton quite a number who would be willing and able to care for some little one.'[89] Within a few days, Watermillock had been acquired and a committee of volunteers (perhaps the same sub-committee of Spanish Medical Aid) was at work transforming the mansion's forty rooms, a chapel 'still equipped for [Anglican] services' and substantial basement into a children's hostel.[90] Help poured in, it was said, 'from people who speak Spanish, people who can cook, people accustomed to looking after children, members of TocH [and] the Youth Hostels Association, the Scouts', women prepared to scrub and clean, and men willing to clear the drains, 'swarm over [sic]' the roof, service the electrical system, oil the locks and repair the fences.[91] Within a few days sixty beds and mattresses had been donated and the first funds raised towards a total cost estimated at £1,400: 'a mere baga-telle', according to the Lord Mayor of Manchester, for 'well-circumstanced men and women'.[92] The warden and matron (a Miss Peel of Leeds, a former social worker), a housekeeper and cook, in place by 7 June, all offered their full-time services without charge: the only likely wage-bill was for a general handyman.[93] Altogether some twenty helpers, their work coordinated by the warden and a small house committee, were gathered together to look af-ter the children's material needs.[94] A photograph of 'squads' of smiling and aproned women helpers appeared in the *Bolton Evening News*.[95] By 2 June, at the request of the volunteers, classes had been set up to teach them enough Spanish to communicate with the children;[96] notices in the children's bed-rooms were in English and Spanish.

There were other indications that the responses of the community justified the belief of Craven Ellis that 'the simple humanitarian gesture' represented by Watermillock would be welcomed 'by all fair-minded people, no matter their political views'.[97] Two dissenting letters in the *Bolton Evening News*, and one in the *Salford City News*, all arguing for the prior claims of 'starving' children in the 'grim Welsh valleys' and 'the stricken areas of the north', met with powerful responses and received short shrift from the editor of the *Evening News*, who noted that 'those who are foremost in this humane undertaking are also prominent in caring for the well-being of English children'.[98] The Boy Scouts of Astley Bridge, looking forward to teaching the Basque children to play cricket, laid out a pitch behind the house.[99] Two Catholic priests, one of whose mother tongue was Spanish, offered their cooperation in ensuring the 'spiritual welfare' of the children.[100] Bolton's Education Committee supplied Watermillock with 120 blankets, carpentry tools and help with devising an educational programme.[101] After some internal debate, the Bolton Trades Council decided to sponsor one child at Watermillock at a cost of 10s a week.[102] Montserrat Fau, the thirteen-year-old daughter of a Spanish father and an English mother, who had herself arrived in Britain with her mother as a refugee in December 1936, offered her services as an interpreter.[103]

On 31 May, as it became clear that Watermillock would form the 'centre of the Manchester district's share of the work' for Basque children,[104] a public meeting in Manchester Town Hall, under the chairmanship of the Lord Mayor of Manchester, and at which the Labour MP Sir Richard Acland spoke on behalf of the NJCSR, transferred control of the arrangements from the Spanish Aid Committee to a more powerful 'non-political and non-sectarian' Manchester and District Committee for the Care of Basque Children at Watermillock (MCCW), with the cotton goods manufacturer (and chairman of the Hallé Concerts Society), Philip Godlee as its treasurer.[105]

A committee of twenty-two[106] included representatives of the Catholic, Anglican and Nonconformist communions, members of Manchester's Liberal Party elite, such 'well-circumstanced' merchants and industrialists as the shipping merchant, Sir Robert Noton Barclay (of Mobberley Hall), the iron merchant, Sir Christopher Needham, and Sir Mathewson Watson; such leading figures from the professional world as the physician Dr Catherine Chisholm and the surgeon Wilson Harold Hey; the mayors of Manchester, Salford, Rochdale and Bolton; representatives of the National Council of Women, the Women Citizens Association and the Manchester and District Spanish Medical Aid Committee, and a handful of academics, including Manchester University's Vice-Chancellor, John Sebastian Bach Stopford, its Professor of Systematic Medicine, Frank Tylecote, and Hilda Buckmaster, an economist (and Liberal Party activist) who had arrived at the university a year earlier to serve as the warden of a student hostel, Ellis Llwyd Hall, and who was already deeply involved in raising funds for Spanish Aid. For politically ambitious members of the local Liberal Party like the textile merchant, Alfred Simon, and the barrister, P.M. Oliver, the national collapse of whose party had deprived them of their seats on the City Council (Simon) or in Parliament (Oliver),[107] the support of refugees offered an alternative outlet for their progressive views and humanitarian energies. Both cut their teeth on Medical Aid and the Basque children.[108] The committee also included

Nathan Laski, although there is no evidence that he used his position to generate Jewish support for Watermillock. Setting itself a target of £1,500 to cover the cost of an assumed six months' stay, in under three weeks the committee had raised £685 and arranged for the 'adoption' (that is, the private sponsorship at 10s a week per child) of three Basque children.[109]

As if the membership of the Watermillock Committee was not enough, there were further attempts to reassure Manchester people that the refugees were not political exiles seeking left-wing support: the rescue operation was 'non-sectarian and non-political'.[110] 'No people had more claim on our sympathy than the Basques', Sir Richard Acland told the Manchester public: they were 'not Bolsheviks or revolutionaries and asked only to be allowed to live their own life according to their own ideas'. Support was needed by the Republicans rather than the insurgents, not for political reasons, but because Franco controlled most of Spain's agricultural land and Nationalist casualties received adequate treatment from German and Italian ambulance units.[111]

With these testimonials, fifty weary Basque children between the ages of seven and sixteen, accompanied by two teachers, arrived at Watermillock late on the evening of 9 June 1937; 400 local people had gathered at the gates to welcome them.[112] They gave 'a rousing cheer' to the drivers of the two coaches which had carried them from Southampton: in the course of their journey they had been stopped for speeding, but 'in the circumstances' the police had taken no further action.[113] Reflecting on her arrival at Watermillock half a century after the event, Elvira Buckley (then Elvira Lopez) remembers that 'we were all welcomed with open arms'.[114] There were none the less signs of anxiety amongst children moving to yet another unknown destination. On the first night they chose to sleep together on the mansion's landings rather than be separated from their friends and siblings.[115]

In the days prior to the children's arrival at the Christian Volunteer Force's 'Harold's Memorial Orphanage' in Seedley, a journalist from the *Salford City Reporter* found the orphanage enveloped in 'an atmosphere of busy happiness' as volunteers prepared five 'bright and cheerful rooms' as dormitories. The staff of the orphanage were 'overwhelmed by offers of help'. An (unnamed) Manchester firm had donated forty high-quality dolls for the girls, sets of tools for the boys, puzzles, games, 'miniature pianos', saucepans and crockery. Large crowds had gathered to await the children's arrival, and when this was delayed by a minor outbreak of typhus at North Stoneham, a Mr J. Hutchinson, a 'staff-captain' in the Christian Volunteer Force, and, with his wife, Elsie, the orphanage's joint warden, had felt compelled to post daily bulletins on its door announcing the 'latest developments'. Visitors had brought their own gifts, including bats and balls and the offer of their cars for taking the children on outings. 'On behalf of the NJCSR', Hilda Buckmaster had undertaken to provide as interpreters two students from the School of Spanish at Manchester University.[116]

The Hutchinsons and their fellow officers, 'Adjutant' McMullen and 'Commodore' Hill, were proud of the daily routines they had planned for the children, and particularly of the meals they had in mind. A breakfast of half a pint of sweetened milk, a quarter pound of bread and butter 'and chocolate', would be followed by 'some kind of instruction' in English and Spanish. Following a midday dinner of 'a stew of beans, potatoes, onions and carrots', two ounces of meat, a quarter pound of bread and butter, and a banana, the afternoons would be 'reserved for play'. For supper, the children would receive two ounces of Dutch cheese, another quarter pound of bread and butter and an orange.[117] It was a diet almost certainly a good deal more wholesome than that of children of many poorer families in a poor city, calculated, it might be thought, to fuel the complaints which occasionally surfaced that refugee children were being pampered while native children starved.[118]

As the typhus scare in North Stoneham subsided, and following an inspection of the orphanage by the Salford Medical Officer of Health, the appointment of a doctor to be in attendance on the children for the first ten days of their stay, and the transfer by Salford Corporation of beds and bedding from one of its recently-closed 'cottage homes', yet more potential sources of native envy, twenty-five children (ten boys and fifteen girls, all aged between six and sixteen) arrived in Seedley on 18 June. Thereafter 'hundreds of onlookers' arrived each day to watch the boys play football and the girls skip, to leave gifts of books, dolls, toys, crockery and other 'useful items', to throw pennies and cigarette cards to the children in the orphanage grounds, and to beg for Basque autographs.[119] When Bilbao fell to Franco's Nationalists on 19 June 1937, it was decided not to tell the children, who, at all events, were 'busy entertaining the crowds'.[120]

Finally, on the evening of 24 June, the last batch of ninety children, also held up by health problems, arrived at London Road Station in Manchester for assignment by Father William J. Sewell, chaplain, secretary and organiser of the Salford diocesan Catholic Protection and Rescue Society, to six orphanages, refuges and convents in the Lancashire districts of Salford Diocese. The largest group, fifty strong,[121] was allocated to Holly Mount Convent at Tottington, near Bury, a school and refuge for homeless children run since the late 1880s by a Belgian Order, the Sisters of Charity of Jesus and Mary, with its mother house in Ghent, which had already housed Belgian refugees during the First World War. Twenty-five were housed in the Home of Our Lady of Lourdes in East Didsbury, twenty in Nazareth House, near Heaton Park in north Manchester, fifteen in the convent in Rumford Street, Chorlton-on-Medlock, of the Sisters of Charity of St. Vincent de Paul; ten in St. Joseph's Home in Patricroft and ten in a crèche attached to St. Vincent's Convent at Facit, near Rochdale. An expected 'further contingent' was to be accommodated at Buckley Hall, a Catholic boys' orphanage in Rochdale.[122] More 'large crowds' gathered, to accompany the Bishop of Salford and the nuns who were to be their protectors, in meeting the first batch to arrive at London Road; from there they proceeded by car and charabanc to their new homes.[123] 'Cheers [had] welcomed the little exiles as the train drew in'.[124]

Everywhere the children, all, it would seem, from the neighbourhood of Bilbao, Tolosa and San Sebastian, attracted interest, evoked generosity and were seen by the press to have created a favourable impression.[125] They were all 'splendid Catholics', according to *The Harvest*, 'very happy and contented', who 'fraternised well with our own children'.[126] Local papers found them highly photogenic; on 10 June, under a heading 'The Peaceful Haven', the *Bolton Evening News* printed a photograph of a party of girls with dolls at Watermillock, some being given rides on her bicycle by Annie Lockwood; another of the young interpreter, Montserrat Fau.[127] Singing and dancing, they were decorative additions to fund-raising events, whatever the cause.[128] For several weeks after the opening of Watermillock, Marguerita Campo, a former Professor of Biology at the University of Barcelona, and one of the adult helpers who had assisted the evacuation of children from Bilbao, was found a place of honour on the platforms of peace meetings in the Manchester area.[129] All the children were seen to have settled at once to educational programmes which included lessons in English: the two Spanish teachers accompanying them had put in an immediate request for pens, pencils, paper, blackboards, chalk, Spanish school texts and [sic] a Spanish translation of H.G. Wells' *History of the World*.[130] A *Manchester Guardian* reporter who visited Watermillock on the day after their arrival found the children happy, contented and talkative: their protectors were 'kind', the food good, and 'though they would rather be in Spain, under the circumstances they were glad to be in England'. Their 'black Spanish eyes glowed', he wrote, at even the suggestion of a joke. At least one child, twelve-year-old Vera O'Ugarte, appeared in a bright mantilla, and clasping castanets, for the sake of her visitors. Although most of the children were said to be atheists, and their two accompanying Spanish teachers, Noemi Marques and Martina Astiazarrain, Protestant, the children had access to two local Catholic priests.[131] Only one child at Watermillock, the sixteen-year-old Dolores Lopez, whose father and three brothers were fighting on the Bilbao front, showed signs of trauma, remaining alone in a corner, weeping constantly;[132] the rest were 'in good spirits and best of spirits'.[133] They accepted the fall of Bilbao to Franco's forces, shortly after their arrival in Bolton, although not without distress, 'very bravely'.[134] In a letter to the *Bolton Evening News*, 'Wanderer', who visited the children soon after their arrival and found two of them to be 'budding footballers', wrote: 'I never saw a bunch of children so happy or so appreciative of the attention shown them.'[135]

Much the same was true of the Christian homes. At Seedley, where the crowds of onlookers showed no signs of waning, Captain Hutchinson reported that the children had settled down quickly and comfortably: they had found the dormitories a pleasant change from the tents at North Stoneham. The girls, who spent their first days sewing garments for their dolls, had proved anxious to help with the housework and the cooking.[136] Hutchinson was 'delighted to see how well they all behaved'. Within a week the children had begun lessons at the Friends Meeting House in Langworthy Road, loaned for the purpose by the Quaker Meeting in Eccles; a local reporter witnessed 'excited' children marching in twos down Langworthy Road for their morning classes with exercise books, pencils and rulers sent over from Watermillock.[137] At the Meeting House, the elder children were taught by Senora Martin, who had accompanied the children from Spain, the younger by Sarita Castro, a native of Panama and a first year student in Spanish at Manchester University, introduced to the hostel by Hilda Buckmaster.[138] Three girls of fifteen considered too old for schooling were 'being trained in housework'.[139] Although they told horrific stories of their experiences – fifteen-year-old Juanita Ibanez y Echarre, an apprentice tailoress from San Sebastian, who had helped make overalls for government troops, spoke of hearing air raid sirens fifteen times a day – they were apparently none the worse for their ordeal: after the first day they asked few questions about the war and showed 'no desire to write to their parents and friends in Spain'.[140]

Official Salford went out of its way to comfort them. At the end of July, two councillors who were also coach proprietors arranged for them a day trip to Blackpool for which the Mayor had raised the money (£7) to pay for their amusement. They were entertained to lunch by the Blackpool Rotary Club; took tea (with the Mayors of Salford and Blackpool) at the fashionable Imperial Hotel; visited the Tower and the Pleasure Beach, to be met in person by their directors; and each left with a stick of Blackpool Rock, a 'Spanish hat', a box of fruit, a surprise gift and a plaster mug inscribed 'City of Salford, England 1937'.[141]

At St Joseph's, where eight children between the ages of eight and fourteen were soon 'happily settled', a reporter from the *Eccles and Patricroft Journal* noted what he saw as their 'absence of shyness', their smiling faces and their love of dancing.[142] The nuns of Holly Mount were equally entranced by the 'refugee guests' who took over one of the convent's dormitories. According to the report of the convent's 'reunion day' in June 1937, 'the little blue-frocked Basque girls' were seen to 'welcome the real English summer with happy laughter and chatter'. With their 'Basque love of music' they formed an 'attentive ring' around the band of the 5th Battalion of the Lancashire Fusiliers. They 'patronised the sweet stall', chatted to the nuns, some in 'perfect English', and entertained the visiting old girls of the school with national music and dances.[143] In another account, the refugees appear as 'wild strangers' who 'danced and sang together to the beating of tambourines'.[144]

There was about these supposed eye-witness accounts a degree of symbolism from which the real Basque children rarely emerged. It is difficult to escape the impression that they were as much icons as people; in their playful and exotic innocence, in their mantillas and with their 'black Spanish eyes', the 'Basque babies' (in the *Daily Worker*, 'the Basque Kiddies') stood as symbols not only of the effects of Fascist aggression but of the ravages of what was seen, particularly after the bombing of Durango, Guernica and other Basque towns during April 1937, and with Italy's Ethiopian campaign as a backcloth, as 'modern warfare'. They were vulnerable 'innocent souls'.[145] Their reception symbolised, by way of contrast, the degree of sympathy available in a democratic state. In its earliest account of the children's arrival in Britain, the *Manchester Guardian* commented: 'The descriptions of the children's arrival ... can scarcely fail to stir sympathy; how they clutched their paper parcels containing their worldly possessions; rejoiced in the white bread and chocolate which was presented as a substitute for their customary diet of black bread and beans in threatened Bilbao; how some of them were frightened by the batteries of cameras and others cried "There are no bombardments here" ... Kindness and time should heal, at least for the younger ones, the scars left by their horrible experiences of modern warfare.'[146]

If not Fascism's earliest victims, they were the first victims of a kind of warfare which, in a popular mind shaped by images of German rearmament, the Japanese bombing of civilians in Shanghai in February 1932, the Nazi occupation of the Rhineland and the invasion of Ethiopia, was associated with Fascist aggression. They were the first escapees from the warfare of modernity. It was in this that the Basque children differed from the German refugees who were making their way into the country as individuals in the same period. Unlike German-Jewish refugees, chiefly, so it was thought, from middle-class families which had the means, talents and contacts to make their personal escapes, and whose suffering did not yet include military assault, the Basque children were powerless working-class innocents caught up in Fascist violence. Unlike Hitler's German-Jewish victims, who might be seen as accepting their fate or, at any rate, as not challenging a Fascist regime, some of the fathers and elder brothers of the Basque children, it was often pointed out, were fighting and dying for democracy.[147] It was perhaps because they could not be portrayed, in contrast to the Basques, as politically motivated class warriors against Fascism that Hitler's Jewish victims appeared so rarely in the anti-Fascist propaganda of the CPGB. Without wishing to question the humanitarian instincts of those who supported the Basque children, it seems clear that they also offered British people a ready and painless means of demonstrating their commitment to democracy and decency and of expressing their abhorrence of Fascist ideals. There was no attempt to link the rescue of German Jews with that of the Basques.

The children's impending arrival spawned fund-raising groups throughout suburban Manchester. One was in the growing middle-class dormitories of Cheadle and Gatley in south Manchester. Here in late May 1937 a small group which soon evolved into the 'Cheadle and Gatley Relief Fund for the Spanish Children' set itself up to draw together local Friendly Societies, churches, sports clubs and Ratepayers Associations for house-to-house collections on behalf of Watermillock. Quakers of national eminence like John Cuthbert Wigham, chairman of the Friends Service Council in London. and leading local pacifists like Canon Thomas Shimwell, chairman of both the South Manchester Peace Council and the Manchester branch of the National Council of Civil Liberties, were drawn in as speakers to public meetings in halls loaned without charge by the local authorities and designed to drum up support. Typically, local Anglican clergy, anxious to demonstrate both their liberalism and their tolerance, were prominent in such groups: the Cheadle and Gatley committee was chaired by A.B. Leaman, the vicar of

St James Church in Gatley.[148] It was said to have attracted the support 'of all the churches in the district ... friendly societies, political organisations, the Peace Pledge Union (PPU), the League of Nations Union (LNU) and other bodies'.[149]

The volunteers, friends and funds necessary to keep the Basque refugee project afloat flowed from a variety of local sources, big and small. In 1937 students from Manchester University's Spanish Department, encouraged by Hilda Buckmaster, helped out with interpreting for and teaching the Basque children at the Harold Memorial Orphanage in Salford. A concert organised by University students, part of what was seen by one observer as part of the growing concern of the student body with 'international affairs' and 'the foreigner' during the inter-war years,[150] is said to have raised a 'creditable sum' for the fund supporting the Basque children.[151] The students' union of the Manchester College of Technology (then also the university's Faculty of Technology) gave expression to 'the responsibilities' it felt towards 'our fellow students who were victims of modern organised brutality' by holding regular collections, 'the proceeds being divided between Central European and Spanish Refugees'.[152] Profits from the sale of programmes and chocolates at a performance of Neil Grant's *The Last War* put on by Fallowfield Central Girls School in south Manchester during Manchester Peace Week in July 1937 were committed to the Basque Children's Fund.[153] In Bolton, a local girl from a nonconformist family who 'felt she would like to do something' for the Basque children at Watermillock invited six of them to her fourteenth birthday party, a fact reported to the press by the minister of her chapel.[154] In early July 1937, at the request of the Eccles branch of the LNU, the Mayor of Eccles opened a fund for the children at St Joseph's Home in Patricroft; to make a start the Mayor transferred a surplus of the funds he had already raised for Spanish Aid.[155] Later that month, a 'strictly non-partisan' garden party in aid of the Basque children was held at Ashton-under-Lyne.[156]

Although not without its reservations – not least that the British government had 'handed the baby' (the Basque children) for maintenance by its citizens rather then by itself – the Bolton Labour movement came to the support of Watermillock to the extent of 'adopting' a child. When, at a meeting of Bolton Trades Council in June 1937, some members expressed their reluctance to commit even a small portion of their limited funds to the sponsorship of a child refugee, one speaker reminded them of their obligations to humanity. The £400 the Council had in the bank was there to be used, he asserted, and not left 'so the treasurer could take pride in leaving the Council in such a healthy position when he relinquished office. The Council had an opportunity to make history. No other scheme of adoption had been attempted in Bolton ... if the delegates were anxious to add to its prestige, they would accept the scheme [for sponsorship] placed before them.' If Fascists gained control of this country, another member added, the £400 would be lost soon enough.[157]

Of Christian bodies within the region, only the Catholic Church remained unconvinced of the necessity of bringing the Basque children to Britain.

Although in the Diocese of Salford the Catholic Protection and Rescue Society had, under orders from the Archbishop of Westminster, orchestrated the settlement of Basque children in six of its diocesan Homes, was meeting the cost of their maintenance from church funds and had mounted its own (admittedly low-profile) appeal, 'For the Spanish Children', the editorial stance of its monthly journal, *The Harvest*, suggests the degree of its suspicion of the whole rescue operation. Virulently anti-Communist and pro-Franco, the need to rescue Basque children 'from a Franco death … to Anglo-life' was, in its view, a 'Red leg-pull' and a costly one at that.[158] Francisco Franco, far from being the 'dictatorship-maker, a monarchist-imperialist [and] a down-treading autocrat' portrayed in the British left-wing press, was 'a Spanish gentleman out for the good of his country', who would offer his own protection to the children of Spain'. Many 'good people' had been 'duped' into protecting the children, just as they had been 'gulled' into contributing to Spanish Aid and into joining the International Brigade: 'the absurd bringing over of these Basque children' was 'the greatest triumph yet of Red Propaganda'. It was 'an intellectual swindle – a bucket shop – and people in this country had been gulled, duped and fooled. There was no necessity of bringing them' to Britain, still less to Russia.[159] Although, out of 'deep-seated sympathy for the little ones' and 'even though our Homes are full and our financial obligations desperate', the Salford Diocese 'would not shirk responsibility for harbouring them kindly and graciously', they 'should never have come' and 'should never have become a charge on the Catholic body, which was not consulted about their coming'.[160] 'Now is not the time,' asserted one Bolton Catholic in June 1937, 'to argue whether they should have been evacuated or not – they are here and we must look after them': donations for these 'innocent souls' should be sent to the Archbishop of Westminster.[161]

Even within the Catholic Church, the official stance did not recommend itself to all the faithful. In May 1937 there emerged a dissident 'People and Freedom Group', made up of Catholics who, while keeping their distance from any critiscism of Franco's wider aims, were ready to protest in public at his 'massacre of non-combatants'. A 'statement' to this effect which first appeared in the *Manchester Guardian* of 11 May had within two weeks attracted eighty-two Manchester signatories.[162]

The backlash

It was perhaps because the children served an iconic purpose as the innocent, vulnerable and apolitical victims of Fascist aggression that support for them, while widespread, was also 'brittle'. Misbehaviour, especially if it defied authority, was liable to be construed by some as evidence of an 'anarchist' violence, and, equally significantly for those charged with their welfare, was likely to diminish the degree of financial support which they attracted.

A rare insight into the realities of a Basque colony is provided by a leading member of Mass Observation's 'Worktown' project who became a participant-observer at the Basque hostel at Watermillock on 10 June 1937, the day after the children's arrival. Joe Willcock, who before joining the Mass Observation team had been a hostel warden in London's East End, was at first struck by how little the children appeared to have been unbalanced by their recent experiences of bombardment and upheaval. They appeared nonplussed by a crowd of 100 local children and thirty adults who had arrived to watch them at play. They 'stared back' at the passengers in a passing bus who 'waved and smiled' at them. The girls coped readily with the attempts of boys from a local Catholic school to impress them. The boys who readily played football with him he found to have 'good ball control and [to be] tricky with it'. They all seemed to him happy, responsive and self-assured; there was only one child he judged to have been 'scared by the memory of recent events in Spain'. The children, he thought, were 'much more co-operative than English children', 'much less strenuously active' and 'less inclined to bicker and shout at each other'. They listened attentively to a lecture from a local doctor on 'the danger of typhoid'. When Willcock raised his right arm in the 'left front [Socialist] salute' to eight girls of twelve sharing a dormitory with their language teacher, all reciprocated. Within twenty-four hours of their arrival the children had 'settled down', the girls unravelling wool for knitting, all presenting 'quite normal expressions of pleasure' at receiving gifts of toys and books from local people, many willingly helping with the housework.[163]

Willcock's only criticism at this stage was of the local volunteers, whose management of the hostel, although they certainly 'slogged at it', he judged to be 'inadequate'; they were, he thought, 'hopelessly inefficient' and 'unsuitable for their jobs'. The warden, 'a large lady of 50', was too old, too inexperienced and too lacking in management skills to cope with the exhausting and sensitive work which the hostel required. Unable to speak Spanish, and unaccustomed to this 'unusual type' of social work, she was, he thought, 'out of touch' as much with the Spanish teachers as with the children's needs. On her first day with the children, she managed to antagonise 'the gentlemen of the press', whose support was necessary to the raising of funds. Willcock had no hesitation in predicting that, with 'no idea how to run the place', she would soon 'fall down' on the job. Of the 100 people who had volunteered their services, only four turned up for the 'slogging work'; in particular, there were no male volunteers on hand to play with the Basque boys.[164] By 12 June, divisions between leading members of the hostel staff generated by petty jealousies, confrontational management and perhaps social differences had created within the hostel itself what one of them described as 'class war'.[165] Within weeks some of the volunteers who had offered their services without reserve had begun to see their roles as excessively onerous, ill-defined, ill-appreciated and, in one instance at least, degrading: it came to seem to the warden as 'rather unfair' that staff and helpers should eat the same food as the children.[166] Such tensions may perhaps be seen as one negative consequence of the wide social spectrum from which volunteers had offered their services.

While never satisfied with what might be seen as the inevitable limitations of hard-working volunteer helpers, Willcock was soon brought face to face with the children's continuing emotional engagement with events in Bilbao. 'Their experiences,' he discovered, 'had not frightened them off the thought of war – but had aroused their more savage instincts.' Given the slightest reference to the war, they would break out 'quite spontaneously' into angry accounts of their menfolks' struggles against the Fascists, of how 'aeroplanes had come and ... their houses had been destroyed,' and 'how the defenders had replied with guns and rifles'. 'Their faces lit up,' Willcock reported, 'and they seemed quite transported at the idea of bringing down the planes and firing the guns'.[167] A group of the girls had composed 'some interesting rhymes about cutting off Mola's or Franco's hair and using it as a broom'.[168]

Willcock's rosy accounts of the children's cooperative attitudes became gradually nuanced by the realities of personal trauma and adolescent rebellion. 'The unruly boys seem[ed] [to Willcock] to be getting unrulier'; on 16 June five of them were caned by a male volunteer for their 'bad behaviour'. Girls offered coronation medals by one of the volunteers 'shouted', 'screamed' and refused to form an orderly queue. By 24 June some of the children had begun to rebel against the high-handedness of the matron, the 'hypocrisy' of some of the women volunteers and attempts by local priests to impose on them a degree of Catholic observance. Priests who had wanted to destroy the red flag were told 'where they got off'; one in particular, 'who spoke Spanish' was 'spoken of with great disgust by all the children'. There was growing anxiety amongst the children about the fate of their parents and the possibility of their having to return to a Fascist Spain; one visitor provoked their anger by telling them in bad Spanish that 'next week they would all go [back] to Bilbao'.[169] Perceptions of a welcoming public had also begun to pale: faced by 'staring' and 'whispering' onlookers, the children had begun to see English people as 'queer and unpleasant'.[170] As to the children's more exotic qualities, in responding to a request from the BBC, the house committee at Watermillock discovered that none of the children could sing and none knew any Basque songs.[171]

Such cracks in the stability of life at Watermillock produced neither the internal breakdown which Willcock had feared nor any sort of confrontation with the Bolton public. In the hostel, with the support of their Spanish helpers, and the resourceful and well-liked Father Morse, the children weathered what they saw as the warden's mismanagement, the matron's 'autocratic' manner, the carelessness of the 'Bolton boy helpers', and the gossip of the 'kitchen women'. Their very limited engagement with the drab cotton town which was Bolton and with English weather which they saw as 'a joke ... carried too far', had its compensations. The manager of a local cinema to which the children were taken on a visit told them that, as 'the Spanish children from Watermillock ... they could always come in the future free with the management's compliments'.[172] Synopses of film plots were provided in Spanish.[173] The hostel shortly developed its own cinema, playrooms and carpentry shop, the children were regularly invited out to tea and to local fetes and garden parties by local people and trips were arranged to Southport.[174] The management of the house was probably typical of BCC hostels dependent on well-meaning but unpaid and inexperienced volunteers drawn from differing political and social sectors of local communities, and on an uncertain income derived from episodic public appeals. Watermillock's relationships with the town were plagued by the (probably equally universal) fragility of civic dignitaries coming to terms with an alternative jurisdiction exercised by voluntary committees: the Mayor of Bolton became 'very annoyed and unhelpful' after the MCCW failed to invite him to speak at an appeal meeting in Manchester. Feeling that the Watermillock project had been foisted on Bolton by Manchester do-gooders, he proved reluctant to sponsor the local appeals upon which the hostel ultimately depended.[175]

A small house committee, as the final link in a chain of humanitarian effort stretching down through region and city from the BCC, struggled with a range of tasks which included the coordination of the hostel's administration, the location of local sources of funds, equipment and furniture, Watermillock's relationship with the local authority, local people and the local press, the children's welfare and education, and the papering over of such cracks as appeared in the hostel's internal harmony and external image. If the meeting attended by the anthropologist and Mass Observer, Tom Harrison, is anything to go by, the committee demonstrated the typical strengths and weaknesses of volunteers of widely differing backgrounds, thrown together by their routine duties, and working a miniscule democracy. The debates, while (in Harrison's somewhat aloof and occasionally contemptuous view) were over-long, repetitive, often inconclusive, and punctuated by acrimony and 'back-chat', decisions were made on a range of matters which, while (to Harrison) seemingly 'petty', effectively kept the hostel afloat.[176] The objects of Harrison's condescension included the Vicar of St Augustine's, A.S. Macdonald, Annie Lockwood of Spanish Medical Aid and Miss Leonard from the National Council of Women, to whose efforts the hostel owed its very existence. Watermillock appears to have owed its survival largely to the flexibility of the powerful MCCW, which late in June 1937 replaced the hostel warden and added experienced and influential new members to the House Committee.[177]

It seems likely that problems related to child behaviour and staff relations were more likely in 'secular' hostels like Watermillock than in Catholic homes and convents, with their settled staff, their long experience of handling homeless and 'difficult' children, and their authoritarian traditions. In most of these, too, the refugees were not separated from native children, but slept in the same dormitories and ate at the same tables as the native children.[178] Children from Catholic backgrounds were also more amenable to a discipline imposed by priests and nuns who commanded a natural respect. A visitor from the BCC to the homes in the north of England in the autumn of 1937 accorded special praise to Holly Mount and to the Nazareth House home at Heaton Park in Manchester; in both the children were said to be settled and happy.[179] Within the Catholic homes in the region the only problem occurred at the Sisters of Charity home in Chorlton-on-Medlock where 'some [unstated] difficulty' led to the dispersal of the fifteen girls to Southampton, Hereford and Tottington.[180] Most problematic were the 'camps' in which the accommodation was in huts and where the facilities were primitive.

It was certainly the case that the first reported instances of 'indiscipline' amongst the Basque children related to more primitive hostels and make-shift camps outside Catholic control. On 16 July 1937 'trouble' was reported amongst the eighty Basques living in a tented camp at Harwood Dale, near Scarborough, where, according to a press report, forty boys, one armed with a knife, 'stormed' the cookhouse, causing 'considerable damage', and forcing the cook to take refuge in a nearby farmhouse, from which he had subsequently to be rescued 'disguised as a sack of potatoes'.[181] Although individually 'quite orderly and well behaved', according to the camp's organising committee in Scarborough, the boys were liable to get out of hand under the influence of 'disturbing elements', six of whom were immediately to removed to another camp.[182] After a *Manchester Guardian* report headed 'The Spanish Situation' five days later had included the further allegation that the Basque boys at Harwood Dale were 'terrifying local children', the camp's management committee at Scarborough was 'disbanded' and its administration taken over directly by the BCC in London.[183] Scarborough Town Council, which had only recently welcomed the boys, now resolved that they 'should be kept out of the town itself'.[184] On 19 July clashes were reported between Basque and local children at a hostel in a 'residential quarter' at Sutton on the outskirts of Hull.[185] Finally what the *Manchester Guardian* described as a 'proper riot' broke out amongst the Basques at a camp for seventy-six children in Brechfa, a remote village in Carmarthenshire, after a number of them were reported by a visiting angler for damaging a window of his car. The rioters descended on Brechfa, breaking all the windows of the hotel where the visitor was staying and the house of the local resident who had reported them to the camp authorities.[186] The 'ringleaders of the disorder' were again 'drafted elsewhere' in Britain before, in their case, being despatched by the NJCSR, via France, to a children's home 'of a Reform School type' in Spain.[187] Staff at camps where the disorder had occurred were replaced by those experienced enough 'to ensure discipline and proper conduct'.[188]

Reports of the activities of the 'Violent Young Refugees'[189] or 'the Bad Basque Boys'[190] had very probably exaggerated the reality, sometimes deliberately. At Sutton local 'hooligans' were said to have set out to 'offend and provoke' the Basque children, whose conduct was subsequently defended by local residents.[191] A travelling inspector from the NJCSR judged that the Basques at Harwood Dale had been 'considerably provoked': it would be wrong, he told an audience in Kendal, to describe the boys as 'young desperadoes'.[192] The NJCSR had been quick to punish the few identifiable offenders and to defend the remainder, many of whom, according to Wilfrid Roberts, had been rendered 'liable to become excited' by the 'shell-shock' they had suffered in their homeland. The Council, he said, was seeking to break up the larger camps into smaller colonies in 'various towns'.[193] The

123

real problem for the Council, however, was not so much the disorder itself, as the ammunition it provided to those sections of the British press and the public who had never welcomed the arrival of the Basques and who by July 1937 were seeking their speedy repatriation, regardless of what might have happened to their parents. In Bilbao, which had fallen to Franco's forces on 19 June 1937, a Fascist press calling for repatriation could speak of 'crimson children ... terrorising every part of England'.[194] In the Salford Catholic Diocese, *The Harvest,* supposedly shocked by the 'gangster attitude' and political militancy of some of the children, added its voice to the demands for repatriation: 'let us pray that soon they may be able to rejoin their parents and resume normal life in their own land'.[195]

Messages of violence, widely diffused through the national and local press, had also affected the humanitarian mood, even amongst some of those working closely with the children. In early August Aileen Moore, once a worker for the Basque children, wrote an article in the *Manchester Guardian,* 'The Basque Children – Aftermath', expressing her anxieties and her disillusionment. The repatriated children had been 'undesirables' who had somehow 'slipped through the meshes of what was actually a very careful combing process [in Bilbao]'. They had placed a 'stigma' around those who remained 'which it will be hard to remove', especially amongst those who had opposed their arrival. There were other difficulties, she wrote, known only to those 'behind the scenes'. The Salvation Army, whose lips were officially sealed, had acted with 'the truest Christian gallantry' in the face of 'the indignities, the ingratitude, and even violence they have had to endure' from their Basque charges.[196] During August 1937 a proposal of the BCC to send twenty-five Basque children to the Queen's Tower in Sheffield, put at its disposal by the Duke of Norfolk, was successfully opposed by the city's Medical Officer of Health. An alternative proposal – a hutted camp at Hollowford, near Castleton, in Derbyshire – was met by protests from the Rural District Council on the grounds of the risks to health, poor sanitation, an inadequate water supply and the potential ill-discipline of the newcomers. 'They had plenty of bad boys in the village', according to one councillor, 'without bringing any more': the presence of the children was likely to scare away the visitors upon whom Castleton's well-being depended.[197]

The NJCSR and the BCC had their defenders, not least the *Manchester Guardian,* which had consistently lent them its backing. Its issue of 14 August 1937, at the height of the controversy, included a powerful editorial defence of the children's behaviour, a favourable account of conditions at Watermillock by a 'special correspondent', and a photograph of a group of smiling, shirt-sleeved Basque boys on their way to gardening; shouldering hoes, spades and forks and pushing two wheelbarrows containing their youngest members. 'Disorder' in only three Basque colonies, seen by the *Guardian* as 'trifling', had wrought only a few pounds' worth of damage: 'surprisingly small' amongst 'nerve-wracked children who had suffered the brutalities of modern warfare', some of whose parents had been shot, and who had experienced 'the broken, lowered life of a bombarded and beleaguered town'. In Britain the children were 'well-taught and well-fed' and 'being shown a little of the country'. At Watermillock, although liable to become excited by the sound of low-flying planes, the revving-up of passing buses and the buzzers of local mills, they were 'losing nervousness and gaining weight'. They were being asked out to tea by local residents and taken on day-trips to Southport. The food was good and plentiful. The hostel now had its own cinema. The children had people around them who spoke Spanish and with whom they could share their worries. Some were beginning to hear from parents and friends in Spain or (as themselves refugees) in France.[198]

Others, with no political or religious axe to grind, found nothing unnatural or unexpected in the 'naughtiness' of young teenage boys. 'It does not matter whether the Basque children are little rascals or not,' wrote one correspondent from London to the *Manchester Guardian*, 'the fact remains that they are children'.[199] To the veteran Labour leader George Lansbury, who visited some of the Basque colonies, the children seemed 'too good. I like children to be naughty.' 'We cannot make up to them what they have lost,' he went on, 'but we should do as much as we can, and be grateful for the chance of doing it'.[200]

The probable truth is that the Basque children and their protectors were now the victims of the romantic imagery which had accompanied the children's arrival: the children, in the NJCSR's own publicity, were 'of naturally fine physique, intelligent, literate, vivacious, responsive [and] affectionate'.[201] The excessive publicity now given to the 'misbehaviour' and ingratitude of the few both deprived philanthropy of its just reward and provided an opening for those who, from motives religious or political, sought to reinvent the children collectively as Catholics at risk or as a new generation of Socialist revolutionaries: at all events, as people who should be returned as soon as possible to their parents and their homeland. To maintain the momentum of humanitarian effort, the NCJSR was forced back increasingly onto such demeaning, and in the long run self-defeating, devices as defensive letters of appeal in the press,[202] assertions of the children's continued popularity in localities like Bolton, or the publication of evidence of the children's gratitude to their helpers.[203] Arrangements were made for Don Jose Ignacio de Lizasco, the Basque government's official representative in Britain, to visit the Basque colonies, including those around Manchester, to assess the truth of critical comment and to report on any difficulties being faced by those controlling the children.[204] At the same time, in the face of a 'whispering campaign' levelled at the children's behaviour and the administration of the hostels,[205] the committee now felt obliged to assert its intention, from which it had 'never deviated', of returning the children once authenticated requests had been received from the parents whose whereabouts were known and whose rights to guardianship could be ascertained.[206]

From late July 1937 the Franco regime in the Basque country, backed by the Spanish Catholic hierarchy, by the emissaries of the Vatican in Spain and by the Fascist press, was applying increasing pressure on the countries of reception for the return of the 'unfortunate children' whose religion was said to be at risk, whose parents were said to be seeking to reclaim them and whose presence in Britain, France, Belgium and the Soviet Union was seen 'to defame the New Spain'.[207] In Britain the call for repatriation, which had begun in some circles soon after the children's arrival, was backed by the Catholic and right-wing press, and, following the fall of Bilbao on 19 June 1937, by the Archbishop of Westminster, the Foreign Office (where Eden believed any delay of the children's return might be construed as a political act), the Home Office and a 'Spanish Children's Repatriation Committee' set up in December 1937 by Franco's supporters in Britain and chaired by the Duke of Wellington.[208]

In Salford, *The Harvest,* supposedly shocked by 'the gangster attitude' and Socialist militancy of some of the children, echoed the Catholic hierarchy and the national Catholic press in pressing for the children's speedy return to Spain, and that at the cost of the NJCSR: 'will those busy bodies', it asked, 'who took the children from their homes now get busy and find the money to return them?'[209]

After a short but forceful rearguard action in the late summer and early autumn of 1937, designed at least to delay the children's return until conditions in Spain were 'sufficiently settled' and applications from the parents' for their children's return could be authenticated by the committee's legal commission,[210] in early November, in the face of concerted pressure, its own 'chronic lack of funds' and divisions within its own ranks, the BCC felt compelled to arrange what turned out to be the long-drawn-out repatriation of all but around 500 of the 'Basque babies'.[211]

The timing of the children's departure from particular colonies depended as much on local circumstances as on parental requests. When, on 21 October 1937, four and a half months after their arrival, twenty-five 'weeping Basque children' were despatched by coach from the Christian Volunteer Force's orphanage in Seedley to new accommodation in a guest house loaned by the Holiday Friendship Association at Froggatt Edge, Grindleford, nine miles out of Sheffield, the reason probably had to do with the changing plans (and perhaps the increasing financial fragility) of the CVF. The Force had first acquired the hostel in 1936 to supplement its two existing hostels in Glasgow. When a third hostel was opened there in June 1937 the Harold Memorial Orphanage, which before the refugees arrived had rarely been full, became a burden it could no longer afford. At the time of the children's departure Hutchinson was already negotiating with Salford Corporation for its sale to them as a remand home.[212] At the same time a committee in Sheffield had begun to raise funds to defray the cost of a six-month stay at Froggatt Edge.[213] Before leaving, the children had been fitted out with new clothes, part of the cost being met by the crew of a Spanish ship, the *Bartolo*, berthed in Salford Dock.[214] Following their departure Hutchinson revealed to the press letters of thanks he had received from the children, some beginning 'Dear Father and Mother' and ending 'Your affectionate Son or Daughter'.[215] At their new home, meantime, the children had received 'a hearty welcome'. The Bishop of Sheffield and the Deputy Mayor had turned out with the Spanish Vice-Consul to meet their train in Sheffield, six 'adoptions' had preceded their arrival, and a public campaign on their behalf was launched a few days later.[216]

Children in Catholic homes were the next to leave the Manchester region. *The Harvest* recorded the departure of the first party on 11 November 1937, to join a contingent of 160 children returning from Britain to Bilbao. Having made 'a wonderful impression on those who met them here', the report read, they left 'loaded with toys', and each with a rosary given by Fr Sewell 'as a souvenir from the Rescue Council'.[217] The *Manchester Guardian* of 8 January 1938 printed, without comment, a photograph of another group leaving the Our Lady of Lourdes convent in East Didsbury. The emptying of Watermillock began on 22 March 1938, when twenty of the fifty-four children (those who could prove they had a home and two parents in Spain) left for London, each with an identity card hanging from his coat, to join a second contingent of 500 returning to Bilbao.[218] The *Bolton Evening News* typically printed a photograph of the children at the station in Bolton under the care of their new warden, a Mr P. Booth.[219] The timing of other departures are not recorded. Twenty-four Basque children and two of their teachers were still at Holly Mount in Tottington in September 1938, when the children, in Basque national costume of red, green and white and black aprons performed folk dances as part of the convent's Golden Jubilee.[220] Those who remained in Britain, including some from Watermillock,[221] were for the most part from working-class homes in the industrial belt around Bilbao, and were chiefly those with strong left-wing sympathies who saw their settlement in Britain as 'political exile'. From the end of 1939, when most of the Basque colonies had been broken up, they had lived either in private foster homes arranged by the BCC, or in one of six designated Catholic group homes, of which one was Our Lady of Lourdes in East Didsbury.[222] The last children to be repatriated before sea communications were interrupted by the exigencies of war left Manchester on a Spanish cargo ship on 26 July 1940,[223] leaving some 470 stranded in Britain.[224]

National memory and the Basque children

It has been argued that the story of the Basque children, along with most other aspects of Spanish Relief, has been largely ignored by 'orthodox historians' infected by the anti-Communism of the Cold War years.[225] There may be some truth in this. At the same time, however, it was also the case that the Basque children failed to leave the kind of indelible mark on British culture achieved by the children who began to arrive on the Kindertransport, just as most of the Basques were departing, in December 1938.[226] This was as much a matter of education as of numbers. Whereas most of the Kindertransport children were drawn from aspiring middle-class professional and commercial families in which their liberal education had been a priority, the Basque children were chiefly members of working-class families which had lacked both the resources and the cultural horizons to foster their children's educational ambitions. Unlike the *kinder*, they were not from backgrounds likely to generate high profile contributions to British life. Nor was there anything in the process of the Basque re-settlement to counter the fact that most of the children had not completed their primary education. At Watermillock education had comprised little beyond lessons in elementary English, sewing classes for the girls, craft lessons for the boys and physical training for all.[227]

Although from the end of 1938 some of the older children had been allowed by the Home Office to enrol in British state schools, the BCC had not seen the children's education as part of its responsibility. The few children who found places at Catholic boarding schools were amongst the first to be repatriated. In the British Basque colonies, where their presence was, at all events, seen as temporary, little was on offer beyond an introduction to the English language. Nor had the Basques the advantage, like the *kinder*, of a British-based community which might have sustained their educational progress. As a result, 'relatively few of those who stayed went on to the secondary school … even fewer to the technical colleges [and] only about thirty went to university'.[228] Few of the Basques who remained, therefore, became equipped to enter the professions or to exercise the kind of influence on the 'high culture' of Britain which might have sustained their memory or attracted the kind of cultural historians who might have perpetuated an awareness of their 'contributions' to British society. As they entered adulthood, most of the boys were qualified only for 'factory jobs',[229] most of the girls for secretarial work, nursing and domestic service.[230] It may be that one cause of their neglect is that in British history it has been for their 'contributions' to the host nation that refugees have been most often valued and remembered.

The arrival of the Basques had also coincided with the anxieties which accompanied Britain's drift into war with Germany. Those who had known the Basques in Britain had little time to maintain contact with those who returned to Spain. Rare exceptions were the two sisters who, as teachers, had accompanied the Basque children to Holly Mount in Bury in June 1937, and with whom the convent's Mother Superior had kept up a correspondence until 1947, even though their father was 'an avowed Communist and therefore in trouble with Franco'.[231] Most of the Basques who returned to Spain, and who were there compelled to make the best of it under a Fascist regime, departed from British consciousness as certainly as those who remained.

Jews and Basques

In Manchester, the suffering and vulnerability of the Basque children attracted a wide swathe of humanitarian support, embracing, if the composition of the Watermillock Committee is any guide, churchmen of every denomination, liberal-minded professionals, academics and industrialists, members of all three political parties, trade unionists, Quakers and other pacifists, members of the organised women's movement, and, at least in a nominal capacity, the leader of the Jewish community, Nathan Laski. Support for the young Basques, moral and financial, was an expression of the compassion and status which had drawn these same people into civic philanthropy. It was a broad front which had no equivalent in the case of Jewish refugees. This was partly because the Basques were children and not only that but innocent working-class children physically endangered by the sophisticated techniques of modern warfare. This is not how the earliest German-Jewish refugees might have been seen. Most were adults. The majority were drawn from middle-class families capable, so it might be thought, of helping their own. Some were industrialists, others academics. Most could not readily be defined in 1937 either as the victims of Fascist politics or the subjects of governmental aggression. However monstrous and well-publicised their exclusion from German life, and however they were seen to suffer from sporadic violence, they were not yet generally regarded as being collectively in physical danger. Unlike the situation of the Basques in 1937, the suffering of the Jews of Germany, increasingly marginalised from mainstream German life, and suffering random violence, was insufficient to evoke the kind of broad humanitarian response which met the children of the Basque country.

They were also Jews and, as such, subject to stereotypes from which the Basque children were free. Apart from the imagery of anti-Semitism, as much part of the cultural tradition in Manchester as elsewhere in Britain, these included, in Manchester, the long-standing and well-publicised notion, and one held with (defensive) pride by the Jewish community itself, that Jews 'looked after their own', a notion no doubt reinforced by the decision of London Jewish leaders in 1933 that they would meet the cost of Jewish refugee settlement in Britain. Since there was no equivalent Spanish community in Manchester, the Basques were from the start dependent upon the charity of native well-wishers. There was no organised equivalent, in the case of Jewish refugees, of the body of liberals who made up the Watermillock Committee.

Nor should the support of the Basque children be taken as evidence that in 1937 the realities of international Fascism were well understood in Manchester outside the narrow confines of the CPGB and the journalism of the *Manchester Guardian*'s German correspondents. The general public in Manchester was scarcely attuned to the realities of National Socialism or to its links with Franco's Spain. In 1937, following the year of the Berlin Olympics, when the Nazi government had moderated its more extreme policies, Germany remained a feature of the holiday routines of Manchester's middle-class families and of the extra-curricular activities of Manchester's schools, colleges and churches. Germany was accessible not simply via the costly Hamburg-American and Norddeutscher shipping companies, but via a direct line to Hamburg and Bremen from the Manchester Ship Canal. In May 1937 four Manchester branches of Thomas Cook and Sons announced fortnightly, and 'incredibly low-cost', fifteen-day tours of Germany, 'in the Grand Manner', with the opportunity of 'really seeing inside Germany'. German students, including members of Hitler Youth, were welcomed in Manchester. Franco had his admirers amongst Manchester Catholics, Hitler amongst

Manchester Germans. 'If only Hitler had embraced the Roman Catholic Church as an ally against Bolshevism', according to one commentator in *The Harvest*, the quarterly periodical of Salford's Catholic Rescue Society, and the nearest the Salford Diocese had to a diocesan magazine, 'he could have had us [the Catholic Church] with him'.[232] Few first-hand observers of Germany made note of the fate being endured by German Jews. The present author has the photograph album of a Salford family which visited Germany in 1937: it includes a photograph of the family's convivial meeting in the German countryside with a unit of Hitler Youth and another of a member of the family holding the Swastika flag with the title, 'Mr … as a Nazi'.

William Hodgkins, minister of the Oldham Road Congregationalist Chapel, had a 'regular repricocity arrangement' with the Bureau of Foreign Students at the University of Bonn for annual visits to Germany by 'youth workers and students' from Manchester and to Manchester of Hitler Youth leaders from Bonn. 'Anyone who may be interested' was invited to join a fortnight of excursions by nine Hitler Youth leaders who arrived in Manchester on 6 July 1937 to places of interest including the major industrial plants of Mather and Platt, Renold's Chains and ICI. Hodgkins' guests, whose declared aim was to study 'social and economic conditions in the [Manchester] district', were entertained by Hodgkins' church and given a farewell party at the Tudor Café.[233] On 6 July a separate party of German schoolgirls were received by Manchester University. Gerhard Kruger, a spokesman for the ten Hitler Youth leaders who had been invited to join the North of England School Camp at Chatsworth in late July was given space to defend the dismissal of Jewish staff from German universities who had 'served their own race only': what use was there in keeping them, he asked representatives of the Manchester press, when German students would not attend their lectures?'

Typical of the reports of such journeys are eulogies of the new Germany, praise for the warm reception received from a German people committed to peace, and the absence of any reference to the nature of the Nazi regime or to its victims. So in June 1937 a Manchester University student spoke, without irony, to the Salford Rotary Club of the 'revolutionary change' wrought by the Nazi regime on German pedagogy. 'Exaggerated intellectualism' had given way to more 'practical' programmes which accorded proper recognition to physical education and a 'political citizenship … tinged with a romantic mystical atmosphere that made it almost a religion'. Schools, the Hitler Youth Movement and the German Labour Service had effectively inculcated children with 'a passionate love of their country', a 'spirit of service', and 'a willingness to make any kind of sacrifice' for the national good, 'no matter what it cost to themselves and others'. Young people were taught 'to be wholehearted supporters of their particular political faith'.[234] One of Salford's senior librarians, after visiting Bavaria, informed the Rotarians that Germany was 'the ideal holiday country of Europe': the atmosphere in Bavaria was particularly friendly.[235] The report of a Salford woman's visit to Berlin was accorded two columns in thee *Salford City Reporter*: at the new Reichstag, to her evident delight, she had been shown the offices of Hitler and Goering.[236]

In July 1937 the Lord Mayor of Manchester was reported to have 'received sympathetically' a suggestion from the Mayor of Stoke-on-Trent that a group of English civic heads visit Germany to promote 'friendly relations'. 'We know little of the German people,' according to the Mayor of Stoke, 'and they of us, and I believe there is a mutual desire for friendship and for the peace of the world.'[237] The seven civic heads, including the mayors of Manchester, Salford and Eccles, who subsequently accepted the invitation, visited Berlin, Cologne and Düsseldorf on a 'Peace Mission' and 'were impressed by all they had seen'; according to the Lord Mayor of Manchester: they had received a 'wonderful welcome', the German people were 'well-clothed and fed' and 'everyone seemed cheerful and happy'. The visit, he believed, had helped to 'cement peaceful relations' between Germany and Britain.[238] The *Eccles and Patricroft Journal* printed a report of the mission by the Mayor of Eccles to the Eccles Men's Forum under the heading 'Clean streets, Modern schools and Smokeless towns'.[239]

Such visitors were perhaps no more self-delusional than a National Government bent on the appeasement of Hitler. They had convinced themselves, and then had their convictions confirmed, of the desire of the German people, as of themselves, for peace. Some were, no doubt, awe-struck voyeurs of the drama of Nazism and the power, and supposed charisma, of its leaders. Few, however, were genuine sympathisers with the Nazi ideology. And yet a characteristic common to the perceptions of Christian visitors is the invisibility of the Jews. The single exception is a report from a representative of the *Bolton Evening News* who made the trip from Grimsby to Hamburg in May 1937. His 'fleeting glimpse' of Germany took in streets full of uniforms, the omnipresence of Hitler's portrait, a 'propaganda press' which attributed Germany's difficulties to the Jews and 'the barricades of windows of shops bearing Jewish names'. It would seem that few, if any, of those involved in aiding the Basque children made a connection between their suffering and the fate of German Jews already deprived of their rights as German citizens.

There is also something prescient in the responses to the Basque children of Manchester Communists, many of them of Jewish origin. While publicising the arrival of the Basque children in the *Daily Worker* as a further example of the human consequences of Fascism, there is no evidence of Communist action on their behalf beyond participation in fund-raising. There was no Communist hostel; only a handful of Basque children not repatriated found a home with Communist families.[240] This may partly have been an act of self-denial to allow space for action by the anti-Communist Catholic Church. It may also have to do with the party's lack of adequate numbers and resources. But it is also tempting to interpret inaction as part of the CPGB's preference, their support for the Spanish Republic apart, for propaganda over action. There are hints of the party's help for German political refugees at this early period. The wife of the Manchester International Brigader, George Brown, is said to have acted as the party's courier from the early 1930s in providing German refugees with the funds to make an escape. Liverpool dock workers are said to have arranged for the clandestine transport of political refugees to Russia. But no proof has yet been offered of such activities which, at all events, did not concern Jewish refugees. Throughout the period of refugee arrival, Manchester Communists were no more than sympathetic and articulate observers, at most providing German KPD exiles with useful contacts in finding employment and accommodation. Their main targets, no doubt identified by their Soviet masters, were the Francoists in Spain and the BUF in Britain.

Jewish refugees received nothing like the waves of humanitarian sympathy and action which greeted the Basque children. There were none the less hints in Spanish Aid of the sectors of Manchester society which, in later years, for reasons of religious belief and political ideology were likely to support Jewish refugees. One was the Quaker community, which, by its support for Spanish Aid, demonstrated its willingness to support victims other than its own. Another was a circle of prominent Liberals. Four of those who were later to lend their support to refugee Jews emerged on the refugee scene as supporters of the Basques. One, the textile merchant, Alfred Simon, was Jewish. Two of the others, the Unitarian barrister, Philip Milner Oliver, and Manchester University's Vice-Chancellor, John Sebastian Bach Stopford, had track records as Judaeophiles. The fourth, Hilda Buckmaster, was a Liberal Party activist recently arrived in Manchester and bringing with her an academic interest in Europe's minority problems. It was the tight-knit circle of middle-class liberals to which these four belonged, rather than militant anti-Fascists of the Left, who, in the last resort, offered Jewish refugees the practical means to escape and survive.

Although Laski, as an influential local dignitary, lent his name to the fund-raising efforts of the Watermillock Committee, there is no evidence that either he or his Jewish colleagues on the Jewish Representative Council made a link between the arrival of the Basque children and the emerging fate of German Jewry. Within the Jewish community at large, it was only the small minority of Jewish Communists, many of whom had joined the International Brigade, who recognised the nature and the breadth of the Fascist threat. There is no reference to Spain in the minute books of the Jewish Representative Council, and no indication of any kind that the Jewish population at large (as distinct from its tiny secularised and politicised minority), while increasingly well-informed of the persecution of German Jews, recognised the relevance of the fate of Spain. Laski was later to claim to the Council, in relation to the threat posed by the BUF, that ' the Fascist question was not a Jewish question', implying, inter alia, that it was a problem for all Mancunians, to be resolved, in case of the BUF, by the police,[241] an implication on which he had failed to act with any semblance of energy in the case of the Spanish Civil War or the Basque children of 1937. As a political Liberal and as a communal leader concerned primarily with the orderly conduct, patriotism and respectability of the Jewish community, and in spite of the leftward movement of his younger son, Harold, he shared the anti-Communism of the Catholic Church. His notable, and otherwise inexplicable, absence from the committee which organised Manchester's Jewish Book Week in April 1938 may have to do with the committee's decision to include, in the 'Political Economy' section, a complete set of Harold's works.

Basque children's colonies in the Manchester region

Buckley Hall, Rochdale (Brothers of Charity, Roman Catholic). Number of Basque residents unknown.
Harold's Memorial Orphanage, Seedly Road, Seedly, Salford (Christian Volunteer Force): 25 boys and girls.
Holly Mount Convent, Tottington, Bury (Sisters of Charity of Jesus and Mary, Roman Catholic): 50 boys and girls.
Nazareth House, Heaton Park, Manchester (Sisters of Nazareth, Roman Catholic): 16 girls.
Our Lady of Lourdes Home, East Didsbury (Missionary Sisters of St Joseph, Roman Catholic): 30 boys and girls.
St Joseph's Home, Worsley Road, Patricroft. Eccles (Missionary Sisters of St Joseph, Roman Catholic): 8 boys and girls.
St Vincent's Convent, near Facit, Rochdale (Roman Catholic): 10 boys and girls.
Sisters of Charity Home, Rumford Street, Chorlton-on-Medlock (Sisters of Charity of St Vincent de Paul, Roman Catholic): 15 girls.
Watermillock, Bolton (BCC): 54 boys and girls.

Notes

1 The Rumanian-born Austrian national, Joseph Eisner, arrived in Hull on 4 April 1938 on a small cargo boat from Gdynia on the Baltic. Since no one was expecting a passenger, 'he walked through the docks without being challenged', and only later registered his presence. He found work in Derby and was followed there by his wife and daughter (information from Joseph Eisner's daughter).
2 The NJCSR was a cross-party and interdenominational body established at the House of Commons on 6 January 1937 as an umbrella body to coordinate fund-raising for the Republican cause.
3 Tom Buchanan, 'The Role of the Labour Movement in the Origins and Work of the Basque Children's Committee, 1937–39', *European History Review*, Vol. 18, April 1988, pp. 155–174.
4 The title of a film of the Basque children made shortly after their arrival by a consortium of companies in the British film industry and first shown at Film House in Wardour Street on 3 November 1937 (MG 2 November 1937).
5 MG 25 May 1937, leader column headed 'The Basque Children'.
6 MG 25 May 1937.
7 BEN 25 May 1937.
8 MG 27 July 1937, commenting in a leader column on the proposal to close the Nansen International Office.
9 MG 14 August 1938.

10 MCN 20 May 1937. The actual number of Basque children accommodated in the region was 180.

11 MG 1 June 1937.

12 MG 26 July 1937.

13 SCR 23 July 1937.

14 Jim Fyrth, *The Signal was Spain* (London and New York 1986), p. 21.

15 MG 31 May 1937.

16 MG 31 May 1937, report of the 14th Congress of the CPGB. The crime of the ILP was to have lent its support to the anarchist formation, Partido Obrero de Unificacion Marxista (POUM). According to Pollitt, 'the worst feature' of the Labour leadership was its 'treatment of Spain'.

17 MG 31 May 1937.

18 MG 16 September 1937. Joe Norman, a member of an AEU branch in Salford, who himself left for Spain when unemployed in October 1937, calculated that ten Salford men had joined the International Brigade, of whom, by January 1939, four had been killed and two were in Fascist prisons in Spain. (Letters from Joe Norman in the SCR, 6 May and 8 July 1938, 20 January 1939.)

19 Christopher Hall, *'Not Just Orwell': The Independent Labour Party and the Spanish Civil War* (Barcelona 2009), pp. 174–175, 197–198.

20 MG 3 May 1937; MCN 7 May 1937. Mossop was minister to the Unitarian chapel in Platt Fields in south Manchester.

21 MG 10 July 1938.

22 MG 12 July 1937.

23 MG 26 July 1937.

24 E.g. MG 7 September 1937: a programme of Sunday films on the Spanish struggle (and later on the Soviet Union and unemployment in South Wales) put on by the Manchester and Salford Film Society (formerly the Workers' Film Society) at the Rivoli Cinema in Rusholme.

25 Fyrth, *The Signal*, p. 199.

26 *Ibid.*, pp. 199–200.

27 MG 26 June 1937.

28 MG 15 and 19 July 1937.

29 MG 21 September 1937, letter from the committee chairman, J. Robinson. The treasurer was Dr Ralston Patterson, a Didsbury GP.

30 MG 23 August 1937.

31 Circular letter from F.E. Walker, Manchester Divisional Secretary of the AEU in the Working Class Movement Library in Salford (n.d. [early 1939?]).

32 SCR 28 May, 11 June 1938.

33 SCR 18 March 1938. One of the speakers was to be Martin Bobker, the Lancashire Organiser of the YCL.

34 E.g. MG 19 July 1937.

35 MG 25 August 1937.

36 MG 5 October 1937.

37 MG 23 August 1937, Report of the TUC at Norwich.

38 MG 3 May 1937.

39 MG 10 May 1937.

40 MG 14 and 17 July 1937.

41 MG 20 July 1937.

42 MG 26 January 1938, letter from Betty de Courcy Ireland, its honorary secretary and secretary also of the Youth Foodship Committee. A Communist Party member, de

Courcy wrote that she had recently visited Catalonia with the delegation from the British Youth Peace Assembly.

43 MG 1 March 1938.
44 MG 9 March 1938.
45 ISC 21 January 1937.
46 ISC 21 January, 18 February 1937.
47 ISC Undated minutes of a meeting in [May] 1937. For an account of Quaker relief work in Spain, see Fyrth, *The Signal*, pp. 158–180.
48 ISC 20 January 1938.
49 ISC 17 February 1938.
50 *Ibid.*
51 ISC 24 February 1938.
52 ISC 22 September and 17 November 1938.
53 They preferred to raise money for their own work in Spain rather than support the fund-raising of the NJCSR, to whose conference in London in September 1937 they felt 'unable' to send a delegate.
54 MG 3 May 1937.
55 ISC 20 January 1938. (MG 2 and 5 November 1937.)
56 Minutes of the Executive Committee of the Manchester branch of the National Council of Women (MCL M271), 7 February 1938.
57 MG 10 May 1937.
58 MG 3 May 1937.
59 In Stockport, Aid for Spain and for the Basque children was taken on by the Stockport and District Peace Council (SA 18 November 1938).
60 MCN 20 May 1937.
61 The conditions were designed in part to prevent an obvious breach of Britain's policy of non-intervention in favour of the Republic: the children were non-combatants and were drawn, notionally at least, from across the Basque political spectrum.
62 *The Harvest: A Monthly Magazine of the Salford Catholic Protection and Rescue Society*, Vol. 50, No. 8, August 1937, p. 25. The magazine had its offices in St Gerard's Home, the Rescue Society's headquarters in Denmark Road in Manchester's Moss Side. The editor was Revd F.W. Kershaw.
63 Buchanan, 'The Role of the Labour Movement', pp. 155–159.
64 *Ibid.*
65 *Ibid.*, pp. 162–165. Footwear for the Basque children was provided by the National Union of Boot and Shoe Operatives and, in the Manchester region, by the Rossendale Union of Boot, Shoe and Slipper Operatives (MG 23 August 1937).
66 Buchanan, 'The Role of the Labour Movement', pp. 164–165.
67 Fyrth, *The Signal*, p. 225.
68 MCN 20 May 1937. On 26 May 1937 the Manchester Liberal Women's Council (MCL M283) urged each of its branches 'to do what it can in giving financial support to this most worthy object [the support of the Basque children]'.
69 Buchanan, 'The Role of the Labour Movement', pp. 160–161.
70 Altogether twenty-six homes were run by the Catholic Church, forty-five organised by the BCC and managed by local committees (Fyrth, *The Signal*, p. 230).
71 MG 25 June 1937: letter from the Duchess of Atholl and Wilfrid Roberts MP.
72 MG 25 May, 19 June 1937.
73 MG 4 June 1937.
74 MG 19 June, 10 July 1937.
75 MG 25 May 1937.

76 MG 10 and 16 July 1937.
77 Hywel Francis, *Miners Against Fascism: Wales and the Spanish Civil War* (London 1984), p. 126.
78 MG 9 July 1937.
79 The final total was 185.
80 MG 25 May 1937.
81 'An undenominational mission movement founded in Glasgow', the Christian Volunteer Force had centres in 'several' northern cities, including an orphanage and mission hall set up in Salford 'sixteen months ago'. Ten children from the Manchester district in the orphanage were transferred elsewhere on the arrival of the Basques (MG 16 and 17 June 1937).
82 MG 26 May 1937.
83 MG 1 June 1937.
84 MG 25 May 1937.
85 [Bolton] *Journal and Guardian*, 7 August 1936.
86 Watermillock was built during 1880–82 for Thomas Thwaites, head of the cotton bleaching firm, Eden and Thwaites of Bolton, and remained in his family until shortly before the First World War, when it was purchased by a local GP, a Dr Schofield, for use as a private hospital. During the war it was in use as a military hospital. In 1919 it passed into the hands of the Manchester Diocese, which equipped it with a private chapel and made use of it as the diocesan retreat house until, in 1935, it was replaced by St. Hilda's Church in Manchester ([Bolton] *Journal and Guardian*, 7 August 1936 as part of a series, 'Bolton's Notable Buildings').
87 *Ibid.*; MEN 7 and 9 June 1937.
88 BEN 20 and 28 May 1937. The woman had been informed by the NCJSR that such adoptions were not possible. The Bolton Spanish Medical Aid Committee had proved highly effective in raising money for both the Manchester and District ambulance and the Save the Children Fund (*ibid.*) A bring-and-buy sale organised by the committee was said to have found support from local churches, unemployed women and the Bolton branch of the Women Citizens Association. A sewing committee had made 156 garments and 366 bandages for despatch to Spain (BEN 28 May 1937).
89 BEN 20 May 1937.
90 BEN 24 May, 2 June 1937.
91 MG 25 May 1937. An appeal for volunteers was made by the Vicar of St Augustine's in BEN 25 May 1937.
92 *Ibid.*
93 MG 4 and 8 June 1937.
94 MEN 9 June 1937.
95 BEN 3 June 1937.
96 BEN 2 June 1937.
97 BEN 25 May 1937, letter from Craven Ellis.
98 BEN 28 and 31 May 1937 (letters from Victor Connor and 'AH'); SCR 16 July 1937 (letter from 'Britain First').
99 BEN 2 and 24 June 1937.
100 BEN 28 May, 9 June 1937: the two priests were a Father W. Turner of St Patrick's Church in Bolton and a Father J.A. Weston, who had been born in South America to a Spanish mother and an English father.
101 BEN 2 June 1937.
102 BEN 17 June 1937.
103 BEN 10 June 1937; [Bolton] *Journal and Guardian* 11 June 1937.

104 BEN 28 May 1937.

105 BEN 1 June 1937. Godlee was a principal in the cotton firm Simpson and Godlee of Quay Street, Manchester. In a private capacity, he was chairman of the Hallé Concerts Society, designed to offer support to Manchester's Hallé Orchestra.

106 The names of the earliest members are attached to a letter calling for support for 'The Watermillock Fund', printed in MG 9 June 1937. Other members were Revd Canon Peter Green, the rector of St Phillip's church in Salford and a canon of Manchester Cathedral; Professor Revd Alex J. Grieve, the Principal of Lancashire Independent College in Whalley Range; Revd Canon Thomas Shimwell, rector of St Crispin's Church, honorary canon of Manchester Cathedral and chairman of the Manchester branch of the National Council for Civil Liberties and of the South Manchester Peace Council, and Dr Joseph Robinson, secretary of Spanish Medical Aid; Sir Noton Barclay, who had served in the Liberal interest on Manchester City Council for twenty years, and was also chairman of the District Bank Limited; the industrialist Sir Christopher Needham, chairman of the Council of Manchester University; Dr Catherine Chisholm, a consultant at the Duke of York Hospital for Babies in the Burnage district of Manchester.

107 Oliver, a leading Manchester barrister, stood for Parliament as Liberal candidate for the Blackley division of Manchester from 1918. He won in 1923, only to be unseated by the Conservatives in the following year. He was elected again in 1929, with a majority of 889, only to be beaten into second place by the Conservatives in 1931 and 1935 (and into third place in 1945).

108 Oliver chaired meetings of the North Manchester and Bury Spanish Aid Committees (MG 11 January, 17 June 1937).

109 Mass Observation Archive, Worktown Collection, Box H, File 8: Tom Harrison's report of a meeting of the Watermillock House Committee on 17 June 1937; BEN 9 June 1937. While the legal adoption of children was ruled out, a form of 'semi-adoption' was possible, according to the *Manchester City News*: the sponsorship of a child at 10s gave the sponsor visiting rights (MCN 11 June 1937).

110 MG 26 May 1937.

111 MG 1 June 1937.

112 [Bolton] *Journal and Guardian*, 11 June 1937. On 17 June 1937 a decision was taken by the Watermillock House Committee to take four more children, all girls aged over fourteen (Tom Harrison's report, MOA, Box H, File 8).

113 [Bolton] *Journal and Guardian*, 11 June 1937.

114 BEN 23 May 1988. Elvira was one of three Spanish women who had arrived as fourteen-year-olds at Watermillock, who were revisiting Bolton in 1988.

115 Adrian Bell, *Only for Three Months: The Basque Children in Exile* (Norwich 1996), p. 85.

116 SCR 18 June 1937.

117 *Ibid.*

118 Letters from 'Britain First' in SCR 16 and 30 July 1937.

119 MG 17, 19, 21 and 24 June 1937.

120 MG 21 June 1937; SCR 18 June 1937.

121 Of these, only twenty-four actually arrived, twenty-one on 24 June, three on 8 August, with two teachers, Maria and Begona Luaces (Sr Brighid Moloney, *Hollymount: The Home on the Hill, Centenary 1888–1988* (n.p. 1988), p. 124.

122 Announcement by the Bishop of Salford, Dr. T. Henshaw, reported in MG 14 June 1937. They had arrived at Buckley by 17 June, when funds were being raised for their maintenance (Tom Harrison's report, 17 June 1937, MOA Worktown Collection,

Box H, File 8).

123 MG 23 June 1937.

124 *The Harvest: A Monthly Magazine of the Salford Catholic Protection and Rescue Society*, Vol. L, No. 8, August 1937, p. 25. The magazine was published from the Rescue Society's headquarters, St Gerard's Home, Denmark Road, Moss Side, Manchester. The editor in 1937 was Revd F.W. Kershaw. Covering local as well as national and international events, it was, in effect, a diocesan magazine.

125 A worker at their reception camp, while acknowledging that some of the older boys might occasionally be 'wild and rough', and inclined to move in 'gangs', found the majority spirited, energetic, highly adaptable, physically 'beautiful', graceful in their movements, 'reasonable' in coping with everyday problems and ever ready to 'sit in the fields at night and sing their folk songs' and to dance to music on the radio (Yvonne Cloud, *The Basque Children in England: An Account of Life at North Stoneham Camp* (London 1937), pp. 26, 30–31, 33–35.

126 *The Harvest*, Vol. L, No. 8, August 1937, p. 25.

127 E.g. MG 3 July (children having an English lesson at the Christian Volunteer Orphanage in Salford) and 10 July 1937 (smiling children grouped in and around a wheelbarrow in Hull); for other press photos BEN 10, 11, 22, 23 and 25 June 1937.

128 MG 10 July 1937: 'some of the 100 Basque children' at Brampton in Cumberland performed English and Basque songs and dances to raise funds for the creation of a children's park in memory of Basil Murray, son of Professor Gilbert Murray, who was killed in Spain.

129 MG 8, 9 and 12 July 1937. At a women's meeting in Leaf Street, Salford, on 8 July 1937 Campo is said to have delivered 'a passionate plea against war'. Each year, she told her audience, 'we learned new ways of killing each other, but no new ways of knowing each other' (SCR 9 July 1937). Campo had begun working with the BCC soon after her arrival in Britain. She worked for a time at the Peace Pledge Union (PPU) colony at Colchester and later became a teacher at Dartington Hall, an independent, progressive school, to which she obtained scholarships for two of the Basque children who later (with her encouragement) trained as teachers (Bell, *Only for Three Months*, pp. 134–135).

130 [Bolton] *Journal and Guardian* 11 June 1937.

131 MG 11 June 1937. According to another account, only three or four of the children were Roman Catholics; the rest were Protestants of various denominations ([Bolton] *Journal and Guardian* 11 June 1937.

132 [Bolton] *Journal and Guardian* 11 June 1937.

133 BEN 14 June 1937.

134 BEN 22 June 1937; Bell, *Only for Three Months*, p. 85.

135 BEN 12 June 1937.

136 SCR 25 June 1937.

137 SCR 2 July 1937.

138 SCR 18 June, 2 July 1937.

139 SCR 2 July 1937.

140 SCR 25 June, 2 July 1937.

141 SCR 28 and 30 July 1937.

142 EPJ 2 July 1937. One of the nuns is said to have been fluent in Spanish.

143 Quoted in John Slawson, *A Labour of Love: Holly Mount, Tottington: Memories of the Children's Home* (Manchester 1995), p. 53. During the First World War the convent had 'sheltered' over 440 Belgian refugees; in 1939 it received a small number of German refugees (*ibid.*, pp. 43–44, 50; and see pp. 184–185 below).

144 Moloney, *Hollymount*, p. 125.
145 Letter from Albert Mather to the *Bolton Evening News*, 7 July 1937.
146 MG 25 May 1937.
147 MG 19 June 1937. The Spanish schoolmistress who had accompanied the children to the Seedley orphanage was said to have three grandchildren who were refugees in France and a son and husband who were fighting in defence of Bilbao.
148 MG 27 May, 1, 11 and 14 June 1937.
149 MG 11 June 1937.
150 Mabel Tylecote, *The Education of Women at Manchester University* (Manchester 1941), pp. 125–127.
151 *The Journal of the University of Manchester*, Vol. 1, No. 3 (1939), pp. 77–78.
152 *Ibid.*, p. 79.
153 MG 8 July 1937.
154 MG 26 July 1937.
155 EPJ 4 July 1937.
156 MG 26 July 1937.
157 BEN 17 June 1937.
158 *The Harvest*, Vol. 50, No. 8, August 1937, pp. 229–230.
159 *The Harvest*, Vol. 50, No. 7, July 1937, p. 198.
160 *The Harvest*, Vol. 50, No. 10, October 1937, p. 287.
161 BEN 7 June 1937: letter from Albert Mather.
162 MG 11 and 27 May 1937.
163 Joe Willcock reports for 10 and 11 June 1937 in Mass Observation Archive (hereafter MOA), Worktown Collection, Box H, File 8. I owe this and other references to correspondence in the MOA to Professor Tony Kushner, who kindly provided photocopies of the relevant items. The interpretation of them is my own. Cf. Tony Kushner, *We Europeans? Mass Observation, 'Race' and British Identity in the Twentieth Century* (London 2004), pp. 66–69.
164 *Ibid.* Miss Peel had been replaced as matron and warden by March 1938, when the warden was a Mr P. Booth ([Bolton] *Journal and Guardian* 25 March 1938.
165 Joe Willcock MOA report 12 June 1937. Another insight into the internal power struggle is provided in Tom Harrison's report, 17 June 1937, MOA Worktown Collection, Box H, File 8.
166 Tom Harrison's report, 17 June 1937 (MOA Worktown Collection, Box H, File 8).
167 Joe Willcock's report, 11 June 1937, *ibid.*
168 Joe Willcock's report, 16 June 1937, *ibid.*
169 Joe Willcock's report, 24 June 1937, *ibid.*
170 Joe Willcock's report, 6 July 1937, *ibid.*
171 Tom Harrison's report, 17 June 1937 (MOA Worktown Collection, Box H, File 8). Twelve of the Watermillock children were none the less persuaded to sing songs as part of the BBC's Northern Programme (BEN 24, 25 and 26 June 1937).
172 Joe Willcock's report of 6 July 1937 (MOA Worktown Collection, Box H, File 8).
173 BEN 23 June 1937.
174 Fyrth, *The Signal*, p. 234; BEN 24 June 1937.
175 Tom Harrison's report, 17 June 1937 (MOA Worktown Collection, Box H, File 8).
176 *Ibid.* The decisions witnessed by Harrison in a meeting lasting two hours twenty minutes included the choice of a gas rather than an electric cooker, spreading the children's bread with butter rather than margarine, the provision of new shoes, the admission to the hostel of four more children, the use of English rather than Spanish as the medium of education, dealing with criticisms of the hostel in the local press

and the selection of a new nominee to the committee from the Bolton Rotary Club.

177 BEN 24 June 1937. The House Committee, increased in size to eighteen, was placed under the chairmanship of the influential local JP and cotton spinner, J. Norman Grierson.

178 For this being the case, for example, at St Joseph's Home, Patricroft, EPJ 2 July 1937.

179 Fyrth, *The Signal*, p. 233.

180 MG 14 August 1937.

181 MG 16 and 22 July 1937.

182 MG 16 July 1937.

183 MG 21 July 1937.

184 MG 22 July 1937.

185 MG 19 July 1937.

186 MG 24 July 1937.

187 MG 26 and 27 July 1937.

188 EPJ 6 August 1937.

189 The heading of a report in MG 27 July 1937.

190 EPJ 6 August 1937.

191 MG 19 July 1937.

192 MG 22 July 1937.

193 *Ibid.*

194 Dorothy Legarreta, *The Guernica Generation: Basque Refugee Children of the Spanish Civil War* (Nevada 1984), p. 204.

195 *The Harvest*, Vol. L, No. 10, October 1937, p. 296.

196 MG 3 August 1937.

197 MG 10 August 1937.

198 MG 14 August 1937.

199 MG 27 August 1937.

200 MG 28 August 1937.

201 MG 25 June 1937.

202 E.g. MG 5 and 9 August 1937, 7 March 1938.

203 MG 17 August 1937: article including excerpts from the letters of children at Hazeldine House in Hull, with a note that the 'bad boys' of Scarborough were mounting a garden party for the townspeople.

204 MG 14 August 1937.

205 MG 4 October 1937.

206 MG 14 August and 1 September 1937, 7 March 1938. Some of the parents were said to be in Bilbao, some in Santander, to which many Basque families had retreated, some in France and 'some are no one knows where'.

207 Legarreta, *Guernica Generation*, pp. 201–204.

208 Wellington's committee also received the support of the Catholic hierarchy. The Archbishop of Westminster was represented on it by Canon Craven, his former representative on the BCC, and Douglas Jerrold.

209 *The Harvest*, Vol. 50, No. 8, August 1937, pp. 229–230.

210 E.g. MG 29 June (the NJCSR reported that conditions in Bilbao were not sufficiently settled 'for it to take responsibility for the children's return'), 7 July (the BCC would continue its work of rescue until it was considered safe for the children to return), 2 August, 1 September 1937. A Legal Commission set up by the NJCSR under the chairmanship of the former Recorder of London, Sir Holman Gregory, reported at the end of October 1937 that 800 of the parents' applications were authentic and

that arrangements should be made for the early return of all the children (MG 2, 9 and 29 October 1937).

211 Legarreta, *Guernica Generation*, pp. 211–225, 251–252. By February 1938, 900 children had been repatriated and a further 400–500 were preparing to leave; 1,155 children remained in Britain at the outbreak of war; about 500 by the middle of 1940.

212 SCR 22 and 29 October 1937.

213 SCR 22 October 1937.

214 *Ibid.*

215 SCR 29 October 1937.

216 MG 20 October 1937.

217 *The Harvest*, Vol. L, No. 12, Christmas 1937, p. 362.

218 BEN 19 and 22 March 1938; [Bolton] *Journal and Guardian* 25 March 1938. According to the report of 19 March other Basque children transferred to Watermillock kept the total living there at 40, likely, it was said, to be in Bolton 'for some time'. I have found no record of the final evacuation. The first batch of 500 children to leave Britain had departed in January 1938; as they boarded the train in London they were heard to shout 'Vivir England'. After again falling into decay, Watermillock was taken over in 1948 by the Bolton Welfare Department to become a hostel for the aged and the physically handicapped. It was put up for auction by Bolton Corporation in 1990 with the hope that it would fetch £400,000, but failed to find a buyer. Plans devised in 1992 to convert it into a Muslim School also came to nothing. Finally, it was purchased in 1993 by Wolverhampton and Dudley Breweries, who opened it in the following year as part of their chain of 'Milestone' restaurants. A Grade Two listed building, it remains a Milestone Restaurant ([Bolton] *Journal and Guardian*, 30 April 1948, 31 March 1968; BEN 28 June 1990, 24 January 1992, 21 July 1993, 11 August 1994).

219 BEN 22 March 1938.

220 *The Harvest*, Vol. L1, No. 9, September 1938, p. 287.

221 Of the three former refugee girls from Watermillock who re-visited it in 1988, two – the sisters Susana and Elvira Lopez – had remained in Britain. Elvira, who was adopted by a Bolton doctor, married an Englishman to become Elvira Buckley and settled in Southport, where she was still living in 1988. Susana was then living in the Bolton area (BEN 23 May 1988).

222 Legarreta, *Guernica Generation*, pp. 252–253. From March 1939 those children over fourteen years of age had been given the option of remaining. An unnamed Manchester convent/orphanage run by 'Irish nuns' was the temporary home of Juanita and Maria Angeles, whose story is told in Bell, *Only for Three Months*, pp. 20–23, 156–157. After leaving their home in Santurce in 1937 they lost contact with their mother until 1942. They remained at the convent, with 'two other Basque girls', throughout the war and then decided to remain in Britain, where Maria began working in the laboratory of the local doctor who had secured their release from the convent, and Juanita trained at night school and day release classes to become a nursery nurse.

223 *Ibid.*, p. 19.

224 Of these, all but 250 left after the war (*ibid.*, p. 8).

225 Fyrth, *The Signal*, pp. 23–24.

226 When I reported this in a talk at the Jewish Museum in London, a member of the audience who had arrived on the Kindertransport, remembered a football match in Brighton in which a team of Kindertransport children were defeated 12–0 by a team

of Basque children from a nearby hostel.

227 BEN 22 June 1937.

228 Legarreta, *Guernica Generation*, p. 255.

229 *Ibid.*, p. 255.

230 Fyrth, *The Signal*, p. 241. Many of the boys were assisted by the Basque Boys Training Committee, set up by the BCC in March 1939 after Sir Samuel Hoare had lifted restrictions on the employment of alien workers, and supported by it until March 1941.

231 Moloney, *Hollymount*, p. 125.

232 *The Harvest*, Vol. 50, January 1937, p. 4.

233 MG 6 and 10 July 1937.

234 SCR 25 June 1937.

235 SCR 10 September 1937.

236 SCR 24 September 1937.

237 MG 13 July 1937.

238 MG 13 July, 25 August 1937; SCR 28 August 1937.

239 EPJ 15 October 1937.

240 'Political hostels' were not out of the question. The ILP housed and maintained forty Basque children from Anarchist families in a hostel in Street, Somerset, provided by the Clarks, the Quaker shoe-making family (Hall, 'Not Just Orwell', pp. 66–68).

241 Neil Barrett, 'The Threat of the British Union of Fascists in Manchester', in Tony Kushner and Nadia Valman (eds), *Remembering Cable Street: Fascism and Anti-Fascism in British Society*, a Special Issue of the journal *Jewish Culture and History*, Vol. 1, No. 2, Winter 1998, p. 66.

7

'The work of succouring refugees is going forward': the Manchester Jewish Refugees Committee, 1939–1940

The decisive factor which drew provincial communities into the more systematic rescue of refugees was the escalating number of those seeking entry to Britain following the Anschluss (March 1938), the German occupation of the Sudetenland (October 1938), the Kristallnacht pogrom (9 November 1938), the British Government's decision to facilitate the entry of unaccompanied children on the Kindertransport (21 November 1938) and the German annexation of Bohemia and Moravia (March 1939). As the sources of emigration multiplied and the Jews of Germany became finally convinced of the permanence of the Nazi regime and the centrality of its anti-Semitic intentions, Britain received a total of around 70,000 refugees, of whom a little over one-tenth (between 7,000 and 8,000) reached Manchester. Around 856 children arriving with the Kindertransport were accommodated in what became Region 10 of the Refugee Children's Movement, a region extending northwards from Manchester, east of Merseyside, through Lancashire, Westmorland and Cumbria. The most likely reading of events is that, as the number of refugees swelled, the London agencies of support, Quaker and Jewish, in danger of being overwhelmed by the case work and financial commitment involved, applied increasing pressure on provincial centres to share the load. In the case of the Jewish community, this was particularly after the London Jewish community came to realise, after Kristallnacht, that it could no longer honour the formal commitment, made in 1933, that it would bear all the expenses in respect of the temporary or permanent sanctuary of refugees granted entry to Britain.

During summer 1938 what had been in Manchester, at best, a half-hearted communal response to refugees, underwent a sudden and dramatic transformation. For Laski, the pivotal moment appears to have been the unmistakable tragedy of the Anschluss and the Jewish exodus which followed. The 'Austrian crisis' also put increasing pressure on Apfelbaum as 'many enquiries' were received 'as to the position of relatives in Austria and the possibility of emigration to Palestine and England'.[1] With the entry of refugees to Palestine now severely restricted, however, Laski was persuaded that the Representative

Council could no longer remain publicly aloof from the needs of those seeking entry to Britain and settlement, if only temporary, in Manchester. At the end of July 1938 he announced that the Council was 'dealing with a large number of cases arising out of the tragic situation of the Jewish communities in Austria' – probably the first public reference to the efforts of Apfelbaum, accorded praise, also for the first time in public, for the work he was doing 'in that connection'.[2] A Manchester Austrian Appeal, steered by Norman Jacobs, who also attracted Laski's praise, had by then already raised £9,200.[3] Laski remained reluctant to entertain Manchester as the destination of those supported by such funds. A minute of the Council's Quarterly Meeting of 2 October 1938 reads: 'Referring to the Jewish Refugees, Mr Laski stated he had a scheme to send some of our Refugees to various countries … He thanked God that we lived in a free country and that we had not these tragedies here.'[4] He, added, however, that, with Jacobs as the 'Liaison Officer between Manchester and London … the work of succouring the Refugees was going forward'.[5]

Jacobs' appointment suggests that Laski was also under pressure from Woburn House to step up the Manchester effort on behalf of refugees. In effect, faced with the prospect of an escalating flow of refugees, and committed since 1933 to responsibility for the cost of their maintenance, Otto Schiff was calling on provincial communities, of which Manchester was far and away the largest, to carry part of the refugee case work which London's German-Jewish Aid Committee could no longer shoulder alone. 'Batches' of trainees and domestic servants were arriving faster than he could deal with them. On 7 November 1938 Bernard Davidson, a key member of the Jewish Refugees Committee in London, visited Manchester as part of a tour of the provinces designed to whip up enthusiasm for refugee work. There he spoke first to a public meeting which Laski had convened in Cheetham Hill, 'with a view to forming a committee to assist German-Jewish refugees'.[6] After giving a 'detailed account' of the work undertaken at Woburn House, particularly 'in the placing of trainees', Davidson sought to persuade an audience of around fifty 'sympathisers' 'to work energetically in placing as many refugees as possible in Manchester'.[7] On the same day he attended a meeting of the Manchester Women's Lodge of B'nai Brith to which Colette Hassan gave a report of 'a refugee meeting' she had attended in London, which had also issued 'an urgent appeal for aid'.[8] Her motion to the meeting that each sister contribute 1s a week for two to three years towards the 'upkeep of refugee children to be adopted by the lodge' was 'enthusiastically received', a collective pledge made to that effect, collectors appointed for north and south Manchester and a sub-committee set up 'to facilitate the working of the scheme'.[9] At the same meeting, a letter was read from the London Women's International Zionist Organisation (WIZO) calling on the lodge for help in 'the placing of German and Austrian women in domestic service in this country'.[10]

The urgency of the situation, as well as the pressures emanating from London, were massively intensified as news of the Kristallnacht pogrom reached Britain and by the decision of the British government on 21

November, in response to a delegation of Anglo-Jewish leaders which included Schiff, to allow the entry of an unknown number of children from Greater Germany. An embryonic Manchester Jewish Refugees Committee (MJRC)[11] set up after the public meeting of 7 November was given a more sophisticated and permanent shape at a further meeting on 22 November, again convened by Laski, and further energised by a meeting in London a week later between its representatives and the 'principals' at Woburn House.[12] Early in December, in the light of information from the MJRC that 'at least 30,000 [sic] children [from the Kindertransport] would have to be placed in this country', the Manchester sisters of B'nai Brith debated an increase in their weekly subscriptions towards the creation of refugee hostels.[13] By this time, at least four other groups in Manchester had announced proposals for the support of refugees.

The very number of such initiatives posed problems for a man like Nathan Laski, still uneasy about giving too great a prominence to work with refugees. His personal commitment, in so far as it can be judged, was to support his over-stretched London peers at Woburn House, with whose objects of containment and selection he was fully in sympathy, while ensuring that refugee work received as low a profile, and was subjected to as high a degree of centralised (and financial) control, as was possible in the circumstances. It was said of him later that he 'exert[ed] himself to bring about the complete unification of all efforts on behalf of Refugees in this city under the auspices of [the MJRC]' and that in this 'he succeeded with the help of all concerned'.[14] The notions which Laski had earlier applied to communal administration – a tight central control, which limited the risk attached to maverick operations, and a rationalisation, which limited the wastage of communal energy and funds – were now to be applied to work with refugees. In achieving these purposes, chiefly from behind the scenes, he delegated the chairmanship of the MJRC to his close friend and dependable ally, the cotton merchant Norman Jacobs. It was Laski's view of the situation, later to lead him into serious conflict with Schiff in London and with the MJRC, that work for refugees was subject to the ultimate control of the Representative Council, of which he remained the president.

The structure of what Laski now saw (and, for a time at least, persuaded others to see) as the umbrella organisation for all refugee support work in Manchester was created at three meetings in November 1938, all convened by Laski but chaired by Norman Jacobs.

Although credit was accorded 'the work done hitherto',[15] and Apfelbaum was present at all three meetings, it soon became clear that his activities were now to be absorbed by a more formal organisation in hands other than his own. The fact that the office-holders in the two sub-committees now set up were called upon 'to work in conjunction with him' and that one of them, the Industrial Committee, was based on his former business network, did nothing to disguise the reality of his demotion. Of the Industrial Committee itself he became only the 'honorary director', real control passing into the hands of its secretary, another local businessman, Leonard Cohen.[16] None the less, the committee continued to make use of Apfelbaum's wide contacts and his exceptional ingenuity in seeking out 'traineeships'. On his arrival in Manchester from Landau in January 1939 the seventeen-year-old Werner Mayer made immediate contact with Apfelbaum, who sent him to Blackpool, to 'a training centre for hotel employment' which proved, on his arrival, to no longer exist. Its former owner had signalled his agreement to employ German (but not Austrian) refugees 'on the understanding that once the promise had fulfilled the purpose of obtaining a visa', the MJRC 'would not expect anything further'. Werner found himself serving food in what had become a shelter for the unemployed.[17]

What was now being set up was a local equivalent of the metropolitan German-Jewish Aid Committee, modelled on its organisation and procedures, and serving, in effect, and in Schiff's view, as its first provincial branch. The MJRC was to be a cog in what was now becoming a national wheel of refugee support, the hub of which was in Woburn House. It was from Woburn House (or, from January 1939, Bloomsbury House) that the Manchester committee was to receive its clients; from its banker, the Central British Fund, that it was to receive the bulk of its funds. The expectation was that, in return, it would provide hospitality for those passed on to it, secure local 'guarantors' or employers to ensure their material support, superintend their welfare while they remained in Britain, and, when the time came, facilitate their departure. At a meeting in London with a delegation from the MJRC on 29 November Schiff gave the committee his 'endorsement' and arrangements were made with the key volunteers at Woburn House for the first batches of male trainees, women seeking posts as domestic servants and 'nurses and probationers over the age of 19' to be sent to Manchester. The Manchester delegates were briefed with 'detailed information regarding all refugee problems' and stress was laid on 'the necessity of closer relations between the London and Manchester Committees'.[18]

In theoretical control of the MJRC was a 'general committee' made up of all fifty of the original 'sympathisers' who had attended the meeting of 7 November. Of these ten were themselves refugees, including Rabbi Dr Altmann, who had arrived in Manchester only a month earlier, Werner Treuhertz, from the Lancashire Tanning Company in Rochdale; the GP, Dr Lazarus Wislicki; the solicitor, Dr Feibelmann, who had arrived in Manchester from Landau in 1933; and Professor Adolf Loewe, one of the 'displaced academics' (in his case arriving from Frankfurt-am-Main in 1933) given Honorary Fellowships at the University of Manchester. Otherwise the committee was made up of a cross-section of Manchester's Jewish mainstream, religiously observant Jewish middle-class: professionals (including six doctors and two rabbis), export merchants and industrialists, chiefly in the clothing, furniture and waterproof trades. A lower-middle class of shopkeepers was not represented; nor were the working-class districts of north Manchester. There was no one with radical political connections, only two (both refugees) from the Reform Synagogue. Twenty lived in Manchester's southern suburbs –

Fallowfield, Withington, Whalley Range, Didsbury and Chorlton-cum-Hardy – all but one of the rest in the Jewish areas to the north of the city, chiefly in the older residential districts of Higher Broughton and Kersal. Only one came from the new area of Jewish settlement in Prestwich. Apart from the refugees, that is, the membership was drawn from longer-established families, if not wealthy then comfortably-off, most of whom had already made their mark in communal life and who might be regarded by a man like Laski, who may well have had a hand in selecting them, as symbolising just those values of respectability, Englishness and patriotism on which he believed the welfare of the community to depend. Twenty-eight of them were women, either wives of male members; women like Margaret Langdon, from families long resident in Manchester with a tradition of communal philanthropy or activists from the local Zionist movement, including Marie Nahum, wife of a Sephardi merchant and Manchester's leading woman Zionist, and the wife of the dentist, Philip Wigoder, president of the Manchester Zionist Central Council.

In reality, this general committee met rarely, if ever.[19] In practice, policy was determined and routine decisions taken by an executive of thirteen, elected, it was said, 'to enable the committee to deal more promptly with the work in hand', and meeting weekly under the chairmanship of Norman Jacobs.[20] Sub-committees, set up by the executive and chaired by its members, increased in number as the refugee influx expanded, continually adjusting in name and function to deal with problems as they emerged.[21]

By the end of November, the MJRC was already fully operational. A register had been compiled of those refugees known to Woburn House to be willing to work as domestic servants or trainees in the Manchester area.[22] An Industrial Committee of thirty-six members, three of them non-Jewish, was putting together a list of local vacancies for trainees.[23] In a telling move, employers in Manchester, including representatives of the vast engineering works, Metropolitan Vickers, in Trafford Park, were persuaded to go down to London to recruit refugees for their Manchester factories.[24] A Guarantee Committee, chaired by Morris Feinmann, and with Lore Phillip, a refugee of 1933 from Berlin as its secretary,[25] had begun to identify sponsors, individual and corporate, who were prepared to treat the material support of middle-aged and elderly refugees 'as a serious responsibility'.[26] If guarantors could be found, Jacobs was led by Woburn House to believe, 'quite a number' of older refugees would be 'allowed into the country' and granted work permits provided they did not interfere with British labour.[27] A search began for 'as many houses as possible' prepared to offer hospitality for unaccompanied children due to arrive shortly from Berlin and Vienna at the Kindertransport holding camp at Dovercourt.[28] This search, Jacobs told his colleagues, was 'undoubtedly the most important' aspect of the MJRC's work.[29] The welfare and placement of children was entrusted to a Children's Committee, under the chairmanship of Margaret Langdon, who pledged to work closely with the inter-denominational Refugee Children's Movement which had been set up nationally to disperse the proceeds of the Baldwin Fund and to coordinate the reception of Kindertransport children.[30] A circular was sent out to 1,700 Jewish homes in Manchester seeking help in providing hospitality for children, openings for domestic servants and opportunities for 'boys and girls' to learn a trade. Early in December, the committee's key volunteers moved, with their 'competent paid secretary', into an office at 3 Spring Gardens in central Manchester, provided free of charge by Leonard Cohen.[31] It was not well-equipped. Rae Barash remembers that it began with her husband's old portable typewriter, one filing cabinet and a card table to deal with applications and phone calls and to serve refugees who formed queues on the road outside.[32] Local police were persuaded to provide protection against BUF activists who 'watched every movement'.[33]

As the pressures on the executive increased exponentially throughout the winter of 1938–39, it became clear that real authority on the MJRC was being exercised informally by four of the executive's most active members: Norman Jacobs, as its chairman, Rae Barash and Morris Feinmann, at first as joint-secretaries of a so-called Hospitality Committee, Margaret Langdon, as chairman of the Children's Committee, and Leonard Cohen, as secretary of the Industrial Committee. Their centrality in no way reflected the distribution of power within the community as a whole; of the four, only Norman Jacobs might have been counted amongst the community's dominant elite. Giving them administrative and secretarial support was Jean Gafan, appointed in February 1939 as the only paid employee of the committee, officially as 'secretary', in fact to take control of its office as a kind of Chief Executive.[34] Born in Bolton to parents of Eastern European origin, she had moved to Manchester with her parents as a teenager, there entering communal life to be the voluntary secretary of the Manchester Jewish Literary Society and an assistant to Margaret Langdon at the Delamere Home.[35]

It seems probable that Jacobs, like Apfelbaum, was Laski's nominee; his father, Hyman Jacobs, a Polish immigrant whose fortunes were made by the export of Manchester textiles to South Africa, belonged to Laski's inner circle of friends and fellow textile exporters.[36] It was as Laski's protégé that Norman Jacobs had gradually emerged as an influential figure on the Representative Council Executive between 1931, when he became secretary of the Nathan Laski Trust,[37] and 1936, effectively managing the four successful appeals for European Jewry, representing the Council on a succession of affiliated bodies and serving as the Council's link with the increasingly important local Zionist movement.[38] Unlike Apfelbaum, however, Jacobs was by 1938 in the front rank of local communal leaders: he possessed the breadth of vision, the administrative skills, the financial expertise and the credibility in the community now expected not simply by Laski, but by Woburn House, in a new era of refugee management.

Born in Manchester in 1902, educated at Manchester Grammar School and at the University of Manchester, where he took a degree in Commerce, Jacobs was a member of that second generation of Russo-Polish immigrant families to which Laski himself belonged, and which by the 1930s was serving as the community's chief source of leaders. Like Laski, too, he belonged to the community's orthodox mainstream. A member of the prestigious Higher Broughton Synagogue, of which his father had been a founder member, he was personally observant: his diaries depict him as a synagogue-goer who kept a kosher home in Upper Park Road, Higher Broughton, the preferred place of residence of orthodox entrepreneurial families of Eastern European origin, regularly laid *tephillim* (phylacteries worn by men over the age of bar-mitzvah for prayers on weekday mornings) and davened (prayed) three times a day. In or about 1930, after a spell as manager of the South African branch of the family business, he returned to Manchester to take charge of the firm, then chiefly exporting cotton shirtings for distribution by other members of the family in South Africa and the Argentine.[39]

He threw himself at once into communal work, securing election to the Representative Council Executive, joining the small group of volunteer offic-ers who managed the Manchester Battalion of the Jewish Lads Brigade and, in particular, committing himself to the Zionist cause, to which other mem-bers of his family had become equally attached. An elder brother, Julius, who had settled in Palestine after the First World War was, by the 1930s, a junior minister in the Government of the British Mandate.[40] In 1938 Jacobs himself was secretary of the Manchester Zionist Central Council, the coordi-nating body for Zionist activity in Manchester, of its Propaganda Committee, and of the Manchester branch of the Jewish Agency, of which Laski was the president.[41] It is possible that he was linked to the Zionist caucus which in the late 1930s, in London as well as Manchester, was intent on both widening the movement's popular base and extending its influence within the repre-sentative organisations of Anglo-Jewry;[42] he was certainly the member of the Council Executive who put the greatest pressure on his colleagues to under-take the protests and lobbies which might keep Palestine open to refugee settlement.

There was a link, too, between Jacobs' dedicated Zionism and his accept-ance of a key role in refugee support. In view of the likelihood, for all the community's protests, of continuing restrictions, at least in the short term, on Jewish settlement in Palestine, Britain offered the possibility of accord-ing refugees a temporary haven from which they might subsequently make *aliya* (leave for Palestine). Like Laski, Jacobs held the view that Palestine represented 'the only solution for the oppressed who were already [during 1938–39] clamouring at the doors of all free countries and finding them barely ajar'. Manchester might serve them as a temporary Zion.[43]

Before 1938 Jacobs was already familiar with the mechanisms of refugee support. He and his wife had been amongst the 'nucleus' of B'nai Brith mem-bers who had enabled the Manchester Women's Lodge to run its Hospitality Committee between 1933 and 1935.[44] As secretary of the Manchester's German and Austrian Appeals, he had effectively served as the community's link with the Central British Fund, with whose leading members and meth-ods he would already have been familiar.[45]

Margaret Langdon owed her role as the first chairman of the Children's Committee to her unrivalled and widely acknowledged experience, sensitivity and skill in managing the welfare of Jewish women and children. Unlike Jacobs, she belonged to one of Manchester Jewry's long-established families of German origin and Reform affiliations. Her paternal grandfather, Henry Moritz Lazarus, was one of a group of textile merchants who arrived in Manchester from Hamburg during the 1830s to obtain 'Manchester goods' at source for export to their European markets. Within the community he became part of a dominant commercial elite which had shaped the community's institutions of education and philanthropy in the mid and late nineteenth century.[46] He was also a founder-member in 1858 of the Manchester Congregation of British Jews, Manchester's first Reform Synagogue, to which the 'Lazarus-Langdons', including Margaret, continued to lend their support. Margaret's father was Edward Henry Langdon, a cotton trader prominent on the Manchester Exchange and in the Manchester Chamber of Commerce, who in 1919 had become the first president of the Council of Manchester and Salford Jews.[47] Both generations had been deeply involved in Jewish communal charity, Margaret's mother as one of the founder-members of the Jewish Ladies' Visiting Association (JLVA), founded in 1884 to organise welfare work amongst the Jewish poor; her father as a member of the Jewish Board of Guardians, the main mechanism of Jewish charity, and, when he became disgusted at the treatment of women by the Board, as the founder of its Jewish Widows and Mothers Fund, which organised weekly allowances for Jewish widows and helped place their children in work.[48] Dr Niven, Manchester's progressive Medical Officer of Health and a man who took a benevolent and active interest in Jewish communal poverty, was a family friend.

Born in 1891, Margaret shared the wide cultural horizons and philanthropic tradition of her parents and grandparents. She was educated first at Ladybarn School, a private institution, based on Froebelian ideas, favoured by the more liberal Jewish merchants of German origin living in south Manchester, where she remembered being taught, in particular, how to observe and learn for herself. From the age of nine she joined her parents and two younger brothers on trips to Switzerland, Austria, Italy, France and Germany (where, in Berlin, she learnt to speak fluent German). In her teens she herself organised trekking and cycling tours on the continent, including in Norway, where she joined the Norwegian Alpine Club and acquired her lifelong interest in botany. The sight of so much dire poverty in the cities of Europe awakened her own interest in the British poor. As a young girl she read Rowntree's study of poverty in York, Charles Booth's work on the London poor, the works of Tawney and the Webbs, and the 'tracts' published by the Fabian Society. She became, in her own view, 'a Socialist', read the *Daily Herald* and joined the Co-operative Women's Guild, for which she became a speaker and an investigator of child welfare. Between 1910 and 1914 she was a committee member of the Manchester and Salford Women Citizens' Association, editing its local journal.

From this background she moved naturally into voluntary social work, first, in the wider society, with organisations interested in the welfare of mothers, babies and 'delicate' children, then in the Jewish community, where she first organised a basement of the Jews School in Derby Street, Cheetham, for the preparation of milk for children at the Jews School and Southall Street Board School, and later became active in the JLVA. Driven on, in her own self-deprecating estimation, by a sense of her 'parasitical existence' as a member of the Jewish 'leisured classes',[49] she went on to play a key role in the foundation of the Jewish Fresh Air Home and School, in effect a retreat for working-class children threatened with TB, which opened in Cheshire's Delamere Forest in 1920, and of which she became the first secretary. She was a co-founder with the Manchester City Councillor, A.P. Simon, the underwear manufacturer, Alex Jacobs, and Rae Barash in the foundation of the [Jewish] School Camps Association, which she helped acquire a permanent base in Prestatyn. On the eve of joining the MJRC she was also chairman of the Jewish Holiday Home for Mothers, Babies and Convalescent Children in Lymm, in the foundation of which she had also played a part.[50] Her interests straddled women's and children's health and welfare in both Manchester and Manchester Jewry. She had been a volunteer at a city Day Nursery later taken over by the Corporation; at Dr Niven's request, she had studied childhood rickets with medical students at Manchester University and spent twenty months helping to treat babies at the Duchess of York Hospital for Babies in Burnage. By 1938 she was well-known in the city and the community, not only for her active sympathies, but for her formidable administrative skills.

She had also shown her concern for Hitler's victims as early as 1936, when she had advertised for a German-Jewish woman to work at the Delamere Home. The successful applicant had been Olga Pfefferkorn, the younger daughter of a Jewish wool and cotton merchant from Frankfurt-am-Main and a recent graduate in eurhythmics of the Conservatoire in Zurich. Impressed by her CV, Langdon had offered her a post teaching eurhythmics and bamboo pipes (a variant on the recorder) for 10s a week with free board and lodgings. Pfefferkorn arrived in Manchester in May 1936 with a work permit negotiated by Langdon, who took an immediate maternal interest in her twenty-year-old employee. She introduced Olga to her wide circle of friends, including the local GP, Bernard Sandler, and in July 1939 acted as one of the witnesses to their marriage at Eccles Registry Office and as one of the *unterfuhrers* at the religious marriage which followed. The second *unterfuhrer* was Langdon's friend, Morris Feinmann.[51]

Of the inner circle of the MJRC, only Feinmann (1891–1944) was himself an immigrant. During the First World War, he had left his home in Koenigsberg for Scotland, moving on later to Manchester, where by the 1930s he had become a successful 'paper, twine and hessian merchant'. In communal affairs, he had committed himself to the support of the Jewish Home for Aged, Needy and Incurable Jews, an institution founded in 1896 for the residential care of the elderly, and in 1938 still housed in cramped, decaying and ill-equipped premises on Cheetham Hill Road. As one of the Home's two honorary secretaries, Feinmann was in the forefront of a campaign to provide the residents with more spacious, more comfortable and better-equipped accommodation, a role which marked him out as one of the community's more progressive *machers* who in the later 1930s acknowledged the need for communal institutions to adjust to the needs and higher expectations of a suburbanising community. Before joining the MJRC executive, his experience of the refugees was limited to the personal; in 1938 he had acted as guarantor for a young refugee from a well-to-do Jewish family in Aachen, Marlies Amberg, whom he had taken into his home in Higher Broughton as a companion for his daughter.[52] It is a tribute to his sensitivity that after Marlies' arrival, he kept in touch with her mother, on one occasional sending her a bouquet of red tulips.[53] At around the same time he befriended Werner Treuherz, a young German-Jewish refugee who in 1936 had been sent by his German firm to create the Lancashire Tanning Company in Rochdale; together they went on Sunday walks in the countryside around Manchester with a group of Jewish ramblers which also included Norman Jacobs' cousin, the underclothing dealer, Alex Jacobs.

Rae Barash, like Langdon, was drawn to refugee work by an active interest, as a volunteer, in the welfare of Jewish women and children. Born in Salford in 1902 to a Polish-born father, Joachim Applebaum, a dealer in incandescent gas mantles, and Roumanian-born mother, Annie Shapiro, she was educated at Grecian Street School in Higher Broughton, at Salford Grammar School and at the Manchester High School of Commerce, where she took a course in languages (in her childhood, German had been the language of her home). She began work in communal institutions at the age of eighteen, when, in 1920, she took on 'the welfare side' of the Manchester Ivrit Society, a Zionist organisation which offered lessons in modern Hebrew to the children of the poor. Two years later she joined Alex Jacobs and Margaret Langdon in founding the Manchester School Camps Association, which sent 'young children each week, throughout the Summer, for a holiday in the country';[54] she was persuaded by Langdon, whose protégée she had by then become, to chair an after-care committee for children leaving Delamere. In longer perspective, she may be seen as one of several younger Manchester Jewish women from middle-class homes moved in the 1920s, largely by Langdon's example, to bring to bear on Manchester Jewry some of the more progressive aspects of women's philanthropy in Christian society. At some time before 1929, when, as a member of the Women's Lodge of B'nai Brith, she began to plead their need for the lodge's support, she was involved in setting up the Cheetham troop of the Jewish Girl Guides.[55] Her first involvement with refugees came in 1933, when she began to raise funds and to mount events for the Lodge's new Hospitality Committee. Many of these events, as well as the English lessons for refugees organised by the lodge, were held, she was to remember, in the home she had set up in Goulden Road, Withington, with Dr Michael Barash, a fuel technician of Polish birth, whom she had married in 1925.[56] In a job application made after the war, she claimed to speak German, Yiddish, French and a little Spanish.[57]

Leonard Cohen was the only newcomer to the organised communal scene. In 1933 he was the owner and managing director of a series of popular clothing stores in central Manchester set up by his Russian immigrant father, Henry Cohen, and known collectively as 'Henry's Stores'. While himself apparently lacking experience of social welfare work, his wife Amy, the daughter of an Austrian immigrant, Dr. Solomon Herbert, a pioneer in Manchester of Freudian psychoanalysis, a specialist in child criminology and a founder-member of the Manchester Fabian Society, was a leading figure in the development of Child Welfare Clinics in Manchester.[58]

Norman Jacobs saw himself chiefly as the public face of the MGJAC , as its mediator with Laski and Schiff and as its financial controller.[59] The committee's routine case-work and its onerous day-to-day dealings with Woburn House and the Refugee Children's Movement were managed by Barash, Feinmann, Langdon and Cohen, at first with minimal secretarial support.

The context of their work was determined in large part by Laski's spectacular conversion to the open, even enthusiastic, support of local refugee settlement. Beginning tentatively after the Anschluss this was driven forward thereafter by a combination of local, national and international pressures. The chain of international events which began with the German occupation of the Sudetenland in October 1938 and reached its climax in the annexation of Bohemia and Moravia in the following March brought home to him the extremity of the threat faced by European Jewry and the imperative of a large-scale resettlement of European Jewry in which Manchester must play its part. Manchester, it was recognised, 'must relieve the considerable pressure on London'.[60] Laski was also moved by changing attitudes in the community at large, symbolised by the massive response to the Baldwin Appeal on behalf of Kindertransport children. In supporting refugees, the Jewish community could now be seen, not as working against the national grain, but as operating in harmony with the popular will. 'The darkness is not completely unrelieved', he told the Representative Council, 'It is, indeed, a matter of happiness to feel that the great heart of this country is still sound, that the causes of tolerance and humanity still make their appeal, and that, in spite of the efforts of our enemies, it is universally recognised that the cause of the refugee is one which must appeal to all. We owe a great debt of gratitude to Lord Baldwin for what he has done, and to our Christian fellow-citizens who have so generously subscribed.'[61] The work of rescue, he now felt, was 'made heartbreaking by the delay and red tape' which it involved.[62]

In these circumstances, as new responses to the refugee crisis evolved spontaneously within the Jewish community during the winter of 1938–39, they could now count on Laski to lend them his own, and the Representative Council's, advocacy, provided only that they accepted the supervision of the MJRC (and, through it, his own ultimate control). In mid-December 1938 he approached Woburn House, on behalf of the MJRC, for a grant towards the creation of refugee hostels in Manchester; if it was refused, he informed the Council, then Manchester would have the right to launch its own appeal to meet its specific requirements. At the end of January 1939 the Council approved an application from the Manchester Union of Jewish Literary Societies to devote the proceeds of its Drama Festival 'to the benefit of

German-Jewish refugees'.[63] By this time he had begun to lose patience with both the Palestine policy of the British government and the bureaucratic immigration procedures of the British Home Office. 'It is obvious,' he told a Quarterly Meeting of the Council on 15 January, 'that we can do nothing for our German co-religionists except get them out of the country as speedily as possible.' He was becoming impatient with the government's bureaucratic delays. He could scarcely understand the Colonial Secretary's refusal to accept the settlement of 10,000 Jewish children in Palestine: 'one cannot protest in too strong terms,' he told his fellow Council members, 'against making so humanitarian a cause the subject of political expediency'.[64]

Towards the end of November 1938, a young Manchester Jewish estate agent and property speculator, Arthur Kershaw, and a group of his 'influential friends', chiefly members of middle-class and traditionally orthodox Sephardi and Ashkenazi families from the south Manchester suburbs, devised a scheme to create what would be the first refugee hostel in provincial Anglo-Jewry. Kershaw was the Manchester-born son of the Polish immigrant, Myer Kersh, who in the early years of the twentieth century had set up in business in Manchester, first as a wholesale clothing dealer and then as a property developer. At the time of his death in August 1938 he had left to his children an impressive portfolio of buildings in north and south Manchester, including a mansion, 'Buena Vista', at 34 Alexandra Road South, Whalley Range.[65] It was this house which, in a 'speech' to the MJRC on 6 December, Kershaw offered as a 'Central Residence ... for a minimum of thirty people' between the ages of sixteen and thirty.[66] He and his friends had already worked out the aims of the residence, its management structure and the kind of purposes it would serve. Whether or not the original intention was to initiate an entirely independent project, its promoters had been persuaded by 6 December, perhaps by Nathan Laski, a fellow office-holder with Kershaw's late father at the Manchester Great Synagogue,[67] to proceed through the official channels of Woburn House and the new MJRC.[68] Once Schiff had expressed his 'delight' with the idea, the plan was refined at a meeting of its supporters on 1 December and accepted formally to the MJRC five days later.[69]

The house was conceived as a hostel offering only short-term accommodation to trainees and prospective domestic servants sent from London for placement in Manchester. It would be, in effect, a point of transition – its first title was the 'Refugees Temporary Shelter' – for young Germans and Austrians (and later Czechs) making their entry into British society. Twenty-four residents – twelve men between the ages of sixteen and nineteen, and twelve women between sixteen and thirty – would each stay for a maximum of six weeks, during which time they would be expected to undertake 'certain duties' at the hostel, to 'acclimatise themselves to this country' and to make themselves available for interview by prospective employers. Volunteers from the community would deliver classes in 'English, Physical Culture, Horticulture and Air Raid Precautions', and 'further instruction' would be given, 'particularly to Females, to adapt themselves for Domestic Service'. As soon as they found work, the residents would be expected to contribute to their own upkeep on a sliding scale of payments: from 25s a week by those earning £2 or more to 10s for those earning between 15s and 25s.[70]

The working of the hostel was supervised by a Kershaw House Executive Committee (KHE), made up of thirteen of its promoters, but working 'in conjunction and jointly' with the MJRC, which would be represented on the KHE and which would assume responsibility both for the cost of the hostel and for the welfare and placement of its residents. The house was offered, initially for two years, free of rent and rates and such 'incidental expenses' as the cost of its conversion, decoration and running repair, all of which would be taken on by Kershaw. Furniture and equipment was 'spontaneously and generously given' by his friends (thirty beds by the furniture dealer, Maurice Freedland), together with regular foodstuffs either free of charge or at cost price. Apart from a House Administrator, chosen from amongst the volunteers on the KHE, there would be a paid caretaker, whose wife would do the cooking, 'a [resident] nurse or two', and three doctors and a dentist on call, each of whom had 'agreed to give his services voluntarily'. The House Administrator would be assisted by three sub-committees of volunteers, for 'Supplies', 'House Administration' and 'Entertainment and Social [Events]'.[71]

The first chairman of the KHE, Robert Breckman, was perhaps typical in age, status and circumstances of those who now devoted themselves to Kershaw House. Aged forty-two, he was a successful furniture manufacturer and agent, with a business in the city and a mansion, Landsdown House, on Wilbraham Road, Withington, close to the South Manchester Synagogue, of which he had once been a member before changing his allegiance to Reform. In the community he was a 'zealous philanthropic and social worker', who was said to have been 'behind the success' of the Fresh Air Home and School for Jewish Children at Delamere and who had served as treasurer of the Manchester Country Club, a centre of leisure (in particular, tennis and bridge) for the middle-class Jewish families living south of the city. He was a member of Whitefield Golf Club, founded by Jewish golfers in 1932 in the face of their exclusion from other clubs, and Worshipful Master of Zion Lodge, established in Manchester by Jewish Freemasons in 1879, and still in 1938 predominantly a 'Jewish lodge'.[72]

On 12 December 1938 satisfactory 'working arrangements' were agreed between the MJRC and the KHE,[73] and the hostel – now officially named Kershaw House – opened in January 1939 for 'Refugees of either sex from the age of sixteen upwards, but excluding elderly people, brought to Manchester under the auspices of the German Jewish Aid Committee [the first title of the MJRC], for whom temporary shelter is required.'[74]

It was, even as a hostel, Lisa Wolfe remembers, a 'fabulous' house, with a ballroom, ornate lounges, a conservatory, spacious dormitories, each with five or six beds, huge gardens, where, in the course of time, chickens were kept, and, leading off the garden, a 'grotto' under the house which served as a venue for unsupervised meeting between the residents and their friends.[75]

It was said to have once been the home of the Slazenger-Moss family, whose eighteenth-century ancestors had been amongst the founders of Manchester Jewry and who, in the course of the nineteenth century, had built up one of Manchester's largest retail clothing firms, with huge premises in Market Street, and branches throughout Lancashire.[76]

The KHE delegated the day-to-day management of the hostel to a voluntary 'House Administrator' drawn from its own ranks. This was Henrietta ('Ettie') Myrans, an experienced and strong-minded communal worker, vice-chairman of the Ladies Committee of Manchester's Victoria Memorial Jewish Hospital and a prominent member (and one-time chairman) of the B'nai Brith Women's Lodge. From the beginning 'Mrs Myrans' ruled Kershaw House with a kind of benevolent despotism. She 'did not approve of anybody', she announced to the KHE, 'particularly men [who] interfere with any work being done'.[77] Members of the executive were asked to keep out of the residents' lounge, 'so as to allow the Refugees to spend the evening in their own company'.[78] 'All refugees must be left to entertain themselves', she told the executive on another occasion, 'and the Committee were not to interfere with their enjoyment'.[79] The placing of refugees she saw as part of her brief: domestic servants were to be given posts only 'after frank discussions … between Mistress, maid and House Administrator'.[80]

The regime she and the executive imposed upon them was strict but scarcely Spartan. 'Call bells' signalled the stages of a closely time-tabled day – reveille at 7a.m. ('all beds to be stripped and windows opened before leaving bedrooms'); breakfast at 8a.m. 'prompt' (followed by bed-making); house duties, carried out by rota; lunch at 12.30; dinner at 6.30p.m.; lights out at 11p.m. on weekdays and 11.30 on Saturday, the only day on which late passes were available.[81] On Sunday evenings, the refugees were allowed guests from outside the hostel in their own lounge for 'quiet entertainment and conversation', although with the caution that 'anyone wishing dancing or excitement had an open invitation to the Grove House Lads Club',[82] the social club set up in 1907 by the officers of the Manchester Battalion of the Jewish Lads Brigade.

Disciplinary measures occasionally deemed necessary in a hostel of young adults uprooted from their native communities and separated from their parents were hardly draconian. In extreme (and rare) circumstances, refugees might be returned to London or (perhaps more ominously) have their behaviour 'investigated' by Nathan Laski.[83] Occasionally the chairman of the KHE was called in 'to emphasise the necessity of keeping to the printed rules and regulations'.[84] In March 1939 reports of secret drinking led the executive to ban the sale or consumption of alcohol on the hostel premises.[85] In May reports of pilfering led Rae Barash to consider the extreme measure of seeking the advice of the Manchester Aliens Officer.[86] In July 1939 fines were imposed on those in breach of the hostel's nineteen 'rules and regulations' – 6d for the first offence, 1s thereafter.[87] There was no sense of panic. Young women who refused posts as domestic servants found for them by the MJRC were persuaded to think again; the advice of Woburn House was sought for the tracing of refugees who went 'missing'.[88]

The refugees were well looked after. On arrival in Manchester, they were met at the station by a member of the MJRC executive and escorted to the Police Station to register (as aliens) their change of address.[89] Routine medical and dental care was available from refugee dentists and from GPs with surgeries nearby, specialist care from local hospitals to which Nathan Laski had negotiated access.[90] During their first week in the hostel, newcomers received travel expenses to get them to work.[91] A barber visited the hostel once a week to give free haircuts; free shoe repairs were available from a local shoemaker.[92] Those not at work received 2s pocket money every Thursday evening.[93]

The executive saw itself as easing newcomers into life and work in an unfamiliar environment. In a letter to Otto Schiff shortly before the hostel opened, Norman Jacobs explained that the short period spent there by refugees would be used 'to give [them] the opportunity of perfecting their knowledge of the English language and … to give [them] some idea of domestic customs so that they will fill their prospective posts very easily'.[94] Lessons in English, instruction on domestic service and lectures on aspects of English life were compulsory.[95] There were 'English Evenings' on selected Sundays, at which only English could be spoken.[96]

When Leonard Cohen, as chairman of the MJRC's 'After-Care Committee', began to devise plans for providing all young Jewish refugees in Manchester with some form of organised leisure, he saw Kershaw House as its natural base. On New Year's Day 1939, he held a party for refugees in the café of Henry's Stores in Market Street (of which he was the owner) at which he announced the opening of a 'Young People's Club'. For 1s a year young refugees would be entitled to meet together on two nights a week between 7 and 10p.m. in the ballroom at Kershaw House for tea and biscuits, conversation and dancing, for which the committee provided a tea urn, two tea trolleys and a cigarette machine.[97] So successful was the experiment that in February 1939 it was refined into what became regular Kershaw House 'Thursday Evening Socials' – evenings of dance, music and sketches to which refugees from all over Manchester were invited, together with their non-refugee Jewish friends.[98] With Ettie Myrans concerned only that those attending should respect the privacy of her resident charges, the socials became one important focus of young Jewish refugee society in Manchester, while by July 1939 Kershaw House itself had become 'a recognised Social Centre for refugees'.[99] In addition to those attending Socials, it became a drop-in centre for domestic servants with nowhere else to go on their half-days and for trainees at a loose end after work; a cup of tea and biscuits were available for 6d, an evening meal for 1s.[100] 'It was our refuge, as it were', Lisa Wolfe remembers, 'Everybody congregated there.'[101]

It was at Kershaw House, too, that refugees were accorded scope for their creative talents. There the executive mounted occasional exhibitions of refugee art and craft work. In March 1939 the refugees formed their own 'theatrical troupe'.[102] A young refugee musician from Vienna, Roman Marik, put together a small band.[103] Another refugee, Kurt Cohn, performed with his brother on the piano at the Kershaw House socials.[104] The highlight of a Viennese Cabaret put together at the hostel to raise cash for the Baldwin Fund was the Tingle-Tangle Concert Party of young refugee singers, dancers and musicians which thereafter performed regularly at Kershaw House on Thursday evenings.[105]

During 1939 Kershaw House became something of a showcase for Manchester's refugee aid. Lord Rothschild was persuaded to visit it during a trip to Manchester in March 1939.[106] Snippits of information about its activities were conveyed to the local press by the MJRC's Press Officer, a Miss Calderon.[107] The executive congratulated itself even on the low cost of maintaining the residents – 12s 8d per head per week as against the 15s to 16s per head spent on the forty boys at the Cassel-Fox hostel in North Manchester.[108] The inherent tragedy in the situation is symbolised by a book of photographs of potential German and Austrian domestic servants, many with high academic qualifications, which the committee circulated in the hope of finding them placements.[109] Most were doomed.

Kershaw House was, at least in the first instance, intended by the MJRC to provide only temporary accommodation for men under nineteen and women under thirty admitted to Britain as domestic servants or as trainees. Under the pressure of events, however, both these age limits and the restrictions on occupation were soon abandoned. Of the twenty-six refugees known to have been admitted to Kershaw House between July 1939 and March 1940 – fourteen Austrians, eleven Germans and one Czech – five were aged over forty, six were in their thirties, nine in their twenties. The oldest was Irma Roth, a forty-seven-year-old domestic servant from Vienna. The residents also included two dressmakers, a machinist, a housewife (said to have two children), a publisher (thirty-three-year-old Theodor Gottlieb from Vienna), a photographic assistant and a 'merchant', Hans Weissenburg, whose wife, Bianca, occupied another of the hostel's rooms.[110] The changes suggest the difficulties experienced by the MJRC in finding accommodation for older refugees and for married couples.

The expectation was that once suitable 'placements' had been arranged, domestic servants and trainees appropriately (and rapidly) introduced to English ways, would be in a position, with the committee's help (or perhaps its direction), to move into private accommodation, either, in the case of domestic servants, with their masters and mistresses, or, in the case of trainees, in lodgings at rents affordable from the small allowances paid to them by their employers. By the beginning of 1939 a Lodgings Sub-committee had been set up under the chairmanship of Morris Feinmann to seek out suitable lodgings at the right price.[111] This did not prove easy. Early in February, in some desperation, Feinmann was approaching the Health Visitors of the city and the management committee of the long-standing communal charity, the Jewish Ladies' Visiting Association, for help in finding lodgings at rents of up to 25s a week.[112] Once the stream of new refugee trainees and domestic servants dried up with the outbreak of war and those who had arrived earlier became self-sufficient, Kershaw House and Cassel-Fox, while retaining their distinction in terms of Jewish observance, became hostels for more general use, without restriction on length of stay, but with a fairly rapid turnover of residents.

Even more problematic was finding accommodation within the means of middle-aged and elderly Jewish refugees whose rescue had, from the beginning, formed part of the brief accorded to the MJRC by Woburn House. The MJRC acted at once both to identify individual guarantors and, when this proved frustrating, to set up a 'Guarantee Fund' which would satisfy the Home Office's concessionary gesture, made in November 1938, that refugees might be brought over under 'block guarantees'.

The reception of elderly refugees was promoted most obviously by Morris Feinmann, with his long experience as a volunteer with the Jewish Home for the Elderly in Manchester. Insufficient evidence exists to show exactly how this Guarantee Fund worked. From fragmentary references in the MJRC's surviving minutes, it appears that donations from the relatives or friends of those seeking guarantees, and perhaps from other well-wishers, were held in a bank account in Manchester administered by a Guarantee Fund Sub-committee, of which Feinmann was the chairman. Once an intending refugee in Germany had obtained a visa from a British Consulate on the strength of this capital, money would be released from the fund for his support in Manchester and, since his visa would typically require it, for his subsequent re-emigration. The order in which those in Germany were chosen for support was apparently determined by a form of lottery such as that applied in Manchester, for example by the Jewish Naturalisation Society.[113] Donors whose relatives, for whatever reason, failed to obtain a visa or failed to reach Manchester, were entitled to a refund of their contributions. To start the fund off, 100 donors each deposited £100.[114] Some sixty people in all were brought to Manchester by a fund which totalled £5,000 by the beginning of May 1939 and £14,000 by the middle of July.[115] The fund effectively provided a means of rescuing those for whom personal guarantors could not be found.

As 'middle-aged and elderly refugees without individual guarantors', or whose individual guarantors failed to honour their commitment to the provision of hospitality, joined young trainees and displaced domestic servants in the search for low-cost accommodation in a congested and increasingly expensive local housing market, the MJRC faced something of a crisis, particularly since, following the opening of Myer Kersh House (see below p. 238), it received no further offers of rent-free houses which might readily be converted into hostels. Its response was to seek, and obtain, permission from Woburn House, for what appears to have been a novel scheme of 'taking houses to be run as Boarding Houses for refugees'.[116]

The idea was to acquire properties which, while offering accommodation at reasonable rents, could be run as self-supporting commercial enterprises by managers appointed by and responsible to the MJRC who might also be refugees. The first, opened that same month, was a property at 250 Great Clowes Street, Lower Broughton, rented by the MJRC and then handed over for management to a Dr Koppenheim, a refugee who had earlier served as the first superintendent at the Cassel-Fox Hostel (see below p. 219). In return for free accommodation for himself and his family, Koppenheim was expected to render his 'boarding house' financially self-sufficient.[117] By mid-July he had received his first trainees from Cassel-Fox,[118] as well as a young refugee from Hamburg whose epileptic fits had led to his being removed from his placement in a family home.[119] Although not without its teething problems, 'Koppenheim's' served as a model for similar ventures, three of which had taken shape by September 1939 – two in Moreton Avenue (one of them, specifically 'for girl trainees and elderly people who would be coming over on guarantee'), one, apparently briefly, at 'Dr. Golber's house', in Northumberland Street, Higher Broughton.[120] In February 1940 the committee was offered a private hotel, 'Fabian's', also in Northumberland Street, which might house refugees on a similar basis and which was finally taken as a refugee boarding house/hostel in the following October. After unspecified 'complaints' from its residents had reached the ear of Nathan Laski, however, in April 1941 it was transformed into a hostel under staff appointed and paid by the committee.[121] By then the committee managed eight hostels/boarding houses, seven of them in north Manchester, only Kershaw House in the south, together providing accommodation for just under 200 refugees.

The distinction between 'hostels' and 'boarding houses' is unclear, even in the MJRC's records. Once the flow of refugees had been halted by the outbreak of war, Kershaw House was itself opened up to wider constituencies and run on a more commercial basis,[122] while the earlier boarding houses were now themselves described in the MJRC's correspondence and accounts, as 'hostels'. Even this impressive complex was placed under strain at such times of crisis as the eviction of 'enemy aliens' from the Merseyside Protected Area after June 1940. Of the 300 Jewish refugees who then arrived in Manchester, some were placed in a house at 270 Great Clowes Street, 'obtained' by Feinmann, where they could be 'kept together'. Boys from a Liverpool Jewish hostel were given temporary accommodation (presumably on the floor, since it had no bedrooms) in Derby Hall, the meeting place of the Jewish Working Men's Club, while more permanent lodgings were found for them.[123] Thereafter the MJRC was constantly juggling with the roles of its hostels to meet the changing circumstances of refugees as they found (or lost) work in the city, as managers came and went, and as enemy aliens were arrested and released. Throughout, the officers of the London Jewish Refugees Committee believed, the MJRC 'had introduced into many of the hostels a homely atmosphere which after all is the most important thing for the well-being of the refugees'.[124]

It is probable that most refugees lived neither in hostels nor in the MJRC's 'official' boarding houses, but in bed-sits in private homes and lodging houses to which they were directed by the committee and where, when necessary, refugees received weekly grants to enable them to afford the rent. On his return from Blackpool early in 1939 Werner Mayer found there was no room for him in the committee's hostels. Apfelbaum directed him to a private (and decrepit) lodging house at 107 Bellott Street, where a Mrs. Fletcher, a Christian woman with a Jewish husband, had already taken six or seven refugee lodgers, whom she supplied with kosher food. The gap between the 15s a week Werner was receiving as a trainee and his rent (£1) and maintenance costs was filled by a grant from the committee of 10s a week. There Werner remained until his wedding to a local Sephardi woman in 1946.[125]

While creating accommodation for the range of refugees who were likely to come under its care, the MJRC was seeking out guarantors and placements for the Jewish children arriving on the Kindertransport from the beginning of December 1938. The terms of their admission to Britain had been spelled out by the government in the previous month. Admissions were simplified and speeded up by means of procedural shortcuts and the employment by the Home Office of additional staff. The usual requirement of a passport and visa was replaced by a single form. At the same time, each child required a guarantor who would defray the cost of its maintenance up to the age of eighteen and of its re-emigration, the latter in the form of a £50 deposit which lay beyond the reach of most working people. While the guarantees of some of the children were financed from the Balfour Fund, a national appeal launched in December 1938 by the former Prime Minister, Earl Baldwin, and which raised a total of £550, about half allocated to Jewish organisations and used largely on helping child refugees, others had to be guaranteed by cash deposits from private sponsors.

In Manchester, the original search for potential guarantors, as well as the local appeal for the Baldwin Fund, was apparently managed by a Manchester Children's Refugee Committee (MCRC), with its offices in Gaddum House, also the headquarters of the Manchester Council for Social Service, and made up chiefly of Jews and Quakers but including also the Anglican clergyman and pacifist, Thomas Shimwell, as the representative of the Manchester, Salford and District Council of Christian Congregations. It included the chairs of the children's committees set up by the Jewish community (Margaret Langdon) and by the Manchester Quakers (Christine Sutherland, the wife of the Principal of Dalton Hall), which were expected, once fund-raising ended, to take on, under the supervision of the London-based Committee for the Care of Children from Germany and Austria (otherwise the Refugee Children's Committee (RCM)), the case-work involved in the settlement and welfare of the *kinder*.[126]

Early in 1939 the MCRC made a special appeal through the *Manchester City News* towards the creation of a hostel for fifteen to twenty children. By the beginning of April, when the 'generosity' of the paper's readers had 'brought the hostel into the realm of practical politics', the appeal was for a donor of a house which might be converted into a hostel with the help of further funds. 'Boys [in Germany] were waiting to begin a new and happy life', the appeal read, 'but until we find a donor of a house we can go no further'.[127] Later in the same month the MCRC joined a nation-wide Mothers Day Appeal to 'mothers of the UK', which was expected to pay for the entry of a further thousand children, 500 of them Jewish, 500 Christian.[128] Another appeal was launched soon afterwards by a small committee set up by the University Vice-Chancellor at the behest of the Quakers, Harold Howard and John Major.[129] In June the MJRC organised a spectacular week-long fund-raising event centred on an exhibition of artefacts made by Austrian refugees (presumably at Kershaw House) – 'exquisite' embroidered satins, gossamer, fine lace and 'gay little Viennese accessories' – and a 'Viennese Café' at 76 Deansgate in which customers were offered Viennese coffee and cakes by young Austrian girls in national dress. A map which formed part of the exhibition provided 'an outline of the refugee problem and the part played by Manchester in its solution'. The programme climaxed with a 'sensationally successful Tingell-Tangel' (song and dance revue) of songs, dances and pieces by an Austrian refugee pianist and opera singer from Vienna working in Manchester as a domestic servant.[130]

In September the Quakers placed collecting boxes in Manchester's 'larger stores', stationed lady collectors outside local cinemas and placed a 'final appeal' in the local press.[131]

By this time the MCRC, which 'had played such a useful part when the children came to this country from Germany',[132] had been wound up, with its hope of setting up a children's hostel unrealised, and responsibility for the reception of the *kinder* had fallen squarely onto the shoulders of the Jewish and Quaker children's committees. The Jewish committee had, at all events, ruled out hostels in favour of private homes, preferably those of relatives.[133] It had also brought a degree of order to the selection of children, by preventing couples from Manchester making their own way to Dovercourt, the initial base of the Kindertransport, to make their own choices from amongst the *kinder*. The children's committee insisted on its sole right to meet the children in person and photographs were taken of those available at Dovercourt for circulation within the community.[134] Responses from Manchester Jewish families were, however, disappointing. Offers to take children were so slow coming in that the committee approached Nathan Laski for his views on Jewish children going to non-Jewish homes. His ambiguous reply that it was acceptable for 'certain special children' was taken to mean that the committee had carte blanche to seek out Christian foster-parents for Jewish children.[135] In July 1939, notwithstanding its earlier decision, the MJRC acquired the loan of a house at 1 Windsor Place in Newton Heath, in East Manchester, from a Mr Godbert, as a children's hostel, an eventuality avoided only when the offer was withdrawn on the outbreak of war.[136]

The details of the search for private placements, as well as the names of those who took on Jewish children, have not survived. A rare window onto the communal response is recorded in the minutes of the Provincial Independent Tontine Society, one of Manchester's leading Jewish friendly societies. On 22 November 1938, the day after the government agreed to receive child refugees, the Society's committee decided to 'forego its annual dance' and instead to donate the usual cost (5s a head, making a total of £80) 'to the bringing over of refugee children from Germany under the wing and care of members of this society'.[137] After the MJRC had delegated Morris Feinmann to follow this up, members willing to 'adopt' a child were asked to give their names to the secretary, who 'would apply on their behalf to the Jewish authorities for the proper transfer of a child or children under the members' care'. Some members then donated a further 5s, while the retiring chairman, M. Kozansky, donated his retirement gift of three guineas to the same cause. He commented that, in devising this scheme, members were 'adding to the prestige of this society, which is already held in high esteem in the community'.[138] It is no longer possible to judge the typicality of such a response.

Finally, some 428 Jewish *kinder* were found homes in what became Region 10 of the RCM, an area stretching northwards from Manchester into Westmoreland and Cumberland, at least fifty of them with Christian families. An now unknown (but small) number of Catholic children, chiefly of Jewish origin, were taken in by at least one Catholic Children's Home in the Manchester Region,[139] while Quaker families offered homes (how many is again uncertain) to 'non-practising Jews'.

The growing pressure on such refugee organisations as the MJRC after the Anscluss, as well as the growing sense of panic within German and Austrian (and British) Jewry, is amply documented. A pamphlet published by the *Jewish Chronicle* in 1939 as 'a guide to those who wish to help' is entitled, ominously, *Salvaging German Jewry*.[140] Young Austrians and Germans were writing to prominent British Jews known to them only by name in a desperate search for sponsorship; so Adalbert Eisner, a fourteen-year-old from Vienna, wrote to Abraham Moss, a city councillor and textile merchant, in his case with success.[141] One document survives which, although its exact provenance is uncertain, was very probably a list compiled by the Domestic Service section of Bloomsbury House but being circulated in Manchester by the MJRC during the summer of 1939.[142]

It is a list of 329 German and Austrian women between the ages of eighteen and forty-six, with their photographs attached, seeking posts as domestic servants in Britain. It includes their names, their ages, their nationalities, their experience, their linguistic skills and their home addresses in Europe. Most had addresses in Germany; twenty-nine were living in Austria, seven in Italy, three in Poland, three in Czechoslovakia, one in each of Holland and Hungary, and two in Zbasyn, the camp between the borders of Germany and Poland occupied by those expelled from Germany by Nazi decree as non-citizens, but not yet allowed into Poland, their place of birth. Some, that is, had managed (or been forced) to leave Germany, but now sought entry to Britain. Of those whose nationalities are recorded 214 were German, twenty-two Polish, fourteen 'stateless' and one Rumanian. Of the 329 only twenty-three on the list are recorded as being 'fixed up' or 'applied for', only one of these in Manchester, with a Jewish family in Vine Street, Kersal. One is noted as wishing to 'remain in Berlin', two as having affidavits for entry to the United States, one for entry to Australia. Four are described as being in 'urgent' need.

Of this substantial body of young Jewish women seeking to escape Nazi rule, in a way which, for most, was nothing less than humiliating, most advertised their skills in some aspect of domestic service: either in 'all kinds of domestic work', or in cooking, cake-making, baking, ironing, washing, needlework, dressmaking, cosmetics, the care of children, even gardening: Annmarie Elias of Berlin had 'perfect agricultural knowledge'. One was a 'perfect cook'; one a 'vegetarian cook'; one a 'dietcook'; two had worked in the kitchens of German-Jewish hospitals. One young Viennese woman, who also spoke English, French, Italian and Spanish, was a 'pianist', but 'fond of children', the typical phrase of those leaving themselves open to work as children's nurses. But the list also includes trained and experienced kindergarten teachers, governesses, nurses, nursery nurses, and welfare workers with experience in German hospitals and orphanages. Some advertised their additional commercial and secretarial skills; one knew shorthand; one was a fashion designer, another a photographer. Forty-five year-old Margareth Silberstein, who had trained as a 'lady's maid', claimed expertise in pedicure, manicure, tailoring and 'kosmetique'. The Rumanian, Ilse Schoenbach, was a 'masseuse'. One described herself as 'not afraid of hard work'; two others were prepared to undertake 'rough work'. Nineteen describe themselves as 'Orthodox', four as 'Very Orthodox', two as 'Strictly Orthodox'. The rest, no doubt wishing to keep their options open, did not define their relationship to Judaism. Most claimed to know English, to know it 'very well' or to be 'fluent' in the language. Only one confessed that her English was 'poor'.

Their self-advertisements, some offering 'good testimonials', reflect not so much the social status, or even, necessarily, the real skills of these women in their home countries, as the degree of their desperation. These were people who were, in effect, begging for their freedom, some might even then have seen themselves as begging for their lives. They were ready to leave their families and homes as skivvies in Britain rather than to further endure Nazi rule. Their likelihood of success depended upon their being 'applied for' by some generous-minded British citizen, probably identified for them by the Jewish Refugee Committees in London, in Manchester and elsewhere in the provinces, or perhaps by the Quakers. There is now no way of knowing how many of them were successful.

Notes

1 JRC Annual Report for 1937–38, p. 1.
2 JRC QM 28 July 1938. The MCC's Annual Report for 1937–38 includes the statement that 'numerous applications have been made to the Home Office Authorities in obtaining extended stay for aliens and in making arrangements for bringing out from Abroad young people on permitted visits to relatives in Manchester and else-

where'. This must refer either to Apfelbaum's work before November 1938 or (more probably) to that of the new MGJRAC.

3 *Ibid.*

4 MJRC QM 2 October 1938.

5 *Ibid.*

6 MJRC Preliminary General Meeting, 7 November 1938.

7 *Ibid.*

8 MWLBB Lodge Meeting 7 November 1938.

9 *Ibid.*

10 *Ibid.*

11 The committee was first called the 'Manchester German-Jewish Aid Committee', and was re-named the Manchester Jewish Refugees Committee only in 'early 1939', but to avoid confusion, the term Manchester Jewish Refugees Committee and its abbreviation, MJRC, is used throughout the present text.

12 MJRC General Meetings, 22 and 29 November 1938. A day later, on 23 November, 1938, the Manchester and District Refugee Committee of the Society of Friends was also formalised.

13 MWLBB Lodge Meeting, 6 December 1938.

14 MJRC Draft of a letter from the chairman to the *Jewish Chronicle*, 7 June 1943.

15 *Ibid.*

16 MJRC List of Members of the Industrial Committee (probably 1938).

17 Werner Mayer, *To Tell the Story: Recollections and Reflections* (Manchester Jewish Museum nd c.1980), pp. 47–49. On his return to Apfelbaum, he was found a 'traineeship' in an electrical components factory ('consisting almost exclusively of refugees) at 15s a week. After failing at this and other factory work, he took employment in a Jewish bakery on Cheetham Hill Road. In later life he became the Deputy Head of King David School and the second chairman of the trustees of the Manchester Jewish Museum.

18 MJRC General Meeting 29 November 1938.

19 No General Meeting minutes after 29 November have survived. Elections for office were apparently held by an executive enlarged in the course of time by numerous co-options.

20 MJRC General Meeting 22 November 1938.

21 The two sub-committees set up on 7 November – an Industrial Committee 'to deal with trainees' and a General Hospitality Committee to assist 'all other refugees' – were rapidly overtaken by events. By the end of December, there existed a Children's Committee, a Trainees After-care Committee, a Domestic Workers Committee and a Guarantee Committee.

22 MJRC EM 29 November 1938. The meeting advised Schiff to refuse any support to young women unwilling to work in Manchester.

23 *Ibid.* The three non-Jews were the architect and surveyor, Percy Cummings; Sir Harry Fildes, Director of the Mosley Construction Company in Cheetham Hill; and the (unnamed) secretary of the Manchester Rotary Club's International Service Committee.

24 MJRC EM 18 April 1939.

25 Lore Philip arrived in Britain from Berlin, where she had been 'bullied by the SA', in September 1933, apparently after convincing an Immigration Officer that she had received an offer (actually fictitious) to study English. It was her original intention to return to Germany, but in 1936 she received a permit to remain in Britain. After working for the Guarantee Committee, she became a welfare officer at one of the

committee's hostels, 'Fabian's Hotel' before replacing Gafan in 1945 as MJRC's paid administrator (notes of a conversation with Mrs Rae Barash c.1977).

26 MJRC EM 29 November 1938.
27 *Ibid.*
28 *Ibid.*
29 *Ibid.*
30 *Ibid.*
31 Apfelbaum's Industrial Committee continued to meet on his business premises until March 1939, when he moved to Spring Gardens, apparently as a paid member of the MJRC's staff (MJRC EM 21 March 1939). In April 1939, as its work expanded, the MJRC moved to larger premises at 42 Deansgate, also in central Manchester.
32 Author interview with Rae Barash (hereafter Rae Barash interview).
33 *Ibid.*
34 MJRC EM 7 February 1939.
35 Greater Manchester County Record Office (hereafter GMCRO), Photos relating to refugees and the Landsberg Displaced Persons Camp. Gafan left Manchester in 1945 to work for the American Joint Distribution Committee at the Landsberg camp, returning to Britain in 1946.
36 Transcript of a lecture in private hands, 'From Lodz to the House of Lords: The Life and Times of a Provincial Jewish Family in England, 1840–1990', based on the diary and personal papers of Norman Jacobs, p. 13.
37 MWLBB CM 25 January 1931.
38 JRC Special Meeting 25 May 1933, EC 18 March and 17 July 1936.
39 *Ibid.*
40 *Ibid.* Norman Jacobs himself left Manchester in 1951 to settle in Tel Aviv.
41 *Jewish Chronicle Year Book*, 1938.
42 In Manchester, Jacobs became vice-president of the Communal Council. He also became a member of the Executive Committee of the Board of Deputies during Selig Brodetsky's presidency and chairman of the Political Committee of the Zionist Federation.
43 Norman Jacobs, 'Manchester', in Cyril Domb (ed.), *Memories of Kopul Rosen* (London 1970), p. 63.
44 MWLBB Lodge Minutes 4 December 1933.
45 He also made himself exceptionally vulnerable. After the war he was to find his name and Laski's, as the only two Manchester Jews on the Black List of British Jews prepared by the Gestapo. A copy of the list, as published by the *Manchester Guardian*, is in the possession of Norman Jacobs' nephew, Leonard Jacobs.
46 Bill Williams, *The Making of Manchester Jewry, 1740–1875* (Manchester 1976), Chapters 4 and 7.
47 Very probably as a compromise candidate agreeable to both a long-established German commercial elite and radical newcomers of Eastern European origin. See John Shaftesley, 'The Origins of the Manchester Jewish Representative Council', unpublished typescript c. 1970.
48 E.H. Langdon joined the Jewish Board of Guardians in 1913. This sentence and the two paragraphs which follow are based, except where noted, on a taped interview made with Margaret Langdon by an unknown interviewer in 1978 and in the possession of Mr Louis Rappaport.
49 Taped interview with Margaret Langdon held by the Manchester Jewish Museum (hereafter Margaret Langdon interview). Rae Barash believed that Langdon committed herself fully to social work only after the death of her younger brother and

her fiancé in the First World War (interview of Rae Barash by Bill Williams in the tape collection of the Manchester Jewish Museum Tape J15).

50 *Ibid.*; *Jewish Chronicle Year Books, passim.*

51 Rosalyn D. Livshin, *Olga Sandler: a Biography* (privately printed, Manchester 2003), pp. 1, 7 and 9.

52 Obituary in *MG* 5 September 1944; Treuherz, *True Hearts*, pp. 86–87. A friend of Marlies from the Aachen Girl Guides, Hildegund Bohn, had met Feinmann during a spell as a courier in Sweden; in 1938 she wrote to ask him to help Marlies. Soon after arriving in Manchester, Marlies also was offered a bursary to study at the Manchester College of Music.

53 *Some letters of Aennchen and Richard Amberg, 1909–1942* (English transcripts in the possession of Julian Treuhertz), letter from Aennchen Amberg to Marlies 15 June 1941. Aennchen was deported and murdered by the Nazis in June 1942.

54 *Jewish Chronicle Year Book, passim.* Alex Jacobs was Norman Jacobs' first cousin. He was a member of the Reform Synagogue and of its Park Place (Reform) Synagogue Social Club (PPSSC). He was later a member of the MGJAC and chairman of its 'Quota Committee', which dealt with refugees living in Manchester while they awaited their quota numbers to come up for emigration to the USA. He also employed two young refugee women as domestic servants at his home (taped interview with his son, Leonard Jacobs).

55 Barash was initiated into the MWLBB on 2 April 1928. Her appeals for money from the lodge to help the Cheetham Jewish Girl Guides rent suitable premises were made on 1 July and 7 March 1929. She gave a talk to lodge members about the Jewish Guides on 4 November 1929. At a lodge meeting on 3 May 1930 she was asked to chair the lodge's 'outings committee'.

56 Rae Barash interview.

57 MJRC Rae Barash's undated [1944–45] application to the Allied Post-War Requirement Bureau. Her husband was then a technical officer with the Ministry of Fuel and Power. She died on 18 December 1987.

58 MCN 3 February 1940.

59 MJRC EM 17 July 1939.

60 MJRC typescript of a speech by Arthur Kershaw to the MJRC 6 December 1938.

61 JRC QM 15 January 1939.

62 *Ibid.*

63 JRC EC 25 January 1939.

64 *Ibid.*, QM 15 January 1939.

65 Information on Myer Kersh from notes made for the author in the early 1970s by his maternal grandson, Vivian Besso.

66 MJRC EM 29 November 1938.

67 Myer Kersh was for many years treasurer of the Great Synagogue, where Laski was president.

68 According to Rae Barash, Laski had at first opposed the opening of the hostel (Rae Barash interview).

69 MJRC typescript of a speech by Mr Arthur Kershaw to the MJRC, 6 December 1938. Kershaw had at first been irritated by a delay which he interpreted as the 'apathy' of the MGJAC towards his plans, a 'misunderstanding' for which Norman Jacobs apologised (MJRC EM 6 December 1938).

70 *Ibid.*

71 *Ibid.*

72 MCN 21 December 1940. Breckman died at his home in December 1940, aged 46.

73 MJRC EM 12 December 1938.
74 Elisabeth (Lisa) Wolfe interview.
75 *Ibid.*
76 Rae Barash interview.
77 MJRC KHE 12 December 1938.
78 *Ibid.*
79 *Ibid.*, 5 March 1939.
80 Arthur Kershaw speech, 6 December 1938.
81 19 Rules and Regulations attached to MJRC KHE 6 February 1939.
82 MJRC KHE 9 May 1939.
83 MJRC EC 14, 21 and 28 March 1939.
84 MJRC KHE 6 February 1939.
85 MJRC KHE 27 March 1939.
86 MJRC KHE 9 and 22 May 1939.
87 MJRC KHE 3 July 1939.
88 MJRC KHE 19 June 1939; MJRC EC 28 March, 18 April, 17 July 1939.
89 MJRC KHE 6 February 1939.
90 MJRC KHE 18 April, 8 May 1939.
91 MJRC KHE 6 February 1939.
92 *Ibid.*
93 MJRC KHE 22 January 1939.
94 MJRC Letter from Norman Jacobs to Otto Schiff 21 December 1938.
95 MJRC KHE 20 March 1939.
96 MJRC KHSC 22 March 1939.
97 Elisabeth (Lisa) Wolfe interview; MJRC KHE 10 January 1939.
98 MJRC KHSC 23 March 1939.
99 MJRC EM 17 July 1939.
100 Elisabeth (Lisa) Wolfe interview.
101 *Ibid.*
102 MJRC KHSC 23 March 1939. The troupe rehearsed in the hostel basement.
103 Elisabeth (Lisa) Wolfe interview. Elisabeth's father played the violin in the band.
104 *Ibid.* Kurt Cohn emigrated to the United States, where he became the composer, Ray Martin.
105 Rae Barash interview.
106 MJRC EC 14 March 1939.
107 MJRC KHE 28 March, 18 April 1939.
108 MJRC EC 1 May, 17 July 1939
109 MJRC book of photographs of the names and experience of potential domestic servants, recently indexed by the archive department at Manchester Central Library.
110 MJRC Entry forms of residents at Kershaw House.
111 MJRC ACC 9 January 1939.
112 MJRC EM 7 February 1939.
113 The Manchester Jewish Naturalisation Society, founded in the 1890s, drew lots on a monthly basis to decide which of its contributing members was next in line to have the cost of naturalisation covered. It is not clear exactly how the guarantee lottery was organised.
114 Rae Barash interview.
115 MJRC EM 1 May and 17 July 1939.
116 MJRC EM 28 February, 7 and 14 March 1939.
117 MJRC EM 28 February, 18 April 1939. The SCR (9 February 1940) reported a fire at

a hostel in Great Clowes Street to which the fire brigade was called by 'a refugee who knew a little English'.

118 MJRC EM 17 July 1939.

119 Interview of Alice Rubinstein by Rosalyn Livshin, 2 October 2003. The young refugee was Alice's elder brother.

120 MJRC EM 18 April, EC 17 July 1939.

121 MJRC EM 16 February, 1 October 1940, 2 April 1941.

122 Thus blurring the distinction between refugee 'hostels' and refugee 'boarding houses', the latter often appearing as hostels in both the MJRC's minutes and in the recollections of refugees who once lived in them.

123 MJRC EM 4 September 1940. The cost of accommodating and maintaining the Liverpool evictees was shared between the Liverpool Refugees Committee, Bloomsbury House and the Public Assistance Board (MJRC EM 1 October 1940).

124 MJRC Leslie Prince to Morris Feinmann 17 November 1941.

125 Mayer, *To Tell the Story*, pp. 49–50.

126 Its other members were a local philanthropist, Dr Erna Reiss, Rose, the wife of a Manchester Jewish cotton merchant; A.P. Simon and an A.C. Wilson. There is no record of its precise remit. The 'regional organiser' of the Baldwin Fund was a Miss Putnam (QRC EC 4 April 1939)

127 MCN 8 April 1939.

128 MCN 22 April 1939; QRC EC 4 April 1939.

129 QRC EC 25 April 1939.

130 MCN 22 July 1939. 76 Deansgate was owned by the mysterious 'Mr. G. Hardy', who later donated property to the Quakers for use as a hostel. I have been unable to trace his identity.

131 MCN 1 July 1939; QRC EC 17 September 1939.

132 MJRC RCM letter from Ida Whitworth to Margaret Langdon, 7 June 1941.

133 MJRC 7 November 1939; Children's Sub-committee 7 December 1938.

134 MJRC Children's Sub-Committee 7 December 1938.

135 MJRC EM 7 February 1939.

136 MJRC EM 17 July 1939; QRC EC 25 April 1939.

137 PI CM 22 November 1938.

138 PI GM 30 November 1938.

139 My research in this respect was hampered by my inability to gain access to the files of the Catholic Rescue and Protection Society for the Salford Diocese.

140 Joseph L. Cohen, *Salvaging German Jewry* (London 1939).

141 The Albert Edwards (once Adalbert Eisner) papers in MCL: letter and card to Abraham Moss, 1939. Eisner later worked for Moss's firm in Manchester, H. and A. Moss, and followed his sponsor into the Labour Party. Eisner arrived in Britain on a children's transport supervised by the SS on 15 May 1939.

142 The document is in the Archive of Manchester Central Library (M533/1/5/1/1). The numbering suggests the document has been revised as some women had already been found employment.

8

'Serious concern': the Manchester Quakers and refugees, 1938–1940

In the face of an increasing number of refugees reaching Manchester, the Quaker ISC could not justify any more than the Jewish community, what was at best a haphazard response to their needs. On 20 October 1938, the ISC declared itself 'seriously concerned with the need to help the increasing number of Refugees in this country. We suggest that a panel of Friends be drawn up showing those able and willing to take refugees for varying periods.' The causes of this sudden 'serious concern' are not clear. The sense of a 'refugee crisis' had been developing since the Anschluss in March 1938. The most likely explanation, as it had been earlier in the case of the Jewish response, was pressure exerted from London.

It seems likely that the foundation of the Manchester Jewish Refugees Committee on 7 November, followed closely by news of the Kristallnacht pogrom (9–10 November), witnessed personally by Roger Carter of the Berlin Quaker Centre, and no doubt accompanied by pressure from the Germany Emergency Committee in London, served to concentrate Manchester Quaker minds. When, on the morning after Kristallnacht, 'a large crowd of frightened Jews gathered outside the [Berlin] Centre' in search of help, Carter was given a list of twenty German Friends 'prepared to give discreet support to Jews' seeking an escape.[1] In Manchester, on 17 November, it was reported to the ISC that the Preparatory Meeting at Mount Street had decided to set up an 'Emergency Refugee Committee'. Six days later what became the 'Refugee Committee of the Society of Friends in Manchester and District' (hereafter, the QRC) held its first monthly meeting, under John Major's chairmanship, to devise an urgent plan of action and to launch an appeal for funds. At Mount Street there was now a dramatic change of mood. Apathy towards refugee Germans was set aside as the Manchester Quakers launched themselves into what was to become Manchester's most impressive non-Jewish effort on behalf of all manner of victims of the Nazi regime.

It took some time for the committee to get its act together, to work out its priorities, and to define a working relationship with both the Friends' GEC in London and, in Manchester, with a Jewish Refugee Committee founded only a week earlier, and which was to be the only other major agency of refugee support in the Manchester region. Initially the QRC's organisation was rudimentary. With John Major as chairman and the long-standing Mount Street elder, Harold Howard, as its secretary, four sub-committees were formed out of the first twenty volunteers: a 'clerical sub-committee', with May Elliott and John Major's wife, Katherine, as its convenors, to oversee day-to-day correspondence and filing; an 'administrative sub-committee', convened by Winifred Garnett, to undertake legal work, Home Office contacts and case-work, and to advise on matters of policy; a social sub-committee under Edmund Emson, to take care of external 'liaison' and internal 'fellowship', and a 'Finance and Publicity sub-committee', with the former China missionary, R. Thornton Smith, as its convenor, and John Major as a member. The QRC became another of those voluntary societies to which the Home Office delegated its case-work: made up of unpaid volunteers and without any form of subsidy from the state, the QRC was expected to share the burden, and attract some of the odium, involved in the implementation of British immigration law. It was substitute, as its members were soon to realise, for a rescue operation orchestrated and financed by the British state.

Its members were typically those who had earlier been attracted by their ideals to welfare work either within the local Quaker community or in society at large. By the end of November 1938 twenty-one Friends had joined the QRC, one from the Bolton meeting, one from Westhoughton, four from Cheshire, the rest from Mount Street.[2] Four had earlier been members of the ISC. All belonged to what might be seen as the major social constituency of British Quakerism: an intellectual and socially-sensitive commercial and professional lower-middle class residing chiefly in the lower reaches of English suburbia. Few were wealthy. The most well-to-do, according to one of their younger fellow-members at Mount Street, was Ida Whitworth (1889–1959), a member of the Cheshire Meeting, daughter of Alfred King, a cotton bleacher by trade and a former Liberal MP for the Knutsford Division of Cheshire, and the widow of a Manchester barrister, Major John Howarth Whitworth, who had also nursed political ambitions, and who had been killed in action during the First World War.[3] Her experience of Quaker international affairs included a spell at the Berlin International Centre with Roger Carter, since April 1938 leader of its 'British section'. In November 1938 she was living with her four daughters and several refugee protégés in a comfortable mansion, 'Woodburn', in the Derbyshire village of Disley.[4] Having 'lived for prolonged periods in various parts of the Continent, including Germany and Italy', she is said to have had personal knowledge of Fascism and its effects; her daughter Julia, who also joined the committee, had studied German and music in Freiburg.[5]

Those of the remainder who can now be identified were petty traders, retailers, social workers, school teachers and 'housewives'. Harold Howard was a cotton yarn agent whose business in 1938 was in the course of 'winding down' under the impact of the Slump,[6] leaving him time for a near-total dedication to the refugee cause. There were two specialist teachers; one, Benia Hesford, working with epileptics, one, May Elliott, with the deaf. Christine

Sutherland, involved with her husband in the welfare of students at Dalton Hall, was also an 'overseer' at Mount Street.[7] Wilfred Garnett was the son of John Garnett, a partner in a long-established firm at 309 Oxford Road, 'opposite the University', dealing in scientific instruments and supplying microscopes, lantern slides and laboratory equipment to the University and to Manchester schools.[8] His mother, Winifred, a former school teacher, was also on the committee, along with three other teachers: two, John Major from Leigh and Edmund Emson from Eccles, from Grammar Schools, one from an inner-city elementary school. There were at least two women without paid occupations: Sophie Brentano, wife of a physics lecturer at the University of Manchester, and Patti Denton, whose husband was a skilled engineering worker. It was a feature of this, as of other Quaker committees, that it included a number of unmarried women of 'strong character' and feminist leanings, some in lesbian relationships well-known to, and deeply respected by, their fellow Quakers.[9]

Millie Uhland, herself unmarried, was co-opted onto the QRC at its second meeting and put her formidable linguistic skills at its disposal. At Mount Street, she and Percy Long, widower of her late friend, Lily, fulfilled the vital functions of translating the German documents of potential refugees and communicating on their behalf with the QRC and the British authorities. Millie's house in Manley Road, Whalley Range, became also a pied-a-terre for newly arrived refugees, put up on her sofa while they awaited the more permanent hospitality of local families or placements as domestic servants.[10]

The QRC was composed of dedicated men and women, chiefly in their thirties or early forties, held together by their powerful and practical commitment to the social implications of 'the Quaker Way'. A handful brought to the committee earlier experience of community work. One, Douglas J.J. Owen, a manufacturer's agent by profession and a member of the Quaker meeting in Stockport, was also employed by the Mount Street meeting to supervise its Centre for Unemployed Men.[11] Another, Margery Wilson,[12] was active in the University Settlement.

Margery Wilson was born into a committed Anglican family in London in 1905, but moved soon afterwards to a village in Berkshire where her father, the theologian Cyril Emmet, was Vicar of the Parish Church and vice-principal of Ripon Hall, a theological college near Oxford. At the age of fifteen, after her father's appointment as Dean and Chaplain of University College,[13] she accompanied him to Oxford, and it was there, after his death in 1921, that she formed a close friendship with a charismatic fellow student, Roger Cowan Wilson, who in 1928 had defeated Quentin Hogg to become President of the Oxford Union. Roger's mother, Edith, was from a long-established Manchester Quaker family; his father, Alex, an engineer, a convert to Quakerism and a voluntary worker with the Mount Street meeting.[14] After her own conversion, Margery married Roger Wilson in August 1931. Following his 'false start' in the textile trade, she followed him to Manchester when, in 1932, he was offered a post in the Talks Department of the BBC. In Manchester the couple, now members at Mount Street, joined the University

Settlement at the Round House in Ancoats, of which the long-serving Warden was another Quaker, Hilda Cashmore,[15] and soon afterwards, on her behalf, set up what they described as a 'Guild of Neighbours' in Newton Heath in East Manchester, where they chose to live.

The Guild was part of a drive by the University Settlement, initiated by Hilda Cashmore, to bring a degree of social warmth and creativity to families moving in the wake of the slum clearances of the early 1930s from cohesive working-class communities to the city's new and soulless municipal housing estates, of which the earliest were in Newton Heath and Wilbraham Road, Fallowfield, and the largest at Wythenshawe. Taking over a derelict hut on the Newton Heath estate, restored, it was said, with the help of subscriptions from three hundred of its residents and the labour of the local unemployed, the Wilsons used it to orchestrate a range of activities which included a library and play centre for children, classes in handicrafts, literature, philosophy, economics and psychology, a hockey club, a 'Wireless Group' and a 'Women's Adult School'.[16] Although the project was later abandoned when the Wilsons left Manchester temporarily for London in 1935,[17] Margery's experience at Newton Heath marked her out for co-option to the QRC at its second meeting. It was an opportunity which Margery also welcomed. A year or two earlier, while on a walking tour in the German Rhineland with her husband, she had looked up the parents of a refugee German-Jewish girl who worked in her mother's house in Oxford; through them she had learnt of the 'appalling things' going on under the Nazi regime.[18]

The QRC was composed at first exclusively of Friends, and only once subsequently used its powers of co-option to bring in a non-Quaker. This was James Henry ('Harry') Wharmby, a man in his late sixties, a publisher's agent by profession and a devout Methodist, who joined the committee in January 1939, after he had volunteered to find guarantors for refugees from within the membership of his own organisation, the Manchester branch of Rotary International.[19] A 'noted Methodist layman' of whom it was said that he 'took religion with almost medieval seriousness', Wharmby had earlier shifted his voluntary interest from the foreign missions supported by his chapel in Styal to 'refugees from foreign oppression'.

The QRC never saw itself, even potentially, as a refugee self-help organisation. Between 1939 and the end of 1941 the QRC co-opted a further twenty Quakers, chiefly from backgrounds and occupations similar to those of its founders. It was not until late in 1939 that it included two members who were themselves refugees, and, of these, one, Herta Israel, who joined the committee in October 1939, was a displaced worker from the Quaker Centre in Berlin.[20]

From the beginning there were some committee members who understood the degree to which, as volunteers, they were being expected to take on roles which more properly were those of the British state. They did so under protest. In January 1939 Ida Whitworth drew attention to the 'large number of refugees [who] were short of [the] necessary money to bring them out even though their papers were in order. The men of 35 and upwards [those, that is, not eligible for work permits] were in a desperate plight with nothing but starvation, prison or suicide ahead … Only intervention by the [British] Government on an appropriate scale would solve the problem.'[21] Sporadic pressure was applied on the Home Office to simplify its procedures, to act with a greater degree of urgency, to place more funds at the disposal of voluntary agencies and generally to open its doors more widely to those seeking a means of escape, always without substantive success.[22] At a public meeting at the Friends Meeting House at Hillgate in Stockport in mid-February 1939, the QRC member Douglas Owen expressed his belief 'that if urged by the people the Government would take over the responsibility of admitting refugees on a larger scale. They were just afraid of how far public opinion would support them'; the meeting was persuaded to pass a resolution 'that the Prime Minister or some other responsible person be urged that this country do whatever it could to co-operate with other nations in finding the necessary money to assist the refugees'.[23] In April 1939 the QRC decided on a public meeting of protest at Manchester's Houldsworth Hall, sending out 3,000 handbills inviting the citizenry to an event to be chaired by the leading Manchester Liberal, P.M. Oliver, and at which the main speakers would be Sir John Hope Simpson and the Manchester University geographer and folklorist, Professor Fleure, both known to have their personal reservations about the direction of British policy towards refugees.[24] In the event, the protest was ineffective, the attendance 'disappointing', the profit negligible.[25]

By this time the QRC had gone some way towards defining its relationships with London Friends and Manchester Jews. Although occasionally jealous of its power to act independently, the QRC saw itself from the start as primarily a sub-committee of the GEC, which, in turn, increasingly embattled by the trend of events, welcomed provincial support. In truth, the GEC, although seen from Manchester to be operating effectively 'in difficult circumstances',[26] was nearing breaking-point: the office at Friends House in Euston Road was said to have been 'transformed' by the 'immensity' of the refugee work that it had taken on since March 1938.[27] Hilda Clark, who negotiated with Mount Street on its behalf, estimated that 'one million persons ought if possible to be brought out of Germany and Czecho-Slovakia'. She too believed that the task was 'too great for voluntary effort … only by Government support can the problem be tackled in the right proportion'.[28] Since this was unlikely to ever be the case, the GEC was anxious to transfer to Manchester some of its work (and some of the refugees who applied to it for help). Harold Howard was co-opted onto the GEC as Manchester's representative; it was his view that in particular cases, 'to economise time', it might be necessary for the QRC to act without consultation.[29]

There were two ways in which it was necessary from the start for the QRC to coordinate its work with that of the Manchester Jewish Refugees Committee, in the event its only major partner in Manchester in the support of refugees. One was the potential of overlap, and possible conflict, in working with refugees of Jewish origin, the vast majority of all refugees, not all of whom were Jewish by religion. The other was how the two committees might work together, if at all, in the reception of the 10,000 unaccompanied children, the first of whom were due to arrive in Britain on the Kindertransport at the beginning of December 1939.

In resolving the 'Jewish issue' the QRC took its lead from the GEC, which since 1933 had been working harmoniously with the Jewish Refugees Committee in London. The agreement reached in London was essentially that while the Jewish Committee registered[30] all 'practising Jews', the GEC took responsibility for non-Jews, 'non-practising Jews' and, in a Nazi terminology sometimes taken on by Friends House (and at Mount Street), 'non-Aryan Christians' (Christians, that is, who would have been defined as 'Jewish' under the Nuremberg Laws).[31] Although it was acknowledged that there would be 'borderline cases', these lines of demarcation were thought to be 'fairly clear'. If, in the rush of emigration, a refugee was wrongly registered, then, after consultation between the committees and with the consent of the refugee, a transfer could be effected. Refugee women who, after their arrival 'married out of their communities' were then to be re-registered with their husbands' committee. The few refugees who changed their religion after their arrival (chiefly, it was said, from Judaism to Christianity) were then re-registered with the committee appropriate to their new affiliation. In the case of the children of those registered with the Jewish committee attending Christian denominational schools, their registration was 'not necessarily changed unless at the request of their parents'.[32] A reference in the QRC minutes to 'amicable working relationships' between the Quaker and Jewish committees, as well as the list kept by the QRC of its clients, suggest that in 1939 the London arrangements were accepted in Manchester, although possibly without any kind of formal agreement.

These arrangements were more readily defined in theory than applied in practice. An exception made from the beginning on the Quaker side, was the registration with the QRC of 'Friends of Friends', whatever their religious affiliation or practice. The Kurer family is one example: the Friend who entitled them to registration with the QRC was Millie Uhland. More significant was the difficulty of defining what constituted a 'practising Jew'. There is ample evidence in the records of the Quaker committee of borderline cases in which neither the Quakers nor the refugee knew how to act for the best. At least eight families whom the Quakers themselves defined as 'practising Jews' chose to register with the QRC, and the list of those supported by the Quakers includes the names of others whom the evidence would suggest were 'practising': one was the kosher butcher, Jonas Halberstadt, brought to Manchester specifically to supply meat to the ultra-Orthodox Machzike Hadass, another Feliz Reich, formerly Principal of the Berlin school for deal and dumb Jewish children, a third described simply as 'related to the Rothschilds'.[33] Members of the same family did not always make the same choice: one entry reads: 'mother is registered with JRC, he prefers FRC [Friends Refugee Committee]', another: 'Jewish, divorced. Chose to register under FRC.'[34] In practice, in 'the rush of emigration', Jews who in normal circumstances might have been judged 'observant', found their way, either from the start, or subsequently, onto the books of the QRC.[35] Mixed marriages brought particular definitional problems: one of those registered with the QRC was described as 'Jewish with an Aryan wife in Germany', another as being Jewish with a Protestant wife.[36] The MJRC itself was not entirely averse to refugees being 'allowed to make their own choice'.[37]

What was unacceptable was the refugee who chose to register with both committees. Dr Rudi Friedlaender, a refugee GP in south Manchester, with many refugees on his books, and a founder-member of the MJRC, believed such people to lack 'scruple' and 'conviction'; for him, even those seeking out the materially more advantageous committee could not be counted amongst 'the best and most characterful elements' of refugee society.[38] Dual registration was to cause 'considerable difficulties' in both London and Manchester until the end of 1941; until the matter was then clarified, there were even cases of refugees registered with the Friends in London re-registering in Manchester with the MJRC.[39] Although roundly condemned, the practise had still not been entirely suppressed in October 1942.[40]

The division to which the MJRC now lent its name was to have significant consequences for the future identities of those Jewish refugees for whom Jewish observance had become in their homelands no more than a peripheral part of their lives. Many (perhaps most) of those from families for whom Jewish practice in Germany, Austria or Czechoslovakia had come to mean no more than a visit to the synagogue on Yom Kippur, the lighting of the candles on Eruv Shabbos, or the celebration, often in some bowdlerised form, of the annual Seder meal, chose, or were advised to choose, to place themselves under Quaker care. This in turn was unlikely to include any measures which might bolster their identities as Jews. What happened for most refugees who came into these categories was that a 'slippage' from Judaism which had begun under the impetus of cultural assimilation in continental Europe was now carried to completion. It is not that the Quakers failed to support Jews; what they failed to support, more often than not with the tacit consent of the refugees themselves, and with the silent complicity of the MJRC, was their Judaism or, more correctly, their Jewishness, their Jewish identity. Many refugees were understandably willing enough to shed what remained of the identity which had caused their flight. The MJRC never felt inclined to explain its position. It is unlikely to have been indifference, although the British Jewish community was not well-known for supporting the non-conformists in its midst. The most probable explanation is the MJRC's sense of its inadequacy, in terms of its human and financial resources, to cope, after Kristallnacht and the beginnings of the Kindertransport, with the task of supporting all those refugees (the vast majority) who were of Jewish origin. Contracting out a share of the burden served both to reshape the identities of many residually religious Jewish refugees and so effectively place them out of reach of a Jewish community of which they might otherwise have become a part.

The understanding between the Quaker and Jewish committees generally worked well enough in practice, however, each applying the rules with what seems to have been an acceptable degree of elasticity, keeping one another informed of important developments, and occasionally launching a joint operation, most notably the setting up of a shoe-making workshop in the basement of the Mount Street Meeting House, a proposal emanating from Norman Jacobs, chairman of the MJRC, in July 1939, and under way by September.[41] In the end, a development for which each committee paid half the cost, and which was expected to provide both a mechanism for refugee training and a cheap means of repairing refugee footwear, lasted less than six months. In April 1940, when the MJRC claimed that the training was 'unsuited to English conditions', the quality of the output poor and the workshop ceasing to pay its way, Harold Howard arranged for its 'satisfactory wind-up'.[42] Rather less is known about what was apparently another joint enterprise: a Viennese café on Deansgate, opened as a fund-raising venture in the summer of 1939.[43]

Apart from non-practising Jews, the QRC chose to concern itself chiefly with refugees from Czechoslovakia – Czechs, Germans from the Czech Sudetenland and German refugees from Germany and Austria who had taken refuge in Prague. Largely because these refugees were chiefly 'politicals' – Social Democrats and Communists – but also because they were already overburdened by their commitment to Jewish Germans and Austrians – the Jewish refugee committees in London and Manchester decided that refugees from Czechoslovakia lay outside their remit. The Quakers took up the slack. The QRC appears to have reached an agreement with the Czech Refugee Trust Fund, the government-supported body responsible for the escape and maintenance in Britain of refugees from Czechoslovakia, by which the Manchester Quakers would provide the accommodation for refugees maintained by the trust. The QRC's hostels were intended chiefly for this category of refugee.

Within the QRC's evolving structure the priority was rescue. Private guarantors, the major resource in opening Britain to refugees, were given to understand that their personal obligations would be backed, wherever necessary, by the QRC: 'it was right and proper that the Committee as a whole should be willing to undertake a moral but not a legal obligation to help individual guarantors, but that the number of such guarantors should be limited'. [44] A letter sent to the Preparative Meeting at Mount Street asked Friends 'to stand behind the guarantors', fifty of whom had put themselves forward by the end of January 1939, with more expected through the Manchester Rotary Club, now working closely with the QRC.[45] The Home Secretary was called on to simplify forms which were 'extremely difficult for people to sign'.[46] Applications were invited from prospective employers of domestic servants, one of the few occupations for which work permits might readily be obtained from the Ministry of Labour. Between sixty and seventy had been received by the middle of December, for which Home Office permits were being sought; their 'hosts' were informed that, given bureaucratic delays, the time of their arrival was 'elastic'.[47] Enquiries were made at the Labour

Exchange as to 'what [other] occupations show[ed] a scarcity of labour'.[48] The committee entered into negotiations with the Czech Refugee Trust Fund (CRTF), which by January 1939 had agreed to pay part of the expenses of refugees accommodated by the QRC. Twenty-four adult refugees arrived in Manchester under the QRC's auspices during January, twelve from the CRTF, twelve sent by the GEC.

By the end of April 1939 guarantors had been found for fifty-five refugees, posts as domestic servants for seventeen, with 200 other applications for entry 'still being dealt with', as the crisis in Nazi Europe deepened and attempts to prise open the doors of bystander nations failed.[49] Margery Wilson reported that the United States was 'practically closed' to refugees, Australia 'almost impossible', New Zealand 'difficult', South Africa 'hopeless', Bolivia 'closed', Canada willing to take only Czech refugees, and Shanghai 'definitely to be avoided'. Only Paraguay was possible for those with £20-£30 'landing money'.[50] In Manchester the QRC had by this time set up a section to deal with agricultural and industrial trainees, a category allowed temporary residence in Britain under one of the few concessions made by the government to Jewish pressure for the liberalisation of the immigration laws, while Czechs and German exiles in Czechoslovakia continued to arrive through the CRTF. With Home Office assent, the QRC had also set up a 'domestic service pool' , which made possible the entry of refugee women with the necessary permits but without posts; some were housed temporarily in a new children's hostel in Newton Heath.[51] In June, 'as an experiment', a refugee couple was added to the pool.[52]

Behind these bureaucratic arrangements were the complex personal stories of men and women desperate to escape from Germany, and who, after exploring other options, and witnessing the involuntary dispersal of their families, now turned to the Quakers for help. One was twenty-nine year-old Margarete Herman, a Roman Catholic convert to Judaism from Konigsberg in East Prussia, with a Jewish husband, Siegfried (Siegie), a manufacturer's agent, and a baby son, Danny. Early in 1939, after failing to obtain visas for Palestine, the United States or any European country, she had bought 'black-market tickets' for Shanghai, the only destination for which no visa was required. ('Shanghai was hell', Margarete thought, 'but better to go to hell together than be separated'.) Soon afterwards, however, Siegfried was offered a place amongst those allowed into Britain as transmigrants and housed at Richborough Camp in Kent. After persuading him to accept, and promising to follow on a domestic permit, Margarete then wrote 'a desperate letter' to a Mrs Shaefer, who had known her family in Konigsberg, and who was then working as a volunteer for the QRC in Manchester. Siegfried's parents, meantime, left Konigsberg in May 1939 to stay with their daughter in Holland. After waiting in vain for four months for her permit to arrive from the Home Office at the British Consulate in Berlin, towards the end of August, Margarete took matters into her own hands. Travelling at some risk through the Polish Corridor to Berlin, with a child suffering from scarlet fever, she persuaded a 'very handsome' consular official, on the point of ending the official issue of visas, to endorse her passport. Travelling on the toilet of an over-crowded train (the last boat-train) to Cologne, she made it to the quayside at Flissingen on 31 August to board a tourist ship bound for Harwich. Arriving in London at midnight the same day, they were met by Quakers and accommodated in a crowded hostel (the children slept on mattresses under their parents' beds).

After being reunited with her husband and staying for eight days in Richborough Camp and in lodgings nearby (on money earned by Siegie for filling sand-bags), Margarete then faced the problem of what she was to do with Danny before taking up her post as a cook-general in Manchester on 1 October. She again wrote to Mrs Shaefer, who put Danny's photo, amongst others, on a notice board at Mount Street. Fortunately a couple visiting the Meeting House, a Mr and Mrs Holmes, took a liking to Danny's photo and agreed to take him into their home in Broadbottom. Margarete's mistress in Manchester, the Russian wife of the French Consul, reluctantly agreed to put up Danny for one night, before he was placed with people Margarete 'had never seen before'. As things turned out, she was fortunate in the choice of foster parents, who looked after Danny with great care and warmth, although less lucky in her work placement, where, from the start, she was 'treated like a slave'. Working from six in the morning until midnight, she was expected to do all the cleaning and cooking for the family and their many guests in an eight-bedroomed house. With the help of Harold Howard, who Margarete saw as a 'wonderful man', always true to his word, ever ready to lend practical help, she was able to move to a more congenial placement and, in the meantime, to receive a loan from the QRC to have her belongings brought to Manchester from Holland. When the luggage arrived, the Hermans were reunited in a rented house in Mabfield Road, Fallowfield, furnished at first with orange boxes and camp beds, which they shared with 'four German refugee girls', one working for a rabbi in Withington, one 'who came to England from Berlin in a fur coat' and now worked 'as a cook for the Argentine Consul and his lady friend'.[53]

Accommodating those who had been saved was a major problem. It may be that at first the hope was that most refugees would find hospitality in the private homes of Friends and friends of Friends. By mid-December 1938, however, when appeals transmitted through all the meeting houses of the Hardshaw East circuit had come up with only thirty suitable offers, and most of them for women, it had become clear that something more than private accommodation was required.[54] This in turn was seen to depend on the one hand on the acquisition of suitable property on manageable terms and, on the other, on the availability of financial contributions and voluntary help from outside the limited Quaker fold. The creation of hostels and the forging of links with allied organisations thus went hand in hand.

One temporary measure, apparently arranged by the Quaker physics lecturer at Manchester University, Dr F.C.M. Brentano, was the taking of rooms at the Lamb Guildhouse, a substantial Gothic mansion in Bowdon, a fashionable commuter township in the Cheshire countryside, some seven miles south of Manchester, then in use for residential courses mounted by Professor R.D. Waller, head of the Extra-Mural Department of Manchester University.[55] Six refugees, described in the QRC's minutes as 'Czechs', but in fact German political exiles brought to London from Prague by the Czech Trust Fund, arrived at the Guildhouse on 19 December 1938.[56] This also marked the beginning of the QRC's contacts with the Manchester branch of the National Council of Women (NCW), which since November had begun to interest itself in 'Czech' refugees from Nazi Europe, perhaps the first of Manchester's women's organisations to do so. An appeal launched by the NCW in November 1938, whether on its own initiative or at the prompting of the QRC, 'for the support of refugees from Czechoslovakia', had met with such a 'very good response' that by the end of the first week in December the branch had received £140 in cash and three promises of hospitality. It was then that it decided to work with the QRC, first by paying, on its behalf, for the rooms at the Lamb Guildhouse in which the 'six Czechs' were now installed.[57]

It was the promise of further help from the NCW which persuaded the QRC to proceed with the acquisition in January 1939 of its first refugee hostel: a Victorian detached property at 14 Birch Polygon in the Rusholme district of south Manchester, offered 'at a nominal rent' by the parents of Roger Cowan Wilson, Alex and Edith.[58] This, in turn, prompted the QRC to look for support from its fraternal pacifist organisations, most of which saw Mount Street as their spiritual home. It was Roger's wife, Margery, who now persuaded 'the Manchester and District IVSP' to contribute £2 10s a week towards the cost of converting it into 'a house for refugees' and to offer voluntary support in its management; two (unnamed) representatives of the IVSP were then co-opted onto the QRC.[59] By mid-February sixteen single men and one married couple had moved into what was now called 'Wilson House', perhaps to honour Roger's parents, perhaps his wife, who now took responsibility for obtaining donations of furniture, finding jobs for the occupants and supervising the hostel's daily routine.[60] Margery described the occupants as 'all Sudeten Germans'; in reality at least two were from amongst the German politicals housed earlier at the Lamb Guildhouse.[61] Edmund Emson, the Eccles teacher and QRC member, offered them lessons in English.[62]

The NCW had meantime provided a further £50 towards the cost of housing nine other Czechs in lodgings prior to the opening of a second hostel.[63] On 30 March 1939, less than a fortnight after the German occupation of what remained of the Czech Republic, the QRC opened this second hostel at 4a Palatine Road, Withington, for 'Czech' refugees arriving under the auspices of the Czech Refugee Trust Fund, with which it had now forged a working relationship. It was the CRTF which was to pay the rent (at 18s a week) of the twenty refugees who arrived at what was now 'Hardy House', loaned without charge by the Manchester businessman, E.W. Hardy.[64] A second pacifist body, the Fallowfield Group of the PPU, was now brought in tow, probably through the mediation of the PPU activist and QRC member, Winifred Garnett, a respected friend of the Fallowfield group's 'leader', the Jewish pacifist Lionel Cowan, and one of its most committed members, Stanley Mossop, the Unitarian Minister at Platt Chapel. It was the QRC's hope that the Fallowfield PPU might be persuaded to 'take charge' of 4a Palatine Road.[65] In the event, Sophie Brentano's further negotiations on the QRC's behalf led only to volunteers from the Fallowfield PPU taking on a number of specific, although important, tasks. These included the establishment of 'a rota for social evenings, sewing etc.', the invitation of refugees into the homes of PPU members ('to get them into a home atmosphere'), the teaching of English, the organisation of rambles, and the offer of occasional gifts of cigarettes and other items. Cowan also appealed to his members for donations of such 'urgent necessities' as a wireless set, gramophone records and copies of Picture Post and other illustrated magazines.[66] In August 1939 Cowan reported that, with the support of his members, the hostel was 'running well' and that visitors were welcome.[67] Its management, however, was in the hands of the QRC's appointees, including an Austrian refugee as its warden.

Most of the volunteers who helped out at the Quakers' two Manchester hostels remain anonymous. One, however, was the twenty-seven year-old Samuel Johnson of Swinton, an assistant secretary at Manchester University, who recorded his work in testimony to the Conscientious Objectors' tribunal in September 1940. An 'admitted member' of the Society of Friends, a member of the League of Nations Union (LNU) since he was sixteen and of the PPU since he was twenty-seven, Johnson noted that over the last two months he had taught English to refugees, 'visited their hostels', arranged discussion groups and collected clothing for them until his activity had been 'curtailed' by internment. Although judged by the tribunal to have been 'truculent, bellicose and studiously offensive', he was duly registered as an objector, 'without conditions'.[68]

By this time, the QRC had called in other allies from Quaker meeting houses on the Hardshaw East and Cheshire circuits. During late winter 1939 and spring 1940 'refugee committees' under the aegis of the QRC were established by Quakers, or under Quaker inspiration, in Bolton in Lancashire, Marple, Sale and Wilmslow in Cheshire, and Disley[69] in Derbyshire, each expected to raise funds, identify guarantors and sympathetic employers, and provide hospitality in their districts.[70] All were immediately active. In February 1939 Ida Whitworth, secretary of the Disley Committee with her fellow Quaker, Margaret Hadfield, reported to the QRC that while offers of hospitality had been 'disappointing', the committee had raised £300 towards the maintenance of refugee children and trainees.[71] By the end of April the Bolton Committee had found accommodation in private houses for 'several refugees', placements for a number of domestic servants and one 'farm trainee', and money enough to help a refugee join her family in Chile.[72] In four of the districts, Salford, Sale, Wilmslow and Marple, small 'houses for refugees' (that is, hostels) had been established, each maintained by its own committee, but accepting refugees sent to it by Mount Street.

In late April 1939 forty-six refugees from Czechoslovakia, forty-three men and three women, all of whom had left their country illegally through

Poland and travelled to Britain through the Polish port of Gydnia with the help of the CRTF, arrived in Marple, where they were met by a committee from the tiny Marple Meeting House and Margery Wilson from the QRC.[73] They were there found accommodation by the QRC, first in Brentwood, a holiday home in Church Lane, Marple, offering summer breaks for unemployed women and their children organised by South East Lancashire and North East Cheshire (SELNEC). In early May this, 'the largest single party of refugees which has yet arrived in the Manchester district', were visited by a reporter from the Stockport Advertiser, who found them traumatised but resilient, preoccupied with 'housework ... cooking and cleaning and putting their gardens in order', as they came to terms with their 'terrible experiences'. In Marple he believed they had been well received. The Vicar of the Parish Church, which many of them attended, gave them a 'warm welcome' and 'urged the congregation to help the refugees make themselves at home ... and also to help them in any way as far as they possibly could'. After the service, 'a number of the congregation made themselves known to the refugees and chatted freely with them'.[74] The Quakers meantime set up classes in English and launched an appeal for clothing 'urgently needed' by those who had arrived 'without money, [with] few personal possessions and with no clothing apart from that in which they had 'escaped'.[75]

On 18 May, when Brentwood was returned to its original use, the refugees were relocated by the QRC, some to a hostel in the town, 'Norwood' in Arkwright Road, rented for £70 a year, eighteen to a house rented by the Quaker committee in Wilmslow.[76] Heinz Vogel, who entered Norwood with his mother in July 1939, after being removed from a 'protected area' on the Kent coast, found several Czech families already in residence, including his relatives, four members of the Slatner family from Zlin, where Hugo Slatner had been a dentist, the Bergmans and the Kohns.[77]

By the outbreak of war, when government policy all but blocked the entry of further refugees, between ninety and 100 refugees from Czechoslovakia – Czechs, Sudeten Germans and German exiles – were being accommodated at hostels managed by the QRC, as well as an unknown number of other refugees, some of them Austrian, in private homes, student hostels, and boarding houses. Of the lodging houses, the one of which most is known was run by a Mrs Mary England at 85 High Street, Chorlton-on-Medlock. Who Mrs England was, and how she made her connection with the Quakers, are both unknown, but, certainly from the end of June 1939, she was being paid by the Quakers for boarding and lodging Czech, German and Austrian refugees, at a rate of £1 a week.[78] Hanna Behrend's recollections suggest that it was used by the QRC for housing those suddenly rendered homeless or 'problematic' refugees judged to be too 'disturbed' for immediate allocation to a hostel or those having difficulty in holding down jobs.[79]

Hanna Siederer, as she then was, a seventeen-year-old Viennese refugee, found a place at Mrs England's when on 1 November 1939, she was dismissed from her post as a trainee nurse at the County Mental Hospital in Prestwich because her work permit was judged by the police to be invalid.

After spending two days and nights roaming the streets of Manchester and sitting in late-night cafés, she sought advice at Manchester Town Hall, where, as a person of Jewish origin, she was directed to Mrs Barash. After being 'bombarded' with questions by a woman she found unfriendly and abrupt, Hanna was passed on (she was a 'non-practising Jew') to the Friends Meeting House, where Harold Howard, after giving her her first meal for two days and a small loan to tide her over, found her a place at 85 High Street. There she found herself amongst what she experienced as a group of refugee eccentrics. 'All these émigrés,' she wrote in her diary on 11 November 1939, 'they're all mad'. They included an elderly German who walked incessantly up and down the room, 'six steps forward, six steps back'; 'crazy' Maria, who believed herself to be permanently ill; a Viennese man lacking the fourteen teeth knocked out in a Nazi camp; and a 'very brutal' Communist chemistry student from Berlin who was constantly engaged in 'bitter' disputes with a member of the German SPD. At house parties which went on until two in the morning, relationships were made and broken by young refugees clearly in desperate need of human warmth. 'Was it just the terrible experiences which made them like this?' Hanna asked herself.[80]

The management of refugees in hostels was a major headache for the QRC. Not all refugees, some of them politically radical, many uprooted from comfortable homes, buckled down to the conditions they now encountered. Even at Mrs England's, protests at the 'unappetising meals' she provided led to the refugee boarders being allowed to cook their own ('more varied and continental') meals out of the money for food allocated by the QRC.[81] In February 1939 two of the 'politicals' from the Lamb Guildhouse, Bruno Kresse and Ernst Hoffmann, moved into 14 Birch Polygon with ten other refugees from Czechoslovakia, including at least one other Communist, Christof Kirschneck. There Kresse and Hoffmann spoke out against what they saw as an unduly strict regime imposed by the Austrian refugee house-manager, a Dr Pappe, installed by the QRC. They also identified him, rightly or wrongly, as a Secret Service agent employed to keep tabs on the political activities of refugees. They were allowed to leave the hostel only with his permission and then only after stating their purpose and the time of their return. Unable to foment a rebellion by their fellow residents, Kresse and Hoffmann left the hostel for private accommodation found for them by local members of the CPGB.[82] Disquiet at the hostel continued. 'Disharmony' at Wilson House forced the QRC into several managerial adjustments, and finally into the dismissal of their house-manager. He was replaced by a house committee, made up of refugee residents as well as volunteers and members of the QRC, a form of limited democracy which the committee applied thereafter to all its hostels.[83]

The immediate work of rescue formed only part of the burden on the unpaid members of the QRC during the first eighteen months of its existence. A calculated stand-off by the agencies of the state meant that between twenty and thirty 'amateurs', many with day-time jobs and families, took responsibility for the social lives, personal welfare and financial viability of their guests. Small loans were offered for anything from a landing fee in Panama to the charge of transporting luggage from Oldham to Manchester. Pocket money, usually around 5s a week, was paid to the unemployed, 'hostel inhabitants' given 1s a head at Christmas.[84] Holidays were arranged for refugees through the Co-operative Holiday Association.[85] Advertisements for posts were placed in the Manchester Guardian on behalf of the German and Austrian domestic servants on its books, even during the months of panic which produced mass internment.[86] A clothing store was maintained at Mount Street on which refugees might draw at will. A panel of local doctors and dentists was set up 'to give their attentions to the refugees': some, like Dr Margarete Helbing, were refugees, some, like Muriel Edwards, Quakers.[87] A Youth Group formed by refugees in March 1939 was allowed to meet at Mount Street once a fortnight.[88] There was liaison with the local police when refugees fell foul of the law, committed (or attempted to commit) suicide, or, on one occasion at least, simply 'disappeared'.[89] There were conflicts with the CRTF over the placement and maintenance of 'its refugees', most of whom had been moved from Quaker hostels by the end of April 1940.[90]

Social and cultural events organised by the QRC's 'social committee', with Edmund Emson as its convenor and Millie Uhland as one of its members, served at once as opportunities for 'fellowship', outlets for refugee creativity and instruments of publicity and fund-raising. One of the first was a garden party at Dalton Hall on 12 July 1939 for 200 people, chiefly potential donors, but including all the adult refugees and thirty of the children on the QRC's books.[91] The first of what were to become annual exhibitions (and sales) of refugee arts and crafts, was mounted in April 1940, when pride of place was given to the young refugee artists, Heinrich Weiss, Ursula Leo and Alex Schwartz.[92]

The QRC had also taken on from the beginning, either by agreement or by default, the support of refugees from other Christian denominations, which, for reasons unknown, had decided against the establishment of northern branches of their London-based agencies of refugee support. This was occasionally problematic. A German Catholic refugee couple, the Kallinanns, who in May 1939 had taken posts as domestic servants in Harrow, had earlier deposited their three children, aged five, three and two, in Holly Mount Convent, a Catholic refuge for homeless children at Tottington, near Bury. Three months later, still speaking no English, they sought help from the Manchester Quakers in making what they saw as the 'complicated' journey to visit their children. Provided by Tom Ellis with a volunteer chauffeur, a Dr Stanley Haydock, they arrived at Holly Mount at the end of July. Their experience, as described to Ellis by Haydock, was traumatic. The Kallinanns were soon in 'great distress' because their children – 'delightful youngsters' according to Haydock – did not remember them: 'they clung to the Sisters ... and regarded their parents as strangers ... They had apparently forgotten most of their German and were speaking English which Mr. and Mrs. Kallinann did not understand.' When he returned to pick up the parents Haydock found them outside the convent gates with their children's belongings, volubly voicing their dissatisfaction with conditions in the convent. After the Mother Superior had tried unsuccessfully to reason with them through 'a German interpreter', they left for Harrow without ceremony, taking the children with them and borrowing the rail fare from the disconsolate Haydock.[93]

Although the QRC remained in existence until 1949, going on to supervise the welfare of those refugees who had registered with it, including their welfare in the British internment camps set up in June 1940 to house 'enemy aliens', and, after 1945, sharing with the MJRC the care of those Holocaust survivors who reached Manchester, its work of refugee rescue ended in 1940, when, like the MJRC, it was called upon to accommodate refugees expelled from the 'protected' coastal areas of Merseyside and the north-east.

On 26 June 1940, after the fate of refugees in the 'protected areas' had become well-known, the QRC accepted the offer made by Emma Tomlinson, an elementary school teacher and a member of the newly formed Quaker meeting in Cheadle, of a large Victorian end-of-terrace house at 2 Madison Avenue, for those evicted from Merseyside 'who might become a charge on us'.[94] The condition was that 'the Cheadle group', not yet formally a 'meeting', would maintain the house, meet the cost of its rent and rates, and 'give such further help as they might feel able'.[95] The first three residents arrived in July; by the end of August it was said to be 'nearly full and getting along well'.[96] One of the refugees, Sophie Rujder, was being paid 5s a week (with free board) to act as warden, her daughter, Hildegard 1s a week pocket money to assist her.[97] A small committee, made up of four members of the Cheadle group and representatives from Mount Street supervised the warden and watched over the welfare of what turned out to be around ten resident refugees.

Sophie Eleanora Rujder, the Viennese woman chosen as the hostel's warden, was a Catholic with a Jewish husband, Friedrich, who in Vienna had been the manager of a drinks manufacturing company. Both alienated from their family's faiths, they had become Lutherans, the religion in which they brought up their only child, Hildegard (Hilde), born in Vienna in 1922. It was only when Hilde came home from her Lutheran elementary school chanting ant-Semitic slogans that her parents decided to tell her that her father was Jewish. The escape of all three was engineered by the Quakers. Hilde travelled first on a kindertransport put together by Austrian Quakers, her parents following to posts as housemaid and butler with the Gladstone family in Hoylake on the Wirral. After a few uncomfortable months with a family in Wells, Somerset, Hilde joined them in Hoylake as an assistant nursemaid to the Gladstone children In Vienna, when Hilde had nursed an ambition for the stage, her parents had entered her for the famous Max Reinhardt Drama School, but emigration meant that she could never take up her place. Early in 1940 the Quakers arranged for her to enrol for drama and drawing classes at the Liverpool School of Art.[98]

It was there, after an episode in a bleak Christian Friendly Society Hostel where she was abused as a 'spy', that she turned for consolation to a fellow

German, Ruth Windmuller, with whom she shared accommodation at the house of the pastor of Liverpool's German Church. Ruth was born in Hamburg in 1919, the daughter of a Manchester Jewish lawyer who was working in Germany and his non-Jewish German wife. Although not strictly speaking a refugee, Ruth had been sent by her parents to the Liverpool School of Art after Nazi legislation had barred Jews from art colleges in Germany.[99]

In June 1940, when they were forced to move out of Merseyside, they found themselves at the Friends Meting House in Mount Street. 'It was full of these people,' Hilde remembers, 'we hadn't a clue what was going to happen and there was Mr. Howard, God bless his soul, who was sitting there and sorting us all out. And what happened was that ordinary Quaker families simply took us into their homes.' After a few weeks in the house of a Quaker couple, William Brown, a bank clerk, and his wife, Jessie, in Cheadle Hulme, Hilde joined a group of around ten refugees to be housed at 2 Madison Road. They included Bruno Tublin, a Catholic of Jewish origin, a puppeteer by vocation and once 'youth organiser for evening classes in Vienna', with his wife and two children, a fragile Czech woman, Catherine Pollack, born in Prague in 1900, Martin Reichenbach, then in his late sixties, who in Germany had been a hat maker, but who had come to Britain as an 'assistant butler, a young man from Stuttgart, Edgar Neuberg, and Ernst Schwarz, a former Viennese businessman, now alone with his two children, Karl Heinz and Vera, after his wife, Helen, had deserted him in Vienna, converted to Catholicism and remarried. Charlotte Pollack was the victim of a defrauding guarantor, a Mr Parker, who informed the QRC that 'he was only a nominal guarantor and refused either to implement his guarantee or assist the committee in any way'.[100] Ruth Windmuller, who, as a British citizen was not compelled to leave Merseyside, chose to join her friend Hilde at the Madison Street hostel.

Hilde and Ruth both have positive memories of the hostel. They were happy in a 'relaxed hostel in which, of an evening, the residents would gather in the lounge to solve the problems of the world'. The only sour note was struck by the local police, who would come in after the end of curfew to check on their refugees, when 'poor Mr. Reichenbach and poor Mrs. Pollack would be got out of bed without their teeth'.[101] Living together in the hostel attic, Hilde and Ruth wrote their journals, read poetry, painted each other's portraits and planned long walks across the Cheshire countryside. While Hilde confirms that the Quakers had no conversionist intent, on Sunday mornings she and Ruth began to attend, with Hilde's parents, what Ruth saw as the 'particularly good' Quaker meetings in Cheadle. Hilde was entranced by a guest appearance of the Quaker MP, Philip Noel-Baker.[102]

Ruth and Hilde were drawn into the enterprise of the ambitious puppeteer, Bruno Tublin, whom they accompanied as his (unpaid) assistants to schools and societies throughout the north-west. By the March of 1941 Tublin had 'played his puppets' in over 300 schools, publicising himself as something of a pioneer, bringing 'the old stagecraft' to the notice of local teachers and children, so keeping a tradition alive.[103] He had entertained 'many hundreds of appreciative kiddies' in Lancashire and Cheshire with puppet plays, some written by Manchester people.[104] During the summer of 1942 he made a name for himself for the 'delightful displays' in local parks during Manchester's 'holidays at home' programme. Ruth and Hilde cycled from place to place with Mr Tublin's equipment, helped in the performances ('blowing smoke through holes', Hilde remembers) and carrying back to the hostel his bags of pennies. Although regarded by both as 'a wide boy', for Ruth, the making of puppet heads turned out to be the first stage in a career at the end of which she remains a world-famous ceramicist, while puppet drama led her into the world of theatre.[105]

It would be difficult to overstate the part played by Quaker individuals to facilitate the rescue of refugees.[106] In the European capitals from which Kindertransports set out, Quakers helped families find places for their children, took part in organisational work, saw off children whose parents were barred from platforms, accompanied some transports to Harwich, and arranged for the children to be met and befriended in London and Manchester. On a personal basis, they provided refugees with homes, guarantees, financial assistance, friendship and placements as domestic servants, trainees, university students and scholars in secondary schools, and they hid Jews trapped in Europe. The mother of Elizabeth Rosenthal and her maternal grandfather had assisted Quakers from Manchester in giving assistance to those starving in Danzig in 1918. When her mother, then in Berlin, renewed contact with the Meeting House in Manchester in 1938, the Quakers arranged for Elizabeth to be accommodated with a Mrs Doxan, the headmistress of a Church of England Infants School in Oldham, and found work for her mother as a children's nurse with a family in Greenfield, near Oldham. Millie Uhland, beyond her work for the QRC, found guarantors for at least six refugees, including, in November 1938, a Roman Catholic family prepared to accommodate four members of the Fessler family from Vienna.

Muriel Edwards was a Quaker GP with her surgery at 45 Yew Tree Lane in Wythenshawe. When, in September 1939, she heard that the German refugee, Dr Gertrude Mueller-Lange, her mother and sister, with an affidavit for entry to the United States, were likely to remain trapped for some time in Manchester, without resources, she rented a house near her own to provide them with accommodation. There they stayed at her expense until their departure for the United States in 1942. Amongst other young refugees housed in Muriel Edwards' house or in its 'annexe' were Ernst Wangermann, whose father had committed suicide in Vienna and whose mother was in domestic service in Mellor in Derbyshire; Hans and Lorelinde Einstein, who had arrived from Stuttgart, and who had neither friends nor relatives in Manchester; and two refugees, Gerda Wolf and Herta Fiebig, who were paid as servants, jobs which, according to Ernst Wangermann, 'neither performed very efficiently'.

Notes

1 Email of Roswitha and Peter Jarman, drawing on Carter's personal correspondence to Nicholas Carter, 4 March 2007.
2 For much of the information about the social and occupational backgrounds of members of the QRC I am indebted to Mrs Margaret Bayes of Romiley who joined the Mount Street Meeting in 1937 (hereafter, Margaret Bayes interview). Margaret was the niece of a leading QRC member, Benia Hesford.
3 SA 9 December 1938. Alfred King won the 1906 election for Knutsford, but subsequently retired from politics. For J.H. Whitworth, see W.L. Mackennal, *Life of John Haworth Whitworth DSO, MC* (Manchester 1918). Whitworth offered himself twice, without success, as a Liberal parliamentary candidate: for Shrewsbury in January 1910 and for Knutsford in December 1910. He married Ida Whitworth, whom he had met during his political campaigning, in 1913. Amongst his close friends in Bowdon, where he spent his early years, was the Liberal party activist and barrister, P.M. Oliver. Whitworth died from his wounds in a casualty centre in Rouen in April 1918.
4 In May 1940 Ida's eldest daughter, Julia, married Roger Carter at the Ring o' Bells Meeting House in Disley. At Woodburn, Ida offered hospitality to several refugees: Gerta Flack and her son, Peter, from Germany; Fritz Pringsheim and his wife, Kathe, from Freiburg im Greisgau; and the child of one of the several families from Guernsey who settled in Disley after the German occupation of the Channel Islands. Pringsheim was later Professor of Roman Law at Oxford (SA 17 May 1940; conversation with Ida's youngest daughter, Joan, and Roger Carter's son, Michael, at Windermere, November 2007).
5 SA 9 December 1938.
6 Howard's first contact with the Quakers is said to have been his imprisonment as a Conscientious Objector during the First World War (Margaret Bayes interview).
7 'Overseers' were those who organised the social work centred on Mount Street.
8 An advertisement in the *Manchester and Salford Official Red Book* for 1932 (p. 216) describes the firm as Flatters and Garnett Limited, 'established over a quarter of a century'.
9 (Margaret Bayes interview.) May Elliott lived with a friend, Katie Croft, also a Quaker, in Ashton-on-Mersey; they are said by Margaret Bayes to have hiked together, with packs on their backs, 'before this was usual'. Emma Tomlinson, an elementary school teacher, lived with her 'companion', Annie Lee, the head teacher of a school in Stockport, in the small Derbyshire town of New Mills.
10 Elisabeth (Lisa) Wolfe interview.
11 Owen, who lived in Heaton Mersey, was also a frequent correspondent to the Manchester Guardian on a range of political and humanitarian issues, including the British presence in Ireland (MG 1 January 1938), conscientious objection and the treatment of refugees.
12 Unless otherwise stated, this account of Margery Wilson's life is based on a recorded interview with her by the author in 2003, when she was ninety-eight years of age and living in retirement at Hartrigg Oaks, an estate in York built by the Rowntree Trust (hereafter Margery Wilson interview). For her husband, Roger Wilson, see Fred Brown, *The Making of a Modern Quaker: Roger Cowan Wilson, 1906–1991* (London 1996).
13 There he was a leading figure in the 'Modern Churchmen' movement. After his death, his family was left penniless; his friends paid for Marjorie to be educated at St

Mary's Hall, a 'school for the daughters of clergymen' in Brighton.

14 Brown, *A Modern Quaker*. Roger's mother was a born Quaker.

15 Cashmore worked for the University Settlement in Bristol from 1911 to 1926. She was Warden of the Manchester University Settlement from 1926 to 1933. Roger Wilson was its joint honorary secretary during 1933 and 1934. Cashmore left Manchester to found, under the auspices of the Quakers, a settlement at Rasula in the Central Provinces of India (MSWC No. 181 April 1932). She died in November 1943, having set up bursaries to help students train for social work at the universities of Bristol and Manchester (obituary in MCN 25 February 1944).

16 *Manchester University Settlement, Autumn Programme for 1931–32*, p. 11; ... *for 1932– 1933*, p. 11; ... *for 1934–35*, p. 15; ... *for 1935–36*, p. 15. For the University Settlement, M.D. Stocks, *Fifty Years in Every Street: A Story of the Manchester University Settlement* (Manchester 1945), *Manchester University Settlement, Diamond Jubilee Souvenir Brochure* (Manchester 1955).

17 Stocks, *Fifty Years*, pp. 100, 108. The Wilsons later returned to Manchester, where in 1939 Roger was the Honorary Organiser of the Manchester and Salford Citizens Advice Bureaux (MSWC No. 252, November 1939, pp. 6–7).

18 Margery Wilson interview. Later, independently of the QRC, Margery helped person- ally to bring out refugees, including these parents and some of their friends from the Ruhr, by persuading her friends to offer work or guarantees. She and her husband themselves took on at least three refugee domestic servants; her house, she remem- bers, 'was full of people for quite a long time'. Looking back, she reckons she saved some thirty-five refugees, 'quite a small number' in her own estimation. Amongst the guarantors arranged by Margery was her sister, Dorothy Emmet, a Professor of Philosophy at the University of Manchester, who was also active, as an official of the Manchester branch of the International Student Service, in facilitating the entry to the University of refugee students. At the time of her work with the QRC Margery was the mother of two small children.

19 Co-opted on 24 January 1939. Later Wharmby was to offer free holidays at the Willesby Guest House of the Rotarians and to inform the QRC of the possibility of the Rotarians setting up their own hostel for twenty refugee boys between the ages of fifteen and eighteen (QRC 17 February, 14 March 1939). There is independent evidence that the Rotarians did, in fact, set up, equip and run a 'Residential Hostel' for refugees (Rotary International 1905–55: *Golden Jubilee Brochure: Supplement on Founder Club No. 4* [ie Manchester] (Manchester 1955) n.p. The brochure dates the beginning of the hostel to 1938, adding that it was in existence 'for several years'). Wharmby's death was announced at a committee meeting on 14 October 1939, when he was replaced by another Rotarian, Clifford Whatmough.

20 QRC 17 September and 14 October 1939.

21 QRC 24 January 1939.

22 E.g. QRC 24 January 1939.

23 SA 17 February 1939.

24 QRC 4 and 25 April 1939.

25 The QRC attributed the poor attendance to the number of other meetings held in Manchester that evening (QRC 25 April 1939).

26 QRC 30 November 1938.

27 *Ibid.*

28 *Ibid.*

29 QRC 30 November 1938.

30 While 'registration' with a voluntary agency of support was not obligatory, refugees

likely to be in need of support were advised by the Home Office to place their names on the list of one or other of the committees. Hence the QRC could later talk of refugees 'on its books'.

31 Such Nazi terms as 'half-Aryan, Protestant', 'Aryan' and 'Non-Aryan' appear occasionally in entries in the QL.

32 MJRC Joan Stiebel and Bertha Bracey of the GEC to Rae Barash 2 January 1942.

33 QL Jonas Halberstadt, Felix Reich.

34 QL Alice Fleischmann, Hanna Judith Warner.

35 The QL describes refugees registered with the Quakers as 'Jewish (Liberal)', 'Jewish Reform', 'Jewish race and religion'.

36 QL H. Otto Schoen, Dr Hans Nathan.

37 MJRC Rae Barash to Joan Steiner 22 December 1941.

38 MJRC Dr Rudi Friedlaender to Morris Feinmann 26 October 1942.

39 MJRC Rae Barash to Joan Stiebel 22 December 1941.

40 MJRC Morris Feinmann to Rudi Friedlaender 27 October 1943. The arrangements made between the Quakers and the Jewish Refugees Committee in London entailed similar difficulties of interpretation (Kotzin, 'Christian Responses in Britain', pp. 70–72).

41 QRC 18 July, 17 September, 25 November 1939.

42 QRC 9 April 1940.

43 QRC 17 September 1939; Elisabeth (Lisa) Wolfe interview.

44 QRC 15 December 1938.

45 QRC 3 January, 24 January 1939.

46 Ibid.

47 QRC 15 December 1938, 3 January 1939.

48 QRC 3 January 1939.

49 ISC 20 April 1939.

50 QRC 4 April 1939. Wilson was reporting on the proceedings of the Oxford Conference.

51 QRC 6 June, 16 December 1939.

52 QRC 26 June 1939.

53 Interview of Margarete Herman by Lynne Jesky 20 February 2002 (hereafter Margarete Herman interview).

54 An undated (late 1938?) card index in MFA of the fifty-five responses to requests from the QRC for refugee hospitality (from which only the thirty deemed suitable had presumably been chosen) also suggests that the full nature and severity of the 'refugee crisis' had not yet been fully appreciated by ordinary Quakers. Ten were willing to accommodate only Christians; twenty-three offered hospitality for three months or less, one 'for several weeks'.

55 Card index, MFA.: two cards for 'Dr. F.C.M.Brentano'.

56 QRC 15 December 1938, 3 January 1939; Kresse, Illegalitat, Kerker, Exil, pp. 220–223; and see below pp. 194–195.

57 Minutes of the Executive Committee of the Manchester Branch of the NCW, 1 November and 6 December 1938, 7 and 28 February and 6 June 1939. The minutes are in the archives of MCL M271.

58 QRC 24 January 1939.

59 Ibid.

60 QRC 17 February 1939; Margery Wilson interview; Kresse, Illegalitat, Kerker, Exil, pp. 245–246.

61 Ibid., p. 225. The two were Kresse himself and Ernst Hoffmann.

62 QRC 6 June 1939.

63 NCW Executive 28 February, 7 March 1939.

64 QRC 14 March 1939. 'Czech refugees' might well have included Czechs, Sudeten Germans and German exiles in Czechoslovakia.

65 QRC 17 February 1939.

66 WCML Cowan papers: Cowan's notes for a meeting of Fallowfield PPU on 27 March 1939.

67 WCML Cowan papers: Circular to Fallowfield PPU members August 1939.

68 MCL M547/2/14 Record of Sittings of the Lancashire Tribunal; Samuel Johnson.

69 The Disley committee is reported to have been set up by the Vicar of Disley Parish Church at a public meeting at St Mary's School in Disley in December 1938, when Mr Penman, a London Rotarian, was one of the two speakers, the other Ida Whitworth, 'from first-hand knowledge of the events [in Germany]'. Both joint-secretaries were Quakers. (SA 9 December 1938).

70 QRC 17 February, 25 April, 16 May 1939.

71 QRC 17 February 1939.

72 QRC 25 April 1939.

73 QRC 25 April 1939. The new Nazi regime in Czechoslovakia, while freely allowing Jewish emigration, was anxious to prevent the departure of political dissidents, who were thus forced back on illegal entry into Poland. After the Polish Government had signalled its reluctance to harbour refugees, emissaries from the CTF arrived to select those it believed to merit the limited number of visas assigned by the Home Office. The meeting house in Marple was one of a row of small terraced houses. It was vacated in 2004 when alternative accommodation was found for surviving Quakers in a local Methodist Chapel.

74 SA 5 May 1939.

75 *Ibid.*

76 QRC 25 April, 16 May, 26 June, 17 September 1939. 'Norwood' was vacated in September 1939 and the refugees found alternative accommodation, some at a hostel in Sale, some with private families. The house still stands, now a hostel for people with learning difficulties.

77 Form completed by Heinz Vogel for a survey made by Peter Kurer of Manchester. Kurer used the AJR journal to distribute forms entitled 'Quakers who helped Jews'. The forms are now in the Archives of Manchester Central Library (hereafter referenced as QHJ). The hostel was closed as the government introduced its internment policy in June 1940. The Slatners were then allowed to purchase hostel furniture for a nominal amount and to use it in a house they rented in Marple.

78 QRC 26 June 1939.

79 Hanna Behrend, 'Autobiography' typescript (unpublished 2004), pp. 19–22.

80 *Ibid.*

81 *Ibid.*

82 Kresse, *Illegalitat, Kerker, Exil*, pp. 245–246.

83 QRC 4 and 25 April, 16 May, 17 September 1939; Kresse, *Illegalitat, Kerker, Exil*, p. 246.

84 QRC 16 December 1939.

85 QRC 19 March 1940.

86 MG 2 July 1940.

87 QRC 6 June 1939.

88 QRC 4 April 1939. In June 1939, after he had been accepted for an honours course at the university, the QRC arranged and paid for accommodation for Hoffman in a

student hostel, Hulme Hall (MFA QRC 6 June, 26 June 1939).

89 QRC 14 October 1939, 31 July, 24 September 1940.

90 QRC 19 March , 9 April 1, 30 April 1940.

91 QRC 6 June, 18 July 1938. It was adjudged a 'great success'.

92 QRC 19 March 1940.

93 MFA letters from W.W. Graddon in Harrow to Tom Ellis 18 July 1939; Dr Stanley Haydock to Tom Ellis 24 July 1939.

94 QRC 26 June 1940. That is those evicted who were not 'practising Jews' three hundred of whom were allocated to the MJRC.

95 Ibid.

96 QRC 31 July, 27 August, 24 September 1940.

97 QRC 31 July 1940.

98 Taped interview of Hilde Brooker (née Rujder) by Bill Williams and Anne Priest (hereafter Hilde Brooker interview).

99 Letter from Ruth Duckworth (née Windmuller) to Anne Priest, 19 March 2004.

100 QRC 24 September, 26 October 1940.

101 Hilde Brooker interview.

102 Letter to Anne Priest, 19 March 2004.

103 MG 24 March 1941. In April 1941 he was doing well enough to offer his 'surplus profits' to the QRC, an offer refused on the grounds that he might better use it for the upkeep of his child (QRC 29 April 1941).

104 MCN 20 June 1941, 18 and 31 July, 20 August 1942.

105 Autobiographical notes in the catalogue of an exhibition of ceramics by Ruth Duckworth (née Windmuller) in the Gallery of American Ceramics, Evanson, Illinois. The exhibition included a puppet head carved by Ruth. The Madison Road hostel closed in the autumn of 1943.

106 The information in this paragraph is taken from replies in QHJ.

9

'Our remaining comrades in Czechoslovakia': the Manchester branch of the KPD

In taking responsibility for refugees from Czechoslovakia, the Quakers were brought into contact with political refugees, Communists and Social Democrats, brought to Britain by the Czech Refugee Trust Fund. Some of them were experienced members of the German KPD who, following the emergence of the Nazi regime, had taken refuge in Prague, from where, at least at first, they had cherished the hope of building an anti-Nazi existence in Germany. Some had been sent on what turned out to be unproductive missions to Germany for just this purpose. Arriving in Britain in 1938, their ideological solidarity, their continuing sense of party loyalty and their well-honed political skills enabled them to re-group and to work for the rescue of their comrades still trapped in Czechoslovakia. One such group of KPD members, helped by the Quakers, found its way to Manchester, where it sought to make contacts and to create accommodation which might provide their comrades with a means of escape. In doing so, they concealed their Communist identities in the hope of enlisting the support of the Quakers and of influential Manchester liberals. While many individuals who had found refuge in Manchester worked to achieve the escape of their relatives and friends, this was a unique example in Manchester of an organised effort by refugees to secure the escape of their fellow victims.

The origins of a Manchester branch of the KPD may be traced to the arrival in London in mid-November 1938, under the auspices of the British Committee for Refugees from Czechoslovakia (BCRC), the precursor of the Czech Refugee Trust Fund, of a body of young Communist refugees who were housed for the first few nights of their stay in Britain in a youth hostel in Highgate. On the morning after their arrival they made a pilgrimage to Marx's grave in Highgate Cemetery, where one of them 'said a few commemorative words' and all of them 'vowed to carry on working for the cause in the spirit of our great teacher'.[1] Already, they had been 'entrusted by the party in Prague' with 'tasks', of which the first was to seek 'a right of asylum for their remaining comrades in Czechoslovakia'.[2] During a stay of one month in London, the men in a BCRC hostel in Putney, the women in private homes, they experienced the sympathetic reception accorded to most refugees from Czechoslovakia by sections of the English public still shocked by the Munich 'betrayal': in preparation for their mission, they readily acquired a wide circle of friends, 'among them many comrades', 'learnt to move with ease among English people of different social classes', mastered the rudiments of English and developed a measured contempt for the 'Pickwickian' men and avaricious women of the English middle-class.[3]

On 19 December 1939, eight of the group – Adolf Buchholz, Alexander Starck and his wife, Johanna, Walter and Lola Struewe, Ernst Hoffmann, Richard Rothe and Bruno Retzlaff-Kresse (otherwise Walter Kresse) – were moved on, for reasons which probably had more to do with BCRC logistics than with politics, to Manchester, where the committee had made arrangements for their reception and support by the Manchester and District Refugee Committee of the Society of Friends (QRC).[4] Apart from Hoffmann, who was a student youth leader, and, at twenty-six, the youngest of the group, they were ordinary German working men and women aged between twenty-eight (Walter Kresse) and thirty-nine (Rothe). Kresse, who from his exile in Prague had acted as a regular cross-frontier courier to Germany, was a clerk, Alex Starck a carpenter, his wife a typist, Walter Struewe a bricklayer, Rothe a plasterer.[5] Johanna Starck was found accommodation with a private family in Manchester, the men in the Lamb Guildhouse, a palatial, Victorian-Gothic mansion in Bowdon, a smart residential suburb in the Cheshire countryside, some nine miles to the south of Manchester, which had recently been converted into a residential centre for adult education,[6] and part of which the Quakers had acquired for temporary use as a refugee hostel. In Bowdon the men were immediately drawn into what they came to see as the typical weekend schools of an English residential college, with their combination of dances, singing, party games and 'harmless' lectures from which current political topics were entirely absent. Their offer of a talk on the anti-Fascist struggle, in which it was their object to touch upon the 'moral duty' imposed on Britain by the Munich Agreement and the urgency of rescuing their comrades, was turned down diplomatically by the Guildhouse's founder and director, Professor R.D. Waller, head of the Extra-Mural Department of Manchester University. Their one achievement was to 'unmask as a Nazi' a German guest lecturer who had come to Bowdon to speak on Dürer.[7]

Posing as Social Democrats, and taken as such by Waller,[8] they used their subsequent few months at the Guildhouse, apart from attending a course in English put on for them by the Quakers,[9] to 'enlist and mobilise' in their cause some of the middle-class men and women whom they met at organised events. These included Norman and Katherine ('Kay') Barnes, secondary school teachers living in Sale, a small town (in effect, a residential suburb) some four miles to the south of Manchester, who, while not party members, were found to be sympathetic to the Communist cause. In gathering support, perfecting their English, and gaining an acquaintance with the 'customs and manners' of the land, the Guildhouse proved to be 'an important station ... on our way to becoming politically active'.[10] In the meantime, one of the women, Lola Struewe, became a typist for the QRC at the Mount Street Meeting House of the Society of Friends, a position which enabled her to provide the group with 'inside information' and with a room for their (clandestine) meetings. There, in January 1939, the eight comrades elected the leaders of what now became formally the Manchester branch of a British-based KPD with its 'central leadership' in London.[11] With 'instructions' and other forms of support from the London headquarters, the branch set about making an impact on the Manchester scene. Concerned at what they saw as the 'half-legal' status accorded to German Communists in Britain, they concealed their party allegiance, parading as trade unionists and Social Democrats expelled for their anti-Fascist activities.

Their links with the CPGB and with other refugee Communists were equally covert. Friendly contact with Austrian Communists in Manchester was hindered by differing perceptions of the future of Austria, for while Austrian Communists strove single-mindedly for the revival of an independent nation, the KPD favoured a Greater Germany converted to Socialism. In the case of the CPGB, Ernst Hoffman was appointed by the branch to maintain permanent contact with Frank Bright, the District Organiser of the Party in Lancashire and Cheshire; Kresse with David Ainley, 'an untiring [CPGB] party worker', and then the northern advertising and distribution manager for the *Daily Worker*.[12]

There is no evidence that such links represented anything more than mutual affection and respect or that they provided the KPD branch with anything more than useful contacts in finding accommodation and seeking funds or the CPGB with anything more than a refugee attendance at its meetings.[13] There is no suggestion of joint meetings, still less of common strategies other than the pursuit of a British Popular Front. At the time of its first contacts with the KPD, the CPGB was preoccupied with an anti-war policy which would have been scarcely to the liking of its German comrades, and with the support of Spanish refugees during the closing days of the Civil War. Although some support had been given by individual party members to particular German and Austrian refugees, the party as a whole had taken no collective action on their behalf, perhaps because they were seen at the time, as well as it retrospect, as 'the more affluent victims of the Nazis',[14] this in spite of the fact that most refugees were Jewish and that the Manchester party had a strong Jewish constituency which included such leading figures as its secretary, Mick Jenkins, David Ainley, and the Manchester agent of the Left Book Club and then the manager of Collet's (radical) book shop in Manchester, Frank Allaun.

Kresse's contact, David Ainley was one of three brothers, all of whom became Communist Party activists, sons of a Lithuanian Jewish immigrant, Solomon Abrahamson, who had arrived in Manchester during the 1880s and there, in 1895, married a recent immigrant from Latvia.[15] While Abrahamson had found work as a skilled artisan in the local manufacture of walking sticks and umbrellas, his wife ran a tiny tobacco and newsagent's shop in Great Ancoats Street, at the heart of a working-class district chiefly inhabited by an Irish and Italian underclass, and where the first of the Ainley brothers was born. A member of the Bund in Russia, Abrahamson celebrated his Socialism in Manchester by naming his first child 'William Morris', or, having already anglicised his own surname, 'William *Maurice*', in deference to what he saw as a proper Englishness. Returning soon afterwards to his religious roots, and moving his family, for this reason, to St James Road, to the north of Hightown, in the Jewish Quarter, the two sons which followed became David and Benjamin. Finally, a conversion to Zionism decided the name of his next-born, Theodore Ainley. While it was, in fact, William Maurice Ainley who carried on the Zionist tradition, becoming, in time, a salaried Zionist official, David, Benjamin ('Ben') and Theodore ('Teddy') were active in the local Communist movement during the 1930s.

It seems that Ben had led the way. After attending the Manchester Jews School, learning Hebrew at his uncle's *cheder* on Rydal Mount, and experimenting with junior Zionism, Ben was one of a group of young secularised Jews, all children of Jewish immigrants from Eastern Europe, and most of them, like Ben, unemployed, who in 1919 began to meet informally at the Ainley home to debate political issues. Calling themselves 'The Pioneers', they were, in fact, in the vanguard of young Jews, born and brought up in Manchester, who had begun to reflect critically upon the social and economic circumstances which were defining the prospects of immigrant Jewish families. Failing to elicit what they saw as meaningful answers from the community's lay or religious leaders, already, towards the end of the war, they had begun to make contact with such non-Jewish radical organisations as the No Conscription Fellowship, the County Forum and the ILP. Gradually driven politically leftwards by their own discussions, which came to centre on Socialist publications, and by such local Jewish Socialists as Moses Baritz of the Socialist Party of Great Britain and, Leon Locker, a Clarion Club activist and a key figure in the local formation of the Labour Zionist movement, Poalei Zion, by 1921 the 'Pioneers' had begun to consider the Communist option. During 1922–23 most, including Ben, David and Teddy Ainley, became founder members of the YCL branch then being set up in Cheetham Hill, a branch which, with the rise of fascism, became dominated by its working-class Jewish members.[16] By the mid-1930s the Ainley brothers had become leading intellectuals within the Manchester branch of the CPGB. Teddy was responsible for giving final shape to the branch's 'social programme', published in 1937 as a pamphlet, *This Our City: A Programme for a Modern Manchester*.[17]

It was probably in his capacity as secretary of the Manchester Area Committee of the CPGB, to which post he had been elected in 1939, that David was put into contact with the KPD.[18] He was, according to Kresse, 'extraordinarily kind and helpful ... Amongst other things, he provided me with valuable connections in the suburbs of Northenden and Wythenshawe.'[19] More informal KPD links were established with 'an ever growing circle of comrades of the brother party'.[20] 'Regular discussions' held with refugee Austrian and Czech Communists also active in the Manchester area, for 'standardising our activities' and the planning of common action, are said to have 'borne great fruit'. 'Though there were at time differences of opinion about tactical matters', according to Kresse, 'they were never serious enough to spoil the harmony'.[21] It seems clear that the small KPD elite (the Manchester branch, cautious in its recruitment, never numbered more than forty members) already saw itself as spearheading a Communist mission within the refugee community and as maintaining a degree of control over refugee Communist activity.

It was a tightly-knit group, 'rigid' in its structure and thinking in the eyes of one observer,[22] in which members were expected to toe the party line without reservation, and which, judging from its treatment of the young Berliner, Hugo Koeditz, had no time for dissent or nonconformity. Koeditz arrived in Manchester in October 1939 from Berlin, where after April 1933 he had undertaken underground work for the banned KPD, including service as a courier between the underground party in Germany and its comrades in Prague. In 1934 his KPD cell was raided by the Gestapo and Koeditz imprisoned and tortured. What appears to have then raised the suspicions of his comrades was his subsequent acquittal by a German court on a charge of High Treason, and, less probably, the relationship which he then formed with a young woman deemed by the party to have Nazi sympathies. In the eyes of the KPD inner circle in Manchester, these misdemeanours were compounded by Koeditz's reluctance to accept the authority and direction of the party, and perhaps by maverick behaviour which was seen to include a dangerously disreputable sexual promiscuity. At all events, in Manchester he was ostracised by his former comrades, who were believed by his then girlfriend, Hanna Siederer, to have subsequently poisoned his relationship with the Home Office, the University, the Czech Trust Fund and local refugee organisations, and to have withheld the references to his ant-Fascist credentials which might have secured him an early release from internment.[23]

What the small Manchester branch described as its 'mass political work' was aimed at 'supporting the anti-Fascist struggle in Germany', winning over German refugees in the region to the Communist cause and securing the friendship, sponsorship and patronage of influential personalities from the British labour movement and 'the progressive middle classes' who might aid their quest for accommodation for those who remained in Czechoslovakia.[24] The threat of a war against Fascism brought to what was clearly an anti-Fascist organisation the support of individuals from all three British political parties, from the local 'intelligentsia' and from 'various Church associations', none of whom were allowed to suspect its true political objectives. Members of the branch, their party credentials again concealed, accepted invitations from unsuspecting sympathisers to speak on anti-Fascist themes to local organisations. In February 1939 Bruno Kresse and Ernst Hoffmann received invitations from the elderly Methodist lay preacher, W.H.B. Wharmby[25] to speak at the Reform Club, the Liberal Party's headquarters in Spring Gardens, and at the Manchester Rotary Club, of which Wharmby was a prominent member.[26] They used the opportunities in this 'entirely alien world', according to Kresse, 'to bring our problems to a circle of influential personalities and, if possible, to win some over as friends, which we succeeded in doing'. From Wharmby, a man who 'radiated dignity and human warmth' (he reminded Kresse of Albert Einstein), they evoked, as the uncomplicated 'German anti-Fascist refugees' he took them to be, 'true friendship', 'great interest', useful advice and further contacts. He was persuaded to send letters to the press on their behalf, drawing attention to refugees still at risk in Czechoslovakia. At the start of their meeting at the Reform Club, short biographies were read out. 'What might have happened', Kresse comments, 'had they been complete ones?' Wharmby spoke up for them as 'marvellous chaps', well worthy of support.[27]

'Deceit' is perhaps the wrong word to apply either to the KPD activists or their British friends. On the KPD's part, the courtship of liberal Manchester was consistent with their pursuit of a Popular Front. On the liberal side, a middle-class professional and devout Methodist like Wharmby might well have been 'duped' into lending his support to militant atheists seeking a Dictatorship of the Proletariat. But in the circumstances, for Wharmby as much as the KPD, the priority was the defeat of Nazism and the support of its victims. An estimate of the extent to which native liberals colluded in their own deception is now beyond reach. Through reputable sponsors acquired at such prestigious meetings, members of the branch obtained engagements to speak to 'groups and clubs of the Labour Party, unions and co-operatives, the Left Book Club, Conservative and Liberal Clubs, the International Club, Church clubs, youth and student clubs, wealthy clubs and poor clubs, refugee hostels and local companies'.[28]

Another element of the Manchester KPD's self-proclaimed 'mass operation among English people' was the creation of sympathetic 'local refugee committees' outside the tightly controlled orbit of the main Quaker and the Jewish organisations. This was part of the branch's 'rescue operations': the creation, with the help of the Czech Refugee Trust Fund (CRTF), of hostels based on local support would perhaps counter the British government's argument that insufficient accommodation and resources existed for further refugees. They would also provide the KPD with malleable groups of English people; it would have a 'more direct influence' on local committees than would have been possible under the direct auspices of the Quakers or the MJRC. Hostels operating under such influence would guarantee for their residents the 'greater freedom of movement essential for carrying out our political tasks'.[29] Although it was never formulated publicly in these terms, local committees would make possible the creation of what were, in effect, KPD cells.

The 'first and largest' local committee was put together in Sale, where a number of German refugees had apparently already settled in private homes,[30] from amongst the circle of friends of Norman and Kay Barnes, the teachers whom the KPD activists had first met at the Lamb Guildhouse. All in their late 1920s or early 1930s, they included the CPGB activists George McKenzie, Bill Maher and Harold and Frances Teel, all members, like the

Barnes, of the lively local branch of the Left Book Club. Seeing the club as 'a favourable starting point for exerting political influence' and given an introduction to the club by Norman Barnes, Kresse then used it, as an 'honorary member', to create a local committee. Fate favoured him. At one of the club's fortnightly meetings, which by chance coincided with the Nazi occupation of Prague (15 March 1939), Kresse seized the opportunity to speak with passion and at length on the 'immediate danger' faced by anti-Fascists from the new regime, and the urgency of their escape. 'The best way they could help,' he told the meeting, 'was to create conditions locally which would guarantee some of the [potential] refugees secure temporary accommodation and means of survival'. He then made 'the concrete suggestion that steps be undertaken to form a local [Sale] committee, whose immediate task would be the creation of a home for refugees'. His suggestion, he remembers, 'found overwhelming approval' and at the same meeting a working party was set up, of which Kresse became a member, to take the idea forward. The secretary of what became the Manchester and District Committee for Refugees from Czechoslovakia (MCRC) was Norman Barnes, its chairman Alfred Stone, a man in his early forties, a Labour Party supporter, a member of the Peace Pledge Union and the Fellowship of Reconciliation, and by profession a sales manager with the Renold and Coventry Chain Company. Although disabled, and already active on other committees, Stone devoted himself to the work of the committee, Kresse recalls, 'with astonishing energy and without ever allowing his interest to wane'.[31]

It was necessary also to maintain a link with the Quakers, who were still responsible for the accommodation of those brought to Britain by the CRTF. William Sparkes, a member of the QRC, was co-opted onto the MCRC as its treasurer, with a brief from the Quakers to report back to Mount Street.[32] Winifred Garnett, a 'born Quaker', and a founder member of the QRC, gave a talk at Field's Café in May 1939 to the Sale branch of the WILPF, of which she was also a member, in support of the Sale hostel, stressing the necessity of the British government giving support to the entry of refugees.[33] The assumption must be that, apart from its own fund-raising efforts, the KPD expected the Quakers to foot the bill for the acquisition and maintenance of the hostel.

The people of Sale, left totally unaware of the political significance of the project that now evolved, reacted at once with sympathy and support. On 25 April, in Sale Town Hall, a public appeal was launched, which the Mayor of Sale agreed to chair, to which the Vicar of Sale and other local notabilities were persuaded to lend their names, and the stated object of which was 'the establishment of a refugee hostel in Sale'. Norman Barnes explained to an audience of around forty that 'in the last few weeks contact with refugees already in Manchester and district has brought to our notice what has been done in the way of hostels and hospitality elsewhere. It is felt that Sale should not be behind in forming an active committee to canalise the generosity and good will which certainly exists and awaits a lead.' The citizens of Sale were called upon to help either 'by offering hospitality in their own homes' or by 'contributing a small sum weekly towards the maintenance of a hostel'. An (unnamed) German refugee, almost certainly Kresse, after acknowledging the 'hospitality and humanity of the British people', told the meeting that though he and his friends 'had been lucky enough to reach England safely, they saw it as their obvious duty to do everything in their power to help rescue the many thousands of their friends – Czechs, Germans and Austrians – now endangered by Hitler's occupation of Czechoslovakia'. A second refugee then put the possible fears of Sale citizens to rest. 'All the refugees allowed to come to England,' he told the meeting, 'had passed rigorous tests' to prove that 'they were genuinely in danger and not Nazi agents. No fear need be felt … that there were spies among the refugees.' Alfred Stone then appealed 'to anyone who knew of a suitable building available rent free or at small cost, to bring it to the notice of the committee'.[34]

By the end of April, just such a house had been identified; by the beginning of May the first refugee residents had been installed.[35] This was a large and handsome double-fronted Victorian mansion called 'Sylvan House', set back in its own grounds off Broad Road, in a fashionable residential district a little over a mile from the centre of Sale:[36] a vacant property whose owners had for years tried in vain to let and which they were now ready to offer rent-free, if only to save it from further decay. Fund-raising for its support then became intense. In an 'Open Letter' published by the *Sale and Stretford Guardian* on 9 June the Mayor called for regular weekly contributions towards rent, rates and other necessaries for the support of 'these unfortunate victims of upheaval in Europe'. Collecting cards were available 'to anyone willing to contribute or to collect'. The period from 10 to 17 June was declared a 'refugee week', advertised by posters in shops and slides in local cinemas, and marked by public street collections. It would begin with a 'Pound Day' at the hostel, on which people were asked to donate either one pound in cash or a stock of groceries to that value. The Mayor was at pains to soothe the understandable anxieties of his citizens. 'To those who feel that unemployment in England precludes any such effort,' he wrote, 'I wish to make clear that we are anxious to further every means of helping the unemployed.' It was his belief, however, that refugees were not only bringing benefits to the nation's industry, but that their presence locally would 'generate an understanding of races and other mentalities [*sic*]' which would 'be of incalculable benefit to ourselves'. Later that month, the creation of a 'mile of pennies', introduced by a small brass band, raised £212 in less than an hour;[37] a whist drive was organised, for which the Mayoress provided the prizes;[38] in mid-July a garden party opened by the headmaster of Haslingden Senior School, and which included a dancing display by Sale Rangers, a local 'character-reader' and 'turns' by the refugee themselves, was attended by ninety people and raised a further £25.[39]

Refugees,[40] most arriving with the help of the CRTF, moved into what Kresse saw as 'the nicest refugee home in the whole of Britain' and 'ideal for extensive mass political activity among the inhabitants of Sale and Manchester'. There was spacious sleeping accommodation for up to forty people,[41] including married couples; a large room on the ground floor which could hold an audience of up to eighty; games rooms; two comfortable day rooms; and a library with hundreds of books, although Kresse noted with regret that the group's own 'Marxist-Leninist texts and obvious party literature' had to be 'hidden away'.[42]

In the months which followed, Sylvan House, under the management of Franz Rennhak, a thirty-five year-old refugee from Pomerania, probably now co-opted into the KPD elite,[43] became the venue for garden parties, film and slide shows, table tennis competitions, song evenings and events to mark such special occasions as what Kresse describes as 'political weddings'. The first of these was his own. On 10 June 1939, after seven months' delay as she evaded arrest by the Gestapo and sought a means to enter Britain, Kresse's Slovak fiancée, Fanny, arrived in Manchester under the sponsorship of the Czech Trust Fund. Although the couple had, in fact, lived together for many years, and were happy to continue to do so, the KDP leadership in Manchester now decided that to please Kresse's English friends, who had looked forward to the marriage of a couple romantically reunited, and so to consolidate the political support which Kresse had built up in Northenden, where, with David Ainley's help, he had been found rented accommodation, that an Anglican marriage ceremony in Northenden Church should be followed by a 'big wedding party' in Sylvan House. And so the wedding ceremony of two KPD comrades, 'using false names', on 21 January 1939, in a church packed with Kresse's English friends and German comrades, was followed three days later by a celebration at Sylvan House attended by some 150–200 people. Kresse judged that a marriage which, for the KPD leadership, had become 'a party matter', and behind which 'the whole party mechanism' had been mobilised, had, in fact, advanced the KPD's political work, 'particularly amongst English people'.[44]

Although the 'precarious' position of the KPD in Britain made it unwise for the KPD to mount openly political events at Sylvan House, the attraction to the house of many English guests (Sylvan House became, in Kresse's words, 'a social centre in Sale'), as well as Jewish and other political refugees, provided the KDP with ample opportunities for a more informal promotion of its anti-Fascist cause. Behind the scenes, there were 'regular party meetings and training courses'.[45]

The immediate and spectacular success of the Sale venture encouraged the KPD to look further afield. One promising target was Salford, where the local Communist Party was particularly strong, which was the home of their 'English friend and comrade', the 'technical chemist' Harold Teel, and where considerable public sympathy for Czech refugees had been evoked by the visit of a Czech free church minister, Revd Joseph Stifter. In January 1939 Stifter, then on a 21-day visit to Britain from Prague, had urged upon a large audience at the Westwood Methodist Church in the Irlams o' th' Height district of Salford, the urgent need of Czech refugees of help from 'foreign friends'.[46]

Early in the spring of 1939, supposedly 'after meeting several refugees at the Manchester International Club',[47] but also at the request of the KPD, Teel put together a Salford Committee for Refugees from Czechoslovakia (SCRC), which first sought out private hospitality and, when this failed, collected funds which, with further help from the CRTF (and presumably the Quakers), would make possible the creation of a refugee hostel.[48] In May 1939 Teel put out a further appeal for furniture for a substantial terraced house in Barfield Road, in Irlams o' th' Heights, which the committee had rented as a hostel for ten men, and to help clothe those who 'had nothing more than the clothing they stand up in'.[49] The local press, unaware of the KPD's existence, let alone its plans for Salford, saw the committee as a group of ordinary citizens: apart from Teel, who served as its secretary, it included two housewives, a school teacher, a joiner, a telephone operator and a stenographer.[50]

The reporter was not to know that the 'German refugee' staying in Irlams o' th' Heights as the guest of Teel at his house in Denstone Road, and 'helping to prepare the hostel', was in fact, Alex Starck, the comrade in charge of 'political education' in the KPD branch, perhaps its leading ideologue and the man regarded by Kresse as the 'founder' of the Salford hostel.[51] He was more impressed by the privations suffered by the refugees in reaching Britain – one couple from Saxony was said to have walked 400 miles from Prague to Poland to make their escape – by the courage of the committee in taking responsibility for the rent, coal and lighting, and by the help being given to the project by the community at large: pupils from Pendleton High School were said to have provided the curtaining and to have helped clean the house.[52] The expectation was that, once installed, the refugees would form a committee to run the hostel themselves, with its own elected chairman, 'a method [it was said] already adopted in Manchester', presumably in Sale, with each member of the committee reaching out for regular monthly contributions from the people and organisations of the area.[53] During the last week in May ten refugees, eight of them Germans, one an Austrian and one stateless, and including two women, took up residence in the hostel, where they elected as their chairman Friedrich ('Fritz') Wetzel, a journalist and another KPD member who had suffered imprisonment in Germany.[54] By the autumn, their numbers had increased to fifteen.[55]

Like Sylvan House, the Salford Hostel became both a venue for 'many events' and a means of 'winning over a few influential personalities'. At the end of May a meeting in support of the hostel was held at the Bolton Road Methodist School in Salford, at which two local Methodist ministers and the Vicar of St John's were present, and which was addressed by Charles Royle, the prospective Labour candidate for the Salford West constituency, and Arthur D. Worsley, president of the West Salford Liberal Association and secretary of the Lancashire, Cheshire and North Western Liberal Federation. In dealing with a question from the audience on whether refugees took employment from British people, both spoke up for the refugees. 'Some of the most prominent people in the world, and some of the best brains in the world', according to Royle, 'were amongst the refugees who had come to Britain'. Far from displacing British workers, Worsley declared, 'capital brought by refugees had started new factories in this country and refugee brains had helped to extend English businesses'. Those who would keep refugees out 'were displaying a spirit of niggardliness and parsimony'. The meeting ended with a group of refugees singing 'a concentration camp song'.[56] Another notability identified by Kresse as having been drawn in to support the Salford project was the prominent barrister, Unitarian lay preacher, former Liberal MP and Liberal Party activist, P.M. Oliver. Oliver became, in Kresse's words, 'a true friend to us', although probably without ever knowing the true nature of the project he had chosen to support. In June 1939 'refugees from Nazi Germany' were amongst the guests at a garden party in Kersal organised by the North Salford, West Salford and Middleton and Prestwich Liberal Associations, presided over by Oliver and addressed by Helen Simpson, the prospective Liberal candidate for the Isle of Wight.[57]

The refugees themselves did what they could to create a good impression. A garden party in the grounds of St Augustine's Vicarage in Pendlebury in late July, organised by the SCRC to raise funds for the hostel, included sketches performed by the refugees, several of whom later 'formed themselves into a band' and played at a social attended by a hundred local people at St Augustine's Senior School.[58] Religion or no religion, they attended Harvest Festival services at the Westwood Methodist Church and volunteered for local formations of the Air Raid Precautions (ARP).[59] On 28 September, three weeks after the outbreak of war, they presented widely publicised and carefully crafted memorials to the Mayor and Chief Air Raid Warden of Salford 'offering their services', and incidentally highlighting the refusal of the British government to accord them an equal place in the war against Hitler.[60] 'English men and women,' they wrote, 'will readily feel our sorrow and shame that still loving our country as dearly as they love theirs we are denied a say in its destiny because we hold views forcibly suppressed by the Nazi Government … Therefore we German and Austrian political refugees from Czechoslovakia now living in Salford through the hospitality of the British people will gladly help with all our powers in the present struggle to end once and for all the tyranny that still threatens us. To this end we place ourselves at your disposal for any work in connection with Civil Defence and National Service and await your command.' Delegates from the hostel informed the Mayor that several of the refugees had training in 'special services' likely to be of particular use in Civil Defence: two were trained in First Aid, two were motorcyclists, one was trained in decontamination work, one in fire drill, one, who had spent two and a half years with the International Brigades in Spain, was a 'motor driver'.[61]

While no doubt such offers were sincere, symbolising the KPD's commitment to Britain's war against Fascism, their publication may also be seen as a means, almost certainly orchestrated by the KPD, of heading-off popular anti-refugee and anti-German sentiment, and perhaps of forestalling government concern over the loyalty of German and Austrian refugees as war with their home countries began and they were transformed overnight into 'enemy aliens'.

Notes

1 Kresse, *Illegalitat, Kerker, Exil*, p. 212.
2 *Ibid.*, p. 213.
3 *Ibid.*, pp. 213–217.
4 QRC 15 December 1939. Expenditure was authorised to share with the Czech Refugee Trust Fund the cost of housing of 'six Czechs' [*sic*].
5 Entries under Kresse, Stark [*sic*], Struwe [*sic*], and Rothe in the QL. Of the five on the QL, Kresse is described as a Protestant, Struewe as a Roman Catholic, Rothe and the Starcks as having no religion. Only two birthplaces are recorded: that of Walter Struewe, in Bielefeld, that of Hoffmann, in Elberfeld.
6 The story of its creation is told in R.D. Waller, *Residential College: Origins of the Lamb Guildhouse and Holly Royde* (Manchester 1954), pp. 1–17. A residential college for adult education with 'an element of cherry activity' and a 'greater regard for the beautiful' than was evident in the WEA's weekend residential schools was the idea of R.D. Waller, a lecturer in English, who was appointed Director of Extra-Mural Studies at Manchester University in 1937. He made use of the offer from Bowdon Council of a mansion recently donated to it by Samuel Lamb, a prominent local Liberal. 'A museum of elaborate late Victorian craftsmanship', according to Waller, the Lamb Guildhouse was formally opened as a college on 25 June 1938. A series of weekend schools began at once, some with such distinguished visitors as Cecil Day Lewis. When, in the late autumn of 1939, the mansion was taken over as a home for expectant mothers, the college moved to another house in The Firs, Bowdon, loaned by one of its supporters. There it remained until 1944, when it moved into its final resting place, Holly Royde, a mansion at 30 Palatine Road, once the home of the cotton merchant Gustave Behrens and his wife, Fanny, and donated to the University by their son, Frederick. Holly Royde was formally opened on 24 January 1945. In the autumn of 1943, while retaining his position at the University, Waller became secretary of the Manchester Regional Committee for Education in the Forces, which provided courses for British and allied troops, and chairman of the North Western District of the WEA. For reasons unknown, his hope for the post-war reconstruction of the Lamb Guildhouse as a 'People's College' came to nothing (MG 28 September and 16 October 1943. 26 June and 2 July 1944).
7 Kresse, *Illegalitat, Kerker, Exil*, pp. 217–220. He was said to have been a lecturer at the University.
8 To Waller (*Residential College*, p. 13) they were 'German social democrats who had had to leave Prague in a hurry and were being assisted by the Society of Friends'. Such deception was common enough amongst refugee Communists, German and Austrian, in part 'to avoid possible difficulties with the British authorities', especially during the years of the Nazi-Soviet Pact (September 1939–June 1941); in part so as not to alienate non-Communist refugees who might otherwise have been attracted to the organisations they created; in part to strengthen their hand in negotiations with the government. Eva Kolmer, secretary of the Austria Centre in London and a member of the unofficial KPO National Executive in Britain, described herself as a 'radical socialist'. (Charmian Brinson, 'Eva Kolmer and the Austrian Emigration in

Britain 1938–46', in Anthony Grenville, *German-speaking Exiles in Britain: Year Book of the Research Centre for German and Austrian Exile Studies,* Vol. 2 (2000), pp. 146–151).

9   QRC 3 January 1940: English classes to be started for four [*sic*] German refugees at the Lamb Guildhouse.

10   Kresse, *Illegalität, Kerker, Exil,* pp. 221–223.

11   *Ibid.,* p. 226. The London leadership is said by Kresse to have included KPD members whose prominence in Germany, some as members of the Reichstag, meant that their political allegiance could not be concealed in Britain. He names Wilhelm Koenen, Hugo Graf, Heinz H. Schmidt and Willi Barth.

12   *Ibid.,* p. 227.

13   Research into possible links is hindered by the loss (or possible destruction) of the records of the Manchester and Salford Communist Party. A possible go-between was Lou Baruch, the child of a German-Jewish refugee couple from Hamburg who settled in Liverpool shortly before the rise of Hitler and who moved to Manchester in 1940 when Merseyside was declared out of bounds to aliens. By this time Lou, a machinist by trade, had joined the CPGB and met and married Hilda Froom, the daughter of a Liverpool Communist tram-driver and secretary first of the Liverpool YCL and then of the North West YCL, with its headquarters in Manchester. In 1942, following his release from internment, Lou and Hilda went to live with the Manchester Communist, Alice Bates, in her house in Chorlton-cum-Hardy. There Alice remembers him having meetings with 'German comrades', from which she was excluded. (Author interview with Alice Bates, 2005. Hereafter Alice Bates interview.)

14   Jim Arnison, *Hilda's War* (Lancashire Community Press, Preston, 1996), p. 4.

15   This and the following paragraph are based on a taped interview by the author with Ben Ainley in March 1976 (MJM Tape M15, hereafter Ben Ainley interview) and notes on interviews with Ben Ainley (1968) and David Ainley (1978) by Edmund Frow, now in the Working Class Movement Library. See also Mick Jenkins' typewritten autobiography, 'Prelude to Better Days' n.d., n.p.

16   Cf. Sharon Gewirtz, 'Anti-Fascist Activity in Manchester's Jewish Community', in the *Manchester Regional History Review,* Vol. 4, No. 1, Spring/Summer 1990, pp. 17–27. Those named in the Williams and Frow interviews as members of the Pioneers who joined the YCL branch were Gabriel Cohen, Joe Cohen, Hymie Lee, Johnny Rosenbloom, and (un-named) young men from the Dublansky, Bulchansky and Schlosberg families,

17   Mick Jenkins, *George Brown – Portrait of a Communist Leader* (Manchester 1937), pp. 18 and 22.

18   Notes of an interview of David Ainley (1978) by Edmund Frow.

19   Kresse, *Illegalität, Kerker, Exil,* p. 227.

20   *Ibid.*

21   *Ibid.*

22   Behrend,'Autobiography' typescript, Chapter One, pp. 45–46.

23   *Ibid.,* Chapter One, pp. 22, 24, 26, 40–48, 61–62. This reading of the KPD's motives is based on Behrend's interpretation of its responses to Koeditz which, in the last resort, and in spite of questioning hi m and her close contacts with KPD members in Manchester, she was unable to fully understand. Following his return to Germany in 1945, Koeditz continued to be treated with mistrust by the party, being finally struck off its membership list in 1951 (*ibid.,* p. 40).

24   Kresse, *Illegalität, Kerker, Exil,* p. 228.

25   For Wharmby and the Rotarian Hostel see p. 322.

26   Bulletin of the Rotary Club of Manchester 7 September 1939. In his talk, Hoffmann

spoke of the appreciation of refugees of 'what was being done for them' and of his admiration for 'the spirit of freedom so much in evidence here'.

27 Kresse, *Illegalitat, Kerker, Exil*, pp. 229–230.

28 *Ibid.*, p. 231.

29 *Ibid.*, p. 232.

30 Kresse (*ibid.*, p. 235) notes the presence of 'refugees from Berlin now resident in Sale' at the public meeting in Sale Town Hall in April 1939.

31 *Ibid.*, pp. 232–234; MG 2 and 24 October 1940; Cowan Papers, Minutes of a meeting of the Wilmslow PPU 5 November 1939: Stone, who had 'spent all his spare time exerting himself on behalf of the peace movement for many years', had been secretary of the Manchester branch of the Fellowship of Reconciliation. One of the few surviving references to the Manchester and District Committee for Refugees from Czechoslovakia is a letter from Alfred Stone, as its chairman, to MG 3 August 1942.

32 QRC 4 April, 6 June 1939.

33 SSG 5 May 1939.

34 Kresse, *Illegalitat, Kerker, Exil*, pp. 235–236; *Sale and Stretford Guardian* (hereafter SSG), 28 April 1939.

35 SSG 9 June 1939.

36 The house still exists, still in excellent condition, although now converted into flats, close to the junction of Temple Road with Broad Road, in what remains an attractive residential district.

37 Kresse, *Illegalitat, Kerker, Exil*, p. 236.

38 SSG 30 June 1939.

39 SSG 14 July 1939.

40 Refugees who are remembered as having stayed at Sylvan House include Oscar Bunemann, a refugee from Hamburg who had arrived in Manchester in October 1935, after eighteen months' imprisonment by the Nazis, to study mathematics at the University of Manchester, who achieved a first class degree and who in 1939 was involved in scientific research at the University towards a Ph.D. which he was awarded in June 1940 (QL Supplement, Oscar Bunemann; MCN 3 October 1941); Joseph Thiele, a German engine stoker from Westphalia, who had received his Communist education in Russia; a German 'orthopaedic shoemaker' and chiropodist, possibly of Hungarian origin, called Geza Papp, and his wife; a German lawyer and his wife with the surname Rechtandvald; and another German known as Walter Zionz (all remembered by Reg Holmes, who visited the hostel as a friend of Bunemann: interview of Holmes by Bill Williams in November 2001 – hereafter Reg Holmes interview); Thiele and Papp appear on the QL, Thiele as a Roman Catholic who in 1939 had left two children in Germany). In a birthday book in the Leonard Behrens Collection, the date of Oscar Bunemann's birth is given as 1913; in September 1941, by which time he was said to be 'doing important research work for the country', he became engaged to Behrens' eldest daughter, Mary Frances (MCN 3 October 1941). Renata Laxova (*Letter to Alexander* (Cincinnati 2001), p. 81), when living in Flixton, was visited by German and Czech refugees from 'a nearby hostel' which was almost certainly Sylvan House.

41 Letter from N.O. Barnes, Honorary Secretary of the Sale Refugee Committee, printed in the *Manchester Guardian* of 3 October 1940. In the latter Barnes states that forty men and women were then resident at the hostel.

42 Kresse, *Illegalitat, Kerker, Exil*, pp. 236–240.

43 On returning to Germany in 1945 Rennhak became BGL chairman at the State Broadcasting Committee in the DDR. Rennhak appears on the QL as having been

born in Pomerania in 1903.

44 Kresse, *Illegalitat, Kerker, Exil*, pp. 248–255. It was a marriage which was also to last for over forty years.
45 *Ibid.*, pp. 239–240.
46 SCR 20 January 1939. Stifter, a native of Bohemia, belonged to the Bohemian branch of the Czech Council of the Free Churches. In Britain, apart from appraising the British public of 'the present problems of his country', he was raising funds for the National Organisation for Non-Aryan Christian Refugees.
47 SCR 5 May 1939.
48 WCML Minutes of the Salford Central Labour Party EC 26 April 1939. Harold Teel of Pendleton is noted as suggesting a 'Salford Committee for Refugee Relief'. The response of the Salford party is not recorded.
49 *Ibid.* Teel himself was said to be providing private hospitality for 'a German refugee'.
50 *Ibid.* Other members whose names are recorded in SCR were J. Jones (chairman), a Liberal Party activist and financial secretary of the West Salford Liberal Association (SCR 2 July 1943), Mrs and Mrs Lea, Mr. J. Toft, Mr and Mrs H. Arthur, Misses E. and G. Dodd, Mrs Vernon Bramhall, Mrs Teel and Miss Monica Heywood
51 SCR 19 May 1939.
52 SCR 5 and 19 May 1939.
53 SCR 5 May 1939. The structure being suggested was not so much that 'already adopted in Manchester', where most refugee hostels were run by refugee support groups and their employees, as that devised by the KPD for its hostel in Sale.
54 The eight Germans are named in the Salford Aliens Register as Hans Kasemann (born in Thuringia), Kurt Dudek (born in Freiburg), Maria Golla, Otto Neitzel, Julius Margules, Friedrich Wetzel, Willi Golla and Paelegrimm Eberhard, the Austrian as Oskar Rosenstrauch (born in Tarnopol), the stateless person as Bela Tobinetz. Three, Dudek and the Gollas, had arrived from Prague, one, Kasermann, from Posnitz, one, Neitzel, from Mor Ostravr, one, Wetzel, from Kyjor, one from 'Czechoslovakia', the rest from Brunn (Brno). Nine are recorded as having 'no religion', Dudek as a Roman Catholic. Dudek is said to have left his wife and two sons in Saxony in July 1938 and to have received no news of them since (Centre for Jewish Studies Refugee Data Base, Salford Aliens Register for 49 Barfield Road). Further detail appears in the QL: in their homelands, Kasemann was a 'rubber worker', Wetzel a scientific instrument maker, Dudek a mental nurse, Neitzel a journalist, Eberhard a baker and confectioner, Rosenstrauch [*sic*] a woollen weaver.
55 SCR 29 September 1939.
56 SCR 1 June 1939.
57 SCR 7 July 1939.
58 SCR 28 July 1939. Sketches were also performed by refugees from the Quaker hostel on Palatine Road. For other local contacts SCR 15 August 1939.
59 SCR 22 September 1939.
60 SCR 29 September 1939, which reprints the memorial in full.
61 *Ibid.*

10

'Not because they are Jews': the Catholic Church in Salford and refugees

[The Quakers have] done golden deeds for the refugees here and the helpless victims of totalitarian brutality abroad ... But why, in heaven's name, do we time and again find these services of elementary good fellowship left only to the Quakers? Do no other religions feel any obligations ...? Or are they all so sanctimonious that they can't do a good turn without wanting to stuff a hymn or sermon down the recipient's throat in return?

From an article on the Manchester Quakers in the *Manchester City News*, 10 February 1940

As this report suggests, the Quakers were the only organised body of Christians in Manchester to take collective measures for the rescue of the victims of Nazism. Individuals of the Christian faith – Methodists, Congregationalists and Unitarians – were to be found in refugee support organisations and amongst the advocates of tolerance towards refugees, but the branches of Christianity to which they belonged engaged in no concerted action on the refugees' behalf. For some this may simply have been a matter of convenience in the absence of refugees of their own denominations in any number. For the Roman Catholic Church in the Salford Diocese, it was a matter of principle. Whatever the feelings of their congregants, the hierarchy of the Church in Salford was disinclined to put itself out in the rescue of refugees, particularly those of Jewish origin.

The response of the Roman Catholic Church to refugees was particularly shaped by the Church's response to the rise of Fascism. Belgian refugees from the German occupation of 1914, some 3,000 of whom are said to have been given help in Manchester, were received sympathetically by the Catholic hierarchy of Salford Diocese. Bishop Casartelli, himself the son of an Italian immigrant, appointed two priests to act as chaplains to the Belgian settlers, helped raise funds on their behalf, and served as one of the patrons of the Belgian Refugees Committee which raised a total of £21,000 for their support.[1] These Belgians, however, were the refugees from Britain's ally threatened by German violence in a pre-Fascist era.

When, in May 1937, the Roman Catholic Church in Britain had agreed to accommodate and support 1,500 of the 4,000 Basque refugees from Fascist violence who arrived in Britain during that month, it was not without some misgivings that it had felt impelled to go along with a decision in which it had played no part. The Church, after all, saw Franco as an ally. There was more than a little resentment that those who had brought the children into the country had not felt obliged to maintain them and that hard-pressed Catholic clergy had found themselves faced with onerous tasks not of their making. Canon George Craven, the Archbishop of Westminster's represent-ative on the Basque Children's Committee, and otherwise director of the Church's Crusade of Rescue, confided to Thomas Henshaw, the Catholic Bishop of Salford, that he 'had been absolutely overwhelmed by this Basque work that has been thrust upon us so suddenly and which I have had to do in addition to my ordinary work, in itself heavy enough. I have hardly had a minute at my desk, to do anything that is not directly connected with these children.'[2] In the Diocese of Salford, which received ninety of these chil-dren, Father William Sewell, secretary and chaplain to the local Catholic Protection and Rescue Society, was equally nonplussed by the expense which the support of Basque children had brought upon the Diocese.[3] The arrival of Basques added to the burden of his own work as Director of St Gerard's Catholic Remand Home in Denmark Road, Moss Side. All in all, in spite of the high level of support actually offered to the children by Catholic nuns, the Diocesan authorities had been put out by their arrival, irritated by their cost and anxious for their return to the bosom of their Catholic families in Franco's Spain.

Following this experience, the capacity of the Church authorities to en-gage supportively with refugees from Central Europe, most of them of Jewish origin, was further undermined, on the one hand, by a blinkered concern for its own faithful and institutions in Britain and Europe, and, on the other, by its negative perception of the Jewish people.

When, on 9 April 1933, Bishop Henshaw lent his support to a public meet-ing at the Free Trade Hall to protest against the persecution of German Jewry, his sympathy for the Jewish victims was tempered by 'the fact that no voice had been raised nor pen put to paper to protest against the very similar and worse persecution against our fellow-Catholics in Mexico, Spain and the Soviet Union'.[4] The failure of the press to address such matters', the Bishop went on, to report 'our own protest' or to offer anything but 'garbled' ac-counts of the facts left the non-Catholic public 'in ignorance of what was re-ally happening'. 'The flag of protest is instantly raised on behalf of the Jews, and in the spirit of sympathy with the Jew in England, for which we are en-tirely grateful. Cannot the same be done for the Catholics in Spain or for us in England? The point of the protest is persecution, not the persecuted. Why give it to one and withhold it from the other?' While he 'wholeheartedly as-sociated himself and the Diocese' with the protest, this was 'not particularly because they were Jews, but particularly because they were persecuted'.[5]

It might be argued that it was the priority it accorded to the safety of its own institutions which had led the Roman Catholic Church in Britain (and in Salford) into sympathy with Mussolini's revolution in Italy and with the Francoists during the Civil War in Spain, and which, but for Hitler's reneging on the Concordat, would have gained its backing for National Socialism. In *The Harvest,* the nearest Salford possessed to a monthly diocesan journal, overt anti-Semitism is rare and second-hand; what is much more obvious is the absence of references to the Jews from the periodical during the years of their persecution.[6]

They were, in fact, irrelevant to what the Church saw as its main theatre of operations in Europe: the battle against Bolshevism. From the perspective of the Church, in Salford as elsewhere, the crucial ideological conflict in the world of the 1930s was not between democracy and Fascism, but between Rome and Moscow; in the words of one Salford Catholic, between 'DEOcracy' and 'DEMONocracy'.[7] 'The world of the future' would have 'only two capitals, Moscow and Rome; only two temples, The Red Square of Russia and St. Peter's; only two tabernacles, The Kremlin and Emmanuel; only two hosts, the rotting body of Lenin and the Living Christ – but only one victor, for if Christ wins, we win, and if … Ah! But Christianity can't lose.'[8] To such a struggle the Jews were, at best, an irrelevance; at worst, the accomplices of Atheistic Communism. When, in July 1938, the Bishop of Salford initiated an investigation into the politics of a 'Manchester and District Youth Peace Council' to which the Diocese had been invited to send a representative, it was enough for one of his informants that the Council's affiliates contained a 'preponderance of Jewish names' for him to judge it to be 'too closely linked with Communism to be healthy'.[9]

Other references in *The Harvest* suggest a profound suspicion of the Jewish people. In February 1934 *The Harvest* reprinted 'An Open Letter to Mr. Samuel Untermeyer' which had first appeared in the American *Catholic Gazette.* In it, Donald MacLean, Professor of Social and Political Ethics at the Catholic University in Washington, posed a series of questions to Untermeyer around his attempt, through a World Jewish Economic Federation, to impose an economic boycott on Germany. Their overall effect is to cast doubt on Jewish perceptions of Nazi policy, to suggest Jewish indifference to 'the brutal and outrageous persecution' of Catholics and other Christians in Spain, Mexico and Russia, and to place Jews at the heart of a conspiracy 'inimical to Christian civilisation'. 'A considerable number of Jews' had been amongst the leaders of the German Communist Party suppressed by Hitler, while 'the Headquarters of Communist World Militant Atheism' was 'in the heart of the Berlin Jewish colony'.[10] In editorial comment on the Anschluss, *The Harvest* speaks of Austria having once been governed 'by a group of Jewish and Masonic Socialists'.[11]

How far such attitudes permeated the Catholic faithful is difficult to judge. It may well be that a gulf existed between an anti-Communist hierarchy and working-class Catholic Salfordians, many of them members of the Labour Party such as had in the 1920s distinguished Bishop Casartelli's anti-

Socialism from the more left-leaning inclinations of many of his flock.[12] That the Church, as an institution, did not reach out to political refugees of the 1930s is understandable enough. Apart from their support for the Basque children during 1937, individual Catholics, particular Catholic churches and priests, and such institutions as the Catholic Social Guild, which sought to study and promote the social teachings of the Church, showed no interest throughout the 1930s in either the plight of the Jewish people in Europe or in the needs of its refugee victims. The only organisation in the Diocese which took any interest in the Jews during the 1930s was the local branch of the Catholic Guild of Israel, a body founded nationally in 1917, in which 'Jewish Catholics and others' came together to promote Christ's teachings amongst the Jews, to pray for the conversion of Israel, to publish Christian literature in Yiddish and to organise public lectures.[13]

A problem for the organised Church, however, was that following the Anschluss, which brought the traditionally Catholic Austria under Nazi domination, the Aryan Laws would, by its own estimation, 'eventually effect over 100,000 Catholics [of Jewish origin] in Greater Germany'.[14] It was for this reason that Cardinal Hinsley, the Catholic Primate in Britain, called into being the Catholic Committee for Refugees from Germany 'to give immediate relief to sufferers, to work with the various relief organisations in this country and above all to co-operate with other Catholic committees abroad'. Like the Jewish Refugees Committee, it was to work within the framework of Home Office regulations. It was 'not primarily the purpose of this committee to bring refugees into this country', except temporarily to 'free places in Catholic schools' where refugees could be given 'that Catholic education which each day is becoming more impossible to obtain in Germany', or as trainees prior to their re-emigration. The 'main purpose' of the committee, it was announced, was 'to prepare and carry through a scheme of controlled Catholic emigration' to lands where, turning the 'German problem' to 'good account', they might 'spread the light of the Gospel'. Meantime British Catholics were invited to 'listen with particular sympathy' to appeals from Catholic refugees and to offer their 'interest, sympathy and concrete financial help' and Catholic business firms to provide openings for refugee trainees. The end result, however, was to offer the Catholic refugee, as the Jewish Refugees Committee had offered to its Jewish clients, 'a new life in a friendlier land' other than Great Britain.[15]

It was this appeal, coupled with the arrival in Britain of the first Kindertransport children in December 1938, which galvanised the Salford Catholic Protection and Rescue Society to revive an interest in refugees which had ended with the return of the Basque children.[16] In February 1939 Father Sewell announced in *The Harvest* that 'a large number of Refugees from Austria are arriving in this country; many of them are Catholics ... Those responsible for their stay here will be glad to hear of any Catholic families willing to give hospitality to these children'. The plan, he noted, was to place the children with individual families rather than in hostels or orphanages.[17] This was followed in Lent 1939 by a 'Declaration of the Hierarchy of England

and Wales' which called upon the Catholic faithful 'to give generously …
to support in the fullest possible way' the Earl Baldwin Fund, on which the
'Catholic body' was represented by Lord Tyrrell of Avon, and the income
from which would be 'apportioned among all the sufferers'. While Catholics
were called upon to support all refugees 'irrespective of their race and their
belief', their attention was drawn to the 'many thousands' of their fellow
Catholics affected by the Aryan Laws. 'It is our duty to do our utmost to assist
the victims of persecution seeking a temporary refuge in this country … To
follow the example of the Good Samaritan is our duty and our privilege.'[18]

In the absence of access to the personal records held by what is now the
Catholic Children's Rescue Society, it is difficult to assess the impact of these
appeals. No Catholic Refugee Committee emerged in Manchester or the
north-west, so that, in so far as the hierarchy's intentions were implemented
in the Salford Diocese, it was by Father Sewell and his Catholic Protection
and Rescue Society.[19] The Catholic hierarchy in Salford failed to launch, or
to back, any movement for the rescue of European Jewry. Although playing a
part, after 1941 on the executive of the RCM for Region 10, he appears to have
delegated the task of visiting the children of Catholic belief and Jewish origin
to the Committee's general body of (non-Catholic) paid and volunteer workers, provided only that their reports were sent to 'the Catholic Committee'.[20]
In other ways the welfare of such children appears to have been low in the
order of Sewell's wartime priorities. The Regional Committee experienced
some difficulty in persuading Sewell's committee to make adequate material
provision for the young refugee, Rolf Hertz, 'a movement [that is, a kinder-
transport] boy', whose mother, a domestic servant, had been reduced to
accepting low-paid part-time work. Its first response the regional secretary
found 'rude and unhelpful'.[21] Lack of evidence renders a more measured
judgement of the Catholic Church's role impossible: Rolf Hertz was one of
an unknown number of refugee children living in the north-west 'guaranteed' and found 'foster-parents' by the Catholic Committee.

Such evidence as exists in other sources suggests that the plan to provide
hospitality for Catholic refugee children with private families gave way to the
reality of their accommodation in some of those same Rescue Society homes
which had earlier housed the Basque children. The details of how this was
arranged, and for how many, as well as the religious identities of the children
are currently not available. Nor is there any record of adult refugees who
might have arrived in the Manchester region under Catholic auspices.

One of the Catholic homes involved by the Catholic Refugee Committee
in Westminster (probably through Sewell) in the rescue of German children
was Holly Mount Convent, a residential home for orphans and abandoned
children in Tottington, a country village near Bury in Lancashire. Set up in
1888 by Herbert Vaughan, Bishop of Salford, for girls of his diocese up to the
age of seventeen or eighteen, Holly Mount consisted by the early 1930s of a
complex of bleak, 'prison-like' buildings – a chapel, a school, separate dormitories, a laundry, an infirmary, a farm, a 'Rosary Hostel for Working Girls'
and miscellaneous outbuildings – under the charge of a Belgian Order, the

Sisters of Charity of Jesus and Mary, whose task it was to receive, support and educate children referred by parish priests and by local authorities to the Salford Diocese's Catholic Protection and Rescue Society. It was an all but self-sufficient rural community of fifteen nuns and 300 children 'from poor homes (or no homes at all)' which provided its charges with all they had by way of a home and a family.

The Home, according to an observer who visited it in July 1939, however gaunt, was 'pleasantly situated' on rising ground in a valley below Holcombe Hill; the Sisters, he thought, were 'charming people [who] show every kindness and sympathy to the children'. The children themselves, who in his view could not 'be called brilliant intellectually', appeared to him 'well and happy, neat and tidy'.[22] Only the wearing of uniforms and the existence of 'a definite [daily] routine' suggested an 'institutional atmosphere'.[23] This was probably the way the home was experienced by the children themselves. The memories of former residents of the 1920s and 1930s, collected by the husband of one of them,[24] suggest a regime that was strict rather than harsh, food that was 'spartan but sound', and nuns who, although one or two might occasionally appear 'cruel', insensitive and 'spiteful', and few offered 'love and real affection' in their surrogate mothering, provided a setting that most of the children came to appreciate as caring and protective: 'some we would come to love; others we would learn to fear'.[25] While denied luxuries, subject to corporal punishment, grouped in 'work squads', sleeping in crowded dormitories with bare polished floors, taught in classes of seventy or eighty, subjected to regular Swedish Drill, and tagged with numbers 'by which the nuns would always call [them]', the girls who were interviewed chiefly saw themselves as having lived 'in secure surroundings', as having been 'adequately clothed and fed' and as having received a 'good' elementary education.[26]

It was a 'cloistered existence'. Apart from occasional day-trips to New Brighton, Southport and Manchester's Belle Vue, and (for the well-behaved) a week in the summer at the convent's holiday home at Ansdell, between Lytham and St Annes, Holly Mount was the only world known to its inmates. It was a very Catholic world: the days began with morning mass, the day was punctuated with prayer, there were 'marches' on all the major Catholic festivals, a 'Lourdes Grotto' stood prominently in the grounds. Girls defined as 'deprived', were essentially steered, some for twelve or thirteen years, through a basic schooling up to the age of fourteen, and Day Continuation Classes for a further two years, into largely menial work as factory workers and domestic servants, when they had a right to reside for a further two years at the Rosary Hostel. In particular they provided another pool of housemaids, cooks, cleaners and companions for priests, for Catholic institutions and for the better-off families of suburban Manchester: for most, marriage was their only route of escape.[27]

Holly Mount represented the Salford Diocese's chief link with refugees of any variety. During the First World War it had 'sheltered and provided for' 440 Belgian refugees.[28] In 1937, it was one of several Lancashire Catholic institutions to offer refuge to children from the Basque theatre of the Spanish

Civil War. On 7 June 1939 it was the only Catholic institution in the diocese to receive a party of 'refugees of Jewish origin' sent, through Sewell, by the Catholic Refugee Committee of the Westminster Archdiocese: 'several children' according to Klaus Berentzen, who, at the age of ten, with his sister and younger brother, was among them.[29] In May 1940, after the German occupation of the Channel Islands, a group of 200 children from Guernsey became boarders at Holly Mount.[30]

A wide social gulf separated refugees, like the Berentzens, who were from 'stable and comfortable' middle-class German homes, 'very well-dressed and cared for', from the homeless working-class children of Holly Mount. Berentzen himself was 'amazed' at 'how often other youngsters sulked and misbehaved', attributing their conduct to the 'privations from which [they] had been delivered'. The Sisters, he felt, must have 'had a difficult time taking care of so many children coming from so many different backgrounds'. It is possible to read the recollections of his two years at Holly Mount[31] as evidence of the favour shown him, not so much as a refugee, but as an unusually orderly, well-educated, refined and diligent child. The nuns put themselves out to teach him English, allowed him to attend cookery lessons because he was 'too young to be taught woodwork', granted him a weekend's stay in Accrington with his cookery teacher, and selected him, probably out of turn, for the annual excursion to Ansdell.[32] The clothes his mother had packed for him 'were looked after with tremendous care' by one of the sisters.[33]

Apart from an unknown (but small) number of nominally Catholic child refugees assisted by Sewell, the Catholic Church left the support of Catholic refugees to the Society of Friends. So, apparently, did the Anglican Church and nonconformist congregations. It has been calculated that of the 2,500 refugees supported by the Manchester Society of Friends between 1938 and 1949, 30% were 'Protestants' and 24% Roman Catholic. In so far as it was necessary for the Manchester Quakers to make contact with other Christian bodies helping refugees, it was with their national headquarters in London. This was chiefly to resolve particularly knotty problems. When a decision was necessary on the religious fate of a young refugee whose family in Austria had been practising Catholics, whose mother had 'Jewish connections', who had become attracted to Quakerism, and both of whose parents had taken their own lives, negotiations were opened by the Manchester Friends with the Catholic Refugee Committee in London. The refugee's own preference ultimately carried the day, and he became a lifelong Quaker.

Notes

1   Martin John Broadley, *Louis Charles Casartelli: A Bishop in Peace and War* (Manchester 2006), pp. 149, 261.
2   SDA Marshall Papers. Un-indexed letter from Canon George Craven to the Bishop of Salford 27 May 1937. Craven was director of the Crusade of Rescue and Homes for Destitute Catholic Children.

3   SDA Marshall Papers. Annual Report of the Salford Catholic Protection and Rescue Society attached to an un-indexed letter from Nairne, Son and Green, accountants, to the society, 27 May 1937; *The Harvest*, Vol. L1, No. 1, January 1938, p. 18.

4   *The Harvest*, Vol. XLV1, No. 6, June 1933, pp. 173–174. The Bishop's speech was not reported by the *Manchester Guardian*. Nor did *The Harvest* have access to 'his actual words'; its report was based on the memory of one who had heard him.

5   *Ibid.* It is with this speech in mind that Nathan Laski's tribute to Henshaw following his death later in 1938 should be understood. According to Laski, Henshaw was 'a broadminded man … who stood very high as a champion of the oppressed and of those who are made to suffer for their faith and religious convictions'. One of his last appearances had been at a lunch in aid of the 'Jewish Women's Effort of the German Fund [the local effort for the CBF]', when he had spoken of his indignation at the treatment meted out to the Jews of Central and Eastern Europe (*The Harvest*, Vol. L1, No. 11, pp. 359–360).

6   The exclusive preoccupation is with the plight of the Catholic Church. A column on 'The New Germany' in November 1938 (*The Harvest*, Vol. L1, No. 11, November 1938, pp. 360–361) makes no reference to the Jews, and in the subsequent issue for Christmas 1938, while there is no reference to Kristallnacht, there is an account of a 'Red' air attack on civilians in Spain (*The Harvest*, Vol. L1, No. 12, p. 390). An account of 'Hitler's War' in November 1939, focuses on the ideologies of Germany and Russia and again makes no reference to the Jews (*The Harvest*, Vol. L11, No. 11, November 1939, p. 335). In the issues of 1942–43 there are no references to the growing evidence of Nazi genocide.

7   SDA Henshaw Papers 205/163: 'DEOcracy versus DEMONocracy', in the Programme of the Catholic Annual Procession (of Salford Diocese) for 1937, pp. 3–11.

8   *Ibid.*

9   SDA Marshall Papers 204/235–236. Letter from Captain T.W.C. Curd of London attached to a letter from the News Editor of the *Universe* (a Catholic weekly newspaper) to the Bishop of Salford 20 July 1938. A further example is 204/246 Letter from M. Rebitt to Father James Fallon, July 1938.

10 *The Harvest*, Vol. XLV11, No. 2, February 1934, pp. 51–53.

11 *The Harvest*, Vol. L1, No. 4, April 1938.

12 Broadley, *Louis Charles Casartelli*, pp. 191–199.

13 Entries under 'Catholic Societies' in the *Almanac for the Diocese of Salford* for 1933 (p. 136) and 1937 (p. 138). No records of the Guild are known to survive. Reports in *The Harvest* of the activities of the Catholic Social Guild, its affiliated 'circles' throughout the diocese, its weekend courses and its 'College of Social Studies in Manchester' (founded in 1937), the Link Society (an 'old students' association … to promote Catholic interests and activities'), the University Catholic Association and the Catholic Women's League contain no evidence of an interest in the Jews.

14 SDA Marshall Papers 204/134–135, typescript headed 'Catholic Refugees' n.d. (but shortly after the Evian Conference of July 1938).

15 *Ibid.*

16 Of the 1,000 children in the Manchester region by 1943 (600 of them in the city and its immediate vicinity), between 20 and 25% were said to have been Christian.

17 *The Harvest*, Vol. L11, No. 1, February 1939.

18 SDA Henshaw Papers 203/146.

19 In the absence of any evidence of an alternative, I have assumed this to have been the body referred to occasionally in the records of the Manchester Quaker and Jewish Refugee Committee and in the minutes of the North West Regional Committee of

the Refugee Children's Movement.

20 MJRC. Minutes of an executive meeting of the North West Regional Committee of the RCM 16 March 1943.

21 *Ibid.* 31 October and 14 November 1944. In a change of tone, the Catholic Committee subsequently agreed to re-consider his case, although with what result is not known.

22 The holiday home at Ansdell – formally, the Stella Matutina Convent – was the former mansion of a wealthy businessman, acquired by the Home in 1934.

23 MFA Dr Stanley Haydock to Tom Ellis 24 July 1939.

24 John Slawson (ed.), *A Labour of Love: Holly Mount, Tottington: Memories of the Children's Home* (Manchester 1995).

25 Testimony of Anne Logan in *ibid.*, p. 5.

26 *Ibid., passim.* The interviewees, mostly from homes 'broken' in various ways, some never or rarely visited by relatives, tended to stress the benefits of living in an alternative family: there were some former residents, however, whose experiences at the home had been so traumatic that they were unwilling to share their memories.

27 The home was run by a Mother Superior and by a Management Committee of nine, made up of two priests, two nuns and five prominent Catholic laymen. It was subject to periodic inspection by the Catholic Rescue Society and by local Public Assistance Committees which between them provided most of the funds. In 1962 Holly Mount was converted into a home for the elderly; in 1991 it was closed for conversion into luxury flats.

28 Annual Report of Holly Mount for 1920, quoted by Slawson, *Labour of Love*, p. 50.

29 Moloney, *Holly Mount*, p. 128.

30 *Ibid.*, p. 132.

31 Slawson, *Labour of Love*, pp. 43–44. Klaus Berentzen's younger brother, whose recollections Slawson did not record, remained at Holly Mount until 1944. The names of most of the other refugees are not known.

32 *Ibid.* and Moloney, *Hollymount*, pp. 128–130. Klaus's mother corresponded with him through the Red Cross before her death in a Nazi concentration camp.

33 Moloney, *Holly Mount*, p. 128.

11

'Inspired idealism': Rabbi Dr Solomon Schonfeld and Manchester

The same meeting of the MJRC on 6 December 1938 to which Arthur Kershaw had been invited to outline his plans for a hostel in south Manchester was attended by another group of friends, this one led by Eli Fox, with proposals for the creation of a hostel to the north of the city. It was probably in late November that the insurance broker, Eli Fox, and the building contractor, Adolf Cassel, paid £8,000 for a house at 20 Upper Park Road, Higher Broughton, set in one-and-a-half acres, which might serve as a hostel, they believed, for fifty young people of sixteen years and over. The *Salford City Reporter* quoted Fox as saying that his plan followed a meeting with the 'Chief Rabbi', at whose school in London the fifty youngsters were said to be.[1]

In fact, the article was a local journalist's misreading of the link which Fox had established, not with the Chief Rabbi, but with the Chief Rabbi's Religious Emergency Council which, its name notwithstanding, was the organisational base for the 'manifold activities' of the 'inspired idealist' and maverick British orthodox rabbi, Dr Solomon Schonfeld. In 1933, at the age of twenty-two, Schonfeld had assumed the leadership of a network of independent orthodox institutions in London established by his father, a Hungarian immigrant rabbi, including the Union of Orthodox Hebrew Congregations (founded in 1928), a Jewish Day School (1929), a youth group, Ben Zakkai, and a synagogue, Adas Yisroel, all of which lay beyond what Shonfeld saw as the religiously suspect jurisdiction of the Chief Rabbi and the United Synagogue. This complex was informed by 'a vigorous Orthodoxy which [the Schonfelds believed] would goad the rest of Anglo-Jewry into renewed life'.[2] Informed late in 1938 by Agudist[3] rabbis in Germany and Austria that those selecting children for the Kindertransport were unduly favouring young Zionists, who could be relied upon to leave Britain for Palestine, and 'openly discriminating against the orthodox',[4] Schonfeld set about establishing 'a one-man rescue, relief and rehabilitation organisation'[5] which, with the Chief Rabbi's assent, became the Chief Rabbi's Religious Emergency Council. Using the Council as his vehicle, Schonfeld went on to invent a 'paper Yeshiva', Ohr Yisroel, in Stamford Hill, north London, as a mechanism for obtaining student visas,[6] and, in December 1938 to negotiate with the Home Office independently of Otto Schiff's Refugees Committee to create a Kindertransport for young, orthodox non-Zionists with 'block guarantees' from the Council. Once in England, the young people were housed in Schonfeld's Day School or in his own home until more permanent accommodation could be found for them.[7] Perhaps 'one of the most difficult people to have operated at an organisational level in British Jewry during the 20th century',[8] Schonfeld was unscrupulous in ignoring the red tape of refugee rescue, often leaving loose ends which, as in Manchester, it was left to local committees to tidy up.

The assumption must be that at some time in November or December 1938, Schonfeld made contact with Fox, himself something of a maverick in Manchester.[9] Fox and Cassel claimed also to have the backing (presumably the financial backing) of the Manchester Jews' Benevolent Society, an important communal charity founded by Fox in 1905, and of which he was still the president.[10] At some point in these negotiations, probably at Schonfeld's bidding, the idea of a hostel for those over sixteen was transformed into plans to house children arriving on Schonfeld's Agudist Kindertransport.

Cassel and Fox were both amongst the Jewish immigrants who had entered Manchester between the 1870s and the First World War. Cassel arrived in Manchester from Odessa as early as the 1870s. Already a builder in his homeland, in Manchester he created a firm of building contractors which by 1938 had become Adolf Cassel and Sons. Amongst the first entrepreneurs to anticipate a movement of Jewish (and non-Jewish) families northwards from the run-down inner suburbs across the northern rim of the city, he built hundreds of houses, detached and semi-detached, in the Broughton Park area of Salford, on the natural line of northwards advance for the population from Cheetham Hill and Straageways. Most of the houses in Stanley Road, Marston Road, Roston Road and Waterpark Road (where he himself lived) were built by his firm. Orthodox and observant, he was proud of his Jewish heritage. When, at some time in the early 1930s, two of his daughters were refused entry to a tennis club in Higher Broughton, he responded by building the Waterpark Club on Stanley Road as a 'Jewish club'. With a ballroom and four tennis courts, the club became a popular resort for the younger members (entrance was limited to the over-16s) of aspiring Jewish families moving 'up the hill'. There were regular Sunday night dances and a Yom Kippur 'breakfast dance' which followed the Fast. Amongst Cassel's other building ventures was a block of shops in Great Clowes Street which included the Higher Broughton Assembly Rooms, a popular dancehall in the 1930s which on Saturday nights attracted such bands of national renown as those of Joe Loss and Ted Heath.[11]

Eli Fox, who had arrived in Manchester from Russia as a young man in 1896, had by 1938 become a highly effective but notoriously independent-minded communal activist. Impatient with what he saw as the assimilationist synagogues and charities of the community in which he had arrived, he had immediately set about creating places of worship and charities more in keeping with what he saw as the true Jewish orthodox tradition. The first was the Russian-Jewish Benevolent Society, founded, quite explicitly, to free new immigrants from reliance on the investigative methods and anglicising objectives of the Jewish Board of Guardians, a charity created and led by the community's official leaders.[12] He worked against the elitist grain, too, in the support he gave to the establishment of a Jewish Hospital in Manchester, a project at first fiercely opposed by Nathan Laski and by his allies in the community's cottonocracy, as being likely to generate images of Jewish exclusivity detrimental to the community's integration. In religious terms, Fox identified himself first with a *stiebl* of his own making on Carnarvon Street, Cheetham Hill, of which he was the 'Honorary Reader', then with the United Synagogue, also in Cheetham, which saw itself as reflecting the purest of Eastern European religious traditions, and finally with the Heaton Park Synagogue, which he himself had founded in 1937 as one of the first places of worship to carry strict orthodoxy into the new areas of Jewish residence in Crumpsall and Prestwich. The Linas Hazedek Sick and Burial Society, which he founded in 1912, ensured the provision of kosher meals to Jewish patients at Crumpsall Hospital.[13] In 1906, sharing the resentment of his Eastern European peers at the hostility directed at new immigrants by the established elite, he became one of the founders of a Manchester Temporary Shelter for the Jewish Poor, of which he later became the 'honorary superintendent'.[14]

It seems that in 1938 Fox saw himself once more as the protector of orthodox refugee newcomers and guardian of their religious standards. In October 1938 he was already seeking to raise funds for Austrian refugees.[15] What he had in mind in the following month, perhaps at Schonfeld's bidding, was a hostel for refugees from more strictly observant German and Austrian families. Like Kershaw, he and his friends were invited to put their proposals to the meeting of the MJRC executive on 6 December, but while Kershaw's plans were immediately taken on board, Fox's were amongst three projects rejected on 12 December as not being 'urgently required'.[16]

No evidence exists to suggest the reasons either for the rejection or for its reversal during the three weeks which followed. It seems hardly likely, in the international circumstances of December 1938, that it was ever really judged to be surplus to potential refugee requirements. What seems much more likely is an initial suspicion on the part of the MJRC (and perhaps of Laski) that in this, as in other communal matters, Fox and his allies were unlikely to work comfortably within an agreed, centralised structure (as, in fact, later proved to be the case). It is not clear why Laski changed his mind. Perhaps he was under pressure from Woburn House to increase hostel accommodation in Manchester. Perhaps he was persuaded in discussions with Fox: later events were to suggest a degree of mutual respect between two equally independent-minded, but also equally orthodox, men. It may be that the decisive moment was the decision to house children arriving on the Kindertransport, for whom the MJRC had no facilities. What is certain is that on 6 January 1939 Fox was able to announce to the local press the imminent opening of Cassel-Fox House, in the management of which his committee had agreed 'to work in conjunction with the German Jewish Aid Committee' (that is, the MJRC).[17] The first fifty residents were already expected, accompanied by a German refugee doctor (a Dr Alfred Koppenheim of Breslau) who was said to speak fluent English and who would serve as the hostel's superintendent.[18] In fact, twenty-six boys from the Schonfeld Kindertransport, aged between ten and sixteen, arrived in January with Koppenheim. By the end of February 1939, Kershaw House and Cassel-Fox were both full, the former 'so full that they have been forced to accommodate boys in rooms reserved for girls'.[19]

Sam Stern, then the sixteen-year-old son of a Viennese Jewish grocer, still remembers vividly the events which led him to Cassel-Fox. Sam belonged to a strictly orthodox family of Eastern European origin (his father was Russian, his mother from Brody in Galicia) associated with the tiny place of worship of Vienna's Chortkover Chassids, Shomrei Hadass, of which his uncle was the *chazan* and *shochet*. Sam attended services at Shomrei Hadass, although, as a talented singer, he also joined the choir at the city's main synagogue, the Central. Sam's three elder brothers all studied at Yeshivoth in Austria or Poland. Following the Anscluss Sam witnessed Hitler's triumphant victory parade in Vienna, and his family was soon caught up in the Nazi regime's violent anti-Semitic policies. The family's grocery shop was confiscated, his father incarcerated in Buchenwald (where he subsequently died), and Sam himself briefly placed under arrest. His brother Max (Moshe) had migrated to Palestine in 1930, and Sam might well have followed him had not his mother heard that Agudas Israel in Vienna, of which Sam was an active member, was giving out forms for the Kindertransport. On the evening of 20 December 1938, Sam walked with his mother (they could not afford a taxi) to the tram stop on Wallenstein Platz, where they said their goodbyes before he left for the station, where 120 young people had already gathered.

After a snowy crossing to Harwich, the boys destined for Cassel-Fox were met at London's Liverpool Street station by Schonfeld, whom Sam remembers as 'a slim man with fiery eyes and a small ginger beard'. He took them by bus to his school in Amhurst Park Road, where, with the pupils away for the Chanukah holidays, every room was full of beds. After a few days, with the school's children due to return, they moved on to the Manchester hostel.[20]

Former members of the Schonfeld Kindertransport have good memories of their lives at the hostel, with its nine bedrooms with bunk beds .There was a table-tennis table, and football was played in the hostel grounds. The boys were taken to swim at Cheetham baths and to play billiards in the saloons in Queens Road and Halliwell Street. They were invited for tea by local Jewish families, the first time that the young refugees got to see English homes, 'with gardens back and front and a fire in the grate'. They were taken to films at the Premier and Shakespeare cinemas in Cheetham. Some attended talks at the Jewish Forum, a communal debating society, in Mamlock House. Pinchus Harris and Chaim Halpern, both from Machzikei Hadas, took them on walks to Heaton Park. In the summer of 1939 ten of the boys were sent (at Joe Mamlock's expense) to the camp of the Jewish Lads Brigade in Penrhyn Bay. On what Sam Stern remembers as a special occasion, organised by Joe Cassel, son of the builder, they were taken in two cars for tea at Whitefield Golf Club.[21] There were no educational facilities at Cassel-Fox. Those of the right age attended the Manchester Jews School, where language proved an obstacle to mixing with their English peers. In the absence of formal tuition, Sam Stern tried to teach himself English by reading *Far From the Madding Crowd* with the help of a dictionary.

Whether by design or by the chance circumstances of their origins, the two hostels came to represent the two poles of Manchester orthodox observance. Siegfried Eimerl, the child of strictly observant German parents, who arrived in Manchester via the Schonfeld Kindertransport, remembers feeling immediately at home at Cassel-Fox. The hostel was run efficiently, he remembers; it was very clean, the food was good, there were play areas for table-tennis, billiards and chess, and, most of all, he found himself amongst children from similar religious backgrounds to his own. There was a regular morning *minyan*. On Sabbath and at the High Festivals, the hostel boys were called upon to make up the *minyan* at Eli Fox's Heaton Park Synagogue, and received regular visits from Rabbi Kopul Rosen of the Higher Crumpsall Synagogue. Like many of the boys, Siegfried attended the Manchester Yeshiva on a part-time basis. Edmund Goldman, born in 1923 in Deutschkreutz, near Austria's border with Hungary, and also one of the original twenty-six hostel residents, remembers the hostel as 'a beautiful' house in which he felt comfortable in an orthodox setting similar to that in his home in Austria. Social life was limited. There were no concerts, dances or 'entertainments' such as took place at Kershaw House. Occasionally the hostel boys took part in events at the Bachad Bayit on Middleton Road. *Bachadniks* from the Thornham Fold *hachsharah* were regular visitors.[22] Jonah Balkin, whose *cheder*, popular with the more orthodox Manchester Jewish families, was in Bignor Street, Cheetham Hill, and a local Jewish minister, Sydney Olsberg, gave regular *shiurim* (religious study sessions) at the hostel. Like Siegfried, Edmund was a part-time student at the Yeshiva and a regular member of the *minyan* at the Heaton Park Synagogue.[23] At Passover, the boys were allocated to orthodox families in the area. A strictly observant regime was enforced by the hostel's new houseparents, Dr Moritz Weinberger, a former teacher of science, maths and Hebrew at the Hamburg Talmud Torah, and his English-born wife, a volunteer charity-worker in the Jewish area of Hamburg,[24] appointed early in 1939 in place of Dr Koppenheim specifically to impose stricter discipline on the boys, some of whom had become 'unmanageable'.[25]

The founders of Kershaw House first publicised it as 'open to Jews and non-Jews'[26] and the House Committee described itself as 'non-sectarian'.[27] In reality it was from the start a Jewish hostel, administered by a committee made up exclusively of Jews, employing only Jewish staff and, in the words of its promoters, 'run on orthodox and Jewish lines'.[28] The food was kosher, the Sabbath strictly observed ('No smoking, music or cards'), a weekly service conducted in the hostel. When the residents requested it, Rabbi Dr Altmann, Manchester's Communal Rav and the hostel's spiritual guardian, sent in the German-speaking rabbi, Dr David Feldman of Machzikei Hadass.[29] On 29 January 1939, at the official opening, Altmann had conducted a form of 'consecration' and blessed the mezuzah attached to its main entrance.[30] When, later that year, he judged the premises to be unsuitable for the proper celebration of Passover, all but its sleeping accommodation was closed down for eight days and the children found appropriate hospitality for the Seder in private homes.[31] The standards of religious observance expected of the residents, however, in spite of Feldmann's occasional presence, was that of the orthodox mainstream of the southern suburbs. Lisa Wolfe, who was a frequent visitor to the hostel remembers the level of observance demanded by the committee was 'strict enough' but 'probably not quite strict enough for some people'. One girl who complained that the food at Kershaw House 'wasn't kosher enough' was transferred at once to the B'nai Brith girls' hostel in Waterloo Road,[32] which, like Cassel-Fox for boys, had a reputation for the strictest orthodoxy. Sam Stern remembers Kershaw House, with pardonable exaggeration, as a 'non-religious hostel'.[33]

The contrast between the two hostels also effected the choice of accommodation for those that left. Whereas those ending their six-week stay at Kershaw House were found bed-sits in Whalley Range and Fallowfield (districts with few Jewish inhabitants and no Jewish facilities, where observance was a matter of no concern), in February 1939 Revd (later Rabbi) J. Vilensky, minister at the Holy Law Synagogue, was asked by the MJRC 'to try to find orthodox homes' for those leaving Cassel-Fox at the end of their period of training.[34] Even in their first places of residence in Manchester, that is, Jewish refugees were effectively steered in different religious directions. The result was two distinct areas of young refugee settlement: for the less observant, the residential suburbs of south Manchester; for those with a commitment to stricter standards, the Jewish Quarter to the north of the city.

At some time in August 1939, as the pressure on Cassel-Fox increased, Eli Fox and ten other potential guarantors came forward with the offer of another 'wonderful residence', next door to the existing hostel, as accommodation for a further forty-two trainees 'who were not able to maintain themselves in lodgings'.[35] A management committee made up of Fox and his fellow guarantors was to work in cooperation with the MJRC, which would subsidise the costs of the hostel; by 22 August, when the plan received Nathan Laski's blessing and its promoters his thanks, a matron and superintendent were being sought.[36] Only the outbreak of war less than a fortnight later prevented the opening of a hostel which was to have been called, with a nod of deference to London, 'Woburn House', and which would undoubtedly have served the more orthodox.

Notes

1   *Salford City Reporter*, 6 January 1939.
2   David Kranzler and Gertrude Hirschler (eds), *Solomon Schonfeld, His Page in History: Recollections of Individuals Saved by an Extraordinary Orthodox Jewish Rescue Hero during the Holocaust Era* (New York 1982), p. 21. I have used Kranzler and Hirschler's biographical essay in this book (pp. 19–33) as my main source for Schonfeld's career. When war broke out he and Dr Judith Grunfeld established a centre at Shefford,

sixty miles from London, to provide 'a total Jewish environment' for children evacuated from the capital (*ibid.*, pp. 25–26). After the war, he facilitated the entry of Holocaust survivors.

3   That is, members of Agudas Israel, the anti-Zionist group within international Jewish orthodoxy.

4   Kranzler and Hirschler, *Solomon Schonfeld*, p. 22.

5   *Ibid.*, p. 25.

6   These enabled him to secure the entry of any Jewish adolescent on an entry permit as a student.

7   Kranzler and Hirschler, *Solomon Schonfeld*, pp. 22–23. Transcript of an interview with Matilda and Edmund Goldman (hereafter Edmund Goldman interview). Edmund Goldman was one of these recruits.

8   Tony Kushner, *Remembering Refugees*, p. 166.

9   A list of names in one of the transports organised by Schonfeld corresponds to those first admitted to the Cassel-Fox hostel.

10   Edmund Goldman interview.

11   Biographical information based on notes of the author's conversations with Ruth Giness, Cassel's granddaughter, in September 2004. In 1940 Cassel advertised for customers for his 'sunshine factories', built to specification (MG 8 June 1940). After the war the firm, under Adolf's son, Joseph Cassel, built a number of factories, some as small industrial estates, particularly in the area of Waterloo Road, to replace those which had been blitzed.

12   Minute Book of the Russian-Jewish Benevolent Society in MCL.

13   Handwritten summary of his 'Fifty Years of Communal Activities' by Eli Fox, now in the author's possession.

14   *Ibid.* The Shelter was later amalgamated with the Manchester Jewish Home for the Elderly. Fox died in November 1946.

15   MJRC EC 14 October 1938. He organised a concert on behalf of both the Linas Hazadek Society and 'the Austrian refugees'.

16   MJRC EM 12 December 1938. The other plans set aside at this meeting as being 'not urgently required' were an unspecified offer from a 'Mr. G. Hardy' and the offer of a hostel in Southport. 'Seven Springs Camp' in Disley, which was also on offer, was turned down as 'unsuitable' (MJRC EM 6 and 12 December 1938).

17   The minutes of a meeting of the Executive Committee of the Manchester Yeshiva (MY EC 26 February 1939) raise an unresolved problem. The minutes state that Fox had recently offered to the Yeshiva a home to accommodate its refugee students. Either Fox was keeping his options open or the home in question was not Cassel-Fox. At all events, the Yeshiva turned down the offer, on the grounds that it would not be able to afford the cost of its maintenance or the wages of a caretaker, 'not to mention the trouble and responsibility entailed by such a scheme'. In his own notes on his life, Fox refers to a branch of the Cassel-Fox hostel which he set up in Blackpool, presumably for young evacuees.

18   SCR 6 January 1939.

19   MJRC EM 7 February 1939.

20   Interview of Sam Stern by Rosalyn Livshin, April–May 2002 (hereafter Sam Stern interview).

21   Author interview with Edmund Goldman, 2006 (hereafter Edmund Goldman interview), and Sam Stern interview.

22   For Bachad, see Chapter 14 below.

23   Edmund Goldman interview.

24 Mrs Weinberger met her husband when he was studying in Heidelberg and she was visiting her aunt and uncle there. She returned to Britain at the beginning of the First World War and then in 1920 married Moritz in Fulda and settled down with him in Hamburg. They had three children, two daughters and a son. In Britain, one of the daughters, Matilda ('Tilly') stayed with relations in London, and was evacuated to Huntingdon before joining her parents in Manchester.

25 MJRC EC 1 May, 17 July 1939.

26 MJRC KHE 4 December 1938.

27 *Ibid.*

28 MJRC KHSC 4 December 1938.

29 MJRC KHE 27 March 1939.

30 MJRC KHE 22 January 1939.

31 MJRC KHE 5 March 1939.

32 Elisabeth (Lisa) Wolfe interview.

33 Sam Stern interview.

34 MJRC EC 7 February 1939.

35 Loose page of minutes of a meeting of guarantors and members of the MGJAC dated 22 August [1939] in the Barash Papers. The guarantors named in the document are Eli Fox, Alfred Goodwin, L.M. Glancy, S. Oppenheim, S. Beenstock, S. Segal, B. Adler, Arthur Fox, John Lee and Jacob Levy. The joint secretaries of the management committee are named as Mr Latin and Charles Green, the treasurer as Arthur Fox. The first reference to the offer is in MJRC EC 17 July 1939.

36 *Ibid.*

12

The Harris House girls: girls from the Kindertransport in Southport, 1938–1940

On 6 December 1938, as it sought to define its remit, the MJRC was given to understand by members of the Livingstone family of Southport that a local committee there had obtained premises at 27 Argyle Road, in a fashionable residential district near the town centre, at a rental of £900 for four years, which it proposed to convert into a hostel for twelve children. Approval had been obtained from Woburn House and the committee now sought the imprimatur of the MJRC, of which it perhaps saw itself as a potential satellite.[1] On 12 December, after the MJRC had delayed its response, Lewis Livingstone, head of the family and chairperson of the committee, wrote that unless an immediate expression of support was received 'enthusiasm could evaporate'.[2] For reasons not disclosed, the MJRC then decided that a hostel in Southport was 'not urgently required'.[3]

The Livingstones [originally Levinsteins] were perhaps typical of those Jewish immigrant families which, having made a marked success of commercial or industrial ventures in Manchester, took advantage of a convenient rail link to reside in what was seen as a particularly attractive and healthy segment of the Merseyside commuter belt – the 'Seaside Garden City', according to its own publicity.[4] Other such families in the Southport of the 1930s were those of Henry Doniger, the wealthy director of a group of factories manufacturing cloth caps in the Cheetham area of Manchester;[5] Isaac Freedland, 'managing director of one of the largest cabinet-making firms in the north of Britain';[6] the Manchester cinema proprietor, Benjamin Henry Franks;[7] the money-lender, Samuel Claff; the fashion fabric manufacturer, Philip Pariser; and Ephraim Marks, the owner of a toy and fancy goods warehouse in Manchester and brother of Michael Marks, the founder of the Marks and Spencer chain.[8] The heads of such families, as the wealthiest Jewish families in the town, all of them orthodox in their religious observance, made up a local elite which dominated the affairs of the Southport Hebrew Congregation in Arnside Road, built during 1924–26 as the successor of the town's first synagogue, opened in Sussex Road in 1893. Of a total Southport population of around 80,000 in 1938, 500 were Jewish.[9] With its large population of hoteliers and retired business people, Southport was already in 1917, according to the editor of the leading local paper, *The Southport Visiter* [sic], 'the wealthiest town in Great Britain for its size … [and] well-known for the munificence of its gifts to deserving objects'.[10]

Of the Jewish elite, the Livingstones were perhaps the most locally influential. Lewis Livingstone, a Lithuanian immigrant who arrived in Manchester, penniless, in the 1890s, was first provided by his *landsleit* in the Central Synagogue with goods to sell as a pack-man in the country districts around Wigan. Graduating first into an independent hawker of jewellery, by 1910 he had established a well-publicised money-lending business, with its head-quarters in Market Street, Manchester, and profitable branches throughout the Lancashire cotton towns. In 1912, on the crest of a wave of success, he moved with his family to a mansion close to the seafront in a select suburb of Southport. Apart from these business commuters, the community was made up of shopkeepers, boarding-house keepers and others engaged in Southport's flourishing tourist trade. Amongst those best-known to the local population were Arthur Jacobson, the musical director of the Floral Hall, a focus of tourist social activity, and the comedian and compère, Samuel Benoliel.

There is ample evidence of the friendly relationship which existed between Southport and its Jewish citizens, although none of them played as central a part in urban development as Nathan Laski in Manchester or Louis Winter in Stockport. The main local weekly, *The Southport Visiter*, provided a full and sympathetic coverage of the escalating persecution of European Jewry and of the fund-raising on its behalf.[11] C. Aveling was president of the Southport Society for the Protection of Trade. Benoliel, 'well-known on the Southport Operatic Society Stage', according to the *Visiter*, regularly organised fund-raising events for Southport's football club, the Operatic Society and Southport Infirmary.[12]

It was apparently Lewis Livingstone's son, Harry, brought up and educated in Southport, his wife, Ruth, and their network of well-to-do friends, most of them traditionally orthodox members of the local synagogue, who in 1938 acquired and contributed to the rent of the 'charming modern house' in Argyle Road put at its disposal by its owner, Miss Jose Harris.[13] They had perhaps been inspired to action by a sermon delivered in the Southport Synagogue on 22 November 1938 by its minister, Rabbi Dr Alec Silverstone, a graduate of the Manchester Yeshiva, delivered during a Service of Intercession for German Jewry following Kristallnacht. The urgency of the situation, Silverstone told his congregants, made necessary 'the co-ordination of all the forces [*sic*] in ameliorating the needs of the stricter Jews of Germany'. He told the story of a little girl struggling to carry a baby that seemed clearly too heavy for her. When a passer-by stopped her and asked 'Isn't the baby too heavy for you?', however, she replied, 'He is not too heavy – he is my brother.' 'Where there is love', Silverstone ended, 'there is no burden. The German Jews are burdened, but their burden is not too heavy for us to take over. They are our brethren and their trouble is our trouble.'[14]

Sensing a lack of enthusiasm from the MJRC, which may well have seen Southport as lying well beyond its realistic sphere of operations, the promoters now converted themselves into the 'Southport branch of the Movement for the Care of Children from Germany', for the reception of children from the Kindertransport, and pressed on without Manchester support. On 29 December their 'first contingent' of ten German and Austrian refugee girls from the Kindertransport, after spending a fortnight in Lowestoft and Dovercourt, arrived in Southport, where, the local press was told, they 'will stay with the "foster parents" until arrangements can be made for them to live in one house, properly controlled and a suitable education given to them, so that they can receive domestic training and be helpful citizens'.[15] At least nine Southport Jewish families provided hospitality[16] into which the girls are said (by the branch secretary, a Mrs Max Cantor of Birkdale) to have quickly settled down with gratitude and relief.[17] They were shown 'every consideration'. Two cousins who had never before been parted were placed in the homes of two married sisters who lived close to one another 'so that the children will be able to see one another frequently'.[18] More generally, 'talking and playing with the children of the homes into which they have been taken, gradually building up a new life, they will be able to live in security and comfort after the hardships they have endured'.[19]

This committee lost no time, however, in removing the girls from private care to a more 'controlled' setting. An 'enthusiastically supported' concert, 'organised by numerous members of the [Jewish] community' at Southport's Garrick Theatre on 8 January 1939, with an all-star cast headed by Stanley Holloway, George Formby and Sid Field,[20] raised a remarkable £600 for their cause; a Bridge Party in the Floral Hall a further £91; while 'generous support' from Jewish families and 'local tradespeople' limited the cost to the committee of furnishing and equipping the hostel to £70.[21] Ruth Livingstone is said to have persuaded her wide circle of friends to commit themselves to paying 10s a week towards the upkeep of the hostel.[22] On 12 February 1939 'Harris House' was opened and consecrated by Rabbi Dr Silverstone as a hostel 'for young ladies up to eighteen years of age'.[23] It was rather more than 'charming'; built in the 1920s for the Jewish company director, Ernest Harris, it was a handsome and substantial detached house in an attractive residential district a mile from the city centre, perhaps half a mile from the sea.[24]

Apart from providing the girls with guarantees and maintaining the hostel, the General Committee of the branch also 'supervised the welfare of refugee children under private guardianship'[25] and served as a means of liaison with the regional headquarters of the movement, in Manchester. The management of the hostel was exercised by a 'House Committee' of eleven women under the chairmanship of Ruth Livingstone,[26] its day-to-day management entrusted to a salaried Matron, the Austrian-Jewish refugee, Dr Margarete Steinberg (known to her charges as 'Mrs. Stone'). A former psychologist and once the superintendant of a large children's home in Vienna, Dr Steinberg moved into the hostel from Manchester with her mother, Wilma Weiss,[27] ('Our Dear Granny' to the girls),[28] also a Viennese refugee, in time for its opening; Mrs Weiss did all the cooking, while 'a weekly domestic' was employed to assist with household tasks on Sabbaths and Holy Days.[29] Their work was supplemented and apparently closely monitored by the House Committee, which purchased 'all foodstuffs, clothing and general household requisites', supervised 'the routine of the Institution' and watched over the girls' physical health: a member of its 'inspection rota' visited the hostel each day, 'so that at no time has there been other than the most regular contact and supervision'.[30]

The girls at the hostel, rising rapidly in number from ten in February 1939 to eighteen in May, were all but one from middle-class professional and business families in Austria and Germany.[31] They were unaccompanied Kindertransport children, aged between fourteen and seventeen, most of whose parents were trapped in their homelands, some of whose fathers had spent time in concentration camps.[32] Members of the Southport branch of the RCM stood as their financial guarantors and, as they reached the age of sixteen, found 'suitable places' for them as 'trainees', the condition on which they had been allowed temporary residence in Britain. During their first few months in Southport, most took up posts as 'apprentices' in local hairdressing salons, pharmacies, gown shops and confectioners chiefly owned by members of the Southport Jewish community, in domestic service, chiefly in Jewish homes, or, in two cases, as assistants in 'Mary Willet's Day Nursery'.[33] They were said by the General Committee to 'be giving their employers satisfaction, as well as deriving the satisfactory benefit from their instruction'.[34] Each girl was also expected to undertake 'specific duties' towards the running of the hostel, 'so that expenditure on staff charges' was 'reduced to a minimum'.[35]

Margarete Steinberg set great store on the employment of her charges. Fourteen to seventeen years, she believed, was a 'difficult age ... even in the most favourable and familiar surroundings ... How much more so in this particular case when the girls are away from home in a far country and separated from their parents.' Guiding them 'towards a profession ... means to give all those uncertain feelings and desires a firm direction and helps more than anything else to make the girls content and happy'.[36] Her intent, too, was their rapid acculturation. 'I allow only English to be spoken here,' she wrote in the Harris House Diary, 'the girls know that I insist on that rule.'

By keeping its expenditure 'carefully watched', eliminating 'all possible waste' and reaching out to the community for support, the branch's Finance Sub-Committee rendered the hostel more than financially viable. Annual subscriptions and donations of £1,092 during its first year raised a surplus income of £220.[37]

At the hostel,[38] at least according to their personal accounts inscribed in what has now become known as 'the Harris House Diary', the girls found only 'kindness, understanding, sympathy and loving care'. Conditions in the hostel were said to be 'just as homely as [in] any private house'. They were housed in 'lovely bedrooms', each sleeping four or five girls. A garden rockery left room for outdoor games; in the garage was a table-tennis set. After work, their day was taken up by an educational programme, organised by an Education and Welfare Sub-Committee, run by volunteers and including

English, elocution, needlework, gymnastics, modern Hebrew, French and cane-work. During August, when there were no lessons, they were taken on picnics to Ainsdale Beach, swimming at Southport Baths, walks in the Botanical Gardens and tea parties at the homes of 'friendly ladies'. The House was 'conducted on strictly orthodox lines'. The religious needs of the girls were met by Rabbi Dr Alec Silverstone, whose Sabbath services they attended regularly, and who conducted classes in biblical studies each Sunday. The synagogue's Reader and Shochet, Revd S. Meisels, also a Manchester Yeshiva graduate, was their teacher of modern Hebrew; over Pesach they became the guests of 'friendly families'. A highlight of the girls' first year in Southport was a Purim Concert in which a play performed by the girls was followed by songs, some of them English, some 'Hebrew and Jewish'.[39] In Southport, they learnt, according to one of them, that 'Jewish children are never altogether homeless amidst fellow Jews':[40] they welcomed invitations to participate in communal events and the 'shelter' accorded them after the trauma of the separation from their families.

They were equally fulsome in their gratitude to Britain and to non-Jewish Southport. In their own accounts, they wrote with appreciation of visits from the Mayor and Mayoress, the offer of free tickets for Southport cinemas and an introduction to Anton Wallbrook at a local theatre. 'After all the excitement and worrying,' wrote Dorothea Frankel from Frankfurt, 'I experienced happily the shelter and security I found here in this country.' Margot Brauer, from Beuthen in Upper Silesia, and Kitty Pistol, from Vienna, both felt happy to arrive in a country that was both 'friendly' and 'free'. Their 'Quaker friend' from the Refugee Children's Movement, Mary Goodwin (of Manchester), was a frequent visitor to the hostel and wrote a poem entitled 'Brotherhood' for inclusion in their Purim Play.[41]

It would seem that the committee had also found stronger support from urban society than its equivalent in Stockport. Early responses to fund-raising by the Jewish community were taken by the *Southport Visiter* to suggest that 'Southport's attitude is most sympathetic towards the Jewish children refugees who are arriving in this country';[42] the fund-raisers themselves found the 'generosity and interest' of Southport people 'amazing'.[43] Certainly, the £600 raised for refugees by the concert at the Garrick Theatre far surpasses other sums raised by single events not only in Stockport, but throughout the country. The Aliens Tribunals before which the older girls were compelled to prove their loyalty, and the police who escorted them to the courts, treated them with genuine sympathy and sensitivity. 'We feel thankful to the police,' the committee reported, 'the more so as we know so well of the help they gave towards the establishment of our hostel.'[44] Early in 1939 the hostel received the 'splendid donation' of £5 from members of the Southport Police Athletic Club.[45] The managers of the Palladium and Regal cinemas provided 'many amusements' for the girls.[46] The Open Air Baths Committee of Southport Corporation offered 'kind assistance whenever the occasion arose'.[47] The heads of the two schools attended by hostel girls gave them 'valuable assistance';[48] at Brentwood Senior School, Dorothea Frankel found the head, her class teachers and her fellow pupils all 'helpful and kind'.[49] The Lady Mayoress sent free tickets for a pantomime at the Garrick Theatre.[50] 'Many tradesmen and townspeople' helped arrange '[the] purchase [of] various requisites on advantageous terms'.[51] Of the seven people who conducted classes at the hostel, three were non-Jewish; one of them, Leonard Holmes, who taught the refugees elocution, deportment and mime, also helped organise parties through which the girls sought to thank their carers.[52] Of the four 'honorary consultants' who looked after the girls' medical needs, one was a non-Jewish doctor.[53] Of the 79 donors who had contributed to the founding of the hostel, at least thirty-five were non-Jewish, and seven non-Jews were amongst its regular subscribers.[54]

There was no local hostility to the refugees. The only sour notes were a sermon by Canon Morris, the Vicar of Southport's All Saints Church, who in February 1939, in response to the Baldwin Appeal, urged the prior needs of Britain's 'under-nourished [and] insufficiently clad children … being brought up under conditions which … would compare with the conditions of some of those we are being urged to contribute our money towards', and a long letter supporting him from a 'J. Jack', printed in the *Southport Visiter*.[55] Neither generated a debate amongst the public or in the press.

The experience of the Southport refugees clearly differed markedly from that of their contemporaries in Stockport.[56] Religious supervision, no doubt orchestrated by an exceptionally orthodox Southport Rabbi (whose initial concern had been for 'the stricter Jews of Germany') left little room for manoeuvre for girls drawn chiefly from assimilated families. Members of the Southport committee were also both more socially involved with the children than their Stockport peers, and, perhaps because, as girls, they were seen as more vulnerable or more worthy of protection, readier to draw them into the bosom of local communal life. They were readier, too, it would appear, to organise links for the refugees with Southport society. It may be that the differences are to be accounted for chiefly in terms of a more confident community in a more confident town. In the town the tourist industry was prosperous and unemployment minimal;[57] within the community, whereas in Stockport there were Jewish individuals of prominence and influence in town life, Southport Jewry embraced a wealthy echelon of retired and commuting businessmen, well-known locally and part of two sources of new residents.

What the young refugees of Stockport and Southport shared, apart from communal support, was a compelling anxiety over the fate of their parents. Much of the free time of the girls at Harris House was taken up trying desperately (and chiefly without success) to find guarantors, permits or funds which would enable their parents to join them.[58] In their entries in the 'Harris House Diary' after a year in Britain, Gerta Herzberg, from Vienna, and Eva Riese, from Magdeburg, both expressed their regret that they had not succeeded 'in getting their parents out', something which Riese thought possible with the help of her Southport guarantors.[59] Lottie Gross records only her hope that her parents in Vienna remained safe. Only one of the hostel girls left to join parents who had also escaped: this was Ruth Hammer, who joined her mother in Colombo en route for a new life in Australia.[60] Other girls' families had become fragmented by Nazi policy and by the urgency in which they had sought means of departure. Hedwig Herzberg's eldest sister was in Chile, her father, deported from Germany as a Polish citizen, was in Warsaw, her mother still in the family home in Vienna. Both her parents, along with those of all the other girls but Ruth Hammer, perished. Apparently it did not occur to the refugee committees in either Stockport or Southport that, at the time of their rescue of younger refugees, channels still existed for the rescue of adults.

The first page of the Harris House Diary begins with a paragraph almost certainly penned by the matron, Margarete Steinberg, which reads: 'We just wished to give a token of gratitude to all those kind people who through their unremitting endeavour enabled us to write this book after a happy year spent in the security of our Home in Southport.' There seems little doubt that, as self-professed 'editor' of the diary, Steinberg was anxious to produce a tribute which the 'kind people' might see as commensurate with their efforts. A more critical perspective on the 'carefree time'[61] supposedly spent by the girls at Harris House is provided by Eva Riese, the daughter of a German-Jewish lawyer, who arrived in Southport from Magdeburg through the Refugee Children's Movement in June 1939 at the age of fourteen.

For Eva, 'Granny' Wilma Weiss was 'the only true, warm-hearted soul surrounding us'.[62] Eva found reason to be deeply suspicious of the motives of the 'nice, local ladies' who visited the hostel on Sundays 'to pick a girl for the weekend'. On the first occasion on which this happened to her, Eva felt that she had been 'paraded' on Southport promenade as 'the lady and the poor refugee girl'; she deserted her 'benefactor' with a 'friendly reminder' that on future walks she should find herself a dog.[63] Harris House she saw as 'a puritanical hostel',[64] offering the girls no scope for entertaining their male friends. In their 'apprenticeships', the girls were hard-worked and ill-paid. Eva was first given 2s a week at a local pharmacy ('largely for cleaning up after the pharmacist'), rising to 5s when she was promoted to 'saleslady'. Unable to afford bus fares, the girls walked to town every morning, returning in the evening to help 'granny' in the hostel kitchen.[65] Eva's most relaxed moments were during lunches at the home of a local boy she had met by chance and whose parents ran a Southport guest house.[66] There was no one in Southport to provide sensitive individual support, to lighten the atmosphere or provide the girls with any real sense of purpose; even Dr Steinberg's daughter did not believe her mother to be well-equipped, by experience or temperament, to handle the teenagers under her care.[67]

The expectation was that the hostel girls would show due gratitude for their place of temporary refuge. After the outbreak of war, they assisted in a Sale of Work and a Bring and Buy Sale organised by the [Jewish] Ladies Aid Committee which raised over £40 for the Southport Mayor's War Comforts Committee.[68] They joined the Southport Zionist and Literary Society and Southport Habonim in mounting a concert at the Temperance Institute in aid of the Mayor's Red Cross Fund.[69] At a time of war Dr Steinberg was anxious to stress the refugees' solidarity with the British people, the Harris House Diary attributing to them the phrase, 'we stand by Britain, we feel with England's people'. In January 1940 the General Committee reported that arrangements were being made to transfer some of the girls to forms of trainee employment 'which will relieve the growing shortage of labour owing to the large volumes that are being absorbed in work of National Importance'.[70]

This does not appear to have happened, perhaps because the cheap labour of the refugee girls had become too valuable to local shopkeepers, perhaps because no munitions factories existed within easy reach of Southport, perhaps because these good intentions were overtaken by events such as had closed the Stockport hostel. In June 1940, shortly after the fall of the Low Countries, and gripped by fear of a Fifth Column, the government designated Southport as part of the Merseyside 'protected area' from which all 'enemy aliens' were now excluded. With only twenty-four hours' notice, and on the demand of the local police, the committee dissolved the hostel and the girls were scattered with some haste in towns beyond the prohibited area, including Manchester. Eva Riese remembers that the girls 'were handed enough money for a train ride' to an inland town, several of them going to London 'in search of another hostel', Eva herself deciding to stay with (refugee) relatives in Manchester.[71] At all events, as in Stockport, the panic of June–July 1940, amongst the other injuries and humiliations it delivered to refugees, effectively put at end to the continuity of a hostel designed for refugee care.

The Harris House Girls[72]

Anon. (that is, no name appears before her entry in the Harris House Diary). She was born on 22 January 1927 in Vienna, where her father, who had been a shoe manufacturer assisted by his wife, had died in 1933. In Southport, before moving into the hostel, she had stayed at the 'nice house' of Mr and Mrs Lewis Livingstone. Mrs Livingstone had 'brought over' her sister.

Gina [Jean] Bauer was born on 10 December 1924 in Vienna, where her father was a comfortably-off businessman. She was helped to enter Britain by a sister working in London. She herself arrived in the country on 10 January 1939 and, after spending her first four months in London, entered Harris House on 18 May 1939. Her sister had made arrangements for the entry of their parents, who were expected to arrive on 6 September 1939. Her placement in Southport was as a trainee hairdresser in the salon of Mrs Crystal.

Frieda Beer (now Allon) was born in Vienna on 21 June 1924. After two weeks in the Kindertransport depot in Lowestoft and a further two weeks in Dovercourt, she spent nine 'happy weeks' at the home of Mrs Jacobs in Southport before entering the hostel. Her placement was with a tailor, Mrs Kaistiff [?]

Margot Brauer (now Barnes) was born on 19 October 1924 in Beuthen in Upper Silesia. Her first six weeks in Southport were spent at the home of Mr and Mrs (Max) Cantor. An orphan at the time of her arrival, her hope was to be reunited with her brother, who was working on a farm in Britain.

Dorothea Frankel was born on 25 August 1922 in Frankfurt, where her father, an ardent Zionist, was a doctor. She herself had been a member of the Zionist youth organisation, Habonim. At some point in the 1930s her parents had moved to Palestine, leaving her in Germany to await a permit to enter Britain. Unable to afford the cost of educating her in Palestine, their hope was that she would receive an education with foster parents in Britain. She left Frankfurt on 3 May 1939, arriving in Southport on 5 May. At the start of the Christmas term, she became a pupil at Brentwood Senior School.

Charlotte Gross was born in Vienna on 6 November 1922 and was brought up on a farm near the city managed by her father. She arrived in Southport with the first nine girls, stayed a few days in the home of Mrs Marks and six weeks with Mrs Livingstone before entering the hostel. Her placement was in a chemist's shop and she herself hoped to become a chemist.

Ruth Hammer left the hostel soon after her arrival to join parents en route for Australia. No details of her life are available.

Gerta Herzberg was born in Vienna on 26 July 1923. She spent her first weeks in Southport in the home of Mrs Nyman. In Southport she was 'trained for housework' but hoped to work in a gown shop. She spent the Pesach of 1939 at the home of Mrs Moss.

Hedwig Herzberg was born in Vienna on 21 January 1925, arrived in Britain on 12 December 1939 and spent her first six weeks in Southport at the home of Mrs Lever. In Southport she was an 'apprentice hairdresser'. Her elder sister had reached Chile, but her mother was still in Vienna and her father in Poland.

Helga Liebeman (spelt Lieberman in the Diary) was born on 26 December 192[?] in Berlin, where her father was an agent in the cotton trade, but was training as a baker and confectioner in order to gain entry to Australia. Relatives in London had found guarantors for Helga and her brother. In Southport, she was doing voluntary work at Mary Willet's Day Nursery.

Gisela Marx was born on 24 April 1925 in Suchteln (Dulken), near Cologne, where her father was the manager of a silk factory. She spent her first week in Britain in London before moving to Southport with Gina Bauer.

Ilse Maurer was born in Vienna on 21 June 1924. She spent two weeks in Dovercourt and Lowestoft before arriving in Southport, where she spent six weeks – 'a lovely time' – at the home of Mrs Caplan before moving into the hostel. Her placement was in the workroom of a gown shop.

Kitty Pistol was born on 25 November 1924 in Vienna, where her father was a doctor.

Eva Riese was born on 6 January 1924 in Magdeburg, where, after the Nazi takeover, her father, a lawyer had become a 'consultant for Jews'. Her guarantors were a Mr and Mrs Royce. Her placement was in a chemist's shop.

Hilde Rojt was born on 30 October 1932 at Borken, Germany.

Frieda Rojt was born on 21 April 1934 at Borken, Germany.

Lea Rojt was born on 23 July 1935 at Borken, Germany.

Rosa Schapira was born in Vienna on 22 January 1924.

Klara Schapira was born in Vienna on 1 February 1926 and arrived on 22 July 1939 in Southport, where she was met by Mr and Mrs Livingstone, the hostel matron and her elder sister, Rosa.

Jutta Schulz was born in Ratibor [*sic*] in Upper Silesia, where her father was a bank manager. A teacher in England had helped her gain entry to Britain. In Southport, she did housework in Harris House and looked after the 'three little ones' (that is, the Rojt sisters).

Notes

1 MJRC 6 December 1938.
2 MJRC Children's Sub-Committee 12 December 1938.
3 MJRC EM 12 December 1938.
4 The title of the *Southport Official Guide* for 1913. According to *The Shorn Lamb*, a novel by W.J. Locke, published posthumously in 1931, Southport was the home of 'thousands' of rich businessmen from Manchester and Liverpool (quoted in Francis A. Bailey, *A History of Southport* (Southport 1955) p. 193. For the Livingstone family, taped interview of Harry Livingstone by Bill Williams in MJM and Harry's unpublished typescript autobiography, '79 Years in Moneylending' (revised edition, 1970). In the late 1930s, with its headquarters still in Manchester, his firm had branches in Rochdale and Wigan. It was ultimately transformed into the present London Scottish Bank Ltd., once directed by Harry's son, Jack Livingstone.
5 MG 26 February 1941 records the death of Henry Doniger in Southport and the size of his estate (£118,150).
6 MG 21 November 1940. His home in Southport was in Lord Street, a mile-long street chiefly of fashionable shops, which was one of Southport's major tourist attractions.
7 MG 9 November 1940 records the bankruptcy of his firm in Brazennose Street in central Manchester. His residence was Cambridge Street, Southport.
8 MG 39 May 1940 records the death of Ephraim Marks in Southport.
9 Southport's population is given as 78,927 in the Census of 1931 and as 85,023 in the Census of 1941. The figure of 500 Jews is taken from the *Jewish Year Book*.
10 MCL M138 Letter from the editor of the *Southport Visiter* to Jon Billinge 30 November 1917.

11   E.g. *Southport Visiter* (hereafter SV) 10, 12, 19 and 22 November, 1, 6, 13, 29, 31 December 1938, 5 and 12 January 1939.

12   SV 1 October 1938.

13   Manuscript bound volume, 'Our First Year in Harris House', written in February 1940, on their last day together before the hostel's closure, by fifteen of the girls who were then still living in Harris House, edited by their matron, Dr Margarete Steinberg. The diary was bought for 20p at a jumble sale at St Philip's Church, Hampton Road, Southport, in the 1980s. It is now in the Manchester Jewish Museum. In 1987 the Harris House girls were reunited by Yorkshire Television at the Prince of Wales Hotel in Southport.

14   SV 22 November 1938.

15   SV 31 December 1938. The *Visiter* printed a photograph of the ten girls, still with identification labels in their buttonholes.

16   Report and Accounts of the Southport branch of the Movement for the Care of Children from Germany for the year ending 31 January 1940, p. 3. A handwritten note on the cover records that the report was compiled by Sampson Goldstone.

17   SV 31 December 1938.

18   *Ibid.*

19   *Ibid.*

20   SV 5 and 7 January 1939. The concert was organised by a committee under the chairmanship of Harry Buxton, 'a well-known [Jewish] theatrical figure' and manager of Prince's Cinema in Wigan. Letters of appreciation from Buxton and Harry Livingstone to the Southport public and the Garrick's owners appeared in SV 14 January 1939.

21   Report and Accounts of the Movement; SV 29 and 31 December, 1938, 5 and 7 January 1939.

22   From an (undated) offprint of an article in the SV by Julia Nason.

23   Report and Accounts of the Movement, pp. 1, 3.

24   The house survives intact in what is still a desirable residential area.

25   Of whom no evidence has come to hand.

26   *Ibid.*, p. 2.

27   Elisabeth (Lisa) Wolfe interview. Elisabeth was Margarete Steinberg's daughter.

28   *Ibid.*

29   Report and Accounts of the Movement, p. 4.

30   *Ibid.*, p. 8.

31   See biographical details below, pp. XX–XX. One girl was the daughter of a shoemaker assisted by his wife.

32   SV 31 December 1938 On 2 September 1939 the girls were joined by three sisters from the Rojt family, aged seven, five and four, refugees evacuated from the Tynemouth Refugee Hostel in Newcastle.

33   'Our First Year'. In the Harris House Diary, three were said to be in tailoring establishments, one in dressmaking, two in hairdressing, five in domestic service and two at school. The nursery was originally set up by Mary Willet for the children of tourists, but in 1939 it was converted for the use of some of the 50,000 evacuees expected in the town, chiefly from the poorer districts of Liverpool.

34   Report and Accounts of the Movement, p. 9.

35   *Ibid.*, p. 8.

36   'Our First Year'.

37   *Ibid.*; Report and Accounts of the Movement.

38   This paragraph is based on 'Our First Year'. Another interpretation of the Harris

House Diary is Tony Kushner's in *Remembering Refugees*, pp. 155–158.

39 'Our First Year'.

40 *Ibid.*

41 *Ibid.* In Manchester, Mary Goodwin had provided accommodation and support to members of the Kurer family, including the children and grandchildren of Wilma Weiss.

42 SV 29 December 1938.

43 *Ibid.*

44 'Our First Year'.

45 SV 10 January 1939; Report and Accounts, p. 5.

46 Report and Accounts of the Movement, p. 4.

47 *Ibid.*

48 *Ibid.*

49 'Our First Year'.

50 *Ibid.*

51 Report and Accounts of the Movement, p. 8.

52 'Our First Year'.

53 Report and Accounts of the Movement, p. 2. This was Dr S. Burns.

54 Report and Accounts of the Movement, pp. 11–12.

55 SV 25 February 1939.

56 See Chapter 15.

57 In October 1938 the unemployment figures stood at 1,936 men and 823 women (SV 8 October 1938). Both towns were dominated politically by the Conservative Party. Southport had been represented in parliament by a Conservative MP since 1924.

58 E.g. Eva Hamlet, *Against All Odds* (Citra, FL 1994) pp. 16, 19–20. In 1943 Eva married another young refugee, Egon ('Eddie') Hamlet, at the Aliens Office in Manchester; the couple left Britain for the United States in 1947.

59 'Our First Year'.

60 Report and Accounts of the Movement, p. 4.

61 The phrase is that of Helga Liebeman in 'Our First Year'.

62 Hamlet, *Against All Odds*, p. 19.

63 *Ibid.*, p. 20.

64 *Ibid.*, p. 30.

65 *Ibid.*, pp. 20–21.

66 *Ibid.*, p. 21.

67 Elisabeth (Lisa) Wolfe interview. Lisa Wolfe believed, however, that her mother was exceptionally skilled in handling the kind of younger children she had been accustomed to dealing with in the home in Vienna.

68 Report and Accounts of the Movement, p. 4. The Report attributes the girls' involvement to the impression made upon them by the Mayor's Appeal. It was they who then 'sought permission' to take part in the sales.

69 'Our First Year'.

70 Report and Accounts of the Movement, p. 9.

71 Hamlet, *Against All Odds*, p. 23.

72 Compiled from information in 'Our First Year' and Report and Accounts of the Movement.

13

'A haven of safety': refugees and the Manchester Women's Lodge of B'nai Brith

A revival of interest in refugees within the Manchester B'nai Brith Women's Lodge, following the collapse of its Hospitality Committee in 1935, was apparently sparked off by the same chain of international events and those same pressures from Woburn House which had brought the MJRC into being. Early in November 1938 Colette Hassan brought back from 'a refugee meeting' she had attended in London an 'urgent appeal for help'.[1] A joint meeting of the Manchester's men's and women's B'nai Brith lodges which followed on 7 November was addressed by Bernard Davidson, from the Jewish Refugees Committee in London, who on that same day spoke at the public meeting in Manchester out of which the MJRC emerged.[2] The response of the women's lodge was a decision to collectively 'adopt' child refugees and to pay for their upkeep by a 1s a week levy on its members.[3] A B'nai Brith Children's Care Committee was put together, with (Sister) Leon as its secretary-treasurer.[4]

A month later, after the Kindertransport had begun, further pressure was placed on the lodge, this time by the MJRC, which stressed 'the need for immediate assistance and outlining a scheme for placing children in hostels in numbers between 20 and 40'.[5] According to the MJRC, local help was required towards the placing in Britain of as many as 30,000 refugee children. The lodge meeting on 6 December which considered this appeal was addressed by a Dr Steuer, a Viennese refugee, who gave a 'very moving' account of 'some of his experiences before leaving Austria' and again emphasised the need of the 'unfortunate Jews of Central Europe' for immediate help. The lodge's response was a call for an increase in the weekly contributions of its members towards its 'refugee care fund' and a canvass for support from 'their friends outside the lodge'.[6] There were still no plans for the lodge to set up a hostel of its own. When requested by the MJRC, a few days later, to help run the proposed Cassel-Fox Hostel, it refused, on the grounds that a hostel intended for boys between the ages of twelve and sixteen 'would leave very little scope for the members of the lodge'; seven volunteers from the lodge agreed nevertheless to help with the 'enormous amount of work' needed to prepare the hostel for occupation, but only on a temporary basis.[7]

237

What transformed the lodge's plans was an offer by Arthur Kershaw, who had also donated Kershaw House to the MJRC, of a large villa at 391 Waterloo Road, rent-free and 'for as long as necessary', for use as a hostel for refugee girls.[8] At an 'Extraordinary Lodge Meeting' called at the request of ten members on 23 January 1939, by which time weekly contributions were yielding £19, a unanimous decision was taken to convert the premises on offer into 'Myer Kersh House'. Even then, it became a matter of debate. There were influential members, including the then president, Flora Blumberg,[9] who doubted the lodge's capacity to raise the £800 a year believed necessary for the support of twenty children, to maintain the level of weekly contributions necessary for their maintenance or to find the money which would be necessary, 'when the time came', for their re-emigration. Blumberg called on the lodge to 'proceed warily' in view of the 'innumerable snags' she had detected in the hostel scheme; the 'responsibility was so enormous' that it might be better, she believed, to hand over the money already collected to the MJRC and to call on it to assume 'all [financial] liability' for a hostel the 'entire administration' of which would be undertaken by the lodge.[10]

It was only when the MJRC, its own resources limited, found such terms unacceptable,[11] that a viable plan, agreeable to the lodge, the committee, Woburn House and the Home Office, was finally put together for the financing and management of a children's hostel with accommodation for a maximum of twenty-two children between the ages of thirteen and sixteen. The absence of girls awaiting placement at Dovercourt (one of the 'snags' identified by Blumberg) was overcome by a decision to work with 'a Dr. Klibansky of Cologne', who was known to Colette Hassan to have a 'well-formulated plan of getting children out of Germany fully clothed and with practically the entire equipment necessary for any hostel'.[12] Since contributions to its refugee fund were now said to be increasing in north and south Manchester, the lodge resolved to offer a block guarantee for sixteen children brought to England under Dr. Klibansky's scheme, leaving room at the hostel for six more children from other sources 'if and when finances would allow'.[13] These 'other sources' included the pool of 500 refugee children whose settlement was collectively guaranteed by the B'nai Brith District Grand Lodge in London, which now also assumed responsibility for financing the re-emigration of those refugees who came to live in Waterloo Road.[14] An arrangement was made with the Manchester Jews School for the younger children to spend one or two years there before going on to training 'according to their capabilities'.[15] It was believed that accommodation at the hostel would be 'for short periods', since the parents of some of the children had already made plans for their re-emigration.[16]

The Dr Klibansky whose name was introduced to the lodge by Colette Hassan, and through whom it now intended to fill its Waterloo Road hostel, was, in fact, Dr Menachem Erich Klibansky (1900–42), the young and energetic headmaster of Yavne School, a private Jewish gymnasium in Cologne, where in 1938 over 400 boys and girls were undergoing an education informed by the strictest values of orthodox Judaism.[17] The school was part of a complex of institutions centred on the Adass Yeshurun, a congregation which, since the 1880s, had held aloof from the liberal Judaism which characterised the bulk of Cologne Jewry. Appointed in 1929, Klibansky's perennial and largely successful efforts to render the school financially viable and to maintain its orthodox integrity in the face of liberal and Zionist pressures, was complicated, after 1933, by the need to navigate the obstacles placed in the way of Jewish education by the Nazi regime. Until the November of 1938 he remained hopeful that by skilful diplomacy, by ingeniously exploiting loopholes in Nazi legislation and by promoting united defensive action by all twelve Jewish secondary schools in Germany, Yavne School might somehow survive. This optimism was undermined by Kristallnacht when, following looting and the seizure of documents during the night of 9/10 November, both the Adass Yeshurun and Yavne came under physical attack, and two of the school's teachers were arrested and despatched to Dachau.

Klibansky then bent his efforts to the preservation of Yavne's traditions by more indirect means. His first thought was for the transfer of the school in its entirety to new premises in Cambridge.[18] By the end of 1938, however, as he came to accept the impossibility (on financial grounds alone) of such a move, he evolved a scheme by which pupils aged between six and fifteen might be transferred to England in successive groups, ideally with their teachers. This was more than a simple plan of human rescue. His hope was also to keep his pupils exiled in what he saw as 'the island of salvation' within the orbit of the kind of Jewish education for which Yavne had been created; taking advantage of the opening of Britain to unaccompanied young children, but working outside the usual channels of the Kindertransports, it was as much the spirit of Yavne which he now sought to export as its human constituents. His search, therefore, was for sponsors who might not only guarantee his pupils' material maintenance but ensure that they be kept together in hostels for the continuance of the kind of religious education which, in Klibansky's view, was the only appropriate response to Nazi anti-Semitism. There they would continue to have access to the 'spiritual resources' which had ensured the survival of the Jewish people 'in such times of distress'. The groups of escapees represented, for Kliblansky, the components out of which Yavne would, in due course, be reconstituted in Britain under his direction and with some, at least, of its teachers. In Cologne he secured the support for the scheme of almost all the parents of the Yavne children, the payments of the richer families helping to meet the travelling expense of poorer children. A similar arrangement was made with the English hostels: payments from the children of better-off families created free places for Yavne pupils.[19]

Klibansky's plans were particularly attractive to potential British hosts, since the children were accompanied by furniture and equipment from the school and were 'well-supplied with clothes, linen etc'.[20] During the Christmas holidays of 1938 Klibansky left Germany for London, with the approval of a German government still anxious to encourage Jewish emigration, to make the necessary arrangements, returning to Britain on two further occasions during 1939 to monitor their progress.

Before war intervened, four groups had been successfully transplanted in this way. On 17 January 1939, thirty boys from the junior classes of Yavne and two of their teachers – a young rabbi from Bonn, Dr Rudolf Seligson, and his wife, Gerda – left Cologne for London, where they found accommodation at a hostel in Cricklewood. Klibansky himself led a second group, made up of fifteen boys and fifteen girls, which arrived in London in February 1939, and a third, consisting of forty-two boys, which left Cologne on 9 May for Liverpool, where, again, guarantees and a hostel (at 19 Linnet Lane) were made available to them by the Liverpool Jewish Refugees Committee. The fourth and, as it turned out, final party was the one sponsored by the Manchester B'nai Brith Women's Lodge: sixteen girls, mainly from the fourth year at Yavne (all aged fourteen to fifteen years), under the supervision of the Yavne teacher, Rabbi Hans Joseph Heinemann (1915–78),[21] and accompanied by a Mrs Kahn of Altona, the prospective warden of the hostel on Waterloo Road, and by furniture and equipment transported to Manchester at the cost of the MJRC.[22] The intention was that the hostel would be managed by a House Committee, made up of members of the women's lodge, of which the chairman would be the lodge president, and which would be responsible to the MJRC, on which it would have one representative.[23] The expectation was that Heinemann would continue the religious education of girls who, for their secular studies, would be placed in the Manchester Jews School.

In the months preceding the opening of the hostel, others had chipped in with offers of support in money and kind. There were gifts of paint, wallpaper, lino and furniture. The curtaining was provided by the Dorcas Society of the Withington Congregation of Spanish and Portuguese Jews; the B'nai Brith Men's Lodge covered the cost of painting the exterior of the building and asphalting the paths. Compassionate builders reduced their first estimate, the Kershaw family donated £50 towards repairs. Dr Shindler offered his services as honorary dentist; the Quaker, Dr Margaret Edwards, as honorary medical officer. A small sum was raised by (Sister) Tescuiba from amongst the members of her private dancing academy. There were delays as the Home Office took its time in agreeing to the block guarantee and issuing entry permits,[24] but finally the hostel opened in mid-July 1939, in the event for sixteen girls.[25]

Heinemann and Mrs Kahn, who arrived with the girls, were joined shortly afterwards by Mrs Kahn's husband, Gotthelf, and by her daughter, Ruth, whose entry permits had been delayed and who were also expected to help with the hostel's management.[26]

In the three months before the girls were unceremoniously evacuated to Blackpool soon after the outbreak of war,[27] the hostel took its place as one of the Women's Lodge's two priority projects, second in its outlay of money and time only to the support of 'convalescent children' at the Lymm Home.[28] A rota of visitors monitored the welfare of the children and, apart from subsidising their maintenance, the lodge arranged an annual *Chanucah* 'treat' and a hostel *Seder*. From the beginning, Myer Kersh House acquired a reputation in the community for the strictness of the religious observance expected of its residents.[29] One of the original sixteen girls was to look back with gratitude on 'the inspiration received from the Jewish atmosphere of the hostel'.[30] This was perhaps the work of the Kahns, strict in their own observance and sensitive to the background of the children in Dr Klibansky's school.[31] The lodge's house committee was more concerned with the girls' social behaviour. Their movements were restricted, not least by pocket money of only 6d a week. No one was to leave the hostel without the committee's permission.[32] Only those who received the lodge's approval for their marriages were entitled to receive a gift.[33] The hostel was subject to occasional inspection by the MJRC, which had accepted ultimate financial responsibility for its upkeep, but what little evidence of these inspections survives suggests that its inspectors were more concerned with the fabric of the building than with its inmates. Otherwise, in spite of initial anxieties, the lodge's levy on its members covered the cost of the children's maintenance. The girls were apparently happy; Mrs Kahn's efficiency was eventually to make her the highest-paid refugee hostel matron in Britain.[34] A class in Ivrit, centred on the hostel, but open also to outsiders, was taught by the *Bachadnik*, Israel Alexander.[35]

If the girls believed that they had cause for complaint, it was of the absence of the kind of education which Klibansky had in mind, particularly after Heinemann's departure in December 1939 for another post in Manchester. Although of secondary age, they found themselves grouped as an extra class in an elementary school which could offer little more than practical commercial skills such as shorthand. 'We were in no way harmed,' one of the girls was to recall, 'we suffered a little, we were hungry at times, we experienced discomfort and did not learn anything. All this was often not easy for us. I still regret to this day that I was not able to study.' The dark side was the absence of parents. On one occasion, a member of the House Committee, May Aubrey, gave voice to the otherwise unspoken 'hope that they will all soon be united with their parents'.[36] In fact, the parents of only one of the children survived.[37]

Following the girls' return from Blackpool in April 1940, a decision had been taken by the lodge that those who were not still at school should 'commence training to enable them to become self-supporting'. A report on 'the present position', probably written late in 1944 or early in 1945, notes that only three of the original girls were left at the hostel, one of them nursing at Crumpsall Hospital, one working at a chemist's shop while studying for her matric, the third an apprentice to a milliner. Of the original thirteen girls 'who have left after their interviews with the Labour Exchange', eight were *chalutzim* on various *hachsharoth*, one was married, one had 'rejoined her parents in Chile', one was 'sent to [a] school for backward children and has remained there helping', and two were engaged on munitions work. Of the newcomers to the hostel, three were young children still at school, two were adults teaching 'at the new Jewish Day Nursery which is being opened' (probably the former Cassel-Fox hostel), two were machinists in factories engaged in war work, one was an apprentice to a dressmaker. The report ends: 'we hope the lodge will flourish and make progress during the coming year so that we may be able to shoulder our responsibilities in these times of stress as Bnai [*sic*] Brith and ... be true to the teachings of our Ritual, Benevolence, Sisterly Love and Harmony'.[38]

The children at Myer Kersh House, however unique the process of their arrival, were classed as Kindertransport children, and as such came within the remit of the Refugee Children's Movement (RCM), which in July 1941 opened a branch in Manchester to supervise work with 'Movement children' in Region 10 (that is, Manchester, Salford, South Lancashire, Cumbria and Westmorland). Their carers were members of the house committee set up by B'nai Brith, but their official guarantor was Lord Gorell, chairman of the RCM in Britain.[39] Until autumn 1944 the RCM had left the B'nai Brith house committee to get on with it, but as the original residents began to move on, and hostels in other parts of the north began to close down, the RCM's regional executive saw the hostel as a resource it might use for children otherwise stranded in Manchester. In October 1944 five children from the Harrogate Hall hostel, which was on the point of closure, were transferred under its auspices to Waterloo Road. This created initial difficulties. Not only were two of the children said to be 'inclined to be difficult' and to need 'careful handling', but two others, Ursel Guterman and Helen Schaffer, were found to be 'much more liberal in their orthodoxy' than the standards set at Myer Kersh House. Within six weeks, however, after Ursel and Helen had held discussions with Mrs Leon (now chairman of the House Committee) and Doris Pogmore (of the regional RCM), the two girls had settled down and all five were 'enjoying life in Waterloo Road'.[40] The standard of orthodox observance was too much, however, for Rosa Schneck, who was transferred to Waterloo Road from Liverpool in January 1945. As soon as she informed the Matron that her work in Manchester demanded her attendance on Saturdays, she was asked to leave and was immediately transferred to the more religiously relaxed hostel at 42 Heaton Road (see Chapter 21 below).[41]

One rare tragedy suggests both the precariousness of life in Britain for young, unaccompanied refugees and the sensitivity of agencies to adverse publicity. In late August 1944 Ruth Schmerler left her room in Myer Kersh house to travel to the *hachsharoth* of the Midlands and the South of England, perhaps with plans to enlist as a pioneer. She is known to have visited training centres in Bromsgrove and Maids Norton in Buckinghamshire. On 20 September she set off to visit the Bachad *hachsharah* at St Asaph in North Wales. A few days later her baggage was found abandoned on Shap Road near Kendal; a little later her strangled body was found near Charlton in Staffordshire. The verdict of an inquest in Manchester on 20 October was that she has been murdered 'by a person or persons unknown'. The decision of the MJRC was that she should be buried 'without publicity'. The only person at her funeral was her younger brother Kurt, then working at the Cleenbite Works and waiting to begin an optics course at Salford Royal Technical College. Although Myer Kersh House, still with twenty residents (eleven of them 'Movement girls'), was finally closed down in April 1945 after it was found to be 'in a dangerous condition', the B'nai Brith's refugee committee was given £250 by the RCM and MJRC between them for the purchase and fitting out of a house at 2 Bury Old Road identified by Rae Barash and reserved for the orthodox.[42] As they moved in with their twenty charges in the summer of 1945, B'nai Brith's attention, like that of the community as a whole, was turning its attention from refugees to survivors of the Nazi genocide.

Notes

1 MWLBB LM 7 November 1938.
2 MWLBB LM 7 November 1938: the meeting she attended was perhaps an early meeting of the (London) B'nai Brith Council for Refugee Children.
3 *Ibid.*
4 *Ibid.*, CM 21 and 24 November 1938.
5 BBMWL LM 6 December 1938.
6 *Ibid.*
7 *Ibid.*, LM 10 December 1938.
8 *Ibid.*, Extraordinary Lodge Meeting 23 January 1939.
9 In November 1936 a 'young and energetic' Flora Blumberg had stood unsuccessfully as Conservative candidate for the City Council for New Cross Ward (MSWC No. 219, November 1936, pp. 1–2).
10 *Ibid.*, Lodge Meeting 6 February 1939. Part of the problem was the president's sense of her initial exclusion from the decision-making process; she began the meeting by expressing her regret that the meeting had been held during her absence in London. She resigned from the Lodge Council in April 1939 because 'details' of the hostel 'did not meet with [her] approval'; she asked that her name be removed from the forms guaranteeing the girls' maintenance.
11 *Ibid.*, Lodge Meeting 6 March 1939. MJRC EM 28 March 1939.
12 *Ibid.*, Lodge Meeting 2 February 1939. It was Colette Hassan who drew Dr Klibansky to the notice of the lodge; she had seen a hostel in Cricklewood set up under his scheme.
13 *Ibid.*, Lodge Meeting 6 March 1939.
14 *Ibid.*, Lodge Meeting 17 April 1939.
15 *Ibid.*
16 *Ibid.* The children were allowed in only for temporary residence and training prior to their departure for other countries.
17 The account of Yavne and of Klibansky's role as its headmaster is based on Dieter Corbach, *Die Jawne Zu Koln: Zur Geschichte der ersten judische Gymnasiums im Rheinland und zum Gedachtnis an Erich Klibansky* (Coln 1990), written to accompany an exhibition mounted in Cologne in November 1990 to celebrate the life of Dr Klibansky, pp. 263–295. Klibansky was born in Frankfurt-am-Main in 1929 into a family, originating in Kovno, which had moved into Frankfurt during the 1860s. He was educated at the Goethe Grammar School in Frankfurt, where he took his Arbitur in 1919. He went on to the universities of Frankfurt, Munich and Marburg, where he was awarded his doctorate in 1925. Following teacher-training in Frankfurt, he became an assistant

teacher at the Judische Reformrealgymnasium in Breslau, where he was teaching when he was offered the post in Cologne. In 1927 he married Meta David, the daughter of a teacher at the Jewish girls' school in Hamburg, and the couple moved into a flat in Cologne in the spring of 1929. Apart from teaching, Klibansky's main interest was in historical research; for a time he was a member of the Historical Commission for Hessen and Waldeck. With 450 pupils Yavne was twice the size it had been during the early 1930s, its numbers swollen by the arrival of Jewish children driven from state schools by escalating anti-Semitism, some from distant towns.

18 The choice of Cambridge may relate to the fact that children in the higher forms were working for certificates accredited by Cambridge University. Between January and July 1938 a Cambridge student, Raphael Loewe, was a teacher at Yavne.

19 Corbach, *Die Jawne*, pp. 284–285. According to a *Jewish Chronicle* report of May 1939 (quoted in *ibid.*, pp. 285–286), children were allowed into Britain provided they were guaranteed £2 a week for their maintenance during their stay. Guarantors were required to deposit the necessary money in the bank for one year in advance.

20 JC 18 August 1939.

21 Born in Germany in 1915, Heinemann obtained his rabbinical semicha from the Mir Yeshiva in Belarus, which he attended from 1935 to 1937, before taking up a teaching post at Yavne. It was the intention that he should be joined in Manchester by his wife, Hilda (née Katz), a fellow teacher whom he had married in September 1938, but she failed to make her escape from Germany and died in Warsaw. Heinemann became a student at the University of Manchester. In 1949 he emigrated to Israel, where, as Yosef Heinemann, he became Professor of Hebrew at the Hebrew University (Corbach, *Die Jawne*, p. 250).

22 MWLBB Lodge Meetings 6 March, 17 April. Jacobs disputed that he had ever agreed to meet the costs of transportation, but ultimately paid up. For details of the Yavne transports, Corbach, *Die Jawne*, pp. 284–285. Although precise numbers are not available, Corbach estimates that Klibansky's scheme saved a total of 127 children, most of them pupils at his school. Other children made their own way to Britain on the official Kindertransports or with their parents.

23 *Ibid.*, Lodge Meeting 10 May 1939.

24 *Ibid.*, Lodge Meetings 10 January–3 July 1939 *passim.*

25 One Yavne pupil, Werner Lachs, arrived separately in Manchester in June 1939 with his parents, on visas issued in Berlin (without guarantors) by Captain Foley (interview of Werner Lachs by Rosalyn Livshin 18 February 2002. Hereafter, Werner Lachs interview). Myer Kersh House was one of seven hostels supported by the B'nai Brith Grand Lodge, five of them in London, each supported financially by local committees (JC 11 August 1939).

26 Heinemann left the hostel December 1939 to take up another post (MWLBB LM 7 December 1939).

27 During the girls' time in Blackpool, the MJRC took responsibility for the hostel. The girls returned to the hostel in April 1940 after it was decided that 'they should return to a Jewish environment and to commence training to enable them to become self-supporting' (MWLBB Report of Lodge Activities from October 1939 to the present day [late 1944 or early 1945]).

28 One reason why the lodge refused a collective contribution to the Austria Appeal in June 1938 was its 'obligations to Lymm'. The other was that its members had already subscribed as individuals.

29 When the closure of the hostel was mooted in 1944, strenuous objections were received by the lodge from Rabbi Dr. Altmann and his Religious Emergency Committee;

Hilda Barrett interview.

30   MWLBB LM 12 January 1944.

31   Barrett interview.

32   *Ibid.*, 11 March 1942.

33   MWLBB LM 6 June 1944.

34   MWLBB LM 12 January 1944, when her annual salary stood at £140. The girls were said to be 'overjoyed' on their return to the hostel from Blackpool (MWLBB LM 2 April 1940). When Mr and Mrs Kahn 'left for Palestine', probably during 1944, a Mrs Lorch, a relative, was appointed Matron (MWLBB Report of Lodge Activities).

35   Shula Jacobs, 'Kibbutz and Cocoa' (bound typescript, n.d.), p. 8. Alexander was later a teacher at the leading Anglo-Jewish boarding school, Carmel College.

36   MWLBB LM 29 December 1940.

37   Klibansky himself was trapped in Germany by the outbreak of war. He, his wife and three sons were arrested and on 20 July 1944 placed on a train in Cologne that was originally destined for Theresienstadt. Redirected to Minsk, the train halted on an estate 20km beyond the town, where 1,000 people (including the Klibansky family and many of the remaining Yavne children) were taken off, marched to pits prepared for them and shot by a death squad under the command of SS-Unterscharfuhrer Arlt. (Corbach, *Die Jawne*, pp. 296–298).

38   MWLBB Report on activities.

39   MJRC RCM EM 14 November 1944.

40   MJRC RCM EM 24 October, 14 November, 28 November 1944.

41   MJRC RCM EM 9 January 1945.

42   MJRC RCM EM 22 August, 12 December 1944, 12 and 19 February, 27 March, 24 April, 10 July 1945.

14

'Outposts of Jewish Palestine': young Zionist refugees in Manchester

In 1933 the Zionist movement in Manchester was already fifty years old. The first Manchester Jewish organisation to promote the colonisation of what was then Ottoman Palestine was founded in 1884, the first body seeking the creation of a Jewish state in 1896, the year of publication of Theodore Herzl's *Judenstaat*. In the following year, at least four delegates from Manchester attended the first Zionist Congress in Basle. Since the 1890s Isaiah Wassilevsky, whose *cheder* in Cheetham was favoured by the well-to-do, had been a leading figure in the revival of Hebrew as a modern language.[1] By 1900 the community had generated twelve Zionist formations, representing most facets of the international Zionist movement, and including one of the first women's Zionist organisations in Britain, the Daughters of Zion. Manchester became the home of the Russian émigré, Chaim Weizmann, already a leading player on the international Zionist scene, when in 1904 he took up a research post in chemistry at the University of Manchester. It was in Manchester that Weizmann made his seminal contacts with C.P. Scott, editor of the *Manchester Guardian*, and A.J. Balfour, then the Conservative MP for North-East Manchester. The 'Manchester School' of Zionists which Weizmann gathered around him during his Manchester years included young men and women – Simon Marks, Israel Sieff, Leon Simon, Harry Sacher, Harry Dagut and Rebecca Sieff – who were to become key figures amongst the leaders and publicists of British Zionism. It was with their backing that Weizmann was able to negotiate the Balfour Declaration, by which the British government in 1917 committed itself to support for the creation of a Jewish homeland in Palestine.

It is by no means clear what point the ebb and flow of Zionist sentiment in Manchester had reached on the eve of Hitler's accession to power in Germany. A Manchester Zionist veteran, speaking in 1937, remembered 'when in Manchester a Zionist dare not show his face in any synagogue' and when he 'had to sneak around when everyone was at prayer to post notices of a Zionist meeting, which otherwise were immediately torn off'.[2] By 1937, however, Zionists and Zionist sympathisers were amongst the community's acknowledged leaders. Nathan Laski, who is said to have been converted to the Zionist cause on the eve of the Balfour Declaration, was by 1933 making his way towards what turned out to be a near-dictatorship of the community. Norman Jacobs, his friend and ally on the Manchester Jewish Representative Council, was by 1933 the leading figure in an emerging local Zionist elite of young business and professional men. The *Jewish Year Book* for 1933–34 records seventeen Zionist formations in Manchester, including branch-es of the two main Zionist fund-raising bodies, the Jewish National Fund (JNF) and Keren Hayesod (the Palestine Foundation Fund), a branch of the British Section of the Jewish Agency for Palestine; a Manchester Zionist Association (MZA), the direct successor of the first Herzlian Zionist bodies in Manchester; a youth section of the religious Zionist Mizrachi Federation, a Hebrew-speaking society; two women's Zionist societies; and a coordinating committee, the Zionist Central Council of Manchester and Salford (ZCC). Within the Manchester rabbinate, the Mizrachi movement[3] had secured the backing of such influential figures as Rabbi Dr S.M. Lehrman, minister of the prestigious Higher Broughton Synagogue, the congregation of which the Marks and Sieff families had been amongst the founder members and which was still favoured by rising entrepreneurs of Eastern European origin; Rabbi H. Freeman, minister of the North Manchester Synagogue, which, as the Brodyer Synagogue, had been created in the 1890s by immigrants from Galicia; and Rabbi Israel Yoffey, who, as minister of the Manchester Central Synagogue since 1896, had laid the basis of religious Zionism in the city and subsequently served as its link with Mizrachi activists throughout the world.[4]

Amongst Manchester Zionists active at a national level was Lewis Namier, Professor of Modern History at the University of Manchester, Honorary President of the Manchester University Zionist Society and a provincial vice-president of the English Zionist Federation, on which the Manchester-born Israel Sieff and Simon Marks, the joint managing directors of Marks and Spencer, were London vice-presidents. Marie Nahum, wife of a wealthy Sephardi cotton merchant trading in Manchester, was president of the Manchester Daughters of Zion and a vice-president of the Federation of Women Zionists of Great Britain and Ireland, of which Manchester-born Rebecca Sieff, Israel's wife, was president.

An optimistic report in the *Manchester City News* described 1932 as 'A Year of Progress' for Manchester Zionism.[5] Membership of the Zionist ranks was said to be 'steadily increasing', especially amongst the young. Local fund-raising by the JNF, through blue collecting boxes in most Jewish homes, the sale of *shekolim*, and an annual Palestine Bazaar, was increasingly produc-tive. During 1932 the blue boxes raised £725, the Palestine Bazaar, held that year in Houldsworth Hall in the city centre, £1750. The sale of shekels at 2s 6d each had come to be regarded in the community, according to the report, as a 'voluntary income tax'.[6] A total of over 2,500 *shekels* had been sold that year by the Manchester Commission of the JNF and by the seven Manchester branches ('Beacons') of the Order of Ancient Maccabeans, a na-tional Zionist Friendly Society founded in Manchester and with its headquar-ters in the city. Towards the end of 1932 fund-raising to celebrate the 70th birthday of Nathan Laski had raised enough to endow a colony in Palestine to be known as Kfar Nathan Laski. A small but steady flow of Manchester Jews made *aliyah*, the most recent the seventy-year-old Hebrew teacher, Mordecai Sortman, a man of Lithuanian origin who, after serving in Manchester as an 'ardent worker for the Zionist cause' for over forty years, retired to Palestine in February 1933.[7]

This is not to suggest that Zionism had attracted the allegiance of the Jewish community at large. It was the more pessimistic view of the local Zionist, David Freeman, that in the years immediately preceding Hitler's rise to power 'a strong and virile Zionism had in Manchester been conspicuous by its absence. A spirit of apathy and indifference prevailed and even the staunchest lost heart.' To him 'it was evident that the Zionist idea had not yet lodged itself firmly with the general [Jewish] public', and that 'any serious endeavour to awaken the Zionist consciousness of the Jewish masses had yet to be made'.[8]

For Freeman the turning point was 'the German catastrophe'. The 'heart-searching' induced by the beginnings of the Nazi persecution of German Jewry evoked public protests in Manchester Jewry out of which a Zionist revival emerged during 1933–34. In 1933 the ZCC set up a Propaganda Committee whose 'slogan posters' and 'weekly meetings in every Synagogue Hall, Education Centre, Social Club and Friendly Society' attracted a 're-markable warm and eager' response from 'the masses'. A number of local synagogues now chose for the first time to affiliate to the English Zionist Federation (EZF). The sale of shekels rose 'materially'. The Order of Ancient Maccabeans, 'perhaps the finest recruiting ground for Zionism in the country', now set up 'junior beacons', the women's Zionist societies 'Ziona' groups, designed to ease the way into the movement for the Jewish young. A Zionist Youth Council was created 'to guide, inform and encourage the restless Jewish youth' of its twelve constituent bodies, 'who had been deeply moved by the violent treatment of their brethren in Western Europe'. Each was invited to send 'three of its most promising speakers' to a Speakers' Training Class out of which there had evolved by April 1934 'a body of speakers second to none in their knowledge, ability and assurance to state a case for the Cause'. Courses of lectures on Zionist history, lantern lectures on Palestine and classes in modern Hebrew were all 'remarkably well-attended'. A 'metamorphosis' of opinion had strengthened the hand of the ZCC in its 'serious endeavour to arouse Jewish consciousness' and to enable Zionism to take 'its rightful place in the heart and mind of the community'.[9] Zionists in Manchester, in common with the leaders of the movement throughout Europe and America, had found in the emergence and progress of an anti-Semitic regime in Germany at once 'a terrible confirmation' of its predictions,[10] a tragic validation of its existence and an urgent reason for strengthening its resolve.

It has been suggested that the prioritisation of Palestine as a destination for those escaping persecution in Germany was one reason for the apparent reluctance of Jewish communal leaders to encourage and support the settlement of refugees in Manchester itself before November 1938. Nathan Laski proclaimed Palestine to be, in 1933, 'the only place ... that the Jew could enter without reproach and with security' and urged even the community's non-Zionists to contribute to Zionist funds.[11] This was the message, too, of the Manchester branch of the JNF: Palestine was 'the sole avenue for the rescue of those co-religionists who are suffering untold miseries under the Nazi iron heel'.[12] It was taken for granted in Manchester that the bulk of the funds collected locally for the Central British Fund (CBF), bankers of the London Jewish Refugee Committee in London, would be devoted to projects designed to strengthen the infrastructure of Palestine and so increase an absorptive capacity upon which the right of Jewish settlement depended.

In 1935, apparently in breach of a 'fund-raising truce' in which Zionists had agreed in 1933 to suspend their routine fund-raising in return for a share of the monies accumulated by the CBF ,[13] the Manchester JNF Commission, in association with the ZCC, set up its own German Jewish Refugees Palestine Bazaar Fund, an extension of the annual Palestine Bazaars, which during that year was said to have raised funds at the rate of nearly £1,000 a week.[14] It was, according to one commentator, Manchester Jewry's answer not only to Hitler, but to a national Jewish leadership 'whose failure to press for government intervention [was] causing dismay'.[15] A programme of events designed to culminate with the Bazaar in May 1936 (which was itself expected to raise at least £3,000) included, in January, a concert at the New Hippodrome of which the leading stars were Robert Donat and George Formby and a 'Cruise Ball' at the Cheetham Assembly Rooms, at which the prizes on offer included a Mediterranean cruise on the luxury liner, the *Lancastria*, and which was expected to raise a further £1,200.[16] The 'meaning' of Palestine for the beleaguered Jews of Germany was spelled out in a powerful piece of propaganda by the Immigration Officer of the English Zionist Federation at a meeting at the Midland Hotel in Manchester on Sunday 12 January 1936. 'The main topic of conversation among them is now Palestine,' he told the meeting, 'and the only Jews who have any hope for the future are those who are waiting to emigrate there'. Palestine Certificates brought 'glad tidings of reprieve from despair and even death'. Desperate German-Jewish women, he asserted, were entering marriages of convenience with their holders. It was up to Britain to curb such illegality and meet such need by adopting 'a more sympathetic policy of granting certificates'.[17]

The editor of the *Souvenir Handbook to the Manchester Palestine Bazaar* of May 1936, after drawing attention to the increasing suffering of German Jewry, added: 'There is one hope for these, our brothers, whose "crime" is their Jewish heritage, and that hope is Palestine ... Side by side with the pity that urges us to their aid, there is the noble ideal and pride of the rebirth of Eretz Israel.'[18] Visitors to the Bazaar were urged to earmark their contributions to the Manchester branch of the Central British Fund, 'JNF': the Jewish National Fund would then 'use Earmarked sums for the purchase of land [in Palestine] upon which German Jews will be settled'.[19] In the handbook to the 1939 Bazaar, by which time the community had begun to make provision for refugee settlement in Manchester, the editor continued to press the prior cause of Palestine: 'Our pity for the persecuted,' he wrote, 'must take a practical form, and Palestine, our eternal ray of hope, offers the only relief to a tortured nation.'[20] There is evidence, too, that the Manchester JNF would approach Jewish bodies which had committed themselves to a regular donation to the CBF to make their contributions available 'for the use of the JNF'.[21]

In the years before the war, as speakers from the ZCC's Propaganda Committee worked to 'maintain Zionist interest' within the community and despatched Manchester delegations to London to press the Zionist case, the tempo of Zionist fund-raising and the intensity of its publicity kept pace with the progress of Hitler's 'war against the Jews'. In 1936 the Manchester Zionist Association, which had fallen into abeyance, was reconstituted to mount its own 'full and vigorous programme'.[22] The ZCC orchestrated communal protests and lobbied the MPs of Manchester, Salford and South Lancashire in the face of government restrictions on Jewish immigration into Palestine which culminated in the White Paper of 1939. A Manchester petition to the government in 1938 received 25,000 signatures.[23] Within the community the institutional structure of Zionism was extended to include three senior Mizrachi organisations and an active branch of the Socialist Zionist Poalei Zion, its constituency to embrace the new Jewish residential districts in Crumpsall, Sedgley Park and Prestwich. In 1939 there were at least twenty-three Zionist organisations within the Manchester community.[24] Zionist collecting boxes were then to be found in 800 Jewish homes, 700 of them in north Manchester, most of the rest in the areas of Jewish settlement in Withington and Didsbury.

A concerted attempt was also made, chiefly by the ZCC, to create a base of support for Zionism in the city, for which the way had long since been opened up by the pro-Zionist reportage of the *Manchester Guardian* and its sister weekly, the *Manchester City News*.[25] A 'Palestine Week' mounted by the ZCC in October 1938 included talks on Zionist topics open to the general public. In February 1939, when the city celebrated the centenary of its incorporation, the ZCC arranged for a 'City of Manchester Grove' to be planted in the King George V Forest in Palestine, for the name of the city to be inscribed in the Golden Book in Jerusalem and for the holding of a celebratory dinner at the Midland Hotel, to which local dignitaries were invited. During 1939 regular talks on Zionism to LNU branches, Co-operative Guilds, Rotary Clubs, local churches and party political bodies throughout the city were accompanied by the Zionist propaganda film, *Homeland in the Making*, for the showing of which Albert Oppenheim, a local Jewish garage proprietor and Zionist activist, offered 'the apparatus and his own services'. The ZCC's chairman, the dentist, Dr Philip Wigoder, was particularly active in spreading the Zionist word.[26] It seems likely that by 1939 this propaganda had made its mark, particularly within middle-class circles already under the influence of Manchester's liberal press. A Pro-Palestinian Committee, in its own words 'a body of non-Jewish sympathisers with the policy of the Jewish National Home as embodied in the Balfour Declaration and the Mandate',[27] was set up, perhaps in late 1938, under the chairmanship of the barrister, Liberal

Party activist and lifelong Judaeophile, Philip Milner Oliver: its propaganda meetings during 1939 included showings of another Zionist film, *Land of Promise*, loaned to it by the ZCC.[28]

In the absence of a large Arab population and of an organised Muslim community, no base existed for any powerful counter-blast to Zionist propaganda.[29] At some time in 1938 Syed M. Haffar,[30] a member of a Syrian merchant family living and trading in Manchester since the early 1920s, a lecturer in Arabic at the Manchester High School of Commerce and a devout Muslim, took it upon himself to 'state the Arab case' to local Rotary Clubs, often in response to earlier talks by Wigoder: an unequal contest in which the content of his talks, unlike those of Wigoder, were rarely reported in detail in the Manchester press.

On the eve of war refugees had only just begun to make what, in the longer term, turned out to be a decisive contribution to the ideological transformation of British Jewry. The most prominent refugee Zionist in 1939 was the Communal Rabbi, Dr Alexander Altmann, then a leading figure in the Manchester Senior Mizrachi Organisation. The chairman of the Senior Mizrachi Zionists was Dr Laser Lazarus Wislicki, who had arrived in Manchester from Breslau in November 1938 and who by the outbreak of war was also a vice-chairman of the Manchester JNF Commission. Refugee business and professional men were amongst the financial contributors to the cause,[31] but, as yet, the young Zionist formations which were to play such an important role in the popularisation of the Zionist ideal in Britain had not yet become part of the cultural baggage of those fleeing Germany.

In the handbook to the 1939 JNF Bazaar in Manchester, the editor wrote: 'Our pity for the persecuted must take a practical form, and Palestine, our eternal ray of hope offers the only relief to a tortured nation'.[32] Although other nations inevitably came to be seen as temporary resting places for refugees from Nazism, it remained the unwavering view of Manchester Zionists throughout the war years, a view continually reinforced by the scale and intensity of Nazi atrocities, that Palestine alone offered a secure and meaningful future for the Jewish people. In any post-war settlement, it was argued, Jews 'must have an area of land sufficient for the settlement of hundreds of thousands, perhaps millions, of people whose livelihood and future in Europe had been ruined by Hitlerism' and one with which it possessed a traditional link, and over which it might exercise 'sovereign control'.[33] Nazi persecution had 'shattered the illusion of saftey in assimilation' and confirmed Zionist belief that 'the abnormal and uncertain position of Jews must lead to tragedy in any world convulsion'. The creation of a Jewish state offered 'the last and greatest opportunity in history to solve the Jewish problem in any way that would secure Jewish survival'.[34]

War and Fascism equally provided Zionist leaders with new opportunities for pressing their case. From the beginning it was argued that in Palestinian Jewry the British Empire had its most dependable, perhaps its only, true friend in the Middle East.[35] Given recognition as an 'ally', and the promise of future sovereignty, the 'Jews of Palestine' could raise a loyal army of 50,000 to fight 'under the British flag', provide sustenance for Allied troops in the Middle East from its newly-cultivated acres, offer high-grade technical expertise, even supply bromide and potash to help Britain herself grow more food.[36] Pressure on the British government to 'accept the offer of Palestinian Jewry' of armed support, beginning with a Jewish battalion in Palestine, became a central theme of Zionist propagandists from early in the war.[37] In a war in which the western allies looked forward to a post-Nazi 'reconstituted humanity', there was room also for new variants on the cherished Zionist perception of a Jewish National Home as the vehicle of 'civilisation' in a barbarous Arab world. A parallel was drawn, by Rebecca Sieff for example, speaking in Manchester in October 1940, between the rebuilding of European civilisation and the 'upbuilding' – a favoured word in Zionist propaganda – of a Jewish nation.[38] The future of the Jewish people was portrayed as being as dependent on those 'principles of humanity and civilisation' for which the Allies were at war as the democratic way of life.[39] The creation of a Jewish state was 'not merely work for the Jewish people', but part of 'the greater cause' of ensuring the survival of 'civilisation itself'.[40] The creation of a Jewish nation would be a means of concentrating and 'cultivating' the 'genius of the Jews' so that its achievements would be 'thrown into the common pool': this was 'true patriotism'.[41]

While in Manchester, the effect of the rise and progress of Nazism was to stimulate Zionist activity, add grist to Zionist propaganda, win more non-Jewish friends to the Zionist cause and perhaps engender new levels of support for Zionism in the Jewish community at large, in Germany one of its immediate effects was to create a growing reservoir of recruits to Zionism, especially amongst the young boys and girls who had not yet been drawn irretrievably into the assimilatory imperatives which dominated the life of German Jewry. For them chalutzic Zionism, in particular, offered a ray of hope in an otherwise desperate situation: an alternative national identity to the one of which they were being exponentially deprived and a creative agenda to offset the well-founded pessimism of their elders. For them and others, Zionist youth movements constituted an alternative to the popular *Wandervogel* movement, as what had once been for German adolescents a form of healthy generational and social protest, fell increasingly under Nazi control.

An important witness to these events was Leon Aryeh Handler,[42] born in 1915 into a German business family of Eastern European background, Chassidic beliefs and Zionist inclinations. Brought up in Magdeburg, Handler received a secular and religious education, both of which culminated in Frankfurt, in the Lessing Gymnasium on the one side and the Mizrachi Yeshiva on the other. It was on his return to Magdeburg in 1931 that he first became involved in religious Zionism, joining the new but growing Zionist youth movement, Brit Hanoar. In 1932 he was one of a group of young Zionist leaders called together in Berlin by a rabbi's wife, Recha Freier, to create what became the prototype of Youth Aliyah, the *Judische Jugendhilfe EV*; looking back on this event, it remains Handler's view that Freier has received insufficient credit as the founder of a German movement dedicated to the training of young Jewish people for resettlement in Palestine which, in cooperation with the better-known Henrietta Szold[43] in Palestine, evolved during 1933–34 into Youth Aliyah: more properly 'The Movement for the Rescue of Jewish Boys and Girls from the Countries of Oppression and their Rehabilitation in Palestine'. Under its auspices German-Jewish children were brought together in groups of between twenty and sixty to train 'as future farmers and craftsmen in Palestine' and to be imbued, at the same time, 'with the spirit of Jewish culture and tradition'. Inspired at training centres (*hachsharoth*) to adopt Hebrew as the language of everyday life, they would be transformed into the citizenry of a Jewish-state-to-be, where they would become part of 'the renaissance of Jewish culture'.[44]

Within the next two years, Handler had taken charge of Youth Aliyah in Germany and of Bachad (an abbreviation of Brit Chalutzim Datiim, the 'Covenant of Religious Pioneers'), that part of the religious Zionist movement imbued with Socialist ideals and designed 'to train and educate religious Jewish boys and girls to be pioneers for Palestine and to settle them after concluded training as *Chalutzim* in Eretz Israel, where they help at the upbuilding of our National Home'.[45] With opportunities for settlement in Palestine limited by British law, Handler had by 1935 begun to travel throughout western Europe in search of alternative temporary placements for religious *chalutzim* (pioneers). The Nazi regime, favouring, at this time, the expulsion of Jews, gave him support, the Gestapo in Berlin allowing him to move into and out of the country without restriction, although with no more than ten marks in his pocket and with the stipulation that he supply eight copies of a ten-page report on his activities on his return. He met with most success, he remembers, in Denmark, Sweden and Holland, where, in the circumstances, local farmers were prepared to aid the rescue of young Jewish children by offering them jobs as 'trainees'. Belgian farmers were rather less accommodating, while in Britain and France legal restrictions on immigration presented him with immovable obstacles.

On a visit to London in 1935 he failed to persuade either the Chief Rabbi or the secular leaders of British Jewry to put pressure on the British government for the easing of entry requirements. They were, he believes, unwilling to challenge a government committed on the one side to the appeasement of Hitler and, on the other, to an economic recovery which an influx of 'alien immigrants' seemed likely to disrupt. It remains his view that a more combative approach could have saved many more German lives. The Chief Rabbi, while declining to act, in part, because he did not believe his role as joint-chairman of the German Boycott Committee would help Handler's cause, offered him instead a thousand free copies of the first volume of his translation of the Torah which Oxford University Press was about to publish. Diplomatically failing to mention his visit to Hertz in his report to the Gestapo, his relationship with the Nazis was all but destroyed by the arrival of the copies in Germany, and their seizure by Nazi officials, soon after his own return.

With the travel of German Jews to Austria banned by the Nazi regime immediately after the Anschluss, Handler became part of a group which made illicit visits to Vienna to keep in touch with the Austrian *chalutzim*. Always a dangerous operation, on one occasion Handler narrowly escaped with his life after a chance encounter on a train with Adolf Eichmann, who either did not recognise the man he had done business with in Berlin or chose, for whatever reason, to take no action.[46]

In the summer of 1938 Handler was called upon by Henrietta Szold to go to Palestine on an extended visit to help her find ways of increasing its limited absorptive capacity for religious *chalutzim*. In the event, with his return journey scheduled for what turned out to be the day after Kristallnacht, Szold alerted him to the danger of returning to Berlin, where orders were out for his arrest, and instead persuaded him to make his way to Britain, where London could become the new base for his activities. In late November 1938, with letters of recommendation to the Chief Rabbi and Chaim Weizmann supplied by Szold, Handler joined the staff at Woburn House as leader of Youth Aliya. There, with the beginnings of the Kindertransport in December 1938, which included some transports despatched under the auspices of Youth Aliyah, he saw it as his task to create, within Britain, *hachsharoth* to which the religious amongst them might be directed. For this purpose, with help from Rebecca Sieff and Elaine Blond, he established a Jewish Agricultural War Committee, with Sieff as its chairman and he as its secretary. It was, he remembers, an independent committee, although working 'in partnership' with the German Jewish Aid Committee and the CBF. It became, in his words, the 'cover' under which both the secular and religious chalutzic Zionist movements acquired land and made their placements. He seems equally to have immediately assumed the task of creating in Britain a religious Zionist youth movement, based on the German Brit Hanoar, which might in time create a pool of *chalutzim*, both refugee and native Jews, for British *hachsharoth*. His base for both sides of his work was Bachad, the headquarters of which were now transferred to London.

In Britain, Handler worked closely with British Jewry's own chalutzic movement, a pale reflection of the movement in Germany, and, as in Germany, in consultation with the secular wing of the chalutzic movement, of which the overarching body was Hechalutz (literally, 'The Pioneer'), an organisation founded in Russia in 1917 to prepare Jewish youth for 'creative settlement' in Palestine.

Although Britain was not the ideal context for the recruitment of *chalutzim* – the general perception by English Jews of the role in Zionism of 'Western Jewry' was as the providers of the finance which would enable the settlement of Eastern European Jews in Palestine[47] – at some time during 1933–34 'a few idealistic young people' in Britain, chiefly dissidents from the (then non-Zionist) youth movement, Habonim, 'made up their minds to relinquish the comforts of their urban lives and to take up agricultural training'.[48] According to one autobiographical account, their initial search for land to turn into a *hachsharah* brought them to Manchester, where, under the leadership of Yehuda Avner, twelve members of the group, who now identified themselves as part of the European Hechalutz, tried, without long-term success, to establish a training centre on an (as yet unidentified) farm on the northern outskirts of the city.[49] Writing in April 1934 the Zionist David Freeman noted the presence of 'twelve Haluzim [*sic*] ... going through a practical course of work on a farm [also un-named] on the outskirts of this city [Manchester]'.[50] It was probably members of this group whose presence in the Manchester area was noted in February 1934 by two leading members of the Manchester Women's Lodge of B'nai Brith, who called on their fellow lodge members to give 'the first [Manchester] *chalutzim*' whatever help they required.[51] Although Freeman suggests that the farm had evinced 'considerable interest',[52] it appears to have been the failure of this and similar initiatives, unsupported at first by the mainstream Zionist movement in Britain, which persuaded the young idealists to constitute themselves in 1935 into a formal British branch of Hechalutz, Histraduth Hechalutz B'Anglia.

In a parallel development, also in 1935, the Agricultural Committee of the German Jewish Aid Committee in London, intent on the rescue of the German-Jewish young, began to experiment in providing agricultural training for refugees (thus securing their entry and temporary residence as agricultural trainees under British immigration law), who were then expected to leave the country for Palestine. This took what was soon found to be the unsatisfactory form of sending individual 'pupils' to (the very few) Jewish farmers throughout the country. In such circumstances, the training soon proved to be both 'technically inadequate' and unduly expensive; it was logistically impossible to bring together the scattered pupils for a coherent education in agricultural theory, while, for their part, the farmers expected payment for their services.[53]

These limitations were an object lesson for Histraduth Hechalutz B'Anglia, which soon after its foundation had become a 'flourishing organisation' with nearly 200 members in London and the provinces. In that year it felt strong enough to sound out the official institutions of the community on the possibility of their setting up and funding a training farm. It seems that it was the Zionist Federation of Great Britain and Ireland (EZF) which took the lead in persuading the community that a 'real need' existed for such an institution and then in raising a loan of £4,000 for its purchase. An impressive communal committee was appointed to seek out suitable land and in mid-June 1935 possession was taken of a farm at Harrietsham, in picturesque country some ten miles from Maidstone in Kent, which was to become the David Eder Farm.[54] The aim was to prepare some 20–25 'young English Jews and Jewesses for life in Palestine':[55] following a year's training they were expected to leave for the Yishuv, where they were to set up 'a special English colony'.[56] The belief was that once it went into full production – in an estimated two years' time – the farm would become self-sufficient, particularly if it could attract a London custom, as it was fully expected to do.[57] In the meantime, an appeal went out for donations. In July 1935 members of the Manchester Women's

Lodge of B'nai Brith were pressed to lend their 'moral and financial support' to an appeal from the District Grand Lodge on its behalf.[58] Amongst the first donors (and the only one from Manchester) was the cotton merchant, Victor Hassan, whose wife was a prominent member of the women's lodge.[59]

It was thus the EZF, although inspired indirectly by European Hechalutz, which played the decisive role in setting up the first *hachsharah* in Britain. While it appears to have acted in response to spontaneous pressure from the communal grass-roots, the establishment of a chalutzic movement in Britain was in keeping with its political agenda in 1935. It was necessary to serve notice on both the British government and the authorities of the Mandate that British Jewry was as committed in a practical way to Jewish settlement in Palestine as its European peers. An 'English colony' might also serve a strategic purpose, it was believed, as an 'intermediary' between Palestinian Jewry and the British authorities 'to clear up such difficulties and misunderstandings which exist on both sides'.[60] In Manchester, meanwhile, a branch of British Hechalutz was in existence by May 1936, when it participated in the annual Palestine Bazaar.[61]

What was then a still relatively minuscule chalutzic movement in Britain was soon provided with a decisive boost by the arrival of refugees already committed to the pioneer movement. In Hitler's Germany, movements dedicated to the preparation of *chalutzim* were both stimulated by Nazi anti-Semitism and tolerated by the regime as one means of promoting Jewish emigration. In July 1936, for example, permission was granted to the Socialist Zionist youth movement Hashomer Hatzair (the 'Young Guard')[62] to hold a national training camp at Porchendorf, a village near Pirna in Saxony, which included, apart from the promotion of *Aliyah*, courses in modern Hebrew, a small library of Zionist texts and a large map of Palestine on the wall of a barn. In Nazi Saxony, which those attending the camp navigated with some difficulty, a blue and white flag with the Star of David was ceremonially raised over the camp every morning.

Members of Hashomer Hatzair were amongst those who were arriving in Britain, together with religious Zionists, on Kindertransports sponsored by Youth Aliyah at the time that Handler set himself up at Woburn House. It has been suggested that at least one thousand of the young transportees had already been involved in chalutzic youth movements in their home countries,[63] and no doubt many more were open to persuasion once they had experienced the rootlessness of their own lives in Britain. At all events, Handler did not see the constituency of his *hachsharoth* solely in terms of refugees. From the beginning it was his intention to 'meet immediately with English Jewish youth and … instil in them the same education for religion and labour. And I must say … we managed then to … bring the foreign Jews together with the English young Jews.'

The chronology of Handler's early activities in Britain remains vague. By the end of 1938, with the help of his assistant, Bob Durlacher, and a young Belgian refugee, Ben Polack, he had set up in London a Bachad Snif (Branch) and two small, but thriving, groups of B'nei Akiva (the 'Sons of Akiva'), a youth movement, based on the German Brit Hanoar, which was to become the junior section of British Bachad. At the same time he toured the country in search of land which, with the help of his London committee, and ideally of local Jewish communities, might be borrowed, rented or purchased for use as *hachsharoth.* Early in the search he turned his attention to Manchester, renowned for the size and piety of its orthodox community, for over fifty years an important focus of European Zionism and the place of origin of the chairman, and some of the members, of his London committee.

The first documentary evidence of his interest is an appeal received by the Manchester Jewish Refugees Committee in December 1938 for help in providing 'hospitality' for 150 *chalutzim* who were to be trained on a farm in the Manchester area.[64] It seems that Handler had already opened negotiations with Arthur Kershaw, the wealthy Manchester Jewish property-owner who had earlier placed Kershaw House at the disposal of the MJRC, and who early in 1939 allowed Bachad the use of a small farm owned by his family in Whitefield, a township some five miles north of Manchester. Although perhaps only a temporary expedient until more extensive property could be acquired, twenty *chalutzim* were settled on the farm by February 1939, when Kershaw resigned his chairmanship of the Kershaw House executive in order to give them his personal attention.[65]

At some time in early March, the Manchester *chalutzim,* now forty in number, moved from Whitefield to Thornham Fold Farm, a neglected dairy farm of 60–70 acres at Castleton, between Manchester and Rochdale, apparently purchased for Bachad by Kershaw, perhaps with the help of Albert Oppenheim, a well-to-do owner of a garage in Prestwich, already active in the propaganda activities of the ZCC.[66]

Oppenheim shared with Dr Isidore Blair, a surgeon at the Manchester Jewish Hospital the nominal 'directorship' of the farm.[67] Although the farm buildings were primitive and ramshackle, it was none the less, in Handler's view, a good training centre, particularly after the members of Whitefield Golf Club had been persuaded to donate all the necessary equipment.[68] By mid-July forty-two young orthodox refugees from Germany, Austria and Czechoslovakia, thirty boys and twelve girls, were living in wooden huts they had built for themselves at Thornham Fold, six boys had found work on other local farms, and the whole operation was 'functioning [so] satisfactorily' that Bachad nursed the hope of a further twenty young people being taken in the near future.[69] They would become, Rabbi Rosen believed, 'messengers to Eretz Israel, to give the Jewish people dignity and self-respect'.[70]

From the beginning the farm was brought within the managerial orbit of the MJRC, which exercised a degree of control through an Agricultural Committee of sixteen members, of which the chairman was the Sephardi merchant, Victor Hassan and the treasurer Hassan's Haifa-born business partner, Joe Leon (whose wives were members of the B'nai Brith Women's Lodge); it was apparently from this committee that a smaller management group was chosen.[71] In 1941 this 'Refugee Farm Committee' was made up of Joe Leon, Albert Oppenheim and Dr Isidore Blain.[72] Handler remembers also the involvement of Dr Laser Lazarus Wislicki, who had arrived in Manchester as a refugee from Breslau in November 1938 and who had rapidly become active in local Zionism.[73] Conditions on the farm, approached from the main road by means of a mud track, impressed one sympathetic observer as involving considerable 'hardship'.[74]

In compliance with Bachad ideals, Thornham Fold Farm was characterised not only by agricultural training, but by intensive educational programmes which embraced modern Hebrew, Judaism, Jewish history, modern Jewish thought, current affairs and Zionist propaganda, and by a simple communal life which the pioneers were expected to replicate in Palestine. The life-style was co-operative and, if not Marxist, then 'anti-bourgeois':[75] a simple routine of work, worship and study was punctuated by *shiurim*, lectures and debates (some of them in German), and by conferences and summer schools which brought together pioneers from throughout the country.

According to one close observer of life on Thornham Fold, 'Chaverim and chaveroth, after having finished their day's work in gardens, fields or stables, return home to their joined meals and finish their day with various studies: Hebrew language, Jewish history, Bible. They have lectures, readings and discussions, music evenings and they talk about the problems of the time, that must be dealt with. Because the Bachad does not only want to train youth in agricultural and manual work, but her aim is to raise the educational standard of her members and to intensify their cultural and social life, much emphasis is laid on tarbut work.'[76] As future *kibbutzniks* the *chalutzim* were encouraged to see their lives in terms of the vocabulary of visionary Zionism: they were *Chaverim* (comrades) chosen for *hachsharah* (training) which would lead, in time, to the creation of an Eretz Israel (Land of Israel) based on social justice and orthodox Judaism.[77]

Beyond these routines, little is known of the inner life of the Thornham Fold kibbutz. In November 1940 it received a grant of £500 from the Jewish Refugees Committee in London, 'to help it to become self-sufficient'.[78] From February 1941 it had 'a paid manager', presumably financed by the MJRC.[79] From Manchester, the Refugee Farm Committee did what it could to coordinate its activities, recruit new *chalutzim* and shore up the farm's finances, although the initial expectation was that it would achieve a high degree of self-sufficiency. Neighbouring farmers who employed the *chalutzim* were expected to pay the equivalent of their wages into the farm's funds. The farm itself sought a market for Kosher and Passover milk amongst Manchester's more orthodox Jewish institutions and families.[80] Amongst the fund-raising devices organised by Joe Leon, the imaginative treasurer of the management committeee, was one which entitled donors to 'name a cow'.[81] Occasionally the MJRC supplied clothes for the boys on the farm.[82] The Manchester branch of the Mizrachi body, the TVA, organised regular visits from the community to the farm, perhaps to encourage donations, perhaps to interest young Manchester Jews in themselves training as pioneers.[83] Shula Jacobs remembers that the *chalutzim* gave occasional talks at Myer Kersh House, the B'nai Brith Children's Hostel at 381 Waterloo Road, only two doors away from the Bachad Bayyit, a form of recruitment which bore some fruit, although not, apparently, for Thornham Fold.[84] According to one account, some members of the management committeee, at least, became personally involved in the work of the *hachsharah*. If Albert Oppenheim's memories are accurate, they travelled to Thornham Fold on a daily basis, as teachers of English, Hebrew and Jewish history and as instructors in the arts of 'settlement-making' and self-reliance.[85] Handler remembers that he received moral support from the members of some of Manchester's haredi families, amongst them Leo Groskopf and Heinz Pfeffer, although they were less than sympathetic towards the mixing of the sexes which life on Thornham Fold entailed. Although the outbreak of war is said to have 'interfered' with the farm's progress, in 1941 it remained, according to the ZCC, 'a source of pride to all who had come into contact with its workers'.[86]

Handler himself kept in close touch, leaving the agricultural management to the local committee, but occasionally visiting the farm to deal with 'human problems'. One that he particularly remembers was the decision of two of the *chaverim*, Heinz ('Heini') Preiss and Johnny Mantel, to leave the farm, abandon their Judaism and join Free German Youth, a local refugee body believed by Handler (correctly) to be under Communist leadership. He spent a whole night in one of the huts, trying, by candlelight (the farm's electrical power supply was fragile), and without success, to dissuade the young *Bachadniks* from leaving the farm and the faith.[87]

Classed by the Home Office as agricultural trainees, the young religious refugees under Handler's care were legally obliged to leave the country for Palestine once their training was complete. In reality, with the closure of the Mediterranean at the end of 1939, only a few were able to leave, none of them, it seems, from Thornham Fold. To deal with those trapped indefinitely in Britain, Handler (and Hechalutz) entered into negotiations with the War Agricultural Executive Committees (WAECs), set up by the government on a county basis to maximise food production. With these he soon developed a good working relationship: not only did they supply equipment and funds to his *hacharoth*, seen now as useful contributors to the cause of British self-sufficiency, they subsidised the wages paid to the *chalutzim* by farmers and became accustomed also to turning to Handler for extra workers at harvest time. By 1943 the government's central WAEC was paying the wages of hundreds of *chalutzim*, religious and secular, spread in groups throughout the country; wages which were then typically pooled to meet the expenses of the *hachsharah*.[88] Teams of experts provided specialist courses, again with the support of the WAEC, on the scientific principles underlying agricultural production, with special reference to conditions in Palestine. Other *chalutzim* were re-deployed, with the help of the Ministry of Labour, the men into industry, the women into nursing. The same was true of the 600 workers on the thirteen secular *hachsharoth* whose activities were coordinated by British Hechalutz. They too were subsidised by the WAECs, and with good grace: the chairman of the Worcestershire WAEC wrote to Hechalutz in 1944 in praise of 'an excellent movement ... which combines ... the maximum help for the war effort and the best possible training for the young people who hope to go to Palestine after the war'. The work of the 'young Jews', he went on, was 'more and more appreciated by farmers seeking to feed the nation and so release cargo space for essential war supplies'.[89]

It is not possible to define the moment at which Thornham Fold Farm was abandoned as being no longer economically viable. The probability is that it was at some time in 1943, when Sam Stern remembers boys from the farm arriving at the Cassel-Fox hostel.[90]

In refugee history, the wartime *hachsharoth* are perhaps best seen as transient phenomena: footprints made by refugees on their chosen and single-minded route from their homelands to Palestine. They offered a degree of stability, perhaps an alternative family, certainly a sense of purpose, to those uprooted and isolated by Nazi oppression. Although a few *chalutzim* lost their Zionist way to tread one or other of the routes of integration into British society, most made *aliyah* as soon as it became possible after the war. They have left few traces on the ground of the English countryside.

More important in its effects in Manchester than the Bachad *hachsharoth* themselves was the orthodox infrastructure which sustained them. As Handler had hoped, Thornham Fold was one element of a comprehensive and distinctive Bachad collective life in Manchester, in which the chief participants, other than the *chalutzim* themselves, were refugee trainees in Manchester industries and refugee domestic servants in Manchester homes. 'Although our chaverim and chaveroth do not live or work together as in the *Hachsharoth*,' wrote one secretary of Manchester Bachad, Toni Szac, herself a refugee, 'the same ideals combine us and bring us together to social gatherings and various studies in the evenings. Many of our chaverim come from *Hachsharoth*, some of them have already been there on the Continent, and many of us [*sic*] hope to go to Hachshara [*sic*]. When we work in factories or in households all day and we come together in the evenings to Shiurim and Sichoth, although tired out from our day's work, we feel new life brought to us in these meetings. We see that not only our body, but also our spirit wants his food, and we feel, wherever we are, whatever we do, we have an ideal in front of us, and we work to come nearer to it. We have been deprived of our homeland on the Continent and we found refuge in this country, but we want to build ourselves a new home in Eretz Israel, and we train and educate ourselves to be good pioneers.'[91] On the High Holydays Bachad organised special services for its members.[92]

Apart from the *hacharoth*, Bachad created in each of major towns with which it forged strong links – London, Glasgow and Manchester – a Beth Chalutz (literally 'House of Pioneers', otherwise the Bachad Bayit), which served not only as its local headquarters and central meeting place, but as a centre for the training of refugees in skills which equipped them for work in local industries, and which, like agricultural expertise, they would be expected to deploy in due course in Jewish Palestine. There too Bachad organised regular programmes for the study of Hebrew, religion and politics, in which a leading part was played by Rabbis Heinemann, Altmann and 'one of the spiritual leaders [of Bachad]', S. Sperber, who, after leaving the Bachad Hachshara at Gwrych Castle in North Wales to become a welfare worker with the Refugee Children's Movement in Manchester, remained in the city until February 1945.[93]

'Joining Bachad in many of its activities' at its Beth Chalutz at 387 Waterloo Road in Cheetham Hill were members of its 'younger group', B'nei Akiva (BA) – 'the youth movement of TVA and Bachad', according to the *Jewish Gazette*[94] – which in 1941 included both young students from the Manchester Yeshiva and around twenty girls between the ages of fifteen and seventeen, many from Myer Kersh House, all said to be 'eager in their work and studies'.[95] Members of Bachad and B'nei Akiva often held meetings at Thornham Fold Farm, which during the summer months they visited 'nearly every Sunday', joining the *chalutzim* 'to play ball games and to enjoy ourselves at [*sic*] the countryside'.[96] It is difficult to overestimate the significance of BA to the future of Manchester Jewry. Its social and religious activities served to sustain the orthodoxy of post-war Jewry, to maintain a link between the orthodox young and the Zionist movement and to provide a committed lay (and Zionist) leadership to the community's many orthodox institutions, even to the community as a whole. It formed part of Handler's ideal of a refugee and native Jewish youth united in their Zionism and in their orthodoxy.

On 27 December 1941, in a rare reference to events in the orthodox, as distinct from the assimilated, Jewish community of Manchester, the *Manchester Guardian* reported the opening by the Manchester Mizrachi Association of a 'residential educational centre' in Great Clowes Street, in the Lower Broughton area of Salford, for 'young refugees training as farmers'. Lectures in advanced Jewish learning, the report read, would be complemented by programmes designed to enable the refugees to complete their interrupted secular education.[97] This was, although the report did not use the word, Manchester's Merkaz Limmud (literally, 'Centre of Learning'), one of three such bodies set up by Bachad (the others were in London and Glasgow) as national training centres to which religious *chalutzim* from throughout the country might be selected for between three and six months of 'solid learning', and which also served as a focus for orthodox social events, religious *shiurim* and Mizrachi Zionist education, in all of which many young refugees outside Bachad were invited to participate; discussions were often conducted in German or in broken English.[98] Betty Rabin, a refugee from Hamburg who, although not connected with the *hacharoth*, attended lessons at Merkaz Limmud with her brother, Beni, and 'joined the Hebrew sing-songs' of the *chaverim*.

She remembers its first principal as being 'an exceptionally intelligent and mature teacher in his middle twenties'. After training as a teacher in Germany, she recalls, he had spent some of his early years in a Lithuanian Yeshivah.[99] This was almost certainly Hans Heinemann, the 'religious

Socialist' who had arrived in Manchester from Cologne in July 1939 as a worker at the Waterloo Road Hostel of B'nai Brith. A fellow teacher at the Merkaz, however, was the London-born Kopul Rosen, the dynamic young rabbi who arrived in Manchester in February 1939 at the age of twenty-six to become the first minister of the recently established Higher Crumpsall Synagogue. Following a religious education from the age of fourteen at Yeshiva Etz Chaim in Whitechapel, Rosen had completed his rabbinical training with four years at the Mir Yeshiva in Lithuania.[100] 'An immensely gifted speaker',[101] he rapidly made a name for himself in Manchester as a preacher, youth leader and dedicated Mizrachi Zionist. Also on the staff of Manchester's Merkaz Limmud, according to Rabin, was a Jewish refugee woman who acted as its matron, and Eva, the eldest daughter of the Chief Rabbi of Hamburg, Dr Joseph Carlebach.[102] The first Merkaz Limmud building, Shula Jacobs remembers, was an 'old grim house', its ice-cold dormitory bare of anything but iron bedsteads.[103] Until the organisation had acquired its own Torah scroll, the services it sponsored were held in the home, at 1 Wellington Street West, Higher Broughton, of Isskar Emanuel, an orthodox refugee who had brought with him a scroll from Hamburg.[104] Once a scroll had been acquired, Merkaz Limmud established its own *minyan*, attracting young orthodox men and women of Zionist inclinations from some of the older Manchester synagogues, including the Roumanian.[105] Unusually for the orthodox, no *mechitza* (screen) separated male and female worshippers: 'in our egalitarian world', according to one of the congregants, 'it was done'.[106] At some time before June 1943 Merkaz Limmud moved into new premises at 3 Middleton Road, which became also the venue of B'nei Akiva 'Study Circles' for boys aged between thirteen and seventeen.[107]

A final component of what was, in effect, Manchester's religious Zionist complex – a complex which certainly existed in embryo by the end of 1939 and which was complete by 1944 – was the Manchester branch of Torah Va'Avodah (TVA), a non-chalutzic study and social group for young adults which, like Bachad, sought to promote the idea of a Jewish state 'based on the letter and spirit of the Torah on social justice and creative labour'. Although founded on the eve of the war by and for young native Jews, the TVA cooperated with Bachad in organising a weekly Oneg Shabbat and Sidra Shiur at the Higher Crumpsall Synagogue, to which 'young religious refugees' were specifically invited.[108] The first Oneg Shabbat, held in July 1939, and attended by about 100, initiated a weekly programme of Sunday meetings designed, according to Rosen, 'to express the spirit of Judaism in modern surroundings'.[109] In 1941 the ZCC judged TVA to have been 'strengthened' by members of Bachad completing their training at Thornham Fold: 'crowded audiences' listened weekly to 'addresses on Jewish subjects and create[d] a truly Eretz Yisrael atmosphere'.[110] TVA's guest speakers brought news of the latest developments in Palestine, including news of the TVA's own Palestinian settlement, Tirath Zvi.[111] Kopul Rosen had worked with TVA in London before coming to Manchester and is credited with the chairmanship or, alternatively, the 'honorary presidency' of the Manchester branch, of which other leading figures were the orthodox merchants, Maurice Grosskopf and Joseph Jaffe.[112]

It was almost certainly Rosen who threw the weight of Manchester TVA behind the strategy then favoured by the British Zionist leadership: in January 1942 a two-day conference of the Manchester TVA ended with the demand 'that the Jewish people be recognised as an Allied nation and that its soldiers be welcomed into the comradeship of Allied arms as a Jewish fighting force under the Jewish flag'.[113] It is a symptom of its rapid rise in influence within the Manchester Jewish community that in December 1942, shortly after news of the Final Solution had filtered through to Britain, it was the Manchester TVA which orchestrated a protest demonstration attended by 'hundreds of Manchester Jewish youth and representatives of every Zionist society': the government was urged to 'alleviate suffering ... by opening the gates of Palestine' and arranging for neutral states to admit as many as could be rescued.[114] In January 1945 Manchester was the venue for the British TVA's national conference: its aim was to promote the idea of a Jewish state 'based on the letter and spirit of the Torah on social justice and creative labour'.[115]

As Handler saw it, B'nei Akiva, which children joined at the age of thirteen, formed the 'base' of a coherent and interdependent structure of which the organising core was Manchester Bachad. A 'smaller part' of those leaving B'nei Akiva at seventeen or eighteen went on to the Thornham Fold *hachsharah*. The 'larger group' went on to participate in TVA.[116]

It is not easy to assess the longer-term influence of these structures. Handler had chosen Manchester as one focus of his activities because it was already known to him by reputation for the strength of its orthodox sector and for the fervour of its religious Zionism. The Mizrachi movement had formed a significant element of Manchester Zionism since the 1890s; it had found a powerful local advocate in Rabbi Israel Yoffey, minister of the Manchester Central Synagogue, member of the Manchester Beth Din and a regular correspondent with Mizrachi activists throughout the world; it was Yoffey who in 1911 persuaded the British Mizrachi Federation to hold its annual conference in Manchester. When Kopul Rosen's biographer credits religious refugees with having 'brought a drive and inspiration in matters affecting Jewish life which had been little evident previously in Anglo-Jewry',[117] he is almost certainly underestimating the strength of the British community's pre-existing religious, and religious Zionist, life, and of native activists,[118] particularly in a 'kosher city' like Manchester. At best it might be argued that Bachad and Merkaz Limmud, both products of refugee endeavour, and of the TVA, its strength reinforced by refugee activists, extended support for the Mizrachi movement, of which all three were affiliates. In February 1945 the Manchester Mizrachi Organisation is said to have had 336 signed-up members, 238 of them men, ninety-eight women.[119] While uncomfortable with some aspects of Bachad – in particular, such 'modernist' tendencies as the mixing of the sexes on the *hachsharoth* and in the residential Merkaz Limmud, the failure to separate them in the Merkaz Limmud *minyan* and a commitment to political Zionism – some of the founding families of the chassidic Machzikei Hadass such as the Yaffes, the Groskopfs and the Pfeffers lent Handler their moral, and perhaps their financial, support. [120]

By the end of the war B'nei Akiva was evolving, under the influence of talented organisers supplied by Bachad,[121] into a national movement, with branches not only in such larger towns as London, Glasgow, Manchester, Birmingham and Liverpool, but in those scattered 'goyische places'[122] in which young Jews had found themselves as a result of evacuation, the arrival of the Kindertransports and the exigencies of British immigration law. It held the first of what were to become its regular winter camps in Windsor at the end of 1940; in return for BA members spending three or four hours a week working on the land, the local War Agricultural Executive Committee supplied the tents. With its scout-like uniform, its conferences, its handbook, its centralised leader (*makzir*) and directorate (*hanhalla*), its local activists (*madrichim*), its monthly magazine and its annual camps, it was becoming the favoured Zionist, orthodox alternative to the assimilatory, and religiously relaxed, Jewish Lads Brigade. By 1945 it was already on the way to becoming the largest Jewish youth movement in Britain: a major source of *aliyah* on the one hand[123] and, on the other, a fertile training ground for a new generation of orthodox communal leaders in Manchester. The post-war possibility of attaching of Palestinian Jewish emissaries (*shilichim*) to BA branches, as organisers and teachers, further underwrote the movement's expansion, itself a symptom of the impact of the war years on the Jewish communal grassroots.

For young, radically inclined and politically ambitious orthodox Jews like Sidney Hamburger, the Salford-born son of an immigrant entrepreneur of Eastern European origin, Bachad, combining, as it did, Socialist theory with orthodox beliefs, provided a congenial means of transition from a vague interest in social welfare into membership of the British Labour Party. Hamburger himself, already, as a young man shocked by the deprivation of working-class families in Salford whose children were his classmates at the Grecian Street Elementary School in the late 1930s, became a volunteer worker for Manchester Bachad soon after its creation and, through it came into touch with publications designed to reconcile secular Socialist theory with Jewish orthodoxy. These included Hans Heinemann's *Torah and Social Order*, published and distributed by Bachad on Handler's initiative.[124]

Bachad ventures may be seen also as having added new elements to the wide spectrum of Manchester orthodoxy. One observer perceived the Merkaz Limmud, for example, as the Mizrachi alternative to the largely Agudist Manchester Yeshiva and the substantially Chassidic Machzikei Hadass, both centres of opposition to the Zionist enterprise.[125] One young refugee who attended classes at the Yeshiva wearing his Bachad badge, with its emblematic luchot and ears of corn, remembers being teased by his fellow-students and warned off the *hachsharoth* by his teachers. In the 'Yeshiva world', he came to believe, 'Zionism was not popular', in part because it was theologically suspect, in part because, particularly in its chalutzic forms, it created a distraction from religious study.[126] Earlier he had been discouraged by his religious teachers from joining B'nei Akiva, seen as promoting religiously dubious behaviour amongst its adherents: at social events, Jewish boys and girls were seen to dance together.[127] It was seen, according to one of its early *madrichim* as 'the slightly rebellious youth movement of Mizrachi'. This was also how they saw themselves: 'we considered ourselves to be Bolshie'.[128]

Notes

1 MCN 4 December 1939.
2 MG 24 August 1937 at a meeting in honour of Nathan Englesberg, chairman of the Propaganda Committee of the Manchester Zionist Central Council.
3 As distinct from the 'general' Zionists of the MZA, who shared no common view of the future political shape of a Jewish homeland, Mizrachi Zionism stood for a political programme 'carried out on the basis of Traditional Judaism'.
4 Yoffey was one of the promoters of the first annual conference of the British Mizrachi Federation, held in Manchester in 1911.
5 MCN 7 January 1933.
6 The purchase of shekels entitled their owners to a vote in the election of deputies to the World Jewish Congress.
7 MCN 11 February 1933.
8 David Freeman, 'Zionism in Manchester' in *The Zionist Review*, April 1934, p. 23.
9 *Ibid.*
10 Selig Brodetsky, president of the Jewish Board of Deputies and an executive member of the Jewish Agency, addressing a meeting of the Order of Ancient Maccabeans in Manchester (MG 29 December 1941).
11 JRC Special Meeting 25 May 1933.
12 MCN 17 January 1936.
13 Amy Zahl Gottlieb, *Men of Vision: Anglo-Jewry's Aid to the Victims of the Nazi Regime 1933–1945* (London 1998), pp. 21ff.
14 MCN 17 January 1936. The total collected during 1935 was £43,000.
15 *Ibid.*
16 *Ibid.*
17 *Ibid.*
18 *Palestine Bazaar, Cheetham Assembly Rooms, 5–7 May 1936: Souvenir Handbook*, p. 3. The annual Manchester Palestine Bazaar was jointly organised by the Manchester JNF and Women and Children's Welfare Work in Palestine.
19 *Ibid.*, p. 40
20 *Palestine Bazaar Handbook*, p. 9.
21 Provincial Independent Tontine Society CM 19 January 1937. The Society decided 'to leave the matter in the hands of the CBF as originally intended'.
22 Typescript of '50 Years of Zionism', a survey headed 'Mr. Margolis', in the possession of the author, p. 10.
23 *12th Joint Report of the Zionist Central Council of Manchester and Salford for the Three Years ended 30th September 1941*, p. 9.
24 *Ibid.*, pp. 6–18.
25 Both papers belonged to the Manchester Guardian Company Limited under the ownership of the Scott family. In January 1945, when the Manchester Zionist Central Council added the name of the *Manchester Guardian*'s late editor, W.P. Crozier, to

the Golden Book of the Jewish National Fund in Jerusalem, its president spoke of Crozier's 'constant support' for Zionism.

26 *Joint Report of Zionist Council*, pp. 9, 10, 12, 14; SCR 21 July 1939.

27 MG 18 April 1942. It was the local equivalent of Wyndham Deedes' London-based British Asociation for the Jewish National Home in Palestine, with which it was in friendly contact.

28 *Ibid.*, p. 9.

29 A rare exception was apparently the maverick decision by members of the Men's Union of Manchester University in February 1930 to invite Jamaal Husseini, a Palestinian and 'secretary of the Arab Delegation to England', to give a talk to students on 'The Arab Case Against Zionism'; this was followed, however, by a 'heated' discussion in which leading Manchester Zionists attacked Husseini's credibility, and, later, by a talk from Selig Brodetsky, then a professor at Leeds University, on 'The Defence of Zionism' (both speeches reproduced in the Manchester student journal, *The Serpent*, Vol. 14, No. 4, April 1930, pp. 110–112). The men's union later decided that 'interest in these meetings' had been 'so dangerously high' that they could not be accepted as a precedent for future debates (*The Serpent*, Vol. 14, No. 5, May 1930, p. 156).

30 I have been unable to discover details of Haffar's life. In November 1943 he was named as honorary secretary of what appears to have been the recently formed 'Moslem Association of Manchester' (MG 9 December 1943). In November 1947, then described as 'a shipper of Whitworth Street', he became the first Consul in Manchester for Syria, which had achieved independence early in 1945, his appointment celebrated in Manchester by the Manchester Muslim Association and 'the Arabic community' with a dinner at which the guests included the head of the Syrian Legation in London (MEN 19 November 1947). A Leila Haffar was one of the artists whose 'promising' work featured in the exhibition of Manchester's Society of Modern Painters in February 1945 (MG 14 February 1945).

31 The ZCC's *12ᵗʰ Joint Report* includes two full pages (pp. 32 and 64) highlighting the United Palestine Appeal, paid for by two refugee firms, Newman's Slippers and Universal Leather Goods, both of Blackburn.

32 *Palestine Bazaar Handbook*, p. 9.

33 Selig Brodetsky, president of the Jewish Board of Deputies, speaking at a regional conference in Manchester of the Zionist Federation of Great Britain and Ireland (MG 16 June 1941).

34 Brodetsky in an address to the OAM in Manchester (MG 29 December 1941).

35 E.g. Brodetsky at a meeting of the Zionist Federation in Manchester (MG 16 June 1941).

36 Lady Reading at a Manchester fund-raising appeal (MG 3 March 1941).

37 E.g. MCN 26 October 1940, in a speech by Rebecca Sieff, national chairman of WIZO, to a meeting of Jewish women in Manchester; JRC QM 30 November 1941.

38 By Rebecca Sieff, for example, at a meeting in Manchester in October 1940 (MG 23 October 1940).

39 Paul Goodman at a conference of the Zionist Federation of Great Britain and Ireland (MG 21 October 1940).

40 Mrs Edgar Dugdale at a lunchtime rally in Manchester (MG 28 May 1941).

41 *Ibid.*

42 This account of Handler's early life and his Zionist activities until 1938 is based on taped interviews with him by Judith Seitner and Bill Williams, an extended interview by the Oral History Department of the Imperial War Museum in London, on a

brief summary of his life in his personal papers, and on an early draft of a proposed biography.

43 Szold was born in Hungary in 1880, the daughter of a rabbi. Accompanying him to the United States, she became a social worker and founder of the Women's Zionist Organisation of America. After joining the executive of the Jewish Agency, she made her home in Palestine in 1920.

44 *Ten Years of Children and Youth Aliyah, 1934–44*, a pamphlet issued by Children and Youth Aliyah in London (London 1944).

45 MJRC: letter, with attachments, from Toni Szac, on behalf of the Manchester Bachad Snif (branch), to the Secretary of the MJRC, 14 September 1941. Handler also participated in the Zionist Congresses in Lucerne (1935), Zurich (1937) and Geneva (1939) in his capacity as an elected member of the Zionist General Council (Vaad Hapoel Hazioni).

46 When asked to testify at the Eichmann trial, Handler declined for this reason.

47 *Hechalutz: How Jewish Youth in Britain Regain New Life on the Land*, an undated pamphlet [1942?] published in London by English Hechalutz, p. 3.

48 'Moggy. The Story of his Life as he told it to Kfar Blumitson in 1973', in *Kol Vatikei Habonim*, Vol. 2, No. 8, September 2003, pp. 10–11.

49 *Ibid.*

50 Freeman, 'Zionism in Manchester', p 23.

51 MWLBB Lodge Meeting 5 February 1934.

52 Freeman, 'Zionism in Manchester', p. 23.

53 *The Jewish Training Farm*, a pamphlet published by the Zionist Federation of Great Britain and Ireland, London 1936, describing the origins and organisation of the David Eder Farm, p. 6.

54 *Ibid.*, pp 6–9.

55 'Moggy', p. 11; *Jewish Year Book*, 1939 p. 297. In 1939 the David Eder Farm was extended to accommodate 45 refugees from Germany, Austria and Czechoslovakia (*The Young Zionist: Organ of the Federation of Jewish Youth*, Vol. XIV, No. 6, June 1939: item on 'Kibbutz Habonim David Eder Training Farm').

56 *The Jewish Training Farm*, p. 9.

57 *Ibid.*, pp. 8, 15.

58 MWLBB July 1935.

59 *The Jewish Training Farm*, p. 19.

60 *Ibid.*, p. 17.

61 *Palestine Bazaar Handbook*, p. 27.

62 The political programme of Hashomer Hatzair was formulated in 1927. It defined itself as part of Histraduth, the General Federation of Jewish Labour, whose Socialist objectives it shared. In its variant on mainstream Marxist ideology, the social revolution which would usher in the millennium would be preceded by the return of the Jewish masses to Palestine, where they would be transformed into a class-conscious proletariat (Stephan E.C. Wendehorst, 'Between Promised Land and Land of Promise; The Radical Socialist Zionism of Hashomer Hatzair', *Jewish Culture and History*, Vol. 2, No. 1, 1999, pp. 44–57). It was also the only 'non-dominational' Zionist youth movement, dedicated to the creation of a bi-national state in which there would be equal rights for returning Jews and Arab Palestinians, prior to their joint participation in class struggle.

63 *Hechalutz: How Jewish Youth in Britain Regain New Life*, p. 4.

64 MJRC EM 28 February 1939.

65 *Ibid.* 28 February 1939; KHE 20 December 1938.

66 MJRC. 28 February, 21 March 1939.
67 JC 14 July 1939.
68 *Ibid.* 28 March 1939. Whitefield Golf Club, founded for Jewish golfers in 1933, was by this time numbered amongst the sporting groups in Manchester affiliated to the Maccabi movement.
69 *Ibid.* EM 17 July 1939. No list survives of those refugees who worked at Thornham Fold. One was Hermann Spielman, who in 1941, overtaken by 'a longing for Jewish learning', applied for entry to the Manchester Yeshiva; his acceptance was followed by discussions between representatives of the Yeshiva and 'Mr. Blain and Mr. Oppenheim, the sponsors of the farm'. (MY CM 2 November 1941).
70 JC 14 July 1939.
71 An undated list of members of the Agricultural Committee is in the Rae Barash Papers, preserved in Manchester City Library.
72 *12th Joint Report of the ZCC,* p. 18.
73 Salford Aliens Register Case Number 1679E, 14 November 1938. Wislicki was born in Dobryn in Russia in 1877 and died in Manchester on 2 October 1944. In 1939 he was chairman of the Prestwich Branch of the JNF (*Jewish Year Book* for 1939).
74 Jacobs, *Kibbutz and Cocoa.*
75 The term 'anti-bourgeois' is used periodically in Shula Jacobs' memoir to indicate a revolt against the materialism and 'show' of an older Jewish generation. Jacobs was unsympathetic to secular Marxism.
76 Letter from Toni Szac, 14 September 1941.
77 Based on Jacobs, 'Kibbutz and Cocoa'.
78 MJRC EM 5 November 1940.
79 MJRC 11 February 1941.
80 Jacobs, 'Kibbutz and Cocoa', p. 5; MJRC EC 20 June 1941.
81 The author's notes of a conversation with Albert Oppenheim, a member of the Thornham Fold Management Committee, November 1971.
82 MJRC EC 20 June 1941: the MJRC decided to purchase suits for the boys on the farm.
83 Jacobs, 'Kibbutz and Cocoa'.
84 In 1942 three young women from Myer Kersh House joined *hachsharoth* at St Asaph and Kynnersley (MWLBB LM 11 March, 5 May 1942); see also the recollections of one of the girls housed in the Waterloo Hostel quoted in Corbach, *Die Jawne,* p. 295.
85 Conversation with Albert Oppenheim, November 1971.
86 *12th Joint Report of the ZCC,* p. 18.
87 In later life, Handler stressed in his interview, both returned to the orthodox fold, Preiss becoming Professor of Languages at Glasgow University; Preiss's son, Edgar Prais QC, became Attorney General in Scotland.
88 Pamphlet, Freda Whittaker, *The Road to a New Life: An Englishwoman approaches the Jewish Problem* (London 1943), pp. 4–5.
89 *Hechalutz* pamphlet, p. 15.
90 Interview of Sam Stern by Rosalyn Livshin, 28 April 2002.
91 Letter, with attachment, from Toni Szac, 14 Moxley Road, Manchester 6, on behalf of the Manchester Bachad Snif, to the Honorary Secretary of the Manchester Jewish Refugee Committee, 14 September 1941, in the Rae Barash papers.
92 *Ibid.*
93 JG 2 February 1945. Manchester's Bachad Bayit was first on Middleton Road, then on Singleton Road (Sam Stern interview).

94 JG 1 December 1944.

95 Letter from Toni Szac, 14 September 1941.

96 *Ibid.*

97 MG 27 December 1941. This was also the only *Manchester Guardian* report of those refugees 'training as farmers', the purpose of the training not being explained. It may be that Bachad was reluctant to release information which suggested the complicity of the government in the training of future settlers in Palestine. The report quoted may well have originated with the British Council, which was said in it to have offered help in the form of lecturers.

98 Jacobs, 'Kibbutz and Cocoa', p. 7; Betty Batya Rabin, 'Friendly Enemy Aliens or Uprooted but not Rootless', an undated typescript autobiography (c. 2000) p. 198.

99 Rabin, 'Friendly Enemy Aliens', p. 198.

100 For a biography of Koppul Rosen, see Cyril Domb (ed.), *Memories of Koppul Rosen* (London 1970), pp. 13–36. He left Manchester in 1944 to become Communal Rabbi of Glasgow. Subsequently he was successively Principal Rabbi of the Federation of Synagogues and the 'creator' and Principal of Carmel College. In 1947 he was elected to the presidency of the Mizrachi Federation of Great Britain, although later in life he was to abandon the Mizrachi cause.

101 *Ibid.*, p. 135.

102 Carlebach sent five of his older children to safety; their four younger siblings remained with him in Germany (Rabin, 'Friendly Enemy Aliens', p. 198).

103 Jacobs, 'Kibbutz and Cocoa', p. 7. Its location is noted as Great Clowes Street by Rabin, 'Friendly Enemy Aliens', p. 197; one interviewer locates it in Singleton Road, more probably the location of the B'nei Akiva Bayyit. By the end of the war Merkaz Limmud had moved to more spacious premises in Middleton Road, Crumpsall, near Half-Way House.

104 Rabin, 'Friendly Enemy Aliens', p. 198: Isskar Emanuel was Betty Rabin's father.

105 The chronology is uncertain. Certainly the *minyan* was under way by 1943, when Yehuda Avner left the Roumanian Synagogue to join it.

106 Yehuda Avner interview. At the end of the war the Merkaz Limmud was transferred to the Bachad hachsharah in Thaxted, and after 1948 to Israel.

107 This is the address given in JG 17 November 1944.

108 Letter from Toni Szac, 14 September 1941.

109 JC 7 July 1939.

110 *12ᵗʰ Joint Report of the ZCC*, p. 17.

111 Taped interview with Revd Gabriel Brodie by Rosalyn Livshin (1983) in MJM (hereafter Gabriel Brodie interview); JC 7, 14 and 21 July 1939.

112 Domb, *Koppul Rosen*, pp. 16 and 177.

113 MG 12 January 1942. At another Manchester meeting Rosen commented that 'only in a Jewish state in Palestine would the solution to their nation's problems be found' (MG 10 November 1941).

114 MG 18 December 1942.

115 JG 12 January 1945.

116 Lem Handler interviews (see n. 42).

117 Domb, *Koppul Rosen*, p. 16.

118 Koppul Rosen himself initiated the first Jewish kindergarten in Manchester, served on the Manchester Beth Din and helped raise funds for the Manchester Yeshiva and the Joint Palestinian Appeal, while writing his MA thesis, subsequently published, on 'Rabbi Israel Salanter and the Musar Movement' (Domb, *Koppul Rosen*, pp. 16, 63–64).

119 JG 9 February 1945.
120 Handler remembers, in particular, the support he received from Ephraim and Yetta Jaffe, Leo Groskopf and Heinz Pfeffer (Leon Handler interviews).
121 These included Rabbi Gastwirth, the national BA organiser in the early 1940s, who designed its uniform and arranged its first camps.
122 The term was used in interview by Handler, who believed very strongly that those who organised the Kindertransports had paid insufficient attention to the religious integrity of their orthodox charges, with disastrous results for their future and that of the community.
123 Handler estimates that B'nei Akiva has been responsible for sending some 5,500 British settlers to Israel. In the immediate post-war years Handler was active in making arrangements for the sending of illegal shipments of immigrants to Palestine on such boats as the *Exodus*.
124 Handler was the editor of the Bachad monthly periodical, *Chayenu*, and had also arranged the publication of Dr Isidore Epstein's *Talmud and Social Legislation*.
125 Handler interview.
126 Gabriel Brodie interview.
127 *Ibid.*
128 *Ibid.*

15

'The most difficult boys to handle': refugees at the Stockport hostel, 1939–1940

On 29 November 1938, David Blank, a prominent solicitor living in Stockport, announced to the MJRC, of which he was a founder member, that the Stockport Hebrew Congregation, of which he was the treasurer, had decided to take responsibility for ten refugee children.[1] It is not clear who took the initiative. David Blank's widow remembers a visit to their home in Heaton Chapel by Norman Jacobs, the MJRC's chairman, followed by a short business meeting at which important decisions had clearly been made. Blank himself had important Manchester connections:[2] his offices were in St Peter's Square in central Manchester; his uncle (his mother's brother) was the Manchester cotton merchant, City Councillor and communal activist, Abraham Moss. The expectation, however, whatever its origins, was that ten refugee children would receive independent moral and financial support from Stockport Jewry.

In the early 1930s Stockport, a Cheshire textile town of some 125,000 people,[3] eight miles to the south of Manchester, typically of the towns of the cotton belt, was in the midst of a slow economic recovery from the impact of world recession, and in the throes of a municipal programme of modernisation which the collapse of the cotton trade had served only to delay. Unemployment, which had peaked in June 1931 at 13,526, had by the end of 1938 been reduced to a little under 5,000.[4] Although in that year much still remained of what Friedrich Engels had seen in the 1840s as the 'truly revolting' social conditions generated by Stockport's rapid transformation during the eighteenth century from a small market town to an important centre of the cotton and hat-making industries, a progressive Borough Council, dominated since 1904 by the Conservative Party,[5] had in hand plans for an urban regeneration which included a further widening of its now dangerously narrow economic base. A central strand of Conservative Party policy was the maintenance of a low level of rates which would encourage new industries and 'so absorb large numbers of our unemployed'.[6] Machine engineering, a factor in the local economy since 1926, when Henry Simon set up his flour milling plant at Cheadle Heath, was by 1938 on the way to overtaking cotton as the staple industry of the town. In 1935 the London-based Fairey

Aviation Company, one of the world's largest aircraft manufacturers, opened a plant in Heaton Chapel, a southern suburb of Stockport, which by March 1938 was producing 'high-speed bombers' as part of Britain's rearmament programme.[7]

A combination of municipal policy and private enterprise sought also to strengthen Stockport's role, based on its long-established covered markets, as a major market place for the population of rural Cheshire and Derbyshire. In 1938, following the covering by the Corporation of a stretch of the River Mersey near the centre of the town, the Council opened Mersey Square as a modern shopping precinct, said to be composed of 'handsome shops with facades of glazed stone and chromium surrounds, great areas of plate glass, illuminated at night with massed vari-coloured and strip electric lighting'.[8] An exceptionally active Stockport Chamber of Trade, made up chiefly of local shopkeepers, was by 1938 dedicated to the creation of 'a sound progressive shopping centre' in the town, furthering the 'needs and aspirations' of 'private traders', negotiating on their behalf with the Corporation, and so encouraging the 'betterment of trade and trade conditions' as to 'tempt people to come to Stockport rather than to neighbouring cities'.[9] Locally, the Chamber was seen as a body of some significance. Some 450 people attended its annual whist drive and diner dance at Stockport Town Hall in February 1939, including the local MP, the Mayors of Stockport and Ashton-under-Lyne, the Chief Constable and a host of other civic notabilities.[10] It was equally to enhance its role as a centre of the regional retail trade that a 'great engineering feat' by the Corporation engineers linked the town centre with the residential suburbs of South Reddish and Portwood.[11]

Stockport was in many ways typical of the many Lancashire and Cheshire towns which during the 1930s were emerging from the years of depression, under the aegis of progressive councils, as dynamic centres of industry with competitive aspirations for modern structures of health-care, education, housing and leisure. Slum clearance, municipal housing estates, a purer water supply and improved leisure facilities were all part of an agenda which Stockport's councillors shared with their urban peers throughout the northwest. In Stockport itself, a new reservoir at Fernilee in the Goyt Valley was completed in 1937,[12] eleven new council estates were built between 1932 and 1939,[13] and by 1937 twelve bus routes had been added by the borough transport department to the town's remaining nine tram services.[14] A six-year programme of school building was initiated in 1937.[15] During 1937–39 planning permission was granted for the building of five new cinemas.[16]

Of all these changes, the leading families of Stockport's tiny Jewish community, said to comprise only 350 individuals in 1939,[17] were amongst both the promoters and the beneficiaries. The first evidence of any Jewish connection with the town was the creation in the 1850s of a cotton-spinning firm at Kingston Mill by two Manchester industrialists, Henry Micholls and Philip Lucas, both leading founders of Manchester's first Reform Synagogue and the latter the first Jewish member of Manchester City Council. Although notable for their donations to Stockport charities, Micholls and Lucas both lived in Manchester, Micholls in a villa in Victoria Park, Lucas at Temple House, a fine mansion set in extensive grounds in the upper reaches of Cheetham Hill. The first Jewish residents of Stockport, the creators of a Jewish communal life, were Eastern European immigrants who from the 1880s saw Stockport, then a thriving town of over 60,000 people, as a viable alternative to Manchester, where they had first made their homes, for retail trading, the manufacture of clothing and itinerant commerce. For the most part they were shopkeepers trading in what had become the staple commodities of the Jewish retail trade – clothing, drapery, furniture, jewellery, stationery, tobacco and fancy goods – in and around the town centre. Others, perhaps twenty or thirty in all, were tailors from the immigrant workshops of Cheetham Hill tempted to Stockport by the search of local hat-makers for skilled cheap labour.[18] The initial successes of both had led by the 1890s to the evolution of a close-knit Jewish colony, which, although maintaining links with Manchester, was bound internally by close ties of commerce and intermarriage, and by their common membership of the Stockport Synagogue, consecrated in 1891 in what had been a Christadelphian Church on Dodge Hill.[19]

By the 1930s Jewish traders in Stockport included the furrier, Max Margolis, who, in regular advertisements in the *Stockport Advertiser*, announced that his 'vast knowledge of the fur trade' was at his customers' disposal and that he offered 'genuine value at unbeatable prices'.[20] Local trades directories for 1938 list some nine Jewish tailors and clothiers, four furriers, two milliners, a dressmaker, a 'corsetier', a furniture broker, three tobacconists, an 'arts and crafts dealer', a 'general dealer' and a picture frame maker. Two stalls in Stockport's popular covered market were rented by Jewish traders, one 'as a toy and fancy goods repository' by the Manchester-based firm, Ephraim Marks and Company, the other by the draper, S. Landau.[21] In the late nineteenth century at least two Jewish entrepreneurs from Manchester had established small clothing factories in Stockport which employed immigrant Jewish workers,[22] but by the late 1930s no trace of such industries, which were still central to the economy of Jewish Manchester, remained, their workers apparently either returning to Manchester or acquiring stalls in one or other of Stockport's flourishing indoor markets.

Probably the longest established and certainly the most prosperous of the Jewish retail traders in 1938 was the jeweller, Louis Winter, a great-nephew of London-born Jacob Winter, who had arrived in Stockport at the age of fifteen in 1880 to work for a local jeweller, and who in 1887 had opened his first shop in Lower Hillgate. On Jacob's death, Louis had inherited a flourishing jewellery, optical and watchmaking business by then housed in handsome double-fronted premises, 'The Clock House', at 23 and 25 Lower Underbank. A mechanical clock installed on the shop front by Jacob in 1903, with painted figurines which emerged to strike the hours and quarters, had become, according to the official guidebook, 'a well-known feature' of the town. In 1938 Louis Winter was both a leading figure in the synagogue and a prominent and respected Stockport citizen: he was a generous donor to local causes, a borough magistrate, president of the Stockport Chamber of Trade, vice-president of the Stockport branch of the British Legion and a prominent Freemason. It was Winter who hosted the Chamber's annual dances, personally presenting the obligatory bouquet to the Mayoress.[23] He was also amongst the wealthiest of Stockport's citizens. Part of his inheritance from his uncle was a substantial portfolio of property which included two cinemas in north Manchester in which Jacob Winter, with considerable foresight, had invested surplus capital in the first decade of the century, as well as two hotels, one in Blackpool, one in North Wales.[24] In 1938 Winter, while still managing the shop, was living in some luxury in a detached mock-Tudor villa on Buxton Road, Disley, opposite the entrance to Lyme Park, some five miles from Stockport, in the Derbyshire countryside.

Also prospering in the late 1930s were the wholesale drapery warehouses of six Jewish immigrant entrepreneurs who, from the 1890s, had made Stockport their base for 'Scotch drapery': men of small means, they had become, in the first instance, itinerant salesmen of clothing and textiles on credit repayable at anything from 1s to 2s 6d a week, before themselves becoming the suppliers of other tallymen. Foremost amongst them in 1938 were Bernard Brown, S. Landau, whose premises were in Union Road, David Faust in Higher Hillgate and Churchgate, and Bernard Clare (formerly Klahr), who had arrived in Stockport from Latvia in 1905, to be initiated into the credit drapery business by Bernard Brown, his brother-in-law. A ledger surviving from the years 1905–09[25] suggests that he journeyed on foot from Stockport to a rural market stretching as far as Dukinfield, Disley and Wilmslow, selling cheap clothing and household textiles. The warehouse which Brown and Clare established in Greek Street, in the Edgeley district of Stockport, in 1909, was by 1938 under the management of Bernard Clare's son, Harry, Stockport's leading supplier of household drapery to the retail trade. Harry Clare's nephew, Samuel Clare, was by the late 1930s the owner of a butcher's shop which supplied the community with its kosher meat.[26]

A handful of men from a second, English-born generation had moved into the professions as doctors, opticians, pharmacists and solicitors. They included Dr Harold Hirsch, a GP in Stockport since 1923, whose surgery in 1938 was in Heaton Norris, on the northern, residential edge of the town. Another was David Blank, whose Russian immigrant father, Max Blank, originally one of the tailoring workers recruited by the Stockport hatting industry, had subsequently created a small chain of tailors' shops in Stockport's town centre and its residential suburbs. Born in Stockport in 1911, David attended Stockport Grammar School, where, although the only Jewish boy, he became Head Boy and Captain of Football and Cricket. After taking a First in Law at the University of Manchester, he became a successful Manchester solicitor, with offices in Century House, a newly built and prestigious office-block in St Peter's Square in central Manchester, with a part-time lectureship in Law at the University of Manchester, a home in Broadstone Road in Heaton Chapel, a mile to the north of Stockport, and the treasurership of the Stockport Synagogue.[27] Making up a tiny Jewish professional elite were two more solicitors, a pharmacist and two opticians.

The religious lives of Stockport Jewry centred on the double-fronted Georgian house at 211 Chestergate, bequeathed to the community by Jacob Winter, which had served as its synagogue since 1903.[28] This was also the focus of the local Zionist Society, founded a year earlier, only six years after the publication of Herzl's *Judenstat*.[29] An attachment to Zionism was very probably one of the bonds which had held the community as a whole together early in the century; it is said that Revd Abraham Dove, who was minister to the congregation between 1905 and 1920, had the garden at the back of the Synagogue divided into plots for cultivation by the cheder boys in preparation for farm work in the Jewish-state-to-be'.[30] An active Zionist elite in the 1930s included the congregational minister, Rabbi Abrahams, who spoke on 'The Jews of Palestine' to the Stockport Rotary Club in March 1937,[31] and the solicitor David Blank. A suggestion in the leader column of the *Stockport Advertiser* of 25 November 1938 that Jewish immigration to Palestine posed a danger 'to the interests of those living in the country' drew from Blank a robust response[32] in which he depicted large-scale Jewish settlement not only as 'a practicable proposition', but one which was already bringing 'extensive benefits' to the native Arab population and which alone offered 'a permanent solution to the problem of the refugees'. 'How better could the Government express practical sympathy with the refugees', he wrote, 'than by opening to them their religious and spiritual home and allowing them, in pursuance of the Mandate, to make Palestine a truly Jewish National Home'.

The Jewish community saw itself equally, and was so seen, as an integral part of Stockport society, committed to its best interests and deeply involved in its social, cultural and political affairs; there is no hint of discrimination in the local press. A local branch of the BUF, initiated by Oswald Mosley in person in April 1937 and including a handful of members drawn from the families of leading Stockport industrialists, failed to attract popular support and apparently thought better of launching an anti-Semitic campaign.[33] In November 1938 Dr Hirsch contested the Hollywood Ward of the town in the Conservative interest, committing himself to the reduction of overcrowding and unemployment, and losing to the sitting candidate, a local magistrate, by only 354 votes.[34] Maurice Mendleson, son of an immigrant tailor, and a member of the Stockport Branch of the Communist Party of Great Britain, returned to the town in December 1938 from Spain, where he had been wounded while fighting with the British Battalion of the International Brigade: on Edgeley Station he was greeted, according to the *Stockport Advertiser*, by 'members of Stockport Jewry, the Stockport Labour Party and the Communist Party with its banners'. He brought news of two non-Jewish Stockport Brigaders, one still a prisoner of Franco, one killed in action in Spain.[35] Mark Berger, the son of a town-centre tailor, and himself a baker and confectioner in Bramhall, in the Stockport commuter belt, was also a boxer well known as an amateur competitor in Stockport's Central Hall.[36] When

Louis Winter was re-elected to the presidency of the Chamber of Trade in January 1939, two other Jewish traders – the clothiers Philip Burman and Joseph Blank – became members of its Executive Council.[37] In his presidential address Winter stressed the Council's determination to tempt shoppers to Stockport 'rather than go to neighbouring cities with their attendant noise and crushes'.[38] At his son David's Barmitzvah, attended by the Mayor and Mayoress and other local dignitaries, and reported, in detail and with respect, in the *Stockport Advertiser*, reference was made 'to the good relations existing between Jews and non-Jews in the town'.[39]

Jewish traders were also well-known as generous contributors to local charities. Beginning in 1935 a 'Jewish Efforts Committee', chaired by Louis Winter, had staged popular and profitable annual concerts in Stockport's Theatre Royal in aid of the Stockport Infirmary, 'the premier institution of the town', raising £120 in 1937 and £150 in 1938. Staged under the patronage of the Mayor, they were said to 'have set up a reputation for the high standard of the turns secured and the huge audience, which included members of the Council and Corporation, doctors, and many prominent citizens'. Jewish artistes, some of them from the town, shared the stage with such talented locals as Dorothy Penny, 'Stockport's own soprano'.[40] The concerts provided the occasion for the kinds of ritual gestures intended to emphasise the solidarity of Jewish and Christian Stockport: in their speeches, Winter expressed his appreciation of the patronage of the Mayor and Mayoress, the Mayor his 'gratitude to the Jewish fraternity in Stockport'.[41]

Such Christian expressions of goodwill did not extend to any dramatic show of support for the growing number of Jewish refugees from Germany, Austria and Czechoslovakia. In late 1938 the campaigns which more obviously attracted the empathy of Stockport citizens were those organised by local branches of the National Joint Council for Spanish Relief and the Stockport and District China Relief Fund; in the local press, it was the 'starving refugees' from the theatres of war in China, and children from the Basque towns under threat from Franco's forces, who received the greatest attention.[42] Stockport citizens gave no more than token contributions to the Czechoslovak Relief Fund or to the Earl Baldwin Fund, even though the collectors for the latter, in local cinemas, for example, were chiefly younger members of the local Jewish community, the sons and daughters of local shopkeepers.[43]

With hindsight, such public statements as were made in Stockport related to refugees – and the topic was never high enough on the local agenda to inspire anything like a debate – appear lukewarm or ambiguous. The local Conservative MP, Norman Hulbert, who spent ten days in Germany in December 1938 'assessing the situation', although emphasising his 'abhorrence' at the treatment meted out to members of a 'racial minority' and his sympathy for those who, in queues of up to 500 people, were to be found outside the British Consulate in Berlin from 9a.m. 'waiting to apply for British visas' (but 'what a compliment to us!', he wrote), found it 'difficult to express an opinion' on 'the Jewish problem' in Germany.[44] A leader column in the Conservative-inclined local weekly, *The Stockport Advertiser*, of 25 November

1938, a fortnight after Kristallnacht, and headed 'Practical Sympathy', used the supposed effects on 'those living in the country' of Jewish settlement in Palestine, to emphasise the danger of encouraging further Jewish immigration into Britain. While sharing the 'universal sympathy for the victims of persecution', the leader read, 'we must not allow our natural sympathy and inevitable indignation to blind us to practical aspects of the question'. In 'industrial countries like our own', it was 'easy to see that ... the influx of a large number of new competitors might cause economic differences and stimulate the very racial feelings which we desire to avoid ... The subject required that we should keep our emotions under reasonable control'.[45]

Of local groups, only the Quakers spoke out unreservedly for the victims: on 12 February 1939, Douglas J.J. Owen, a prominent and articulate member of the Stockport Society of Friends, addressed a public meeting at the Friends Meeting House at 91 Hillgate on 'why we should welcome refugees'.[46] 'The claim of humanity', he argued, as much as the teachings of Christ and the dictates of democracy, placed upon the British Government a moral obligation to concern itself with those who had 'lost their freedom', particularly when they had done so under a regime for the creation of which Britain itself bore 'a certain responsibility'. The arguments against opening Britain's doors more widely were spurious. Unemployment 'did not increase or decrease by [the] influx of population': far from exacerbating the problem, refugees would generate new opportunities for native workers and 'extra trade to the shopkeepers, wholesalers, factories and so on'. Money currently spent on armaments would be better used in providing houses and camps for refugees. The government was inhibited, he believed, by a mistaken belief that in easing the entry of refugees it could not count on public support: 'if urged by the people the Government would take over the responsibility for admitting refugees on a large scale'. The meeting ended with a unanimous resolution 'that the Prime Minister or some responsible person [sic] be urged that this country do whatever it could to co-operate with other nations in finding the necessary money to assist the refugees'. In the meantime, Owen urged those present to come forward with offers of guarantees, individual or corporate, or of hospitality.[47]

From such statements Blank and his fellow members of what, by late December, had become the Stockport Jewish Refugee Committee, drew some encouragement. They were in no way phased by the *Stockport Advertiser*'s notion of 'practical sympathy'. In response to its claim of the supposed threat of refugees to the British workforce, Blank quoted the Home Secretary's comment that refugees 'had been instrumental in employing 15,000 British workmen in the industries which they have set up', while adding, diplomatically: 'no one ... realised better than the Jewish Community the difficulties in the way of large-scale immigration ... [and] that nothing should be done which might intensify England's own economic difficulties'. The leading article he chose to see as 'yet more evidence of the goodwill [towards the Jewish community in its efforts for refugees] which is so deeply appreciated'.[48] As to Owen's speech, his failure to mention the persecution of Jewry was perhaps taken as typical of Quaker perceptions of refugees. From the Quaker perspective refugees warranted empathy and rescue not primarily for their particular fate as Jews or political dissidents but as fellow human beings each with 'the Divine Spark within'. It was 'the claim of humanity' which, in Owen's words, demanded that the victims of persecution should be rescued to become 'additions to our human family'.[49] Quakers might still be relied upon to support the Jewish community in its efforts. More a cause of anxiety was the reporter's note that 'the meeting was not well-attended'.[50]

In the absence of the congregational records of the Stockport Synagogue, the narrative of the events which follows can be pieced together only from occasional references in the local press and from the memories of those of the participants who have survived and are within reach.

On 6 December 1938 a letter with the signatures of Louis Winter, David Blank, Harry Clare and Leslie Solomon, a well-to-do property dealer, as members of a Stockport Jewish Refugee Committee (SJRC), was published in the *Stockport Advertiser*. The aim of the committee was 'to make arrangements for the accommodation of a number of German children, Jewish and non-Jewish', brought over to England by the British Inter-Aid Committee, '[in] temporary homes in Stockport', and for them to be kept there 'until they can be restored to their parents or trained in some occupation which will enable them eventually to emigrate either to the Colonial Empire or to Palestine'.[51] In offering their help to other bodies which might arise with 'the same purpose' as their own, they noted that, if they themselves could not provide assistance, they were in contact with the 'appropriate organisations' in Manchester and London 'to whom such cases would be referred without delay'. Although 'primarily concerned with children', they hoped eventually to 'do what we can for other refugees also'.[52] The letter called on sympathisers, Jewish and non-Jewish, to 'group their offers in one or more of [three] categories': 'offers of homes, temporary or otherwise' for refugee children; offers of financial assistance towards their maintenance; offers of 'other kinds of help' – gifts of clothing, training for older children 'in some manual occupation to fit them for emigration', and 'any other assistance or suggestions' which would cushion 'the unhappy lot of the European refugees, whether Jewish or non-Jewish'.[53] Louis Winter, almost certainly the prime mover on the committee, had himself offered hospitality to a child refugee, thirteen-year-old Gudula Cahn, who arrived in Britain with the Kindertransport in June 1939 and whom he had escorted from London to his home in Disley.[54] Gudula herself was impressed with the deferential way in which Winter was greeted on the Stockport streets.

The SJRC clearly saw itself, like the Jewish Refugee Committees in London and Manchester, as a voluntary organisation seeking to support the entry of refugees within the framework of British immigration law and Home Office regulations. The inclusion in its remit of non-Jewish children was no more than what was expected of committees working under the aegis of British Inter-Aid, a Christian-inspired predecessor of what became the Refugee

Children's Movement. It may be, however, that talk of the emergence of 'other bodies' with 'similar aims' reflected the expectation of men like Winter and Blank that Jewish child refugees could rely upon the practical empathy of Christian Stockport.

In late December, a fortnight after the letter's publication, the committee held its first fund-raising event: a bring-and-buy sale at the home of Mrs F. Freedman at 263 Wellington Road North, apparently organised by the tiny Stockport lodge of B'nai Brith. The eight stallholders included the wives of Louis Winter, Dr Hirsch, Philip Burman and Usher Roseman: the Mayoress of Stockport paid a flying visit.[55]

It must have been around this time that the idea of providing homes for children gave way to that of providing a refugee hostel. The occasion was the offer, rent-free, by Simon Freedman, a local tailor and property-dealer and one of Stockport's longest-established Jewish residents, of a large, detached Victorian mansion in Whitefield, a secluded and remarkably rustic cul-de-sac running off Wellington Road North, the main thoroughfare linking Stockport to Manchester, perhaps a mile from Stockport town centre.[56] This was almost certainly the house noted at a MJRC meeting on 28 February 1939 as being ready for occupation. On 2 March 1939 the *Stockport Advertiser* noted that the Stockport Jewish Refugee Committee had made arrangements with the town's Education Committee for the placing of ten German children in local schools.

It must have been soon after this that, in searching for someone to take care of the hostel, the committee chanced upon Marianne Prager, a refugee herself, and a young woman of exceptional humanitarian instincts, social work skills and experience in the care of children. Intending to open the hostel soon after Easter 1939, the committee had at first selected a German couple as wardens, but when their entry to Britain was delayed, an alternative had been sought through Woburn House. Their enquiries coincided with Prager's own search through refugee organisations for more fulfilling work than the domestic service for which she had been accorded an entry permit.[57]

Born in Vienna in 1902, the daughter of a Medical Officer in the Austrian Civil Service, and brought up in a cultured but largely non-observant Jewish middle-class home, Marianne Prager trained for three years at what was the first training college for social workers in Vienna, before taking up a variety of posts in education and child care, the last, to which she was appointed in 1928, as matron of the Bondi-Heim, a residential home in Vienna for Jewish girls between the ages of five to eighteen who, for one reason or another, could not live with their parents. There, for eleven years, she was effectively 'mother and father' to twenty-five girls from broken homes, with single parents or from Jewish families in the rural hinterland of Vienna who wanted their children to attend city schools. As she remembered it twenty years later, she watched over their 'bodily and mental growth' during their formative years, keeping in touch with their teachers, supervising their homework, introducing them to 'swimming, walking, mountain climbing ... games ... skating, skiing [and] tobogganing', taking them to 'concerts, theatres, cinemas and art galleries', and in other ways supporting their growth, as she saw it, into 'responsible human beings'. Paid staff were kept to a minimum: the girls 'not only helped with the housework, but the older ones looked after the younger ones and these in turn did small tasks for the older ones who had lots of homework to do and little free time'. 'It was strenuous work,' she remembered, 'but also a great deal of pleasure'.[58]

With the arrival of the Nazis, however, such a life became increasingly untenable. Following the closure of Jewish schools in the wake of Kristallnacht, the Bondi-Heim offered sanctuary to Jewish teachers who continued to hold classes on an informal basis.[59] As the danger to the home increased, Prager first made 'arrangements for many of the children to find homes in other countries', and then, after acquiring a domestic service permit through English friends she had met on a previous visit to Britain, herself left for Britain, arriving in London on 15 February 1939. It was after spending a month there, as a 'lady's maid in big house in Kensington', altering dresses, dusting the furniture, filling hot water bottles and taking the dog for walks, that a sense of uselessness, 'at a time when so much should be done',[60] led her to seek work from Woburn House as a hostel warden. Put in touch with the Stockport Committee, she arrived in the town a fortnight before Easter to help prepare the way for the expected '8–10 refugee boys of school age'.[61] On 15 April two members of the committee travelled to London 'to select the children and bring them to Stockport'.[62]

Prager recalled the events which followed to an audience of local women in Manchester in 1957: 'I got all the beds ready, cooked a nice dinner and became quite excited in expectation. Suddenly there was a commotion outside the house and I went to meet them. I had an awful shock. Instead of schoolchildren there were nine young men on my doorstep who ... were between 16 and 17 years of age. I realised at once that this was the most difficult age group to handle.' Their schooling interrupted and speaking little English, the boys 'were neither able nor willing to make headway' at Stockport Technical College, at which Louis Winter, perhaps as surprised as Prager at their ages, arranged places for them for training which would ease their re-emigration. In the meantime they led Prager 'a terrible life'. 'I only prayed,' she remembered, 'that the couple from Germany would soon arrive, because I thought that these boys needed a strong man to keep them in order. Had it not been for a number of people in the neighbourhood who started to befriend us and with whom I could spend a few peaceful hours, I would have given up there and then.'[63] It was only when, one by one, the boys decided, with the committee's help, to leave the college and take up jobs in the town that a 'rowdy crowd turned into a nice lot of young people'.[64]

With what those who knew her would have seen as typical self-effacement,[65] Prager failed to mention her own central role in this transformation. The Refugee Committee took responsibility for the financing and maintenance of the hostel; its representatives paid weekly visits to the boys and distributed pocket money of 2s 6d;[66] Usher Roseman supplied the hostel with free fruit and vegetables; Annie Williams (who was Jewish) taught the boys English; members of the local branch of the Peace Pledge Union took them on out- ings once a month;[67] members of the Stockport Hebrew Congregation oc- casionally took boys into their homes on Shabbat; they were invited to the synagogue on the High Holydays and to Stockport Parish Church for social and sporting events; other 'friends', including the three 'charming and in- telligent' Smith sisters, Quakers who ran a private school at 194 Wellington Road North nearby, acted as volunteers, visiting the hostel, entertaining the boys and providing Prager with the occasional respite. The Smith sisters, in particular, are said to have been 'very very supportive of her and her efforts': in their own home, they mounted play readings 'through which Marianne could escape into culture from the challenges of running the hostel'.[68] But it was Prager, without any daily help, who bore the brunt, as she had in the Bondi-Heim, not only of the washing, mending and cleaning,[69] but of turn- ing these awkward boys, their early lives shattered, separated from parents trapped in Germany or Austria, some of them deeply traumatised,[70] into 're- sponsible human beings'. It is a tribute to her sensitivity, skill, tenacity and care that five of the boys – the Germans Albert Freimann, Helmut Beck, from Breslau, and the cousins Rolf and Egon Hamlet, and the Austrian Rudolph Friedlansky, from Vienna – came to see her (under her nickname 'Maschi') as their surrogate mother and kept in touch with her for the rest of their lives; even after their marriages, they went on holiday with her, with their wives, three times a year.[71] Friedlansky's daughter remembers that he talked of Prager with 'reverence and respect'.[72] She was in fact far and away the most professional and talented 'carer' amongst Manchester refugees.

The SJRC supervised the hostel from a distance and with so light a touch that none of the boys, at all events from more or less assimilated Jewish homes, retained a religious identity in later life. Of the six boys of whose lives any evidence has emerged, four married out of the Jewish faith, two to women they met at social events at Austria House towards the end of the war.[73] Prager herself, perhaps the major influence on the boys' identity at this stage, was herself not religiously observant.[74]

The house at 30 Whitefield served as a refugee hostel for only fourteen months. In July 1940, all its inmates but Helmut Beck, who, although born and brought up in Germany, retained the Czech nationality of his father, were interned on the Isle of Man. Helmut himself was found accommodation with the Tapp family of Heaton Moor, members of the Peace Pledge Union. The hostel was closed, the SJRC disbanded, never to be reconstituted. All links between the boys and Jewish Stockport were effectively severed. Finding herself unemployed without warning, Marianne Prager found employment as matron of a Quaker refugee hostel on Palatine Road, where she worked for two years before serving as a welfare visitor for the Refugee Children's Movement and then training in London for a career in social work.[75]

The temporary residence of nine young Jewish refugees from Central Europe in the Stockport of 1938–39 made scarcely a ripple on the life of the town or the Jewish community. It was probably by mutual choice that the boys did not become active members of Stockport Jewry. From German and Austrian families which had retained, at most, only the vestiges of Jewish religious ritual, they attended the Stockport synagogue only on festival days, and then with some reluctance. They had little else in common with the Stockport Jewish families to whose houses they were occasionally invited for a Sabbath meal. For their part, while managing its affairs and providing the funds for its maintenance, and so providing a temporary haven of safety, Stockport Jews played little part in the social and cultural life of the hostel.

This was left to Prager and her volunteer supporters, most of them non-Jewish. Lisa Wolfe remembers that the Quakers 'took more interest in us than the Jews: a lot more interest'.[76] Shortly after the outbreak of war, a number of leading Stockport Jewish families had, at all events, moved to safer havens, particularly in North Wales: David Blank, concerned at the proximity of his house in Heaton Chapel to the Fairey Aviation Works, moved his family to Prestatyn, where he visited them at weekends.[77] Within the small Jewish community of Stockport, there scarcely existed a tradition of philanthropy out of which Jewish volunteer social workers of the calibre of Rae Barash or Margaret Langdon in Manchester might have emerged. In view of the backgrounds of those for whom it had unwittingly taken on responsibility, the community, and the refugees, may be counted as exceptionally lucky to have chanced upon Marianne Prager.

The town had other things on its mind, not least the thousands of evacuees whose arrival closely followed that of the Whitefield refugees, the intensive bombing which began during the winter of 1939–40 and the general privations and responsibilities of a community at war. It seems likely that the secluded hostel largely escaped public notice; certainly it attracted no hostility, even as its inmates were taken off for internment. What is clear also, however, is that, closely knit though it was into urban Stockport, and treated consistently with public respect, the local Jewish community could not count on local institutions to support its refugee co-religionists on any scale. There are signs of friendship and acceptance of the Whitefield boys – by the Parish Church, by individual Quakers (although not, apparently, by the Friends Meeting House), and by the employers of refugee 'apprentices' – but no evidence that any body of Stockport citizens came forward, as the SJRC believed they might, with the offer of other mechanisms for the reception of refugees or, for that matter, to offer a collective welcome to the nine who did arrive.

For those nine, short though it was, the stay in Stockport left a significant imprint on their lives. They were young men from middle-class professional and commercial families whose education and hopes had been dashed by the Nazi regime and who in 1938 had been abruptly separated from their families. The vulnerability of the families they had left behind was the backcloth against which they sought to remake their lives. Rolf Hamlet was born in Bad Salzuflen, where his well-to-do parents owned a small lakeside hotel. With money saved from his work as a trainee plumber in Stockport, Rolf

Hamlet took out an advert in *The Times* which read 'Married couple, still in Germany, former proprietors of boarding house; wife excellent cook, housework; husband good handyman, driver; both willing to do every work. Hamlet, 30 Whitefield.'[78] Following a short spell at Stockport Technical College, which scarcely made up the ground lost in their earlier education (Rolf Hamlet had attended a fee-paying Gymnasium, or secondary school), all nine were placed by the Refugee Committee, largely, it seems, through the extensive contacts of Louis Winter, as 'trainees' with local tradesmen, after which the expectation was that, in accordance with Home Office regulations, they would re-emigrate. The work found for them had nothing to do either with their backgrounds and expectations in their homelands or with their aptitudes.[79] Rolf Hamlet became first a plumber, then an upholsterer; Helmut Beck, who in his home town, Breslau, had been expected to join his father and elder brother in a prosperous timber business, became a repair man for a local firm of radio retailers; Hahn, Friedlansky and Rolf's cousin, Egon Hamlet, the son of a farmer and timber merchant from Bad Salzuflin, became motor mechanics in local garages. Although none of them remained in Stockport, in later life all made something of this unlikely pool of new occupations. With Egon's help, Rolf Hamlet opened up a radio repair and retailing business in Cheadle, the success of which was assured in the late 1940s by the advent of television; following service in the British Army, Hahn became a garage proprietor; Helmut Beck continued to work as a radio repairer for firms in Manchester and Ashton, and subsequently as a tester for fail-safe devices; Egon (now Eddie) Hamlet became a specialist car dealer in Florida, where he settled with his wife Eva, herself a Jewish refugee who had spent a year at Harris House, the refugee hostel in Southport.[80]

For most of the nine, the days in Stockport strained what remained of their links with their Jewish origins to breaking point. Rudi Friedlansky (later Fenton) married a practising Christian, Anne Cotton, whom he had met when she was working as a volunteer at Austria House, the social and cultural focus of Austrian-Jewish refugees, then seen by Manchester women as a likely useful point of contact with eligible refugees; their daughter Rita was christened in a Catholic church. Helmut Beck married Anne's friend, Dorothy, whom she had introduced to Austria House. Gerhardt Hahn married another Christian woman, Winnie, from Stoke-on-Trent, where he subsequently settled and opened his own garage. Only one of the boys, Albert Freimann, who settled in Israel after the war and worked for the El-Al Airline, is known to have built his later life around a Jewish identity, although Helmut Beck, after distancing himself from Judaism throughout his married life, insisted on a Jewish funeral, arranged for him by his Christian wife with Rabbi Eli Tov, minister of the Sha'are Sedek Synagogue in Didsbury.[81]

Notes

1   MJRC 29 November 1938.
2   Taped interview of Hettie Blank by Bill Williams, 2004 (Hereafter Hettie Blank interview).
3   The borough population stood at 123,309 in 1922 and 125,505 in 1932 (John Christie-Miller (ed.), *The Development of Stockport 1922–1972 and the History of the Stockport Advertiser* (Stockport 1972) p. 13; *Stockport Advertiser* (hereafter SA) 9 December 1938.
4   Christie-Miller, *Development of Stockport*, p. 29.
5   There were thirty-six Conservative and thirteen Labour Councillors in 1932. The Conservatives also held the borough's parliamentary seat from 1931 with a large majority over Labour.
6   SA 28 October 1938, from a speech by the [Jewish] Conservative candidate, Dr. Hirsch.
7   *Stockport as an Industrial, Commercial and Residential Centre: the Official Handbook of Salford Corporation* (4th edition, 1935) p. 42; MEN 24 and 28 March 1938: the report is of an attempted sabotage of four bombers.
8   *Stockport as an Industrial ...*, p. 5.
9   From a speech by Louis Winter, then president of the Chamber, reported in SA 27 January 1939.
10 SA 10 February 1939.
11 Christie-Miller, *The Development of Stockport*, p. 103.
12 *Ibid.*, p. 43.
13 *Ibid.*, p. 47.
14 *Ibid.*, p. 36.
15 *Ibid.*, p. 65.
16 *Ibid.*, p. 89.
17 This was the estimate in the *Jewish Year Book* for 1939.
18 Hettie Blank interview.
19 Clare Hilton, *The Stockport Jewish Community* (Stockport MBC 1999), pp. 14–15.
20 E.g. *Stockport Advertiser* (hereafter SA) 6 January 1939.
21 There had been Jewish stallholders in the Stockport covered market since the 1890s, perhaps a dozen or so in 1930 (Hilton, *Stockport Jewish*, p. 35.)
22 Hilton, *Stockport Jewish*, p. 17.
23 SA 10 February 1939.
24 For Winter and the history of the shop at 23 and 25 Little Underbank, *Stockport Official Handbook*, pp. 45–47; Hilton, *Stockport Jewish*, pp. 13, 64.
25 Preserved in the MJM. For details of the Brown and Clare enterprises, see Sue Sargent, '50 Years of the Tallyman', unpublished dissertation, BA Hons History of Design and Visual Art, University of Manchester, 1991, pp. 10–11.
26 Hettie Blank interview.
27 *Ibid.* In 1936 David Blank married Hettie Rueck, the Manchester-born daughter of Eastern European immigrants, who had attended Manchester High School for Girls and who had qualified as a designer at the Manchester School of Art. Hettie's mother, Sophie Moss, a Romanian by birth, was the sister of the Manchester cotton merchant, Manchester City councillor and communal activist, Abraham Moss.
28 Hilton, *Stockport Jewish*, p. 21. This was the community's third successive synagogue. The first, consecrated in 1891, was in a former Christadelphian Chapel on Dodge Hill. The second, in the former hall of the Stockport Spiritualist Society, collapsed

only months after its acquisition in 1903 (*ibid.*, pp. 14–15, 19).

29   JC 10 January 1902.

30   Hilton, *Stockport Jewish*, p. 29.

31   SA 12 March 1937.

32   SA 9 December 1938.

33   SA 16 and 23 April 1937, cited by Hilton, *Stockport Jewish*, p. 63. Of the four Stockport fascists arrested in July 1940 under the Emergency Powers Act, one had been a director of a well-known local hat-making firm (SA 7 July 1940).

34   SA 28 October and 4 November 1938.

35   SA 23 December 1938. Mendleson's father was then one of the few remaining Jewish working tailors in Stockport. His family are described by Hettie Blank as 'not educated people … very, very foreign' (Hettie Blank interview).

36   SA 18 November 1938, when the paper recorded in some detail (with a photograph) his marriage to Gertrude Ruben of Cheetham Hill under the heading 'Stockport Jewish Wedding'.

37   SA 27 January 1939.

38   *Ibid.*

39   Hilton, *Stockport Jewish*, p. 61. In an interview with Olivia Blechner in 2004 (hereafter *Leigh*) George Leigh, who as a young boy had played football with the boys at the Whitefield Hostel, remembers that Jewish boys on their way to cheder at the Chestergate Synagogue were occasionally subject to verbal abuse by local 'louts'.

40   SA 24 February 1939. See also Hilton, *Stockport Jewish*, p. 26.

41   SA 24 February 1939.

42   SA 18 November, 2 December 1938. In November 1938 Eleanor Rathbone was in Stockport speaking on the Spanish crisis to the Stockport and District Peace Council. The Peace Council and the Stockport branch of the League of Nations Union were both active on behalf of Spanish refugees. In December, the China Relief Fund raised £350 at a single event.

43   SA 20 January 1939. On a Saturday evening, collections taken at three Stockport cinemas, in which Viola Freedman, Enie Rubins, H. Landau and Cecil Levene took part, raised £15 between them.

44   SA 9 December 1938.

45   SA 25 November 1938. In other ways the column reiterated the policy of appeasement then being pursued by the National Government. There should be no 'tirade' against Germany; the German government, whose 'declaration of war on Jewry' was 'their own affair', should rather be persuaded to cooperate in 'dealing with the problem', for example by enabling intending emigrants to take with them their property and possessions', and by cooperation with the powers represented at the Evian Conference. As regards refugees, Britain should respond 'with caution', offering only 'what practical aid we can'. In a letter published by the SA on 23 December 1938, the only letter printed by the SA relating to Germany and German Jewry, a certain 'Gunner', while expressing his hatred of persecution and emphasising the contributions made by Jews to German life, suggested that the German people themselves hated persecution 'as much as the rest of the world', and that Hitler, who didn't want war, should be persuaded to join Britain, France and the United States in defending the world against 'the Yellow Peril'.

46   SA 10 and 17 February 1939. The meeting was chaired by Alderman Charles Hoyle, who expressed his own empathy with those 'who had been driven ruthlessly away from the things they had held dear'.

47   SA 17 February 1939.

48 SA 9 December 1938.
49 *Ibid.*
50 *Ibid.*
51 *Ibid.* The Inter-Aid Committee was the voluntary body which had brought children to Britain before the inauguration of the Kindertransports; by the time of the letter it had become part of the Refugee Children's Movement.
52 *Ibid.*
53 *Ibid.*
54 Gudula's wartime correspondence with her parents is in the possession of a member of the Winter family.
55 SA 23 December 1938.
56 Simon Freedman arrived in Grimsby from Russian Poland in 1885 and set up his tailoring business in Stockport in the early 1890s (Hilton, *Stockport Jewish*, pp, 11, 26). The hostel's address was 30 Whitefield.
57 'Marianne Prager (1902–1982)', the 22-page typescript of a speech delivered by Prager at 'a women's meeting' in Manchester on 4 July 1957, in the possession of her nephew, David (copy in the Centre for Jewish Studies, University of Manchester), p. 15.
58 *Ibid.*, pp. 11–13. The Bondi-Heim was founded by the Bondi family of Vienna in memory of their daughter, Lillian. Prager's charges at the home included Lisa Wolfe, whom she was later to meet again in Manchester (Elisabeth (Lisa) Wolfe interview).
59 (Elisabeth (Lisa) Wolfe interview); taped interview with Prager's sister-in-law and friend, Heidi Johnson (hereafter Heidi Johnson interview).
60 *Ibid.*, pp. 14–15.
61 *Ibid.*, pp. 15–16.
62 *Ibid.*, p. 16.
63 *Ibid.*, pp. 16–17.
64 *Ibid.*, p. 17.
65 Transcript of an interview of David Prager by Olivia Blechner, 2004 (hereafter David Prager interview).
66 Author interview with Dorothy Beck (hereafter Dorothy Beck interview).
67 Elisabeth (Lisa) Wolfe interview.
68 David Prager interview. According to David Prager one of the sisters became a representative for a chocolate firm and was involved in the introduction of the Mars Bar in the late 1930s; in later life she would visit the Prager home, always with a box of chocolates in the boot of her car.
69 According to Lisa Wolfe, 'she did everything, she washed and mended and cleaned'. Lisa's abiding vision of her at the hostel is sitting with a basket mending the boys' socks (Elisabeth (Lisa) Wolfe interview).
70 Letter re Helmut Beck, concerning his claim for compensation from the German government, from Dr S. Shafar, Consultant Psychiatrist, Crumpsall Hospital, Manchester, to Dr Eckstein, 17 August 1965.
71 Elisabeth (Lisa) Wolfe interview.
72 Dorothy Beck interview.
73 Dorothy Beck interview; David Prager interview; Elisabeth (Lisa) Wolfe interview.
74 David Prager interview.
75 'Marianne Prager', pp. 18–22. In London. Prager undertook a three-month training course as a youth leader and served for a year as a youth leader in Marylebone before returning to Manchester to become a welfare worker with the Refugee Children's Movement. As an RCM welfare worker for two years, her task was to visit children in

foster homes in Lancashire, Cheshire, Cumberland and Westmorland. In 1948 she took a course in mental health at the London School of Economics and went on to become a Psychiatric Social Worker at Springfield Hospital in Manchester, a post from which she retired in 1971.

76   Elisabeth (Lisa) Wolfe interview.

77   Hettie Blank interview.

78   From an undated receipt preserved by his widow, Dorothy Beck (copy in the Centre for Jewish Studies, University of Manchester). In fact, his parents were deported to Theresienstadt, from where they were transferred to Auschwitz, where they were murdered. For more of Beck's attempts to rescue his parents, see below pp. 352–355.

79   In later life Helmut Beck was to attribute his depression in part to his placement in a job to which he was unsuited, a fact later confirmed by a consultant psychiatrist (letter from D.S. Shafar, 17 August 1965).

80   Eva Hamlet, *Against All Odds* (Florida 1994).

81   Dorothy Beck interview.

16

'By the grace of the Almighty': refugees and the Manchester Yeshiva

Of all the reversals of attitude which followed the changing international situation after March 1938, the most dramatic was that of the Manchester Yeshiva. Between 1933 and early 1938, in the face of severe financial restraints and the pressure of communal concerns, the natural empathy of the Yeshiva's managers with their beleaguered co-religionists abroad persuaded them to accept only three foreign students, two from Germany, one, a Roumanian by birth, from Czechoslovakia. Less than eighteen months later, at the beginning of the summer term of 1939, its student body comprised fifty-six young foreigners, thirty-two from Germany, twenty-three from Czechoslovakia and one from Vienna.[1] This is not to be explained in terms either of the Yeshiva's greater financial stability or of any lull in its ideological campaigns on behalf of Jewish orthodoxy. On the contrary, the admission of refugees contributed to an already critical financial deficit and was accompanied by fresh campaigns against such long-term latitudinarian opponents as the Talmud Torah. The explanation lies rather in the Yeshiva's open and unapologetic defiance of financial logic, communal policy and Home Office regulations, even of what might have seemed the reasonable caution of some of its own committeemen, to pursue a campaign of rescue based as much on the humanitarian dictates of Jewish orthodoxy as its more routine battles for the religious integrity of the community.[2]

Although, in the end, a matter of near-consensus, such idealism was initiated and driven forward by four men in particular: the Rosh Yeshiva, Rabbi M.I. Segal, who deployed his moral authority with consummate strategic skill, and three of the lay volunteers who served on the Yeshiva's committee of management – Saul Rosenberg, who had succeeded Israel Libbert to the Yeshiva's presidency; Mark Bloom, a long-serving and independent-minded committeeman, the eldest son of one of the Yeshiva's most generous patrons and himself a donor of some significance; and Syney Needoff, Bloom's son-in-law, a local Liberal Party activist and chairman of the Yeshiva's Finance Committee. Their efforts were tempered and their achievement limited (and then marginally) only by the near-inevitable intervention of Nathan Laski (backed by his son Neville as president of the Jewish Board of Deputies) in the cause of central coordination, deference to authority and economic rationality. Looking back on the events years later, however, those who had promoted substantial refugee admissions believed that they had received rather weightier support; the survival of the Yeshiva through those years of 'huge' over-expenditure was deemed a miracle wrought by the Almighty.[3] With the seats of Jewish learning in Europe 'closed down by hostile forces', it had 'preserved the fountain head from which, when the time came, would spring forth the life stream for the revival of Torah and the Jewish people'.[4]

A train of events which was to slowly gather momentum in the year which followed began in a small way on 20 March 1938, only days after the Anschluss, when the Yeshiva committee considered a request from the Reader and Shochet of the Southport Synagogue, Revd S. Meisels, for the admission as a student of a friend in Austria, 'where', he told the committee, 'the conditions did not require any emphasising'.[5] Still wary of the financial implications of accepting refugees, the committee granted the request only after Meisels had promised £1 a week to cover his friend's board, lodgings and expenses.[6] Contributing to a sense of near-insolvency was the Yeshiva's persistent failure to dispose of the building on Cheetham Hill Road it had vacated in 1936; plans to sell, convert, auction and raffle the building, or to transfer it to the bank as security for its overdraft, all came to nothing.[7]

Finance remained a constraint for the committee even in the face of Rabbi Segal's initial, and shrewdly constructed, intervention in the cause of greater liberality. On 3 July 1938 Segal complained to his Education Committee of 'the shortage of students' at the Yeshiva, urging both 'a drive to enrol more schoolboys in the Preparatory Classes with a view to having them continue as students', and pointing up the experience of the Etz Chaim Yeshiva in London which, 'suffering from the same complaint … as a remedy were taking in students from Germany'. The Manchester Yeshiva, he believed, should follow London's example, particularly in view of the Talmud Torah's continued refusal to pass on its more promising students.[8] In dealing with the Talmud Torah, the committee decided, nothing could be done before the (impending) arrival from Germany of the newly elected Manchester Communal Rav, Rabbi Dr Alexander Altmann, in the hope that he would bring a measure of coordination to Jewish education in Manchester.[9] On the matter of refugees, the Finance Committee decreed that the Yeshiva must still tread warily: applicants could be accepted only when the Yeshiva was not called upon to pay for their maintenance.[10] The Yeshiva was none the less sufficiently attracted to the idea of accepting more students from Germany for whom sponsors could be found, to draft (early in September) 'a formula for a document to be signed by parties undertaking to keep a student' at a standard rate of £1 a week.[11]

Less than a month later, deteriorating conditions for the Jews of Greater Germany, in particular for those of Polish origin most likely to be attracted to a higher religious education, and the Yeshiva's 'inundation' by German and Austrian applicants,[12] brought a further softening of its stance towards refugees. The die was cast at a general meeting of the Yeshiva subscribers on 2 October 1938, when, following a general review, initiated by Saul Rosenberg, on the 'terrible plight' of Jewish students in Nazi Europe, Mark Bloom made an impassioned plea on their behalf: 'he depicted their appalling treatment in their native countries and said it was the duty of everyone to come to their assistance'.[13] A fortnight later when, within the management committee, Saul Rosenberg announced that the Yeshiva had 'already applied for ten boys to be admitted to England from Austria and Germany', Bloom commented that 'the Yeshiva had room for another hundred. The community should be appealed to especially for bringing over and keeping these refugee students.'[14] Within a fortnight plans were in place for a fund-raising concert by the community's major charity entertainers, the Manchester Jewish Amateur Minstrels, and for a prestigious dinner at which an appeal would be launched for contributions to a Manchester Yeshiva Refugee Students Fund.[15] The Yeshiva was effectively committing itself to the collective maintenance of an unknown number of young refugee students at a time when the managers of both its banks were pressing for a reduction of its overdrafts.[16]

News of the Kristallnacht pogrom strengthened the hand of the pro-refugee caucus. At a meeting of the Finance Committee on 13 November, after moving a vote of sympathy with the Jews of Germany, Rosenberg 'expressed the hope that the conscience of the world would be moved to some action, as it was not a question of race or politics, but of humanity'. A week later he pressed the urgency of the work of rescue on his fellow committeemen; it was necessary, he told them, for the dinner launching the appeal 'to be held as early as possible, while public sympathy with the victims of German oppression was at its height'.[17] In the face of some calls for caution, Needoff called on his colleagues 'to strike the iron while it is hot [sic]'.[18] Other charitable institutions, he believed, should 'try to extend their benefactions to refugees'; the Yeshiva 'had blazed the trail'.[19] Early in December 1938, even before the dinner had been held, Rosenberg announced that the Yeshiva had admitted twenty-eight students from Germany for whose maintenance it was solely responsible.[20]

In the event, and even without the charismatic presence of Nathan Laski, who had been invited to attend 'as a distinguished guest',[21] the Appeal Dinner, held in the Congregational Hall of the Higher Crumpsall Synagogue on 8 January 1939, raised an impressive £260, and this before the dinner had been followed up by 'personal approaches' to those who attended.[22] Other fund-raising devices were deployed, even, to the dismay of Rabbi Segal, who believed it would interfere with their studies, the sending out of refugee students to place collecting boxes in Jewish homes and seek out subscribers.[23] On 12 February 1939 the Manchester Jewish Amateur Minstrels were persuaded to put on a new version of its 'Coloured Capers' at the Odeon Cinema in Prestwich; its advertisement in the *Jewish Gazette* ended, 'An Effort in Aid of Refugee Students at the College. It will be a pleasure for you and a salvation for others'.[24] Lists of donors to the appeal were published in the *Jewish Chronicle* with the reminder, 'Is your name here? If not send your donation to the Honorary Treasurer. Save the Refugees, and Save them for

Judaism'.[25] A deputation was despatched to London to seek (in this case, without success) support from the Chief Rabbi's Emergency Fund.[26]

By mid-March, although still against the better judgement of the more earth-bound committeemen,[27] German admissions had arisen to sixty, although not all were expected to arrive and, in fact, most did not.[28] On 19 March the Yeshiva committee, emphasising its 'sympathy with the Refugees', empowered the executive officers to grant admissions at their discretion.[29]

By this time, the focus of the Yeshiva's concern had moved from Germany to Czechoslovakia, where the occupation of the Sudetenland was followed, on 15 March 1939 by the German invasion of what remained of the Czech state and by the creation of the Protectorate of Bohemia and Moravia and the Nazi puppet-state of Slovakia. In her home town of Bratislava, meanwhile, the wife of the chazan of the Manchester New Synagogue, Solomon Stern, on holiday in Czechoslovakia, spread the word of the favour shown by the Manchester Yeshiva towards foreign applicants.[30] Another difficult moment of decision had arrived. The Yeshiva Executive had already decided in February 1939 that that there could be no more foreign admissions 'except in exceptional circumstances'.[31] Even Rosenberg accepted the reality that, with the arrival of German students, even in numbers less than anticipated, the Yeshiva 'would have its hands full';[32] notwithstanding the successful dinner, 'expenditure was increasing enormously while the income was not growing correspondingly'.[33] It would be 'impossible', he believed, to accept all twenty of the Czech students who had applied to the Yeshiva by 12 March.[34]

It was at this point that Rabbi Segal's intervention proved decisive. Even as Rosenberg informed the Executive that the Czech applicants would have to be refused, a message was received from the Rosh Yeshiva to the effect that unless they were accepted at once, their very departure from Czechoslovakia would be placed in jeopardy by the decision of the British government, to take effect on 1 April, that the holders of Czech passports would henceforth require visas to enter the country. In these circumstances, Segal urged that the applicants be accepted at once.[35] Within a week the refusals had been reversed and a fresh drive was under way to support the expected Czechs. Dr Altmann was approached to use his influence to persuade Manchester synagogues to participate in fund-raising, a full-time Collector was appointed on a commission basis and a Refugee Student Fund Committee set up under the chairmanship of Sidney Feather, the son of another of the Yeshiva's major donors, Alexander Feather.[36] The decision was taken to admit up to 100 Czechs; by the end of April forty of them had arrived in England en route for Manchester.[37]

News of these events soon reached Nathan Laski, who, for whatever reason, had kept his silence as the Yeshiva, consulting no one outside itself, had taken on board its twenty-eight German students. In his presidential address to a meeting of the Communal Council on 30 April, at which Saul Rosenberg and Walter Wolfson were both present as the Yeshiva's representatives, Laski now visited the full force of his wrath on the Yeshiva authorities. Ignoring the Refugee Committees of Manchester and London, they had set themselves up, quite wrongly, in his view, 'as an authorised Refugee body'.[38] Even the Chief Rabbi's Emergency Committee, from which they might otherwise have expected some sympathy, had written to him to deplore their action. Since the Yeshiva was ill-equipped to bear the costs of its decision, the burden of supporting the students would now inevitably fall on the community. 'Did they really think,' he stormed, 'that the Manchester Jewish Community could support these young people [the cost of whose annual maintenance he estimated to be £5,000], in addition to all the local Jewish institutions?'[39] Laski doubted also the prospects of these young Czechs finding their feet in Britain. The Yeshiva was 'very wrong' to facilitate their arrival, he believed, 'since they have not the slightest chance of making headway in this country'.[40] Nathan's eldest son, Neville, then President of the Jewish Board of Deputies and a guest at the Council meeting at which these thoughts were expressed, backed his father's condemnation of the Yeshiva in terms which suggest the convergence of London and provincial thinking on the treatment of potential refugees. The Yeshiva had broken 'the rules worked out by the Government and the Jewish organisations dealing with the refugee question'.[41] Emigration, Neville Laski asserted, needed to be 'of an orderly character. Discipline had to be maintained in the community and they must not allow their administrative and financial arrangements to be upset by sentiment.'[42]

Rosenberg responded at once to what he later described as 'very unkind words'.[43] He called on Laski to retract his statement: 'Were there not enough of our brethren drifting homeless', he asked the meeting, 'that ... Manchester Jewry should refuse to open their doors to a number of young men, many of whom had suffered terribly in concentration camps?'[44] The Yeshiva was being condemned for 'something of which we felt very proud'.[45] The minutes do not record the details of the 'lengthy discussion' which followed. Rosenberg and Wolfson both believed that Laski had cut them off abruptly before they were able to make complete statements of the Yeshiva's case.[46] At a meeting of the Yeshiva committee a week later Rosenberg struck a conciliatory note. He believed, he said, in Laski's feelings of goodwill towards the Yeshiva and hoped that he would come to realise that these were 'abnormal times'; 'no one, not even Mr. Laski, would contend that they [the German and Czech students] had better opportunities [than in Manchester] in those countries from which the Yeshiva had rescued them'.[47] Six had been in concentration camps 'while others would have been if not for the Yeshiva'. The Yeshiva authorities, he went on, had not been driven by 'sentiment alone'. They had fully realised the financial commitment they had taken on; already steps were being taken with the Home Office to have some of the students redesignated as 'trainees', a capacity in which they would have their earnings supplemented by the MJRC. The committee as a whole was more palpably angry; in a heated atmosphere they endorsed everything Rosenberg had said at the Council meeting 'as well as what he had not been allowed to say'.[48]

Laski defended himself in a lengthy press release published in the *Jewish Chronicle* on 2 June 1939. 'All who know me,' the release began, 'are aware of the large amount of refugee work with which I have been dealing and of the sympathy which I endeavour to show towards all who pass through my hands.' In elaborating on his speech to the Council, he went on to make some play, in the context, it may be suggested, of what he had always seen as the Yeshiva's 'backwardness', of its political naivety, its ignorance of the law and the recklessness of its financial management. British immigration regulations dictated that young refugees brought over as students would have to leave the country when they were eighteen: 'what will be their future in any country they are sent to if they have no trade? Knowledge of the Talmud alone will not enable them to make a living in a new country.' For two or three months, the students might expect public sympathy, but for 'how long will this continue?' Since he knew that the Central British Fund had declined to accept financial responsibility for 'these importations', the Yeshiva would then be forced back on its own resources, from which it could currently scarcely afford to pay its teachers' salaries. In making a communal appeal to help it out of such an impasse, it would be effectively depleting the funds available to other institutions. Like other communal bodies concerned with refugees, the Yeshiva should 'have worked through the Council of Manchester and Salford Jews, with the close co-operation and financial support of the CBF'.

The most probable reading of what happened next is that Laski now used the Yeshiva's inexperience of Home Office procedures, and his own 'official' government contacts, to try to force on the Yeshiva a partial retreat. By the end of July 1939 he and Otto Schiff, 'after much trouble', according to Laski, had obtained from the Home Office trainee permits for fourteen of the Czech students; the price to be paid by the Yeshiva was that only the remaining twelve, and those to be selected by the Communal Rav, might be taken on as students.[49] It was presumably on Laski's prompting that help was now sought by the Yeshiva, which was, in truth, by then in desperate financial straits (salaries were in arrears, bills unpaid, supplies running out)[50] from Eli Fox. Seen, perhaps, as the member of the MJRC most likely to be sympathetic to its cause,[51] the Yeshiva looked to Fox to find trainee placements for fourteen young Czechs, all of them, much to Fox's displeasure, 'extremely reluctant' to take them up.[52]

In this they had the unqualified backing of Rabbi Segal, who was more than equally reluctant to lose them. For Fox the transfer was 'the Yeshiva's only way out'. For Segal it was a surrender of principle: 'Yeshivas abroad,' he told a meeting of the Education Committee, 'had been closed down by hostile forces, and here the Yeshiva was contemplating what amounted to a partial closure.'[53] His word, once again, carried the day. All twenty-six Czechs, seventeen of them from the Slovak city of Bratislava, were accepted as students and a letter to this effect written to the Communal Council.[54] Laski's response is not recorded; on the Communal Council he kept his silence. Rumour has it that Rosenberg then sent him a request for a substantial donation;[55] for its part the Yeshiva donated £5 10s to 'Mr. and Mrs. Laski's Golden Wedding Presentation Fund'.[56]

Although the Yeshiva's volunteer managers, its teachers and its Principal were justly proud of this result and of the college's subsequent miraculous survival to uphold the cause of Jewish orthodoxy (the executive had done 'a great thing', Segal believed),[57] the truth is that for the next three years the college tottered uneasily on the brink of insolvency, lurching, in some panic, from one fund-raising strategy to the next without ever wiping out its considerable debts or reducing its overheads. The impact of the Czech admissions had raised the weekly outlay on student maintenance from £40 to £90.[58] By April 1940 the Yeshiva balance sheet showed a deficit of more than £400.[59] The payment of salaries was in arrears, £70 of lodging money owed to the students; [60] the burden, Rosenberg believed was 'unshoulderable'.[61] Symbols of the Finance Committee's desperation included the planning of a charity cricket match, provided only that the Yeshiva's name did not appear on the tickets,[62] the sending out (against Rabbi Segal's better judgement) of senior students to earn fees by making up *minyanim* at local *shivas*,[63] a decision to dispose of its now dilapidated former premises 'for almost any price'[64] and the distribution of local mail by students to save on postage.[65] The Jewish public was informed that new collecting boxes on offer to Jewish homes and workshops were 'attractive in design', 'in well-toned colours which will harmonise with all surroundings'; they were 'pleasing to the eye, good for your soul and good for the Yeshiva'.[66] In his plea that the Yeshiva take on the full complement of Czech students, Segal had received some sympathy from Altmann, who believed that, by using his influence with Manchester's synagogues, 'something would materialise' to support them.[67] Thereafter he was pursued relentlessly by the Yeshiva committee for help that, in the event, he was unable to provide.[68] In May 1940, using the experience of the Liverpool Yeshiva as their precedent, they applied to the Manchester Shechita Board (without success) for 'a substantial annual grant'.[69]

For all its initial determination, the Yeshiva had been forced back by spring 1940 into placing (with Fox's help) a handful of its students in employment as trainees, if only on a part-time basis and 'where their orthodox scruples would not be violated';[70] other students made their own choice to go out to work, some in Manchester's many Jewish-owned rainwear factories,[71] as their more viable option;[72] one, 'a deformed youth ... who felt he would do better in life with a university degree' had signed on for a full-time course at the University of Manchester.[73] During 1941 the Yeshiva's alumni association, the Agudas Lomdei Torah, was reinvigorated by its secretary, one of the German refugee students, Sigmund Margulis (later Margolis), to ensure that those who remained at the Yeshiva were properly and sensitively maintained.[74] By what was seen as a combination of the 'superhuman' efforts of its committee,[75] the inspirational leadership of its Principal and Divine Providence, the Yeshiva *did* survive, its teaching (and some of its debts) intact. At a committee meeting in April 1942 Saul Rosenberg announced the receipt of a warm letter of thanks from three former refugee students who had recently left to take up work in London. The committee minutes then read: 'They now felt that they were being rewarded for the enormous responsibility they had accepted in bringing over these refugees and for the strenuous efforts they were obliged to make to meet the increased expenses. They had taken the Rosh Yeshiva's advice and the Al—ty had helped and now they felt happy and proud at the achievement.' When two of the newer committeemen struck a sour note by advocating 'preference for English students', Mark Bloom responded simply that 'it was our duty to look after foreign boys'.

Little record remains of the experiences of the 'boys' themselves. Most received maintenance payments on the same flat rate as that which applied to local students: 9s a week to cover their lodgings and other regular expenses, with free midday and evening meals prepared by the Yeshiva's cook, except on Sabbath and Festivals, when they were expected, in the Eastern European manner, to find local Jewish families, from a list kept by the Yeshiva, which would provide them with free meals.[76] Little of the 9s was left over for luxuries, even for clothing which would bring 'dignity and prestige to the Yeshiva and the students', particularly during their first months in England, when they were lucky to receive maintenance payments one week in five.[77] There was accommodation at the Yeshiva only for the caretaker and the cook; the students, again on the Eastern European model, were found lodgings with private orthodox and religiously observant families in North Manchester at rents (mostly around 4s a week) which reflected the commitment of the host rather than the values of the market.

This appears to have worked well. Gabriel Brodie (then Bledy), who arrived in Manchester from Bratislava at the age of fourteen with his brother, Alexander, towards the end of March 1939, was put up, as a temporary measure, by the Fisher family, only to remain with them in Heaton Street, off Leicester Road, until his marriage six years later.[78] There he and his brother were treated as members of the family throughout the war years, experiencing the Manchester Blitz together in the public shelter in nearby Manley Park.[79] Taking his Sabbath meal with the Rabbinovitz family likewise began on Gabriel's first Friday in Manchester and ended only with his marriage in 1945; other students, he remembers, were less fortunate. After the initial trauma of his departure, Gabriel does not recall having experienced any great difficulty adjusting to a life in England rather more exciting than the one he had experienced in Bratislava. He was one of a group of more rebellious students who, flaunting the official ban on cinema-going imposed by the Yeshiva authorities, visited a little picture house round the corner from the college at least once a week. The following morning would be spent by the rebels discussing its plot over breakfast at the Yeshiva, to the disgust of the 'more pious' students, before the compulsory eight o'clock morning service. This, he remembers, was his introduction to the English language. In other ways Gabriel was more relaxed in his religious observance than his teachers would have wished. Although remaining always *Shomrei Shabbat* (Sabbath observant) and regularly wearing his *tephillim,* in Manchester he at first 'gave himself the benefit of doubt' in taking a cup of tea and a bun, and maybe a vegetable salad in Lyons Corner House after Sunday evening Hallé Concerts (in wartime, the cinemas were closed on Sundays), for which he could usually afford the 1s entrance charge. Heaton Park was the centre of activity for all the Yeshiva boys: on Friday afternoons, which were free of lessons, they played football there, on the afternoon of Shabbos they went for walks in its extensive grounds.

He now feels some pangs of shame that, 'having a reasonably good time here among friends of my own age with a similar outlook and sharing the same sort of activities', he was reminded of the plight of his parents, younger brother and sister, all still trapped in Czechoslovakia, only by rare three-line Red Cross messages in which they sought help in making their escape. 'What was happening in Europe we were not aware of and so we managed to put it to the back of our minds without being constantly aware of what turned out to be this great tragedy.'[80]

Gabriel Brodie recalls his time at the Yeshiva with affection. Its managers, he believes, were 'good to them within financial limits'. Rabbi Segal he remembers as 'a gentle, kind man', well able to cope with traumatised refugee students; his own first teacher in a class of 10 to 12 students, Rabbi I. Dubov, as 'a wonderful teacher'. With his knowledge of German, Gabriel had no difficulty picking up Yiddish, still the main language of instruction. The financial restraints were not onerous; after a year at the Yeshiva, it became possible for boys to supplement their basic (and uncertain) maintenance money by earning small amounts for giving private lessons, for example, or for serving as minyan men in shiva houses (at a fee, Gabriel Brodie remembers, of 2s or 2s 6d for attending every morning and evening of the six days of mourning). Gabriel was able to save up for his first English clothing – an air-force blue striped suit costing 55s at Montague Burton's.[81]

Within the Jewish community, he was drawn into the new complex of institutions then taking shape around Bachad. He was introduced to B'nei Akiva by an English Yeshiva student, Herbert Laster, becoming an active member and ultimately one of its *madrichim*.[82] He attended BA camps, including one held under canvas in St. Asaph in North Wales in 1942, where amongst his companions in the movement was Gubi Haffner.[83] Many weekends were spent at conferences in one or other of Bachad's five Hachsharoth, with whose *chalutzim* Gabriel also attended the Manchester Merkaz Limmud. From his own experience as a participant, with fellow Yeshiva students, in these blossoming Mizrachi chalutzic youth movements, and, as a married man, in TVA, Gabriel believes that 'much of the credit' for the revival of Jewish orthodoxy in Manchester in the post-war years rightly belongs to the refugees.[84]

Another factor in this revival, however, was the evacuation to Salford in September 1944 of the Yeshiva in Staines, thought to be vulnerable to Germany's new flying bomb assault, with its thirteen young students, all of them 'Movement boys'. Considered strong on religious education, but weak on its 'general' side, the RCM executive sought help from the Educational Authorities in Salford, which confirmed it. The Hebrew education, Salford's Chief Inspector accepted, was 'excellent', but the time given to secular education (ten hours a week) fell far short of the Board of Education's requirements, while the living accommodation of the thirteen students was 'far from satisfactory'. When Marianne Prager, visiting on behalf of the RCM in November, agreed about the building, the Principal, Rabbi Weingarten, sought out a new property in Manchester, where he announced his intention 'to stay'.[85]

Notes

1 The subsequent claim by the Yeshiva committee that it had 'brought over 60 or 70 students' is not substantiated by the official lists of entrants.

2 I can find no evidence of the subsequent claim (*Manchester Talmudical College, 40th Anniversary Souvenir Report* (1951), p. 75) that the Yeshiva brought over 120 refugee students 'up to the outbreak of war'; the entrance lists suggest around sixty.

3 MY GM 22 December 1940.

4 MY GM 14 March 1943.

5 MY CM 20 March 1938.

6 MY FC 10 April 1938.

7 MY FC 5 May and 12 September 1937, EC 2 January and 1 May 1938, CM 2 July 1939, 12 May 1940, EC 5 October 1942.

8 MY Education Committee 3 July 1938.

9 *Ibid.*

10 MY FC 27 July 1938; JC 26 August 1938.

11 MY EC 4 September 1938.

12 MY GM 2 October 1938; JC 14 October 1938.

13 *Ibid.*

14 MY CM 16 October 1938.

15 MY CM 30 October 1938, FC 13, 20 and 27 November 1938.

16 MY CM 16 October 1938.

17 MY FC 20 November 1938.

18 MY 27 November 1938.

19 Undated cutting from the JG (late November 1938).

20 MY CM 4 December 1938.

21 The decision had been taken to invite Laski in this capacity 'as otherwise there may be some resentment in certain quarters'.

22 MY CM 22 January 1939; JC 13 January 1939.

23 MY EC 30 January 1939, CM 5 February 1939.

24 Undated advertisement from the Yeshiva's cuttings book.

25 JC 10 February 1939. In this edition, 48 donors are listed.

26 MY CM 5 February 1939, EC 12 March 1939.

27 These included the former president, Israel Libbert, who feared 'that the Yeshiva was undertaking more than it could carry out. The primary object of the Yeshiva was to teach and not to maintain.' (MY EC 26 February 1939.

28 MY EC 12 March 1938.

29 MY CM 19 March 1939.

30 Information from Revd Gabriel Brodie, one of the Czech boys to arrive at the Yeshiva in 1939, and now Secretary of the Manchester Yeshiva and the minister of the Great and New Synagogue in Steencourt, Crumpsall.

31 MY EC 26 February 1939. At this meeting it actually refused to accept and

maintain thirty German refugees pressed upon it by the Chief Rabbi's Emergency Committee.

32 MY EC 12 March 1939.
33 MY CM 19 March 1939.
34 MY EC 12 March 1939.
35 *Ibid.*
36 MY 19 March 1939.
37 JRC AGM 30 April 1939.
38 MY CM 7 May 1939. Laski's comments are pieced together here chiefly from the official minutes of the meeting, but also from the reports of Saul Rosenberg and Walter Wolfson, who were both present as the Yeshiva's representatives, and from the JC 5 May 1939.
39 *Ibid.*
40 *Ibid.*; JRC MM 19 April, 17 May 1939, AGM 30 April 1939.
41 JC 5 May 1939.
42 *Ibid.*; JRC AGM 30 April 1939.
43 JC 5 May 1939; the Yeshiva minutes report it as 'harsh words' (MY CM 7 May 1939).
44 *Ibid.*
45 JC 5 May 1939; JRC AGM 30 April 1939.
46 JC 5 May 1939.
47 *Ibid.*
48 *Ibid.*
49 MCC EC 19 July 1939; MY CM 23 July 1939: report of a joint meeting between representatives of the Yeshiva and of the Communal Council; JC 21 July 1939.
50 MY CM 13 August 1939. Asked by the MJRC for a grant of £250, the Shechita Board replied that it had earmarked part of it to the Yeshiva and the Jewish Home for the Aged (MSB EC 12 July 1939).
51 In March 1939 the Yeshiva had accepted as students two boys from the Cassel-Fox Hostel on condition that the MGJAC pay 10s a week towards their maintenance and expenses (MY EC 5 March 1939, CM 19 March 1939).
52 *Ibid.*
53 MY Education Committee 24 September 1939.
54 *Ibid.*
55 Relayed to the author by a former Yeshiva student, Revd Gabriel Brodie.
56 JC 28 July 1939.
57 MY Education Committee 16 April 1939.
58 MY GM 22 December 1940.
59 MY CM 14 April 1940.
60 MY EC 31 March 1940. Gabriel Brodie remembers that during his first months at the Yeshiva he was paid his maintenance money only one week in five.
61 MY 14 April 1940.
62 MY FC 11 June 1939.
63 MY 19 November 1939.
64 MY CM 12 May 1940. It remained unsold in 1943.
65 MY FC 19 May 1940.
66 JG 28 July 1939: letter from Rabbi E. Golditch.
67 MY Education Committee 24 September 1939.
68 MY CM 1 October 1939, 14 January, 14 April and 12 May 1940. Altmann's help has all the appearance of a deal in which, in return for his help in calling a public meeting of local synagogues and encouraging them to subscribe to the Yeshiva's funds,

Altmann expected Segal and Rosenberg to accept 'a measure of control' over its financial affairs from a 'special synagogue committee' and to cooperate with him 'in effecting desirable reforms'. Only two years into his Communal Rabbinate, Altmann may have seen the Yeshiva's discomfort as a means of bringing it within his jurisdiction and within the scope of his modernising programme. The meeting was, in fact, convened, under the chairmanship of R. Barrow Sicree, and did in fact recommend support for the Yeshiva's refugee fund, but it led neither to an access of funds to the Yeshiva nor to any change in the Yeshiva's structure and independence (JC 21 July 1939).

69   MY CM 2 July 1939, 12 May 1940.
70   MY GM 22 December 1940.
71   Taped interview with Revd Gabriel Brodie conducted by Rosalyn Livshin in 1983, in MJM (J 318) (hereafter, Gabriel Brodie interview). On taking work the students' maintenance payments from the Yeshiva ceased; most would then initially find subsidised accommodation at the Cassel-Fox Hostel.
72   MY EC 5 May 1940.
73   MY EC 5 May 1940. Regarding him as a 'special case', 'out of consideration for his deformity' and to keep him out of the Yeshiva kitchen, which he was using 'as a restaurant' the Yeshiva agreed to give him 15s a week to take his meals elsewhere.
74   MY CM 21 December 1941, EC 14 January 1942. Margolis saw a proposal by the Yeshiva to set up a Students' Clothing Fund as an act of charity; better would be fixed grants. Margolis was later secretary of the Manchester Shechita Board.
75   MY GM 22 December 1940.
76   MY CM 2 November 1941, 21 December 1941. At the end of 1942 this was increased to 12s 6d and to 15s for a few of the older boys (MY CM 31 December 1942).
77   MY CM 21 December 1941.
78   Gabriel Brodie interview. Revd Gabriel Brodie became the long-serving and highly-respected minister of Manchester's Great and New Synagogue (otherwise known, from the former name of its premises, as Stenecourt) and secretary of the Manchester Yeshiva. He was a student at the Yeshiva until 1944.
79   *Ibid.*
80   *Ibid.* Gabriel's parents, younger brother and sister were all deported to Auschwitz, where only his sister survived by hiding during the Death March; after the war, Gabriel brought her to Manchester.
81   *Ibid.* Gabriel went on to serve in the Yeshiva office and then (in July 1944) to lead prayers at Stenecourt, of which he later became the minister.
82   *Madrich*: a role involving a mix of team leader, teacher, helper and brother.
83   Later to become Yehuda Avner, Israel's Ambassador to the Court of St James.
84   Gabriel Brodie interview.
85   MJRC RCM EM 5 May, 26 September, 14 and 28 November 1944, 23 January, 27 February, 27 March, 18 June 1945.

17

'From slavery and persecution to freedom and kindness': refugees at the Manchester Jewish Home for the Aged

Late in 1938, 'after careful consideration and after consultation with the Council of Manchester and Salford Jews', and almost certainly at the prompting of its secretary, Morris Feinmann, the Home for Aged, Needy and Incurable Jews and Temporary Shelter in Cheetham Hill, which had served the community since 1896, and which then regarded itself as 'one of the foremost institutions of its kind in this country', decided to offer accommodation to thirty German Jewish refugees. With the purchase of a house next to its existing buildings and adjacent to the Spanish and Portuguese Synagogue, the Home's Board of Management[1] believed that its facilities now made it possible to 'undertake this humanitarian work both efficiently and economically', that the gesture would 'receive the good will of the community', and that 'the necessary financial support' would be readily raised.[2]

The Home and Shelter, in two donated houses at 198 and 200 Cheetham Hill Road, themselves aged, was then maintaining around twenty men and women over the age of sixty and thirty-five 'incurables' over the age of eighteen, offering a three-day stop-over to over 750 'casuals' a year, providing meals for almost 7,000, and 'entertaining' 40 to 50 homeless people at Passover. With its costs escalating throughout the 1930s, it was already in debt to the bank to the tune of £7,700: adding the refugees would mean that £9,000 would somehow have to be found during 1939 – from donations (of £2,327 in 1938), legacies, annual subscriptions (raising £1,490 in 1938), the sponsorship of rooms, wards (at £500) and beds (at £250), collecting boxes in the community, and the sale of *kiddush* tablets for the departed (at £25) – simply to meet its expenditure. The Board was none the less optimistic: 'it is not conceivable', its annual report read, 'that there should be a single Jew in this community who would withhold his support'.[3] As something of an incentive, beds sponsored during 1939 would be named 'Beds of Peace'.[4]

Permission was obtained from the Home Office for the admission of forty [*sic*] elderly German Jews, who arrived in the spring of 1939. Twenty were housed in the 'refugee annexe' at 202 Cheetham Hill Road, officially opened by Otto Schiff and consecrated by Rabbi Altmann on 18 June,[5] the rest placed in lodgings (the rent paid by the Home) in the immediate vicinity, from which they were to come to the Home for their (free) meals. The whole operation, the Board pointed out diplomatically, had the backing of Nathan Laski, whose 'judgement was sought on any major problem'.[6] One beneficiary of the arrangement was Dr Ludwig Hammelburger, the religious teacher from Wurzburg am Main, who had arrived in London with his family in March 1939 on a visa arranged by the Chief Rabbi's Emergency Committee. Since Hammelburger's intention was that both his grandparents would come to the Home for the Aged, in June or July 1939 he moved to Manchester, where he first found accommodation at Lerner's (Kosher) Hotel, directly opposite the Home. There he was contacted by the Home's salaried secretary, a Mr Ribatsky, who found the Hammelburgers a large house in Heywood Street, promising to send them elderly refugee lodgers to help pay the rent. This marked the beginning of what, for the Hammelburgers, became a successful business venture. Their house at 74 Heywood Street became a boarding house for refugees, only some of them from the Home; the others included the Bachadnik, Rabbi Hans Heinemann, and Benno Reich, a refugee of Polish origin who made a living in Manchester as a private teacher of Ivrit.[7]

Little evidence survives of the individuals who now found refuge in 'the Refugee Home'.[8] It may be that they included Karl Aufrichtig who, with his wife, Irma, had fled Vienna in January 1939, and who are said to have been admitted to a 'Jewish Old Age Home in Manchester'. Karl's son had arrived in Manchester earlier. It is said that shortly after the Anschluss he and his friend, Victor Liebl, had tried to enter Britain illegally, that they had been picked up on the coast and imprisoned in Manchester, before 'regularising their status' and being allowed to stay.[9]

Another may be identified with greater certainty as Rabbi Dr Moritz David (1875–1956), once Rabbi of Bochum and of Dortmund. Moritz David was born in Gimbsheim, a small town in Rheinhessen, in 1875, the son of a local merchant. After a secondary education at a Jewish Gymnasium in Worms, he entered the rabbinical seminary in Breslau, one of three centres for the training of rabbis in Germany, followed by study for his Ph.D. at the University of Erlangen, and four semesters at the Hochschule fuer die Wissenschaft des Judentus, where he qualified as a rabbi in December 1900. In 1901 he was appointed rabbi of the small farming community in Bochum, where, although he identified himself with the Liberal-Reform tradition, he earned a reputation for a 'non-partisan attitude towards all religious orientations'. A skilled teacher, 'an orator of the highest order' and a leader 'in all charitable organisations', he served the community until his retirement in 1934. Deprived of his pension by the Nazis, however, in June 1938 he took a position as Rabbi of the Jewish community in Dortmund, where he was arrested by the Nazis on Kristallnacht and imprisoned for four weeks in Oranienburg. In spring 1939, then aged sixty-four, he emigrated to Britain with his wife, Charlotte, as one of the forty elderly refugees guaranteed by the Manchester Home for the Aged.[10] In Manchester, in December 1939 he was invited to address the congregation of the South Manchester Synagogue, said to include 'some members of his former congregation in Bochum', in German: the first time in the north of England, according to the *Manchester City News*, that a refugee had addressed an English congregation in that language.[11] On 2 February 1940, the *City News* reported that he had conducted the first marriage service ever held at the Home for the Aged, between a bride from Berlin and a groom from Vienna, before a congregation 'composed of the small colony of refugees now resident in the home'.[12]

For the Board of Management there was room for self-congratulation. In the words of its annual report, 'whilst the number admitted had to be limited, there is no limit to the happiness this created amongst those who were fortunate enough to be chosen. From slavery and persecution and to freedom and kindness is the fortunate lot of our German guests. May they remain with us for many years to come, should they so decide.'[13] In September 1939, after death had taken an immediate toll, there were eighteen residents in the Refugee Annexe and fifteen in lodgings; a further twenty-six elderly refugees, who had arrived in Manchester to stay with their own guarantors, came to the Home only for their meals.[14] Their supposed 'happiness' was muted: 'taking into consideration the physical and mental handicaps these co-religionists have suffered before they came to this country, it is difficult to restore happiness so soon, particularly in these difficult times, but the Board is doing everything possible to make them forget the misfortune which has befallen them'.[15] There were initial problems with the matron 'Miss A. Haas'.[16] by whom the refugees felt they were being 'badly treated'.[17] The 'difficult times' included the evacuation of forty-three inmates to Southport in September 1939 and the internment of eight aged 'enemy aliens', one, Rabbi Dr Moritz David, on the notorious *Dunera* to Australia, where he continued his rabbinical ministry to his fellow internees. The Home's Board of Managers launched an immediate appeal,[18] but it was not until mid-1942 that their releases had been secured. Only then were the Home's 'Continental guests' said to be 'in good health' and 'fully acclimatised'.[19]

The Home also had its problems, not least the cost of entertaining refugees in the face of what turned out to be 'sparse support' from the community.[20] With its debt to the bank spiralling towards £10,000, stiff measures were required. The refugees were at first refused pocket money;[21] even after further consideration only 2s a week was allocated, and only to those found to be in need.[22] After first ruling out the admission of refugees whose relatives made a donation to the Home (some had offered as much as £500) – on the grounds that a 'money feeling' would poison 'the atmosphere' and undermine the Home's good name – the Board decided to consider such cases 'on the merits of [the] general suitability of the applicant', although 'under no circumstances' to allow them to constitute more than 10% of the total number of refugees.[23] Rooms were made available in the (native) 'aged section' of the Home to such paying guests.[24] In November 1939 it was decided that 'native' residents and 'the German people', who had previously taken their meals separately, should eat together in the Rest Room, 'to avoid making any fires in the annexe'.[25] For the same reason, in February 1940 the refugees were transferred to the 'incurables section' while the cold weather lasted.[26] Help was sought, without result, from the MJRC and the German Refugee Committee in London.[27] The problem was solved only by the decision of the government, after the outbreak of war, to part-fund the maintenance of refugees.

A potentially more serious problem was posed early in 1942 by widely publicised complaints from the six German refugee[28] nurses at the Home that they had experienced 'anti-Semitism' from the Matron and from some of her non-Jewish staff. The outrage of the Board of Management was exacerbated by the way the complaint surfaced. At the end of January the six nurses had, without explanation, placed adverts in the 'Situations Wanted' column of the *Jewish Chronicle*.[29] A *Chronicle* reporter, sensing a 'serious grievance', added a short paragraph to its 'Provincial News' section to the effect that the advertisements were the consequence of 'the alleged militant attitude of some Irish nurses towards the refugee nurses'. Within the Home, meantime, recognising the danger, Morris Feinmann had 'thought [it] advisable' that the girls should speak 'to three refugees in whom they had confidence rather than [an] English person'. In the event, only one refugee, the respected GP, Dr Rudolf Friedlaender, spoke to the nurses, although in the presence of Feinmann, the Home's president, Laurence Kostoris, and Rae Barash from the MJRC.[30] It was Feinmann's expectation that Friedlaender would inform the nurses that their applications had been 'in extreme bad taste' and were likely to reflect badly not only on the Home but on 'other members of the German community'.[31] In the event, although Friedlaender appeared to accept at the meeting that the nurses' grievances were too 'insignificant' to justify them in placing their adverts, after it he had sufficient a change of heart to write to the *Jewish Chronicle* expressing his own concern at the 'unhappy atmosphere' in the Home and effectively endorsing the nurses' complaints: there was, he wrote, reason to believe that there was 'anti-Jewish feeling within the nursing staff'.[32]

The Board, now incensed as much by Friedlaender as by the nurses, made its wrath felt at its meeting on 8 February. Friedlaender's 'enquiry' had been 'one-sided'. He had written to the *Jewish Chronicle* without consulting the senior of the Home's honorary physician, Dr Bernard Hirson. As to the nurses, who had now extended their complaint to embrace their senior English colleague, Sister Dodgson, 'the fault lay', according to Hirson, 'in the fact of the German nurses thinking they were superior to the English nurses'. No German nurse, he asserted, had experienced anti-Semitism. He supported the matron in her refusal to allow free access to the drug cupboard, the 'main cause', he believed, of the nurses' actions. After considering alternative ways of saving the Home's good name, including a public statement by Kostoris and a meeting of Feinmann with the editor of the *Jewish Chronicle*, the Board settled, diplomatically, on an investigation by a special committee made up of representatives of the Home and of the Manchester Jewish Representative Council, under the chairmanship of Neville Laski, now back in Manchester as president of the Jewish Hospital, at which Drs Hirson and Friedlaender, and a 'representative' of the *Jewish Chronicle* (actually its Manchester reporter,

David Freeman) would be present, and to which the Matron, Sister Dodgson and the nurses, native and refugee, were allowed to give evidence.[33]

The 'ad hoc committee', which was expected to exonerate the Home, went on to do so. Dr Friedlaender should not have been asked to interview the nurses and should not have written to the *Jewish Chronicle*. He was advised by Neville Laski to write to the Home's secretary saying he was satisfied with the enquiry and that there was no element of anti-Semitism at the Home. There was no justification for the nurses' complaint or for any of the allegations made 'against the administration or atmosphere in the Home'. The Matron was no anti-Semite; nor was Sister Dodgson, who was 'aggressive to everyone'; the refugee nurses had been unable to provide a single instance of anti-Semitism.[34] The *Jewish Chronicle* now applauded. The Home had 'set an example' which other Jewish institutions might take to heart. Rather than 'sulk in silence' or 'scream' at its critics, the Home had held what the *Chronicle* saw as a 'full and free enquiry'. As a result, the matter had been 'cleared up without a trace of scandal attaching to the Home'.[35]

The reality appears to have been, as the Matron suggested, 'professional jealousy', although whether resulting from the German nurses' sense of their superiority or the English nurses' feeling of inferiority, or even from international rivalry, is not clear. Certainly two of the 'Christian' nurses (there was no further reference to them being 'Irish') were, according to Feinmann, from 'only [a] low domestic class of girls', one of them 'with no previous training'.[36] Although a degree of friction had been detectable over 'a few weeks', the final spark was the refusal by the Matron and Sister Dodgson to allow the German nurses free access to the 'linen room and medicine cupboard'.[37] Whether there was any element of anti-Semitism in the way the nurses were treated can no longer be assessed. At all events, a prominent refugee who had recently been appointed to the Home's Board of Management, Leopold Lindemann, a well-to-do industrialist, and who had been 'perturbed' by the whole affair, appears now to have taken the aged refugees under his wing, voicing their complaints and ensuring the proper upkeep of their annexe.[38] As to the six nurses, they were all given a month's notice, only one of them being later persuaded to return. The matron, after 'constantly applying for new positions' tendered her resignation on 30 June 1942, after which the Board rejected a proposal that Sister Dodgson might replace her.[39] Whether Dr Friedlaender, who soon afterwards volunteered for the British army, ever wrote his letter of apology is not known. He had remained obdurate to the last, pointing out at the end of the ad hoc enquiry that while the Christian nurses all received Christmas cards from the Board, no cards were sent to the Jewish nurses on Rosh Hashana.[40]

The presence of refugees at the Home, whether as resident or as nurses, apparently created no further cause for concern. Rather, they are rendered invisible in the later minutes of the Board.[41] They were perhaps in the audience when, on 13 August 1944, 'artistes' from the play, *The King of Lampadusa*, based on the real-life surrender of the Italian occupiers of Lampadusa to Sergeant-Pilot Sydney Cohen, provided a 'memorable concert' at the Home.

Notes

1 In 1938 the Board, which supervised the routine business of the Home and employed its staff, consisted of fifteen members: the president of the Home, three life vice-presidents, three vice-presidents, a chairman, an honorary treasurer, two honorary secretaries and four trustees. The inmates were served by eight honorary medical officers: two consulting physicians, two consulting surgeons, a consulting ophthalmic surgeon, two physicians and an honorary masseuse. The paid staff was made up of a superintendent, a matron, a Sister, at least eight nurses and a kitchen staff of five. Apart from its own fund-raising efforts, the Home received a grant of £416 a year from Manchester Corporation. Fund-raising included the 'endorsement' of brass *kiddush* tablets (at £25 each), which were attached to the inside walls of the Home's synagogue, where thirteen ministers from the community, in rotation, conducted the service. Kashruth was supervised by the communal Beth Din.

2 Home for Aged, Needy and Incurable Jews and Temporary Shelter (hereafter HATS); 41st Annual Report for the year ending December 1938, pp. 9–10.

3 *Ibid.*, p. 12

4 *Ibid.*, p. 20.

5 HATS 42nd Annual Report p. 7.

6 HATS 44th Annual Report.

7 Taped interview of Michael Hammelburger by Rosalyn Livshin, 18 March 2002 (hereafter Michael Hammelburger interview). Continuing after the war, another lodger at 74 Heywood Street was the Holocaust survivor, David Jonisz.

8 The only record of admissions to the Home is in the form of photographs of those admitted, preserved at the present Manchester Home for the Jewish Elderly, Heathlands Village. Unfortunately the refugees were not photographed. Refugees at the Home are known to have included Bertha Benjamin and a Mr Feldheim, who had a daughter in Manchester. The Hammelburger parents never made it to Britain (Michael Hammelburger interview).

9 Letter from Charlie Roberts (né Aufrichtig) to the author, 26 August 2005.

10 For Moritz David, Manfred Keller and Gisela Wilbertz, *Spuren im Stein: Ein Bochumer Friedhof als Spiegel jusischer Gesthicht*, pp. 316–322 (article from an unidentified German journal, its translation entitled 'Carved in Stone: Jewish History mirrored in a Bochum Cemetery'). I am grateful to Mr John Chillag of Leeds (and formerly of Bochum) for this reference. Rabbi David died in Manchester on 16 January 1956. Also MCN 16 December 1939.

11 MCN 16 December 1939.

12 MCN 3 February 1940.

13 HATS 42nd Annual Report p. 7.

14 HATS EC 24 September 1939.

15 HATS 43rd Annual Report p. 3.

16 Possibly to be identified as Herte Haas, an Austrian Protestant born in 1918, who in June 1940 was a nurse at the Royal Children's Hospital in Pendelbury, Salford (QL).

17 HATS EC 26 November, 10 and 17 December 1939.

18 HATS 43rd Annual Report for the year ending December 1940 p. 3.

19 HATS 46th Annual Report p. 3.

20 HATS EC 21 August 1939.

21 HATS EC 17 December 1939.

22 HATS EC 4 February 1940. The fund was made up of a special collection by two of the Board's members.

23 HATS EC 3 July and 21 August 1939.

24 HATS EC 9 and 26 November 1939.

25 HATS EC 9 November 1939.

26 HATS EC 4 February 1940.

27 HATS EC9 November 1939.

28 The nurses' names appear in the Board's minutes or in their advertisements in the *Jewish Chronicle*. A. and R. Maier, R. Goldschmid, A. Cohn[?] Fuchs and Hanna Seiderer's former colleague at Prestwich Mental Hospital, Evi Raikover. Three of the nurses had been transferred to the Home from the Manchester Jewish Hospital, when the latter was taken over by the Military.

29 JC 23 January 1942. Most of the advertisements were for nursing posts in London, one for work as a doctor's receptionist. One (R. Goldschmid) added that she had previously been Matron at a convalescent home and that 'she had excellent English references'.

30 HATS Rough notes made by Morris Feinmann for a meeting of the Board of Management.

31 HATS EC 8 February 1942.

32 JC 6 February 1942.

33 HATS EC 8 February 1942.

34 HATS Special Meeting 8 February 1942; JC 13 January 1942.

35 JC 20 February 1942.

36 HATS Rough notes by Feinmann.

37 *Ibid.*

38 E.g. HATS House Committee 31 December 1943, I May 1944.

39 HATS Rough notes by Feinmann; EC 27 April, 2 July 1942. The returning nurse was Goldsmid.

40 For Rudolf ('Rudi') Friedlaender, obituary in the AJR newssheet for January 1969, p. 11. Born in 1906, he was one of the five children of Dr Moses Friedlaender, once the general secretary of the Jewish community in Berlin, who was killed in France in 1917. Thereafter Rudi lived in the Jewish Orphanage in Berlin managed by a friend of his family. After an education in the Sophien Gymnasium, he studied medicine at the University of Berlin, financing himself by coaching pupils for their matric and occasionally driving taxis. Specialising in surgery, he became a general assistant to Professor Freyer at the Medical Academy in Düsseldorf. Dismissed on 1 April 1933, at the end of the month he left Germany for Manchester. Through family connections with Nathan Laski, he obtained a post as House Surgeon at the Manchester Jewish Hospital. In 1934 he obtained British qualifications in medicine and surgery at the University of Edinburgh. After four years at the Jewish Hospital, he set up in private practice in Didsbury, where in July 1936 he married Eva Stern, a refugee from Berlin. In February 1943 he volunteered for the RAMC, becoming, by 1945, a Lieutenant Colonel. After leaving the army, he became a founder and trustee of the Morris Feinmann Home, where he served the residents as Senior Medical Officer. In October 1969 friends in Manchester set up a Memorial Trust in his name which enabled GPs to travel and study new treatments and techniques.

41 Even their names are not known and the photographing of those entering the home was not extended to the refugees. The word 'Germans' was probably used to embrace Austrians. Refugee inmates may have included Karl Aufrichtig and his wife,

Irma, who fled Vienna in January 1939 and are said to have been admitted to a 'Jewish Old Age Home' in Manchester (letter to the author from their grandson, Charlie Roberts (né Aufrichtig) 26 August 2005).

18

'Bright young refugees': refugees and schools in the Manchester region

One way in which young refugees might gain the right of entry to Britain was by offering proof of their acceptance by a British school, although they still required a British sponsor who would guarantee to cover the cost of their accommodation, their maintenance and such fees as the school demanded. Britain's twelve Quaker boarding schools are said to have offered, between them, 100 scholarships to refugees, although some, like Peter and Hans Kurer, among the forty refugee scholars at Great Ayton School in Yorkshire, had already arrived in Britain with their parents.[1] Winchester College offered five free places to refugees, which were advertised by the Earl Baldwin Fund, and one of which was given to Carl Amberg, a refugee from Aachen, members of whose family later settled in Manchester.[2]

Amongst the prestigious private, fee-paying secondary schools in the Manchester region which offered places to refugees during 1938–39 either at no cost or at a reduced rate, were Manchester High School for Girls, Kingsmoor School in Glossop, Culcheth Hall School in Bowdon, and Bury Grammar School. Of these, only Manchester High School for Girls, which had long been the chosen secondary school for the children of Jewish families living in the southern suburbs, and Bury Grammar School, some five miles north of the newer areas of Jewish residence in Prestwich and Crumpsall, already had Jewish pupils, although at Bury still only a handful. For the most part the acceptance of young Jewish refugees was an act of humanity by those emotionally engaged with the escalating suffering of European Jewry, some of them head teachers, others with a degree of influence in local schools.

Amongst the latter was the academic and Liberal Party activist, Hilda Mary Adela Buckmaster, who became responsible for the rescue of the young German refugee, Wolfgang Plessner. It was once again a fact that the chances of young Germans and Austrians depended very much on their families having the right contacts at the right time. Those contacts also represented a network within which a young refugee like Plessner might find safety and comfort.

Hilda Buckmaster was born in Brentford, Middlesex, in 1897[3] into a family with long-standing Liberal and academic traditions. Her grandfather, John

Charles Buckmaster, beginning life as an agricultural labourer in Slapton in Buckinghamshire, became in his later years, and largely through self-help, a platform speaker against the Corn Laws and a Professor of Chemistry at Imperial College. His third son, Hilda's uncle, Stanley Owen Buckmaster, following a junior studentship in Mathematics in Christ's College, Oxford, became a Chancery Barrister. Returned as MP for Cambridge in the Liberal landslide of January 1906, and later representing Keighley, he was briefly, as the first Viscount Buckmaster, Lord Chancellor in Asquith's coalition government of 1915–16. Following Asquith's defeat, although never again acquiring public office, he became the powerful advocate in the House of Lords and on public platforms of a raft of radical causes which included improved housing for the poor, the abolition of capital punishment, women's suffrage and divorce reform.[4]

While sharing her family's enterprise and radical instincts, Hilda's early life took a more unconventional, not to say adventurous, turn. In 1914, at the age of seventeen, she abandoned her secondary education at Haberdashers' Aske's Girls School in Acton to join the war effort, first as a volunteer with the Red Cross, then, in 1917, as a recruit to the newly formed Women's Royal Navy Service (WRNS), with which she served as a motor mechanic until 1919.[5] She subsequently enrolled at the London School of Economics, where, as a student of Economics, she is said to have been 'concerned with the foundation of the NUS (the National Union of Students)', in which she later held a number of honorary posts.[6] Graduating in 1924 with Public Administration as her special subject, she began research of a particularly practical kind towards a doctorate in International Relations. In the course of this work, and already an active Liberal, she was chosen by Lloyd George's last administration to serve as one of the British commissioners sent to study municipal affairs in post-war Germany. This was followed by eighteen months with the Quaker Relief Service in Eastern Poland and by further fact-finding expeditions which included service as a deck hand on the SS *Panape*, one of the last sailing ships trading in grain between Australia and Finland. In the course of her travels, she became particularly interested in minority questions and acquired a good working knowledge of French, German and Russian.

From this experience she emerged in the early 1930s as an active Liberal, a convinced feminist, a propagandist for social reform, and, while never a pacifist, an internationalist with a determined belief in the peace-keeping mechanisms of the League of Nations. She became active in the League of Nations Union, in which she served for three years as the County Organiser for Essex, and began a lifelong and ardent association with the Liberal Party just as it was entering its terminal descent into political impotence. In November 1935, then still a doctoral student and research assistant at the LSE, she stood as Liberal candidate for Maldon in Essex, only to be badly beaten into third place.[7]

Arriving in Manchester in the following September, to take up an appointment as warden of the Ellis Llwyd Jones Hall of Residence at Manchester University,[8] she threw herself at once into the local Liberal politics and peace movement of Manchester and south Lancashire, making contact with, amongst others, the prominent Manchester Liberals, Leonard Behrens, Philip Milner Oliver, the former Liberal MP for the Blackley Division of Manchester, and Thomas Hudson, secretary of the Eccles branch of the LNU. In April 1937 she was present with Hudson at a meeting of the LNU in Eccles chaired by the Mayoress.[9] In July 1937, in a speech to the Rochdale Women Liberals she condemned government expenditure on armaments when half the population was 'undernourished': what was required instead, she argued, was the raising of wage levels and the end of sweating.[10] In that year, she was an active speaker for the Liberal Party in the run-up to the municipal elections in Manchester, urging constituency parties, in a speech to the 95 Club, to start preparing for the General Election as 'evangelists of the party'.[11] Thereafter, she was a speaker sought after by Liberal Party bodies throughout Manchester.[12]

It was perhaps through the LNU, in which she was a critic of Germany's expanding overseas claims, that she first became interested in refugees. When she first met him in 1937 Hudson was involved in the early stages of a process which would lead to the creation of the Manchester International Club. In October 1937, drawing on her research into Minority Questions, she spoke out at the LNU branch in Rusholme against Germany's claim to territories in which her colonists happened to live. There was 'more German blood in Milwaukee and Wisconsin', she told the meeting, 'than in [the] Polish Corridor'.[13] In June 1937 she became a member of the Manchester committee supporting the Watermillock hostel for Basque children It was Buckmaster who also acted as the intermediary in 1937 between the Harold Memorial Orphanage in Salford and Manchester University's Spanish department in the provision of teachers and interpreters for the Basque children then under the protection of the Christian Volunteer Force. She was active too in gathering support for Spanish Aid, which she believed to warrant support from 'people of all shades of political opinion'.[14]

In some way that can no longer be identified – but perhaps as a tutor on a language course in London – she had made contact before 1938 with Rose Bluhm, the wife of a German-Jewish mathematics teacher living in Breslau. It was through Buckmaster's mediation that in late 1938 Rose's son, Michael, was found a place as a pupil at Dartington Hall in Devon, and Michael's friend, Karl Wolfgang (now 'Tony') Plessner, the son of a Breslau Jewish doctor, a place at Bury Grammar School, then a private, fee-paying school, where since November 1936 Buckmaster had represented the university on the Board of Governors.[15] It appears that in Plessner's case, with the help of the school's headmaster, Lionel Lord, she also identified those who became the boys' hosts and guarantors, in Plessner's case a Jewish GP, Dr M.J. (Max) Maxwell, living in Bury, a cotton town of some 56,000 people eight miles north of Manchester, and with a child of his own at Bury Grammar.[16]

The school itself (hereafter BGS), with separate boys' and girls' departments, and a total in the 1930s of around 700 children, was a seventeenth-century Anglican foundation which by 1939 had acquired a high reputation both for its 'tone' and for its academic standards. It was the school favoured by aspiring parents from Bury, Ramsbottom, Tottington and other smaller towns in south Lancashire, just as Manchester Grammar, which the BGS Governors regarded with a mixture of jealousy and respect, attracted the children of Manchester and the Cheshire and Derbyshire towns to the south of the city. Lord 'considered that the standard of the Bury Grammar School was on a par with that of the Manchester Grammar School, which was very high'.[17] Lord himself, appointed headmaster in November 1936, had aspirations to enhance the image of the school, introducing, for the first time, a school uniform, the compulsory wearing of the school cap, 'even at weekends', and a Founders' Day reception for parents and local dignitaries.[18] The school had forged particularly strong links with the University of Manchester, where in the late 1930s there were seldom less than ten of its alumni, but also with Oxford and Cambridge, which the school typically supplied with two or three scholars a year. Entrance was by examination and by the payment of fees of seven guineas a term; the fact that all parents were obliged to sign a contract with penalties if their children left before the end of their schooling meant that there were always a handful of defaulters relentlessly chased up by the Board's Fees and Removals Sub-committee; modest bursaries, most dating from the nineteenth century or earlier, were available on the same terms to children of poorer families.[19]

In so far as can be judged, it was a school with a radical liberal tradition not dissimilar to that of Manchester Grammar. At the time of Lord's appointment, there was a school branch of the LNU with 100 members; at the time of Japan's invasion of Manchuria in 1931 many boys were said to have been allowed to wear bomb-shaped badges inscribed 'Refuse to Buy Japanese Goods'; collections were authorised by the Governors for the victims of the Sino-Japanese and the Spanish Civil wars.[20] A teacher appointed to the school in 1934, J.E. De Courcey Ireland, a graduate of New College, Oxford, who became joint chair of the school's LNU branch, was prominent in Manchester as a supporter (with his wife, Betty) of the victims of international events. In January 1938, Betty De Courcey Ireland was secretary of the District Joint Council for Spanish Relief. Her husband resigned from BGS in July 1938 to become the organising secretary of the China Relief Fund.[21] Given his practical empathy with German-Jewish refugees, Lionel Lord, thirty-eight at the time of his appointment, the son of an official of the Indian Service, an old boy of Clifton, a graduate of Emmanuel College, Cambridge, and, before he came to Bury, a Housemaster and teacher of Classics at Plymouth College, was apparently a man in this same liberal mould: the historian of the school describes him simply as 'a thoughtful and kindly man' who 'safeguarded the school's academic standard'.[22] The school was always short of its full complement, Lord doing what he could to attract new entrants.

Since Bury lay some three miles north of the Jewish Quarter, in 1939 it had not yet attracted the children of Jewish families in any number. Class records in the school's yearbook for 1939 suggest only two Jewish boys (D. Cohen and S.R. Rosen) other than Max Maxwell's son, Victor. The first

Jewish Governor, Alderman A.E. Goldstone, was appointed in 1940.[23] There were only a handful of 'foreign' children at the school prior to the arrival of refugees, a German girl whose parents, fearing the outbreak of war, removed her in November 1938 to a school in Switzerland,[24] and (in 1931) at least one child from each of India, Norway and Czechoslovakia.[25]

The evidence does not exist to clearly define the separate roles in refugee support played by Buckmaster; by the progressive headmaster of Bury Grammar Boys' School, Lionel Cornwallis Lord; by the headmistress of the Girls' School, Nellie Nield; and by other members of the school's Board of Governors, chaired by the Anglican Rector of Bury, Canon Hugh Leycester Hornby MC, MA,[26] particularly since Buckmaster's first attendance at a meeting of the Board all but coincided with Lord's appointment as headmaster,[27] and since the minutes of the Board make no reference of any kind to the admission of refugees. It seems likely that Buckmaster was, at the very least, influential in guiding Lord's hand and in persuading the Board to commit itself to the support of Jewish refugees. The part played by Lord himself, however, need not be underestimated. With a brother working in 'either the Home or the Foreign Office',[28] he was in a strong position to understand the needs of German Jews and the processes required for their rescue.

According to Max Maxwell's son, Victor, 'the Board of Governors decided in 1938 that the situation of Jewish people in Europe was becoming so bad that they must do something to help the children there get out to the safety of England. They agreed to pay all the expenses of bringing eight Jewish children of about fifteen, four boys and four girls, to Bury and to pay for their fees at the school'. They then approached the parents of some of the children, including Max Maxwell, as both a Jew and a 'prominent citizen'.[29] In the letter to Plessner's parents, informing them of his readiness to offer her son a free place 'for such time as he is in England', Lord added that he had 'one or two other boys in similar circumstances coming to the school shortly'. Of Plessner, who believes that the headmaster went out of his way to inform the rest of the school of the circumstances of refugees and to make a plea for their welcome, he wrote: 'apart from natural grief at parting, I hope he will not be too lonely or miserable'.[30] Between them, Buckmaster and Lord appear to have engineered a network of refugee support: in April 1939 Wolfgang Plessner was followed as a free scholar to Bury Grammar by Ernst Fraenkel of Berlin, whose guarantee and accommodation were provided by a patient of Dr Maxwell.[31]

Wolfgang arrived in Manchester in late January 1939, when he was met at the station by Buckmaster – identifying herself, he remembers, by a white handkerchief tied around her arm – and driven by her to his guarantors in Bury.[32] In helping him, Buckmaster and Lord, or both, had begun a chain reaction which also saved his parents. A highly intelligent and articulate young man, Wolfgang, with their help, and with Dr. Maxwell's cooperation, was able to provide his parents with the contacts and advice which made their entry possible at the end of August 1939, on the last pre-war flight out of Breslau, and supposedly in transit for Chile.[33] An internationalist by training, impatient with convention by instinct, Buckmaster's energetic humanity had readily surmounted the barriers of ethnicity and nationality at the beginning of what was to become a distinguished military career in Britain and Canada.[34]

In March 1939 she and P.M. Oliver were amongst the signatories to a letter to the *Manchester City News* seeking support for the Council for the Boycott of German Goods. Her close links with Manchester and the north-west ended, however, in autumn 1939, when she returned to the WRNS, apparently as Third Officer (and later as Chief Officer) in charge of training, in which capacity she initiated a process which led to the creation of a centralised structure of pre-entry and specialist training with depots in London and Glasgow.[35] Her resignation from her university post was noted in the *Manchester City News* of 21 October 1939. The Board of Governors of BGS, from which she was replaced in November 1939 by Miss (later Professor) E.M. Butler, thanked her for 'the great interest' she had shown in the school and for her 'great help' to the Governors.[36] Thereafter she returned to Manchester only on short visits, one, in September 1942, to speak to the students at the Manchester College of Domestic Economy on the formation of a (WRNS) Girls Training Corps.[37]

Meanwhile, Wolfgang Plessner was fortunate in his other personal contacts in Manchester, Jewish and non-Jewish. He was received with unreserved warmth into the 'kindly, affluent and well-connected' family of his guarantor, the Jewish GP, Dr Max Maxwell and his wife, Ada, at 'Springwells', the Maxwell family home at 94 Manchester Road, Bury, with its 'very large lounge' and 'enormous club chairs'.[38]

He was made to feel at ease in a family whose social status, cultural horizons and (modest) levels of Jewish observance[39] were not unlike those he had experienced in Germany. He shared a bedroom first with Dr Maxwell's assistant, Dr Gold, then with Maxwell's son, Victor; he accompanied the family on trips to Blackpool or Southport in the Maxwell's Studebaker, and on their summer holidays in 1939 at St Annes-on-Sea; space was set aside for him in a utility room to pursue his growing interest in handicrafts and 'things electrical' (where he immediately began to construct a battery-powered model motor boat); the family's neglected grand piano was re-tuned especially for him to play; in the evenings he joined the Maxwell children, Victor and Elaine, for Monopoly, on a board sent over from Germany by his parents; together they went regularly to the local cinema. He joined the Maxwells also on visits to their family's relatives in London and Leeds, where on Pesach 1939 he attended the local 'Temple' (Synagogue) and joined a family Seder, conducted, he informed his parents, 'in almost the same manner as at our house [in Breslau], there are also eggs and salt water, only that each one reads for him/herself and not the father of the house alone'.[40]

On his first birthday in Britain, his sixteenth, on 5 February 1939, a lavish party was laid on for him at the fashionable, 400-year-old Royal George Hotel in Knutsford, which belonged to a cousin of Mrs Maxwell. In a private room, he wrote to a friend in Breslau, 'a marvellous long table' was laid out for tea, 'with a large gateau in the shape of a dice (or maybe a cube)' with sixteen candles and the words, 'Many Happy Returns for Victor's friend'.[41] In letters to Breslau Mrs Maxwell kept Wolfgang's mother fully informed of his health and progress in Bury.[42] He 'seems very well with the Maxwell's family, who are most kindly folk', Lionel Lord wrote to Wolfgang's mother in March 1939.[43] 'I get on very well with them', Wolfgang himself wrote to his parents in July.[44]

At Bury Grammar School, where Wolfgang found that he was 'up to standard' in a Fifth Form preparing for the School Certificate, he also found 'everybody ... very kind'. The boys, prompted by the headmaster, were sympathetic: they 'did their best', Wolfgang believes, to rein in their 'dreadful Bury accents' and rapid speech, 'to speak slowly and in simple words'. Within a month he saw his spoken English as 'moderate to bearable' and was able to read the Manchester morning and evening papers delivered to the Maxwell home. He 'enjoyed life under canvas' with his 300 fellow pupils at the school camp in Fleetwood in the early summer of 1939. Lionel Lord who clearly took the young refugee under his personal wing, according him long private audiences to discuss his academic future, sending him a book token on his sixteenth birthday, and negotiating with the Home Office for extensions to his visa, wrote in March 1939 that he was 'doing very well' and was 'popular with his fellows'.[45] Learning to play cricket, Wolfgang himself believed, had 'markedly improved his relationships'.[46] Other teachers, he wrote to his father, were 'particularly nice' to him: his German teacher, a Mr Bagshawe, took him on long Sunday walks in the countryside around Bury and Manchester, and once invited him to a performance of St Joan by the Bury Stage Society. None the less, he saw himself as having 'something to prove': he resented the presence of a fellow refugee, Ernst Fraenkel, whose unruly conduct, he believed, had, by suggesting ingratitude, let the side down.[47] Wolfgang himself became a deputy prefect.

Following announcements of his arrival in the local press, and the appearance of his photograph, with Lionel Lord, in the *Daily Herald*, Wolfgang remembers that he began to receive random calls from local children, 'offering to befriend him'.[48] One, Wolfgang told his parents, was from a boy rather older than himself, who lived in Radcliffe, a township five or ten minutes away by bus from the Maxwell home. This boy had written 'to Mr. Lord ... that he would like to meet me, because he is learning German. Mr. Lord gave me the letter and I answered in German. One day I shall get together with him, because it'll do my English good.'[49] In fact, Wolfgang began a close friendship with 'the Radcliffe boy', Arthur Salisbury, who worked in the office of a local silk factory, until Arthur was conscripted into the army, probably in 1940. They went on walks and cycle rides together, met casually in the evenings and travelled together by train on excursions to Windermere and Southport. Once, after being shown round the silk factory, Wolfgang was invited to supper at Arthur's home.[50]

Another stroke of good fortune for Wolfgang was the presence, near the Maxwell home, of a refugee household which was exceptionally welcoming to fellow refugees. This was the home of Franz Nagelschmidt, the versatile and internationally renowned German 'pioneer of physical medicine', who had left Germany for Britain in 1933. Born in Berlin in 1876 and qualifying there as a doctor, he went first to Copenhagen to work with Finsen, the founder of light therapy, and then returned to Berlin, where he established a light treatment clinic at the Charité, installing there in 1903 the first X-Ray unit for therapeutic purposes. In 1904 he founded a light treatment institute in Breslau, where, for the first time, he applied radium rays to treatment. In 1906 he returned to Berlin, where he founded the Finsen Clinic, of which he was in charge until 1933. There he developed diatherapy, a name coined by him to describe the creation of heat inside the tissue by the external application of electrical currents. He also designed and introduced an ultra-violet lamp without water cooling, the prototype of modern ultra-violet lamps. In 1911 he designed an apparatus to produce an electro-rhythmic current for electrical vibrations treatment. In 1912 he invented the neon lamp, originally for medical purposes.

In 1933 he left Berlin for Britain, where he was immediately made an honorary consultant in physiotherapy at the London Jewish Hospital. In 1934 he was awarded the 'Golden Key' of the American Congress of Physical Therapy for 'outstanding service to the science of physical medicine'. In 1936 he re-qualified as a medical practitioner in Edinburgh, then moving to Manchester as honorary consultant in physiotherapy at the Manchester Jewish Hospital. At his home in north Manchester he also ran a private clinic, equipped with the many physiotherapeutic instruments he had brought from Germany. A man interested in 'arts as well as in science', he was a talented violinist who in Berlin had run a quartet in which the child prodigy Edi Kurtz had played the cello.[51]

Franz's wife, also a refugee, was a psychiatrist and a popular speaker on psychological matters to women's groups in Manchester. After she had spoken to the Cheetham and Crumpsall branch of the Manchester and Salford Women Citizens Association in December 1937 on 'Some Fundamentals of Individual Psychology', the Association persuaded her to set up in the following July a group which met at her home on Tuesday evenings for the study of individual psychology.[52] The Nagelschmidts also set up what was, in effect, a refugee social group, at which their guests enjoyed music, games evenings, bridge parties and chess matches.

Wolfgang had got to know the Nagelschmidts 'through a friend in Bury' early in his university career, when he was looking both for new lodgings and for a physician who might help with a suspected bout of rheumatic fever. The Nagelschmidts had responded by introducing him to 'a first-class heart specialist' and offering him a room in their house, vacated by their daughter, Carla, who had taken a job as a photographer with Gaumont British Instructional Films in London. The house, Wolfgang remembers, 'was full of electrical equipment – several X-Ray machines, Diathermy machines, electrical muscle stimulation gadgets and so on. My room had a rather smaller diagnostic X-Ray unit in it, the big machines for X-Ray therapy were in the so-called dining room', where Franz Nagelschmidt was continuing his research.[53]

When Carla returned from London late in 1943, to be directed to a job in the laboratories at Metropolitan Vickers (for work on the development of jet engines), Wolfgang moved into one of his host's treatment rooms, which the highly methodical student left 'in a respectable state every week day, just in case it was needed'. In the Nagelschmidt house, Wolfgang was introduced to other refugee families, including, he remembers, the Rosenstiels and the Loebingers, who were also regular members of the Abendstern refugee circle in Rochdale. Michael Bluhm, Wolfgang's friend from Breslau, and Carla's refugee friend in Manchester, Eva Roditti, were also regular visitors.[54]

Wolfgang's autobiography moves the story on: 'Carla and I became good friends and when early in 1946, she was invited by her brother to visit Brazil, and did not really want to go, I suggested marriage instead, which was accepted.' Their marriage took place in the Registry Office in Salford, after which they moved to London; Carla as a photographer with Common Ground, which made educational films, Wolfgang to continue his research with his Manchester professor, who had moved in that year to Imperial College. Completing his Ph.D. in 1947, Wolfgang began his career in industry with a job at the newly established AEI Research Laboratories at Aldermaston Court.[55]

There is no indication in Wolfgang's autobiography or in his letters to his parents that such cordial personal relationships between German-Jewish refugees and native non-Jews had been damaged by the approach or the outbreak of war. Officialdom was another matter. At the end of September 1941, when in his last year at school, although Plessner was acknowledged to have been 'one of the most brilliant scholars in the history of the school', and was in receipt of an entrance scholarship (the Mathew Kirtley Open Scholarship in Mechanical Engineering) to study at Manchester University, he was refused a 'town grant' by Bury Education Committee by twenty votes to three, on the grounds that he was ineligible under the Council's Standing Instructions.[56] Although it was clear to at least one Labour member of a Conservative-dominated Council that the real reason for the refusal was 'because the boy was a German Jew', the decision was roundly condemned by the Bury Women's Liberal Association as 'without wisdom, without generosity and without humanity', 'deprecated' by the clergy of the Bury Rurideconal Chapter, and given a rough ride by the *Manchester City News*, the refusal was endorsed by the full Council, on the casting vote of the Mayor.[57] In the event, no doubt through Lord's influence, the school's Board of Governors awarded Plessner a grant (the Kay bursary of £25 a year, for three years) from its own funds.[58] 'We have still a lot to learn', the *Manchester City News* mused: 'how is it of greater importance that a boy who has won a scholarship to the university should have a good brain, or a good ratepayer as a father'.[59]

At the school prize day in November 1941 Wolfgang made what one local paper described as a 'dramatic farewell speech', another as 'a fine gesture'. After receiving his own prize, he spoke for eight minutes to a hall crowded with scholars and parents 'on the need for freedom in education': 'he betrayed no complaint at the treatment he had received in the borough[!]', but expressed his thanks to the governors, headmaster, and staff and all his friends among the boys 'for the many kindnesses they have shown me'. He expressed best wishes for those who are fighting today for freedom and liberty – especially 'the liberty to learn, to teach and to understand, which are necessary for the extension of knowledge'.[60] According to *The Bury Times*, his speech was 'loudly applauded'.[61] At the University, Plessner felt equally well-received by both students and lecturers, only on one occasion experiencing even a hint of prejudice.[62]

His experience, both of entry to Britain, of the support he received, and of the success he achieved, was not necessarily typical. He was a young man of exceptional talent and confidence, who fell on his feet at Bury Grammar School. But, above all, he had the benefit of the support and protection of six 'people of compassion': Hilda Buckmaster, Lionel Lord, Dr and Mrs Max Maxwell and the Doctors Nagelschmidt.

With his own impressive academic record and personal charm, and no doubt with help from Buckmaster and Lord, Plessner had also helped open the door of BGS to refugees.[63] Other refugee children followed Plessner to the school before and after Buckmaster's departure. In July 1941 the school offered a temporary post as a teacher of Modern Languages to Dr Arnold Meier, a German-Jewish refugee from Cologne who, before moving to Bury, had qualified as a teacher in London.[64] Meier went on to be a respected full-time teacher at the school where, immediately after the war, he led groups of children to Germany, Switzerland and France.[65] One was the first school party to visit Switzerland after the war;[66] another was to his own old school in Cologne, the Stadt Neusprache Gymnasium, beginning what was to become the longest continuous exchange visit (it still takes place) by any school in Britain.[67]

Less is known of the refugees who found places in other schools in and round Manchester. One of these was Culcheth Hall, a 'High Class Day and Boarding School' in Ashley Road, Bowdon: a private school which, since 1891, had provided a secondary education to girls from well-to-do families, including many Manchester commuters, some of German origin, in this fashionable Cheshire township. It was probably in 1938, after the beginning of the Kindertransport had been announced, that a group of Bowdon women led by May Pickard, an old girl of the school and the wife of its chairman of governors, set up a committee which persuaded the headmistress, Ruth Brownson, to offer free boarding places to five German girls, brought to Britain with guarantees from the committee: Marianne David, Elspeth Gaertner, Margret Heidenheim, Margot Wassermann and Liselotte Wolfskehl. When war broke out, May Pickard's committee assumed responsibility for the girls' welfare, arranging their holidays and providing birthday parties until most were reunited with their relatives in the United States and South Africa. All five were apparently impressed with the friendliness and kindness of 'every English person'.[68]

Another fee-charging school which offered places at reduced rates to refugees was Manchester High School for Girls, the sister school of Manchester Grammar, with whom it shared a liberal tradition and strong links with the Jewish community, particularly of south Manchester, dating from its foundation in 1871, in which Abigail Behrens, the wife of a wealthy Jewish cotton merchant, was deeply involved. By the mid-1930s forty Jewish girls attended the school out of a total pupil population of 400. Kosher meals were available and a special assembly had been organised for the Jewish girls, at which attendance was compulsory. Between 1934 and 1940 the school offered places to ten refugee Jewish girls, three of them 'Movement children' – Lore Bravmann and Erica Hecht, both from Stuttgart, and Ursula Friede, from Bocholt, all three from acculturated middle-class families – at just over half the regular fees.[69] An attempt was made to find members of the local community who could further subsidise their fees. Special arrangements were made to introduce them to the English language; they were helped to find accommodation with the children of other parents; from 1936 all received free meals. All three left for America during the war, Friede, who had stayed at the home of Geoffrey Sutherland, the principal of Dalton Hall (whose daughter, Hilary, was a pupil at the school) and Hecht in 1940, Bravman (who had been fostered by Dr William Chadwick (a member of the 'general committee' of the MJRC, and whose daughter was also at the school), 'to join her family', in December 1944. At the school, although no special pastoral care had been organised, the refugee girls were well treated by staff and other pupils, and settled in without problems. Lore Bravmann was Head Girl during 1944–45; another refugee girl was leader of the school orchestra.[70]

At some time early in 1939 Kingsmoor School, a private, fee-charging, co-educational school run by a Quaker couple, the Swains – 'a rambling old mansion on bleak Derbyshire moors' near Glossop – offered 'pretty, blue-eyed' Lotta Spitz, a young refugee from Vienna, a post as a domestic servant at the school, work which had secured her entry to Britain. There she awaited the arrival of her husband, the 21-year-old Desiderius (Deszo) Spitz, who in April 1939 was still seeking to overcome 'obstacles' (by implication his lack of personal funds or a guarantor) in seeking a visa from the British Home Office. 'Lotta still waits,' the *Daily Express* reported, 'every day she gets a letter from him'.[71] Deszo did, in fact, follow within months, apparently with a trainee placement organised by the school, for which he wrote an article in the school magazine, *The Arrow*, entitled 'Am I not lucky to be here?'[72]

It was almost certainly the Quaker connection which accounted for the rescue of the Spitzes and of two refugee children taken in by the school in March 1939. These were Rudolph Diamant, the son of Max Diamant, a manager of the Austrian National Bank, still trapped in Vienna after his dismissal by the Nazis, and a fourteen-year-old girl (her name unknown) from Berlin. Rudolph had persuaded the MP for Newcastle-under-Lyne, the refugee-friendly Quaker, Josiah (later Sir Josiah) Wedgwood, to ask the Home Secretary in the House of Commons if he intended to issue a visa for Max.[73] Since the school has now closed and its records have not survived, it is now impossible to say how many more refugees (if any) were found places or whether Rudolph's father actually made his escape.

Notes

1 Margaret Taylor, 'The Missing Chapter – How the British Quakers helped save the Jews of Germany and Austria from Nazi Persecution' (draft typescript, Manchester 2009), pp. 8–9.
2 'Some Letters of Aennchen and Richard Amberg, 1909–42' (typescript of English translations in the possession of Julian Treuhertz): letter from Irmgard Amberg of Aachen to her relatives 31 July 1939.
3 The minutes of a meeting of the Ellis Llywd Jones Hall Delegacy of the University of Manchester, 28 February 1936, include a brief biography of Buckmaster on her appointment as the Hall's warden. She is said to have then been thirty-nine years of age. The biographical details which follow are based on these minutes and on an obituary notice which appeared in the newsletter of the Haberdashers' Aske's Old Girls Club at the time of her death, at the age of 97, in April 1993, a copy of which was kindly provided by Mrs Gywin Notley, the Club's secretary.
4 DNB entry, 'Stanley Owen Buckmaster, First Viscount Buckmaster, 1861–1934'.
5 The formation of a women's naval service to be known as the WRNS was announced in *The Times* on 29 November 1917.
6 Ellis Llywd Jones Delegacy Minutes.
7 She received 5,680 votes (17.7% of the poll) as against 17,072 votes cast for the winning Conservative candidate, Sir Edward Ruggles-Brise, and 9,264 cast for Labour. She was already well thought of in Liberal circles, however, receiving invitations to attend the annual meetings of the Liberal Social Council in 1935 and 1936 (*The Times* 11 July 1935, 21 March 1936) In Essex she was also for five years secretary of an ex-service charity (possibly the Disabled Officers' Garden Homes, near Watford) and had 'an active interest in athletics' (Ellis Llwyd Jones Delegacy Minutes). She never completed her doctorate, appearing in the official record only as holding a B.Sc.
8 A post to be held until her 65th birthday at a stipend of £200 per annum plus board and residence (*ibid.*)
9 EPJ 25 April 1937.
10 MG 9 July 1937.
11 MG 9 September, 9 October 1937.
12 E.g. Minutes of the Barlow Moor and Didsbury Women's Liberal Council (in MCL) 10 May and 14 June 1938, 28 February, 16 May 1939. She was guest speaker at the Council's AGM, chaired by Leonard Behrens.
13 MG 28 October 1937.
14 MCN 1 April 1939: during her speech at the inaugural conference of the Stretford Aid for Spain Conference at Stretford Town Hall.
15 *The Serpent*, XX1, No. 1, November 1936, p. 30; Wolfgang Plessner, 'My Life Story', an incomplete autobiographical typescript, pp. 4–6. In conversation with the author (in

2003), Plessner confessed that he had no idea who the 'Miss Buckmaster' who had helped him was: he had a vague (and erroneous) idea that she was connected to the Jewish Refugee Committee in Bloomsbury House. It was perhaps the case that she used contacts at Bloomsbury House to obtain visas for Michael and Wolfgang. During the Second World War, Michael Bluhm was a member of the British Intelligence Corps, and later acted as an interpreter at the Nuremberg War Crimes Trials. After the war he went into medical physics, working in Glasgow and London.

16 The parents of Dr Max Maxwell (formerly Yehuda Abrams) were born in a village near Mogilev, in 1904. His father left the village for America in 1905 but perished in a shipwreck off the coast of Scotland. His widow, Sara, with her two children, Yehuda (later Max Maxwell) and Hannah, emigrated to Leeds in 1907, where she married Solomon Abrahams, a shoe manufacturer. When Solomon's business failed, he became a shoe repairer and, to make ends meet, Sara sold shoes on markets around Leeds. In 1922 Yehuda won a scholarship to study medicine at Leeds University and qualified as a doctor in 1927. He married Ada in Leeds in 1928. That same year he moved to Manchester and set up as a GP in Butler Street, Ancoats, where he and Ada lived in a small terraced house in what was a poor working-class district. In 1932, while keeping up the Butler Street surgery, he moved his main office to 398 Great Cheetham Street, Salford, a better part of the Jewish Quarter. In 1935 he bought a larger practice at 94 Manchester Road ('Springwells'), Bury, where, at that time, 'Jewish people were unknown', changing his name by deed poll to the less Jewish-sounding Maxwell Julius Maxwell. There he employed an assistant, two living-in maids, a nanny who was also a receptionist for the surgery and a chauffeur who drove him on his rounds. He was also part-time Ear, Nose and Throat specialist at the Manchester Jewish Hospital (typescript by Victor Maxwell, 'My Father's Family', pp. 2–22).

17 Minutes of the School Governors, Bury Grammar School (hereafter MBBGS) 27 March 1939. The Minute books of the Board are in the possession of the school.

18 MBBGS 31 May 1937, 28 March 1938.

19 The Kay Bursary, which Plessner was later to receive, dated from 1887.

20 I.B. Fallows, *Bury Grammar School: A History c.1570–1976* (XXX), pp. 416, 423.

21 *Ibid.*, p. 423; MBBGS 25 July 1938; his wife Betty De Courcey Ireland was in 1938 honorary secretary of the Manchester Youth Foodship for Spain Committee (MCN 29 January 1938).

22 Fallows, *Bury Grammar*, p. 432. Fallows' chapter on Lord makes no reference to his political beliefs. He became president of Bury Rotary Club and Warden of Bury Parish Church.

23 His name first appears in the list of Governors in the BGS Year Book for 1940–41. It was not until the late 1950s that Jewish families moved in any number from Cheetham and Crumpsall to Whitefield, to the immediate south of Bury: the number of Jewish children at the school multiplied throughout the 1960s and 1970s.

24 MBBGS 5 November 1938.

25 In 1931 the headmistress of the girls' school, Nellie Nield, took a party of girls to Geneva under the auspices of the LNU; on their return the girls organised a mock League of Nations on which India. Norway and Czechoslovakia were represented by 'natives' of those countries (Fallows, *Bury Grammar*, p. 481).

26 The minute books suggest a Board membership of twenty-one, which included the two school heads, at least five Councillors drawn from Lancashire Country Council and from the civic authorities of Bury, Ramsbottom and other Lancashire towns, a representative of Manchester University, and a handful of unattached local

dignitaries, one of whom always served as deputy-chairman to H.L. Hornby. Late in 1945 Hornby left the Board after his appointment as Bishop of Hulme.

27 Buckmaster's first appearance at a Board meeting was on 23 November 1936; Lord was appointed headmaster on 27 November (MBBGS). The minute books are in the possession of the school. They record the Board's decisions, regrettably not its debates.

28 Plessner, 'My Life', p. 6.

29 Maxwell, 'My Father's Family', p. 33. If this is correct, the arrangement must have been made informally, since there is no reference to it in the Board's minutes. In the school's records I can find references to only two refugees at the Boys' School (Plessner and Bluhm) and three at the Girls' School (a Viennese, Elizabeth Wangerman a German, Mary Lewey, who in 1942, at the age of fourteen, came to live with her parents in Bury and a French refugee, Yvette Gruner, who left in September 1941 to join her mother, who was with the Free French forces in Syria). MBBGS Fees and Removals Sub-committee 24 November 1939, 24 January and 23 September 1941, 23 January 1942). Wangerman was offered a free place, Mary Lewey and Yvette Gruner places at the reduced fee of three guineas a term (MBBGS Fees and Removals Sub-committee 24 November 1939, 24 January and 23 September 1941, 23 January 1942). Another boy who *might* have been a refugee (there is no evidence either way) was Hans Fessler, who in September 1946 was awarded a West Riding County Major Scholarship on his school examination results (MBBGS 23 September 1946).

30 Plessner Papers at MCL: Mr L.C. Lord to Mr and Mrs Plessner in Breslau 30 December 1938. The Plessner Papers include letters and post-cards written by Wolfgang Plessner to his parents and friends in Germany between February and late August 1939. I am indebted for their translation from the German to Nachman Herz of Cheadle, himself a refugee from Germany.

31 Plessner Papers: Wolfgang Plessner to his parents 28 April 1939. Wolfgang described Fraenkel as 'moderately nice and not all too gifted' (Wolfgang Plessner's letter to his parents on 2 May 1939).

32 *Ibid.* Victor Maxwell remembers that Wolfgang arrived with 'large travelling trunk ... a full-size table-tennis table [and] his German bicycle' (Victor Maxwell, 'My Father's Family', p. 33).

33 Wolfgang's parents lived with the Maxwells, his father acting as Max's assistant, until they found a house of their own in Bury, where Wolfgang joined them. After his internment on the Isle of Man, Dr Plessner had a nervous breakdown and was confined for a time in a mental hospital in Dumfries. His wife meantime took a living-in job as a cook at a student hostel where Wolfgang also had a room. On his recovery, he and his wife left Bury to open a guesthouse at Abersoch in North Wales, where Dr Plessner died. To be nearer to Wolfgang, his wife then went to live in Belsize Park in London, where she died there in about 1992.

34 Buckmaster left Manchester soon after the outbreak of war, when she was recruited as Third Officer in the WRNS, apparently in charge of developing training facilities for new recruits. As the war drew to a conclusion, she renewed her interest in Liberal politics, in January 1945 attending the annual conference of the Women's Liberal Federation in Caxton Hall, where she spoke on the need to provide service-women with an early release which would make it possible for them to undertake professional training (MG 1 February 1945). The first women member of the armed forces to be adopted by the Liberal Party as a candidate in the General Election of July 1945 (MG 27 March 1945), she stood for Chelmsford, where she refused the invitation of the Commonwealth candidate to stand down in the interests of 'progressive unity':

it was the Commonwealth Group rather than the Liberals, she declared, which constituted the 'splinter group' (*The Times* 3 July 1945). She again lost heavily, securing
5,909 votes (10.1% of the poll) compared with the Commonwealth's 27,309 and the
Conservatives' 26,229. On her demobilisation, she became warden of Crosby Hall,
the residential hostel of the British Federation of University Women. In 1954 she emigrated to Canada to be nearer her younger sister, Elizabeth, becoming a Canadian
citizen in the following year. She became an officer in the Toronto branch of the
WRNS Ex-service Association, in which capacity she attended the 50th anniversary of
the Canadian WRNS in Halifax in 1992. A week following her death in April 1993,
her sister received on her behalf a silver medal from the Canadian Government for
Hilda's outstanding service to city and country (Obituary, Haberdashers' Aske's Old
Girls newsletter).

35 Vera Laughton Mathews, *Blue Tapestry* (London, 1949), p. 178.
36 MBBGS 27 November 1939.
37 MCN 18 September 1942.
38 Dr Maxwell had two surgeries, one in a separate wing of his house, where his assist-
    ant, a Dr Gold, also lodged, one on the other side of Bury at 112 Walmersley Road.
39 The family had a 'special dinner' on Friday nights, when Ada lit the candles and Max
    made *kiddush*. The family spent Friday nights together, playing games and listening
    to music (Victor Maxwell, 'My Father's Family', p. 21).
40 Plessner Papers: letter from Wolfgang Plessner, Bentcliffe Drive, Leeds, to his par-
    ents in Germany, 5 April 1939.
41 *Ibid.*, undated letter [February 1939?] from Wolfgang Plessner to his friend Peter
    Weissenberg in Breslau. The Royal George was a long-established hostelry in which
    Queen Victoria is said to have stayed. In April 1939 Mrs Maxwell's cousin opened an-
    other hotel, this one newly built in south Manchester, 'fabulously modern and posh'
    (Wolfgang Plessner to his parents in Germany 2 April 1939).
42 *Ibid.*, undated letter from Mrs Maxwell to Mrs Plessner. Wolfgang, she wrote, was 'very
    sunburnt' and 'looking better than he has done all the time he has been in England'.
    Between the lines of the letter is Wolfgang's translation of it into German.
43 *Ibid.*, L.C. Lord to Frau Plessner 26 March 1939.
44 *Ibid.*, Wolfgang Plessner to his parents in Germany 11 July 1939.
45 *Ibid.*, L.C. Lord to Frau Plessner 26 March 1939.
46 *Ibid.*, Wolfgang Plessner to his parents in Germany 11 July 1939.
47 Notes of author's conversation with Wolfgang Plessner.
48 Plessner Papers: 'Tales of a Refugee at BGS' by Wolfgang Plessner.
49 *Ibid.*, Wolfgang Plessner to his parents in Germany 14 February 1939.
50 *Ibid.*, Wolfgang Plessner to his parents in Germany 10 March 1939.
51 Information on Nagelschmidt from an obituary by W. Roman in *Nature*, 3 January 1953.
    His first diatherapy apparatus is in the Science Museum in London. Nagelschmidt
    died in Manchester on 4 October 1952. His son, Gunter, who arrived in Britain with
    his father in 1933, became a distinguished mineralogist who worked closely with the
    Medical Research Council.
52 MSWC Nos 231 (December 1937) and 238 (July 1938).
53 Plessner, 'My Life', p. 8.
54 *Ibid.*, pp. 6–8.
55 *Ibid.*
56 According to one report, Plessner's parents (refugees who had arrived from Breslau
    in August 1939) were not ratepayers in Bury; according to another, the difficulty was
    that Wolfgang had not attended the school for three years immediately preceding

the date of the award. J.B.S. Stopford, the University Vice-Chancellor, informed the press that in the scholarship examination 'Plessner came out top of a considerable number of entrants'(Plessner Papers: undated and unattributed photocopies of press reports). The Governors of BGS recorded simply (MBBGS 22 September 1941) that Plessner had been recommended by his examiners for a Bury Corporation Scholarship, but 'if not awarded' to 'give him a Kay Leaving Scholarship of £25 a year for three years'. The minutes (diplomatically) make no reference to any controversy.

57 MG 30 September, 3 and 27 October 1941; MCN 26 September 1941.
58 MG 27 October 1941.
59 MCN 26 September 1941.
60 Plessner Papers: undated and unattributed photocopies of press reports.
61 *Bury Times* 29 October 1941.
62 Notes of author's conversation with Wolfgang Plessner. Plessner went on to obtain a Ph.D. and to a successful career as an industrial engineer in Britain first with AEI, then with BICC, working on superconductors and fibre optics.
63 The school kept track of Plessner's university career, sending him letters of congratulation at each stage (MBBGS 23 March 1942, 24 January 1944); he, in turn, sent letters of thanks to the Governors for the Kay Scholarship and 'for their generosity in allowing him free schooling while at BGS and for all the liberal help given him' (MBBGS 26 January 1942, 23 March 1943). The Governors also received a letter of thanks from his parents (MBBGS 22 November 1943).
64 MBBGS 28 July 1941.
65 MBBGS 22 July 1946, 9 June 1947. Meier spent the rest of his teaching career at Bury Grammar and is well-remembered by his former pupils. He died in Bury, where his widow still lives. His son David is a British High Court judge (Fallows, *Bury Grammar*, pp. 428, 434, 449).
66 *Ibid.*, p. 434.
67 *Ibid.*, p. 447; oral testimony from a Governor of the school, Mr Laurence A. Goldberg FRPharmS.
68 *Culcheth Hall, 1891–1991*, centenary brochure compiled and published by members of Culcheth Old Girls' Union Committee, 1991, p. 52. The five refugee girls later donated funds for the establishment of the May Pickard Trust, to provide help to those pupils who required it. The money was later invested to provide books for the school library.
69 Other refugees at the school were Waltraud Feibelmann and her cousin, Trude Feibelmann (in 1934), Doris and Eva Loewenstein, the daughters of a refugee industrialist, Marianne Katzenstein, Susie Lammie (in 1936) and Rosette Levy (in 1940).
70 I owe this information to the kind support of the school's archivist, Christine Joy, and to her generosity on allowing me access to her paper on 'The Care of Jewish German Refugees at Manchester High School for Girls', delivered to the History of Education Society conference in November 2006. This paragraph is based on Joy's paper and research.
71 *Daily Express* 26 April 1939. The Nazis marched into Vienna while Lotta and Desiderius were in Italy on their honeymoon. It was from there that they negotiated their entry to Britain. Desiderius eventually found a way of joining his wife in Glossop, finding work with the help of the School at a power-tool factory in Dukinfield. In 1965 their daughter, Jean, who was born in Glossop, and was then studying for her B.Sc. at London University, married the son of the (non-Jewish) sales manager at the firm where Desiderius worked, the marriage taking place at the Manchester Reform

Synagogue. Their son John, aged sixteen, was a pupil at Glossop Grammar School (*JT* 2 April 1965). During the war five German and Austrian refugee industrialists acquired sites and set up industries in Glossop, where a tiny refugee colony evolved, linked by attendance at the Manchester Reform Synagogue.

72 Form completed by Jean Etherton (née Spitz) in QHJ. *The Arrow, Kingsmoor School Magazine*, Vol. 2, No. 3, December 1939.

73 *Daily Express* 26 April 1939.

19

'Humanitarianism of the greatest value': Manchester Rotarians and refugees

It does not appear than any other Christian denomination but the Quakers set up a refugee committee or in other ways reached out consistently to refugees. William Hodgkins, minister of the Congregationalist Chapel in Oldham Road, wrote articles in support of refugees in the *Manchester City News*, including one which lavished fulsome praise on the refugees for their contribution to Manchester life, but there is no evidence that he or his chapel were otherwise active on their behalf. There is reference in the minutes of the QRC to a 'Catholic Committee', but it seems likely that this was either the Catholic Committee in Westminster or the Catholic Rescue and Protection Society, which in 1939, under the directorship of Father William Sewell, sought placements for the *kinder* in Catholic homes and institutions. The Catholic hierarchy in Salford, like that of Westminster, prioritised the Church's battle with Bolshevism over the needs of refugees, particularly Jewish refugees. A strong current of anti-Semitism, in which, inter alia, Jews are pictured as the allies of the Bolsheviks, runs through the Salford Diocese's magazine, *The Harvest*, of which Sewell was the editor.

It was the not unreasonable belief of the World Alliance Against Anti-Semitism in 1933 that the consciences of 'right-minded' British men and women would generate support for those threatened by Nazi anti-Semitism. One possible perspective on responses to refugees in Manchester is the degree to which individuals and institutions in Manchester were prepared to apply what were otherwise their guiding moral principles to refugees in general and to Jewish refugees in particular; to embrace 'outsiders' with the humanitarian ideals, whether religious or secular in their origins, around which they believed their conduct towards the deprived, the needy and the suffering in their own society to be based. Were the barriers created by xenophobia, anti-Semitism and 'indifference' so great as to dilute or undermine native philanthropic intent when its potential recipients were seen to be 'Jews and other foreigners'? It was an issue which challenged, whether or not they were prepared to acknowledge it, both the consciences of otherwise 'civilised' citizens and the collective strategies of Manchester's many philanthropic societies.

The Jewish and Quaker communities carried by far the largest burdens of refugee support in Manchester. The contributions of other groups were, at best, marginal. The Manchester branch of the National Council of Women supported the Quakers with funds which helped them accommodate their first refugees at the Lamb Guildhouse, and perhaps elsewhere. In October 1939 the pastor of the Salford branch of TocH, Laurence Davis, provided accommodation and a meeting room for young Austrian refugees working in the Pendleton and Higher Broughton districts of Salford. Amongst them was the sixteen-year-old Edouard Friedlander from Vienna, who owed his entry to Britain to the sponsorship of the Manchester and District Boy Scouts, and who in October 1939 used the TocH hostel as the base of a short-lived Salford Austrians Youth Group, which, at its height attracted forty members.[1]

But the philanthropic body which became most active on the refugees' behalf was the Manchester branch of Rotary International, whose members concluded, in April 1939, after 'careful consideration', that 'assistance of Refugees should be regarded as a Rotary activity'.[2] Rotarians had none the less to be kept reminded by their more idealistic members, if only to maintain the necessary flow of funds, of just how, as part of their 'international service', they had come to find themselves, from July 1939, offering material and moral support to German refugees, most of them of Jewish origin, in a hostel of their own creation.

One such reminder was offered by Clifford Whatmough, a leading figure in the hostel's foundation, in an address to his own club members in October 1939 on 'International Service: Refugee Hostels'.[3] In what he described as an 'apologia' for the hostel, Whatmough laid emphasis on the contrast between 'Rotarian ideals of international fellowship and service' and the 'vile persecutions and diabolical attacks on human liberties' of 'the German form of statecraft'. 'The German refugees in this country', he told his audience, 'are in one sense our greatest asset on the moral side, because they are proof positive of the justice of the cause we [the British people] represent'. After assessing their loyalties in tribunals, he believed, the government intended to allow German refugees to join the British army. 'If the British government can take that long-sighted view, surely we Rotarians can be big enough to embrace these people as fellow human beings and give them asylum as long as they do not materially interfere with the welfare of the British people.' He appealed to Manchester Rotarians to see the work of the hostel 'through to a happy and successful conclusion'.

In such a view, put together at the beginning of Britain's military confrontation of the German Reich, the Manchester Rotary Club was conceptualised as a vehicle for the delivery of those values with which the British nation and her allies confronted European fascism. It was part of what many saw as the ideological battle which underlay the military conflict. How accurate was such a perception of the context and of the Manchester Rotary Club's place within it?

The Manchester Rotary Club

Manchester Rotarians had first been propelled into the international arena of the 1930s by the imperatives of their founding principles. First established in Chicago as a luncheon club by a group of liberal-minded American businessmen in February 1905, Rotary International evolved very rapidly into an 'idealistic' fraternity, open to 'professional and business men of executive standing', and bound together by simple rituals of initiation, an inner social life, of which the basic element was a weekly luncheon, and a set of humane and philanthropic 'objects' symbolised by the motto, 'Service above Self'. It was to be the means by which each member enhanced his service to his fellow men by 'widening his circle of friends', adopting 'high standards of business and professional morality', developing 'a sense of duty towards the community' and, as the 'Fourth Object', committing himself to 'the advancement of international understanding, goodwill and peace through a world fellowship of business and professional men united in the ideal of Service'.

While men of means in the real world might well have been attracted to Rotary International by motives less lofty than those embraced by its 'Four Objects' – a desire to share the status, influence or contacts of a local business and professional elite (only one member of each occupation was selected for membership of a particular club), a means of assuring themselves or persuading others of the soul within capitalist endeavour and material success, even as a means of entry into an idealised male camaraderie – the expectation within any Rotary club was that members would actually undertake 'good works'. Each club was expected to adopt its own specific causes and to put in place structures which would guide members to appropriate openings for philanthropic endeavour and encourage them to disciplined involvement. By the 1930s each club was part of a wider District, the elected committees of which added their weight to the moral guidance of their members; typically, at Club and District level, separate committees existed to promote 'vocational', 'community' and 'international service'. Members, that is, were expected to seek out openings for the unemployed, to support those in need within their local communities and to contribute, whenever possible, to the peace of the world. Exactly how they did so was a matter for each club to decide.

Rotary was perhaps seen by aspiring business and professional men as a more open and democratic route to male bonding, social status and moral cleansing than the Masonic Lodge, with its code of secrecy, its complex rituals, specialised regalia and finely-tuned hierarchies. Rotary itself was anxious to distinguish itself from Masonry.[4] Its weekly luncheons, the backbone of its programme, were open to the press and to the friends of members. From 1924 it made provision for the active participation of women, if only the wives and daughters of Rotarians; although relegated to separate and clearly inferior 'Inner Wheels', they were expected to engage in joint enterprises with their menfolk. A motto on the cover of a Rotary Bulletin of 1940 reads: 'Rotary has no Politics, no Creeds, no Secrets and no Signs'.[5] As a kind of reassuring and un-threatening Social Democracy for the capitalist lower-middle classes, 'Rotary International' made fairly rapid progress from its American bases, reaching Canada by 1910, England by 1911, Italy by 1923 and Germany by 1927. Although by the mid-1930s, 82% of its members were still concentrated in the United States and Britain, there were Rotary clubs in almost every country in the world, forty-two of them in Germany when the Nazis assumed power.

In Manchester, a visit to the city by a Chicago Rotarian had been followed by a meeting of eight local businessmen at the Mosley Hotel on 25 September 1911 to create 'Founder Club Number 4'.[6] By the mid-1930s Manchester's had become far and away the biggest of the fifty Rotary clubs in 'Number Five District', a vast area of the north-west including Cumberland, Westmorland, most of Lancashire and Cheshire, and part of Derbyshire, in which some 2,000 Rotarians were said to live. With a membership of over 170, the Manchester Club was more than twice the size of the next largest clubs in the District; it was seen to occupy 'a very prominent position on the Rotary Wheel'. Its headquarters were in Chapel Walks, its weekly luncheons held at the Victoria Hotel in Blackfriars, both in central Manchester.

During the First World War Manchester Rotarians had given 'service' by the reception and accommodation of Belgian refugees, by setting up, equipping and staffing an Auxiliary Hospital for British troops and by work with alien internees and war orphans. After it, they became particularly associated with work in boys clubs in working-class districts of Manchester, in prison and hospital visiting, and in work with disabled children. By the late 1930s their chosen 'causes' included the Collyhurst Lads Club in East Manchester, the Rosamund Street Day Nursery, the Crippled Children's Association, an annual Boys Camp in Buxton and an organisation entitled 'Wireless for the Bedridden'. Members of its very active Inner Wheel raised funds for all these causes, held annual 'garment rallies' for the poor, and knitted clothes for babies' hospitals. International Service by the Manchester Club in the harmonious years of the 1920s was limited, like that of all the other clubs in District Five, to 'inter-country visiting' by individual members, and to the occasional exchange of programmes, speakers and ideas.[7]

The rise of Nazism did not immediately inspire a more creative role. While struck with horror at the excesses and militarism of the Nazi regime, the Manchester Rotary Club was not at first inclined to intervene on behalf of its victims. Nazism was seen, rather, as a temporary phenomenon, which might ultimately yield to the voice of reason, and which, at all events, was not to hinder other work devoted to international harmony. Even the direct threat to its own clubs in Germany did not move Manchester Rotarians to a more militant stance. When, in the late summer of 1937, the German government called on Nazi party members to resign from German Rotary clubs – 'permeated', it was said, 'by Jews and Masons'[8] – the inclination of the District Five Council was 'to keep the doors open' for their possible return.[9] An only mildly ironic 'Open Letter to Adolf Hitler' was printed that winter in the magazine of District Five; adressed to 'Dear Adolf' and written in a friendly, intimate style appropriate to a conversation between war veterans, it called on him not to destroy German Rotary clubs, 'for we were getting on so well together'.[10] At all events, Germany was not necessarily the major focus of Rotary's International concerns: later that same year the District Five Council was encouraging its constituent clubs to send financial help to China, 'a victim of unprovoked aggression', in which Rotary International had no vulnerable presence.[11] The subjects chosen for debate at an International Service Rally in Blackpool in October 1938, attended by 100 members from twenty-six clubs, were 'Anglo-Eire and Anglo-American Understanding'.[12] When, during 1938, Rotary clubs in Italy and Germany were forcibly disbanded, District Five chose to believe that this 'may be pro tem'.[13]

Manchester Rotarians did not see themselves, however, as passive in the face of aggressive totalitarianism. World peace remained their 'ultimate objective'.[14] 'Resigned helplessness', the District Five Council told its members, was neither 'right nor justified'; it was the 'plain duty' of Rotarians 'to keep alive within every member the spirit of Internationalism'.[15] To this end, Rotary's International Service Committee might be of 'real value' as a 'focal point and clearing house for the study and understanding of international affairs'. It did not surrender hope for a harmonious Europe. From late in 1937 and throughout 1938, although well aware that, in its own words, 'until the statesmen of Europe have decided how the present series of crises is to end, contacts with our nearest Continental neighbours can scarcely bear much fruit',[16] the International Service Committee of District Five, on the initiative of the Manchester Club, pressed ahead with plans for exchange visits between the sons and daughters of local Rotarians and their peers in France, Holland and Belgium. On the very eve of war eleven Belgian boys were put up for six days at the Manchester YMCA at the expense of the Rotarians, entertained by Manchester industrialists and taken on a trip down the Manchester Ship Canal, before moving on for a few days in Blackpool. They 'had to hurry back,' the report reads, 'before the storm broke'.[17]

It is not clear when or why the Manchester Club made its decision to move from such optimistic and conciliatory gestures to the active support of refugees. Refugees received their first cursory mention in Rotarian circles in a report on the annual conference of District Five Rotary in Douglas, Isle of Man, during summer 1938, when 'the problem of political refugees' is noted, but apparently only as one of the subjects which came up for discussion.[18] No action appears to have followed. Nor is there any evidence of pressure being applied from above, by precept or example, either by the District Committee or by any one in the higher echelons of International Rotary.

The origins of work with refugees may well lie in a set of circumstances unique to Manchester, although the evidence is insufficient to rank such circumstances in a way which would reveal a prime cause other than the generalised hope of 'mitigating in some degree, the sorrows and hardships of refugees who had fled from Nazi oppression'.[19] One was the co-option of James 'Harry' Wharmby, a publisher's agent and a Rotarian living in Wilmslow, onto the Refugee Committee of the Society of Friends in January 1939, although, even here, it is not clear from the records on whose initiative the decision was taken or, for that matter, how the link was made.[20] At all events, Wharmby is said to have then shifted his interest, perhaps because of what he heard at Mount Street, from the foreign missions supported by his Methodist Chapel in Styal to 'refugees from foreign oppression'.[21] At around the time he joined the Quaker committee, he had given work in his office and hospitality in his home to a young refugee from Frankfurt;[22] a fellow Rotarian was later to credit him with pressing the case that 'something should be done' by the club for the victims of Nazi oppression.[23] Another local circumstance, however, was the offer to the Manchester Rotarians of a house, 'Springfield', at 19 Northumberland Street, Higher Broughton, 'in a good state of repair', on loan 'for such time as it may be required', rent-free, for use as a hostel for refugees,[24] although whether the offer was the coincidental and spontaneous gesture of a well-known philanthropist, or the result of a Rotarian approach, is a matter for conjecture, as is the link between the donor, the highly respected and well-to-do orthodox Jewish calico printer and communal philanthropist, Laurence Kostoris,[25] and Rotary International. Finally, there is evidence that the International Service Committee (ISC) of the Manchester Rotary Club was being approached, from late 1938, by Rotarians in lands under Nazi rule for aid in finding a way out for their children.[26]

Whatever the way in which such eventualities knitted together, it was Wharmby, a man of legendary selflessness in Rotarian circles,[27] who comes across as at least a major player in the chain of events which followed. In February 1939 he reported to the Quakers that the Manchester Rotarians had 'probably decided' to set up a hostel for about twenty refugee boys between the ages of fifteen and eighteen.[28] On 8 March, he was one of a small group of Rotarians, all members of the International Service Committee of the Manchester Club, who met at the Victoria Hotel, the local headquarters of Manchester Rotary, 'to appoint a Refugee Assistance Committee'.[29] On 21 March it was announced that, as a result of this meeting, the Manchester ISC had not only 'formed themselves into a Refugee Aid Committee', but co-opted onto it 'the whole of the ISC of Number Five District'. The aim was 'to establish and control a hostel for the accommodation of any refugee approved by the committee, irrespective of creed or race, and to afford a place of residence for youths of fifteen to nineteen years of age who are suitable for recommendation to employers as trainees'. The necessary funds – it was calculated that £1,250 was required to cover the cost of decorating, furnishing and equipping Springfield and of maintaining twenty refugee trainees during their first year in Britain – were to be raised from 'individual donors' – 'a considerable sum', it was said, 'had already been provided' – so that no financial liability would devolve on the club'.[30] It was apparently the reluctance of the club to accept financial responsibility for the project which led to the creation of a separate Aid Committee 'for this specific object'.[31]

The size and make-up of this committee is unknown. Wharmby was certainly an active member. It was to his office at 22 Lloyd Street in central Manchester that donors were asked to deposit items of furniture and hardware for use by the hostel; it was he who made periodic appeals to members at weekly luncheons; and, judging by the frequency of his visits to London in the late spring and early summer of 1939,[32] it was he who negotiated the formal authorisation of the committee by the Co-ordinating Committee for Refugees at Bloomsbury House. The chairman, however, was Clifford Whatmough, the owner of a firm in Ancoats manufacturing tailors' 'eyelets' and the convenor of the ISC of District Five; the treasurer, Edgar Eady, was the owner of a small chain of tobacconists, with branches in Harpurhey, Blackley and Newton Heath. Another Manchester Rotarian, Stephen Holmes, by trade a haulage contractor, was deputed to collect donated goods and deliver them to Wharmby's depot. The committee included from the beginning at least two members of the Manchester Inner Wheel – Kate Sanders, then its chairman, and Mrs. E.S. Watts[33] – later thanked by Whatmough 'for gifts whether of cash or kind [and] services rendered'.[34]

Although it was not until early May that the President and Council of Manchester Rotary, 'after careful study', gave it their 'complete approval and support';[35] what was now the Springfield Refugee Aid Committee (hereafter SRAC) was immediately seen as the club's agent for dealing with all matters relating to refugees. Early in April 1939 the secretary of the Manchester Rotary Club received a letter from a Rotarian in Czechoslovakia, asking the club 'to help him emigrate his two sons to our country'. In passing the letter on to the SRAC, the editor of the *Manchester Bulletin* commented: 'Thank goodness our ISC decided to take a live interest in this intensely human problem.' The request, he added, had generated 'a feeling of anger that such should be the state of humanity in an apparently civilised world'.[36] The Spring issue of *District Five Rotary* reported: 'The Refugee problem is being tackled vigorously; here is Rotary work if ever there was any! We congratulate one club [almost certainly Manchester's] upon its initiative and very prompt action in rescuing and bringing to Britain at the last moment a young refugee who was in dire peril. This is only one case amongst thousands; but it is humanitarian work of the greatest value.'[37] That Spring the Rotarians opened up their guest house, Willesby Castle, to the Quaker Refugee Committee, offering one week each to eight people, either refugees or office workers at Mount Street.[38]

Early in May the existence of the SRAC was endorsed in a strong 'Statement' in the *Manchester Bulletin* by the club president, the Congregationalist minister, Ernest Hamson, which went on to define its role, to invite Manchester Rotarians to lend it their full support and to comment in passing that 'RIBI has left no doubt that assistance to Refugees should be regarded as a Rotary activity'.[39] In selecting refugees 'of any nationality and creed', his statement read, preference would be given to 'the sons of Rotarians ... and in this respect, communications from ex-Rotarians in Czecho-Slovakia have already been received'. Following their 'vocational training' in Manchester, the refugee trainees would be, as immigration law demanded, 'assisted to emigrate to America or the Dominions'. The Council, it added, had given the SRAC 'permission to circulate and/or approach our membership for financial aid, and, further, recommends whole-heartedly and without reserve your sympathy and help'; offers of furniture and equipment were 'more than welcome'.[40]

The evidence suggests a project to which the club then devoted all its energies. By mid-June 'the very necessary cleaning and decorating [had] started … the furniture acquired … china, linen and kitchen utensils begged or bought … the Warden and his wife installed'.[41] The Warden appointed by the committee was an Eduard Wollheim, himself a Jewish refugee from Germany; with him, as the hostel cook, was his wife, Judith: 'a Turkish lady', according to Whatmough, and 'a very talented' woman, a 'distinguished pianist' and harpist, who spoke seven languages fluently.[42] Early in July, while thanking members for their donated goods and 'financial gifts', the editor of the *Manchester Bulletin,* called for further 'White Elephants … [and] to those still wishing to help, there is the larder and the upkeep of the Home. May we suggest a personal weekly or monthly financial contribution? Articles immediately required are: Gardening Tools (rake, spade, clippers, lawn mower etc), Kitchen Table, Easy Chairs [and] Mirrors'.[43] A week later, with the 'garden tools thankfully received', a final appeal went out for 'clocks and alarm clocks, a mincing machine [and] a wringer'.[44] 'Don't let the matter escape your minds', the *Bulletin* urged, 'see what you can do, will you?'[45]

Finally, on 17 July 1939 the Springfield Hostel was 'formally opened' for its first five boys, with 'ten more expected', bringing the number of its residents up to what was then to remain its maximum.[46] Rotarians could now help, *The Mayflower* told its readers, not only by providing urgently needed funds (many clubs, it was said, had still not sent in a donation), but by offering places in their businesses for 'these unfortunate fellows'.[47]

The Rotarians saw their hostel as part of the network of voluntary refugee support which had by then been created in London and Manchester. 'The object', according to Whatmough, 'was to co-operate with other organisations such as the Jewish Refugees Committee and the Society of Friends, but more particularly with the Co-ordinating Committee at Bloomsbury House', which by then was seeking to generate a degree of cooperation between the many voluntary committees at work throughout the country and to rationalise their links with the Home Office and the Ministry of Labour. Only in this way could the Manchester Rotarians secure the entry and temporary residence in Britain of the trainees who were to become its charges.

Immediate responsibility for the boys' maintenance and care, and for their placement in suitable occupations, was taken by the SRAC, of which Whatmough remained the chairman throughout the hostel's existence. In the absence of minutes, the degree of the committee's concern may be judged only by occasional references to its work in the *Manchester Bulletin.* In August 1939 Whatmough put out an appeal for clothing: 'undervests and stockings for two younger boys; shoes and handkerchieves, ties, raincoat, hat and suit for one boy'. In September, the editor of the *Bulletin* wrote: 'if you have an abundant crop of apples, more than you require, would you be kind enough to bear "Springfield" in mind'; apples and vegetables 'would make an excellent harvest festival'.[48] Individual Rotarians worked as volunteers in the hostel: one 'regular helper' until his death in October 1939 was Harry Wharmby, 'a universal favourite' with the trainees.[49]

There is evidence that the SRAC went to some pains to find traineeships for their charges, whom they came to see as 'a particularly fine type of young men', and to monitor their progress, which was apparently generally satisfactory. Bob Craigford, the Personnel Officer of the Manchester club, with responsibility for guiding its 'vocational service' now took the employment of refugee trainees under his wing. 'Some of them have already been successful [in finding work]', he reported in early December, 'and their employers speak highly of the way they are tackling their jobs'. Craigford decided 'from time to time [to] publish [in the *Bulletin*] particulars of boys needing positions as trainees. Will you see if you can help them?'[50] Such notices followed, and by mid-January 'only three or four boys' were said to be 'without prospect of trainee employment';[51] most of the rest were employed by Manchester Rotarians.[52] By early April 1940, as nine out of the twelve boys then in the hostel were able to pay for their keep, Springfield had become 'practically self-supporting'; all that was required to complete its self-sufficiency was 2s 6d a week from every club in District Five.[53]

Of the trainees themselves very little is known. From Craigford's notices, only six in all, and which safeguarded the anonymity of the applicants, it would appear that most were German or Austrian: Frankfurt am Main, Krefeld, Hamburg, Danzig and Vienna are the only named places of origin. Their social origins were mixed. One is described as the son of 'an Attorney in a large Frankfurt House'; another, a 'cultured type of youth', is said to have spent five years in secondary school and two in 'professional training', after which he became a 'salesman of silks and wools' in a Vienna store of 'the highest class'; the remainder were artisans, one a garage mechanic in Vienna, one trained as a plumber and electrician, one a painter and decorator in Hamburg. Once in Manchester, they had been directed to courses which would help them find jobs; all attended classes in English, one had enrolled on a course in shorthand and typing at Pitman's College, another had taken night classes in sign-writing. Most had probably arrived unaccompanied in Manchester, their parents trapped in Nazi Europe; one boy's father had escaped to Dublin, however, and the parents of another were said to be awaiting his joining them in Cuba. One of the trainees is described as Roman Catholic; most, if not all the rest, were Jewish.

All were hedged in by aliens regulations which, inter alia, demanded that they initially register their addresses and workplaces with the Salford police, notify them of any journey out of the city and seek permission from the Home Office for any change in their place of employment. There is evidence of only one breach of the Aliens Order by a Springfield trainee. This was in February 1940, when a young German refugee, Aaron Iwanier, was brought before the Salford City Police Court for failing to seek the assent of the Home Office when he moved to a new job 'where he could earn more money', and for subsequently making a false statement to a Constable checking alien registrations. Although Iwanier claimed that he had misunderstood the question put to him, he received a fine of £3. Iwanier told the court that he was born to Austrian parents, who had subsequently obtained Romanian nationality and finally settled in Germany: he himself was classified as 'a stateless citizen'.[54]

What little evidence we have of the trainees' responses to their carers and employers suggest their unqualified gratitude. In January 1940 one employer received 'a letter from a refugee to a representative of the people who offered kindest hospitality for me, who has been forced to leave the country I loved'. The letter continued: 'it is your kindness, the kindness of the English, to give us everything as presents not as alms … it will be a great aim of ours to be able to repay to anybody who is in danger, what you gave us. Our ideal will be to help people without looking at their relations or origin first. For this aim you will be our greatest examples.'[55]

By the end of April 1940, the Rotarians had been financing and managing a refugee hostel for almost nine months. The Manchester Rotary Club and its Inner Wheel had raised most of the money and put in most of the effort, with occasional support from individual Rotarians and Rotary clubs of District Five. Only two clubs, however – Lymm and Stretford – sent in regular contributions.[56] Offers of help from outside Rotary circles were rare.[57] There is little evidence of sustained Rotarian support for refugees outside the Manchester region.[58] They had described their commitment as taking no account of 'nationality or creed'. They had found work for the 'boys' in their hostel and apparently looked after them with sensitivity and warmth.

According to one who was present, on a 'memorable' Christmas Day in 1939 Rotarians and Inner Wheelers treated their charges to some particularly 'happy hours'. Women of the Inner Wheel had prepared 'a huge turkey', mince pies, plum puddings, sausage rolls 'and I don't know what'. 'Handsome presents' arrived from the family of the late Harry Wharmby; the dinner table was decked with fruits, nuts, figs, dates, chocolates, sweets and 'huge crackers'. Games, music and songs followed. One of the boys proposed a toast to 'The Providers of the Feast', 'followed by one with a poignant significance in such a home, "Absent Relatives and Friends"'. 'The warmest glow,' the report ends, 'may well have been in the hearts of those selfless souls who had conceived and carried out, so happily, a full day of joyful service'.[59] Christmas, sausage rolls 'and I don't know what', that is, for trainees who were, for the most part, of Jewish origin.

There seems little doubt that a wide cultural gulf separated the middle-class Rotarian business and professional men, secure in their standing in English society, from the refugee youngsters whose sufferings they were intent on mitigating. Part of this had to do with the narrow horizons of even the most sympathetic of Manchester Rotarians. In July 1939 Harry Wharmby was seeking out reading matter for the new arrivals at Springfield; particularly appreciated, the *Manchester Bulletin* told its readers, would be 'illustrated papers … such as "Sphere", "Tatler", "Punch" and so on'.[60] More serious were Rotarian perceptions of Jews and their Jewishness.

It seems likely that, although there was no apparent bar to their entry, Jews constituted only a tiny proportion of the membership of the Manchester Rotary Club. Chance references in the *Manchester Bulletin* reveal six, two of whom were accepted as members during the crisis years, 1938–39. Long-standing Rotarians included the well-to-do haulage contractor, Nathan Fine, whose firm had branches throughout the cotton districts of south Lancashire, and who in 1939 was secretary of the Manchester Country Club, a major social centre for Jewish families in south Manchester; the furrier, M. (Mark) Cohen; the 'neckwear manufacturer', Abraham Bernstein; and a Maurice Saffer, who represented the Manchester Club at the Rotarian Conference in Brighton in March 1939.[61] They were joined in February 1938 by Jack Meek, one of Manchester's leading manufacturers of waterproof garments,[62] and, in the early summer of 1939 by the barrister, Cecil Quixano Henriques, a younger member of one of Manchester Jewry's leading families. All were, in Quaker terms, 'practising Jews'; five were Ashkenazi members of orthodox synagogues in Cheetham Hill, Henriques from a family of Sephardi origin long attached to Reform Judaism. The entry of Henriques was clearly regarded by the club as a major coup. A brief biography noted his collection of Chinese porcelain, his interest in Bridge, dancing, tennis and winter sports (for which he made annual trips to Switzerland), his captaincy in a Manchester Cadet Battalion (in fact, the Jewish Lads Brigade), and, in a rare religious ascription, his membership of the Board of Deputies of British Jews.[63] In October the *Manchester Bulletin* summarised a talk he had given to members on 'The Bar as a Profession'.[64] There is no evidence of any endemic friction between Jewish and non-Jewish Rotarians. In November 1937 the Manchester Inner Wheel entertained a speaker on 'Jewish Homes and Customs', a report in the DFR recording an offer from the speaker 'to take members over a Jewish Church'.[65]

Springfield itself, at the junction of Northumberland Street and Legh Street, Higher Broughton, was at the heart of what was then evolving as the most orthodox sector of Manchester Jewry. Next door to the hostel was the Yesode Hatora Synagogue, the place of worship of Manchester's nascent *haredi* community, Machikei Hadass. A few houses away, at 35a Northumberland Street, lived Saul Rosenberg, lay president of the Manchester Yeshiva. At 23 and 25 was Annie Acker's Fabian's Hotel, a kosher boarding house used by the Jewish Refugees Committee to house some of its more orthodox clients; at 43 Dr Lazarus Wislicki, a refugee, a leading religious Zionist and chairman of the 'Manchester Senior' branch of the Mizrachi Federation. Only a handful of non-Jewish families remained in a street destined to become the backbone of an orthodox *kehilla* in Broughton Park. The Manchester Jewish Rotarian, Jack Meek, lived round the corner in Upper Park Road.

For all this, it is clear that within the Manchester club there was some suspicion of Jews in general. In the build-up towards the formation of the Refugee

Aid Committee, no reference is made to the Jewish origins of Hitler's victims; in so far as the victims of Nazi oppression are identified at all, it is as political dissidents. Nor is there any evidence that Jewish Rotarians were co-opted (as they could have been) onto the Aid Committee. Like the Quakers, and no doubt other non-Jewish groups in Manchester, Rotarians in the region had mixed feelings about the Zionist enterprise, a subject of much public debate as the government's support for Jewish settlement in Palestine was seen to waver in the successive White Papers of 1935 and May 1939. While local Rotarians took pride in the role of the Rotary club in Palestine as the 'only common meeting ground for Jews and Arabs',[66] their ambivalence towards Zionist responses to Palestinian Arabs is exemplified, as it was in the case of the Quakers, by a perceived imperative of putting both sides of the case.

When, in March 1939 Dr Bernard Sandler, a leading Zionist activist in Manchester, and a member of the Stretford Rotary Club, was invited to talk to Sale Rotarians on the subject of 'Palestine', he naturally chose to emphasise the validity of Zionist claims and the good intentions of the movement towards the Arab people. The Arabs, he argued, had never been promised this 'tiny area', within which, at all events, were it not for German and Italian machinations and the selfishness of Arab landowners, Arab peasants would have been perfectly willing to work for Jews. The Fascists, he concluded, were using 'the cover of the Arabs' to obstruct the creation of a settled Jewish community in Palestine which they feared would become 'the best friend of the British Empire'. Without a Jewish nation, the 'homelessness' of the Jews would continually set them up as 'the scapegoat for social decay' in the countries in which they lived. There was nothing new about Hitler's barbarity other than his 'diabolical ingenuity' in 'robbing the Jews and then selling their naked bodies to the humanitarian peoples of the world'.[67] In July 1939, these messages were underscored when another leading local Zionist, Dr P.I. Wigoder, appealed to Salford Rotarians to use their influence to persuade the British government to arrange further Jewish immigration to Palestine.[68]

During June 1939 at least three Rotary clubs in the region felt impelled to provide a platform for Manchester Muslim [and Syrian] merchant, S.M. Haffar, to put 'an Arab's point of view'.[69] In a talk to the Warrington Rotary Club at the end of June, which reads very much like a direct response to Sandler, Haffar savaged the Zionist case. Until recently, he argued, 'Jews had had their own way in Parliament, in the pulpits and in the press ... they had represented or misrepresented the facts just as they pleased. They had purposely misled the world in the essential facts, until the Arabs were driven to despair.' Now, with Arabs engaged in articulate protests which had found some purchase in British government circles, Zionists might experience more difficulty in destroying the White Paper of 1939 than that of 1930. There were, in fact, only a 'small minority' of Jews 'who make a genuine claim to settlement in Palestine'. As to the accusation that Arab protest was being driven (and armed) by Rome and Berlin, 'Arabs had stood up for themselves long before Mussolini and Hitler came to power'. Arab-Jewish cooperation was certainly possible, but only if Jews would 'give up their ambition of political supremacy'.[70]

It may be that within Rotarian circles there existed also a more visceral anti-Jewish sentiment. In a luncheon address on 'Refugee Hostels' on 19 October 1939, Whatmough found it necessary, as part of what was a general 'apologia' for the hostel already quoted, to defend his committee from 'some criticism [that] has been levelled at the fact that most of our refugees are Jews'. He delivered a robust response. While pointing out, with a note of apology, that it was 'not as Jews that they claim our interest and our help, but simply as human beings who need it', Whatmough also launched into 'a fervent defence of the Jews, reminding us of those in our own ranks and of the great men of that race who have contributed so much to the sum of human knowledge and human welfare'.[71] While it seems likely, then, that Judeophile and anti-Semitic sentiments co-existed within Rotarian ranks, Whatmough, in the absence of Wharmby, who died at the end of September 1939,[72] was able to muster sufficient support, and to ward off sufficient hostility, to keep the hostel project afloat.

What brought it to an abrupt end in July 1940 had nothing to do with the Manchester Rotary Club or with its Aid Committee. 'Within a few days' of the general order for the internment of enemy aliens, the warden of Springfield and all but three of its residents found themselves behind barbed wire, and this at a time, Whatmough announced with some irritation, when 'every refugee in the Hostel had been placed in employment, and from all reports were doing good service'. Whatmough was angered, too, by the internment of Wollheim: 'concerning his integrity and desire to help Britain to victory', he told his fellow Rotarians, 'there was and is no doubt'. Wollheim saw his German nationality as the unfortunate accident of his birth in a part of Poland then under German rule; his assertion, however, that 'he was of Polish stock and desired to be so regarded', did not save him from internment. Whatmough called on his fellow Rotarians to help Judith Wollheim find pupils for her piano lessons, which were the means of her survival during her husband's internment. Of the three young men who were left at liberty, one was a 'Danziger boy', Hans Ruhm; one, Hans Heymann, escaped because 'his emigration papers [for the United States] had already arrived'; the third, Karl Heinz Levy, a Jewish Berliner working in Manchester as an electrical fitter, was ' a boy of barely sixteen years' on whose behalf the Quaker Harold Howard, secretary of the Refugee Committee of the Manchester Society of Friends, had successfully intervened, taking him instead, after a 'special appeal', into his own home. On 9 August Whatmough announced that the hostel had been 'officially closed' and the Aid Committee disbanded.[73]

All that remained was to tidy away the loose ends. A sub-committee of Inner Wheelers arranged for the sale of the hostel's 'household effects and equipment', preferably to those prepared to present them to other charitable organisations.[74] Although the Aid Committee's remaining funds were kept liquid 'in order to meet emergencies which may arise in connection with the possible release of the Warden and Refugees',[75] in fact the Springfield

(Refugee) Hostel was never revived. By the time Wollheim and the refugees had been released, the Manchester club had moved on to other projects more closely linked to wartime 'National Service', including support for the YMCA Serviceman's Hostel and Canteen in London Road.[76] After August 1940 District Five limited its refugee work to the provision of 'help and advice' whenever it was sought.[77] A chart of the District's Commmunuity Service Activity during 1941–42 indicates that only 30% of its clubs had members engaged in work of any kind with refugees.[78] Springfield itself disappears as an entry in local trade directories, perhaps because it was incorporated into the growing orthodox *austreit gemeinde*, Machizei Hadass.

There can be no doubting the sincerity and commitment of those who created and managed the Springfield Hostel, or their genuine empathy with the fate of refugees. 'None of us can forget,' Whatmough wrote in August 1940, 'those early days before the war when the ugliness of the crime of Nazism filled our souls with loathing and disgust, and the enthusiasm of the late Harry Wharmby that something should be done to heal the sorrow of those who were the first victims of this frightful menace which has since besmirched so great a part of the world by its infamous and criminal ideology'.[79] The Rotarians who comprised the Refugee Aid Committee were those Rotarians who lived up to their ideal of service and who judged refugees to be amongst its worthy recipients. For a little under a year a group of Rotarian men and women Inner Wheelers dedicated themselves to the care of between twelve and fifteen young men in desperate need of support. They worked, Whatmough believed, in 'happy fellowship'. The hostel was supported primarily by the Manchester club, but also by the voluntary efforts and donations of individual Rotarians and Rotary clubs from throughout District Five. As the only British Rotary club to commit itself to the sustained support of refugees, it paid its way without impinging on the capital resources of Rotary International.

In its treatment of refugees who were also Jewish, however, the club resembled the Society of Friends. Both saw their refugee enterprises as free from considerations of race, nationality or religion; the refugees attracted their support, as Whatmough put it, 'not as Jews', but as 'human beings'. Neither group was collectively anti-Jewish, although there is evidence that neither group was entirely free of traditional anti-Jewish sentiment. There is reason to believe, however, that in the case of the Rotarians, as of the Quakers, a well-meaning liberal egalitarianism, however humane, ran the risk (sausage rolls at Christmas is iconic in this respect) of robbing its recipients of their religious and/or cultural specificity. Like the Quakers, and many other well-intentioned Christian observers, the Rotarians viewed 'the Jewish identity' as something unalterably fixed over time, so that the secular Jews under their protection would inevitably remain so for the rest of their lives. By their apparent indifference to the cultural baggage of Jewish refugees, the Rotarians were also effectively undermining part of the heritage upon which their identities were based. It was with this calculated disinterest, rather than traditional anti-Semitism, that many refugees were compelled to engage in adjusting themselves to life in Britain.

None the less, of the rich galaxy of charitable bodies which existed in the Manchester of 1939, the Rotary Club was one of very few which felt obliged to extend their humanitarian briefs to the rescue and active support of refugees. The evidence does not exist to explain why the club allowed internment to put an end to their efforts. It may be that those within the club who had always nursed doubts about the support of Jewish refugees found in the stigma attached to refugees by internment a means of winning the day. At all events, after June 1940 Rotarians disappear from the scene of local refugee support of any kind. Typically it was the Quakers who picked up the pieces: in this case by providing accommodation and pocket money to those Springfield residents left at large.[80]

The Rotarian experience might give those inclined to portray the late 1930s and early 1940s in simple terms as a battleground between European Fascism and democratic values exemplified by British institutions, further cause for thought. Although leading Manchester Rotarians were prepared to thus contextualise their club's policies, it seems clear that not all Manchester Rotarians were free from the kind of prejudice which, in its more intense form, had inspired Nazism. Of those who were, not all were prepared to pay respect to the particular heritage of the Jewish people. Nor was Manchester Rotarian interest in refugees of any kind sustained in a time of war in the face of more obviously patriotic causes, once the circumstances of a less than liberal British government policy had brought about the closure of the Springfield Hostel. Humanitarian intent towards refugees, whether of the British state or of British voluntary organs of philanthropy, however real, however valuable in its results and however conceptualised as an expression of a distinctively British tradition, was tempered by equally traditional concerns about the character and impact of 'Jews and other foreigners'.

It may also be doubted whether a British humanitarian institution like the Manchester Rotary Club would have turned its attention to refugees without the prompting of committed idealists within their own ranks. More impressive in the British society of the late 1930s than any collective re-focussing of humanitarian effort was the influence exerted by individuals prepared to reach out beyond local and national boundaries to such vulnerable outsiders as refugees. Nationally, the archetypal figure in this respect was Eleanor Rathbone. In the Manchester region, they included Harry Wharmby and Clifford Whatmough.

Notes

1   SCR 20 October 1939.
2   President's Statement in the Manchester Rotary Club Bulletin (hereafter MRCB) 9 May 1939.
3   MG 20 October 1939.
4   *Rotary International 1905–1955: Golden Jubilee Brochure* (Manchester 1955), with a

supplement on Rotary Club Number Four, n.p.

5   *RCMB* 20 August 1940.

6   *Rotary International 1905–1955*.

7   *Ibid*.

8   MG 25 August 1937.

9   *District Five Rotary* (hereafter *DFR*), Vol. 1, No. 5, Autumn 1937, p. 10. The DFR was the magazine reporting on the activities of the clubs of District Five; from the summer of 1939 it changed its name to *The Mayflower*.

10   *DFR*, Vol. 1, No. 6, Winter 1937, pp. 10–12. At one point Hitler is addressed as 'old man'.

11   *Ibid.*, p. 5.

12   *DFR*, Vol. 1, No. 9, Autumn 1938, p. 13.

13   *DFR*, Vol. 1, No 10, Winter 1938, p. 1.

14   *DFR*, Vol. 1, No. 9, Autumn 1938, p. 7.

15   *DFR*, Vol. 1, No 10, p. 5.

16   *DFR*, Vol. 1, No. 9, Autumn 1938, p. 13.

17   *DFR*, Vol. 1, No. 6, p. 5; Vol. 1 No. 7, Spring 1938, pp. 3–4; Vol. 1, No. 8, Summer 1938, p. 6; Vol. 1, No. 9, Autumn 1938, p. 13; Vol. 1, No 11, Spring 1939, pp. 6–7; *The Mayflower*, Vol. 2, No. 2, Autumn 1939, p. 15.

18   *DFR*, Vol. 1, No. 9, Autumn 1938, p. 8.

19   Report on the closure of the Springfield Refugee Hostel by Clifford Whatmough, chairman of the Springfield Refugee Aid Committee, 9 August 1940, attached to *District Five Rotary*, Vol. 2, No 5, Summer 1940.

20   The only known refugee Rotarian in the Manchester area in 1939 was the industrialist, Werner Treuhertz, who in 1936 or 1937 had joined the Rochdale Rotary Club. There is no reference in his autobiography to any role in the creation of the Springfield Hostel.

21   *Ibid*.

22   *RCMB* 5 December 1939.

23   Report by Clifford Whatmough 9 August 1940 op.cit.

24   *RCMB* 9 May 1939; JC 25 July 1939. The house had either been newly acquired by Kostoris or recently vacated by his tenants. The local trade directories show that until 1939 it was the home of the Lever family, including the three Lever brothers, all of them lawyers, Leslie (a solicitor and later an MP), Dennis (another solicitor) and Harold (later Lord) Lever, a barrister. The family moved in 1939 to 4 Castle Hill Road, Prestwich.

25   Kostoris' firm in Portland Street produced 'prints, whites, dyes etc suitable for all markets'; he lived in a mansion, Alton Brook, in the distant and fashionable suburb of Hale (Kelly's *Directory for Manchester, Salford and Suburbs*, 1940). In 1939 he was president of the Homes for Aged, Needy and Incurable Jews, with which he had been associated as a volunteer worker since 1924 (JG 5 January 1945). It seems that Kostoris had already offered hospitality to refugees in his home. In the Salford Aliens Register (1664E and1685E) 19 Northumberland Street is given as the address in December 1938, of Alfred Model, a doctor of medicine from Freiburg, who had earlier lived with his wife, Kache, in Belfast and Liverpool. The Models left Northumberland Street in January 1939 for Burton Road, Didsbury.

26   *RCMB* 11 April 1939.

27   *RCMB* 3 October 1939 for an obituary, 10 October 1939 for a further tribute. Another obituary is in *The Mayflower*, Vol. 2, No. 2, Autumn 1938, p. 17.

28   QRC 17 February 1939.

29   *RCMB* 7 March 1939.
30   *RCMB* 21 March 1939.
31   *RCMB* 9 May 1939.
32   *RCMB* 18 and 25 July 1939. The *RCMB* regularly reported visits by Manchester Rotarians to other clubs.
33   Kate Sanders and Mrs Watts were the wives of leading Manchester Rotarians G. Purvis Sanders and Ernest Swann Watts, both described in the local trade directory for 1940 as 'householders'.
34   Report on closure of Springfield by Whatmough 9 August 1940.
35   *RCMB* 9 May 1939.
36   *RCMB* 11 April 1939.
37   *DFR*, Vol. 1, No 11, Spring 1939, p. 6.
38   QRC 14 March 1939.
39   *RCMB* 9 May 1939.
40   *Ibid.*
41   *RCMB* 11 July 1939.
42   Report on closure of Springfield by Whatmough, 9 August 1940. Eduard Wollheim was born in what was then Prussian Poland on 14 October 1896; his wife was born (the place is not known) on 17 August 1903. After the hostel's closure, the couple left for London, where Eduard became a teacher of handicrafts and Judith, a teacher of the harp and the piano and later a 'BBC monitor' (Quaker List, which defines Eduard Wollheim as 'Jewish').
43   *Ibid.*
44   *RCMB* 25 July 1939.
45   *RCMB* 18 July 1939.
46   *Ibid.*
47   *The Mayflower*, Vol. 2, No 1, Summer 1939, pp. 12–13.
48   *RCMB* 19 September 1939.
49   Obituary in *MCN* 7 October 1939.
50   *RCMB* 5 December 1939.
51   *RCMB* 5, 12, 19 December 1939, 16 January 1940.
52   *RCMB* 5 December 1939.
53   *RCMB* 9 and 16 April 1940. The second entry was clearly intended to offset the implicit suggestion in the first that no further help from Rotarians was required. The Rotarians were then hoping also to receive a government grant towards the hostel's overheads.
54   *SCR* 2 February 1940.
55   *RCMB* 16 January 1940.
56   *The Mayflower*, Vol. 2, No. 2, Autumn 1939, p. 14.
57   *RCMB* 30 January 1940 records a 'surprise gift' of £10 from the Mayor of Banbury's Refugee Fund.
58   There is a note in *The Mayflower* (Vol. 2 No 2 Autumn 1938 pp. 18–19) that members of the Lancaster Inner Wheel had 'decided to support the Rotarians in their efforts to provide a home for a family of German refugees'. That same issue noted (p. 19) that the Manchester Rotary Club had passed on to District 13 (the London area) the request of an Austrian banker that 'friendship' be offered his daughter, who was living in London. District 13 had then decided to invite her 'to all their social meetings'.
59   *RCMB* 2 January 1940.
60   *RCMB* 25 July 1939.

61 *RCMB* 21 March 1939.
62 The RCMB (22 August 1939) printed communications from Meek during a visit to Hollywood (USA), where he visited the local Rotary club, during the summer of 1939.
63 *RCMB* 6 June 1939.
64 *RCMB* 3 October 1939.
65 *DFR*, Vol. 1, No 6, Winter 1937, p. 12.
66 Manchester Rotary Club, Secretary's Report, March 1939.
67 SSG 3 March 1939.
68 SCR 21 July 1939.
69 SA 23 June 1939; SSG 27 June 1939.
70 SSG 27 June 1939.
71 Bulletin of the Manchester Rotary Club, 24 March 1939. In its own report of the same speech, the *Manchester Guardian* (20 October 1939) made no reference to the Jewish issue, perhaps because it did not wish to advertise the presence of anti-Jewish feeling in one of Manchester's leading philanthropic bodies and so taint the image of a tolerant city.
72 MG 2 October 1939 for a tribute to Wharmby by Eduard Wollheim: 'There never appeared to be a wish or desire of ours but what he foresaw and provided. Our spiritual, mental and physical welfare must have been his constant thought … his influence has [also] been exerted for the comfort and help of our relatives and friends in the oppressed areas.'
73 Report on closure of Springfield by Whatmough, 9 August 1940.
74 Notices of sale were placed in the *Manchester Bulletin*, 13 August 1940.
75 Report on closure of Springfield by Whatmough, 9 August 1940.
76 *RCMB* 1 June, 18 June 1940; MCN 20 July 1940. The 'full part' played by Rotarians in 'wartime activities', co-ordinated by a war services committee, included meeting soldiers arriving in Manchester at night and work with young people of 14 to 18 whose fathers were in the armed services: they were encouraged to continue their studies at night school and to engage only in such 'healthy activities' as would help them develop 'character and useful citizenship' (MCN 20 July 1940, 23 May 1941).
77 *DFR*, Vol. 2, No. 10, Autumn 1941, pp. 8–9.
78 *DFR*, Vol. 2, No. 12, Spring 1942, p. 4.
79 Report on closure of Springfield by Whatmough, 9 August 1940.
80 QRC 31 July, 26 October, 24 November 1940, 25 January 1941.

20

The saved and the trapped: refugees and those they left behind

Scattered throughout the earlier chapters are references to the anxieties of unaccompanied child refugees about the fate of their parents. This is, in fact, a theme in refugee history most often marginalised by those who wish to emphasise the humanity of the British state in the rescue of refugees. Such concessions as the government sanctioned need to be measured against the desperation of those seeking entry from Germany, Austria and Czechoslovakia after March 1938.

Between July and September 1939 the columns of 'refugee advertisements' in the *Manchester Guardian* and the *Jewish Chronicle* included cries for help of increasing (and heart-breaking) desperation as war approached and Nazi persecution intensified. 'Must leave Germany', 'urgent case' and 'only hope' became common refrains, often with reference to concentration camps, 'anxiety' and fears of arrest. 'Philanthropists' and 'the noble hearted' in Britain are literally begged for guarantees and traineeships. One advert from a young refugee in Chinley, Derbyshire, reads: 'SOS Who would kindly guarantee for my old parents, who are still in Vienna'. Another: 'willing to accept any employment to get them from Czechoslovakia: very handy'. Yet another, 'Any job anywhere.' One would-be refugee from Vienna advertised herself hopefully as 'the only surviving sister-in-law of Theodore Herzl'.[1] In mid-August, Shanghai, 'the last unrestricted place of refuge', closed its doors to refugees from Central Europe.[2]

This desperation, and the obstacles in its way, is best illustrated by the evidence left in the hands of those who were saved, most often young people, by those who were trapped, most frequently, but not exclusively, their parents and older relatives. What such evidence suggests is not simply 'the anguish, despair and panic of German Jews after Kristallnacht', as they sought to identify any country which would accept them[3] but the source of that anguish in doors which remained at least partially closed, particularly to those who lacked the knowledge, contacts, skills, funds and energy to prise them open. They suggest also the degree to which the elderly and the infirm, and those linked to them by what they took to be unbreakable bonds of family and friendship, became dependent for their rescue on younger members of their families who, in general, and through no fault of their own, lacked the maturity, the judgement, the understanding of world politics, the contacts and the negotiating skills to fulfil the tasks assigned to them. In the case of Britain, these young people, too, were the victims of the 'liberalising' but still labyrinthine and long, drawn-out Home Office procedures which hard-pressed voluntary agencies were seeking to implement. From afar, with their family lives already disrupted, they became the vulnerable and inappropriate witnesses to tragic chains of events which they could do little or nothing to control and which overtook parents who persisted, against all the odds, in roles of distant care and in the hope of a future reunion.

What most distinguishes the letters written to Ruth Schneier, a young refu-gee living with relatives in Manchester, by her parents, first from Austria, then from Yugoslavia, is the juxtaposition of a natural concern for the very ordinary minutiae of their only child's welfare and the increasing despera-tion of their search for a route of escape.[4]

Ruth's parents, Isak and Josephine ('Peppy') Schneier, were both mem-bers of families of Eastern European origin which, in search of economic and cultural betterment, had settled in Vienna soon after the First World War. The assimilated Austrian Jewish majority would have seen them still, at the time of Ruth's birth in 1926, as typical Ostjuden: working-class, Yiddish-speaking, religiously observant, socially exclusive and with only tenuous links – in the Schneiers' case, a second-hand piano – to the learning and culture of the Austrian majority. Isak Schneier's income as a rag merchant – he bought 'bits and pieces' of cloth from tailoring workshops and sorted them into wool and cotton for selling on, his business premises consisting of an allot-ment hut – enabled the family to rent only a tiny and primitive three-roomed apartment on the Brigittgassen in the 20th District of Vienna: a 'zimmer, kueche, kabinett' without an inside toilet or bathroom. Ruth remembers, as a young girl, walking through the courtyard of her tenement block to the toilet and to fetch water from a communal pump.

The family's religious observance had been only marginally modified by the forces of assimilation at work in inter-war Vienna. The home was strictly kosher, Isak worshipped at the local *stiebl* of the Chassidic Machizei Hadas, and he insisted that his daughter supplement the minimal Hebrew she learnt from a visiting teacher at her state elementary school by attending a private *cheder* on three afternoons a week. Every Sunday afternoon Isak Schneier took Ruth to a children's service at his synagogue.

Ruth grew up in one of the working-class districts of Vienna favoured by religious Jewish families like her own, with few non-Jewish friends, as part of a materially poor but emotionally close-knit extended family, and within a world of narrow cultural and political horizons. Amongst relatives who lived within walking distance was her maternal grandfather, Beresch Byk – the be-loved 'Opapa' to his family – who taught Ruth to embroider tablecloths and to play chess and who every day brought to her home *gefilte* fish and *lockshen* cooked by his wife. There was no radio in the apartment, no books other than those Ruth brought home from school, no newspapers. The theatre lay beyond the family's means, visits to the cinema were rare; Ruth's only luxuries were Sunday walks with her father, when they visited the fun-fair and watched the mechanical toys in a toy shop on Konigsstrasse, and twice-weekly piano lessons which her mother deemed necessary to her development into a marriageable young woman. Her parents nursed no cultural or educational ambitions for their only child: the expectation was that after leaving elementary school, she would find some minor position in the business world before marrying an appropriately orthodox Jewish spouse.

On the morning after Kristallnacht, Isak Schneier, along with most of the other adult male Jews in Vienna, was arrested by the SA and incarcerated in Dachau. The price paid by his wife for his release was the purchase of a visa for Shanghai which would underwrite his undertaking to the authorities to leave the country within six weeks. With no great desire to reach Shanghai, however, the couple began what became a frantic search for an alternative. In the meantime, on the advice of friends, they took immediate steps to get Ruth out of the country. Approaching an uncle of Isak, Samuel Schneier, who had settled in Manchester many years earlier, they were offered a guarantee and hospitality by his son and daughter-in-law, Nathan and Lena Press. After what Ruth remembers as 'six months of paper work' to obtain a visa, she left Vienna on 14 February 1939 and two days later arrived by taxi from Piccadilly Station at the Press home in Heywood Street in Cheetham Hill, at the heart of what was still Manchester's Jewish Quarter.[5]

Her last, but still vivid, memory of her parents, both then in their mid-forties, is of them standing with her in the train at Vienna's Central Station, her mother in a black coat with a light-brown fur collar, her father in a black overcoat. With 'everybody crying', she remembers her mother turning nervously to her father shortly before the train's departure with the words, 'perhaps she doesn't want to go'. Before any of them could change their minds, however, the train left: 'it was a good thing that it was quick', Ruth now recalls.

Looking back, she believes she found the transition from Vienna to Manchester easy enough. Since her mother had already sent on 'seventeen paper parcels' of clothing and linen – an 'enormous' collection which filled half the attic of the Press house – her own tiny suitcase contained only one change of clothes and 'bits and pieces' from her childhood treasures: a yo-yo, a bird-shaped pin-cushion, a doll and a pencil sharpener shaped like a frog.[6] Her expectation, she remembers, was that in six or seven months at most she would be reunited with her parents. She felt fully accepted by her cousins, who fitted her out with new shoes, a navy raincoat and a school uniform, and by their relatives and friends: in those first months of exile, she was 'surrounded by people', all solicitous for her well-being. Lena arranged for two girls to take her to the neighbourhood elementary school in Grecian Street, attended by the children of many local Jewish families, where she found two or three other Viennese girls who had arrived a week or two earlier, and where again she was well-received by teachers and children alike. One teacher set aside time to teach her refugee pupils the rudiments of English.[7]

Cheetham itself also provided what in some ways was a safe landing: like the 20th District of Vienna, it was the home of orthodox Jewish families, chiefly of Eastern European origin, amongst whom Yiddish, although no longer the lingua franca, was still in common use; close by was a network of neighbourhood synagogues and *stieblich*, rows of kosher shops, and all the familiar sights and sounds of a Jewish Quarter. On Friday nights she went with friends to the Lower Broughton Synagogue in Sabrina Street, the congregation of which the Press family were members, to hear the choir sing songs familiar to her from Vienna. Ruth marvelled only at the way in which seemingly ordinary Jewish families like her hosts – Lena Press earned only a small wage as the manager of a wallpaper shop, her husband Nathan £2 10s a week as a machinist in a clothing factory – could each afford its own 'villa'.[8] At school she quickly made friends with local Jewish girls, including Betty Levy, daughter of the waterproof clothing manufacturer, Daniel ('Dan') Levy, a member of the MJRC, who had himself provided guarantees and hospitality for refugees,[9] and whose home in Great Cheetham Street was open to them after Shabbat: Ruth remembers 'lovely Saturday evenings' spent at the house with Betty and her other Austrian and German refugee friends, sharing 'loads of lemonade … crisps and nuts'. That first summer in Britain the Press family took her to meet her other distant relatives in South Wales.[10]

All this she shared with those she had left behind: 'I was surrounded by everything new. I was in a different world, and all I did was write, write, to tell [my mother] everything. I used to write 16, 17 letters in a week, all my family I used to write to, friends … all I did in the evenings was just write letters.'[11] Such letters were both prized by her parents ('Your lines keep me alive', her mother wrote) and passed on to relatives and friends in the 20th District, themselves hoping to emulate her experience, and, in some cases, to draw on her support.[12]

In the replies sent by her father and mother, the first of which was posted in Vienna on 18 February 1939, Ruth appears both as a twelve-year-old child, still seen by her solicitous parents as being in need of their daily admonition and advice, and, in an adult role, as a potential instrument of their escape. Their own position was already desperate. Following Isak's decision not to take up his visa for Shanghai, his legal right to reside in Vienna expired at the end of March 1939. In her very first letter, Ruth's father, while giving thanks for his daughter's 'nice' welcome in a 'good home', wishing her success at school, and passing on good wishes from her friends and '1000 kisses' from her grandfather (her 'Opapa'), presses her to 'keep on trying' to find ways of getting them out. To Samuel Schneier, who had arranged Ruth's escape, he wrote, on the same day, 'We want to leave Vienna and then the world will be big enough to go anywhere.' In the same envelope was a brief note from Ruth's teenage friend in Vienna, Edith Neumann, also asking for help in being 'taken over': 'I will not be a burden on you', she writes, 'because my Uncle Ernst will pick me up'.

The first letters from Ruth's parents set what became the regular pattern and tone of their early correspondence with their 'Ruthi', 'Mausi'and 'Madi' questions about British relatives, about Manchester ('How is the weather in Manchester?') and about Ruth's activities and welfare ('where do you sleep, where do you go and who helps you take a bath?' Was she 'per du' or per Sie' to her hosts? 'Can you already speak English?', How was 'her first day in school?'); news of friends and relatives in Vienna ('Grandpa comes to us every day', 'Nurnberg's son is in Manchester'); maternal advice ('Be a good girl, keep your things in order and study a lot ... Don't take the cat into your room because cats are unpredictable'); calls, at first muted, but increasingly strident, for help in 'coming over'. In anticipation of their reaching Manchester, Isak was already sending parcels of clothes to Ruth, with jewellery (referred to in the letters as 'pieces') in the linings and seams.

Although their preference was for joining their daughter, the Schneiers, short on information, short on resources, low on literacy, were already pursuing whatever leads came to their notice. In a letter of 25 February, Ruth is asked by her father 'to be so kind' as to press the Jewish Refugee Committee in Manchester for an answer to her mother's request for help in finding a job. 'She can do everything', he writes. At the same time, he has clearly not ruled out other possibilities. 'We did not get an answer from America', he writes, and then: 'Dear Ruthi! I have heard that if a relative deposits £30 with a bank another person would be allowed to stay in England for three months. The money would be given back on leaving. That would be really convenient for us because we are thinking about going to Palestine after leaving England'. By early March, they both had Austrian passports and had sold most of the furniture from their flat in Vienna. On 10 March, Ruth's mother wrote: 'We have no idea where to go and that is our biggest worry. Time is short and we have to leave, but we still don't know how.' Her father wanted the name of a 'rich man' Ruth had mentioned in a letter: 'Maybe he can help us.' Already by the beginning of March he was toying with the idea of leaving Austria illegally and waiting 'outside' for an opportunity to emigrate.

Somehow Ruth's mother, her health seriously undermined by a medically botched stillbirth, continued to find the emotional space for Ruth's needs. 'Dear Madi! Put *Naftalin* [a moth killer] ... in your knitted clothes and in your fur coat. Keep everything in order. Do your nails still break? Buy a manicure set ... What about your hair style? Do you have your hair cut? Please do it if possible ... Do you play the piano well? Do you practise a lot? Be obedient, do what they say and be thankful that these people freed you from such misery and that they are so good to you ... Be careful when you take a bath and don't let the water be too cold ... Good night, sleep well and don't forget to say the evening prayer.'

The day this letter was written by Ruth's mother, 25 March 1939, her father, 'very upset and worked up' according to his wife, made an illegal crossing into Yugoslavia to take refuge with relatives on a farm near Zagreb while he sought the help of the local Jewish community in gaining entry to Palestine or 'to some other place'. While unable to register his presence with the Yugoslav authorities, and so to work or to 'walk in the streets', he was able to survive by selling jewellery he had brought with him and on the 10M a week he received from the local Kultusgemeinde. He was 'happy', he wrote to Ruth, 'and I thank God every day for not seeing the faces of the enemy ... I can sit down in every park and nobody says anything'. He spent his time 'writing lots of letters to all our relatives', in the hope that one of them might help him, and learning the rudiments of Croatian.

The plan was for his wife to follow him across the border after Pesach, which she spent alone in Vienna for the first time in 35 years, giving notice on the apartment and putting the family's affairs in some sort of order. 'Here the spring is coming,' she wrote to Ruth, 'and everything is beginning to look nice and green. In my heart, too, there is hope that everything will turn out right.' A week later, the date now fixed for her border crossing as 28 April, she wrote to Ruth: 'You know that Mama likes music very much and I ask you to study [the piano]. God will help you. You will be with us and you will play something for me.'

There was a sense in which mother and child were now each sustaining the morale of the other. Ruth's letters gave her mother 'new strength to live and not to give up'. To Ruth she wrote of her optimism that the family would be reunited and 'you will be our "Maus" again ... Don't give up, my dear child, you are still young and the world is so beautiful.' In Vienna, however, nerves were fraying. As she prepared to give up the family apartment on 1 May and move in with relatives, Peppy Schneier was already 'very nervous'; as the date for her border crossing was continually put off, she was approaching paranoia. Some of her friends in Vienna, she believed, were no longer prepared to help her: 'they don't care how I am. I have to do everything by myself and I have to queue everywhere'. 'Don't write to anyone,' she wrote to Ruth, 'they are not worth it.' Ruth was chided for not remembering her birthday or Mother's Day, relatives for not answering her letters; her letters to Ruth, although still expressing maternal concern for her well-being and curiosity about her new life, were increasingly dominated, and occasionally embittered, by the urgency and frustrations of her search for an avenue of escape.

In Manchester, Ruth also received other pleas for help, one, on 16 May, from her cousin Ella. 'I don't feel very good,' Ella wrote from Vienna, 'I can't go to America because the Consulate refused me ... Maybe you could do something for me ... Nobody else cares. Please, dear Ruth, maybe you can ask your relatives or friends in the club if they can do something for me. You could also talk to your teachers and ask them for such advice ... I have already done the test and all my things [papers] are already sent to London to the Woburn House. I am good in handwork ... especially in knitting, that's why I would like to work as a domestic servant ... When I am in England my relatives from America will try to help me. But unfortunately I am still here ... Maybe Josefs can do something for me. I won't be a burden on anybody because I know how to work and I can speak English ... Please write something to me soon. Maybe you will be successful.' Part of her fear was that unless some personal pressure could be brought to bear, her papers would 'lie around in Woburn House' for three or four months: perhaps 'Mr [Daniel] Levy could accelerate the whole process'. She added, 'How often do I have to get up on the table and jump around? Is it worth it? Bad Mouse.'

Tensions were high as in Vienna the search for means of departure took on a competitive edge. While Peppy Schneier accompanied Ella's letter with a plea to her daughter 'to do something for dear Ella', a week later she wrote with anger that nothing should be done. The earlier note had been written, she confessed, only because she and Opapa had been lodging with Ella's parents. To her and to Ruth's beloved grandpapa, they had been nothing but 'mean', not even keeping him supplied with water. Earlier they had not looked after her when she was sick. They had failed to use their contacts to enable the Schneiers to gain entry to the United States. They had spoken ill of Ruth. Ella had written to her after three months' silence only because of the urgency of her need for help. 'Maybe answer her. That is alright', Peppy wrote. 'But don't do anything.' Later, she added, 'I don't allow you to do anything for Ella and these people are not allowed to send her a permit … If Ella gets a permit these will be my last lines … Try to do something for me, not for other people. I want to get out of here alive.' In Manchester Ruth was expected to use whatever contacts she had only to expedite the issue of a visa for her parents: 'all these people [seeking your help] are not like parents to you', her father wrote. She was to find someone who would not only provide a guarantee, but 'accelerate' the processing of her documents in Woburn House.

In what followed a wide gulf is evident between the unfolding plans and high expectations, even optimism, of her parents in Europe, and the reality of what, with the best will in the world, Ruth, as an eleven-year-old girl still herself adjusting to life in Britain, might achieve for them in Manchester. The Press family believed that it lacked the means to help. Ruth recalls that she went to 'many [other] places' without success. She set some store on help promised by a Glasgow Jewish family related to Nathan Press: 'they could have helped', Ruth still believes, had they responded 'a little earlier'.

In Europe, in the meantime, on 13 June Peppy moved from Vienna to Graz, an industrial town within twenty miles of the border with Yugoslavia, where, with the help of a supportive Kultusgemeinde, she spent eleven days of comparative luxury in a local hotel. From there she wrote to Ruth: 'I am happy that I shall see you soon. Let God make it happen … God will help me and he won't punish me because I have already gone through so much … Amen.' On 26 June, after a clandestine three-day journey by car through the mountains and forests of the Yugoslav borderland, much of the time in hiding and 'without anything to eat or drink', a 'weak and excited' Peppy was reunited with her husband in Zagreb. There, while rendered cautious by the deportation to Italy of a fellow 'unregistered' refugee ('I wish I had some-where to walk around as a free person and not be afraid of being watched all the time', she wrote to Ruth), they continued to 'hope for the best', passing on to Ruth news of their friends in Vienna and their own 'happiness', while pressing her for details of a life of which they still fully expected to be a part. On 18 February 1940, perhaps for greater safety, Peppy and Isak moved from Zagreb to Urata, 'a very small [mountain] village' with 'about a hundred inhabitants', near the Italian border, in a 'romantic environment' close to the sea at Susak. 'There are huge mountains,' Peppy and Isak wrote to Ruth, 'and the air is very good, so we are recovering very well and we are not nervous at all … We pray to God for peace so that we will be together soon. Amen.'

In reality time was running out for them. In Manchester Ruth's efforts were effectively ended by the outbreak of war and by her evacuation in September 1939 to a non-Jewish home in Accrington, where for three months she was obliged to adjust to yet another unfamiliar, although friendly, setting. At some time that spring Peppy and Isak appear to have themselves given up hope of reaching Britain. For a time Palestine seems to have emerged as a viable alternative, although this, too, soon proved abortive. 'What will happen to us,' Peppy wrote to Ruth, 'we don't know.' And later, while still clinging to the consolation of wanting to know 'everything' about Ruth's new life ('Please write every detail'): '[Yugoslavia] is not even a cemetery because we are not allowed to die. But we have enough to eat. Papa and me are quite fat. Maybe you won't recognise us any more … But as long as we have something to eat. Maybe a different time will come.'

The last letters Ruth received from her parents are dated 2 March 1941. The messages were of both panic and hope. They call on Ruth's help yet again, this time to contact yet another uncle: 'He shall get us out of here,' Peppy wrote, 'before it is too late … We are not bad but we want to get out of here. Maybe it will be possible for us to be with you soon.' Her letter ends: 'Please write everything to me, my little Mausi. I would like to get a long, nice letter so I have something to read. We are quite well and we are happy when we get letters from you. I give you a big hug.'

At 5.15a.m. on 6 April 1941, with the help of troops from Italy, Rumania, Hungary and Bulgaria, the Wehrmacht crossed the frontier of Yugoslavia. Zagreb fell on 10 April, Belgrade on the 12th and six days later Yugoslavia capitulated. As the young King Peter fled into exile in Britain, the Nazis proceeded to dismantle the Yugoslav state and dismember the Yugoslav nation. On 10 April the Independent State of Croatia was proclaimed, with its capital in Zagreb, under the control of the ultra-nationalist Utasha movement and its leader, Ante Pavelic. Within weeks, the Utasha regime had initiated a bestial onslaught on 'the enemies of the Croatian nation': the Christian Orthodox Serbs and a Jewish population of around 40,000, of whom some 5,000 were refugees.[13] How the Schneiers responded and survived is not recorded; nor did Ruth in Manchester have any immediate information on their fate.

It was only after the war ended that, after searching through the lists of survivors which circulated within the Manchester community, she received a card from the International Red Cross in Sarajevo: 'Sorry, we must send you the sad news that Schneier, Pepi and Isak, are killed by the Utasha, 1941'.

She never finds out how they died and lives with the speculation that, like many other Jews, they were shot down on the streets of Zagreb. From other sources she learnt that her beloved grandfather, Beresh Byk, had been deported from Vienna to his death in Auschwitz.[14]

What the correspondence suggests very clearly, is the difficulty faced by ordinary, ill-educated, ill-informed and unsophisticated members of an Austrian Jewish family like the Schneiers in prising open the doors of their potential saviour-states. In the case of Britain, their chosen priority, this was not only a matter of the regulations surrounding 'alien immigration' which faced potential refugees. These restrictions, while not without a growing 'liberal' element from late 1938, remained during 1938–39 selective, restrictive and informed throughout by the perceived self-interest of the British state. The government may have kept its door ajar for certain categories of refugee; there was no way in which it mounted the kind of humane and comprehensive rescue operation which the Manchester Quakers, for example, believed the circumstances demanded.

Escape was dependent, too, on the class, culture and circumstances of potential refugees. A way through Home Office restrictions depended also in part on voluntary case-working committees, such as the Jewish Refugee Committees in London and Manchester, with which the young Ruth Schneier was called upon to deal, which from November 1938 were increasingly overburdened with applications and which, in the absence of governmental support, lacked the resources and the expertise to deal with them as swiftly and efficiently as the circumstances demanded. The 'acceleration' of their procedures was one of the services which Ruth's parents expected her contacts to fulfil. Peppy and Isak Schneier did not survive because their daughter was unable to activate in time the contacts which might have eased them through Britain's partially-closed doors. This might be construed as human failure: the failure of Isak and Peppy to gain an adequate understanding of British immigration law and of their daughter's powers of persuasion. Even more, however, it might be construed as the consequence of legal barriers which, whatever their liberal loop-holes, were difficult for such very ordinary and such very well-intentioned people as the Schneiers to surmount in the time and space available to them after November 1938.

For one of the saved, Ruth Schneier, the potential consequences of her parents' experiences were catastrophic. As a young girl she had been asked by her parents (and, incidentally, by others) to take substantial responsibility for their survival. She had been left to cope, virtually without support, not only with detailed information about their whereabouts, activities and desperation, and with their increasingly insistent requests for help, but with a role as their 'surrogate survivor' in which they had unknowingly cast her. They were buoyed up, even kept alive, by detailed news of the distant happiness in Manchester of their only daughter. She was asked to take responsibility, that is, as much for their emotional as for their physical survival. She was, in her mother's words, 'balm for my heart'.

It is a tribute to Ruth's inner strength that she was able to deal with such exceptional pressures. She did so, as she sees it, by the very practical device of 'getting on with life' in Manchester. She did not sit and mope. She did not dwell on her misfortune as a displaced child separated from her parents. She made friends; she coped in practical ways with work at school, with the English language, with evacuation, and with the demands of her foster family. Once a week she went to the local cinema; once a week she went to unpretentious 'parties' at the home of Dan Levy; occasionally she listened to the choir at the South Broughton Synagogue. And, as what might be seen as a last line of defence, from the beginning of 1940, she kept a daily record of her own life, entering into a tiny pocket diary in three or four sentences, first in German, then in English, the bare details of the way she had filled her days: the places she had visited, the friends she had met, the films she had seen. Only on one occasion – 'Today [10 May 1940] Hitler marched into Belgium' – did she allow international events to intrude on the personal. Neither her parents, nor her efforts on their behalf, receive any mention. Nor do her feelings, about her parents or about anything else: the contents of the diary represent, rather, a narrative of the 'ordinary' in Manchester which served as a form of self-protection against the overwhelming emotions which might otherwise have been summoned up by the quite extraordinary events in Europe in which she knew her parents to be caught up.[15]

In sharing with Ruth their experiences in the Vienna of 1938–39, her parents, while certainly communicating their general anxiety and the degree of their desperation to depart, were relatively restrained. Ruth is spared the details of the atrocities committed in Vienna by the Nazi regime, of the early deportations to 'the East' and, with one exception, of the restrictions placed on the lives of Jewish families. The Nazis are referred to only once, and then in passing, as 'our enemies'. Nowhere do the letters dwell upon the minutiae of personal suffering: the enforced poverty, the slave labour, the hunger, the immobility and the humiliations involved in seeking hand-outs from the beleaguered Jewish communal authorities. Like Ruth herself, her parents lived life as they found it. Rather like her diary, their letters mirror the determination of two resilient, stoical and still relatively young people not to be submerged by their misfortunes but to take whatever practical steps were available to sustain their morale and shape their futures. Equally, much as they drew on Ruth's support, they were determined to shield their daughter from the direst extremes of Jewish life in Nazi Europe.

Much the same is true of the three surviving letters, all written in August 1939, from Rudolph and Hildegard Beck in Breslau, to their son Walter who, with his younger brother Helmut, had reached Britain during December 1938.[16] In August 1939, after spending some weeks in the 'Mad Hatter's Castle' in Manchester's Whalley Range,[17] Walter was a trainee worker on a farm at Ashford in Kent, and Helmut, then fifteen, one of the ten young men under Marianne Prager's care at the Jewish refugee hostel in Stockport. Typically,

Prager had written to Helmut's mother 'in a very nice way' to assure her that her son had found refuge in 'a good home'.[18]

The letters depict not so much a site of Nazi brutality, which Breslau had certainly become, but a city shedding its Jewish population at an increasing pace and leaving a residue of which the Becks feared they would become a part. Around them, relatives, friends and acquaintances were on the move. Hugo Aufricht, 'Teacher Czollak' and Erna Hirschfield had left for Britain; Walter's friend, Heinz Cohn was on the point of departure; Klaus Tarnowski was going to Sweden; 'Uncle Georg, Aunt Trude and Ms Anne' had received their certificates to enter Palestine; Heinz and Hede Nothman, already there, had written to Hildegard from Petach Tikwah; 'Headmaster Apt' was 'going to South Africa', where other local teachers had already found refuge; 'Hans T' was in Holland, from where he was planning to reach Britain; Mrs Silbermann's son was in Bolivia. 'A lot of people have emigrated during the last two weeks', Hildegard wrote at the end of August.[19] 'We all were very happy [at Uncle Georg's departure] but we also will be sad about all these people leaving and we will stay behind ourselves'.[20] Even the person teaching them English prior to their own anticipated emigration was 'going to England and we will again be left behind'.[21]

In this atmosphere of panic, the Becks themselves, as ill-informed as the Schneiers of the openings available in the West, and as ill-equipped to achieve them, were clutching at straws. Through the friends of a former business partner, with whom they had never seen eye-to-eye at the best of times, they were seeking entry to Chile, where they had deposited funds to ensure their survival. They were in correspondence with a friend in the United States who might stand as surety for an American visa. They were engaged in elaborate plans to join their children in Britain. Once the well-to-do owners of a timber yard, but now impoverished, they were turning to relatives and friends for help towards paying their passage and expenses, whatever their destination. Their awareness of the possibilities was, at best, partial. 'They say that there are barriers to immigration in several countries', Rudolph wrote to Walter at the beginning of August.[22]

By the end of the month what few hopes they had nursed were all at the point of collapse. Chile was 'closed at the moment'; at all events, negotiations for a visa were likely to take 'several months' and, in the last resort, depended on the efficiency of the Chilean consul in Bremen, Hamburg or Berlin.[23] Their former partner, whom they had once believed to be 'a most trustworthy' person, had lost interest in their case: 'we will have to wait and see how things develop', Hildegard wrote to Walter on 29 August. Their friend in America lacked the financial means to act as their sponsor. In response to their requests for further help, one uncle had put fifty dollars at their disposal, another could give only 'a small sum', a nephew in America had nothing to offer: they still needed further help from 'our relatives and good friends'.[24] 'Everybody has to look after themselves at the moment', Hildegard concluded.[25]

Their hopes of making Britain their destination, however, were entirely dependent on their children, and particularly on fifteen-year-old Helmut Beck, who in Stockport had apparently made contact with a group of potential supporters attached to the parish church.[26] The basis of his negotiations, apparently through the mediacy of a Mrs Tapp, a member of the PPU active as a volunteer at the Stockport hostel, is not absolutely clear. What seems likely is that the parishioners were ready to offer a corporate guarantee provided the Becks were able to meet part of its cost. Discussions on this basis between Helmut, the Becks in Breslau and a committee of three representing church[27] were proceeding painfully slowly. From Breslau, Rudolph Beck urged his son Walter to write to the committee pressing their case. 'It doesn't make any sense to me', Hildegard wrote to Walter. 'They meet and discuss all the time but they should finally make a decision ... We don't know if the people can or want to raise the money. We don't know what their intention is. Do they want to help us to get a visa?'[28] At the end of August she added: 'Keep on trying to do something for us. Write to Helmut and talk to him about it. But don't accuse him that it is not going fast enough. He is not to blame, it is only the committee.' 'It is not his fault', Rudolph Beck wrote as a postscript. 'He is trying his very best. Everything takes such a long time.'[29]

Like the Schneiers in Vienna, the Becks combined distant parenting with the use of their children, however sensitively, as the instruments of their rescue. At some expense, with some difficulty with the German authorities, and while clearly preoccupied with their departure, they managed to send a new typewriter to Walter in Ashford, complete with rubber and replacement ribbons. Hildegard called on him to make a wooden cupboard for Helmut in the Stockport hostel, in which he 'might put his things'. She chides him for not having had the foresight to pack the 'velvet carpenter's trousers', which he was now asking her to send on. She worries about her children's health. She corresponds with Helmut about his holiday in Wales. 'Please keep your clothes and shoes in order', Rudolph Beck writes to his eldest son. Hildegard's most 'terrible thought', she confides to Walter, is that she might never see her children again.[30]

This proved to be the case. Four days after Hildegard's last letter, the outbreak of war ended any possibility of the Becks reaching Britain. With other possibilities equally closed to them, they were trapped in Breslau, from where they were ultimately deported to their deaths.

Helmut Beck had been brought up in Breslau 'in a very protected environment, his parents showering affection and solicitude on him', and with the expectation of sharing with his brother the inheritance of a flourishing timber business. Like his elder brother, he had been sent at some expense to a fee-paying Gymnasium.[31]

In December 1938 his education and the promise of a successful career as a businessman were shattered by his departure on the Kindertransport. Like Ruth Schneier, Helmut Beck lived the rest of his life (he died in 1989) with the consequences not only of separation from his parents, and of work found for him by the Stockport Jewish Refugee Committee, for which he was totally unsuited, but of his 'failure' to rescue his mother and father. Lacking Ruth's stoicism, he never fully recovered. In spite of his undoubted aptitude for a life in commerce, he remained in relatively low-paid work as a radio and television repair man. In later life, according to psychiatric reports, 'worrying about his family' and 'the effect of losing his parents' contributed to the 'chronic anxiety' and 'extensive amnesia' which led him to seek psychiatric help.[32]

What trapped the Becks was in part the reality of Chile's closed doors, of Britain's continuing demand for guarantors and of an American quota system they lacked the resources and the contacts to penetrate. But in any *real* world, beyond the speculative heights of academia, people overcome by desperation are prey as much to their perception of 'barriers' as to the barriers themselves. There *were* ways, in an objective reality they were unable to reach, in which the Becks might have escaped, even in August 1939. But access to those ways depended on a reflective calm the Becks, like many others of their age and in their circumstances, were unable to achieve. Instead, they were impelled by their very sense of rapidly contracting havens of safety, to seek out routes of escape, substantially chimerical, which neither they, nor their young son in Stockport, possessed the resources, the time or the expertise to open up. The *image* of closed doors, sustained not only by gossip, hearsay and ignorance in the lands of departure, but by the negative publicity of the western democracies themselves, was as much a cause of entrapment as the doors themselves.

There were other circumstances which made it inherently difficult for the 'saved' to ease their trapped loved ones through doors which might legally, and in ideal circumstances, have been opened sufficiently for their entry. Adolf Rochman arrived in Britain from Leipzig in March 1939 with the help of a guarantee organised by his uncle, Zelig Schmulewitsch, who had earlier in the 1930s established a small textile business in Guisborough in Yorkshire. Before leaving Germany he had promised his mother, Lina Rochman, a woman of fifty-nine, whose occupation – she was a 'hat decorator – did not qualify her for entry and who lacked both the resources and the contacts which might have secured her own immediate immigration, that, as soon as he had established himself in Britain, he would take steps to ensure that she would follow him. Both fully believed this to be a matter of only two or three weeks.[33]

In reality, Adolf Rochman, living and working first in Middlesbrough and later in Leeds and Manchester, encountered a chain of problems which ultimately made her escape impossible. One was his own unfamiliarity with things British. 'I don't know my way around', he wrote to his mother that March; 'I don't know to whom and where to go. Worst of all, my English is not good enough'. Until jewellery smuggled into Britain by a friend of his mother had been pawned, he added, he did not 'have enough money to pay for a lawyer'. Nor did his own sponsor, a local Jewish industrialist, 'have the time' to deal with her case.[34] Others to whom Adolf turned had their own reasons for not coming forward with help. Lina's brother, David Oberman, who had arrived in Britain in 1938, and was then an accountant in London, wrote: 'when you try to talk to people about this [gaining entry for Jewish refugees from Germany], they say that "the Germans that have come over have caused us enough anti-Semitism as it is". What's more is that they can't see what is so desperate about the situation.' What was needed, he believed, was 'a good lawyer with good contacts in the Home Office'.[35] But a lawyer cost money – at least £100 he was told – which Adolf did not have and could not raise.[36] The wife of Zelig Schmulewitsches, who himself wrote to Adolf that he was 'no magician or a millionaire who can wave his wand and bring Aunt Lina here', believed, at all events, that 'the whole thing' (that is, the Nazi persecution of the Jews), would 'be over soon'.[37] 'I'm standing against a brick wall', he wrote to his sister in December 1939. 'No one is interested … and they [his contacts in Middlesbrough] get irritated every time I bring it up.'[38]

What all this suggests is that the impact of immigration legislation is not confined to its literal provisions; it includes equally the circumstances surrounding those seeking to secure its favourable implementation. At least until the outbreak of war, legal openings existed for a woman in Lina Rochman's circumstances to gain entry to Britain. What prevented her were the circumstantial restrictions on the efforts of a son on whom she placed the main burden of her rescue: 'Don't leave my case in someone else's hands', she admonished him, 'Do it yourself'.[39] One such restriction was the human fallibility of a man seeking, at the same time, to secure his own foothold in a potentially hostile society,[40] while short on the funds, the confidence, the contacts and the experience which might otherwise have eased his mother into Britain. Another was the apparent failure of Adolf's Jewish friends and relatives in Yorkshire, even of the refugees amongst them, to fully appreciate the consequences of their inaction: a failure of the imagination common enough in British Jewry and which might occasionally take the form of irritation that help was being asked of them.[41]

The consequences were, in fact, tragic. Following an increasingly humiliating existence in Nazi Leipzig, Lina died in February 1942 on the train deporting her to Riga. Adolf's sister, Berta Gusman, who, with her husband and daughter had earlier found refuge in Romania, and who from April 1941 had also sought his help in reaching Britain, was murdered by German troops or Romanian irregulars in July or August of 1941.[42] One indication of the impact of these events is the way in which Adolf Rochman, like Helmut Beck and Ruth Edwards, preserved for a lifetime the correspondence in which they are recorded.[43]

Notes

1   JC 7, 14 and 25 July, 4 , 11, 18 and 25 August, 1 September 1939.
2   JC 18 August 1939.

3   *Ibid.*, p. 43.
4   The details of Ruth Schneier's family history which follow are taken from an inter-view conducted with her in 2003 by Rosalyn Livshin, augmented by further interviews conducted during 2004–05 by Stephanie Haug and by Ruth's granddaughter, Victoria Edwards, a postgraduate student of Religions and Theology at the University of Manchester. Ruth married a fellow refugee and is now Ruth Edwards (hereafter Ruth Edwards interview).
5   Lena was the daughter of Samuel Schneier, one of Ruth's father's uncles, who had made his home in Llanelli in South Wales.
6   Ruth still has the case and its contents.
7   Ruth Edwards interview.
8   *Ibid.* In fact, the Press family lived in a 1920s semi-detached house, part of the ground floor of which had been turned into a shop.
9   He was the founder and owner of Dannimac. Amongst the refugees for who he of-fered guarantees were the Viennese sisters, Rita and Fred Stark. Amongst the other refugee friends who gathered at his house was Marie Flash.
10 These were the families of her father's uncles, Samuel and Moshe Schneier, who had settled in South Wales.
11 Ruth Edwards interview.
12 Ruth's letters have not survived. These comments and following section are based on letters sent to Ruth between February 1939 and March 1941 chiefly from her parents, but also from relatives and friends. Most are in German, two in Yiddish. The translations used here are by Stephanie Haug, an Erasmus student in Manchester for one semester from the University of Heidelberg, with the help of Mr Norbert Herz of Manchester. Copies of the letters and their translation are available in the archive department of Manchester Central Library.
13 Jonathan Steinberg, 'Types of Genocide? Croatians, Serbs and Jews, 1941–45', in David Cesarani (ed.), *The Final Solution: Origins and Implementation* (London and New York 1994), pp. 175–193.
14 Ruth Edwards interview.
15 Ruth Schneier's later life has been equally marked by positive pragmatism. In June 1949 she married Sidney Edwards, also from a religiously observant Viennese family, who had arrived in Manchester as a Kindertransport child in December 1939. She believed that, as a fellow refugee, he would best be able to empathise with her expe-riences. At the age of 77, as his business partner, she continued to work the markets of Yorkshire and Lancashire selling ladies' handbags. They have three children, all brought up as observant Jews.
16 The three letters, perhaps the last Walter received, were written in Breslau on 1, 14 and 29 August 1939, and are now in the possession of Dorothy Beck, Helmut Beck's widow. Copies, with translations by Stephanie Haug, upon which the references here are based, are accessible at the Centre for Jewish Studies, University of Manchester.
17 See below, pp.XXX.
18 Hildegard Beck to Walter Beck 29 August 1939.
19 Hildegard Beck to Walter Beck 29 August 1939.
20 Hildegard Beck to Walter Beck 14 August 1939.
21 *Ibid.*
22 Rudolph Beck to Walter Beck 1 August 1939.
23 Hildegard Beck to Walter Beck 14 and 29 August 1939.
24 *Ibid.*
25 Hildegard Beck to Walter Beck 14 August 1939.

26   The following reconstruction is based on fragmentary evidence throughout the Beck correspondence.

27   It is possible to deduce that the three were made up of Mr Tapp, a 'Captain H', seen as its most influential member, and the Vicar (Rudolph Beck to Walter Beck 1 August 1939). Following the closure of the Stockport hostel following the internment of most of its residents, Helmut, spared internment by his Czech nationality, stayed for several months with the Tapp family in Stockport prior to their departure for Somerset. Dorothy Beck remembers the family as having 'Quaker connections' (Dorothy Beck interview).

28   Hildegard Beck to Walter Beck 14 August 1939.

29   Hildegard and Rudolph Beck to Walter Beck 29 August 1939.

30   Beck correspondence, *passim.*

31   Dr S. Shafar to Ludwig Eckstein, 19 August 1965.

32   Letters relating to Helmut's claim for compensation from the German government in the possession of Mrs Dorothy Beck, copies of which are accessible in the Centre for Jewish Studies, University of Manchester: an unnamed correspondent to Dr Rudolf Friedlaender 31 October 1964, Dr S. Shafar, consultant psychiatrist at Crumpsall (now the North Manchester) Hospital, to Ludwig Eckstein in Berlin 19 August 1965.

33   The letters on which this account is based are in Anne Joseph (ed.), *From the Edge of the World: The Jewish Refugee Experience through Letters and Stories* (London and Portland, OR 2003), pp. 3–68.

34   *Ibid.*, p. 14. Letter from Adolf Rochman to his mother 25 March 1939.

35   *Ibid.*, pp. 21–22. Letter from David Oberman to Adolf Rochman 24 April 1939.

36   *Ibid.*, pp. 29–30. Letter from Dora Schmulewitsch to Adolf Rochman 14 September 1939.

37   *Ibid.*

38   Joseph, *From the Edge*, pp. 37–38. Letter from Adolf Rochman to his sister, Berta 28 December 1939.

39   *Ibid.*, pp. 27–29. Letter from Lina Rochman to Adolf Rochman 2 September 1939.

40   Adolf himself felt restrained by what he saw as the strength of anti-German feeling. Soon after arriving in Britain, he changed his name from Adolf to 'Peter'. In July 1940, after the hostel in which he had been living in Manchester had come under attack from 'thuds screaming anti-Semitic and anti-German slogans', he commented: 'It's really not the time to go and talk to people about a visa for Mama.' (*Ibid.*, Adolf Rochman to his sister Berta 28 July 1940.)

41   For an example of this irritation, *ibid.*, pp. 41–42. Letter from Max Schmulewitsch to Adolf Rochman 18 January 1940. For the wider context of Jewish responses, Tony Kushner, 'Different Worlds: British perceptions of the Final Solution during the Second World War', in Cesarani (ed.), *The Final Solution*, pp. 246–267.

42   Joseph, *From the Edge*, pp. 53–54, letter from Berta Gusman to Adolf Rochman 30 April 1941, pp. 61–63, letter from 'Marissa' to Adolf Rochman 15 August 1941.

43   *Ibid.*, Introduction by Chaim Rockman, pp. 3–4.

21

'The Dutch orphans': war refugees in Manchester

Following the outbreak of war, when the flow of refugees from Nazi Europe came to an abrupt end, both major refugee committees in Manchester turned their attention to the task of supporting, morally and financially, some of the 8,000 refugees who had already arrived in the region. Recognising that the funds of voluntary agencies had been all but exhausted by the work of reception, and accepting, for the first time, direct responsibility for the welfare of refugees, the government now stepped in with increasingly substantial subsidies. Within the voluntary bodies themselves, case work for intending refugees gave way to a range of philanthropic activities which effectively converted the QRC and the MJRC into refugee branches of the state agencies of public welfare.

This work, apparently proceeding smoothly enough, although not without some internal adjustments, was interrupted by the crisis of confidence which overcame the British state following the German invasion of the Low Countries and France. While fear of a 'Fifth Column' led finally to the whole-sale interment of 'enemy aliens', whose welfare behind wire, and potential release, now became an urgent concern of both committees, the turn of events during spring and early summer 1940 generated new and unexpected waves of refugees who required immediate accommodation and support. One such wave arrived from Liverpool and Gateshead during May 1940, as coastal districts in the north-west and north-east were declared 'protected areas' in which the residence of all aliens was prohibited. Another consisted of more than 200 of the German and Austrian refugees who managed to escape from Holland and Belgium in the wake of the German army and who were earmarked by the Ministry of Health for support in Manchester.[1]

In receiving refugees uprooted from Merseyside and the north-east, the refugee committees were left to their own devices. In providing hospitality for the 'war refugees', the QRC and the MJRC were expected only to provide additional support to that offered by 'War Refugee Committees' set up by local authorities under a national scheme worked out by the Ministry of Health. It marked, inter alia, the first occasion on which the agencies and resources of the state were mobilised for the reception of refugees.

Preparations in the north-west for the reception of 'war refugees' began immediately after the invasion of Holland on 10 May 1940, with local authorities throughout Lancashire and Cheshire being called upon by the Ministry of Health to provide hospitality for an estimated 20,000 refugees. Interpreters throughout the region, it was said, would be provided by the Manchester Dutch Society.[2] In Manchester, where a war refugee committee under the chairmanship of the Town Clerk was at work by 16 May, preparations were made for the reception of up to 5,000 Belgian and Dutch refugees, at first in the Exhibition Hall at Belle Vue Zoo, where they would be housed, fed and given medical attention, and subsequently in empty houses or in private homes, 650 of which had been offered to the Town Clerk by 27 May.[3] Following an assessment of their needs, those refugees 'with private resources' would be expected to support themselves; the rest would be found accommodation by the Corporation's reception and billeting officers. Voluntary organisations were encouraged to supplement the Council's efforts. In particular, the Women's Voluntary Service (WVS) set up a Manchester War Refugees Clothing Committee which on 20 May opened a depot and 'distributing centre' at 230 Deansgate. Around the sorting racks on the depot walls were the flags of Belgium, Holland and Poland.[4] The Clothing Committee, of which Lord Derby became the honorary chairman, put out an immediate appeal, with the slogan, 'Don't put off till tomorrow what the refugees need to put on today.'[5]

From the Jewish communal perspective of Nathan Laski the situation both called for measures which would ensure the welfare of the German and Austrian Jews who, having earlier taken refuge in Holland, were now amongst the war refugees, and provided an opportunity for offering further proof, and this at a time of potential anti-German feeling, of the dedication of the Jewish community to the national cause. At a meeting he arranged on 27 May between representatives of the Town Clerk and the Manchester and Salford Jewish Representative Council (JRC) he signalled the community's willingness to help, but (and this typified Laski's outlook) 'as citizens not as Jews'. While not willing to accept collective financial responsibility for any body of refugees, the JRC would supply interpreters, transport facilities, volunteer workers, subscribers to the War Refugee Committee's funds and billets in private houses, 'it being understood that this was not a Jewish question'. All that the Council required of the city in return was that Jewish refugees would be 'kept together'.[6] The JRC went on to set up its own 'representative committee ... to make provision for Belgian and Dutch refugees expected in Manchester', with Morris Feinmann as its 'liaison officer' with the city, and to recruit men and women volunteers from within the community 'willing to help non-Jews as well as Jewish refugees'.[7] Of a list of eleven volunteers initially presented to the Town Clerk, at least half were already active on the MJRC, but they included also such newcomers to refugee work as the cotton merchant, Manuel Cansino, and the solicitor, Lawrence Marks.[8]

While thus providing a new and unexpected channel between the Jewish community and the voluntary sector of the city, the JRC committee's first tasks included the reception of a group of 169 Jewish war refugees who on 27 May were due to move to Manchester from temporary accommodation in Wigan, and which included seventy-one unaccompanied Jewish children from an orphanage in Amsterdam. In the last reckoning, the committee found private accommodation for forty-two adult war refugees and lodged sixty-five of the children in two vacant houses in Heaton Road, Withington, identified by Hettie Myrans and Mrs Horace Black, both members of the South Manchester and District Women's Zionist Society, and rented by the city.[9]

Number 42 Heaton Road, which became the boys' hostel, was also the base of what was now the Manchester Jewish War Refugees Committee, a body independent of the MJRC, with its own secretary, Elja Baruch, and responsible to the Manchester and Salford Jewish Representative Council.[10] Relationships between the two committees were eased, however, by the personal friendship of Baruch with Rae Barash and her daughter, Joan. Born in Berlin, Baruch's training as an interior designer was interrupted in the early 1930s by the emergence of the Nazi regime. Also a Communist, 'the deciding factor', according to Ruth Schlesinger, 'that pushed her into emigrating in the early 1930s', she was found a placement in Manchester as a domestic servant by the Hospitality Committee of the Manchester Ladies Lodge of the Order B'nai Brith, on which Barash was the key figure. Shortly before the outbreak of war, she had put her life at risk to attend the funeral in Berlin of her brother, who had been killed in a motorcycle accident, only to return safely to Manchester. Outside her domestic work, Baruch made 'attractive lampshades', which she first sold at events organised by the Hospitality Committee and later through Lewis's department store in Market Street.[11] Leaving domestic service after the outbreak of war, she worked as a secretary, for a time to the refugee GP, Dr Friedlaender.[12]

Elja Baruch is one of those refugee social workers, well-loved by their charges, of whom little information had survived. Ruth Schlesinger, who knew her well, judged her to have been 'a stylish young women who had enjoyed the café culture and bohemian life-style of the German capital'. When Ruth first met her as a carer in 1948, however, while living in a stylish flat in Sherringham Road, strewn with beautiful rugs and fabrics, she had come to 'resemble Mole in *The Wind in the Willows*', 'small and squat', 'signally honest and unpretentious [with] no side or vanity at all', 'with grey frizzy hair, clad in brown trousers, [a] long brown cardigan and cream-coloured blouse'. 'Signally unmaterialistic', she once told Ruth that 'she wished she could go through life with only the possessions she had in her pocket'. It was Baruch's warmth, Schlesinger remembers, that gave younger refugees a sense of security. Baruch herself kept close, empathetic relationships with the refugees who came under her care, keeping in touch with them long after their return to their home countries. These included some of the 'Dutch Orphans' who arrived in Manchester in June 1940.[13]

The escape of the children who, on the grounds of their accommodation in the former municipal orphanage in Amsterdam became for ever after known (wrongly) as 'the Dutch Orphans', was engineered by Mrs Geertruida ('Truus') Wijsmuller-Meijer, the non-Jewish wife of a prosperous Catholic banker in Amsterdam, and a Socialist city councillor, who in 1940 was chairman of the Jewish Refugees Committee in Amsterdam. Mrs Wijsmuller, from a family with a long-standing tradition of philanthropy, and then in her early fifties, was already deeply committed to the saving of Jewish lives. In the mid-1930s she had taken responsibility for the reception of German refugees seeking safety in Holland and from late 1938 for Kindertransports from Germany as they crossed the Dutch border. In December 1938 she had been called upon by Norman Bentwich to negotiate with Adolf Eichmann the evacuation of Austrian Jewish children. After what became a humiliating meeting with Eichmann[14] at his Vienna headquarters, she successfully secured the departure of the first Kindertransport from Vienna on 11 December 1938. Thereafter she had worked incessantly to transport Jewish children arriving from Berlin, Vienna and Prague to the Dutch coast; it was she who met the sixty-six children on the last Kindertransport from Berlin, which arrived in Holland on 31 August 1939, moments before the closure of the border by the German authorities, and transferred them by bus to the coast, from where they sailed to Britain on 1 September.[15]

There then remained in Holland, apart from its native Jewish population of 110,000, some 26,000 non-Dutch Jews sheltering in and around Amsterdam, including seventy-one unaccompanied German and Austrian children who, after staying in a series of hostels and vacant 'holiday homes' during the winter of 1938–39, had ended up in spring 1939 in a city orphanage in Amsterdam (the Burgherweeshuis) which Mrs Wijsmuller had converted into a refugee hostel, and which was under the direction of her close friend, Gertrud Van Tijn.[16] All were young people whose parents believed that in sending them to Holland they had secured their safety.

Elsbeth, Hans and Oskar were the children of an orthodox and observant Jewish couple, Helena and Salomon Levy, who had sold their grocery shop in Gladbeck following the violence which had accompanied the Nazi boycott of Jewish businesses in April 1933, and who had subsequently sought safety with relatives, first in the spa town of Hamm in Westphalia, where Salomon Levy became a travelling salesman for a local wine firm, and where his family was treated to escalating anti-Semitic abuse, and, five years later, in Herzeborck, a small village near Bielefeld. It was the ransacking of their home in Herzeborck on Kristallnacht that finally persuaded them to register their children, then aged between eleven and fourteen, for a Kindertransport which left Bielefeld for Holland on 19 January 1939. Soon afterwards Hans and Oskar were placed in an orphanage in Gouda which was serving as a holding post for Jewish child-refugees. With them was fourteen-year old Heinz Martin Hirschberg, a member of a highly assimilated Berlin Jewish family, who in February 1939 had gained entry to Holland under a guarantee from an uncle, Louis Jacobi, who had himself left Germany for Holland in 1934.

Hirschberg remembers that at the Gouda orphanage newly arrived young refugee boys were subjected by the warden and matron to a Spartan regime which involved heavy manual work and punishments which included the stopping of meals and the confiscation of incoming mail. After all being refused evening meals for not completing their work tasks, the boys rebelled, tying their two tormentors to chairs in their office. In May 1940 the children were transferred to the orphanage at 27 Luciensteeg in central Amsterdam.[17]

Hirschberg and Levy recall that in Amsterdam they were treated with great kindness. Wijsmuller found them places in local schools or, in Hirschberg's case, in the Organisation for Resettlement and Training (ORT) training centre (where he was prepared for resettlement in Palestine/Israel by being trained as a baker of confectionery), accompanied them on weekly visits to the town's swimming baths, arranged for them to be taught Dutch, allowed them to visit relatives, provided religious lessons conducted by a fellow refugee, and had them taken regularly to Sabbath services at the Sephardi synagogue. There Levy was barmitzvahed with another of the 'orphans', Alfred Salomon, on 17 February 1940.[18] Truus Wijsmuller's husband, 'Uncle Wijsmuller', took the children on boat trips and to the zoo.[19]

As news broke of the German invasion of Holland on 10 May 1940 Mrs Wijsmuller acted swiftly to save the hostel children and as many other Jewish refugees as she could muster. On 14 May, hearing that an ageing coal freighter, the SS Bodegraven, was tied up at the port of Yjmuiden, to the immediate south of Amsterdam, she hired three coaches, obtained permits for their use from the Aliens Police and, leading the procession in her own car, transported some 170 Jewish people through barricades and check points to the dockside. She then persuaded the captain of the ship to take on board her human cargo. On the dockside, she tore strips off her underwear and used them to sew into the children's coats their names, their dates of birth, their last known addresses in Germany or Austria, and the names and addresses of any of their parents who were living in neutral countries or who had already reached Britain.[20] By the time of its departure at 7p.m., some 270 people were crammed onto the deck of the Bodegraven, with cabin accommodation only for its Indonesian crew of fifty.[21] They included an Amsterdam antiques dealer, Jacques Goedstiker, the wealthy director of an Amsterdam textile firm, Louis Springer, and a Mrs de Groot, who had worked as a clerk with the Jewish Refugees Committee in Amsterdam. As the boat put out to sea – the last refugee transport to leave Holland – the docks were engulfed by black smoke as British troops, still arriving as the Bodegraven departed, destroyed the reserves in Amsterdam's oil refineries. Two hours later Holland capitulated.[22]

The cross-Channel journey was itself eventful. Half an hour out to sea, the Bodegraven was strafed by German planes, only narrowly failing to find a human target. Jacques Goedstriker, was killed in a shipboard accident and buried at sea.[23] The rest were moved into the hold, where Hans Levy remembers that the children slept in coal sacks on an iron floor.[24] As the boat arrived off the south coast of Britain on 15 May, suspicious port authorities refused it permission to dock. For a further five days the Bodegraven sailed northwards along the coast; without supplies, Hans Levy recalls, and forbidden by orthodox Jewish adults to share the rations offered them by the crew, the children were compelled to survive on dog biscuits and cups of tea without sugar or milk.[25] Finally the boat was allowed to dock in Liverpool on the evening of 20 May, under 'stringent precautions'; press reporters were kept at bay, the refugees searched, interrogated and medically examined before being herded into an abandoned seamen's hostel, where, surrounded for two days by police, they slept on mattresses spread across the floor.[26]

It was an irony of the situation that just as these 'heroic' fugitives from the German forces were arriving, fear that a Fifth Column might be harboured within the refugee community in Britain was impelling the government towards the imposition of increasing restrictions on the movement of refugees. By 22 May war refugees from Belgium and Holland were being interned, some on information provided by the French authorities; Hans Levy recalls that, in Liverpool, some of the older passengers from the *Bodegraven* were separated from the rest and transported immediately to internment camps on the Isle of Man.[27] It was later rumoured that amongst the passengers had been two Nazi spies.[28] With Liverpool part of the Merseyside 'protected area', the remainder of the refugee 'aliens' on the *Bodegraven* were moved inland without ceremony to 'neutral areas', 150 of them, including 'elderly men', 'well-to-do merchants and professional men with their wives', a young blind musician and seventy-one children, to the Lancashire coal town of Wigan, some twelve miles from the coast, where they arrived by train on 22 May.[29]

Here again their enthusiastic welcome by the Wigan public as the victims of Nazism, news of whose dramatic escape had already reached the Liverpool and Wigan press, coincided with changing governmental attitudes towards refugee aliens. Wigan already had its experience of refugees. Nine refugee students, five Austrians, two Germans and two Czechs, 'whose credentials had been closely scrutinised', had been admitted to courses at the Wigan and District Mining and Technical College, where the Principal, J.F.S. Ross, had been impressed by their behaviour. They had 'devoted themselves to their studies with great assiduity, behaved well and entered into the general life of the college in a very satisfactory way'.[30] Other refugees had arrived as trainee agricultural workers at Upholland, on the outskirts of Wigan.

A sympathetic crowd now awaited the newcomers from the *Bodegraven*, cheering, clapping and waving handkerchiefs as they arrived at Wigan Wallgate.[31] At a formal ceremony in the Wigan Drill Hall they were welcomed by the Mayor of Wigan in a speech translated into Dutch and French by Fr Turner, a professor of languages at the Catholic seminary at nearby Upholland. Wigan was to be only a temporary resting place, however; arrangements had apparently already been made for the refugees to move on to Manchester. Margaret Langdon was despatched to Wigan by the Lord Mayor of Manchester, in part, it seems, to look after the children's religious needs, in part to make the arrangements for the next stage of their journey. She had 'notes' from the Lord Mayor, she remembered in later life, for food and transport for the children and for the use of a priority phone line to Manchester Town Hall. She found the children in a dreary old Sunday

School, darkened by black-out curtains, with the younger ones crying, and women from the Women's Voluntary Service (WVS) standing around dismayed that the children would not eat the sandwiches and pork pies they had provided.[32]

With her typical efficiency, she took the matter in hand, sending out for milk, bread and butter, before a vegetarian meal was laid on, with a menu put together by members of Wigan's miniscule local Jewish community and with the advice of the Manchester rabbi, Bernard Casper, the newly appointed minister of the Higher Broughton Synagogue, who had been invited to Wigan to offer the newcomers spiritual support.[33] Accommodation was then provided, for the adults in the halls of local Baptist and Methodist chapels, for the 'orphan' girls at the All Saints Institute of the Anglican Sisters of Mercy, attached to the Parish Church, and for the boys in St Michael's Parish Hall.[34] There Langdon explained to the children the plans that had been made for them: in Manchester those aged seven and over would be placed temporarily in two hostels in South Manchester, children under seven in the Lymm Home for [Jewish] Mothers and Babies. Girls and boys would be housed in separate hostels, but close enough together for brothers and sisters to be within easy reach of one another. At this, a seven-year-old girl 'flew at her', pulling her hair and screaming that she had promised her mother that she would not be parted from her three-year-old brother. Langdon used her own authority to allow both to join the Lymm contingent.[35]

Hans Levy's recollection is of a month spent with the 'wonderful and generous people' of Wigan. The day after their arrival, the girls were taken to play games with local children on the lawn of the Rector's house. Boy Scouts and other volunteers guided the children around the town. Local families 'adopted them', inviting them to tea in their homes and accompanying them to local events; the Levy brothers, Hans remembers, were taken by the Barlow family to their first cricket match. The Buxton Theatre Circuit gave out free tickets for performances at Wigan's Princes Cinema. Hans Levy, who in Germany had been banned as a Jew from all cinemas, saw his first film in Wigan: *The Hunchback of Notredame*.[36] When it became known that they were leaving Wigan, a farewell party was arranged for them, at which each refugee child received half a crown.[37]

As a gesture of thanks from the refugees, on Sunday 2 June, one of them, a Mrs Van Voolen, 'a professional vocalist of high repute', sang the evening service at Queen's Hall.[38] The same edition of the *Wigan Examiner* which announced her appearance carried a government warning of the latest restrictions imposed on the possession of enemy aliens. In July 1940 two Wigan women were fined by the Wigan Borough Bench for failing to report the presence of alien lodgers to the local police.[39]

On 22 June, as Wigan geared itself up for the reception of 600 Channel Islanders, the *Bodegraven* refugees were moved on, with WVS escorts, to Manchester, where the Corporation's War Refugee Committee and the Jewish War Refugees Committee had between them made arrangements for their reception: forty-two adults with private families, six children of seven and under at the Lymm Home for [Jewish] Mothers and Babies,[40] the rest in the newly-acquired houses at 40 and 42 Heaton Road in Withington, fitted out with furniture begged and borrowed by Baruch from members of the community. Within weeks, by what appears to have been an arrangement worked out with the city, the details of which are now lost, the Jewish War Refugees Committee assumed responsibility for the Jewish children, the girls at 40 Heaton Road, the boys at 42, the staff appointed by the Jewish War Refugees Committee, which was responsible to the Home Office for their welfare and maintenance, and paid from funds derived ultimately from the Ministry of Health.[41] While Elja Baruch visited the hostels to watch over the welfare of their residents, support was also given to the children by Jewish volunteers, some of them members of the South Manchester and District Women's Zionist Society.[42] Doris Angel remembers that her mother, Helene Loewenstein, wife of a refugee industrialist, 'cooked, washed, ironed and mended' for the children of both hostels, which were only ten minutes' walk from her own home in Mauldeth Road.[43]

These arrangements lasted until December 1941 when, very probably on the grounds of rationality,[44] the Jewish War Refugees Committee was disbanded and the management and financing of the two hostels was taken over by the MJRC, with help from the funds of Refugee Children's Movement (RCM) and with Elja Baruch kept on as a welfare officer.[45] Early in 1942, with the houses on Heaton Road full to overflowing, the MJRC was offered a large detached Victorian villa at 9 Wilmslow Road, rent-free, by its owner, the widow of the Manchester businessman, Mark Rubin, who died in June 1939; in 1942 Mrs.Rubin was apparently living outside the city as an evacuee.[46] After some debate, and with the approval of Bloomsbury House, the decision was taken to accept and to give notice on 40 Heaton Road; 9 Wilmslow Road now became the boys' hostel, with number 42 kept on for the girls.[47] In the event it took some months for 9 Wilmslow Road to be made ready. 'Shaken' during the Blitz, the fabric of the front of the house required extensive repairs, and since, on their departure, the Rubins had failed to protect their wine cellar, German bombing had caused the corks to pop and the wine to run out, causing layers of fungus.[48] It was not until December 1942 that the hostel was ready for occupation, the furniture supplied by Bloomsbury House.[49] Ruth Schlesinger remembers that its ground floor was made up of a 'big kitchen with a scullery at one end, a separate kitchen reserved for washing the dishes, a large sitting room and an even bigger dining room looking out onto the front garden'.[50]

Although the 'Dutch Orphans' were thus brought within the orbit of the MJRC's control, this was exercised with a light touch, Heinz Hirschberg remembers, by Rae Barash in person. Rabbi Altmann, who in February 1941 had given talks 'on Jewish subjects' to the residents at 42 Heaton Road, had found them 'hungry for spiritual food'. On these grounds, he proposed to Rae Barash that he should deliver religious lessons once a fortnight and that the teaching of Hebrew be accorded to a Mrs Klein, a refugee who had been a teacher in her home town, Frankfort-am-Main.[51] Barash was surprisingly reluctant to accept. Arrangements had been made, she wrote to Altmann, for the boys to receive regular Hebrew lessons from 'Mr. Morris' at the Wilbraham Road (that is, the South Manchester) Synagogue and the girls from Revd Pereira Mendoza of the Withington Congregation of Spanish and Portuguese Jews. The boys, she added, had proved a problem, and she promised to call on Mrs Klein for help.[52]

Whether she ever did so is not known. Barash was apparently prepared to work on the assumption that her new charges at the Wilmslow Road hostel were from German and Austrian families with only a tenuous link with Jewish religious observance. Although the younger children were invited to attend the Hebrew classes at the Withington Congregation of Spanish and Portuguese Jews and Sabbath services either there or at Manchester's Reform Synagogue, they were under no obligation to do so. Food at Wilmslow Road, although prepared by a Viennese Jewish refugee cook, Martha Strauss, who lived at the hostel with her son, Kurt, was not strictly kosher.[53] In November 1942 Rabbis Altman and Papo complained that at 42 Heaton Road the matron 'appeared to be obstructing Jewish education'.[54] From the perspective of both the MJRC and the executive of the regional branch of the RCM, 42 Heaton Road became a haven (for Rabbi Dr Altmann something of a dumping ground) for less observant Jewish girls moving into the area or seeking to escape the strict religious discipline of Myer Kersh House.

For boys, the alternative was the new Wilmslow Road hostel. The house-parents, Siegfried Alexander, a former actor and artist from Berlin, and his wife, Erna, both non-practising Jews (and both themselves refugees), made no attempt to ensure that the lives of the boys were set within a religious framework.[55] Given Alexander's ignorance of Jewish ritual, the annual *Seder* was conducted by Hirschberg.[56] An attempt by Rabbi Altmann to impose a more observant regime on the hostel was rejected by Barash,[57] who placed greater emphasis on the maintenance of a relaxed atmosphere for children whom she regarded as having already suffered extreme pressures and whose welfare she had clearly taken under her own wing. On 13 July 1940, after hearing that German propaganda had reported the sinking of the *Bodegraven*, she had spoken about the children's experiences as part of a BBC Home Service series, *Northcountry Women*.[58] Heinz Hirschberg remembers that she took some of the children, who came to know her as 'Aunty Rae', on visits to her cottage in Leicestershire.[59] Under her gentle guidance, they were, Hans Levy believes, 'a happy family'.[60] Martha Strauss, too, was 'really a mother to us'.[61] There were few organised events; the boys did their own thing, reading books borrowed from Withington Library, playing chess, listening to the radio or just hanging around.[62] Siegfried Alexander transformed popular British plays and musical hall scenarios into dramatic events performed at Chanukah under his own direction.[63]

The relaxed and caring approach of the hostel management also accorded its thirty boys a wide degree of freedom. Hirschberg was supported by Alexander in his interest in classical music, taken by Mrs Strauss, a 'very cultured woman', to Manchester Opera House and encouraged by both to cycle to Wilmslow for performances by the Hallé Orchestra at the Rex Theatre.[64] Hans Levy regularly took one of the Heaton Road refugee girls to Sunday dances at the Ritz Ballroom in city-centre Manchester.[65] He continued the violin lessons which he had begun in Germany and made contact with local amateur orchestras. At one of these he was befriended by a local man, Arthur Ellis, a fellow violinist (and guitarist), with whom he went on to play folk music at the Little Robin, a pub off Great Western Street, the Town Hall Clock near Albert Square, the Black Lion in Blackfriars Street, and a local folk club. With Arthur he also joined Manchester's experimental theatre, The Unnamed Society, of which Leonard Behrens was one of the patrons, and where he met his future wife, Elfrida Gainsboro, a work colleague of Arthur Ellis.[66] When one of the boys, Ernest Growald, put himself forward to the committee as a 'potential novelist', arrangements were made for his work to be read when complete by Dennis Cohn of Cresset Press.[67]

Amongst the boys, only Hirschberg, who, at the hostel had been given tuition in Hebrew by Rabbi Dr Papo, had made contact with the institutions of the Jewish Quarter, becoming an active member of the Zionist youth organisation, Habonim, with its Bayyit (headquarters) in Cheetham Hill.[68] At least two of the girls at 42 Heaton Road joined the irreligious left-wing Zionist body, Hashomer Hatzair, which also had a base in Manchester.[69]

The running of the hostels was otherwise unexceptional. The boys slept in five-person dormitories. Their health was cared for by a refugee doctor, Dr Billigheimer, and a refugee dentist, Dr Lewinski. Children under the age of fourteen were found places at Old Moat Primary School in Withington, two of them later moving on to Levenshulme High School for Girls; the rest were expected to find jobs and work permits (chiefly through the junior labour exchange) which would help pay for their keep.[70] Given the restrictions on the employment and movement of enemy aliens at this stage in the war, such jobs consisted essentially of low-paid work, supposedly as 'trainees' in local businesses. Gerd Goldman, who had left Frankfurt-am-Main with his mother before parting from her in Holland, became a trainee chef (a 'cook's apprentice') at Prince's Restaurant on Oxford Road, on '9/8 a week with food';[71] Hans Saloman, from the village of Seibersbach in the German Rhineland, a baker; Hirschberg first (in September 1940) was a delivery boy for the local 'high-class fish, poultry, fruit and flower' dealers, A. and S. Judge, on Wilmslow Road, and then (in February 1942) as a 'trainee mechanic' at the Grosvenor Garage in Burnage Lane, Levenshulme (in 1939 the Manchester agents for German Opels), for £1 a week.[72] In both he acquired a reputation for dedication, hard work and scrupulous honesty, progressing at the Grosvenor Garage from assistant store-keeper to motor mechanic.[73] Hans Levy and another of the boys found work with a cabinet-making firm at Knott Mill, where their main task, he remembers, was to make tea for the older employees, for 10s a week; when the premises was burnt down in the Blitz, he became an apprentice machine-engraver.[74] An appeal from the MJRC in the *Jewish Chronicle* of 28 June 1940 for other employers had come up with no work which was either more challenging or more suitable.

Locally the hostel and its refugees were well received. They were welcomed by 'very friendly and hospitable' local families and local employers:[75] Hirschberg was given a loan by the Burton family of Withington, with whom he briefly lodged, to pay for his first bicycle; he was treated with great kindness by the families to whom he delivered groceries (they gave him hot drinks and an occasional shilling), and found his fellow workers in the garage 'very, very friendly and helpful'.[76] Several local craftsmen offered their services to the hostel free. The cinema in Withington gave the children free tickets for one performance a week. Burton's fitted them out with occasional free suits, Freeman, Hardy and Willis with free shoes. Volunteers from the University gave free English lessons. Arthur Williams, in charge of the ARP station which adjoined the girls' hostel on Heaton Road, took lessons in German at the Berlitz School to enable him to converse with his refugee neighbours. He allowed his daughters to stay overnight at the hostel, while providing tea and entertainment for some of the refugee girls at his home in Barnstead Avenue, on a Withington Council Estate.[77] Hans Levy was surprised when it turned out that the police who arrived at the hostel after an air raid in October 1940 had come not to arrest them but to enquire after their welfare.[78] Anti-Semitism played no part in the children's experience, anti-German sentiment was rare.[79] Hirschberg was both disappointed and favourably impressed when his application to join the RAF was turned down in 1944 on the grounds that he could not be expected to bomb a country in which his parents still lived.[80]

Most of the *Bodegraven* child refugees, whose initial hope was for an ultimate reunion with their families,[81] lost touch with them as the war progressed. Hans and Oskar Levy maintained contact through the Red Cross with their parents in Dortmund until July 1942, when what turned out to be their last message read: 'Dear boys, We have no news from you, please write soon. We will travel in a few days. Be healthy and keep up the good mood. Warm kisses. Mummy and Daddy.'[82] Their 'travel' was, in fact, their deportation to Theresienstadt, from where they were subsequently transported to their deaths in Auschwitz.[83] Only Hans' sister, Elsbeth, survived the death camps to be reunited with her brothers. His desperate search after the war for news of his family's whereabouts led him, he remembers, not only to the Red Cross, but to Blue Cross Motor Insurance and the NSPCC.[84] Heinz Hirschberg, who now, as Harry Jacobi, is 'proud to be English', still cannot forget the Home Office regulations which he believes were responsible for his mother's death; in abandoning his own birth name, he adopted her maiden surname, Jacobi.[85]

In August 1941 the MJRC made a decision to send sixteen of its child protégés, twelve girls from the Heaton Road hostel and four boys from Cassel-Fox, to Whittingehame Farm School, a school for the vocational training of Jewish child refugees between the ages of fourteen and sixteen, on what had been the Scottish estate of Lord Balfour, given for use by Jewish refugees by his nephew, Lord Traprain, in 1939, and reckoned by the *Jewish Chronicle*'s Manchester correspondent, Lucien Harris, to be 'one of the finest establishments working under the auspices of Anglo-Jewry'.[86] It was particularly useful for the MJRC, Morris Feinmann believed, since it would be an economic way of dealing with young refugees in 'blind-alley jobs [with] no plans for the future': their costs would be met by their guarantors.[87]

Harris, who visited the school in September 1941, saw it as both 'permeated with a thoroughly Jewish and idealist spirit' and 'doing a precious piece of work in preparing … young refugees for practical occupations'. It was a particular 'blessing', he believed, in preparing young refugees not engaged in 'useful courses of study or training' for a future occupation which, inter alia, 'was most likely to procure their entry to Palestine [Harris was an active Zionist] or any overseas country at the end of the war'. It was run by expert staff 'with comradely and friendly firmness'; the children were 'well-mannered, courteous and reliably efficient'; those with Jewish foster parents lukewarm towards things Jewish, or evacuated to Christian billets, would be encouraged to strengthen their attachment to Judaism and Jewish traditions. He reassured Morris Feinmann that the children who had arrived recently from Heaton Road and Cassel-Fox 'had settled down well in their new work and were obviously enjoying it'.[88]

This was not quite the case. While the 'Dutch Orphans' from Heaton Road certainly appear to have settled in, some of the boys from Cassel-Fox were more restive: a result, Dr Altmann believed, of 'outside influences [from] relatives in Manchester'.[89] Whether this had to do with the level of orthodoxy at Whittingehame, or with the attachment of Cassel-Fox boys to Manchester, some of the boys were returned to the hostel and the decision was taken to place no further pressure on the residents at Cassel-Fox.[90] At all events in December 1941 the Whittingehame Farm School announced its closure, on the grounds of the 'poor response' of the community to its advertised facilities; British Jewry, its Board of Governors believed, did 'not fully appreciate the benefit to Jewish youth of an agricultural life and training in a Jewish environment'.[91] After the school actually closed, early in 1942, the remaining Cassel-Fox boys presumably returned to Manchester, while the girls may well have taken up the offer of Hechalutz D'Anglia to take them on as members of a new Hachsharah.[92]

The reception of the Durch orphans proved to be Margaret Langdon's last work with the MJRC. Why is not clear. Certainly the work with children was far from complete. It may be that she had fallen out with her former protégée, Rae Barash, as powerful a woman as she was herself. At all events, as the 'orphans' settled in. She moved on to the WVS,[93] with whom she had first made contact in Wigan, and was asked in May 1940 to serve as secretary of the War Refugees Clothing Committee,[94] created under the chairmanship of Lord Derby to provide second-hand clothing to war refugees arriving at ports on the west coast between the Midlands and the Scottish border, with Ruth Rappaport, a close friend who had worked with her on the Refugee

Children's Committee, as her assistant. Her base was to be a car showroom at 230 Deansgate, and the three floors above it, offered to the committee by the architect and Jewish communal worker, Joseph Sunlight.[95]

The venture was a spectacular success.[96] Equipped only with requisitioned trestle tables, wall racks and an office with a desk and chair donated by her father, Langdon used the local press, and Lord Derby's name, to appeal for clothing and for women volunteers. 'An ample store of clothing,' she wrote, 'may be a vital necessity for the region'.[97] She was 'trying to pile up reserves against an unknown future'. It was vital, according to Ruth Rappaport, that the depot 'was able to answer the demands just as soon as they are made'.[98] Within a few hours the depot had received 300 parcels and £140 in cash,[99] and had begun to send clothing to the refugees' ports of entry on the west coast; in the first months of the operation Langdon attracted twenty-six volunteers, two or three of them as drivers of the committee's collecting van. She remembered that, in the war-time absence of road signs, she created a road map of the city's pubs as an effective guide to her drivers. She ruled her volunteers with a road of iron, insisting on a regular rota: any volunteer who failed to attend for her allotted hours was immediately asked to leave, especially after the committee's work was extended during autumn 1940 to embrace evacuees and the victims of bombing in 'the more seriously raided coastal areas' of the north-west.[100] Being a volunteer, she wrote in one letter to the *Manchester Guardian,* 'calls mainly for common sense and a willingness to treat the job as a duty'.[101] By late January 1941, when the committee had already distributed over 144,000 garments, and its work for refugees, evacuees and air raid victims was said to be 'growing daily', she had become its 'regional clothing organiser',[102] with another Jewish volunteer, Mrs Evelyn Harris as her deputy. It was Harris who found a way of dealing with the seriously old-fashioned items which appeared amongst the donations: first placed on a shelf marked 'Impossibilities and Funnyosities', they were then sold off, in the absence of takers, to the rag and bone men.

Amongst their consumers were refugees from the Channel Islands, who began to arrive in Britain in late June 1940, and many of whom were billeted in Manchester and the towns of south-east Lancashire.[103] One day, as Langdon remembered it, a smart, be-suited man appeared at 230 Deansgate with a cheque for £10,000, with which she was expected to purchase new clothing for the Channel Islanders. Taking over and fitting out an adjacent building, Langdon obtained sample garments and prices from firms recommended by the Manchester Chamber of Commerce before beginning her purchases. She placed Ruth Rappaport, whom she had found to be 'an organiser of exceptional ability', in charge of the 'new garments'. It was their proud boast that they were always able to deliver clothing on the day they received a requisition.

While still working for the Clothing Committee, Langdon was asked to inspect hostels in the north-west housing those of the homeless considered by the authorities to be 'unbilletable': a boys' hostel in the Lune Valley in north Lancashire and a girls hostel on the Wirral. In the case of the former, sensing that something was wrong, she delivered new clothing into which the Master and Matron were expected to dress the children immediately. Returning half an hour later to retrieve a notebook she had left (deliberately) at the hostel, she found this had not been done. Subsequent enquiries showed that the Master and Matron had already been dismissed from another hostel for theft. In the case of the girls' hostel, run by capable wardens, she found that the girls had little to do in their spare time. Collecting toys and games from her south Manchester friends, she had them delivered in a WVS van.[104]

The story of the Dutch orphans is more than a narrative of heroism and salvation, although it is certainly that. It is equally a reminder of the tragic (and often permanent) dispersal and (more often than not) the destruction of German and Austrian Jewish families. Gerd Goldman's father had died at the hands of the Nazis in November 1939, his mother was in Switzerland, other relatives in New York and the Argentine. Heinz Hirschberg's divorced parents were both trapped in Berlin; a sister of his mother had arrived in New York from Berlin in the mid-1930s. Although all were legally allowed only temporary residence in Britain,[105] few of the Dutch Orphans had any hope of a family reunion. In a summary of the activities of the MJRC in June 1943, Morris Feinmann wrote: 'It is moving to speak to so many young people whose uppermost idea is to earn and save as much money as they can to enable them to help their parents when the war is over. One is bound to wonder how many of them have become orphans in the last year.'[106]

Notes

1 MG 15 May 1940: the expectation at this stage was that 20,000 Dutch and Belgian refugees would be allocated to Lancashire and Cheshire.
2 MG 15 and 16 May 1940.
3 MG 21, 24 and 27 May 1940.
4 MG 22 May 1940.
5 *Ibid.*
6 JRC EM 27 May 1940.
7 *Ibid.* and JRC Annual Report for 1939–40.
8 JRC EM 27 May 1940. The volunteers were Mrs Alec Jacobs, Mrs [Philip] Wigoder, Rae Barash, Mrs Dan Kostoris, Hettie Myrans, Mrs Horace Black, Abraham Moss, Manuel Cansino, Eli Fox, Lawrence Marks and Morris Feinmann.
9 JRC Annual Report for 1939–40; papers of the Zionist Federation: Annual Report of the South Manchester and District Women's Zionist Society (MCL M350/1/8/10).
10 The chairman was Hettie Myrans, the treasurer Mrs. Horace Black.
11 Ruth Schlesinger, 'The world I have lost' (2007), pp. 87–88.
12 *Ibid.*
13 *Ibid.*, pp. 89–90; after the MJRC had closed its doors, Baruch went on to aid Jewish refugees arriving from Egypt When she died in Manchester in her nineties, a funeral oration was read by Walli Maier, a refugee who had first met her in Rae Barash's house in the early 1930s.

14 Supposedly to confirm her 'Aryan status', Eichmann had asked Mrs Wijsmuller to remove her gloves and show her hands, then to remove her shoes, raise her skirt and walk around the room. He then addressed her: 'So pure Aryan and yet so completely crazy' (Yad Vashem Archive M-31/0266).

15 Biographical information on Mrs Wijsmuller from the archives of Yad Vashem, kindly provided by Mr Solly Kaplinski; Barry Turner, *And the Policeman Smiled: 10,000 Children Escape from Nazi Europe* (London 1990), pp. 40–42, 101–102; Sir Martin Gilbert, *The Holocaust: A Jewish Tragedy* (London 1986), p. 120.

16 Turner, *And the Policeman Smiled*, p. 101.

17 Taped author interview with Harry Jacobi (the name which Heinz Hirschberg subsequently assumed) at his home in London, 28 November 2003 (hereafter Harry Jacobi interview).

18 Harry Jacobi interview; taped interview of Hans Robert Levy by Laura Silcock at his home in Brighton 23 January 2004 (hereafter Hans Levy interview).

19 Harry Jacobi interview.

20 Taped interview with Margaret Langdon in 1978 by an unknown interviewer and now in the possession of Mr Louis Rappaport (hereafter Margaret Langdon interview). Only the first of two tapes is complete. On the second tape, the greater part of Margaret Langdon's memories of the Delamere Home appear to have been deleted. Margaret Langdon's memory of these events (in 1978) is that the Home Office had called the Lord Mayor and the Lord Mayor had called her at 6.45a.m. on the morning of the children's arrival in Wigan.

21 They included a Mrs de Groot, a clerk from the refugee office in Amsterdam and Louis Springer, the 'wealthy director' of a textile firm in Amsterdam who 'had to leave everything'. According to Hans Levy, some families who arrived too late or who could not be fitted in were left on the dockside (Hans Levy interview).

22 After the sailing of the *Bodegraven*, Mrs Wijsmuller continued her work for persecuted Jewry by smuggling Jews (and British soldiers) into neutral Spain and Switzerland. Following the war, she was honoured for her work in France, Holland, Germany and Britain, where a lunch in her honour was held at the House of Commons (MJRC Undated cutting MCL M533/26/2). In 1966 she received recognition from Yad Vashem as one of the 'Righteous Among the Nations'. In 1961 she was a witness at Eichmann's trial in Jerusalem. Throughout her life she maintained contact with the 'Dutch Orphans': Heinz Hirschberg (Harry Jacobi) often visited her in Holland and she was a guest at his wedding at the London Progressive Synagogue. On her death in Holland on 30 August 1978, aged 82, Hirschberg wrote an obituary which was published in the *Jewish Chronicle*.

23 MG 20 May 1940.

24 Autobiographical notes by Hans Levy, Imperial War Museum, London.

25 *Ibid.*; Hans Levy interview.

26 MG 20 May 1940.

27 MG 23 May 1940; Hans Levy autobiographical notes.

28 Harry Jacobi interview.

29 *Wigan Examiner* (hereafter WE) 23 May 1940.

30 MG 9 August 1940, 22 May 1941: letters to the editor from J.F.S. Ross.

31 WE 25 May 1940.

32 Margaret Langdon interview.

33 WE 25 May 1940. Rabbi Casper was inaugurated as minister of the Higher Broughton Synagogue in July 1939. He left the synagogue in February 1942 to become a Chaplain to the Forces (JC 7 July 1939, 6 February 1942).

34 *Ibid.*

35 Margaret Langdon interview.

36 Hans Levy autobiographical notes.

37 Hans Levy interview; Hans Levy autobiographical notes: a few children are said to have remained in Wigan (information from Mrs Ruth McKinnon).

38 WE 1 June 1940.

39 *Wigan Observer* 6 July 1940.

40 The home was created by members of the Jewish community shortly after the First World War in Lymm, a village some twelve miles south of Manchester. Amongst those now placed there was Mr Goestriker, widow of the businessman who died on the *Bodegraven,* and her 18-month old child.

41 MJRC EM 14 November 1941.

42 Annual Report of the South Manchester and District Women's Zionist Society for 1940–41 (MCL M350/1/8/10).

43 Doris Angel interview.

44 It made little sense for the two new hostels to be managed by a committee responsible to the Jewish Representative Council, while all other refugee work, including the welfare of the children in Heaton Road, was in the capable hands of the MJRC.

45 MJRC 14 November, 4 December 1941. The MJRC had financial help in this regard from the RCM at Bloomsbury House (MJRC RCM EM 17 February 1942) The narrative of reorganisation given here may be a simplification. It is possible that the Jewish War Refugees Committee co-existed with the MJRC for much longer, in some way dividing their remit. Ruth McGuiness, who entered the hostel at 42 Heaton Road in 1948 remembers Elja Baruch as 'superintendent' of both that hostel and 9 Wilmslow Road (Schlesinger, 'The World I have Lost', pp. 87–89).

46 MJRC EC 3 February 1942. For the death of Mark Rubin MSB AGM 21 June 1939: he had been a long-serving member of the Manchester Shechita Board. There is some confusion in the records relating to the address of the house on Wilmslow Road. In the minutes of the MJRC it becomes number '13' (MJRC EM 3 February 1942).

47 MJRC EC 7 May, 3 June 1942. Following the death of Ettie Myrans in May 1942, 42 Heaton Road became officially 'Ettie Myrans House' (MJRC EM 7 May, 3 June 1942). Of the Ettie Myrans Memorial Fund, which had raised £120 by June 1942, £100 was set aside 'to assist necessitous refugees' (MJRC EM 3 June 1942).

48 MJRC Correspondence: Rae Barash to Mrs Philip Gross, Welfare Department, Bloomsbury House, 4 November 1942.

49 MJRC EC 30 September 1942: the hostel would be ready 'in the next few weeks'.

50 Schlesinger, 'The World I Have Lost', p. 71.

51 MJRC Letter from Dr Alexander Altmann to Rae Barash, 18 February 1941 (MCL M533/25/33).

52 MJRC [Rae Barash] to Dr Altmann, 25 February 1941.

53 Harry Jacobi interview; Hans Levy interview: the collection includes a certificate from the West Didsbury Hebrew Class dated March 1941 which records that Hans had received excellent grades in rabbinics, that he was sixth in the class and a steady worker.

54 MJRC EC 17 November 1942,

55 Harry Jacobi interview. According to Harry Jacobi, Rae Barash secured Alexander's release from internment in Belfast to become the hostel housefather. A friend of Hugo Koeditz during his internment, and of Hanna Siederer afterwards, he was one of the two witnesses at their wedding in Manchester on 13 March 1942. On one occasion in December 1941 he took six of the boys from the Wilmslow Road hostel to

a meeting of Young Austria (Behrend, 'Autobiography', pp. 88–89).

56 Harry Jacobi interview.

57 *Ibid.*

58 Transcript in MJRC.

59 Harry Jacobi interview.

60 Hans Levy interview.

61 Letter from Hans Levy to Laura Silcock 16 March 2004, in the possession of the Centre for Jewish Studies, University of Manchester.

62 Harry Jacobi interview.

63 Schlesinger, 'The World I Have Lost', p. 79.

64 *Ibid.*

65 Hans Levy interview.

66 Hans Levy autobiographical notes; e-mail correspondence between Hans Levy and Laura Silcock 15 March 2004.

67 MJRC Correspondence (MCL M533/25/25): Leslie Prince at Bloomsbury House to Rae Barash 26 April 1943.

68 Harry Jacobi interview.

69 Information from Mrs Ruth McKinnon (née Schlesinger), who spent some time at 42 Heaton Road when her mother, Charlotte Schlesinger, worked out of Manchester as a domestic servant.

70 Hans Levy autobiographical notes.

71 MJRC M533/10/1/1: RCM Welfare Report on Gerd Goldemann [*sic*], 24 September 1944.

72 Harry Jacobi interview; MJRC: Case Papers of Heinz Martin Hirschberg (MCL M533/10/2).

73 Letters in the possession of Harry Jacobi from A. and S. Judge, 21 February 1942, and the Works Manager of Grosvenor Garage, 19 September 1945. Copies at the Centre for Jewish Studies, University of Manchester.

74 Hans Levy autobiographical notes; Hans Levy interview; Harry Jacobi interview.

75 Harry Jacobi interview.

76 *Ibid.*

77 Notes of an interview with his daughter, Audrey Jones, then Lord Mayor of Manchester 20 January 2004. Audrey's only complaint was of the way in which the refugees, once they had found their feet in Manchester, 'no longer wanted to know her'; JC 22 August 2003.

78 Hans Levy interview.

79 Hirschfield stayed for a time with the Burton family in Withington, but returned to the hostel when he found the anti-German taunts of their son intolerable (Harry Jacobi interview).

80 *Ibid.*; letter of refusal, which makes no mention of the cause, in his possession from the RAF Section, Combined Recruiting Centre, Dover Street, Manchester, date 4 February 1944.

81 Hans Levy interview.

82 Hans Levy interview: Red Cross messages from Salomon Levy to Hans and Oskar Levy 18 June 1942 and 25 July 1942; from Lina Kleeblatt and Elsbeth Levy to Hans and Oskar Levy 4 March 1943. Elsbeth Levy survived Theresienstadt, Auschwitz and slave labour to be reunited with her brothers after the war. The Levy brothers left the Wilmslow Road hostel for private accommodation in 1948. Both were subsequently successful businessmen, Oskar (later Oscar Lawson) as managing-director of his own market-gardening company in Rugby, Hans as a machine engraver and subsequently

as manager of branches of True Form Shoes. In 1949 he married Elfrida Gainsboro and moved with her to Watford. In 1972 they settled in Brighton, where Hans is an active member of the Brighton Synagogue. Heinz Hirschberg (now Harry Jacobi), after being refused entry to the RAF on psychological grounds, went on in 1945 to serve in the Jewish Brigade and in the British Army. In 1961, after several adventures in the business world, and a belated return to education, he became rabbi of the Liberal Synagogue in Southgate. At the time of his interview in 2003 he was part-time minister of a Liberal congregation in Amersham, vice-president of the Union of Liberal and Progressive Synagogues, and Senior Dayan of its Beth Din. He kept in contact with Mrs Wijsmuller, whom he often visited in Holland and who attended his wedding in London. In 1978 he wrote her obituary for the Jewish Chronicle (JC 29 September 1978).

42 Heaton Road was given up as a hostel in 1950 and the girls moved in with the boys at 9 Wilmslow Road. The Wilmslow Road hostel was passed to Siegfried Alexander and Martha Strauss for use, under the supervision of the MJRC, as a self-financing lodging house (renamed Dunwood House and re-numbered as 401 Wilmslow Road) for refugees, Holocaust survivors and other Jewish children in need of accommodation. It finally closed late in 1954, when the CBF gave Alexander and Strauss £200 each as compensation for the ending of their link with the MJRC and in appreciation of their services (Jacob Papers in MCL M102/2/1 and M102/2/3; information from Mrs. Ruth McGuiness, who, as Ruth Schlesinger, was moved into 42 Heaton Road hostel after her mother, a refugee, had been certified blind, and later moved to Wilmslow Road hostel; letters from the CBF to Siegfried Alexander and Martha Strauss 16 and 23 November 1954, 7 January 1955 in the possession of the author). Mr and Mrs Alexander, the 'houseparents' at the Wilmslow Road hostel, separated soon after the war. After the closure of Dunwood House in 1954 Siegfried became a cartoonist for a British newspaper before returning to Berlin in the 1960s. Erna Alexander emigrated to the United States; Martha Strauss bought a house for herself and Kurt in Withington, where she died in October 1958. Her son, Kurt, became an engineer and emigrated to the United States.

Bodegraven child refugees other than those named in the text included Elfrida Berger, from Vienna, who in later life became secretary to the radio talent-show presenter, Carol Leavis; Eva Stravinsky, who while at the girls' hostel attended Levenshulme High School and later married the Manchester music teacher, Aubrey Black; two Germans, David Werner and Wilhelm Flehner; Ernst Growald, who now lives in San Paolo, Brazil; Rosa Schneinmann (now Rosa Treibach), who also attended Levenshulme High School and now lives in the United States, and her brother, Feodor; later a professor of science at Salford University; Ernst Weinberg, who became a dentist and emigrated to the United States; and eight others of whom no information is currently available: Ya'acov Fiedler, Ilse Wertheimer, Alfred ('Bodo') Saloman, and (less probably) Ruth and Inga Adametz and Raisie and Miriam Shapiro.

Adults who escaped on the *Bodegraven* and who are not named in the text included Lenne Gerd Badman, born in Frankfurt on 5 June 1924, who on arrival in Manchester lived at 2 Hayfield Street, Broughton, and who later settled in London; Elias Moos, born on 5 January 1866, who also lived at 2 Hayfield Road; Rachel Badman, born on 29 October 1862, who on arrival in Manchester lived at 108 Bignor Street, Cheetham Hill; Mrs. De Groot, who had been a clerk with the Jewish Refugee Committee in Amsterdam; Louis Springer, in 1940 the director of a Dutch textile firm; and Mrs Goestriker, wife of the antiques dealer who died on the *Bodesgraven*, and who in 1940 was taken with her child to the Home for [Jewish] Mothers and Babies in Lymm.

83 Hans Levy autobiographical notes; Hans Levy interview.

84 Hans Levy autobiographical notes.

85 Harry Jacobi interview.

86 MJRC EC 28 August 1941; MJRC Correspondence: Lucien Harris to Morris Feinmann 23 September 1941.

87 *Ibid.*

88 *Ibid.*

89 MJRC EC 28 October 1941.

90 *Ibid.*

91 MJRC EC 12 December 1941; JC 6 February 1942.

92 MJRC EC 12 December 1941.

93 The WVS was set up in 1938 by Stella, Marchioness of Reading, at the request of the Home Office. Designed at first to assist the ARP, it rapidly expanded to include such other tasks as the collection and distribution of clothing. 'In its national system of stores, depots and dumps it held the major part of the country's gift clothing for emergency issue' (Angus Calder, *The People's War: Britain 1939–1945* (London 1969), pp. 194–195).

94 The Clothing Committee was made up in the first instance of Lord Derby (chairman); Mrs Harold Baerlein of Bowdon (honorary secretary), the assistant regional organiser of WVS services; Sir Christopher Needham (treasurer); Lady Howarth; Lady Burrows; a Miss Scowby; and Miss D. Foster Jeffreys, formerly organising secretary of the Electrical Association for War and then regional organiser of the WVS (MCN 25 May 1940).

95 Margaret Langdon interview; it was probably her work for the WVS which caused Langdon to resign from her role on the RCM.

96 The next three paragraphs are based on the 1978 Margaret Langdon interview, except where otherwise indicated.

97 MCN 8 June 1940.

98 MCN 6 July 1940. Rappaport herself later wrote a letter of appeal to the MCN (MCN 14 September 1940).

99 MCN 1 June 1940.

100 MG 6 September, 2 and 9 October 1940.

101 MG 9 October 1940.

102 MG 25 and 29 January 1941.

103 This work does not embrace refugees from the Channel Islands, who, at some time before 1944 set up a Manchester and District Channel Islands Society. In September 1944 the Society staged an 'entertainment' by children from the Channel Islands for their 'friends and relatives' at Dale Street Methodist Church in Miles Platting, in east Manchester (MCN 29 September 1944).

104 Margaret Langdon received an MBE and the Silver Medal of the American Red Cross for her work with the WVS. After the war, while remaining active at the Delamere Home, she continued her interest in refugees, working with local committees which in 1956 brought Jewish refugees to Britain from Egypt and Hungary. Between 1956 and 1959 she served on the National Insurance Tribunal of the Ministry of Pensions. In 1962, she was given an honorary MA by the University of Manchester, speaking at the presentation of the link between practical social work and academic theory. In the same year she received the Henrietta Szold Award from the Henrietta Szold Foundation, which included her first visit to Israel, which won her admiration for its work with recently arrived Moroccan Jews. She retired from active work at the Delamere Home in 1975.

105 On the RCM's Report forms, all young people were asked to name the country to which they intended to travel after the war: for Gerd Goldman, this was the Argentine.

106 MJRC: report of the activities of the MJRC for June 1943 (MCL M533/1/1/2/11). According to Margaret Langdon (Margaret Langdon interview), the labels sewed into the children's clothing by Mrs Wijsmuller made it possible to reunite a few of the 'orphans' with relatives in Britain, the USA, South Africa and South America.

22

Pacifism and rescue: the case of
Lionel Cowan

Already in this book we have met many 'exceptional people': people, that is, who went far beyond the ordinary bounds of compassion to concern themselves with those with whom, for the most part, they had no close personal ties. They include the volunteers who worked for the Jewish, Quaker and Rotarian refugee committees. In a paper delivered in 1944 Rae Barash posed the question of why volunteers like herself had committed themselves to work with refugees. She answered: 'My own reason as a Jewess: "There but for the grace of God" ... [but] the reason for all of us, whatever our belief, Refugees matter not only to themselves but to us all – economically, politically (though I am not dwelling on these aspects as they are covered by experts ...) but they also matter as human beings – to themselves but also to all other human beings.'[1]

A Quaker, while not disagreeing, might have added as a motive 'the imperatives of pacifism'. For most members of such organisations as the Peace Pledge Union (PPU), the International Voluntary Service for Peace, and the Fellowship of Reconciliation, as for the Quakers, Pacifism represented rather more than a negative attitude to war. It consisted also of what one former PPU activist in Manchester described as 'the application of non-violent methods to every field of human relationships', with the object of fomenting a 'social revolution' which would generate 'a society in which war [was] unthinkable because war and its progenitors – ignorance, oppression, hate and fear – have no place in it'.[2] Opposition to armed conflict went hand in hand with humanitarian effort on behalf of the oppressed, and on behalf of the victims of war.

From February 1939 the Manchester branch of the Women's International League for Peace and Freedom, the largest Manchester body of women pacifists, perhaps 600-strong by 1939, taking a lead from their national headquarters, began to seek out placements for Czech Jewish women seeking positions as domestic servants. The third, and the only one of whom any record remains, was Erna Fischl, an 'unorthodox Jewess', according to a press report, and a tailoress by training, who was found a post with a family in Dickenson Road, Longsight.[3]

Another pacifist, Derek Senior, a twenty-eight year-old staff reporter on the *Manchester Guardian* brought together a number of his fellow journalists 'and their friends', to acquire a house at 1 School Lane, on the edge of Didsbury village, to accommodate 'four or five' Czech refugee journalists 'in decent comfort'. Following a successful appeal in the press for 'mattresses, blankets, linen, carpets, easy chairs, cupboards, a dining table and wardrobes', the hostel opened in October 1939 with Senior as its manager. It is not clear what happened to it when, at his tribunal in August 1940, he was registered as a Conscientious Objector only on the typically perverse condition (he mentioned his hostel at the tribunal) that he undertook farm work.[4]

A leading Manchester proponent of pacifism was Lionel Cowan, a Manchester Jew who in 1929 was converted to the cause at a meeting he attended at the Friends Meeting House in Mount Street on the evils of war: for him, pacifism 'deepened into a positive philosophy of daily life'.[5] His subsequent efforts on behalf of refugees may be seen in part as a result of his reading of the pacifist creed, an unusual ideology for a man brought up in an orthodox Jewish home; in part as a result of his own background in a family of immigrant (and perhaps refugee) origin; in part as the consequence of the personal links he established in the early 1930s, largely through the peace movement, with Jewish families in Nazi Germany. Most of all, however, they were the outcome of an emotional empathy with the suffering which had triggered his pacifism, which informed his Judaism and which transformed the influences at work on him into determined action.

The context of his 'absolutist' pacifism was a broader peace movement which, beginning with a revulsion against the horrors of the First World War and a determination to prevent their recurrence, was given added momentum by Fascist aggression and probably reached the peak of its popular support in Britain between spring 1936 and the German occupation of Austria in March 1938. A Manchester and Salford Joint Peace Committee, formed in May 1936, constituted, it was said, 'a united front of every shade of peace opinion in the city', with representatives from ten separate organisations,[6] including local branches of such major peace movements as the Society of Friends, the Fellowship of Reconciliation (FoR), the International Women's League of Peace and Freedom (WILPF),[7] the Peace Pledge Union (PPU),[8] the International Voluntary Service for Peace (IVSP),[9] the War Resistors International and the 'Peace Fellowships' of the Congregationalist, Methodist, Baptist and Anglican communions. Although anecdotal evidence suggests that all were growing in size during 1937, when Manchester institutions could be seen as central to the national peace movement, precise estimates of their constituencies are rare: in October 1937 Muter Wilson, secretary of the Manchester branch of WILPF, put the total number of its members at 600.[10]

During 1937–38 Manchester could be spoken of by its Lord Mayor, the Labour politician Joseph Toole, as 'a leader in the movement towards peace'. During his mayoralty he carried a Manchester Manifesto for Peace, of which he had been the chief author, to meetings in France, Czechoslovakia and the

United States.[11] At the Friends Meeting House in Mount Street, the epicentre of Manchester pacifism, where many organisations dedicated to peace held their meetings, a separate Quaker Peace Week was staged at the end of September 1937.[12] In January 1938, when the Manchester PPU assumed responsibility for the Union throughout the north of England, a movement was said to be afoot for the opening of a peace bookshop in the city.[13] The more dedicated pacifists were active on every organisational front. Maude Brayshaw, a Quaker 'by convincement' rather than birthright, a member of the Friends' Wilmslow meeting and from 1936 deputy clerk to the Society in Britain, was active also in the PPU, the Fellowship of Reconciliation and WILPF, of which she was a member of both the Manchester and the national executive.[14]

There were many more local bodies, some of them ephemeral. The 'Area Council' of the International Peace Campaign, which, under the chairmanship of Leonard Behrens, organised Manchester's 'Peace Week' in early July 1937, was said to represent 114 organisations in Manchester and Salford.[15] They included a small 'Peace Group' formed in 1936 at the Union Chapel of the Baptist communion on Oxford Road, next to the Manchester Royal Infirmary, by Frank Robinson, one of the worshippers, with the support of the minister, Revd George Evans. Between six and twelve of the chapel-goers met fortnightly to hear visiting speakers, mount fund-raising events and propagate the cause of peace. One regular speaker at Union Chapel was Lionel Cowan.[16]

Cowan's upbringing was in many ways conventionally Jewish. The son of Morris Cohen,[17] a Jewish bricklayer, and his wife Phyllis ('Polly'), both British-born but from families of probable Polish origin, Cowan was born (in 1905) and brought up in one of the poorer segments of Manchester's Jewish Quarter. His mother cooked kosher meals and sang Yiddish songs. From the age of nine Cowan was sent to learn Hebrew at the *cheder* of a local *rebbe*, whose tiny *stiebl* in Elizabeth Street his parents attended. He was drawn into the social life and leisure pursuits of the Jewish mainstream. He attended those local elementary and secondary schools in north Manchester favoured by Jewish families. In 1915, with his elder brother, and like most young working-class Jews, he joined the communal cadet force, the Manchester Battalion of the Jewish Lads Brigade (JLB): he attended the Brigade's annual summer camps, and 'for four nights out of five' attended its youth centre, the Grove House Lads Club. His early life centred, too, on what had become the more informal centres of north Manchester Jewry: Manley Park, only ten minutes walk from his home, 'where you could watch the old gentlemen … playing bowls [and] the young ladies playing tennis and … even go in the library if you were very quiet and look at the magazines', and Heaton Park, a short tram-ride away, with its bandstand and ornamental boating lake, where by the time of the First World War Jewish families went on Sundays to see and be seen by their neighbours.[18]

As a teenager, however, Lionel largely abandoned the religious beliefs and observances to which his parents had been, at all events, only loosely and erratically committed. His link with Judaism thereafter amounted only to the occasional attendance at the synagogue on the High Holydays. When, in 1918, the time came for his barmitzvah, he remembers that he 'wasn't particularly keen. It was still wartime, my mother wasn't particularly pushing and it went by default.' From then on, while never losing pride in his identity as a Jew, he abandoned not only Jewish religious observance, but, for many years, his links with Jewish communal organisations. As an apprentice compositor from 1923 with a non-Jewish printing firm, Taylor Garnett Evans, in Cheetham Hill he rapidly distanced himself from Sabbath observance, synagogue attendance and Jewish dietary laws. His links with his extended Jewish family 'sort of slipped into the background' and he 'began to enjoy' the wider milieu of working-class Manchester. He attended classes and made close non-Jewish friends at the Manchester College of Technology. He was taken by his 'left-leaning' workmates at Taylor Garnett Evans to Saturday afternoon football matches, to Gilbert and Sullivan operas, in which some of them took part, and to public meetings at which he was expected 'to absorb what they believed was the true way of politics'.[19] He remembers that at his brother's wedding at the Manchester Great Synagogue in 1928 he and his mother, who had by then separated from her husband, 'were isolated – nobody wanted to talk to us and I remember we got out as quickly as we could'.[20] When his father died later that same year, Cowan knew nothing of Jewish funeral customs, had 'no idea' how to organise the Shiva, and could barely 'struggle through the Kaddish'.[21]

What distinguished Cowan from hundreds of other children of Jewish immigrants who in the 1920s, whether through apathy or conviction, were distancing themselves from the *Yiddishkeit* of their parents, was his choice of pacifism, rather than Socialism, as his alternative. For most of the others the preference was for membership of the youth movements of the political Left, particularly the Young Communist League, of which a Cheetham branch was in existence by 1922. Cowan too was attracted to the Left. He remembers that with the General Strike, which found solid support from his fellow workers, he 'began to realise that politics was a very important part of life'. As his interest in the Jewish Lads Brigade 'began gradually to fade', he took to attending Labour Party meetings and to furthering his political education through the *Daily Herald*, the *Manchester Guardian* and *The New Statesman and Nation*.[22]

The major turning point in his political development, however, as 'internationalism, the Labour Party, politics, peace and war' had all begun to 'move around in [his] head', was his attendance in 1929 of an exhibition at the Friends Meeting House on 'the wicked side of war, both economically … socially and internationally'. 'It dawned on me', he later remembered, 'that I must take up some sort of position. I decided I must work for peace.'[23] It was for this reason that a year later, now working as a compositor in the advertising department of the Renold and Coventry Chain Company Limited[24] (otherwise Renold Chains), then in Burnage, he made contact with International Tramping Tours (ITT), a pacifist body set up in 1930 by Frank Happold, a

Quaker professor at the University of Leeds, and intended to promote peace by enabling young people of different nations, 'at minimum cost ... to travel, to unite, to live together, to get to know each other, to sing each other's songs, and appreciate that they're human beings together'.[25] He signed up in Leeds for ITT's first tour of the Rhineland, and on his return, in October 1931, he joined the organising committee of a new branch of ITT in Manchester which, over the next three or four years, mounted a series of walking tours in Britain and Europe: by 1935 he had become one of their regular leaders.[26]

The decision of the government to rearm, which Cowan witnessed at first hand at Renold Chains (the company, he believed, was saved from ruin by re-armament) drew him further into what he saw as the 'local peace movement'. He joined the FoR and the IVSP. He was amongst the signatories in 1934 of Canon 'Dick' Sheppard's Peace Pledge. In the mid-1930s, as the pace of re-armament increased, he was one of those who brought together members of the Labour and Communist Parties, the ILP and the Society of Friends in an informal pacifist grouping which by January 1937 at the latest had become the South Manchester Peace Council (SMPC), under the chairmanship of Canon Thomas Shimwell, the rector of St Crispin's Church in Moss Side.[27] Itself a local branch of the National Peace Council, the aim of the SMPC was 'to co-ordinate [the] activity of all peace-minded groups' in the South Manchester district, bringing together, according to Cowan, 'branches of the League of Nation Union, churches, political parties, co-operative guilds [and] trade unions' for protests against rearmament, poster parades, peace meetings, and the lobbying of local councillors in the cause of peace.[28] It was Cowan's first campaigning group: 'we concocted pamphlets,' he remem-bered, 'we had poster parades and ... I had my first experience of appearing in public, and feeling very strange at being projected into public view.' By 1938, after Cowan had apparently succeeded Shimwell as chairman of the SMPC,[29] he had been 'pressed' by his colleagues into speaking regularly on the Council's behalf to peace groups, church groups and to the public from platforms in Manchester's 'speakers' corner' in Platt Fields.[30]

In February 1937, as the PPU's headquarters in London set about organ-ising signatories to the peace pledge throughout the country into effective campaigning groups, Cowan was called upon to create a Fallowfield PPU, of which he then became 'group leader' and for which he was soon equally active as a speaker and propagandist.[31] During April 1937 its fifteen founder members were busy with open-air meetings, the canvassing of signatories and street sales of the PPU's journal, *Peace News*.[32] In November 1937 Cowan rep-resented the group at a mass meeting in Stevenson Square organised by the Manchester Anti-War Council, the peace arm of the CPGB in Manchester, to protest against Japanese aggression in China, to press the government to adopt a less 'accommodating' attitude and to orchestrate a boycott of Japanese goods.[33] By May 1938 an average of fifty copies of *Peace News* were being sold each week at the street corners, churches, offices and workshops of Fallowfield, a largely lower middle-class residential area some four miles south of the city centre.[34] By October 1938 the group, in Cowan's view, was 'bursting with energy, spreading leaflets like snow, shouting its message on the streets, telling its friends everywhere': Fallowfield was, he believed, gradually becoming 'PPU-conscious'.[35]

Cowan's effective withdrawal from the orthodox mainstream of Manchester Jewry made it that much easier for him to pursue a pacifist ideology not favoured by traditional Judaism. At the time of Manchester's Peace Week, the community's leading orthodox rabbi, Dr S.M. Lehrmann of the Higher Broughton Synagogue,[36] had gone out of his way to express the solidarity of local Jewry with those fighting the cause of peace. On 28 June 1937 the *Manchester Guardian* announced that a 'peace service' was to be held at Lehrmann's synagogue on 10 July, in the middle of Peace Week, to which Christian ministers would be invited.[37] Lehrmann himself laid out the Jewish position in a long letter to the *Guardian* on 7 July in which he explained 'how wholeheartedly we Jews of Manchester and Salford join in the [peace] campaign'. 'Every true Jew', he wrote, nursed 'a total abhorrence of war'. Citing a number of particular Jewish contributions to the cause of European peace – from Dr. Zamendof, the inventor of Esperanto, to the 'Jew of Chicago' who was the prime mover of the Kellogg Pact – he concluded that a 'vision of peace' was 'perhaps one of the greatest contributions of Israel ... to the treasury of civilisation'.[38]

For Lehrmann, the service, which was, in fact, attended by 'a number of Christian ministers and workers', including Canon Shimwell of the SMPC, served several purposes: it was at once a token of the Jewish love of peace, a symptom of local Jewry's acceptance by Christian society and a gesture of Jewish-Christian solidarity in the face of Fascism. It was, he told the congregation, 'a manifestation of the goodwill and harmony which prevail between all sections in Manchester and Salford', a 'trenchant protest against the intolerance and social bigotry which have emptied Nazi Germany of all reason and justice ... Nothing could be more encouraging to those suffering in other lands for a liberty no longer theirs than to learn of such a sweeping away of barriers as this service exemplified.' The 'suffering and patience' of Israel down the years served as an inspiration to Jews 'to stand firm for humanitarian ideals and be prepared to suffer for them'. They 'would always be on the side of those who sought to extricate the world from the present wreckage' and rebuild it, 'not on 'the shifting sands of greed and selfishness, but on the firm foundations of law and righteousness'. 'Years would elapse', however, 'before the whole world renounced war.'[39]

For Jewish pacifists like Cowan, who sought the complete renunciation of war (it was, he wrote later, 'mutual mass murder'),[40] and as a matter of urgency, the sting was in the tail of such sentiments. Orthodox Jewry had itself not 'renounced' war: while preferring the settlement of international dispute (the 'present wreckage') by diplomacy, and certainly committed to a peaceful world and to 'law and righteousness', the orthodox rabbinical leadership saw war as, in the last resort, a necessary safeguard against just those kinds of injustice on which Lehrmann had placed emphasis. Unlike Cowan, who no longer felt bound by their teaching, Orthodox commentators in

Britain, including Chief Rabbi J.H. Hertz, interpreted Judaism as committed to peace rather than to pacifism, a stance increasing fortified by the failure of diplomacy to halt the anti-Semitism of the Nazi regime.[41] For Cowan, even the worsening predicament of German Jewry was an insufficient justification of war.[42] He realised, however, that as a Jewish pacifist he was 'a rare bird'.[43]

In private correspondence, Rabbi Lehrman, while sympathising, 'as a friend and well-wisher', with Cowan's 'dilemma', praising the 'nobility' of his stand, and reiterating Judaism's condemnation of wars in general and his own 'staunch pacifism', declined to accept the idea of peace 'at any price'. Non-resistance might be justifiable, he wrote, in the case of an enemy 'likely to be won over by a policy of justice and sweet-reasonableness', but the Nazis were the implacable enemies of 'poor broken Jews'. He could not tell his fellow Jews 'not to crush our worst enemies in history'. 'If pride of race means anything to you,' he challenged Cowan, 'you will agree that there will be no idealism left in the world at all, if Jews the world over are exterminated'.[44]

Meantime, the prime function of Fallowfield PPU under Cowan's leadership during 1937–38 was to fulfil the wishes of the national PPU executive that 'a relentless pressure' be exerted on public opinion, 'forcing it to face the alternatives – re-armament or pacifism' and to dispel any notion that there might be some 'middle course'.[45] Never far from Cowan's mind, however, was what he described as 'the running sore' of the refugee problem.[46]

This was partly for personal reasons. On an ITT tour through Germany and Austria in 1932, Cowan had met a young German-Jewish woman, Ilse Maass, then acting as 'hostess' to an equivalent party organised from Berlin. On 24 December 1934, in the presence of Ilse's family, the couple married, first in the Town Hall of the Schoneberg district of Berlin, later under a *chuppah* in Ilse's parents' Berlin flat. It was through Ilse, who returned with him to Manchester, that Cowan now became fully aware of the desperation of German-Jewish families. 'By 1935,' he remembered, 'things in Germany were beginning to get really hot, and numbers of Ilse's friends, and some relatives, wanted to make contact with us ... because we represented the possibility of their getting out from difficult conditions ... So letters began to arrive [and] we began to prospect what possibilities there were for Ilse's brothers, and for her parents, to get out and come to England ... Some of the elderly relatives ... decided that they would stay because they had all their possessions, and their pensions and their roots ... [and because] they didn't believe it was going to be so dangerous for them'. By 1936, however, some of Ilse's younger friends and relatives had begun to visit the Cowans at their home in Edgeworth Road, Withington, 'either for interviews [with Manchester firms] or to prospect what should be done'. 'We began to get quite busy', Cowan remembered, finding 'ways and means' of getting Jewish families out of Germany.[47]

This included Cowan's mobilisation of his friends to find the work or the guarantees which might secure the entry of refugees. Ilse's brother-in-law was found work by relatives of Bill Allport, Cowan's colleague in the advertising department at Renold Chains.[48] The 'rich relative' of another colleague offered a guarantee and later a job to Walter Bendix, a brother of Ilse's sister-in-law, Eva Maass.[49] In 1936 Cowan himself put up the guarantee and offered the hospitality which brought Ilse's parents to Manchester. In 1937, using the Quakers as his intermediaries, he was able to arrange papers for Erich Treitel, a Jewish Socialist and a German contact of the ITT who had led the tour through Germany and Austria in 1932 of which Cowan had been a member. Treitel had earlier left Germany for Spain, only to be arrested by the Spanish authorities and put on a boat for Germany. However, he had 'got off the boat' in Italy, from where Cowan had arranged his rescue. Subsequently Cowan used £200 from a legacy of £900 left by his mother to arrange for the re-settlement of the Treitel family in South America.[50] In 1938, after Ilse's elder brother, Helmut (later Herbert), and his wife, Eva, had made several unsuccessful applications for entry, Cowan went in person to Whitehall, where he conducted a personal 'sit-in' on the steps of the Home Office until the necessary documents had been obtained.[51] After Kristallnacht, Cowan remembers, 'quite a bit' of his free time was taken up mediating on behalf of intending refugees with the Quaker and the Jewish refugee committees in Manchester, in both of which he had personal contacts.[52] Within the peace movement there were people 'providing money and doing things to get money, like coffee mornings and so on, in order to try to get refugees out of Germany, to go wherever they could get a visa'.[53]

Meantime, in his official capacity as chairman of the SMPC and group leader of the Fallowfield PPU he was already directing their members' attention to the victims of war. In January 1937 he was one of the SMPC executive which urged the British government and the League of Nations to do all in their power to evacuate the civilian population from Madrid.[54] In May 1938 he directed the attention of his members to the 'suffering folk ... already embroiled in the hell of war' in Spain and China.[55] Amongst the earliest activities of the Fallowfield group was 'collecting for Spanish Relief work ... [and] assisting in the adoption of at least one Basque child refugee': members were encouraged to take out regular subscriptions to the Spanish Relief Fund.[56] A year later all his members were subscribing to the Spanish and Chinese appeals.[57]

From early November 1938 he was speaking at group meetings of the fate of Czech, Polish and German-Jewish refugees. It 'wrings [the] heart to read of [the] sufferings of Czech and Polish and Jewish refugees', he told a meeting on 6 November. 'Can they be helped? Can they be protected?'[58] On 11 November he was reminding his members of such 'refugee victims of peace' as Niemoller, Taglus and von Ossietzley, and 'all the unknown who have suffered for peace and freedom'.[59] On 4 December he spoke of the appropriate response to the persecution of German Jewry. '[The] best. reply', he told his members, 'is help! Let [the] doors of Great Britain and [the] Empire be opened. Settle [the] Palestine problem by discussion and give [a] place to tortured Jewry in its national home.'[60]

Cowan was particularly incensed by what he saw as the ignominy of the British government in 'handing over [Czechoslovakia] on a plate' to Hitler.

At the end of March 1939 he was urging on the group the offer of practical support to 'Czech refugees'[61] housed in a hostel recently established by the Manchester Quakers (with support from the Czech Refugee Trust Fund) at 4a Palatine Road in Fallowfield. The offer followed an initiative by the Quaker Refugee Committee, which in February 1939, at the suggestion of Winifred Garnett, herself a PPU member, had opened negotiations with the Fallowfield PPU with a view to its 'taking charge' of the hostel.[62] In mid-March Sophie Bentata was delegated to contact the PPU with regard 'to the running of the hostel'.[63]

This the PPU apparently declined to do. Rather, under the auspices of a house management committee set up by the QRC, and chaired by Margery Wilson, the Fallowfield members took on a series of specific tasks. These included the establishment of 'a rota for social evenings, mending etc', the invitation of refugees into members' houses ('to get them into [a] home atmosphere'), the teaching of English, the organisation of rambles, and the offer of occasional gifts of cigarettes and other items. Amongst the hostel's 'urgent necessities', Cowan told his members, were a wireless set, gramophone records and copies of *Picture Post* and similar illustrated magazines.[64] It was help the hard-pressed Quakers were only too pleased to accept. In August 1939 Cowan reported that, with the support of PPU volunteers, the hostel was 'running well'; visitors were welcome.[65]

In his application for registration as a Conscientious Objector in November 1940, Cowan summarised his role in these activities in this way: '1933 on. Refugee work with the co-operation of my wife, including organising a hostel, teaching English, translating documents, making applications based on appeals from Germany, giving hospitality, guaranteeing for five refugees, subscriptions to many funds and individuals. Subscriptions, collections and clothing to Spanish, Chinese, Polish and Czech relief.'[66]

For the PPU the outbreak of war represented a severe test. In the light of Nazi aggression, the conspicuous creation of a British Home Front and the escalating persecution of German Jewry, could its members be relied upon to keep the pacifist faith? Lionel Cowan was in no doubt. 'Nothing can justify war', he told members of the Fallowfield group: the government must be urged to convene an international conference at which a new peace treaty would 'redraw frontiers by tearing up the vindictive Treaty of Versailles'. The group would pay its share towards the salary of a paid PPU organiser for peace.[67]

Meantime, it was important that members should not 'cut themselves off from the world': it was now their duty to engage in 'humanitarian pacifist work'. While never ceasing to campaign for peace, or to maintain their fellowship and morale, they could undertake voluntary work at unemployment centres, give blood, study First Aid, learn Esperanto or help conscientious objectors now likely to face 'the brunt of a cowardly attack'.[68] They could also continue their work for refugees: by taking in a 'foreign guest' over the summer; by collecting cash, food, clothes and medical aid for Spanish refugees; or by continuing their support for the Palatine Road hostel.[69] At all events, it was necessary for pacifists to plan ahead to see the country through the chaos which would follow the war.[70] He himself, while in November 1940 seeking registration as a Conscientious Objector, noted that he would 'continue to give voluntary service wherever I am able towards life, progress and the making of a better world'.[71]

Following the first night of the Manchester Blitz – 22 December 1940 – PPU members were directed by Cowan and others to work for those made homeless by the bombing and to offer their services as firewatchers at Manchester hospitals. 'I am sure pacifists can be trusted', he wrote, 'to be courageous, tolerant and kindly to all folks, whatever the future has in store for us'.[72] He himself organised a Pacifist Service Unit (PSU) which offered squads of pacifist firewatchers to the Duchess of York Hospital for Sick Babies at Burnage and the Hospital for Incurables at Mauldeth.[73] Following discussions with a suspicious management committee at Burnage, the hospital accepted Cowan's offer only 'on condition that each volunteer was British born'. When a refugee from Central Europe (the puppeteer Bruno Tublin) offered his services, however, Cowan and his squad were able to convince the hospital authorities, if only after protracted negotiations, of his good character and patriotic intentions.[74]

In spite of his own troubles – he was at first refused registration as a conscientious objector by the Manchester Tribunal, and, on the basis of a press report of the hearing, forced to resign from his post at Renold Chains[75] – Cowan continued throughout the war to work for the welfare of refugees and to speak on their behalf.

On 2 September 1939, the day before war was declared, he had moved with his wife Ilse from Edgeworth Road in Withington, the house from which he had conducted his PPU campaigns, to Dean Drive in Wilmslow, a Cheshire village some ten miles south of Manchester then rapidly developing into a dormitory for the Manchester middle-classes. At Edgeworth Road, he and Ilse had retained a loose connection with Judaism through their membership of the Withington Congregation of Spanish and Portuguese Jews, the major Sephardi synagogue in south Manchester, which Lionel had occasionally attended on the High Festivals.

In Wilmslow, cut off also from their PPU friends, Lionel remembered, 'we were pretty isolated, and when it came to the Jewish festivals, particularly … Rosh Hashanah and Yom Kippur, what did we have to do ? … We decided that to take part in any kind of religious activity in Manchester was not possible, due to the conditions of travel and you never know when the bombers were coming over … We knew there were a number of Jewish refugees in the area: we didn't know them or where they were, so we got on our bicycles, we started enquiring, and eventually we were able to get together about 20 to 25 people, who were mostly refugees in the area working as domestics, and we had one or two people, English people, who were prepared to help with the organisation.'[76] One refugee couple, Mr and Mrs Hans Weiniger, Cowan remembered, worked as housemaid and butler to the Liberal industrialist, Sir Noton Barclay and his wife, Adrienne;[77] other refugee women worked as servants in some of the larger houses of Wilmslow, Handforth, Cheadle Hulme, Alderley Edge and Prestbury.[78]

The remarkable 'Wilmslow and District Jewish Community' which arose in late 1940 out of this unlikely body of people lies beyond the parameters of this book. Suffice it to say that it represented Cowan's typical recognition of refugees as people in need of a safe community in which they might recreate their identities.

Notes

1 MJRC Notes for a paper delivered by Rae Barash (M533/27/26).
2 Lionel Cowan Papers deposited by Lionel's son Kenneth in the Working-Class Movement Library in Salford (hereafter Cowan Papers): article by Lionel Cowan, 'Pacifist Values in FSU Work', in the Annual Report of the Family Service Unit (FSU) 27 August 1987. Another collection of Lionel Cowan papers was deposited in the archives of Manchester Central Library (M599), distinguished in these footnotes as Cowan Papers (MCL).
3 MCN 4 February 1939.
4 MCN 23 February, 30 October 1939, 3 August 1940.
5 Cowan Papers (MCL M599/1/13): application for registration as a Conscientious Objector.
6 MG 7 June 1937, commenting upon the issue of its first annual report.
7 WILPF was founded in April 1915 as an attempt to stop the war. A Manchester branch, opened in the same year, had its headquarters in the late 1930s at 1 Princess Street, near the city centre. A founder member was the pacifist, feminist and Manchester City Councillor, Margaret Ashton, who as a conscientious objector during the First World War, had been branded a traitor and deprived of her seta on the Council. She was chairman of the branch from 1915 to 1922 and its president from 1922 until her death in 1937 (WC January 1929 (No. 134) and December 1937 (No. 231)). At a memorial service held at Manchester Cathedral in October 1937 the Dean of Manchester described her as 'the incarnation of all that was best and most distinctive in Manchester life' (MG 21 October 1937).
8 The Peace Pledge Union grew out of a letter sent to the press by Canon 'Dick' Sheppard, Rector of St Martin-in-the-Fields in central London. The Union was made up, at first very loosely, of those who had accepted Sheppard's invitation to send him a postcard in which they pledged themselves to join him in the renunciation of war. By the time of his death in October 1937, 140,000 had done so and the national membership was growing at a rate of 400 a week. Early in 1938 the Manchester PPU office assumed responsibility for the whole of the north of England.
9 A Manchester branch of the IVSP was in existence by the beginning of 1935, when a long description of its work was placed in a Manchester student journal, *The Serpent.* The aim defined by its constitution was 'to create a spirit of friendship and a constructive attitude towards peace among all peoples by giving practical help on the occasion of natural catastrophes, or by carrying out work of public utility'. It recruited volunteers who, provided with 'simple accommodation and food', and avoiding separation into 'national or linguistic groups', would undertake work of practical social value'. The hope was that by working with people 'who rarely hear Pacifist principles' they would give them 'a better impression of their national neighbours'.

Volunteers were paid expenses from the ISVP's funds (article by Maurice Schofield in *The Serpent: the Official Organ of the Manchester University Unions,* Vol. X1X, No. 3 (February 1935), pp. 62–63).

10   MG 9 October 1937.

11   MEN 1 June 1937.

12   MG 25 September 1937.

13   MG 3 January 1938.

14   MG 6 August 1943: a report of Brayshaw's appointment at the Friends House in London as the first woman clerk of the Society's Yearly Meeting. She was then also an elder of the Society and a member of the executive of the Meeting for Sufferings.

15   MG 12 October 1937, quoting a report on the Manchester Peace Week by the area council. The Peace Week in Manchester, held from 4 to 11 July 1937, was one of many being held that year all over the country as part of an international peace campaign. It included rallies, processions, exhibitions and a 'peace shop' at the junction of Deansgate and Blackfriars Street.

16   Pat Starkey, *I Will Not Fight: Conscientious Objectors and Pacifists in the North West during the Second World War* (Liverpool 1991), pp. 7–8.

17   He changed his surname to Cowan in about 1935 (letter from his son, Kenneth Cowan, to the author, 23 February 2006).

18   'The Life Story of Lionel Cowan', a typewritten transcript of interviews conducted with Lionel Cowan by his son Kenneth between 1977 and 1994, kindly made available to the author by Kenneth Cowan, pp. 1–19. The remainder of this biography, unless otherwise stated is based on this manuscript.

19   *Ibid.,* pp. 21–22.

20   *Ibid.,* p. 26.

21   *Ibid.,* pp. 28–29. Lionel's father left his mother some time before 1921 and, when his elder brother left home four years later, Lionel became solely responsible for supporting 'an ailing and neurotic woman' (undated [November 1940] statement of support by T.B. Waddicor to the tribunal hearing Cowan's conscientious objection (Cowan Papers MCL M599/1/19).

22   *Ibid.,* pp. 38–39.

23   *Ibid.,* p. 39. He was later to attribute his first movement towards pacifism to his reading about the horrors of the First World War. The Quaker influence on his thought is none the less clear. Mankind, he wrote, was 'a brotherhood under the Fatherhood of God': the flame that might be ignited by 'that spark of essential goodness in human beings' was 'smothered and extinguished' by war (application for registration as a Conscientious Objector, 29 November 1940: Cowan Papers (MCL M599/1/11).

24   Founded in Manchester by the Swiss engineer, Hans Renold.

25   *Ibid.* pp. 37–38; MG 22 October 1937.

26   Cowan, 'Life Story', p. 54. By autumn 1937, according to a report at its 'annual gathering' in Overton Hall, Matlock, ITT was organising visits by seventy international parties a year to different parts of Britain and Germany (MG 22 October 1937).

27   MG 7 January 1937.

28   Cowan Papers: Speech by Lionel Cowan to the Ladybarn Church Guild, 15 March 1937, explaining the role of the South Manchester Peace Council.

29   In Cowan, 'Life Story' he makes no mention of Shimwell, who is identified as chairman in several references in MG.

30   *Ibid.,* p. 54.

31   Cowan Papers: Circular letter from Lionel Cowan, February 1937, calling a meeting at St Aidan's Presbyterian Church in Fallowfield on 2 March 1937 to create the

Fallowfield PPU; circular from Lionel Cowan (n.d.) outlining the group's work since April 1937.

32   Cowan Papers: Circular from Lionel Cowan to members of the Fallowfield PPU n.d. [April–May 1937]. In 1937 Manchester City Council barred *Peace News* from the reading rooms of municipal libraries on the grounds that it provided a precedent for others intent on using local libraries for the distribution of political propaganda (MG 17 June 1937).

33   MG 11 November 1937.

34   Cowan Papers: circular from Lionel Cowan to Fallowfield PPU members, May 1938.

35   Cowan Papers: circulars from Lionel Cowan to Fallowfield PPU members, May and October 1938

36   Lehrmann had been minister at Higher Broughton since leaving Emmanuel College, Cambridge, where he had been the Tyrwhitt Scholar in Semitic Languages, in 1925. His departure from Manchester in March 1938 to become minister of the Greenbank Drive Synagogue in Liverpool was seen by one observer as 'a serious blow' to the religious life of Manchester Jewry (MG 7 March 1938).

37   MG 28 June, 3 July 1937.

38   MG 7 July 1937.

39   MG 12 July 1937.

40   JC 4 February 1940: letter from Lionel Cowan. As an absolutist pacifist, Cowan also rejected the right of the state to compel its citizens to undertake an alternative form of service in time of war (Cowan Papers (MCL 599/1/10).

41   MG 7 June 1940 reporting a speech by Hertz in which he declared that there was no basis in Judaism for exemption from military service on the grounds of conscientious objection: on the contrary, Judaism ranked 'defence of the country' as among the 'supreme duties' of every citizen. The JC denounced conscientious objection by Jews on 2 February 1940.

42   In Manchester, there were only a handful of Jewish Conscientious Objectors during the Second World War. Apart from Cowan, they included David Rebeiro, son of Emmanuel Rebeiro, a Manchester CO jailed during the First World War (SCR 7 February 1941); Louis Sukonic, an upholsterer living in Leicester Road, Higher Broughton, both of whose parents were Jewish, and whose father had arrived in Manchester from Russia in 1913, but who himself, he told his Tribunal, 'belonged to no religious body': he was 'not a practising Jew' and did not attend synagogue (Lancashire Tribunal for Conscientious Objectors (MCL M547/2/5) 22 January 1940); Nathan Rosenberg, a 'Jewish Deist' (MG 1 October 1940); Morris Rosner, a Jewish raincoat machinist, Esperantist and 'advocate of a world state' (MG 19 October 1940); and a Mr Goldberg, who failed to turn up for his tribunal hearing and whose written submission was dismissed (MG 7 November 1939).

43   JC 9 February 1940 letter from Lionel Cowan.

44   Cowan Papers (MCL M599/1/1/7–8) letters from Lehrman to Cowan 9 February and 22 July 1940. Lehrman had by then left Manchester to become the minister of the Greenbank Drive Synagogue in Liverpool.

45   Cowan Papers: PPU circular 31 December 1937.

46   Cowan Papers: Lionel Cowan's speech to the Ladybarn Church Guild 15 March 1937.

47   Cowan, 'Life', pp. 51–52. In his application for registration as a Conscientious Objector (Cowan Papers (MCL M599/1/13) Cowan noted that he had visited Germany at least once a year between 1931 and 1937.

48   Cowan, 'Life', p. 52.

49 *Ibid.*, pp. 69–70.

50 *Ibid.*, p. 70.

51 *Ibid.*, p. 69; Letter from Lionel Cowan's son, Kenneth, to the author 23 February 2006. Kenneth Cowan wrote: 'Apparently the civil servants had no idea how to cope with this and gave him the required paper work to get rid of him.'

52 Winifred Garnett of the QRC had worked closely with Cowan in pacifist bodies; Norman Jacobs and Alex Jacob of the MJRC had been amongst his officers in the Jewish Lads Brigade.

53 Cowan, 'Life', p. 71.

54 MG 7 January 1937.

55 Cowan Papers: circular from Lionel Cowan to members of the Fallowfield PPU May 1938.

56 Cowan Papers: circular from Lionel Cowan to members of the Fallowfield PPU n.d. [April–May 1937].

57 Cowan Papers: circular from Lionel Cowan to members of the Fallowfield PPU May 1938.

58 Cowan Papers: speakers' notes [by Lionel Cowan] for 1938.

59 *Ibid.*

60 *Ibid.*

61 Most of the hostel's residents were in fact Germans, some from the Sudetenland, some from the German refugee community in Prague.

62 QRC 17 February 1939. Garnett had suggested contacting the Fallowfield PPU through Stanley Mossop, the minister of the Unitarian Platt Chapel, himself a member and a friend of Cowan.

63 QRC 14 March 1939.

64 Cowan Papers: Lionel Cowan's notes for a meeting of Fallowfield PPU on 27 March 1939.

65 Cowan Papers: circular by Lionel Cowan to members of the Fallowfield PPU August 1939.

66 Cowan Papers (MCL M599/1/13).

67 Cowan Papers: circular from Lionel Cowan to Fallowfield PPU members 27 September 1939.

68 Cowan Papers: notes by Lionel Cowan for a speech to the Alderley Edge [PPU] Group Formation Meeting 6 November 1939; circular by Lionel Cowan to the Fallowfield PPU August 1939.

69 Cowan Papers: notes by Lionel Cowan for a speech to the Alderley Edge [PPU] Group Formation Meeting 6 November 1939.

70 Cowan Papers: notes by Lionel Cowan for a PPU meeting on 'Pacifists in Wartime' at Portland Grove 8 March 1941.

71 Cowan Papers (MCL M599/1/13)

72 Cowan Papers, 8 March 1941, notes for a PPU meeting op.cit.

73 The Fire Watchers Log Books for both hospitals have survived (Cowan Papers MCL M599/2/1/1 and M599 ?2/2/1).

74 Starkey, *I Will Not Fight*, pp. 21–22. The PSUs of Liverpool and Manchester were set up in 1940 under the auspices of a national Pacifist Service Bureau. They went on to care for families displaced by the Blitz, evolving in 1948 into the Family Service Units (for so-called 'problem families') which were subsequently added to the welfare services of the state. Bruno Tublin joined the fire-watching squad in Burnage in August 1941 and remained a member until the end of January 1942 (Log Book

of the Voluntary Fire-watching Squad at the Duchess of Work Hospital for Babies (Cowan Papers (MCL 599/2/2/1))

75 Cowan, 'Life', pp. 62–63. At Renold Chains, the management forced the issue by calling on Cowan to participate in the production of a catalogue advertising the armaments made by the firm. When he refused, as they knew he would, he was given the choice between dismissal and resignation; he chose the latter since it 'gave him the initiative'. Cowan made his first application for registration as a CO 'on humanitarian grounds' on 29 November 1940 (Cowan Papers (MCL M599/1/13). At an Appeal Tribunal in August 1941 Cowan was granted unconditional exemption from military service. After leaving Renold Chains, he worked as a salesman for an advertising firm (Cowan, 'Life', pp. 63–65).

76 *Ibid.*, p. 88.

77 On the Weinigers' departure after the war, Cowan wrote to Sir Noton and Lady Barclay thanking them for employing them 'over such a long period' and for allowing the community to use his house and garden (undated letter from Lionel Cowan Papers (MCL M599/3/5/91)).

78 *Ibid.*, p. 91. An undated list of members (forty 'regular' and twenty-two 'occasional' or 'very occasional') of the Wilmslow Jewish Community (Cowan Papers MCL M599/3/3), probably covering the years 1942–46, names Sir Noton Barclay's servants as Mr and Mrs Hans Weiniger. The list includes at least sixteen unmarried women and married women without their husbands who were almost certainly refugee domestic servants. In all, it is possible to identify twenty-one persons on the list (sixteen 'regular' members and five 'occasionals') as refugees. The deletion of some of the names is indicative of the community's decline as its members left the district.

23

Conclusion: the victims of Fascism and the liberal city

It was probably the case with the Manchester of the 1930s, as it certainly was in earlier years, that the parts did not quite add up to the desired whole. The city cannot be described, without strong reservations, as the 'liberal city' which Manchester's articulate middle-class believed it to be. In the 1880s and 1890s immigrants from Eastern Europe, while welcomed by a liberal paper like the *Manchester Guardian*, and by a liberal-minded elite, had been met by an outburst of anti-alien and anti-Semitic sentiment by other elements in the population and in other sections of the local press. A scurrilous and sometimes vicious anti-Semitic journal, *Spy*, published in Manchester, found a readership in the city between 1891 and 1899. There had always been segments of the Manchester population which, for what they would have seen as justifiable reasons, had reacted badly to the arrival of immigrants on any scale. The liberalism of Manchester had never been other than flawed, and so it was in the 1930s.

At one extreme there were sectors of the population in sympathy with Hitler's regeneration of Germany and Mussolini's recreation of Italy and for whom the welcome of refugees would have represented a form of betrayal. This included those Mancunians who chose to join the Manchester branch of Oswald Mosley's British Union of Fascists, a branch sufficiently large in its beginnings as to almost persuade Mosley to move the headquarters of the party from London to Manchester. Opposition to refugees formed part of the BUF's agenda, more particularly because a majority of the refugees were Jewish. Rae Barash remembers members of the BUF keeping watch over the offices of the Jewish Refugees Committee. BUF street meetings targeted refugees as a threat to the well-being of Manchester's working population. A favoured meeting place was Albert Croft, off Waterloo Road, at the heart of the Jewish Quarter, and within easy reach of the BUF's branch headquarters in Northumberland Street, Higher Broughton. Such meetings were readily disrupted by Jewish left-wingers, one of whose operational bases was in the house of the Clyne family in Waterloo Road.

Less easily countered were BUF meetings in and around the city centre. In March 1939, as 200–300 people, most of them Jews, queued at the New Manchester Hippodrome in Ardwick for a concert in aid of the Baldwin

Fund, they were faced by a gang of men and boys (presumably a BUF squad) with anti-Jewish posters and shouting anti-Jewish insults, while parading up and down the pavement and 'crossing and re-crossing' Stockport Road. Some forced their way into the hall and 'had to be rejected'. Their posters read: 'Keep Yids out of the British Theatre', 'Justice not coffins for the unemployed', 'Britain for the British', and 'British unemployed before alien refugees'. [1]

The precise membership of the local branch and the extent of local sympathy for its causes are unknown. A propaganda film made by the BUF of a demonstration in Manchester (probably in Hulme), with Mosley present, probably dating from 1938, and portraying a crowd of sympathetic onlookers, is probably far from the reality. The BUF rarely appear in refugee testimonies, only one refugee being sufficiently moved by a BUF demonstration in St Peter's Square soon after his arrival to throw in his lot with refugee Communists. Another refugee couple, who in 1940 found accommodation in a flat in Didsbury, where they were well-treated by their non-Jewish landlady, were invited into her basement flat on the eve of their departure. To their amazement, it turned out to be a Fascist shrine.

Local Jewish and left-wing opposition to the BUF was strong, both on the streets and, more diplomatically, through the Jewish Representative Council. In 1938 Mosley himself had abandoned the idea of moving to Manchester, the BUF's local base in Northumberland Street in the Higher Broughton being then sold in 1939 (ironically) to a patron of the burgeoning Jewish ultra-orthodox movement, Machzikei Hadass, whose own headquarters it then became and, in time, the focus of a substantial *haredi* community.

Other admirers of Fascism were members of Manchester's Little Italy and the remnant – perhaps fifty families in all – of what had once been a large and influential German colony. Although only a tiny segment of Manchester's population, their sympathies removed from the local scene some of those who were otherwise well-placed to have been amongst the powerful supporters of the victims of European Fascism. The reality of their attitudes suggests a down-side of Manchester's cosmopolitan make-up: the possibility that immigrants might reflect the politics of their home countries, all very well when those countries were fighting for democracy, as Italy was during the First World War, but less so in the 1930s, when Manchester Germans and Italians were being encouraged by powerful propaganda from their home countries to support the Fascist regimes of their homelands. For the Italians, who, it has been argued, association with the Fascist regime in Italy was one means of addressing their low socio-economic status and sense of marginalisation in their lands of exile; no such claim could be made for Manchester Germans, most of them middle-class merchants, manufacturers, shopkeepers and professional men. There were also German students at the University of Manchester, some of whom are said to have attempted (unsuccessfully) in January 1933 to take over Manchester's German Lutheran Church for conversion into the headquarters of a Manchester branch of the National Socialist Party.[2]

This German Church, in Wright Street, in the Greenheys district of Chorlton-on-Medlock, dating from 1855 and with a membership said to number 400 in 1930, and its social club in nearby Ducie Street, had become the cultural and social centre of what was left of German Manchester after the intense anti-German feeling generated by the First World War. Although never coming out in public with pro-Nazi sympathies, its members included a handful of 'fervent Nazis': Carl Goedecke, a textile merchant from Bremen with his factory in Trafford Park; Otto Baumbach, a manufacturer of glass instruments (including test-tubes for the young physicist Ernest Rutherford) and (less probably) Franz Brumme from Brandenburg, who had opened a delicatessen in central Manchester specialising in 'foreign delicacies', and who in 1933 was the leading layman of the Church and secretary of its social club. Baumbach was one of the Manchester Germans who, in the early years of the Nazi regime, travelled regularly to Germany on the *Eilenau*, a steamer which ran a cheap service from the Port of Manchester to Hamburg and Bremen. His son Geoffrey, who returned briefly to Germany in 1937 there became an enthusiastic member of Hitler Youth, before returning to Manchester on the eve of war.[3]

While there is no conclusive evidence that such local Germans engaged in espionage[4] or indulged openly in anti-Semitism, their sympathies ruled them out as possible mediators for German refugees and as the potential employers of German refugee labour. The German refugee Kurt Grunwald, who was refused employment at Goedecke's factory in 1939 sensed a hostility based on his Jewish origins.[5] The only German Confessional Christian who found refuge in Manchester, Dr Arnold Ehrhardt, 'a friend of Niemoller', owed his rescue not to the German Church but to members of Manchester's Anglican communion.[6] Only one German refugee family made contact with the German Church before its dissolution in 1940: Dr Martin Weinbaum, a German historian of Jewish origin but Christian practice, who was found a post at the University of Manchester in 1933: his daughter Maria was baptised in the German Church in October 1933.[7] Among the Germans imprisoned in 1939 as Category A aliens was a young German au pair and member of the German Church, Edith Schnitzler, whose father in Elberfeld was known for his pro-Nazi sympathies.[8]

Manchester's Italian colony was sharply divided between poor immigrants living in a network of streets in the New Cross area of Ancoats, and subsisting largely as itinerant ice-cream sellers, barrel organists and manual workers, and an elite of academics, lawyers, sculptors and entrepreneurs in the catering, biscuit-making and mosaic industries spread more widely throughout suburban Manchester. It was members of this commercial and cultural elite, no more than twelve in all, who met together in March 1924, very probably at the behest of Dr Piero Rebora, the recently appointed Professor of Italian Studies at the University of Manchester, and already a committed Fascist in Italy, to found the *Fascio*, the Manchester branch of the Fascist Italian League.[9] Prominent amongst these Manchester 'Fascists of the First Hour', apart from Rebora, were Azeglio Valgimigli, also a teacher of Italian at the University (and in 1932 to become the author of a history of Italian Manchester); Enrico Fontana Jucker, an industrialist and Manchester's honorary Italian consul; Domenico Antonelli, who had risen from poverty to become a prosperous manufacturer of the wafers and cones used in the ice-cream industry, and his son Romolo.

Valgimigli's comment that the founders had included 'a good number of Italians from Ancoats' needs to be read with caution. Although the *Fascio* organised classes for black-shirted Ancoats children, it seems likely that Fascism as an ideology was confined largely to the Italian middle classes. Some poorer families may have shared Valgimigli's admiration of Mussolini as 'the man of destiny' who had restored order and self-respect to a nation in chaos. Others were attracted by the offer of free holidays for children in Fascist Italy. In some Italian biscuit and ice-cream factories membership of the party was seen (and perhaps imposed) as a condition of employment. By 1932 the *Fascio* had attracted only 140 members of a colony numbering at least 800.[10] Nor was the party in Manchester, any more than in Italy, characterised by anti-Semitism or by public hostility to refugee settlement. At most, as was the case with Manchester Germans, sympathy for Fascism closed down another potential root into Britain for Italian Jews. Only one Italian Sephardi family was amongst the refugees arriving in Manchester after 1938, and that one gaining entry through the efforts of a relative long-established in Manchester.

Sympathy for Fascism as the potential saviour of the Church from the threat of atheistic Bolshevism was a factor also in the response of the Salford Diocese of the Catholic Church to potential refugees. The hierarchy of Church in Salford, which had only reluctantly supported the arrival of the Basque children from Franco's Spain in 1937, and which had been only too pleased to see most of them return home, also carried a burden of traditional anti-Semitism which outweighed any sympathy it might have felt for Jewish refugees from Germany and Austria. No Catholic Committee emerged in the region to facilitate the entry of refugees. And no more than a handful of Catholic children of Jewish origin on the Kindertransport were welcomed to the region. Judging from the tone of *The Harvest*, the monthly journal of the Salford Diocese's Rescue and Protection Society, it may even be that in the tiny and remote Salford fragment of world Catholicism traditional attitudes towards Jews were at their most intense. A surviving photograph album kept by a Salford Catholic family who visited Germany in 1935 (and now in the author's possession) includes celebratory snaps of Hitler Youth, a Nazi Folk Festival and one of the family holding the Nazi flag.

Until 1938 it is probable that a majority of Manchester citizens, outside the radical Left, remained unaware of the meaning and the full implications of Fascism. Most of those outside organised left-wing formations who lent their support to the Basque children of 1937, did so for reasons of humanity rather than of politics. Their prime impulse was the suffering of Guernica rather than the ideology of Franco. No linkage was made with the victims of Nazism, so that the spectrum of local support for the Basque children and for the maintenance of the Watermillock hostel did not generate anything like the same level of organised sympathy for Hitler's victims, at least until the arrival of the Kindertransport in December 1938, when, once again, the fate of children evoked waves of popular sympathy. Nor did the situation of the Basque children generate within the Jewish community any sense of shared victimhood. Outside the Jewish recruits to the CPGB and its youth formations, some of whom joined the International Brigade, Franco's advance in Spain evoked no response from the leaders of local Jewry; Nathan Laski, in particular, as the community's unchallenged leader, was unwilling to lead the community into what he would have seen both as a breach of Britain's policy of non-intervention and as lending support to the most dangerously obstreperous segment of the Jewish community.

The fear of disloyalty was, in fact, the Achilles heel of the Jewish community in the face of the early victims of Fascism. Laski was later to confess that until 1938, while well-knowing the predicament of German Jewry, he felt unable to give it local publicity for fear of endangering Britain's policy of appeasement. It was partly for this reason too, that, while mounting appeals for German Jewry, he felt unable to lead the community in staking out Manchester as a haven of safety for refugees. His concern, it has been argued, was as always, for the 'image' on which he believed the safety of the community to depend, so that he had no problem in countenancing the 'secret' operations of Isidore Apfelbaum on behalf of refugee trainees. He gave no official backing to those communal bodies, like the Manchester Ladies Lodge of B'nai Brith, which had taken it upon themselves to give a measure of support to those seeking settlement in Manchester before 1938. By and large, the community followed his lead. To have associated the community with public support for the unlimited entry of refugees would, Laski believed, have risked the kind of anti-Semitic backlash which had greeted the immigrants from Eastern Europe, amongst whom had been his own family; an anticipated backlash which was at the heart of the government's immigration policy. It could be argued that behind such thinking lay deeper anxieties, both of Laski and the government, around the injurious impact of immigration on the well-being of a nation with which Laski had identified himself and the community.

It was only after the Anschluss and Kristallnacht that, in the face of public opinion, governmental concession and an escalating flow of refugees, Laski felt empowered to lead the community into the rescue of refugees. He was also pressed into action by metropolitan Jewish agencies of refugee support which might otherwise have been overwhelmed. From 1938, however, the main thrust of his communal policy was to keep the flow of refugees under his own control (and therefore efficiently organised and financially manageable) and to do all within his power, and again the priority was 'image', to press upon refugees a show of loyalty to the British state. As 'communal dictator by consent' he effectively defined, as his spat with the Manchester Yeshiva suggests, the timing, the degree and the methods of rescue.

Within a Jewish community of some 40,000, the work of rescue was placed in the hands (a selection in which Laski almost certainly played the most powerful part) of the communal mainstream, partly no doubt, because this was what Laski regarded as his proper constituency, but also because it was only within the mainstream that there existed the experience of communal activism and philanthropy which might now be turned to good account on behalf of Jewish refugees. Margaret Langdon, Rae Barash, Henrietta Myrans and Morris Feinmann were amongst those who moved readily from the traditional support of the communal needy to the rescue of refugees.

It may also have been a matter of time and resources, particularly in years of an economic depression which enveloped the Jewish working classes in the garment and furniture industries, still anchored by poverty to the least salubrious segments of the Jewish Quarter. Of the fifty volunteers who composed the 'general committee' of the MJRC, all lived in the suburbs of north or south Manchester. Those communal radicals, most of them working-class men and women, who had been involved in such actions as the Kinder Scout Mass Trespass in 1932, who had later advocated (and undertaken) direct action against the BUF and pressed the cause of Republican Spain, found (and perhaps sought) no place on the Manchester Jewish Refugees Committee or within the administrative structures of its hostels. This may have been largely a matter of class, but for Laski they were also the element of the community most likely, by their propensity for violence and their commitment to revolutionary change, to endanger the communal image for respectability, stability and subservience to the civic and national authorities.

The Manchester Quakers, although having little regard for their external image, were also slow off the mark. Although as pacifists and egalitarians they were naturally inclined to help the victims of violence and discrimination, until late in 1938 they were reluctant to endanger the hope of avoiding war and of a harmony with Germany for which they were still working in September 1939. It was the prompting of the overburdened Germany Emergency Committee in London, the collapse of Britain's policy of appeasement, and perhaps the example of the local Jewish community, which finally persuaded them to create a refugee committee in November 1938. Members of the Manchester and District Refugee Committee of the Society of Friends were drawn equally from the Quaker middle classes, its most active members equally exchanging internal philanthropy and communal activism for the support of outsiders. 'Exchanging' is probably not the right word. For while rescuing refugees, the Quakers maintained the momentum of their other concerns, supporting those arraigned at Manchester tribunals as Conscientious Objectors, attacking the atrocities (including the British atrocities) of war, promoting the idea of an early peace and establishing a network of hostels for those displaced by the Blitz. A 'religion for intellectuals' with strong philanthropic traditions, Quakerism appears not to have attracted a working-class or politically radical following such as existed within the Jewish community. The Quaker volunteers on the refugee committee, and within the meeting houses of Lancashire, Cheshire and Derbyshire were a cross-section of the Quaker membership.

The petit-bourgeois composition of both committees was one, but only one, of the factors which defined those who were saved. Since those with suitable contacts, adequate resources, wide intellectual horizons and negotiating skills were the most likely to find the necessary guarantors and placements which made entry to Britain possible, the rescued were drawn chiefly from the assimilated middle class of German and Austrian Jewry. It was they too, or their unaccompanied children, who were seen by Jewish institutions in Europe, by British consulates abroad and by the British Home Office as the most likely to integrate readily into British society and so escape the potentially hostile gaze of native Britishers. It was only the efforts of individualists like Shonfeld in London and Eli Fox in Manchester who ensured the survival of some at least of the *Ostjuden*.

It is also the case that the rescue efforts mounted in Manchester, and which were powerful enough to bring around 8,000 refugees from Nazism to the city, were no more free of self-interest than the policies of the British government. This is not necessarily a criticism. 'Pure' altruism is rare; perhaps no more than a figment of the liberal imagination. In the circumstances it may be that, for most, a degree of self-interest is what gave the work of rescue its momentum, whether that self-interest was material, as it was, for example, in the case of the Manchester academy, local industrialists and the Zionist movement, or ideological, as it was for Quakers, Rotarians, pacifists and men like Solomon Schonfeld and Eli Fox, for whom it represented another expression of the strongly-held beliefs and ideals in which their self-identity was rooted. It was perhaps only with the additional charge of self-interest and self-fulfilment that non-Jewish organisations might have been persuaded to lend their support to Jewish refugees.

The question also arises, in the case of non-Jewish bodies like the Quakers, the Rotarians and the Catholic Church of *who* it was that they thought they were rescuing. Most would probably have subscribed to some variant of Bishop Henshaw's comment in 1933 that the victims of Fascism demanded sympathy 'not particularly because they were Jews, but particularly because they were persecuted'. It was the humanitarian 'universalism' of the Quakers and the Rotarians which had led them to take up the cause of refugees and which had determined also the nature of their support. Although both had Jewish clients, however 'non-practising', neither saw itself as part of a rescue operation on behalf of Jews. The flip-side of this coin was that neither saw itself as in any way protecting the Jewishness of those it supported. The comic extreme of this approach had Jacques Kurer, a dentist from Vienna whose family had retained vestiges of their Jewish observance, dressed up by the Quakers as Father Christmas for a Christmas Party at Mount Street. More seriously it was an attitude which failed to take into account either the secular heritage of European Jewry or the fluidity and complexity of the Jewish identity. As the example of German Jewry itself might have amply shown, the Jewish identity was readily propelled by changing circumstance in many directions, including a movement from variants of 'non-practice' to variants of religiosity. While there is a danger here of reading back into the past a more recent 'multi-cultural' valuation of identity, set against this is the reality that it was their Jewish identity, however secularised or overlaid by conversion to Christianity, which had brought refugees to Manchester and placed them in Quaker or Rotarian hands. The failure to pay any regard to their distinctive heritage may be seen as one of several factors making for the erosion of the Jewish community during the years of war.

This can, of course, in no way be equated with anti-Semitism, with its plethora of long-standing negative images of Jews, and yet, although Manchester generated no organised anti-Semitic group outside the BUF, which was never large, and which was probably in decline before the outbreak of war, anti-Semitism, or, at any rate, an innate suspicion of Jews, was a factor of sufficient influence to complicate in various ways the processes of rescue. It seems otherwise inexplicable that Jews were not represented on the Lancashire Industrial Development Council, which included so many representatives of the business community and local authorities, or that Manchester University's mechanism of assisting displaced academics, like the Academic Assistance Council, was anxious not to define a major part of its task as the rescue of *Jewish* academics. The Jewishness of Hitler's victims, however much the source of their persecution, was not seen as conducive to their rescue. Members of the Manchester Rotary Club clearly found it difficult to stomach the fact that those it was rescuing during 1939–40 were Jewish and its rescue efforts were kept on course only by the exceptional humanity of a man like Harry Wharmby. At the Jewish Home for the Aged, Jewish refugee nurses experienced what they saw as anti-Semitism from the non-Jewish matron and her non-Jewish staff. The slow start of the Quaker campaign owed something, too, to the anti-Semitism which can be detected even within the Manchester Friends, as well as to a suspicion of expansionist Zionism.

Rescue also carried conditions, as had the settlement of Eastern European Jews in the late nineteenth century, not simply the conditions laid down in the Aliens Acts, which had arisen out of responses to immigration from Eastern Europe, but conditions which were inherent in the expectations loaded onto refugees by their rescuers, and particularly by their Jewish rescuers. Just as Russian and Polish immigrants had been pressed by the Manchester Jewish leadership to abandon the 'patois' of Yiddish, to shed their 'foreign ways', to settle for the supposed sobriety and respectability of the British people and to express their pride in the city and their loyalty to the nation (a programme to which the young Nathan Laski had become attuned), so 'anglicisation' was pressed upon the refugees of the 1930s, a pressure which comfortably equated with the expectations of liberal Britain and which has become written into the Whig narrative of refugee history.

At their crudest and most explicit, these conditions were written into a handbook in German and English, published by the German Jewish Aid Committee in London in January 1939[11] and given to refugees as they registered their presence at Woburn House. Even making an allowance for a

fear of anti-German sentiment as Britain's relationship with Germany deteriorated and war loomed on the horizon, it reflects the subservient relationship to British culture and the British state which the leaders of British
Jewry had come to accept as the price of communal acceptance. At its core
is the demand that in return 'for the traditional tolerance and sympathy of
Britain and the British Commonwealth', and the supposed welcome they
had received from the British Jewish community, refugees from Germany
and Austria should follow eight 'lines of conduct' to which they were 'honour bound' and which they should 'carry out faithfully'.

Some of these 'lines of conduct' – to learn 'immediately' the English language and its correct pronunciation, to speak in public places in 'halting
English rather than fluent German' and to refrain from criticising the British
government – might have appeared appropriate for a moment of national
anxiety when fear of espionage was abroad and anti-German feeling high.
Others represented cultural dictates which, inter alia, represented a tragic
and deferential caricature of the British way of life. So refugees were urged
not to 'talk in a loud voice'; in the light of the Britisher's supposed modesty,
respect for 'understatement rather than overstatement' and dislike of ostentation and 'unconventionality', not to make themselves conspicuous by their
dress or manners or to display 'the evidence of wealth'; 'to follow the manners and customs of this country in social and business relations', to 'maintain dignity' and 'to help and serve others'; not to expect 'to be received immediately' in British homes. In an echo of the fears of alien revolutionaries
which followed the First World War, the refugees were urged not to join 'any
Political organisation or take part in any political activities'. The loyalty to
Britain 'in word and deed' which 'the British Jew ... does all in his power to
express' was now the price to be paid by the refugees for the 'new and better
future' they could expect in Britain.

Such advice, offered to vulnerable refugees from on high, was reinforced
at local level by the pronouncements of men like Nathan Laski, and by the
Jewish agencies of refugee support, manned, as they were, by those who had
already passed through the anglicising and embourgeoising processes of
communal life into the Jewish middle classes. The 'After-Care Committee'
set up by the MJRC in late 1938 and chaired by Leonard Cohen, offered
classes in English, 'special talks to refugees' on the British way of life, guided
tours to such local places of interest as the *Manchester Guardian* building,
rambles in the Cheshire countryside, and advice on which organisations in
the city and the community refugees might usefully join. In the April 1939
issue of the monthly newsletter in which the Committee gave this advice, at
its height to 600 young refugees, it began: 'We are glad to welcome you to
Manchester! We hope you will be happy here and that you will be able to fit
yourself into the life of the community.' The organisations to which refugees were directed, some with cut-price terms of entry, were the eminently
reputable institutions of middle-class Manchester and anglicised Jewry; omitted were political bodies (the Cheetham branch of the YCL) and popular

venues (dance halls and cinemas) which Cohen might have seen as the unduly vulgar and hedonistic. Evolving by stages into the north and south Manchester branches of the Association of Jewish Refugees, the After Care Committee and its ancillary bodies were most obviously attempts to guide refugees onto the English straight and narrow and perhaps to keep them away away from refugee national organisations, most of them under the influence of refugee radicals.

For the most part, given the class composition of their Jewish, Quaker and Rotarian rescuers, the refugees were at first rarely brought into contact with left-wing organisations, which, at all events, their anti-Fascism notwithstanding, appear not to have played a central part in the work of rescue. There are hints that the dock workers of Liverpool played a role in transporting German and Austrian Communists to a safe haven in Russia. Margaret Taylor, the wife of George Brown, a prominent Manchester member of the CPGB who died as an International Brigader in Spain, is said to have made several trips to the continent during the 1930s to ease the escape of German Communists, although to which destinations is unclear.[12] At all events, the secrecy surrounding such operations, if they actually took place, has equally concealed from the historian the kinds of evidence by which they might be substantiated. The regional branches of the CPGB, at all events small in size and limited in their resources, despite their substantial Jewish membership, appear not to have established a rescue operation. It may be that while support of the working-class Basque children was unmistakeably emblematic of proletarian anti-Fascism, support for Jewish refugees, seen as coming from comfortable, non-political, middle-class families, carried no such cachet. At most the party liaised with the refugees in the KPD, helped Communist refugees find private accommodation and later work (for Kresse, for example), 'adopted' some of the Basque children who remained in Britain and, late in the war, helped Spanish Republicans who had been imprisoned in France in 1939 and who arrived in Lancashire as POWs in 1945.

With all these caveats, Manchester facilitated the escape of some 8,000 refugees from Germany, Austria and Czechoslovakia, most of them of Jewish origin, but including also Communists, Social Democrats, Liberals, pacifists and Confessional Christians, targeted by the Nazi regime. Could more have been rescued by Manchester efforts? Very probably: if the government had yielded earlier to demands for concessions on the right of entry pressed upon it by Jewish and Quaker agencies and by such figures of national stature, but minimal influence, as Eleanor Rathbone, Josiah Wedgwood and Norman Angell; if the Jewish community and the Quakers had taken action earlier to bring Jewish refugees to Manchester; if the world of Manchester philanthropy had turned its attention earlier, and more comprehensively, to the victims of Fascism; if the LIDC had focused on the escape of Jewish industrialists; if the Manchester academy had been more generous and less discriminating; if war had not broken out when it did. After 3 September 1939 the MJRC was forced to abandon some of those whose escape it had been in the process of negotiating. A document survives which consists of the names, occupations and photographs of hundreds of German and Austrian women still seeking placement as domestic servants on the eve of war.

But the history of refugees is a compound of 'ifs'. What this study suggests is what was possible (and what impossible) within the circumstances and constraints of the time and within the framework of real events and personalities, before the realities of genocide had made themselves known. In retrospect, of course, nothing was 'enough'.

Notes

1   MCN 4 March 1939.
2   Curt Friese, 'Some thoughts on the History of the Germans and their Church Communities in Manchester, especially in the 19th Century' (undated and unpublished typescript in the author's possession), p. 25. Friese does not quote his source for this information. The records of the German Church, other than a baptismal register, are lost, presumed to have been seized by the security services during the arrest of enemy aliens in 1940.
3   Interview of Geoffrey Baumbach by Bill Williams 9 May 2005; Norman Feather, *Lord Rutherford* (London and Glasgow 1940), p. 125.
4   For a note of suspected espionage by Germans in Manchester, National Archive, File on Carl Kuchenmeister (KV2/286) and file on 'Charlie' (KV2/454).
5   Author interview with Kurt Greenwood (né Grunwald). Grunwald described Goedecke as a 'fervent Nazi'.
6   For Ehrhardt MCN 12 February 1943; Kresse, *Illegalitat, Kerker, Exil*, pp. 305, 309–310. In March 1943 Ehrhardt was ordained as an Anglican priest by the Bishop of Manchester at St James Church in Rusholme.
7   Number 676 of the baptisms listed in the surviving register of the German Church.
8   Autobiographical typescript by Edith Froebel (née Schnitzler) in the author's possession. Edith was imprisoned in Holloway prior to her return to Germany on an exchange scheme in September 1944. She returned to Manchester after the war to marry Alfred Froebel, a fellow member of the German Church.
9   Azeglio Valgimigli, *La Colonia Italiana di Manchester 1794–1932* (Manchester 1932), pp. 45, 63.
10 *Ibid.*, p 66.
11 *While you are in England. Helpful Information and Guidance for Every Refugee* (London 1933).
12 Information from Jack Jones, who Margaret Taylor married after the death of George Brown in Spain.

Bibliography

Archival Sources

Bury Grammar School

Minutes of the School Governors

Friends Meeting House, Manchester

Correspondence relating to refugees
List of refugees supported by the Manchester Friends
Minutes of the Manchester International Service Committee
Minutes of the Refugee Committee of the Society of Friends for Manchester and District

German Lutheran Church, Stretford

Register of Baptisms, Marriages and Deaths

Heathlands Village (Manchester Jewish Home for the Elderly)

Annual Reports
Minute Books
Photographic record of admissions

Imperial War Museum, London

Autobiography of Hans Levy

Local Studies Department, Manchester Central Library

Scrapbook of articles, letters etc belonging to G.W. Armitage
The Lionel Cowan Papers
The Ruth Edwards (nee Schneier) Correspondence
Papers of Adalbert Eisner [Albert Edwards]
The Jacob Papers
Correspondence of Wolfgang Plessner
The Wright Robinson papers
Brochure and correspondence relating to Jewish Book Week, 1938
Minute Book of the Manchester Jewish Benevolent Society
Minutes of the Barlow Moor and Didsbury Women's Liberal Council
Minutes of the B'nai Brith Women's Lodge of Manchester
Minutes of the Manchester Branch of the National Council of Women
Minute books of the Manchester Jewish Representative Council
Minutes of the Manchester Liberal Women's Council
Minutes of the Manchester Shechita Board
Minutes of the Park Place Synagogue Social Club
Minutes of the Provincial Independent Tontine Society
Minutes of the South Manchester and District Women's Zionist Society
Minutes of the Wilmslow and District Jewish Community

Papers relating to the 'Mad Hatter's Castle'
Programmes of the Manchester University Settlement
Records of the Manchester Jewish Refugee Committee
Responses to a survey of Quakers who helped Jews
Transcripts of the proceedings of the Lancashire Tribunal for Conscientious Objectors

Manchester High School for Girls

School Archives

Manchester Jewish Museum

Brochures of the Manchester Palestine Bazaars, 1936–39

Manchester Police Museum

Aliens Register for Salford

The Manchester Yeshiva

Book of press-cuttings
Minutes of meetings of the management committee

Mass Observation Archive

Boxes in the Worktown Collection related to the Watermillock Hostel

National Archive at Kew

HO 144/22463 Advisory Committee to the Home Office (Italians)
HO KV2/286 File on Carl Kuchenmeister
HO KV2/454 File on 'Charlie'

Parkes Library, University of Southampton

Papers of Rabbi Dr Solomon Schonfeld

Salford Diocesan (Roman Catholic) Archive

Annual Almanac for the Diocese of Salford
The Diary of Bishop Casartelli
The Henshaw Papers
The Marshall Papers

Salford Local History Library

Papers related to the Lancashire Industrial Development Council

University of Manchester, John Rylands Library

The Leonard Behrens papers
Vice-Chancellor's Archive

The Working Class Movement Library, Salford

The Lionel Cowan Papers
The Ehlert Papers
Minutes of the Manchester Branch of the AEU
Minutes of the Salford Central Labour Party

In private hands

The Walter Beck Correspondence (with his widow, Dorothy)
The Gudula Kahn Correspondence, translated by Monika Sonker (with her grandson, Ben Forman)
Results of survey conducted by Peter Kurer, 'Quakers who helped Jews'
Papers relating to Marianna Prager (with her brother, David)

Oral testimonies

Refugee Voices: the Association of Jewish Refugees Audio-Visual History Collection

Interviews by Rosalyn Livshin of Doris Angel, Hannelore Cohen, Lilly Crewe, Alice Rubinstein, Walter Sondhelm and others at the Association of Jewish Refugees, London

Transcripts/notes of interviews with refugees at the Centre for Jewish Studies, University of Manchester, conducted by Bill Williams unless otherwise stated

George Abendstern, Hanna Abendstern (by Michelle Abendstern), Dr Robert Abendstern, Doris Angel, Fred Arlsberg, Hilda Barrett, Paula Bitzberg (née Rosner) (e-mail correspondence with Lynne Jesky), Fanni Bogdanov (by Lynne Jesky), Reverend Gabriel Brodie, Marga Brodie, Hilde Brooker (with Anne Priest), Lily Crewe (formerly Krug), Sara Doggart, Lita Edwards, Ruth Edwards (née Schneier), Grete Einstein, Eva Frumin, Edmund Goldman, Matilda Goldman, Helga Gorney, Kurt Greenwood, Arieh Handler, Kurt Heilbronn, Hans Heimer, Ronald Hene, Sophie Hirn (e-mail correspondence with Lynne Jesky), Harry Jacobi (né Hirschfield), Mavis Jaffe, Heidi Johnson, Freda Klein, Peter Kurer, Hans Robert Levy (by Laura Silcock), Klein, Wolfgang Plessner, Margaret Rose (by Michelle Abendstern), Robert Rosner, Alice Rubinstein, Tony Russell, Leon Stein (by Michelle Abendstern), David Taubmann, Otto Taubmann, Francis Treuhertz, Julian Treuhertz, Otto Wangerman, Rene Wolf, Elisabeth (Lisa) Wolfe

Transcripts/notes of other interviews and typescripts at the Centre for Jewish Studies, University of Manchester (interviews by Bill Williams unless otherwise stated)

Celia Babsky (native Jewish member of the Manchester International Club), Rae Barash (chairman, Manchester Jewish Refugees Committee), Geoffrey Baumbach (son of a German glass manufacturer in Manchester), Margaret Bayes (Quaker), Hettie Blank, Lionel Cowan (interviewed by his son Kenneth, 1977–94), Ruth Giness (granddaughter of Adolf Cassel), Robin Greaves, Aslan Hamwee (former solicitor of the Lancashire Tanning Company), Reg Holmes (Manchester friend of political refugees), Hazel Howard and Fred Pawsey (former employees of the Lancashire Tanning Company), Leonard Jacobs (employer of a refugee domestic servant), Audrey Jones (witness to refugees in south Manchester), Victor Maxwell (typescript, 'My Father's Family'), Alice Mellalieu (typescript 'Living at the Mad Hatter's Castle 1944–1947'), David Prager (transcript of interview by Olivia Blechner), John Rizza (resident of the Manchester Italian colony), Neil Roberts and John Keith Wilson (former employees of Bevingtons and Sons), Margery Wilson (former member of the Quaker Refugee Committee)

Transcripts of interviews at the Manchester Jewish Museum

Margaret Langdon

Refugee autobiographies/biographies

Unpublished

Behrend, Hanna, 'Autobiography' (2004)

Cowan, Lionel, 'The Life Story of Lionel Cowan' (typewritten transcript of interviews with Lionel Cowan by his son Kenneth from 1977–94)

Froebel, Edith, autobiographical typescript

Jedwab, David, 'Stalybridge, Lancashire' and 'Reminiscences of a Bevin Boy', typescripts

Levy, Hans, autobiographical typescript

Maxwell, Victor, 'My Father's Family', typescript

Plessner, Wolfgang, 'My Life Story', incomplete typescript

Schlesinger, Ruth, 'The World I Have Lost' (2007)

Weisl, Hans, 'Recollections' (including 'My Experiences as a refugee from Czechoslovakia')

Weiss, Meir, 'Memoirs 1923–74' (typescript autobiography)

'Our First Year in Harris House' (collective memories of the girls and their matron 1940), typescript at Manchester Jewish Museum

Published

Behrend, Hanna, 'A Political Refugee in Manchester', *North West Labour History: Journal of the North West Labour History Group*, No. 18, 1993–94, p. 31

Crewe, Franz and Lily, *Lives* (privately printed n.d.)

Epstein, T. Scarlett (née Trude Grunwald), *Swimming Upstream: A Jewish Refugee from Vienna* (London 2005)

Furst, Desider and Lilian R., *Home is Somewhere Else: Autobiography in Two Voices* (New York 1994)

Hamlet, Eva, *Against All Odds* (Florida 1994)

Laxova, Renata (née Polgar), *Letter to Alexander* (Cincinnati 2001)

Lindemann, Rolf , *Be Careful in the Choice of your Parents* (privately printed, Miami n.d.)

Mayer, Werner, *To Tell the Story: Recollections and Reflections* (Manchester 1990)

Peierls, Sir Rudolf, *Bird of Passage: Recollections of a Physicist* (Princeton, NJ 1985)

Retzlaff-Kresse, Bruno, *Illegalitat, Kerker, Exil: Erinnerungen aus dem antifaschistischen* (Berlin 1980)

Rossi, Bruno *Moments in the Life of a Scientist* (Cambridge 1990)

Tanner, Heather and Dietrich Hanff, *Out of Nazi Germany* (London 1995)

Treuherz, Julian (ed.), *True Hearts: the Memoirs of Werner and Irmgard Treuherz* (privately printed 2000)

Wolf, Dr Arthur, *Personal Recollections 1930–1938* (privately printed Manchester 1976)

Zadek, Gerhard and Alice, *Mit dem letzten zug nach England* (Berlin 1992)

Newspapers

Bolton Evening News

Bolton Journal and Guardian

Bury Times

Eccles and Patricroft Journal

Glossop Chronicle
Jewish Chronicle
Manchester City News
Manchester Evening News
Manchester Guardian
Rochdale Observer
Sale and Stretford Guardian
Salford City Reporter
Southport Visiter
Stockport Advertiser
Wigan Examiner
Wigan Observer

Periodicals

Association of Jewish Refugees newssheet
The Bulletin of the Manchester Rotary Club
The Friend
The Harvest: A Monthly Magazine of the Salford Catholic Protection and Rescue Society
The Daltonian
District Five Rotary (from summer 1939, renamed *The Mayflower*)
Journal of the University of Manchester
Manchester and Salford Women Citizen
Old Yealanders Newsletter
The Serpent: the Official Organ of the Manchester University Unions
Shofar: Newsletter of the North Cheshire Reform Congregation

Secondary sources

Abbey, William (ed.), 'Alerting the English', in *Between Two Languages: German Speaking Exiles in Great Britain 1933–1945* (London 1995)

Adi, Hakim and Marika Sherwood, *The 1945 Pan-African Congress Revisited* (London 1995)

Almond, Michael, Peter Hope and John Turner, 'Humphrey Procter-Gregg, 1895–1980: Two Memoirs and a List of Compositions', *Manchester Sounds*, Vol. 4, 2003–04

Angell, Sir Norman and Dorothy Buxton, *You and the Refugee* (London 1939)

Anon., *Manchester Talmudical College: 40th Anniversary Souvenir Report* (Manchester 1951)

Arnison, Jim, *Hilda's War* (Preston 1996)

Association of Jewish Refugees *Britain's New Citizens: The Story of Refugees from Germany and Austria* (London 1951)

Bailey, Francis A., *A History of Southport* (Southport 1955)

Bell, Adrian, *Only Three Months: The Basque Children in Exile* (Norwich 1996)

Bell, G.K.A., *The Church and Humanity, 1939–1946* (London 1946)

Bentwich, Norman, *The Rescue and Achievement of Refugee Scholars: the Story of Displaced Scholars and Scientists, 1933–52* (The Hague 1953)

Bentwich, Norman, *Jewish Youth Comes of Age*

Berghahn, Marion, *Continental Britons: German-Jewish Refugees from Nazi Germany* (second edition, Oxford, Hamburg and New York 1988)

Bernstein, Jeremy, Obituary of Hans Bethe, *Physics World*, Vol. 18, No. 4, April 2005

Beveridge, Lord, *A Defence of Free Learning* (London 1959)

Bevington, Geoffrey, *Bevingtons and Sons, Bermondsey 1795–1950* (privately printed, London 1993)

Birtill, George, *The War and After* (Chorley 1976)

Bloxham, Donald and Tony Kushner, *The Holocaust: Critical Historical Approaches* (Manchester 2005)

Bowden, Tom, *Community and Change* (Manchester 1974)

British Council Guide to Manchester and Salford for the US Armed Forces (Manchester 1943)

Brown, Fred, *The Making of a Modern Quaker: Roger Cowan Wilson, 1906–1991* (London 1996)

Buchanan, Tom, 'The Role of the Labour Movement in the Origins and Work of the Basque Children's Committee', *European History Review*, Vol. 18, April 1988

Buxton, Dorothy, *The Economics of the Refugee Problem* (London n.d. [1939?])

Catterall, Peter and C.J. Morris (eds), *Britain and the Threat to Stability in Europe* (Leicester 1993)

Children and Youth Aliyah, *Ten Years of Children and Youth Aliyah 1934–44* (London 1944)

Christie-Miller, John, *The Development of Stockport 1922–1972 and the History of the Stockport Advertiser* (Stockport 1972)

Cloud, Yvonne, *The Basque Children in England: An Account of Life at North Stoneham Camp* (London 1937)

Cohen, Susan, 'Eleanor Rathbone and her Work for Refugees' (unpublished Ph.D. thesis, Faculty of Law, Arts and Social Sciences, University of Southampton, 2004)

Cooper, R.M., *Refugee Scholars*

Corbach, Dieter, *Die Jawne Zu Koln: Zur Geshichte der ersten judische Gymnasiums im Rheinland und zum Gedachtnis an Erich Klibansky* (Cologne 1990)

Donaldson, Frances, *The British Council: the First Fifty Years* (London 1984)

Domb, Cyril (ed.), *Memories of Kopul Rosen* (London 1970)

Duckworth, Ruth (née Windmuller), autobiographical notes in a catalogue of an exhibition of her work held in the Gallery of American Ceramics, Evanston, Illinois

English Hechalutz, *Hechalutz: How Jewish Youth in Britain Regain New Life on the Land* (London n.d. [1942?])

Fallows, I.B., *Bury Grammar School: A History c.1570–1976*

Fleure, H.J., *The Geographical Background of Modern Problems* (London 1932)

Fleure, H.J., *Race and its Meaning in Europe* (Manchester 1940)

Foulds, Elfrida and A, Neave Brayshaw, *Mount Street, 1830–1930: An Account of the Society of Friends in Manchester together with short essays on Quaker Life and Thought* (Manchester 1930)

Fox, Eli, *Fifty Years of Communal Activities* (handwritten summary n.d.)

Francis, Hywel, *Miners Against Fascism: Wales and the Spanish Civil War* (London 1984)

Frangopulo, Nicholas, *Rich Inheritance: A Guide to the History of Manchester* (Manchester 1962)

Freeman, David, 'Zionism in Manchester', *The Zionist Review*, April 1934.

Friese, Curt, 'Some Thoughts on the History of Germans and their Church Communities in Manchester' (undated typescript, 1970s)

From Idea to Ideal: The International Club, Manchester: 10th Anniversary Brochure (Manchester 1948)

Fuchs, Carl, *Musical and Other Recollections of Carl Fuchs* (Manchester 1937)

Fyrth, Jim, *The Signal was Spain* (London and New York 1986)

Geras, Norman, *Solidarity in the Conversation of Humankind: the Ungroundable Liberalism of Richard Rorty* (London and New York 1995)

Glees, Anthony, *Exile Politics during the Second World War. The German Social Democrats in Britain* (Oxford 1982)

Gottlieb, Amy Zahl, *Men of Vision: Anglo-Jewry's Aid to the Victims of the Nazi Regime 1933–1945* (London 1998)

Grenville, Anthony, *Jewish Refugees from Germany and Austria in Britain 1933–1970: Their Image in AJR Information* (London 2010)

Grenville, Anthony (ed.), *German-Speaking Exiles in Britain: Year Book of the Research Centre for German and Austrian Exile Studies Vol. 2* (London 2000)

Hayes, Louis, *Reminiscences of Manchester and Some of its Surroundings from the year 1840* (Manchester 1905)

Herbert, Michael, *Never Counted Out! The Story of Len Johnson* (Manchester 1992)

Hilton, Clare, *The Stockport Jewish Community* (Stockport 1999)

Hinsley, F.H. and C.A.G. Simkins, *British Intelligence in the Second World War, Vol. 4: Security and Counter-Intelligence* (London 1990)

Israel, Giorgio and Pietro Nastasi, *Scienza e razza nell'Italia fascista* (Bologna 1998)

[Jacobs, Norman], 'From Lodz to the House of Lords: The Life and Times of a Provincial Jewish Family, 1840–1990' (typescript based on the diaries of Norman Jacobs)

Jacobs, Shula, 'Kibbutz and Cocoa' (Privately bound transcript n.d.)

Joseph, Anne (ed.), *From the Edge of the World: the Jewish Refugee Experience through Letters and Stories* (London and Portland, OR 2003)

Kotzin, Catherine, 'Christian Responses in Britain to Jewish Refugees from Europe, 1933–1939' (unpublished Ph.D. thesis, History Department, University of Southampton)

Kranzler, David and Gertrude Hirschler (eds), *Solomon Schonfeld: Recollections of individuals saved by an extraordinary orthodox Jewish rescue hero during the Holocaust era* (New York 1982)

Kushner, Tony, *The Persistence of Prejudice: Antisemitism in British Society during the Second World War* (Manchester 1989)

Kushner, Tony, *We Europeans? Mass Observation, 'Race' and British Identity in the Twentieth Century* (London 2004)

Kushner, Tony, *Remembering Refugees: Then and Now* (Manchester 2007)

Kushner, Tony, 'H.J. Fleure: A paradigm for Inter-War Race Thinking in Britain', *Patterns of Prejudice*, Vol. 42, No. 2, May 2008

Kushner, Tony and Katharine Knox, *Refugees in the Age of Genocide: Global, National and Local Perspectives* (London 1999)

Lancashire Industrial Development Council, *Lancashire, Industrial and Commercial* (Manchester 1935)

Lancashire Industrial Development Council, *Lancashire Builds: Being a Pictorial Survey of the Introduction and Development of many new Industries and Factories in the Lancashire Area since 1930* (Manchester 1938)

Legarreta, Dorothy, *The Guernica Generation; Basque Children of the Spanish Civil War* (Nevada 1984)

Lewis, Anne, *Quakers in Cheadle Hulme* (Manchester 1988)

Livingstone, Harry, '79 Years in Moneylending' (unpublished typescript, revised 1970)

Livshin, Rosalyn, *Dr. Bernard Sandler: A Biography* (privately printed, Manchester n.d.)

Livshin, Rosalyn, *Olga Sandler: A Biography* (privately printed, Manchester 2003)

London, Louise *Whitehall and the Jews 1933–1948: British Immigration Policy, Jewish Refugees and the Holocaust* (Cambridge 2000)

Mackennal, W.L., *Life of Major John Haworth Whitworth DSO, MC* (Manchester 1918)

Malet, Marian and Anthony Grenville (eds), *Changing Countries: The Experiences and Achievements of the German-speaking Exiles from Hitler in Britain from 1933 to today*

(London 2002)

Manchester Talmudical College, *40th Annual Report* (1951)

Mellalieu-Campbell, Alice, *My Story* (privately printed, Manchester 2006)

Moloney, Sister Brighid, *Hollymount: The Home on the Hill, Centenary 1888–1988* (n.p. 1988)

Mosse, Werner E. (ed.), *Second Chance: Two Centuries of German-speaking Jews in the United Kingdom* (Tubingen 1991)

Namier, Julia, *Louis Namier: A Biography* (London 1971)

Oliver, P.M., *Back to Balfour* (London n.d. [1944?])

Panayi, Panikos, *German Immigrants in Britain during the 19ʰ century, 1815–1914* (Oxford 1995)

Parkes, James, *Voyages of Discovery* (London 1969)

Pedersen, Susan, *Eleanor Rathbone and the Politics of Conscience* (Yale 2004)

People, Places and Politics: Paintings by Georg Eisler (Manchester City Art Galley 1988)

Political and Economic Planning, *Are Refugees an Asset ?* (London n.d. [1945?])

Presland, John (Gladys Bendit), *A Great Adventure: The Story of the Refugee Children's Movement* (London 1944)

Rea, Anthony, *Little Italy: Memories of the Italian Colony of Ancoats* (Manchester 1988)

Rea, Antonio, *Italians in Manchester: History, Traditions, Work* (Quart, Italy 1990)

Retzlaff-Kresse, Bruno *Illegalitat, Kerker, Exil: Erinnerungen aus dem antifashistischen Kampf* (Berlin 1980)

Rotary International 1905–1955: Golden Jubilee Brochure (Manchester 1955)

Rubinstein, William, *The Myth of Rescue* (London and New York 1997)

Salway, C., *Refugees and Industry* (London 1942)

Shaftesley, John, 'The Origins of the Manchester Jewish Representative Council' (typescript c. 1970)

Shatzke, Pamela, *Holocaust and Rescue: Impotent or Indifferent? Anglo-Jewry 1938–1945* (London 2002)

Sherman, A., *Island Refuge: Britain and Refugees from the Third Reich 1933–1939* (London 1973)

Sherwood, Marika, *Manchester and the Pan-African Congress* (London 1995)

Singer, Peter, *Pushing Time Away: My Grandfather and the Tragedy of Jewish Vienna* (London 2003)

Slawson, John, *A Labour of Love: Holly Mount, Tottington: Memories of the Children's Home* (Manchester 1995)

A 'Special Correspondent', 'How Refugees Help Lancashire: New Industries with Secret Processes' (reprinted from the *Manchester Evening Chronicle*, 16 May 1939)

Sponza, Lucio, 'The British Government and the Internment of Italians', in David Cesarani and Tony Kushner (eds), *The Internment of Aliens in 20th Century Britain* (special issue of the journal, *Immigrants and Minorities*, Vol. 11, No. 3) (London 1992)

Starkey, Pat, *I Will Not Fight: Conscientious Objectors and Pacifists in the North West during the Second World War* (Liverpool 1991)

Stocks, M.D., *Fifty Years in Every Street: A Story of the Manchester University Settlement* (Manchester 1945)

Sutherland, George A., *Dalton Hall: A Quaker Venture* (London 1963)

Turner, Barry, *And the Policeman Smiled: 10,000 Children Escape from Nazi Europe* (London 1990)

Tylecote, Mabel, *The Education of Women at Manchester University* (Manchester 1941)

Uhlman, Fred, *The Making of an Englishman* (London 1960)

Valgimigli, Azeglio, *La Colonia Italiana di Manchester, 1794–1932* (Manchester 1932)

Waller, R.D., *Residential College: Origins of the Lamb Guildhouse and Holly Royde* (Manchester 1954)

Wendehorst, Stephan, 'Between Promised Land and Land of Promise. The Radical Socialist Zionism of Hashomer Hatzair', *Jewish Culture and History*, Vol. 2, No. 1, 1999

Williams, Bill, *The Making of Manchester Jewry, 1740–1875* (Manchester 1976)

Wise, Zalkind Yaacov, 'The Rise of Independent Orthodoxy in Anglo-Jewry: The History of Machzikei Hadass Communities, Manchester' (unpublished Ph.D. thesis, Department of Religions and Theology, University of Manchester, 2006)

Wortmann, Wilhelm Eberhard, 'Die Geschichte des Hauses Adler and Oppenheim' (offprint, source unknown, in the possession of Julian Treuherz)

Zionist Federation of Great Britain and Ireland, *The Jewish Training Farm* (London 1936)

Index